The Oxford Book of
Nineteenth-Century
English Verse

The Oxford Book of Nineteenth-Century English Verse

Chosen by

John Hayward

Oxford

At the Clarendon Press

1964

Oxford University Press, Amen House, London E.C.4

GLASGOW NEW YORK TORONTO MELBOURNE WELLINGTON
BOMBAY CALCUTTA MADRAS KARACHI LAHORE DACCA
CAPE TOWN SALISBURY NAIROBI IBADAN ACCRA
KUALA LUMPUR HONG KONG

PRINTED IN GREAT BRITAIN

PREFACE

THE climate of thought and sensibility, created towards the end of the eighteenth century by western man's revolutionary struggle for the basic human rights to 'Life, Liberty, and the Pursuit of Happiness', had a liberating influence on the poetic imagination and on the language of poetry that extended far beyond the period of the so-called Romantic Revival. This influence persisted throughout the nineteenth century and made itself felt with varying degrees of emotional intensity at every level of poetic experience—from the poetry of passionate affirmation to that of sentimental introspection. Romanticism, in its shifting and confluent moods of confidence and misgiving, of illusion and disenchantment, of speculation on the mystery of human existence and personal destiny, of nostalgic yearning for the 'glory and loveliness' of the past, of belief in a future of endless progress, inspired the production of an immense amount of English verse during the hundred years that passed between the appearance of *Lyrical Ballads* in 1798 and *Wessex Poems* in 1898. It was, one might say, an attitude to life that tended to bring out the best and worst of Keats in almost every poet of the century.

In so far as the present collection of some 600 poems and extracts by 85 poets of this period (allowing for some extension at each end) represents within the compass of a single volume the poetic achievement of the nineteenth century, it does so of course in the light

v

of the taste and critical opinion of a later age. Considered in this light, its contents are found to reflect those variations in standards of appreciation that occur between one age and another. If value judgements were not subject to periodical revision it would contain little, for example, of Blake and Clare, of Meredith and Hardy, and a great deal, for example, of Southey and Campbell, of Mrs. Browning and Bailey. Appetencies change, and what was once accepted and acclaimed as poetically valuable (or at least fashionable) is subsequently devalued and rejected. Who now reads *The Curse of Kehama*, *Gertrude of Wyoming*, *Aurora Leigh*, or *Festus*?

There are, of course, many poems in this collection which have stood the test of time and no longer abide our question. Their selection presents little difficulty. But there are also many whose right to a place must largely depend upon balancing the conflicting claims to representation of poets who appear retrospectively to have been overvalued in their day and of those who appear to a later generation to have been undervalued or even, like Darley, scarcely recognized by their contemporaries. This is a tricky process but also a fascinating one, for it gives rise to much curious speculation on the character and influence of the *Zeitgeist*, on the nature of poetic sensibility, and on the validity or otherwise of Dr. Johnson's dictum that 'by the common sense of readers uncorrupted with literary prejudice . . . must be finally decided all claim to poetical honours'. Why was *The Prelude* a flop and *Festus* a best seller in Victorian England? Why was 'Love in the

Valley' preferred to 'Modern Love' and 'The Hound of Heaven' to 'The City of Dreadful Night'? Who knows, one might add, whether the future in its turn will not judge *The Testament of Beauty* to have been underrated and Pound's *Cantos* overrated (or vice versa) in their time? How much space, one may wonder, will the *Oxford Book of Twentieth-Century English Verse* allot a hundred years hence to Dylan Thomas and Betjeman?

Inevitably, much of the material originally chosen for an anthology has to be discarded in the course of its compilation in order to ensure a proportional representation of major as well as minor poets and of long as well as short poems. Selection must always involve some calculated sacrifice and compromise: minor work by a major poet must make way for major work by a minor poet: poems too long to be printed in full must perforce be represented by extracts; and even extracts themselves curtailed. It is, in effect, much more than one would expect a matter of using simple arithmetic—addition, subtraction, division—to work out an equitable distribution of available space.

Some room has been saved in the present volume by the omission of dramatic verse (hence the exclusion of *Prometheus Unbound*, *Atalanta in Calydon*, &c.), dialect verse (as practised by Scott, Tennyson, and Barnes), and translated verse (with the traditional exception of Fitzgerald's 'Rubáiyát'), but not enough, needless to say, to allow more than three long poems, masterpieces of their kind—'The Ancient Mariner',

'Bishop Blougram's Apology', and 'The Hunting of the Snark'—to be printed in full. Other long poems, notably *The Prelude*, *Don Juan*, and *In Memoriam*, are represented as fairly, it is to be hoped, as such treatment allows, by substantial excerpts. Extracts, particularly short passages from long poems, are often and misleadingly printed in anthologies as if they were separate poems; here they are clearly shown to be extracts, and where allusive or descriptive titles have been supplied editorially for convenient reference they are enclosed in distinctive brackets.

As a general rule the text (too seldom treated with respect for authority and accuracy in anthologies) reproduces that of the first edition in book form—the version, that is to say, originally approved by the poet for publication and so presented to his earliest readers. Exceptions to this rule are indicated in the list of Contents, where the primary printed source of every poem and extract is given. The most important exception is the 1806 text of *The Prelude*, which was not published until 1926; others relate to poems first printed posthumously or to those more or less substantially altered for later editions. Although it is rare for a poem once in print to be improved by subsequent tinkering or for the first fine careless rapture to be enhanced by second thoughts, some deference must be shown to later readings expressly authorized by the poet. Some revised versions and variant readings have consequently been adopted here. But, in view of the deplorable practice of some anthologists of reprinting poems with lines and even whole stanzas surreptitiously and silently cut out in order to 'improve' them, it may be well to conclude with an assurance that the textual integrity of every poem or passage in this collection has been strictly observed.

I wish to thank the following for the generous loan of original texts and for supplying photographs: Mr. Nicolas Barker, Mr. John Carter, Mr. E. H. Dring (Bernard Quaritch Ltd.), Mr. Rupert Hart-Davis, Mr. B. C. Harding-Edgar (Charles Rare Books Ltd.), Mr. Dudley Massey (Pickering & Chatto Ltd.), Mr. John Grey Murray (John Murray Ltd.), the Oxford University Press, the University of London Library; and the following for their valuable help with the preparation of the copy text: Mr. David Foxon, Mr. R. J. Roberts, Mr. I. R. Willison (Assistant Keepers of Printed Books at the British Museum), Mr. Simon Nowell-Smith.

JOHN HAYWARD

Chelsea, 1963

ACKNOWLEDGEMENTS

FOR PERMISSION TO REPRINT AND PUBLISH COPYRIGHT MATERIAL:
The Syndics of the Fitzwilliam Museum, Cambridge, for the
extract from 'Esther' by Wilfrid Scawen Blunt; the Clarendon
Press, Oxford, for the poems by Robert Bridges; the Lady Alden-
ham for the poems by Digby Mackworth Dolben; the Oxford
University Press for the poem by Austin Dobson; the Very
Reverend Father Prior, Blackfriars, Oxford, for the extract from
'The Flying Fish' and the other poem by John Gray; the Trustees of
the Hardy Estate, Macmillan & Co. Ltd., the Macmillan Co. Inc.,
New York, for the poems by Thomas Hardy; the Oxford Univer-
sity Press for the poems by Gerard Manley Hopkins; the Society
of Authors, Jonathan Cape Ltd., Holt, Rinehart, & Winston, New
York, for the poems by A. E. Housman; Mrs. George Bambridge,
Methuen & Co. Ltd., Macmillan & Co. Ltd., the Macmillan Co.
Inc., New York, Doubleday & Co. Inc., New York, for the
poems by Rudyard Kipling; Mrs. Sylvia Mulvey for the poem by
Alice Meynell; Secker & Warburg Ltd. for the poems by Arthur
Symons; George Harrap & Co. Ltd. for the poem by Sir William
Watson. Titles and sources of the poems in question are given in
the list of Contents.

CONTENTS

TITLES of poems originally published separately are in italics. Titles supplied by the editor for extracts from longer poems are in square brackets —and in quotation marks if their wording is derived from the text or its context. Publication in a periodical is recorded as the earliest printed source only if a poem was not printed otherwise in its author's lifetime.

CONTENTS

CONTENTS

CONTENTS

CONTENTS

CONTENTS

CONTENTS

CONTENTS

CONTENTS

CONTENTS

CONTENTS

CONTENTS

CONTENTS

CONTENTS

CONTENTS

CONTENTS

CONTENTS

CONTENTS

CONTENTS

CONTENTS

CONTENTS

CONTENTS

CONTENTS

CONTENTS

CONTENTS

CONTENTS

GEORGE CRABBE

[The Pauper's Funeral]

Now once again the gloomy scene explore,
Less gloomy now; the bitter hour is o'er,
The Man of many Sorrows sighs no more.—
Up yonder hill, behold how sadly slow
The Bier moves winding from the vale below;
There lie the happy Dead from trouble free,
And the glad Parish pays the frugal fee;
No more, oh! Death, thy victim starts to hear
Churchwarden stern, or kingly Overseer;
No more the Farmer gets his humble bow,
Thou art his lord, the best of tyrants thou!

Now to the Church behold the Mourners come,
Sedately torpid and devoutly dumb;
The Village Children now their games suspend,
To see the Bier that bears their antient Friend;
For he was one in all their idle sport,
And like a monarch rul'd their little court;
The pliant Bow he form'd, the flying Ball,
The Bat, the Wicket, were his labours all;
Him now they follow to his grave, and stand
Silent and sad, and gazing, hand in hand;
While bending low, their eager eyes explore
The mingled relicks of the Parish Poor:
The bell tolls late, the moping owl flies round,
Fear marks the flight and magnifies the sound;
The busy Priest, detain'd by weightier care,
Defers his duty till the day of prayer;
And waiting long, the crowd retire distrest,
To think a Poor Man's bones should lie unblest.

[The Lady of The Manor]

NEXT died the Lady, who yon Hall possess'd;
And here they brought her noble Bones to rest.
In Town she dwelt;—forsaken stood the Hall:
Worms ate the Floors, the Tap'stry fled the Wall;
No Fire the Kitchen's cheerless Grate display'd;
No cheerful Light, the long-clos'd Sash convey'd!
The crawling Worm, that turns a Summer-Fly,
Here spun his Shroud and laid him up to die
The Winter-Death:—upon the Bed of State,
The Bat shrill-shrieking woo'd his flickering Mate;
To empty Rooms, the curious came no more,
From empty Cellars, turn'd the angry Poor,
And surly Beggars cursed the ever-bolted Door.
To one small Room, the Steward found his way,
Where Tenants follow'd to complain and pay;
Yet no Complaint before the LADY came,
The feeling servant spar'd the feeble Dame;
Who saw her Farms with his observing Eyes,
And answer'd all Requests with his Replies;
She came not down, her falling Groves to view;
Why should she know, what One so faithful knew?
Why come, from many clamorous Tongues to hear,
What One so just might whisper in her Ear?
Her Oaks or Acres, why with care explore,
Why learn the Wants, the Sufferings of the Poor,
When One so knowing, all their Worth could trace,
And One so piteous, govern'd in her Place?

Lo! now, what dismal Sons of Darkness come,
To bear this Daughter of Indulgence home!
Tragedians all and well arrang'd in Black!
Who Nature, Feeling, Force, Expression lack;—
Who cause no Tear, but gloomily pass by,

And shake their Sables in the wearied Eye,
That turns disgusted from the pompous Scene,
Proud without Grandeur, with Profusion, mean!
The Tear of Kindness past, Affection owes;
For Worth deceas'd, the Sigh from Reason flows;
E'en well-feign'd Passion for our Sorrows call,
And real Tears for mimic Miseries fall:—
But this poor Farce, has neither Truth nor Art,
To please the Fancy, or to touch the Heart;
Unlike the Darkness of the Sky, that pours
On the dry Ground, its fertilizing Showers;
Unlike to that, which strikes the Soul with Dread,
When Thunders roar and forky Fires are shed;
Dark but not aweful, dismal but yet mean,
With anxious Bustle moves the cumbrous scene;
Presents no Objects, tender or profound,
But spreads its cold, unmeaning Gloom around.

  When Woes are feign'd, how ill such Forms appear,
And oh! how needless, when the Woe's sincere.

  Slow to the Vault they come with heavy tread,
Bending beneath the Lady and her Lead;
A Case of Elm surrounds that ponderous Chest,
Close on that Case, the Crimson Velvet's press'd;
Ungenerous this, that to the Worm denies,
With niggard-caution, his appointed Prize;
For now, ere yet he works his tedious way,
Through Cloth and Wood and Metal, to his Prey;
That Prey dissolving, shall a Mass remain,
That Fancy loaths and Worms themselves disdain.

  But see! the Master-Mourner makes his way,
To end his Office, for the coffin'd Clay;
Pleas'd that our rustic Men and Maids behold
His Plate, like Silver, and his Studds, like Gold;
As they approach to spell the Age, the Name,

3

And all the Titles of th'illustrious Dame.—
This as, (my Duty done,) some Scholar read,
A Village-Father look'd Disdain, and said:
'Away, my Friends! why take such pains to know
What some brave Marble, soon in Church shall show?
Where not alone, her gracious Name shall stand,
But how she liv'd, the Blessing of the Land;
How much we all deplor'd the noble Dead,
What Groans we utter'd and what Tears we shed;—
Tears, true as those, that in the sleepy Eyes
Of weeping Cherubs, on the Stone shall rise;
Tears, true as those, that, ere she found her Grave,
The noble Lady to our Sorrows gave.'

3   ['An Ancient Virgin']

  DOWN by the Church-way Walk, and where the Brook
Winds round the Chancel, like a Shepherd's Crook;
In that small House, with those green Pales before,
Where Jasmine trails on either side the Door;
Where those dark Shrubs that now grow wild at will,
Were clipt in Form and tantaliz'd with Skill;
Where Cockles blanch'd, and Pebbles neatly spread,
Form'd shining Borders for the Larkspurs' Bed;—
There liv'd a LADY, wise, austere, and nice,
Who shew'd her Virtue, by her Scorn of Vice;
In the dear Fashions of her Youth she dress'd,
A pea-green *Joseph* was her favourite Vest;
Erect she stood, she walk'd with stately Mien,
Tight was her Length of Stays, and she was tall and lean.
  There long she liv'd in Maiden-State immur'd,
From Looks of Love and treacherous Man secur'd;

Though Evil-Fame—(but that was long before)
Had blown her dubious Blast at CATHERINE's Door:—
A Captain thither, rich from *India* came,
And though a Cousin call'd, it touch'd her Fame;
Her annual Stipend rose from his Behest,
And all the long-priz'd Treasures she possess'd:—
If aught like Joy awhile appear'd to stay
In that stern Face, and chase those Frowns away;
'Twas when those Treasures she dispos'd for View,
And heard the Praises, to their Splendour due;
Silks beyond Price, so rich they'd stand alone,
And Diamonds blazing on the buckled Zone;
Rows of rare Pearls, by curious Workmen set,
And Bracelets fair, in Box of glossy Jet;
Bright polish'd Amber precious from its Size,
Of Forms, the fairest Fancy could devise;
Her Draw'rs of Cedar, shut with secret Springs,
Conceal'd the golden Watch, the Ruby-Rings;
Letters, long Proofs of Love, and Verses fine
Round the pink'd Rims of crisped Valentine.
Her China Closet, cause of daily Care,
For Woman's Wonder, held her pencill'd Ware;
That pictur'd Wealth of *China* and *Japan*,
Like its cold Mistress, shunn'd the Eye of Man.

　　Her neat small Room, adorn'd with Maiden-Taste,
A clipt French-Puppy, first of Favourites, grac'd.
A Parrot next, but dead, and stuff'd with Art;
(For Poll, when living, lost the Lady's Heart,
And then his Life; for he was heard to speak
Such frightful Words as ting'd the Lady's Cheek;)
Unhappy Bird! who had no power to prove,
Save by such Speech, his gratitude, and Love.
A grey old Cat his Whiskers lick'd beside;
A Type of Sadness in the House of Pride.

The polish'd Surface of an India-Chest,
A glassy Globe, in Frame of Ivory, prest;
Where swam two finny Creatures; one of Gold,
Of Silver one; both beauteous to behold:
All these were form'd, the guiding Taste to suit;
The Beasts well-manner'd, and the Fishes mute:
A widow'd Aunt was there, compell'd by Need,
The Nymph to flatter and her Tribe to feed;
Who, veiling well her Scorn, endur'd the Clog,
Mute as the Fish and fawning as the Dog.

   As years increas'd, these Treasures her Delight,
Arose in value, in their Owner's sight:—
A Miser knows that, view it as he will,
A Guinea kept, is but a Guinea still:
And so he puts it to its proper Use,
That something more this Guinea may produce:
But Silks and Rings in the Possessor's Eyes,
The oft'ner seen, the more in Value rise,
And thus are wisely hoarded to bestow
The kind of pleasure that with years will grow.
But what avail'd their Worth,—if Worth had they,—
In the sad Summer of her slow Decay?
Then we beheld her turn an anxious Look
From Trunks and Chests, and fix it on her Book;
A rich-bound Book of Prayer, the Captain gave,
(Some Princess had it, or was said to have;)
And then once more, on all her Stores, look round,
And draw a sigh so piteous and profound,
That told 'Alas! how hard from these to part,
And for new Hopes and Habits form the Heart!
What shall I do (she cried) my Peace of Mind,
To gain in dying, and to die resign'd?'

[The Vicar]

BUT let applause be dealt in all we may,
Our Priest was cheerful, and in season gay;
His frequent visits seldom fail'd to please;
Easy himself, he sought his neighbour's ease;
To a small Garden with delight he came,
And gave successive Flowers a Summer's fame;
These he presented with a grace his own
To his fair Friends, and made their beauties known,
Not without moral compliment; how they,
'Like Flowers were sweet, and must like Flowers decay.'

Simple he was, and lov'd the simple Truth,
Yet had some useful Cunning, from his youth;
A Cunning never to Dishonour lent,
And rather for Defence than Conquest meant;
'Twas fear of Power, with some desire to rise,
But not enough to make him enemies;
He never aim'd to please; and to offend
Was ever cautious; for he sought a friend;
Yet for the friendship never much would pay,
Content to bow, be silent, and obey,
And by a soothing suff'rance find his way.

Fiddling and Fishing were his arts: at times
He alter'd Sermons, and he aim'd at Rhymes;
And his fair Friends, not yet intent on Cards,
Oft he amus'd with Riddles and Charades.

Mild were his Doctrines, and not one Discourse
But gain'd in softness what it lost in force;
Kind his Opinions; he would not receive
An ill report, nor evil act believe;
'If true, 'twas wrong; but blemish great or small
'Have all Mankind, yea, Sinners are we all.'

If ever fretful Thought disturb'd his breast,
If aught of Gloom that cheerful mind opprest,
It sprang from innovation; it was then
He spake of Mischief made by restless Men;
Not by new Doctrines: never in his life
Would he attend to controversial Strife;
For sects he car'd not; 'They are not of us,
'Nor need we, Brethren, their concerns discuss;
'But 'tis the change, the Schism at home I feel;
'Ills few perceive, and none have skill to heal;
'Not at the Altar our young Brethren read
'(Facing their Flock) the Decalogue and Creed;
'But at their Duty, in their Desks they stand,
'With naked Surplice, lacking Hood and Band:
'Churches are now of holy Song bereft,
'And half our antient Customs chang'd or left;
'Few Sprigs of Ivy are at Christmas seen,
'Nor crimson Berry tips the Holly's green;
'Mistaken Choirs refuse the solemn Strain
'Of ancient *Sternhold*, which from ours amain
'Comes flying forth from Aisle to Aisle about,
'Sweet links of Harmony and long drawn out.'

These were to him Essentials; all things new,
He deem'd superfluous, useless or untrue;
To all beside indifferent, easy, cold,
Here the fire kindled, and the woe was told.

Habit with him was all the test of Truth,
'It must be right: I've done it from my youth.'
Questions he answer'd in as brief a way,
'It must be wrong—it was of yesterday.'

Though mild Benevolence our Priest possess'd,
'Twas but by wishes or by words express'd:
Circles in water as they wider flow
The less conspicuous in their progress grow;

And when at last they touch upon the shore,
Distinction ceases, and they're view'd no more:
His Love, like that last Circle, all embrac'd,
But with effect that never could be trac'd.

Now rests our Vicar—They who knew him best,
Proclaim his Life t'have been entirely rest;
Free from all Evils which disturb his Mind,
Whom Studies vex and Controversies blind.

The Rich approv'd—of them in awe he stood;
The Poor admir'd—they all believ'd him good;
The Old and Serious of his Habits spoke;
The Frank and Youthful lov'd his pleasant Joke;
Mamma approv'd a safe contented Guest,
And Miss a Friend to back a small Request;
In him his Flock found nothing to condemn;
Him Sectaries lik'd—he never troubled them;
No trifles fail'd his yielding Mind to please,
And all his Passions sunk in early Ease;
Nor one so old has left this World of Sin,
More like the Being that he enter'd in.

5   ['Winter Views Serene']

THE Ocean too has Winter-Views serene,
When all you see through densest Fog is seen;
When you can hear the Fishers near at hand
Distinctly speak, yet see not where they stand;
Or sometimes them and not their Boat discern,
Or half-conceal'd some Figure at the Stern;
The View's all bounded, and from side to side
Your utmost Prospect but a few ells wide;
Boys who, on Shore, to Sea the Pebble cast,
Will hear it strike against the viewless Mast;

While the stern Boatman growls his fierce disdain,
At whom he knows not, whom he threats in vain.
   'Tis pleasant then to view the Nets float past,
Net after Net till you have seen the last;
And as you wait till all beyond you slip,
A Boat comes gliding from an anchor'd Ship,
Breaking the silence with the dipping Oar,
And their own Tones, as labouring for the Shore;
Those measur'd Tones which with the Scene agree,
And give a Sadness to Serenity.

6   ['Sailing upon the River']

   AMONG those Joys, 'tis one at Eve to sail
On the broad River with a favourite Gale;
When no rough Waves upon the Bosom ride,
But the Keel cuts, nor rises on the Tide;
Safe from the Stream the nearer Gunwale stands,
Where playful Children trail their idle Hands,
Or strive to catch long grassy Leaves that float
On either side of the impeded Boat:
What time the Moon arising shows the Mud,
A shining Border to the silver Flood;
When, by her dubious Light, the meanest Views,
Chalk, Stones and Stakes obtain the richest Hues;
And when the Cattle, as they gazing stand,
Seem nobler Objects than when view'd from Land:
Then anchor'd Vessels in the way appear,
And Sea-boys greet them as they pass—'What cheer?'
The sleeping Shell-ducks at the sound arise,
And utter loud their unharmonious Cries;
Fluttering they move their weedy Beds among,
Or instant diving, hide their plumeless Young.

7

[A Slum Dwelling]

Say, wilt thou more of Scenes so sordid know?
Then will I lead thee down the dusty Row;
By the warm Alley and the long close Lane,—
There mark the fractur'd Door and paper'd Pane,
Where flags the noon-tide Air, and as we pass,
We fear to breathe the putrifying Mass:
But fearless yonder Matron; she disdains
To sigh for Zephyrs from ambrosial Plains;
But mends her Meshes torn, and pours her Lay
All in the stifling Fervour of the Day.

Her naked Children round the Alley run,
And roll'd in Dust, are bronz'd beneath the Sun;
Or gamble round the Dame, who, loosely dress'd,
Woos the coy Breeze, to fan the open Breast:
She, once an Handmaid, strove by decent art
To charm her Sailor's Eye and touch his Heart;
Her Bosom then was veil'd in Kerchief clean,
And Fancy left to form the Charms unseen.

But when a Wife, she lost her former Care,
Nor thought on Charms, nor time for Dress could spare;
Careless she found her Friends who dwelt beside,
No rival Beauty kept alive her Pride:
Still in her bosom Virtue keeps her place,
But Decency is gone, the Virtue's Guard and Grace.

See that long boarded Building!—by these Stairs
Each humble Tenant to that Home repairs—
By one large Window lighted—it was made
For some bold Project, some design in Trade:
This fail'd,—and one, an Humourist in his way,
(Ill was the humour), bought it in decay;
Nor will he sell, repair, or take it down;
'Tis his,—what cares he for the talk of Town:

'No! he will let it to the Poor;—an Home
Where he delights to see the Creatures come:'
'They may be Thieves;'—'Well, so are richer Men;'
'Or Idlers, Cheats, or Prostitutes:'—'What then?'
'Outcasts pursued by Justice, vile and base;'—
'They need the more his Pity and the Place:'
Convert to System, his vain Mind has built,
He gives Asylum to Deceit and Guilt.

   In this vast Room, each Place by habit fixed,
Are Sexes, Families, and Ages mixt,—
To union forc'd by Crime, by Fear, by Need,
And all in Morals and in Modes agreed;
Some ruin'd Men, who from Mankind remove;
Some ruin'd Females, who yet talk of Love,
And some grown old in Idleness—the prey
To vicious Spleen, still railing through the Day;
And Need and Misery, Vice and Danger bind
In sad Alliance each degraded Mind.

   That Window view!—oil'd Paper and old Glass
Stain the strong Rays, which, though impeded, pass,
And give a dusty Warmth to that huge Room,
The conquer'd Sunshine's melancholy gloom;
When all those Western Rays, without so bright,
Within become a ghastly glimmering Light,
As pale and faint upon the Floor they fall,
Or feebly gleam on the opposing Wall:
That Floor, once Oak, now piec'd with Fir unplan'd,
Or, where not piec'd, in places bor'd and stain'd;
That Wall once whiten'd, now an odious sight,
Stain'd with all Hues, except its antient White;
The only Door is fasten'd by a Pin,
Or stubborn Bar, that none may hurry in:
For this poor Room, like Rooms of greater pride,
At times contains what prudent Men would hide.

Where'er the Floor allows an even space,
Chalking and Marks of various Games have place;
Boys, without foresight, pleas'd in Halters swing;
On a fix'd Hook Men cast a flying Ring;
While Gin and Snuff their female Neighbours share,
And the black Beverage in the fractur'd Ware.

On swinging Shelf are things incongruous stor'd,—
Scraps of their Food,—the Cards and Cribbage-board,—
With Pipes and Pouches; while on Peg below,
Hang a lost Member's Fiddle and its Bow;
That still reminds them how he'd dance and play,
Ere sent untimely to the Convicts' Bay.

Here by a Curtain, by a Blanket there,
Are various Beds conceal'd, but none with care;
Where some by Day and some by Night, as best
Suit their Employments, seek uncertain Rest;
The drowsy Children at their pleasure creep
To the known Crib and there securely sleep.

Each end contains a Grate, and these beside
Are hung Utensils for their boil'd and fry'd—
All used at any hour, by Night, by Day,
As suit the Purse, the Person, or the Prey.

Above the Fire, the Mantel-Shelf contains
Of China-Ware some poor unmatch'd remains;
There many a tea-cup's gaudy fragment stands,
All plac'd by Vanity's unwearied hands;
For here she lives, e'en here she looks about,
To find some small consoling Objects out:
Nor heed these Spartan Dames their House, nor sit
'Mid Cares domestic,—they nor sew nor knit;
But of their Fate discourse, their Ways, their Wars,
With arm'd Authorities, their 'Scapes and Scars:
These lead to present Evils, and a Cup,
If Fortune grant it, winds Description up.

High hung at either end, and next the wall,
Two ancient Mirrors show the forms of all,
In all their force;—these aid them in their Dress,
But with the Good, the Evils too express,
Doubling each look of Care, each token of Distress.

8   ⌜ Peter Grimes ⌝

THUS by himself compell'd to live each day,
To wait for certain hours the Tide's delay;
At the same times the same dull views to see,
The bounding Marsh-bank and the blighted Tree;
The Water only, when the Tides were high,
When low, the Mud half-cover'd and half-dry;
The Sun-burn'd Tar that blisters on the Planks,
And Bank-side Stakes in their uneven ranks;
Heaps of entangled Weeds that slowly float,
As the Tide rolls by the impeded Boat.
When Tides were neap, and, in the sultry day,
Through the tall bounding Mud-banks made their way,
Which on each side rose swelling, and below
The dark warm Flood ran silently and slow;
There anchoring, *Peter* chose from Man to hide,
There hang his Head, and view the lazy Tide
In its hot slimy Channel slowly glide;
Where the small Eels that left the deeper way
For the warm Shore, within the Shallows play;
Where gaping Muscles, left upon the Mud,
Slope their slow passage to the fallen Flood;—
Here dull and hopeless he'd lie down and trace
How side-long Crabs had scrawl'd their crooked race;
Or sadly listen to the tuneless cry
Of fishing *Gull* or clanging *Golden-Eye*;

What time the Sea-Birds to the marsh would come, ⎫
And the loud *Bittern*, from the Bull-rush home, ⎬
Gave from the Salt-ditch side the bellowing Boom: ⎭
He nurst the Feelings these dull Scenes produce,
And lov'd to stop beside the opening Sluice;
Where the small Stream, confin'd in narrow bound,
Ran with a dull, unvaried, sad'ning sound;
Where all presented to the Eye or Ear,
Oppress'd the Soul with Misery, Grief and Fear.

9   ⌈Jonas Kindred's Household⌉

PEACE in the sober house of *Jonas* dwelt,
Where each his duty and his station felt:
Yet not that peace some favour'd mortals find,
In equal views and harmony of mind;
Not the soft peace that blesses those who love,
Where all with one consent in union move;
But it was that which one superior will
Commands, by making all inferiors still;
Who bids all murmurs, all objections cease,
And with imperious voice announces—Peace!
    They were, to wit, a remnant of that crew,
Who, as their foes maintain, their Sovereign slew;
An independent race, precise, correct,
Who ever married in the kindred sect;
No son or daughter of their order wed
A friend to *England*'s king who lost his head;
Cromwell was still their Saint, and when they met,
They mourn'd that Saints were not our Rulers yet.
    Fix'd were their habits; they arose betimes,
Then pray'd their hour, and sang their party-rhymes;
Their meals were plenteous, regular, and plain;
The trade of *Jonas* brought him constant gain;

Vendor of Hops and Malt, of Coals and Corn—
And, like his father, he was Merchant born:
Neat was their house; each table, chair, and stool,
Stood in its place, or moving mov'd by rule;
No lively print or picture grac'd the room;
A plain brown paper lent its decent gloom;
But here the eye, in glancing round, survey'd
A small Recess that seem'd for china made;
Such pleasing pictures seem'd this pencill'd ware,
That few would search for nobler objects there—
Yet, turn'd by chosen friends, and there appear'd
His stern, strong features, whom they all revered;
For there in lofty air was seen to stand
The bold Protector of the conquer'd land;
Drawn in that look with which he wept and swore,
Turn'd out the Members and made fast the door,
Ridding the House of every knave and drone,
Forc'd, though it griev'd his soul, to rule alone.
The stern still smile each Friend approving gave,
Then turn'd the view, and all again were grave.

    There stood a Clock, though small the owner's need,
For habit told when all things should proceed;
Few their amusements, but when Friends appear'd,
They with the world's distress their spirits cheer'd;
The nation's guilt, that would not long endure
The reign of men so modest and so pure:
Their town was large, and seldom pass'd a day
But some had fail'd, and others gone astray;
Clerks had absconded, wives elop'd, girls flown
To Gretna-Green, or sons rebellious grown;
Quarrels and fires arose!—and it was plain
The times were bad; the Saints had ceas'd to reign!
A few yet liv'd, to languish and to mourn
For good old manners never to return.

10 ## ['The Sad Lover']

THAT evening all in fond discourse was spent,
When the sad lover to his chamber went,
To think on what had past, to grieve and to repent:
Early he rose, and look'd with many a sigh
On the red light that fill'd the eastern sky;
Oft had he stood before, alert and gay,
To hail the glories of the new-born day:
But now dejected, languid, listless, low,
He saw the wind upon the water blow,
And the cold stream curl'd onward as the gale
From the pine-hill blew harshly down the dale;
On the right side the youth a wood survey'd,
With all its dark intensity of shade;
Where the rough wind alone was heard to move,
In this, the pause of nature and of love,
When now the young are rear'd, and when the old,
Lost to the tie, grow negligent and cold—
Far to the left he saw the huts of men,
Half hid in mist, that hung upon the fen;
Before him swallows, gathering for the sea,
Took their short flights, and twitter'd on the lea;
And near the bean-sheaf stood, the harvest done,
And slowly blacken'd in the sickly sun;
All these were sad in nature, or they took
Sadness from him, the likeness of his look,
And of his mind—he ponder'd for a while,
Then met his Fanny with a borrow'd smile.

11 ## His Mother's Wedding Ring

THE ring so worn, as you behold,
So thin, so pale, is yet of gold:
The passion such it was to prove;
Worn with life's cares, love yet was love.

WILLIAM BLAKE

12 ## Song

How sweet I roam'd from field to field,
  And tasted all the summer's pride,
'Till I the prince of love beheld,
  Who in the sunny beams did glide!

He shew'd me lilies for my hair,
  And blushing roses for my brow;
He led me through his gardens fair
  Where all his golden pleasures grow.

With sweet May dews my wings were wet,
  And Phœbus fir'd my vocal rage;
He caught me in his silken net,
  And shut me in his golden cage.

He loves to sit and hear me sing,
  Then, laughing, sports and plays with me;
Then stretches out my golden wing,
  And mocks my loss of liberty.

13   ## Song

My silks and fine array,
    My smiles and languish'd air,
By love are driv'n away;
    And mournful lean Despair
Brings me yew to deck my grave:
Such end true lovers have.

His face is fair as heav'n,
    When springing buds unfold;
O why to him was't giv'n,
    Whose heart is wintry cold?
His breast is love's all worship'd tomb,
Where all love's pilgrims come.

Bring me an axe and a spade,
    Bring me a winding sheet;
When I my grave have made,
    Let winds and tempests beat:
Then down I'll lie, as cold as clay.
True love doth pass away!

14   ## Introduction [to *Songs of Innocence*]

PIPING down the valleys wild,
Piping songs of pleasant glee,
On a cloud I saw a child,
And he laughing said to me:

'Pipe a song about a Lamb!'
So I piped with merry chear.
'Piper, pipe that song again;'
So I piped: he wept to hear.

'Drop thy pipe, thy happy pipe;
'Sing thy songs of happy chear:'
So I sung the same again,
While he wept with joy to hear.

'Piper, sit thee down and write
'In a book, that all may read.'
So he vanish'd from my sight,
And I pluck'd a hollow reed,

And I made a rural pen,
And I stain'd the water clear,
And I wrote my happy songs
Every child may joy to hear.

15

The Divine Image

To Mercy, Pity, Peace, and Love
All pray in their distress;
And to these virtues of delight
Return their thankfulness.

For Mercy, Pity, Peace, and Love
Is God, our father dear,
And Mercy, Pity, Peace, and Love
Is Man, his child and care.

For Mercy has a human heart,
Pity a human face,
And Love, the human form divine,
And Peace, the human dress.

Then every man, of every clime,
That prays in his distress,
Prays to the human form divine,
Love, Mercy, Pity, Peace.

And all must love the human form,
In heathen, turk, or jew;
Where Mercy, Love, & Pity dwell
There God is dwelling too.

16 ## The Little Black Boy

MY mother bore me in the southern wild,
And I am black, but O! my soul is white;
White as an angel is the English child,
But I am black, as if bereav'd of light.

My mother taught me underneath a tree,
And sitting down before the heat of day,
She took me on her lap and kissed me,
And pointing to the east, began to say:

'Look on the rising sun: there God does live,
'And gives his light, and gives his heat away;
'And flowers and trees and beasts and men receive
'Comfort in morning, joy in the noonday.

'And we are put on earth a little space,
'That we may learn to bear the beams of love;
'And these black bodies and this sunburnt face
'Is but a cloud, and like a shady grove.

'For when our souls have learn'd the heat to bear,
'The cloud will vanish; we shall hear his voice,
'Saying: "Come out from the grove, my love & care,
' "And round my golden tent like lambs rejoice." '

Thus did my mother say, and kissed me;
And thus I say to little English boy.
When I from black and he from white cloud free,
And round the tent of God like lambs we joy,

I'll shade him from the heat, till he can bear
To lean in joy upon our father's knee;
And then I'll stand and stroke his silver hair,
And be like him, and he will then love me.

17   The Clod and the Pebble

'LOVE seeketh not Itself to please,
Nor for itself hath any care,
But for another gives its ease,
And builds a Heaven in Hell's despair.'

So sung a little Clod of Clay
Trodden with the cattle's feet.
But a Pebble of the brook
Warbled out these metres meet:

'Love seeketh only Self to please,
To bind another to Its delight,
Joys in another's loss of ease,
And builds a Hell in Heaven's despite.'

18   The Sick Rose

O ROSE, thou art sick!
The invisible worm
That flies in the night
In the howling storm,

Has found out thy bed
Of crimson joy:
And his dark secret love
Does thy life destroy.

The Tyger

19

TYGER! Tyger! burning bright
In the forests of the night,
What immortal hand or eye
Could frame thy fearful symmetry?

In what distant deeps or skies
Burnt the fire of thine eyes?
On what wings dare he aspire?
What the hand dare sieze the fire?

And what shoulder, & what art,
Could twist the sinews of thy heart?
And when thy heart began to beat,
What dread hand? & what dread feet?

What the hammer? what the chain?
In what furnace was thy brain?
What the anvil? what dread grasp
Dare its deadly terrors clasp?

When the stars threw down their spears,
And water'd heaven with their tears,
Did he smile his work to see?
Did he who made the Lamb make thee?

Tyger! Tyger! burning bright
In the forests of the night,
What immortal hand or eye,
Dare frame thy fearful symmetry?

20

Ah! Sun-flower

Ah, Sun-flower, weary of time,
Who countest the steps of the Sun,
Seeking after that sweet golden clime
Where the traveller's journey is done:

Where the Youth pined away with desire,
And the pale Virgin shrouded in snow
Arise from their graves, and aspire
Where my Sun-flower wishes to go.

21

London

I wander thro' each charter'd street,
Near where the charter'd Thames does flow,
And mark in every face I meet
Marks of weakness, marks of woe.

In every cry of every Man,
In every Infant's cry of fear,
In every voice, in every ban,
The mind-forg'd manacles I hear.

How the Chimney-sweeper's cry
Every black'ning Church appalls;
And the hapless Soldier's sigh
Runs in blood down Palace walls.

But most thro' midnight streets I hear
How the youthful Harlot's curse
Blasts the new born Infant's tear,
And blights with plagues the Marriage hearse.

22 ## Infant Sorrow

My mother groan'd! my father wept.
Into the dangerous world I leapt:
Helpless, naked, piping loud:
Like a fiend hid in a cloud.

Struggling in my father's hands,
Striving against my swadling bands,
Bound and weary I thought best
To sulk upon my mother's breast.

23 ## A Divine Image

CRUELTY has a Human Heart,
And Jealousy a Human Face;
Terror the Human Form Divine,
And Secrecy the Human Dress.

The Human Dress is forged Iron,
The Human Form a fiery Forge,
The Human Face a Furnace seal'd,
The Human Heart its hungry Gorge.

24

NEVER seek to tell thy love
Love that never told can be;
For the gentle wind does move
Silently, invisibly.

I told my love, I told my love,
I told her all my heart,
Trembling, cold, in ghastly fears—
Ah, she doth depart.

Soon as she was gone from me
A traveller came by
Silently, invisibly—
O, was no deny.

25   I ASKED a thief to steal me a peach:
He turned up his eyes.
I ask'd a lithe lady to lie her down:
Holy & meek she cries—

As soon as I went
An angel came.
He wink'd at the thief
And smil'd at the dame.

And without one word said
Had a peach from the tree,
And still as a maid
Enjoy'd the Lady.

26   Eternity

HE who bends to himself a joy
Does the winged life destroy;
But he who kisses the joy as it flies
Lives in eternity's sun rise.

27   MOCK on, Mock on Voltaire, Rousseau:
Mock on, Mock on: 'tis all in vain!
You throw the sand against the wind,
And the wind blows it back again.

And every sand becomes a Gem
Reflected in the beams divine;
Blown back they blind the mocking Eye,
But still in Israel's paths they shine.

The Atoms of Democritus
And Newton's Particles of light
Are sands upon the Red sea shore,
Where Israel's tents do shine so bright.

28 ## The Crystal Cabinet

THE Maiden caught me in the Wild,
Where I was dancing merrily;
She put me into her Cabinet
And Lock'd me up with a golden Key.

This Cabinet is form'd of Gold
And Pearl & Crystal shining bright,
And within it opens into a World
And a little lovely Moony Night.

Another England there I saw,
Another London with its Tower,
Another Thames & other Hills,
And another pleasant Surrey Bower.

Another Maiden like herself,
Translucent, lovely, shining clear,
Threefold each in the other clos'd—
O, what a pleasant trembling fear!

O, what a smile! a threefold Smile
Fill'd me, that like a flame I burn'd;
I bent to Kiss the lovely Maid,
And found a Threefold Kiss return'd.

I strove to sieze the inmost Form
With ardor fierce & hands of flame,
But burst the Crystal Cabinet,
And like a Weeping Babe became—

A weeping Babe upon the wild,
And Weeping Woman pale reclin'd,
And in the outward air again
I fill'd with woes the passing Wind.

29   Auguries of Innocence

To see a World in a Grain of Sand
And a Heaven in a Wild Flower,
Hold Infinity in the palm of your hand
And Eternity in an hour.

A Robin Red breast in a Cage
Puts all Heaven in a Rage,
A dove house fill'd with doves & Pigeons
Shudders Hell thro' all its regions.
A dog starv'd at his Master's Gate
Predicts the ruin of the State.
A Horse misus'd upon the Road
Calls to Heaven for Human blood.
Each outcry of the hunted Hare
A fibre from the Brain does tear

A Skylark wounded in the wing,
A Cherubim does cease to sing.
The Game Cock clip'd & arm'd for fight
Does the Rising Sun affright.
Every Wolf's & Lion's howl
Raises from Hell a Human Soul.
The wild deer, wand'ring here & there,
Keeps the Human Soul from Care.
The Lamb misus'd breeds Public strife
And yet forgives the Butcher's Knife.
The Bat that flits at close of Eve
Has left the Brain that won't Believe.
The Owl that calls upon the Night
Speaks the Unbeliever's fright.
He who shall hurt the little Wren
Shall never be belov'd by Men.
He who the Ox to wrath has mov'd
Shall never be by Woman lov'd.
The wanton Boy that kills the Fly
Shall feel the Spider's enmity.
He who torments the Chafer's sprite
Weaves a Bower in endless Night.
The Catterpiller on the Leaf
Repeats to thee thy Mother's grief.
Kill not the Moth nor Butterfly,
For the Last Judgment draweth nigh.
He who shall train the Horse to War
Shall never pass the Polar Bar.
The Begger's Dog & Widow's Cat,
Feed them & thou wilt grow fat.
The Gnat that sings his Summer's song
Poison gets from Slander's tongue.
The poison of the Snake & Newt
Is the sweat of Envy's Foot.

The Poison of the Honey Bee
Is the Artist's Jealousy.
The Prince's Robes & Beggar's Rags
Are Toadstools on the Miser's Bags.
A truth that's told with bad intent
Beats all the Lies you can invent.
It is right it should be so;
Man was made for Joy & Woe;
And when this we rightly know
Thro' the World we safely go.
Joy & Woe are woven fine,
A Clothing for the Soul divine;
Under every grief & pine
Runs a joy with silken twine.
The Babe is more than swadling Bands;
Throughout all these Human Lands
Tools were made, & Born were hands,
Every Farmer Understands.
Every Tear from Every Eye
Becomes a Babe in Eternity;
This is caught by Females bright
And return'd to its own delight.
The Bleat, the Bark, Bellow & Roar
Are Waves that Beat on Heaven's Shore.
The Babe that weeps the Rod beneath
Writes Revenge in realms of death.
The Beggar's Rags, fluttering in Air,
Does to Rags the Heavens tear.
The Soldier, arm'd with Sword & Gun,
Palsied strikes the Summer's Sun.
The poor Man's Farthing is worth more
Than all the Gold on Afric's Shore.
One Mite wrung from the Labrer's hands
Shall buy & sell the Miser's Lands:

Or, if protected from on high,
Does that whole Nation sell & buy.
He who mocks the Infant's Faith
Shall be mock'd in Age & Death.
He who shall teach the Child to Doubt
The rotting Grave shall ne'er get out.
He who respects the Infant's faith
Triumphs over Hell & Death.
The Child's Toys & the Old Man's Reasons
Are the Fruits of the Two seasons.
The Questioner, who sits so sly,
Shall never know how to Reply.
He who replies to words of Doubt
Doth put the Light of Knowledge out.
The Strongest Poison ever known
Came from Caesar's Laurel Crown.
Nought can deform the Human Race
Like to the Armour's iron brace.
When Gold & Gems adorn the Plow
To peaceful Arts shall Envy Bow.
A Riddle or the Cricket's Cry
Is to Doubt a fit Reply.
The Emmet's Inch & Eagle's Mile
Make Lame Philosophy to smile.
He who Doubts from what he sees
Will ne'er Believe, do what you Please.
If the Sun & Moon should doubt,
They'd immediately Go out.
To be in a Passion you Good may do,
But no Good if a Passion is in you.
The Whore & Gambler, by the State
Licenc'd, build that Nation's Fate.
The Harlot's cry from Street to Street
Shall weave Old England's winding Sheet.

The Winner's Shout, the Loser's Curse,
Dance before dead England's Hearse.
Every Night & every Morn
Some to Misery are Born.
Every Morn & every Night
Some are Born to sweet delight.
Some are Born to sweet delight,
Some are Born to Endless Night.
We are led to Believe a Lie
When we see not Thro' the Eye
Which was Born in a Night to perish in a Night
When the Soul Slept in Beams of Light.
God Appears & God is Light
To those poor Souls who dwell in Night,
But does a Human Form Display
To those who Dwell in Realms of day.

30   *THE BOOK OF THEL*

THEL'S MOTTO

Does the Eagle know what is in the pit?
Or wilt thou go ask the Mole?
Can Wisdom be put in a silver rod?
Or Love in a golden bowl?

I

THE daughters of Mne Seraphim led round their sunny flocks,
All but the youngest: she in paleness sought the secret air,
To fade away like morning beauty from her mortal day:
Down by the river of Adona her soft voice is heard,
And thus her gentle lamentation falls like morning dew:

'O life of this our spring! why fades the lotus of the water,
'Why fade these children of the spring, born but to smile & fall?
'Ah! Thel is like a wat'ry bow, and like a parting cloud;
'Like a reflection in a glass; like shadows in the water;
'Like dreams of infants, like a smile upon an infant's face;
'Like the dove's voice; like transient day; like music in the air.
'Ah! gentle may I lay me down, and gentle rest my head,
'And gentle sleep the sleep of death, and gentle hear the voice
'Of him that walketh in the garden in the evening time.'

The Lilly of the valley, breathing in the humble grass,
Answer'd the lovely maid and said: 'I am a wat'ry weed,
'And I am very small and love to dwell in lowly vales;
'So weak, the gilded butterfly scarce perches on my head.
'Yet I am visited from heaven, and he that smiles on all
'Walks in the valley and each morn over me spreads his hand,
'Saying, "Rejoice, thou humble grass, thou new-born lilly flower,
' "Thou gentle maid of silent valleys and of modest brooks;
' "For thou shalt be clothed in light, and fed with morning manna,
' "Till summer's heat melts thee beside the fountains and the
        springs
' "To flourish in eternal vales." Then why should Thel complain?
'Why should the mistress of the vales of Har utter a sigh?'

She ceas'd & smil'd in tears, then sat down in her silver shrine.

Thel answer'd: 'O thou little virgin of the peaceful valley,
'Giving to those that cannot crave, the voiceless, the o'ertired;
'Thy breath doth nourish the innocent lamb, he smells thy milky
        garments,
'He crops thy flowers while thou sittest smiling in his face,
'Wiping his mild and meekin mouth from all contagious taints.
'Thy wine doth purify the golden honey; thy perfume,
'Which thou dost scatter on every little blade of grass that springs,

'Revives the milked cow, & tames the fire-breathing steed.
'But Thel is like a faint cloud kindled at the rising sun:
'I vanish from my pearly throne, and who shall find my place?'

'Queen of the vales,' the Lilly answer'd, 'ask the tender cloud,
'And it shall tell thee why it glitters in the morning sky,
'And why it scatters its bright beauty thro' the humid air.
'Descend, O little Cloud, & hover before the eyes of Thel.'

   The Cloud descended, and the Lilly bow'd her modest head
And went to mind her numerous charge among the verdant grass.

II

'O little Cloud,' the virgin said, 'I charge thee tell to me
'Why thou complainest not when in one hour thou fade away:
'Then we shall seek thee, but not find. Ah! Thel is like to thee:
'I pass away: yet I complain, and no one hears my voice.'

The Cloud then shew'd his golden head & his bright form emerg'd,
Hovering and glittering on the air before the face of Thel.

'O virgin, know'st thou not our steeds drink of the golden springs
'Where Luvah doth renew his horses? Look'st thou on my youth,
'And fearest thou, because I vanish and am seen no more,
'Nothing remains? O maid, I tell thee, when I pass away
'It is to tenfold life, to love, to peace and raptures holy:
'Unseen descending, weigh my light wings upon balmy flowers,
'And court the fair-eyed dew to take me to her shining tent:
'The weeping virgin, trembling kneels before the risen sun,
'Till we arise link'd in a golden band and never part,
'But walk united, bearing food to all our tender flowers.'

'Dost thou, O little Cloud? I fear that I am not like thee,
'For I walk thro' the vales of Har, and smell the sweetest flowers,

'But I feed not the little flowers; I hear the warbling birds,
'But I feed not the warbling birds; they fly and seek their food:
'But Thel delights in these no more, because I fade away;
'And all shall say, "Without a use this shining woman liv'd,
' "Or did she only live to be at death the food of worms?" '

The Cloud reclin'd upon his airy throne and answer'd thus:

'Then if thou art the food of worms, O virgin of the skies,
'How great thy use, how great thy blessing! Every thing that lives
'Lives not alone nor for itself. Fear not, and I will call
'The weak worm from its lowly bed, and thou shalt hear its voice.
'Come forth, worm of the silent valley, to thy pensive queen.'

The helpless worm arose, and sat upon the Lilly's leaf,
And the bright Cloud sail'd on, to find his partner in the vale.

III

Then Thel astonish'd view'd the Worm upon its dewy bed.

'Art thou a Worm? Image of weakness, art thou but a Worm?
'I see thee like an infant wrapped in the Lilly's leaf.
'Ah! weep not, little voice, thou canst not speak, but thou canst
        weep.
'Is this a Worm? I see thee lay helpless & naked, weeping,
'And none to answer, none to cherish thee with mother's smiles.'

The Clod of Clay heard the Worm's voice & rais'd her pitying
        head:
She bow'd over the weeping infant, and her life exhal'd
In milky fondness: then on Thel she fix'd her humble eyes.

'O beauty of the vales of Har! we live not for ourselves.
'Thou seest me the meanest thing, and so I am indeed.

'My bosom of itself is cold, and of itself is dark;
'But he, that loves the lowly, pours his oil upon my head,
'And kisses me, and binds his nuptial bands around my breast,
'And says: "Thou mother of my children, I have loved thee
' "And I have given thee a crown that none can take away."
'But how this is, sweet maid, I know not, and I cannot know;
'I ponder, and I cannot ponder; yet I live and love.'

The daughter of beauty wip'd her pitying tears with her white
    veil,
And said: 'Alas! I knew not this, and therefore did I weep.
'That God would love a Worm I knew, and punish the evil foot
'That wilful bruis'd its helpless form; but that he cherish'd it
'With milk and oil I never knew, and therefore did I weep;
'And I complain'd in the mild air, because I fade away,
'And lay me down in thy cold bed, and leave my shining lot.'

'Queen of the vales,' the matron Clay answer'd, 'I heard thy sighs,
'And all thy moans flew o'er my roof, but I have call'd them down.
'Wilt thou, O Queen, enter my house? 'Tis given thee to enter
'And to return: fear nothing, enter with thy virgin feet.'

IV

The eternal gates' terrific porter lifted the northern bar:
Thel enter'd in & saw the secrets of the land unknown.
She saw the couches of the dead, & where the fibrous roots
Of every heart on earth infixes deep its restless twists:
A land of sorrows & of tears where never smile was seen.

She wander'd in the land of clouds thro' valleys dark, list'ning
Dolours & lamentations; waiting oft beside a dewy grave
She stood in silence, list'ning to the voices of the ground,
Till to her own grave plot she came, & there she sat down,
And heard this voice of sorrow breathed from the hollow pit.

'Why cannot the Ear be closed to its own destruction?
'Or the glist'ning Eye to the poison of a smile?
'Why are Eyelids stor'd with arrows ready drawn,
'Where a thousand fighting men in ambush lie?
'Or an Eye of gifts & graces show'ring fruits & coined gold?
'Why a Tongue impress'd with honey from every wind?
'Why an Ear, a whirlpool fierce to draw creations in?
'Why a Nostril wide inhaling terror, trembling, & affright?
'Why a tender curb upon the youthful burning boy?
'Why a little curtain of flesh on the bed of our desire?'

The Virgin started from her seat, & with a shriek
Fled back unhinder'd till she came into the vales of Har.

from *VALA or THE FOUR ZOAS*

31   ['The Lamentation of Enion']

WHY does the Raven cry aloud and no eye pities her?
Why fall the Sparrow & the Robin in the foodless winter?
Faint, shivering, they sit on leafless bush or frozen stone

Wearied with seeking food across the snowy waste, the little
Heart cold, and the little tongue consum'd that once in thought-
    less joy
Gave songs of gratitude to waving cornfields round their nest.

Why howl the Lion & the Wolf? why do they roam abroad?
Deluded by summer's heat, they sport in enormous love
And cast their young out to the hungry wilds & sandy desarts.

Why is the Sheep given to the knife? the Lamb plays in the Sun:
He starts! he hears the foot of Man! he says: Take thou my wool,
But spare my life: *but* he knows not that winter cometh fast.

The Spider sits in his labour'd Web, eager watching for the Fly.
Presently comes a famish'd Bird & takes away the Spider.
His Web is left all desolate that his little anxious heart
So careful wove & spread it out with sighs and weariness.

32 [Enitharmon Revives with Los]

I sieze the sphery harp. I strike the strings.

At the first sound the Golden sun arises from the deep
And shakes his awful hair,
The Eccho wakes the moon to unbind her silver locks,
The golden sun bears on my song
And nine bright spheres of harmony rise round the fiery king.

The joy of woman is the death of her most best beloved
Who dies for Love of her
In torments of fierce jealousy & pangs of adoration.
The Lovers' night bears on my song
And the nine spheres rejoice beneath my powerful controll.

They sing unceasing to the notes of my immortal hand.
The solemn, silent moon
Reverberates the living harmony upon my limbs,
The birds & beasts rejoice & play,
And every one seeks for his mate to prove his inmost joy.

Furious & terrible they sport & red the nether deep;
The deep lifts up his rugged head,
And lost in infinite hum[m]ing wings vanishes with a cry.
The fading cry is ever dying,
The living voice is ever living in its inmost joy.

Arise, you little glancing wings & sing your infant joy!
Arise & drink your bliss!
For every thing that lives is holy; for the source of life
Descends to be a weeping babe;
For the Earthworm renews the moisture of the sandy plain.

Now my left hand I stretch to earth beneath,
And strike the terrible string.
I wake sweet joy in dens of sorrow & I plant a smile
In forests of affliction,
And wake the bubbling springs of life in regions of dark death.

O, I am weary! lay thine hand upon me or I faint,
I faint beneath these beams of thine,
For thou hast touch'd my five senses & they answer'd thee.
Now I am nothing, & I sink
And on the bed of silence sleep till thou awakest me.

33 ['Enion Replies from the Caverns of the Grave']

LISTEN. I will tell thee what is done in the caverns of the grave.
The Lamb of God has rent the Veil of Mystery, soon to return
In Clouds & Fires around the rock & the Mysterious tree.
And as the seed waits Eagerly watching for its flower & fruit,
Anxious its little soul looks out into the clear expanse
To see if hungry winds are abroad with their invisible army,
So Man looks out in tree & herb & fish & bird & beast
Collecting up the scatter'd portions of his immortal body
Into the Elemental forms of every thing that grows.
He tries the sullen north wind, riding on its angry furrows,
The sultry south when the sun rises, & the angry east
When the sun sets; when the clods harden & the cattle stand

Drooping & the birds hide in their silent nests, he stores his
    thoughts
As in a store house in his memory; he regulates the forms
Of all beneath & all above, & in the gentle West
Reposes where the Sun's heat dwells; he rises to the Sun
And to the Planets of the Night, & to the stars that gild
The Zodiac, & the stars that sullen stand to north & south.
He touches the remotest pole, & in the center weeps
That Man should Labour & sorrow, & learn & forget, & return
To the dark valley whence he came, to begin his labour anew.
In pain he sighs, in pain he labours in his universe,
Sorrowing in birds over the deep, & howling in the wolf
Over the slain, & moaning in the cattle, & in the winds,
And weeping over Orc & Urizen in clouds & *flaming* fires,
And in the cries of birth & in the groans of death his voice
Is heard throughout the Universe: wherever a grass grows
Or a leaf buds, The Eternal Man is seen, is heard, is felt,
And all his sorrows, till he reassumes his ancient bliss.

from *MILTON*

34   ⌈Prelude⌉

    AND did those feet in ancient time
    Walk upon England's mountains green?
    And was the holy Lamb of God
    On England's pleasant pastures seen?

    And did the Countenance Divine
    Shine forth upon our clouded hills?
    And was Jerusalem builded here
    Among these dark Satanic Mills?

Bring me my Bow of burning gold:
Bring me my Arrows of desire:
Bring me my Spear: O clouds unfold!
Bring me my Chariot of fire.

I will not cease from Mental Fight,
Nor shall my Sword sleep in my hand
Till we have built Jerusalem
In England's green & pleasant Land.

35 ['A Vision of the Lamentation of Beulah over Ololon']

THOU hearest the Nightingale begin the Song of Spring.
The Lark sitting upon his earthy bed, just as the morn
Appears, listens silent; then springing from the waving Cornfield,
    loud
He leads the Choir of Day: trill, trill, trill, trill,
Mounting upon the wings of light into the Great Expanse,
Reechoing against the lovely blue & shining heavenly Shell,
His little throat labours with inspiration; every feather
On throat & breast & wings vibrates with the effluence Divine.
All Nature listens silent to him, & the awful Sun
Stands still upon the Mountain looking on this little Bird
With eyes of soft humility & wonder, love & awe.
Then loud from their green covert all the Birds begin their Song:
The Thrush, the Linnet & the Goldfinch, Robin & the Wren
Awake the Sun from his sweet reverie upon the Mountain.
The Nightingale again assays his song, & thro' the day
And thro' the night warbles luxuriant, every Bird of Song
Attending his loud harmony with admiration & love.

Thou percievest the Flowers put forth their precious Odours,
And none can tell how from so small a center comes such sweets,
Forgetting that within that Center Eternity expands
Its ever during doors that Og & Anak fiercely guard.
First, e'er the morning breaks, joy opens in the flowery bosoms,
Joy even to tears, which the Sun rising dries; first the Wild Thyme
And Meadow-sweet, downy & soft waving among the reeds,
Light springing on the air, lead the sweet Dance: they wake
The Honeysuckle sleeping on the Oak; the flaunting beauty
Revels along upon the wind; the White-thorn, lovely May,
Opens her many lovely eyes listening; the Rose still sleeps,
None dare to wake her; soon she bursts her crimson curtain'd bed
And comes forth in the majesty of beauty; every Flower,
The Pink, the Jessamine, the Wall-flower, the Carnation,
The Jonquil, the mild Lilly, opes her heavens; every Tree
And Flower & Herb soon fill the air with an innumerable Dance,
Yet all in order sweet & lovely. Men are sick with Love.

from *JERUSALEM*

36   [Prelude to Chapter 2]

THE fields from Islington to Marybone,
To Primrose Hill and Saint John's Wood,
    Were builded over with pillars of gold,
And there Jerusalem's pillars stood.

Her Little-ones ran on the fields,
The Lamb of God among them seen,
    And fair Jerusalem his Bride,
Among the little meadows green.

Pancrass & Kentish-town repose
Among her golden pillars high,
  Among her golden arches which
Shine upon the starry sky.

  The Jew's-harp-house & the Green Man,
The Ponds where Boys to bathe delight,
  The fields of Cows by Willan's farm,
Shine in Jerusalem's pleasant sight.

  She walks upon our meadows green,
The Lamb of God walks by her side,
  And every English Child is seen
Children of Jesus & his Bride.

  Forgiving trespasses and sins
Lest Babylon with cruel Og
  With Moral & Self-righteous Law
Should Crucify in Satan's Synagogue!

  What are those golden Builders doing
Near mournful ever-weeping Paddington,
  Standing above that mighty Ruin
Where Satan the first victory won,

  Where Albion slept beneath the Fatal Tree,
And the Druid's golden Knife
  Rioted in human gore,
In Offerings of Human Life?

  They groan'd aloud on London Stone,
They groan'd aloud on Tyburn's Brook,
  Albion gave his deadly groan,
And all the Atlantic Mountains shook.

Albion's Spectre from his Loins
Tore forth in all the pomp of War:
  Satan his name: in flames of fire
He stretch'd his Druid Pillars far.

Jerusalem fell from Lambeth's Vale
Down thro' Poplar & Old Bow,
  Thro' Malden & across the Sea,
In War & howling, death & woe.

The Rhine was red with human blood,
The Danube roll'd a purple tide,
  On the Euphrates Satan stood,
And over Asia stretch'd his pride.

He wither'd up sweet Zion's Hill
From every Nation of the Earth;
  He wither'd up Jerusalem's Gates,
And in a dark Land gave her birth.

He wither'd up the Human Form
By laws of sacrifice for sin,
  Till it became a Mortal Worm,
But O! translucent all within.

The Divine Vision still was seen,
Still was the Human Form Divine,
  Weeping in weak & mortal clay,
O Jesus, still the Form was thine.

And thine the Human Face, & thine
The Human Hands & Feet & Breath,
  Entering thro' the Gates of Birth
And passing thro' the Gates of Death.

And O thou Lamb of God, whom I
Slew in my dark self-righteous pride,
   Art thou return'd to Albion's Land?
And is Jerusalem thy Bride?

   Come to my arms & never more
Depart, but dwell for ever here:
   Create my Spirit to thy Love:
Subdue my Spectre to thy Fear.

   Spectre of Albion! warlike Fiend!
In clouds of blood & ruin roll'd
   I here reclaim thee as my own,
My Self-hood! Satan! arm'd in gold.

   Is this thy soft Family-Love,
Thy cruel Patriarchal pride,
   Planting thy Family alone,
Destroying all the World beside?

   A man's worst enemies are those
Of his own house & family;
   And he who makes his law a curse,
By his own law shall surely die.

   In my Exchanges every Land
Shall walk, & mine in every Land,
   Mutual shall build Jerusalem
Both heart in heart & hand in hand.

37   ['Male & Female Loves in Beulah']

BEULAH

Where every Female delights to give her maiden to her husband:
The Female searches sea & land for gratifications to the
Male Genius, who in return clothes her in gems & gold
And feeds her with the food of Eden; hence all her beauty beams.
She Creates at her will a little moony night & silence
With Spaces of sweet gardens & a tent of elegant beauty,
Closed in by a sandy desart & a night of stars shining
And a little tender moon & hovering angels on the wing;
And the Male gives a Time & Revolution to her Space
Till the time of love is passed in ever varying delights.
For all Things Exist in the Human Imagination,
And hence in Beulah they are stolen by secret amorous theft
Till they have had Punishment enough to make them commit
    Crimes.

38   [Epigraph to Chapter 4]

I GIVE you the end of a golden string,
    Only wind it into a ball,
It will lead you in at Heaven's gate
    Built in Jerusalem's wall.

39   [Prelude to Chapter 4]

ENGLAND! awake! awake! awake!
    Jerusalem thy Sister calls!
Why wilt thou sleep the sleep of death
    And close her from thy ancient walls?

Thy hills & valleys felt her feet
    Gently upon their bosoms move:
Thy gates beheld sweet Zion's ways:
    Then was a time of joy and love.

And now the time returns again:
  Our souls exult, & London's towers
Recieve the Lamb of God to dwell
  In England's green & pleasant bowers.

40   [Epilogue to *The Gates of Paradise*]

To The Accuser who is
The God of This World.

TRULY, My Satan, thou art but a Dunce,
And dost not know the Garment from the Man.
Every Harlot was a Virgin once,
Nor can'st thou ever change Kate into Nan.

Tho' thou art Worship'd by the Names Divine
Of Jesus & Jehovah, thou art still
The Son of Morn in weary Night's decline,
The lost Traveller's Dream under the Hill.

SAMUEL ROGERS

41   Captivity

CAGED in old woods, whose reverend echoes wake
When the hern screams along the distant lake,
Her little heart oft flutters to be free,
Oft sighs to turn the unrelenting key.
In vain! the nurse that rusted relic wears,
Nor moved by gold—nor to be moved by tears;
And terraced walls their black reflection throw
On the green-mantled moat that sleeps below.

42 ['Another and the Same']

BORN in a trance, we wake, observe, inquire;
And the green earth, the azure sky admire.
Of Elfin size—for ever as we run,
We cast a longer shadow in the sun!
And now a charm, and now a grace is won!
We grow in stature, and in wisdom too!
And, as new scenes, new objects rise to view,
Think nothing done while aught remains to do.
    Yet, all forgot, how oft the eye-lids close,
And from the slack hand drops the gathered rose!
How oft, as dead, on the warm turf we lie,
While many an emmet comes with curious eye;
And on her nest the watchful wren sits by!
Nor do we speak or move, or hear or see;
So like what once we were, and once again shall be!
    And say, how soon, where, blithe as innocent,
The boy at sun-rise whistled as he went,
An aged pilgrim on his staff shall lean,
Tracing in vain the footsteps o'er the green;
The man himself how altered, not the scene!
Now journeying home with nothing but the name;
Way-worn and spent, another and the same!

43 [Man's Going Hence]

O THOU all-eloquent, whose mighty mind
Streams from the depth of ages on mankind,
Streams like the day—who, angel-like, hast shed
Thy full effulgence on the hoary head,

Speaking in Cato's venerable voice,
'Look up, and faint not—faint not, but rejoice!'
From thy Elysium guide him. Age has now
Stamped with its signet that ingenuous brow;
And, 'mid his old hereditary trees,
Trees he has climbed so oft, he sits and sees
His children's children playing round his knees:
Then happiest, youngest, when the quoit is flung,
When side by side the archers' bows are strung;
His to prescribe the place, adjudge the prize,
Envying no more the young their energies
Than they an old man when his words are wise;
His a delight how pure . . . without alloy;
Strong in their strength, rejoicing in their joy!

  Now in their turn assisting, they repay
The anxious cares of many and many a day;
And now by those he loves relieved, restored,
His very wants and weaknesses afford
A feeling of enjoyment. In his walks,
Leaning on them, how oft he stops and talks,
While they look up! Their questions, their replies,
Fresh as the welling waters, round him rise,
Gladdening his spirit: and his theme the past,
How eloquent he is! His thoughts flow fast;
And while his heart (oh can the heart grow old?
False are the tales that in the World are told!)
Swells in his voice, he knows not where to end;
Like one discoursing of an absent friend.

  But there are moments which he calls his own.
Then, never less alone than when alone,
Those that he loved so long and sees no more,
Loved and still loves—not dead—but gone before,

He gathers round him; and revives at will
Scenes in his life—that breathe enchantment still—
That come not now at dreary intervals—
But where a light as from the Blessed falls,
A light such guests bring ever—pure and holy—
Lapping the soul in sweetest melancholy!
—Ah then less willing (nor the choice condemn)
To live with others than to think on them!

And now behold him up the hill ascending,
Memory and Hope like evening-stars attending;
Sustained, excited, till his course is run,
By deeds of virtue done or to be done.
When on his couch he sinks at length to rest,   ⎞
Those by his counsel saved, his power redressed,   ⎬
Those by the World shunned ever as unblest,   ⎠
At whom the rich man's dog growls from the gate,
But whom he sought out, sitting desolate,
Come and stand round—the widow with her child,
As when she first forgot her tears and smiled!
They, who watch by him, see not; but he sees,
Sees and exults—Were ever dreams like these?
They, who watch by him, hear not; but he hears,
And Earth recedes, and Heaven itself appears!

'Tis past! That hand we grasped, alas, in vain!
Nor shall we look upon his face again!
But to his closing eyes, for all were there,
Nothing was wanting; and, through many a year,
We shall remember with a fond delight
The words so precious which we heard to-night;
His parting, though awhile our sorrow flows,
Like setting suns or music at the close!

SAMUEL ROGERS

44   [Byron recollected at Bologna]

MUCH had passed
Since last we parted; and those five short years—
Much had they told! His clustering locks were turn'd
Grey; nor did aught recall the Youth that swam
From SESTOS to ABYDOS. Yet his voice,
Still it was sweet; still from his eye the thought
Flashed lightning-like, nor lingered on the way,
Waiting for words. Far, far into the night
We sat, conversing—no unwelcome hour,
The hour we met; and, when Aurora rose,
Rising, we climbed the rugged Apennine.

Well I remember how the golden sun
Filled with its beams the unfathomable gulphs,
As on we travelled, and along the ridge,
Mid groves of cork and cistus and wild fig,
His motley household came—Not last nor least,
BATTISTA, who, upon the moonlight-sea
Of VENICE, had so ably, zealously,
Served, and, at parting, thrown his oar away
To follow thro' the world; who without stain
Had worn so long that honourable badge,
The gondolier's, in a Patrician House
Arguing unlimited trust.—Not last nor least,
Thou, tho' declining in thy beauty and strength,
Faithful MORETTO, to the latest hour
Guarding his chamber-door, and now along
The silent, sullen strand of MISSOLONGHI
Howling in grief.

He had just left that Place
Of old renown, once in the ADRIAN sea,
RAVENNA! where, from DANTE's sacred tomb
He had so oft, as many a verse declares,

Drawn inspiration; where, at twilight-time,
Thro' the pine-forest wandering with loose rein,
Wandering and lost, he had so oft beheld
(What is not visible to a Poet's eye?)
The spectre-knight, the hell-hounds and their prey,
The chase, the slaughter, and the festal mirth
Suddenly blasted. 'Twas a theme he loved,
But others claimed their turn; and many a tower,
Shattered, uprooted from its native rock,
Its strength the pride of some heroic age,
Appeared and vanished (many a sturdy steer
Yoked and unyoked) while as in happier days
He poured his spirit forth. The Past forgot,
All was enjoyment. Not a cloud obscured
Present or future.
                    He is now at rest;
And praise and blame fall on his ear alike,
Now dull in death. Yes, BYRON, thou art gone,
Gone like a star that thro' the firmament
Shot and was lost, in its eccentric course
Dazzling, perplexing. Yet thy heart, methinks,
Was generous, noble—noble in its scorn
Of all things low or little; nothing there
Sordid or servile. If imagined wrongs
Pursued thee, urging thee sometimes to do
Things long regretted, oft, as many know,
None more than I, thy gratitude would build
On slight foundations: and, if in thy life
Not happy, in thy death thou surely wert,
Thy wish accomplished; dying in the land
Where thy young mind had caught ethereal fire,
Dying in GREECE, and in a cause so glorious!
    They in thy train—ah, little did they think,
As round we went, that they so soon should sit

Mourning beside thee, while a Nation mourned,
Changing her festal for her funeral song;
That they so soon should hear the minute-gun,
As morning gleamed on what remained of thee,
Roll o'er the sea, the mountains, numbering
Thy years of joy and sorrow.
                       Thou art gone;
And he who would assail thee in thy grave,
Oh, let him pause! For who among us all,
Tried as thou wert—even from thine earliest years,
When wandering, yet unspoilt, a highland-boy—
Tried as thou wert, and with thy soul of flame;
Pleasure, while yet the down was on thy cheek,
Uplifting, pressing, and to lips like thine,
Her charmed cup—ah, who among us all
Could say he had not erred as much, and more?

45   [An Interview near Florence]

A NARROW glade unfolded, such as Spring
Broiders with flowers, and, when the moon is high,
The hare delights to race in, scattering round
The silvery dews. Cedar and cypress threw
Singly their depth of shadow, chequering
The greensward, and, what grew in frequent tufts,
An underwood of myrtle, that by fits
Sent up a gale of fragrance. Thro' the midst,
Reflecting, as it ran, purple and gold,
A rain-bow's splendour (somewhere in the east
Rain-drops were falling fast) a rivulet
Sported as loth to go; and on the bank
Stood (in the eyes of one, if not of both,

Worth all the rest and more) a sumpter-mule
Well-laden, while two menials as in haste
Drew from his ample panniers, ranging round
Viands and fruits on many a shining salver,
And plunging in the cool translucent wave
Flasks of delicious wine.—Anon a horn
Blew, thro' the champain bidding to the feast,
Its jocund note to other ears addressed,
Not ours; and, slowly coming by a path
That, ere it issued from an ilex-grove,
Was seen far inward, tho' along the glade
Distinguished only by a fresher verdure,
Peasants approached, one leading in a leash
Beagles yet panting, one with various game
In rich confusion slung, before, behind,
Leveret and quail and pheasant. All announced
The chase as over; and ere long appeared,
Their horses full of fire, champing the curb,
For the white foam was dry upon the flank,
Two in close converse, each in each delighting,
A Lady young and graceful, and a Youth,
Yet younger, bearing on a falconer's glove,
As in the golden, the romantic time,
His falcon hooded. Like some spirit of air,
Or fairy-vision, such as feigned of old,
The Lady, while her courser pawed the ground,
Alighted; and her beauty, as she trod
The enamelled bank, bruising nor herb nor flower,
That place illumined.

ROBERT BLOOMFIELD

46   ['Moonlight . . . Scattered Clouds']

IN part these nightly terrors to dispel,
GILES, ere he sleeps, his little Flock must tell.
From the fire-side with many a shrug he hies,
Glad if the full-orb'd Moon salute his eyes,
And through the unbroken stillness of the night
Shed on his path her beams of cheering light.
With saunt'ring step he climbs the distant stile,
Whilst all around him wears a placid smile;
There views the white-rob'd clouds in clusters driv'n,
And all the glorious pageantry of heav'n.
Low, on the utmost bound'ry of the sight,
The rising vapours catch the silver light;
Thence Fancy measures, as they parting fly,
Which first will throw its shadow on the eye,
Passing the source of light; and thence away,
Succeeded quick by brighter still than they.
For yet above these wafted clouds are seen
(In a remoter sky, still more serene),
Others, detach'd in ranges through the air,
Spotless as snow, and countless as they're fair;
Scatter'd immensely wide from east to west,
The beauteous 'semblance of a *Flock* at rest.

47   from 'SHOOTER'S HILL'

HEALTH! I seek thee;—dost thou love
    The mountain top or quiet vale,
Or deign o'er humbler hills to rove
    On showery June's dark south-west gale?

If so, I'll meet all blasts that blow,
   With silent step, but not forlorn;
Though, goddess, at thy shrine I bow,
   And woo thee each returning morn.

I seek thee where, with all his might,
   The joyous bird his rapture tells,
Amidst the half-excluded light,
   That gilds the fox-glove's pendant bells;
Where, cheerly up this bold hill's side
   The deep'ning groves triumphant climb;
In groves Delight and Peace abide,
   And Wisdom marks the lapse of time.

To hide me from the public eye,
   To keep the throne of Reason clear,
Amidst fresh air to breathe or die,
   I took my staff and wander'd here.
Suppressing every sigh that heaves,
   And coveting no wealth but thee,
I nestle in the honied leaves,
   And hug my stolen liberty.

O'er eastward uplands, gay or rude,
   Along to Erith's ivied spire,
I start, with strength and hope renew'd,
   And cherish life's rekindling fire.
Now measure vales with straining eyes,
   Now trace the church-yard's humble names;
Or, climb brown heaths, abrupt that rise,
   And overlook the winding Thames.

I love to mark the flow'ret's eye,
   To rest where pebbles form my bed,
Where shapes and colours scatter'd lie
   In varying millions round my head.

ROBERT BLOOMFIELD

The soul rejoices when alone,
    And feels her glorious empire free;
Sees GOD in every shining stone,
And revels in variety.

★

Sweet Health, I seek thee! hither bring
    Thy balm that softens human ills;
Come, on the long-drawn clouds that fling
    Their shadows o'er the Surry-Hills.
Yon green-topt hills, and far away
    Where late as now I freedom stole,
And spent one dear, delicious day
    On thy wild banks, romantic *Mole*.

Aye, there's the scene![1] beyond the sweep
    Of London's congregated cloud,
The dark-brow'd wood, the headlong steep,
    And valley-paths without a crowd!
Here, Thames, I watch thy flowing tides,
    Thy thousand sails am proud to see;
But where the *Mole* all silent glides
    Dwells Peace—and Peace is wealth to me.

[1] Box-Hill, and the beautiful neighbourhood of Dorking, in Surry.

48   [The Coracle Fishers]

HUSH! not a whisper! Oars, be still!
Comes that soft sound from yonder hill?
Or is it close at hand, so near
It scarcely strikes the list'ning ear?
E'en so; for down the green bank fell,
An ice-cold stream from MARTIN'S WELL,

Bright as young beauty's azure eye,
And pure as infant chastity,
Each limpid draught, suffus'd with dew,
The dipping glass's crystal hue;
And as it trembling reach'd the lip,
Delight sprung up at every sip.
  Pure, temperate joys, and calm, were these;
We tost upon no Indian seas;
No savage chiefs, of various hue,
Came jabbering in the bark canoe
Our strength to dare, our course to turn;
Yet boats a South Sea chief would burn,[1]
Sculk'd in the alder shade. Each bore,
Devoid of keel, or sail, or oar,
An upright fisherman, whose eye,
With Bramin-like solemnity,
Survey'd the surface either way,
And cleav'd it like a fly at play;
And crossways bore a balanc'd pole,
To drive the salmon from his hole;
Then heedful leapt, without parade,
On shore, as luck or fancy bade;
And o'er his back, in gallant trim,
Swung the light shell that carried him;
Then down again his burden threw,
And launch'd his whirling bowl anew;
Displaying, in his bow'ry station,
The infancy of navigation.

[1] In Cæsar's Commentaries, mention is made of boats of this description, formed of a raw hide, (from whence, perhaps, their name Coricle,) which were in use among the natives. How little they dreamed of the vastness of modern perfection, and of the naval conflicts of latter days!

Soon round us spread the hills and dales,
Where GEOFFREY spun his magic tales,
And call'd them history. The land
Whence ARTHUR sprung, and all his band
Of gallant knights. Sire of romance,
Who led the fancy's mazy dance,
Thy tales shall please, thy name still be,
When Time forgets my verse and me.
    Low sunk the sun, his ev'ning beam
Scarce reach'd us on the tranquil stream;
Shut from the world, and all its din,
Nature's own bonds had clos'd us in;
Wood, and deep dell, and rock, and ridge,
From smiling ROSS to MONMOUTH BRIDGE;
From morn, till twilight stole away,
A long, unclouded, glorious day.

49   ['Meandering Wye']

    HOW placid, how divinely sweet,
The flow'r-grown brook that, by our feet,
Winds on a summer's day; e'en where
Its name no classic honours share,
Its springs untrac'd, its course unknown,
Seaward for ever rambling down!
Here, then, how sweet, pelucid, chaste;
'Twas this bright current bade us taste
The fulness of its joy. Glide still,
Enchantress of PLYNLIMON HILL,
Meandering WYE! Still let me dream,
In raptures, o'er thy infant stream;
For could th'immortal soul forego
Its cumbrous load of earthly woe,

And clothe itself in fairy guise,
Too small, too pure, for human eyes,
Blithe would we seek thy utmost spring,
Where mountain-larks first try the wing;
There, at the crimson dawn of day,
Launch a scoop'd leaf, and sail away,
Stretch'd at our ease, or crouch below,
Or climb the green transparent prow,
Stooping where oft the blue bell sips
The passing stream, and shakes and dips;
And when the heifer came to drink,
Quick from the gale our bark would shrink,
And huddle down amidst the brawl
Of many a five-inch waterfall,
Till the expanse should fairly give
The bow'ring hazel room to live;
And as each swelling junction came,
To form a riv'let worth a name,
We'd dart beneath, or brush away
Long-beaded webs, that else might stay
Our silent course; in haste retreat,
Where whirlpools near the bull-rush meet;
Wheel round the ox of monstrous size;
And count below his shadowy flies;
And sport amidst the throng; and when
We met the barks of giant men,
Avoid their oars, still undescried,
And mock their overbearing pride;
Then vanish by some magic spell,
And shout, 'Delicious WYE, farewell!'

50 ['My heart leaps up']

My heart leaps up when I behold
   A rainbow in the sky:
So was it when my life began;
So is it now I am a man;
So be it when I shall grow old,
   Or let me die!
The Child is father of the Man;
And I could wish my days to be
Bound each to each by natural piety.

[Lucy]

51 [1]

Strange fits of passion have I known:
And I will dare to tell,
But in the Lover's ear alone,
What once to me befell.

When she I lov'd looked every day
Fresh as a rose in June,
I to her cottage bent my way,
Beneath an evening-moon.

Upon the moon I fix'd my eye,
All over the wide lea;
With quickening pace my horse drew nigh
Those paths so dear to me.

And now we reach'd the orchard plot;
And, as we climb'd the hill,
The sinking moon to Lucy's cot
Came near, and nearer still.

In one of those sweet dreams I slept,
Kind Nature's gentlest boon!
And, all the while my eyes I kept
On the descending moon.

My horse mov'd on; hoof after hoof
He rais'd, and never stopp'd:
When down behind the cottage roof,
At once, the bright moon dropped.

What fond and wayward thoughts will slide
Into a Lover's head!
'O mercy!' to myself I cried,
'If Lucy should be dead!'

52

[11]

SHE dwelt among th'untrodden ways
    Beside the springs of Dove,
A Maid whom there were none to praise
    And very few to love.

A Violet by a mossy stone
    Half-hidden from the Eye!
—Fair as a star, when only one
    Is shining in the sky!

She liv'd unknown, and few could know
    When Lucy ceas'd to be;
But she is in her Grave, and, Oh!
    The difference to me.

53   [III]

I TRAVELL'D among unknown Men,
    In Lands beyond the Sea;
Nor, England! did I know till then
    What love I bore to thee.

'Tis past, that melancholy dream!
    Nor will I quit thy shore
A second time; for still I seem
    To love thee more and more.

Among thy mountains did I feel
    The joy of my desire;
And She I cherish'd turn'd her wheel
    Beside an English fire.

Thy mornings shew'd—thy nights conceal'd,
    The bowers where Lucy play'd;
And thine too is the last green field
    That Lucy's eyes survey'd.

54   [IV]

THREE years she grew in sun and shower,
Then Nature said, 'A lovelier flower
On earth was never sown;

63

This Child I to myself will take;
She shall be mine, and I will make
A Lady of my own.

'Myself will to my darling be
Both law and impulse: and with me
The Girl, in rock and plain,
In earth and heaven, in glade and bower,
Shall feel an overseeing power
To kindle or restrain.

'She shall be sportive as the fawn
That wild with glee across the lawn
Or up the mountain springs;
And hers shall be the breathing balm,
And hers the silence and the calm
Of mute insensate things.

'The floating clouds their state shall lend
To her; for her the willow bend;
Nor shall she fail to see
Even in the motions of the Storm
Grace that shall mould the Maiden's form
By silent sympathy.

'The stars of midnight shall be dear
To her; and she shall lean her ear
In many a secret place
Where rivulets dance their wayward round,
And beauty born of murmuring sound
Shall pass into her face.

'And vital feelings of delight
Shall rear her form to stately height,
Her virgin bosom swell;

Such thoughts to Lucy I will give
While she and I together live
Here in this happy dell.'

Thus Nature spake—The work was done—
How soon my Lucy's race was run!
She died, and left to me
This heath, this calm, and quiet scene;
The memory of what has been,
And never more will be.

55   [v]

A SLUMBER did my spirit seal,
  I had no human fears:
She seem'd a thing that could not feel
  The touch of earthly years.

No motion has she now, no force;
  She neither hears nor sees;
Roll'd round in earth's diurnal course
  With rocks and stones and trees!

56   [The Daffodils]

I WANDERED lonely as a cloud
That floats on high o'er vales and hills,
When all at once I saw a crowd,
A host, of golden daffodils;
Beside the lake, beneath the trees,
Fluttering and dancing in the breeze.

Continuous as the stars that shine
And twinkle on the milky way,
They stretched in never-ending line
Along the margin of a bay:
Ten thousand saw I at a glance,
Tossing their heads in sprightly dance.

The waves beside them danced; but they
Out-did the sparkling waves in glee:
A poet could not but be gay,
In such a jocund company:
I gazed—and gazed—but little thought
What wealth the show to me had brought:

For oft, when on my couch I lie
In vacant or in pensive mood,
They flash upon that inward eye
Which is the bliss of solitude;
And then my heart with pleasure fills,
And dances with the daffodils.

57   Lines

COMPOSED A FEW MILES ABOVE TINTERN ABBEY, ON
REVISITING THE BANKS OF THE WYE DURING A
TOUR. JULY 13, 1798

FIVE years have passed; five summers, with the length
Of five long winters! and again I hear
These waters, rolling from their mountain-springs
With a soft inland murmur.—Once again
Do I behold these steep and lofty cliffs,

That on a wild secluded scene impress
Thoughts of more deep seclusion; and connect
The landscape with the quiet of the sky.
The day is come when I again repose
Here, under this dark sycamore, and view
These plots of cottage-ground, these orchard-tufts,
Which, at this season, with their unripe fruits,
Are clad in one green hue, and lose themselves
'Mid groves and copses. Once again I see
These hedge-rows, hardly hedge-rows, little lines
Of sportive wood run wild: these pastoral farms,
Green to the very door; and wreathes of smoke
Sent up, in silence, from among the trees!
With some uncertain notice, as might seem
Of vagrant dwellers in the houseless woods,
Or of some Hermit's cave, where by his fire
The Hermit sits alone.
                              These beauteous forms,
Through a long absence, have not been to me
As is a landscape to a blind man's eye:
But oft, in lonely rooms, and mid the din
Of towns and cities, I have owed to them,
In hours of weariness, sensations sweet,
Felt in the blood, and felt along the heart;
And passing even into my purer mind,
With tranquil restoration:—feelings too
Of unremembered pleasure: such, perhaps,
As have no slight or trivial influence
On that best portion of a good man's life,
His little, nameless, unremembered, acts
Of kindness and of love. Nor less, I trust,
To whom I may have owed another gift,
Of aspect more sublime; that blessed mood,
In which the burthen of the mystery,

In which the heavy and the weary weight
Of all this unintelligible world,
Is lighten'd:—that serene and blessed mood,
In which the affections gently lead us on,—
Until, the breath of this corporeal frame,
And even the motion of our human blood
Almost suspended, we are laid asleep
In body, and become a living soul:
While with an eye made quiet by the power
Of harmony, and the deep power of joy,
We see into the life of things.

                  If this
Be but a vain belief, yet, oh! how oft—
In darkness, and amid the many shapes
Of joyless day-light; when the fretful stir
Unprofitable, and the fever of the world,
Have hung upon the beatings of my heart—
How oft, in spirit, have I turned to thee,
O sylvan Wye! thou wanderer thro' the woods,
How often has my spirit turned to thee!

   And now, with gleams of half-extinguish'd thought,
With many recognitions dim and faint,
And somewhat of a sad perplexity,
The picture of the mind revives again:
While here I stand, not only with the sense
Of present pleasure, but with pleasing thoughts
That in this moment there is life and food
For future years. And so I dare to hope,
Though changed, no doubt, from what I was when first
I came among these hills; when like a roe
I bounded o'er the mountains, by the sides
Of the deep rivers, and the lonely streams,
Wherever nature led: more like a man

Flying from something that he dreads than one
Who sought the thing he loved. For nature then
(The coarser pleasures of my boyish days,
And their glad animal movements all gone by)
To me was all in all.—I cannot paint
What then I was. The sounding cataract
Haunted me like a passion: the tall rock,
The mountain, and the deep and gloomy wood,
Their colours and their forms, were then to me
An appetite; a feeling and a love,
That had no need of a remoter charm,
By thought supplied, nor any interest
Unborrowed from the eye.—That time is past,
And all its aching joys are now no more,
And all its dizzy raptures. Not for this
Faint I, nor mourn nor murmur; other gifts
Have followed; for such loss, I would believe,
Abundant recompence. For I have learned
To look on nature, not as in the hour
Of thoughtless youth, but hearing oftentimes
The still, sad music of humanity,
Not harsh nor grating, though of ample power
To chasten and subdue. And I have felt
A presence that disturbs me with the joy
Of elevated thoughts; a sense sublime
Of something far more deeply interfused,
Whose dwelling is the light of setting suns,
And the round ocean and the living air,
And the blue sky, and in the mind of man:
A motion and a spirit, that impels
All thinking things, all objects of all thought,
And rolls through all things. Therefore am I still
A lover of the meadows and the woods,
And mountains; and of all that we behold

From this green earth; of all the mighty world
Of eye, and ear,—both what they half-create,
And what perceive; well pleased to recognize
In nature and the language of the sense,
The anchor of my purest thoughts, the nurse,
The guide, the guardian of my heart, and soul
Of all my moral being.
               Nor, perchance,
If I were not thus taught, should I the more
Suffer my genial spirits to decay:
For thou art with me, here, upon the banks
Of this fair river; thou, my dearest Friend,
My dear, dear Friend; and in thy voice I catch
The language of my former heart, and read
My former pleasures in the shooting lights
Of thy wild eyes. Oh! yet a little while
May I behold in thee what I was once,
My dear, dear Sister! and this prayer I make,
Knowing that Nature never did betray
The heart that loved her; 'tis her privilege,
Through all the years of this our life, to lead
From joy to joy: for she can so inform
The mind that is within us, so impress
With quietness and beauty, and so feed
With lofty thoughts, that neither evil tongues,
Rash judgements, nor the sneers of selfish men,
Nor greetings where no kindness is, nor all
The dreary intercourse of daily life,
Shall e'er prevail against us, or disturb
Our chearful faith, that all which we behold
Is full of blessings. Therefore let the moon
Shine on thee in thy solitary walk;
And let the misty mountain-winds be free
To blow against thee: and, in after years,

When these wild ecstasies shall be matured
Into a sober pleasure; when thy mind
Shall be a mansion for all lovely forms,
Thy memory be as a dwelling-place
For all sweet sounds and harmonies; Oh! then,
If solitude, or fear, or pain, or grief,
Should be thy portion, with what healing thoughts
Of tender joy wilt thou remember me,
And these my exhortations! Nor, perchance,
If I should be where I no more can hear
Thy voice, nor catch from thy wild eyes these gleams
Of past existence, wilt thou then forget
That on the banks of this delightful stream
We stood together; and that I, so long
A worshipper of Nature, hither came,
Unwearied in that service: rather say
With warmer love—oh! with far deeper zeal
Of holier love. Nor wilt thou then forget,
That after many wanderings, many years
Of absence, these steep woods and lofty cliffs,
And this green pastoral landscape, were to me
More dear, both for themselves and for thy sake.

58   Resolution and Independence

THERE was a roaring in the wind all night;
The rain came heavily and fell in floods;
But now the sun is rising calm and bright;
The birds are singing in the distant woods;
Over his own sweet voice the Stock-dove broods;
The Jay makes answer as the Magpie chatters;
And all the air is filled with pleasant noise of waters.

All things that love the sun are out of doors;
The sky rejoices in the morning's birth;
The grass is bright with rain-drops; on the moors
The Hare is running races in her mirth;
And with her feet she from the plashy earth
Raises a mist; which, glittering in the sun,
Runs with her all the way, wherever she doth run.

I was a Traveller then upon the moor;
I saw the Hare that rac'd about with joy;
I heard the woods, and distant waters, roar;
Or heard them not, as happy as a Boy:
The pleasant season did my heart employ:
My old remembrances went from me wholly;
And all the ways of men, so vain and melancholy.

But, as it sometimes chanceth, from the might
Of joy in minds that can no farther go,
As high as we have mounted in delight
In our dejection do we sink as low,
To me that morning did it happen so;
And fears, and fancies, thick upon me came;
Dim sadness, & blind thoughts I knew not nor could name.

I heard the sky-lark singing in the sky;
And I bethought me of the playful Hare:
Even such a happy Child of earth am I;
Even as these blissful Creatures do I fare;
Far from the world I walk, and from all care;
But there may come another day to me,
Solitude, pain of heart, distress, and poverty.

My whole life I have liv'd in pleasant thought,
As if life's business were a summer mood;
As if all needful things would come unsought
To genial faith, still rich in genial good;
But how can He expect that others should
Build for him, sow for him, and at his call
Love him, who for himself will take no heed at all?

I thought of Chatterton, the marvellous Boy,
The sleepless Soul that perish'd in his pride;
Of Him who walk'd in glory and in joy
Following his plough, upon the mountain-side:
By our own spirits are we deified;
We Poets in our youth begin in gladness;
But thereof come in the end despondency and madness.

Now, whether it were by peculiar grace,
A leading from above, a something given,
Yet it befell, that, in this lonely place,
When I with these untoward thoughts had striven,
Beside a pool bare to the eye of heaven
I saw a Man before me unawares:
The oldest man he seem'd that ever wore grey hairs.

My course I stopped as soon as I espied
The Old Man in that naked wilderness:
Close by a Pond, upon the further side,
He stood alone: a minute's space I guess
I watch'd him, he continuing motionless:
To the Pool's further margin then I drew;
He being all the while before me full in view.

As a huge Stone is sometimes seen to lie
Couch'd on the bald top of an eminence;
Wonder to all who do the same espy
By what means it could thither come, and whence;
So that it seems a thing endued with sense:
Like a Sea-beast crawl'd forth, that on a shelf
Of rock or sand reposeth, there to sun itself.

Such seem'd this Man, not all alive nor dead,
Nor all asleep; in his extreme old age:
His body was bent double, feet and head
Coming together in life's pilgrimage;
As if some dire constraint of pain, or rage
Of sickness felt by him in times long past,
A more than human weight upon his frame had cast.

Himself he propp'd, limbs, body, and pale face,
Upon a long grey Staff of shaven wood:
And, still as I drew near with gentle pace,
Upon the margin of that moorish flood
Motionless as a Cloud the Old Man stood,
That heareth not the loud winds when they call;
And moveth altogether, if it move at all.

At length, himself unsettling, he the Pond
Stirred with his Staff, and fixedly did look
Upon the muddy water, which he conn'd,
As if he had been reading in a book:
And now a stranger's privilege I took;
And, drawing to his side, to him did say,
'This morning gives us promise of a glorious day.'

A gentle answer did the Old Man make,
In courteous speech which forth he slowly drew:
And him with further words I thus bespake,
'What kind of work is that which you pursue?
This is a lonesome place for one like you.'
Ere he replied, a flash of mild surprise
Broke from the sable orbs of his yet-vivid eyes.

His words came feebly, from a feeble chest,
Yet each in solemn order follow'd each,
With something of a lofty utterance drest;
Choice word, and measured phrase; above the reach
Of ordinary men; a stately speech!
Such as grave Livers do in Scotland use,
Religious men, who give to God and Man their dues.

He told, that to these waters he had come
To gather Leeches, being old and poor:
Employment hazardous and wearisome!
And he had many hardships to endure:
From Pond to Pond he roam'd, from moor to moor,
Housing, with God's good help, by choice or chance;
And in this way he gain'd an honest maintenance.

The Old Man still stood talking by my side;
But now his voice to me was like a stream
Scarce heard; nor word from word could I divide;
And the whole Body of the Man did seem
Like one whom I had met with in a dream;
Or like a Man from some far region sent,
To give me human strength, by apt admonishment.

My former thoughts return'd: the fear that kills;
And hope that is unwilling to be fed;
Cold, pain, and labour, and all fleshly ills;
And mighty Poets in their misery dead.
—Perplexed, and longing to be comforted,
My question eagerly did I renew,
'How is it that you live, and what is it you do?'

He with a smile did then his words repeat;
And said that, gathering Leeches, far and wide
He travelled; stirring thus about his feet
The waters of the pools where they abide.
'Once I could meet with them on every side;
But they have dwindled long by slow decay;
Yet still I persevere, and find them where I may.'

While he was talking thus, the lonely place,
The Old Man's shape, and speech, all troubled me:
In my mind's eye I seem'd to see him pace
About the weary moors continually,
Wandering about alone and silently.
While I these thoughts within myself pursued,
He, having made a pause, the same discourse renewed.

And soon with this he other matter blended,
Cheerfully uttered, with demeanour kind,
But stately in the main; and, when he ended,
I could have laugh'd myself to scorn, to find
In that decrepit Man so firm a mind.
'God,' said I, 'be my help and stay secure;
I'll think of the Leech-gatherer on the lonely moor!'

59   ## The Solitary Reaper

BEHOLD her, single in the field,
Yon solitary Highland Lass!
Reaping and singing by herself;
Stop here, or gently pass!
Alone she cuts, and binds the grain,
And sings a melancholy strain;
O listen! for the Vale profound
Is overflowing with the sound.

No Nightingale did ever chaunt
More welcome notes to weary bands
Of Travellers in some shady haunt,
Among Arabian sands;
A voice so thrilling ne'er was heard
In spring-time from the Cuckoo-bird,
Breaking the silence of the seas
Among the farthest Hebrides.

Will no one tell me what she sings?
Perhaps the plaintive numbers flow
For old, unhappy, far-off things,
And battles long ago;
Or is it some more humble lay,
Familiar matter of today?
Some natural sorrow, loss, or pain,
That has been, and may be again?

Whate'er the theme, the Maiden sang
As if her song could have no ending;
I saw her singing at her work,
And o'er the sickle bending;

I listened, motionless and still;
And, as I mounted up the hill,
The music in my heart I bore,
Long after it was heard no more.

60   Composed upon Westminster Bridge

SEPT. 3, 1803

EARTH has not any thing to shew more fair:
Dull would he be of soul who could pass by
A sight so touching in its majesty:
This City now doth like a garment wear
The beauty of the morning; silent, bare,
Ships, towers, domes, theatres, and temples lie
Open unto the fields, and to the sky;
All bright and glittering in the smokeless air.
Never did sun more beautifully steep
In his first splendor, valley, rock, or hill;
Ne'er saw I, never felt, a calm so deep!
The river glideth at his own sweet will:
Dear God! the very houses seem asleep;
And all that mighty heart is lying still!

61   WHERE lies the Land to which yon Ship must go?
Fresh as a lark mounting at break of day,
Festively she puts forth in trim array;
Is she for tropic suns, or polar snow?
What boots the enquiry? Neither friend nor foe
She cares for; let her travel where she may,
She finds familiar names, a beaten way
Ever before her, and a wind to blow.

Yet still I ask, what Haven is her mark?
And, almost as it was when ships were rare,
(From time to time, like Pilgrims, here and there
Crossing the waters) doubt, and something dark,
Of the old Sea some reverential fear,
Is with me at thy farewell, joyous Bark!

62   The world is too much with us; late and soon,
Getting and spending, we lay waste our powers:
Little we see in Nature that is ours;
We have given our hearts away, a sordid boon!
This Sea that bares her bosom to the moon;
The Winds that will be howling at all hours
And are up-gathered now like sleeping flowers;
For this, for every thing, we are out of tune;
It moves us not.—Great God! I'd rather be
A Pagan suckled in a creed outworn;
So might I, standing on this pleasant lea,
Have glimpses that would make me less forlorn;
Have sight of Proteus rising from the sea;
Or hear old Triton blow his wreathed horn.

63   On the Extinction of the Venetian Republic

ONCE did She hold the gorgeous East in fee;
And was the safeguard of the West: the worth
Of Venice did not fall below her birth,
Venice, the eldest Child of Liberty.
She was a Maiden City, bright and free;
No guile seduced, no force could violate;
And, when She took unto herself a Mate,
She must espouse the everlasting Sea.

And what if she had seen those glories fade,
Those titles vanish, and that strength decay,
Yet shall some tribute of regret be paid
When her long life hath reach'd its final day:
Men are we, and must grieve when even the Shade
Of that which once was great is pass'd away.

64   To Toussaint L'Ouverture

TOUSSAINT, the most unhappy Man of Men!
Whether the whistling Rustic tend his plough
Within thy hearing, or thy head be now
Pillowed in some deep dungeon's earless den;—
O miserable Chieftain! where and when
Wilt thou find patience? Yet die not; do thou
Wear rather in thy bonds a chearful brow:
Though fallen Thyself, never to rise again,
Live, and take comfort. Thou hast left behind
Powers that will work for thee; air, earth, and skies;
There's not a breathing of the common wind
That will forget thee; thou hast great allies;
Thy friends are exultations, agonies,
And love, and Man's unconquerable mind.

65   London: 1802

MILTON! thou should'st be living at this hour:
England hath need of thee: she is a fen
Of stagnant waters: altar, sword and pen,
Fireside, the heroic wealth of hall and bower,
Have forfeited their ancient English dower
Of inward happiness. We are selfish men;
Oh! raise us up, return to us again;
And give us manners, virtue, freedom, power.

Thy soul was like a Star, and dwelt apart:
Thou hadst a voice whose sound was like the sea:
Pure as the naked heavens, majestic, free,
So didst thou travel on life's common way,
In chearful godliness; and yet thy heart
The lowliest duties on itself did lay.

66   Inside of King's College Chapel, Cambridge

TAX not the royal Saint with vain expense,
With ill-matched aims the Architect who planned—
Albeit labouring for a scanty band
Of white-robed Scholars only—this immense
And glorious Work of fine intelligence!
Give all thou canst; high Heaven rejects the lore
Of nicely-calculated less or more;
So deemed the man who fashioned for the sense
These lofty pillars, spread that branching roof
Self-poised, and scooped into ten thousand cells,
Where light and shade repose, where music dwells
Lingering—and wandering on as loth to die;
Like thoughts whose very sweetness yieldeth proof
That they were born for immortality.

67   Elegiac Stanzas

SUGGESTED BY A PICTURE OF PEELE CASTLE, IN A
STORM, PAINTED BY SIR GEORGE BEAUMONT

I WAS thy Neighbour once, thou rugged Pile!
Four summer weeks I dwelt in sight of thee:
I saw thee every day; and all the while
Thy Form was sleeping on a glassy sea.

So pure the sky, so quiet was the air!
So like, so very like, was day to day!
Whene'er I look'd, thy Image still was there;
It trembled, but it never pass'd away.

How perfect was the calm! it seem'd no sleep;
No mood, which season takes away, or brings:
I could have fancied that the mighty Deep
Was even the gentlest of all gentle Things.

Ah! THEN, if mine had been the Painter's hand,
To express what then I saw; and add the gleam,
The light that never was, on sea or land,
The consecration, and the Poet's dream;

I would have planted thee, thou hoary Pile,
Amid a world how different from this!
Beside a sea that could not cease to smile;
On tranquil land, beneath a sky of bliss:

Thou shouldst have seem'd a treasure-house divine
Of peaceful years; a chronicle of heaven:—
Of all the sunbeams that did ever shine
The very sweetest had to thee been given.

A Picture had it been of lasting ease,
Elysian quiet, without toil or strife;
No motion but the moving tide, a breeze,
Or merely silent Nature's breathing life.

Such, in the fond delusion of my heart,
Such Picture would I at that time have made:
And seen the soul of truth in every part,
A steadfast peace that might not be betray'd.

So once it would have been,—'tis so no more;
I have submitted to a new controul:
A power is gone, which nothing can restore;
A deep distress hath humaniz'd my Soul.

Not for a moment could I now behold
A smiling sea and be what I have been:
The feeling of my loss will ne'er be old;
This, which I know, I speak with mind serene.

Then, Beaumont, Friend! who would have been the Friend,
If he had lived, of Him whom I deplore,
This Work of thine I blame not, but commend;
This sea in anger, and that dismal shore.

Oh 'tis a passionate Work!—yet wise and well;
Well chosen in the spirit that is here;
That Hulk which labours in the deadly swell,
This rueful sky, this pageantry of fear!

And this huge Castle, standing here sublime,
I love to see the look with which it braves,
Cased in the unfeeling armour of old time,
The light'ning, the fierce wind, and trampling waves.

Farewell, farewell the Heart that lives alone,
Hous'd in a dream, at distance from the Kind!
Such happiness, wherever it be known,
Is to be pitied; for 'tis surely blind.

But welcome fortitude, and patient chear,
And frequent sights of what is to be borne!
Such sights, or worse, as are before me here.—
Not without hope we suffer and we mourn.

68

Ode:

Intimations of Immortality from Recollections
of Early Childhood

> The Child is father of the Man;
> And I could wish my days to be
> Bound each to each by natural piety.

I

THERE was a time when meadow, grove, and stream,
The earth, and every common sight,
    To me did seem
  Apparell'd in celestial light,
The glory and the freshness of a dream.
It is not now as it hath been of yore;—
  Turn wheresoe'er I may,
    By night or day,
The things which I have seen I now can see no more.

II

    The Rainbow comes and goes,
    And lovely is the Rose,
    The Moon doth with delight
Look round her when the heavens are bare,
    Waters on a starry night
    Are beautiful and fair;
  The sunshine is a glorious birth;
  But yet I know, where'er I go,
That there hath pass'd away a glory from the earth.

III

Now, while the Birds thus sing a joyous song,
    And while the young Lambs bound
    As to the tabor's sound,

To me alone there came a thought of grief:
A timely utterance gave that thought relief,
    And I again am strong.
The Cataracts blow their trumpets from the steep;
No more shall grief of mine the season wrong;
I hear the Echoes through the mountains throng,
The Winds come to me from the fields of sleep,
    And all the earth is gay;
      Land and sea
   Give themselves up to jol'ity,
    And with the heart of May
   Doth every Beast keep holiday;—
     Thou Child of Joy,
Shout round me, let me hear thy shouts, thou happy Shep-
  herd-Boy!

IV

Ye blessèd Creatures, I have heard the call
  Ye to each other make; I see
The heavens laugh with you in your jubilee;
   My heart is at your festival,
    My head hath its coronal,
  The fullness of your bliss, I feel—I feel it all.
     Oh evil day! if I were sullen
     While Earth herself is adorning,
      This sweet May-morning,
    And the Children are culling
      On every side,
    In a thousand valleys far and wide,
    Fresh flowers; while the sun shines warm,
And the Babe leaps up on his Mother's arm:—
    I hear, I hear, with joy I hear!
    —But there's a Tree, of many, one,
A single Field which I have look'd upon,
Both of them speak of something that is gone:

The Pansy at my feet
Doth the same tale repeat:
Whither is fled the visionary gleam?
Where is it now, the glory and the dream?

V

Our birth is but a sleep and a forgetting:
The Soul that rises with us, our life's Star,
    Hath had elsewhere its setting,
      And cometh from afar:
      Not in entire forgetfulness,
      And not in utter nakedness,
But trailing clouds of glory do we come
    From God, who is our home:
Heaven lies about us in our infancy!
Shades of the prison-house begin to close
    Upon the growing Boy,
But He beholds the light, and whence it flows,
    He sees it in his joy;
The Youth, who daily farther from the East
    Must travel, still is Nature's Priest,
    And by the vision splendid
    Is on his way attended;
At length the Man perceives it die away,
And fade into the light of common day.

VI

Earth fills her lap with pleasures of her own;
Yearnings she hath in her own natural kind,
And, even with something of a Mother's mind,
    And no unworthy aim,
    The homely Nurse doth all she can
To make her Foster-child, her Inmate Man,
    Forget the glories he hath known,
And that imperial palace whence he came.

VII

Behold the Child among his new-born blisses,
A six years' Darling of a pigmy size!
See, where mid work of his own hand he lies,
Fretted by sallies of his Mother's kisses,
With light upon him from his Father's eyes!
See, at his feet, some little plan or chart,
Some fragment from his dream of human life,
Shap'd by himself with newly-learned art;
    A wedding or a festival,
    A mourning or a funeral;
    And this hath now his heart,
    And unto this he frames his song:
    Then will he fit his tongue
To dialogues of business, love, or strife;
    But it will not be long
    Ere this be thrown aside,
    And with new joy and pride
The little Actor cons another part,
Filling from time to time his 'humorous stage'
With all the Persons, down to palsied Age,
That Life brings with her in her Equipage;
    As if his whole vocation
    Were endless imitation.

VIII

Thou, whose exterior semblance doth belie
    Thy Soul's immensity;
Thou best Philosopher, who yet dost keep
Thy heritage, thou Eye among the blind,
That, deaf and silent, read'st the eternal deep,
Haunted for ever by the eternal mind,—
    Mighty Prophet! Seer blest!
    On whom those truths do rest

Which we are toiling all our lives to find,
In darkness lost, the darkness of the grave;
Thou, over whom thy Immortality
Broods like the Day, a Master o'er a Slave,
A Presence which is not to be put by;
    To whom the grave
Is but a lonely bed without the sense or sight
    Of day or the warm light,
A place of thought where we in waiting lie;
Thou little Child, yet glorious in the might
Of heaven-born freedom on thy Being's height,
Why with such earnest pains dost thou provoke
The Years to bring the inevitable yoke,
Thus blindly with thy blessedness at strife?
Full soon thy Soul shall have her earthly freight,
And custom lie upon thee with a weight,
Heavy as frost, and deep almost as life!

IX

    O joy! that in our embers
    Is something that doth live,
    That nature yet remembers
    What was so fugitive!
The thought of our past years in me doth breed
Perpetual benediction: not indeed
For that which is most worthy to be blest;
Delight and liberty, the simple creed
Of Childhood, whether busy or at rest,
With new-fledged hope still fluttering in his breast:—
    Not for these I raise
    The song of thanks and praise;
    But for those obstinate questionings
    Of sense and outward things,
    Fallings from us, vanishings;

Blank misgivings of a Creature
Moving about in worlds not realiz'd,
High instincts, before which our mortal Nature
Did tremble like a guilty Thing surpriz'd:
    But for those first affections,
    Those shadowy recollections,
  Which, be they what they may,
Are yet the fountain-light of all our day,
Are yet a master-light of all our seeing;
    Uphold us, cherish, and have power to make
Our noisy years seem moments in the being
Of the eternal Silence: truths that wake,
    To perish never;
Which neither listlessness, nor mad endeavour,
    Nor Man nor Boy,
Nor all that is at enmity with joy,
Can utterly abolish or destroy!
    Hence, in a season of calm weather,
    Though inland far we be,
Our Souls have sight of that immortal sea
    Which brought us hither,
    Can in a moment travel thither,
And see the Children sport upon the shore,
And hear the mighty waters rolling evermore.

x

Then sing, ye Birds, sing, sing a joyous song!
    And let the young Lambs bound
    As to the tabor's sound!
We in thought will join your throng,
    Ye that pipe and ye that play,
    Ye that through your hearts to-day
    Feel the gladness of the May!

What though the radiance which was once so bright
Be now for ever taken from my sight,
   Though nothing can bring back the hour
Of splendour in the grass, of glory in the flower;
     We will grieve not, rather find
     Strength in what remains behind,
     In the primal sympathy
     Which having been must ever be,
     In the soothing thoughts that spring
     Out of human suffering,
     In the faith that looks through death,
In years that bring the philosophic mind.

XI

And O, ye Fountains, Meadows, Hills, and Groves,
Forebode not any severing of our loves!
Yet in my heart of hearts I feel your might;
I only have relinquish'd one delight
To live beneath your more habitual sway.
I love the Brooks which down their channels fret,
Even more than when I tripp'd lightly as they;
The innocent brightness of a new-born Day
     Is lovely yet;
The Clouds that gather round the setting sun
Do take a sober colouring from an eye
That hath kept watch o'er man's mortality;
Another race hath been, and other palms are won.
Thanks to the human heart by which we live,
Thanks to its tenderness, its joys, and fears,
To me the meanest flower that blows can give
Thoughts that do often lie too deep for tears.

69   [To Catherine Wordsworth 1808-1812]

SURPRISED by joy—impatient as the Wind
I turned to share the transport—Oh! with whom
But Thee, deep buried in the silent tomb,
That spot which no vicissitude can find?
Love, faithful love, recalled thee to my mind—
But how could I forget thee? Through what power,
Even for the least division of an hour
Have I been so beguiled as to be blind,
To my most grievous loss!—That thought's return
Was the worst pang that sorrow ever bore,
Save one, one only, when I stood forlorn,
Knowing my heart's best treasure was no more;
That neither present time, nor years unborn
Could to my sight that heavenly face restore.

70   After-thought

I THOUGHT of Thee, my partner and my guide,
As being past away.—Vain sympathies!
For, backward, Duddon! as I cast my eyes
I see what was, and is, and will abide:
Still glides the Stream, and shall for ever glide;
The Form remains, the Function never dies;
While we, the brave, the mighty, and the wise,
We Men, who in our morn of youth defied
The elements, must vanish;—be it so!
Enough, if something from our hands have power
To live, and act, and serve the future hour;
And if, as toward the silent tomb we go,
Through love, through hope, and faith's transcendent dower,
We feel that we are greater than we know.

71   Written in the Album of a Child

SMALL service is true service while it lasts;
Of Friends, however humble, scorn not one:
The Daisy, by the shadow that it casts,
Protects the lingering dew-drop from the Sun.

72   [The Wanderer Recalls the Past]

I SEE around me here
Things which you cannot see: we die, my Friend,
Nor we alone, but that which each man loved
And prized in his peculiar nook of earth
Dies with him, or is changed; and very soon
Even of the good is no memorial left.
—The Poets, in their elegies and songs
Lamenting the departed, call the groves,
They call upon the hills and streams to mourn,
And senseless rocks; nor idly; for they speak,
In these their invocations, with a voice
Obedient to the strong creative power
Of human passion. Sympathies there are
More tranquil, yet perhaps of kindred birth,
That steal upon the meditative mind,
And grow with thought. Beside yon spring I stood,
And eyed its waters till we seemed to feel
One sadness, they and I. For them a bond
Of brotherhood is broken: time has been
When, every day, the touch of human hand
Dislodged the natural sleep that binds them up
In mortal stillness; and they ministered
To human comfort. Stooping down to drink,

Upon the slimy foot-stone I espied
The useless fragment of a wooden bowl,
Green with the moss of years, and subject only
To the soft handling of the elements:
There let it lie—how foolish are such thoughts!
Forgive them;—never—never did my steps
Approach this door but she who dwelt within
A daughter's welcome gave me, and I loved her
As my own child. Oh, Sir! the good die first,
And they whose hearts are dry as summer dust
Burn to the socket. Many a passenger
Hath blessed poor Margaret for her gentle looks,
When she upheld the cool refreshment drawn
From that forsaken spring; and no one came
But he was welcome; no one went away
But that it seemed she loved him. She is dead,
The light extinguished of her lonely hut,
The hut itself abandoned to decay,
And she forgotten in the quiet grave.

from *THE PRELUDE*

73   Childhood and School-time

FAIR seed-time had my soul, and I grew up
Foster'd alike by beauty and by fear;
Much favour'd in my birthplace, and no less
In that beloved Vale to which, erelong,
I was transplanted. Well I call to mind
('Twas at an early age, ere I had seen
Nine summers) when upon the mountain slope
The frost and breath of frosty wind had snapp'd
The last autumnal crocus, 'twas my joy

To wander half the night among the Cliffs
And the smooth Hollows, where the woodcocks ran
Along the open turf. In thought and wish
That time, my shoulder all with springes hung,
I was a fell destroyer. On the heights
Scudding away from snare to snare, I plied
My anxious visitation, hurrying on,
Still hurrying, hurrying onward; moon and stars
Were shining o'er my head; I was alone,
And seem'd to be a trouble to the peace
That was among them. Sometimes it befel
In these night-wanderings, that a strong desire
O'erpower'd my better reason, and the bird
Which was the captive of another's toils
Became my prey; and, when the deed was done
I heard among the solitary hills
Low breathings coming after me, and sounds
Of undistinguishable motion, steps
Almost as silent as the turf they trod.
Nor less in springtime when on southern banks
The shining sun had from his knot of leaves
Decoy'd the primrose flower, and when the Vales
And woods were warm, was I a plunderer then
In the high places, on the lonesome peaks
Where'er, among the mountains and the winds,
The Mother Bird had built her lodge. Though mean
My object, and inglorious, yet the end
Was not ignoble. Oh! when I have hung
Above the raven's nest, by knots of grass
And half-inch fissures in the slippery rock
But ill sustain'd, and almost, as it seem'd,
Suspended by the blast which blew amain,
Shouldering the naked crag; Oh! at that time,
While on the perilous ridge I hung alone,

With what strange utterance did the loud dry wind
Blow through my ears! the sky seem'd not a sky
Of earth, and with what motion mov'd the clouds!

*

The moon was up, the Lake was shining clear
Among the hoary mountains; from the Shore
I push'd, and struck the oars and struck again
In cadence, and my little Boat mov'd on
Even like a Man who walks with stately step
Though bent on speed. It was an act of stealth
And troubled pleasure; not without the voice
Of mountain-echoes did my Boat move on,
Leaving behind her still on either side
Small circles glittering idly in the moon,
Until they melted all into one track
Of sparkling light. A rocky Steep uprose
Above the Cavern of the Willow tree
And now, as suited one who proudly row'd
With his best skill, I fix'd a steady view
Upon the top of that same craggy ridge,
The bound of the horizon, for behind
Was nothing but the stars and the grey sky.
She was an elfin Pinnace; lustily
I dipp'd my oars into the silent Lake,
And, as I rose upon the stroke, my Boat
Went heaving through the water, like a Swan;
When from behind that craggy Steep, till then
The bound of the horizon, a huge Cliff,
As if with voluntary power instinct,
Uprear'd its head. I struck, and struck again,
And, growing still in stature, the huge Cliff
Rose up between me and the stars, and still,
With measur'd motion, like a living thing,

Strode after me. With trembling hands I turn'd,
And through the silent water stole my way
Back to the Cavern of the Willow tree.
There, in her mooring-place, I left my Bark,
And, through the meadows homeward went, with grave
And serious thoughts; and after I had seen
That spectacle, for many days, my brain
Work'd with a dim and undetermin'd sense
Of unknown modes of being; in my thoughts
There was a darkness, call it solitude,
Or blank desertion, no familiar shapes
Of hourly objects, images of trees,
Of sea or sky, no colours of green fields;
But huge and mighty Forms that do not live
Like living men mov'd slowly through the mind
By day and were the trouble of my dreams.

    Wisdom and Spirit of the universe!
Thou Soul art the eternity of thought!
That giv'st to forms and images a breath
And everlasting motion! not in vain,
By day or star-light thus from my first dawn
Of Childhood didst Thou intertwine for me
The passions that build up our human Soul,
Not with the mean and vulgar works of Man,
But with high objects, with enduring things,
With life and nature, purifying thus
The elements of feeling and of thought,
And sanctifying, by such discipline,
Both pain and fear, until we recognize
A grandeur in the beatings of the heart.

    Nor was this fellowship vouchsaf'd to me
With stinted kindness. In November days,

When vapours, rolling down the valleys, made
A lonely scene more lonesome; among woods
At noon, and 'mid the calm of summer nights,
When, by the margin of the trembling Lake,
Beneath the gloomy hills I homeward went
In solitude, such intercourse was mine;
'Twas mine among the fields both day and night,
And by the waters all the summer long.

    And in the frosty season, when the sun
Was set, and visible for many a mile
The cottage windows through the twilight blaz'd,
I heeded not the summons:—happy time
It was, indeed, for all of us; to me
It was a time of rapture: clear and loud
The village clock toll'd six; I wheel'd about,
Proud and exulting, like an untir'd horse,
That cares not for his home.—All shod with steel,
We hiss'd along the polish'd ice, in games
Confederate, imitative of the chace
And woodland pleasures, the resounding horn,
The Pack loud bellowing, and the hunted hare,
So through the darkness and the cold we flew,
And not a voice was idle; with the din,
Meanwhile, the precipices rang aloud,
The leafless trees, and every icy crag
Tinkled like iron, while the distant hills
Into the tumult sent an alien sound
Of melancholy, not unnoticed, while the stars,
Eastward, were sparkling clear, and in the west
The orange sky of evening died away.

    Not seldom from the uproar I retired
Into a silent bay, or sportively

Glanced sideways, leaving the tumultuous throng,
To cut across the image of a star
That gleam'd upon the ice: and oftentimes
When we had given our bodies to the wind,
And all the shadowy banks, on either side,
Came sweeping through the darkness, spinning still
The rapid line of motion; then at once
Have I, reclining back upon my heels,
Stopp'd short, yet still the solitary Cliffs
Wheeled by me, even as if the earth had roll'd
With visible motion her diurnal round;
Behind me did they stretch in solemn train
Feebler and feebler, and I stood and watch'd
Till all was tranquil as a dreamless sleep.

74   [Intimations of Sublimity]

    MANY are the joys
Of youth; but oh! what happiness to live
When every hour brings palpable access
Of knowledge, when all knowledge is delight,
And sorrow is not there. The seasons came,
And every season to my notice brought
A store of transitory qualities
Which, but for this most watchful power of love
Had been neglected, left a register
Of permanent relations, else unknown,
Hence life, and change, and beauty, solitude
More active, even, than 'best society',
Society made sweet as solitude
By silent inobtrusive sympathies,
And gentle agitations of the mind
From manifold distinctions, difference

Perceived in things, where to the common eye,
No difference is; and hence, from the same source
Sublimer joy; for I would walk alone,
In storm and tempest, or in starlight nights
Beneath the quiet Heavens; and, at that time,
Have felt whate'er there is of power in sound
To breathe an elevated mood, by form
Or image unprofaned; and I would stand,
Beneath some rock, listening to sounds that are
The ghostly language of the ancient earth,
Or make their dim abode in distant winds.
Thence did I drink the visionary power.
I deem not profitless these fleeting moods
Of shadowy exultation: not for this,
That they are kindred to our purer mind
And intellectual life; but that the soul,
Remembering how she felt, but what she felt
Remembering not, retains an obscure sense
Of possible sublimity, to which,
With growing faculties she doth aspire,
With faculties still growing, feeling still
That whatsoever point they gain, they still
Have something to pursue.

75   ['Consummate Happiness']

IF ever happiness hath lodg'd with man,
That day consummate happiness was mine,
Wide-spreading, steady, calm, contemplative.
The sun was set, or setting, when I left
Our cottage door, and evening soon brought on
A sober hour, not winning or serene,
For cold and raw the air was, and untun'd:

But, as a face we love is sweetest then
When sorrow damps it, or, whatever look
It chance to wear is sweetest if the heart
Have fulness in itself, even so with me
It fared that evening. Gently did my soul
Put off her veil, and, self-transmuted, stood
Naked as in the presence of her God,
As on I walked, a comfort seem'd to touch
A heart that had not been disconsolate,
Strength came where weakness was not known to be,
At least not felt; and restoration came,
Like an intruder, knocking at the door
Of unacknowledg'd weariness. I took
The balance in my hand and weigh'd myself.
I saw but little, and thereat was pleas'd;
Little did I remember, and even this
Still pleas'd me more; but I had hopes and peace
And swellings of the spirit, was rapt and soothed,
Convers'd with promises, had glimmering views
How Life pervades the undecaying mind,
How the immortal Soul with God-like power
Informs, creates, and thaws the deepest sleep
That time can lay upon her; how on earth,
Man, if he do but live within the light
Of high endeavours, daily spreads abroad
His being with a strength that cannot fail.
Nor was there want of milder thoughts, of love,
Of innocence, and holiday repose;
And more than pastoral quiet, in the heart
Of amplest projects; and a peaceful end
At last, or glorious, by endurance won.

76

['There was a Boy']

THERE was a Boy, ye knew him well, ye Cliffs
And Islands of Winander! many a time
At evening, when the stars had just begun
To move along the edges of the hills,
Rising or setting, would he stand alone
Beneath the trees, or by the glimmering Lake,
And there, with fingers interwoven, both hands
Press'd closely, palm to palm, and to his mouth
Uplifted, he, as through an instrument,
Blew mimic hootings to the silent owls
That they might answer him.—And they would shout
Across the watery Vale, and shout again,
Responsive to his call, with quivering peals,
And long halloos, and screams, and echoes loud
Redoubled and redoubled; concourse wild
Of mirth and jocund din! And when it chanced
That pauses of deep silence mock'd his skill,
Then sometimes, in that silence, while he hung
Listening, a gentle shock of mild surprize
Has carried far into his heart the voice
Of mountain torrents; or the visible scene
Would enter unawares into his mind
With all its solemn imagery, its rocks,
Its woods, and that uncertain Heaven, receiv'd
Into the bosom of the steady Lake.

77

[The Shepherd]

THERE 'tis the Shepherd's task the winter long
To wait upon the storms: of their approach
Sagacious, from the heights he drives his Flock
Down into sheltering coves, and feeds them there

Through the hard time, long as the storm is lock'd,
(So do they phrase it) bearing from the stalls
A toilsome burden up the craggy ways,
To strew it on the snow. And when the Spring
Looks out, and all the mountains dance with lambs,
He through the enclosures won from the steep Waste,
And through the lower Heights hath gone his rounds;
And when the Flock with warmer weather climbs
Higher and higher, him his office leads
To range among them, through the hills dispers'd,
And watch their goings, whatsoever track
Each Wanderer chooses for itself; a work
That lasts the summer through. He quits his home
At day-spring, and no sooner doth the sun
Begin to strike him with a fire-like heat
Than he lies down upon some shining place
And breakfasts with his Dog; when he hath stay'd,
As for the most he doth, beyond his time,
He springs up with a bound, and then away!
Ascending fast with his long Pole in hand,
Or winding in and out among the crags.
What need to follow him through what he does
Or sees in his day's march? He feels himself
In those vast regions where his service is
A Freeman; wedded to his life of hope
And hazard, and hard labour interchang'd
With that majestic indolence so dear
To native Man. A rambling Schoolboy, thus
Have I beheld him, without knowing why
Have felt his presence in his own domain,
As of a Lord and Master; or a Power
Or Genius, under Nature, under God,
Presiding; and severest solitude
Seem'd more commanding oft when he was there.

Seeking the raven's nest, and suddenly
Surpriz'd with vapours, or on rainy days
When I have angled up the lonely brooks
Mine eyes have glanced upon him, few steps off,
In size a giant, stalking through the fog,
His sheep like Greenland Bears; at other times
When round some shady promontory turning,
His Form hath flash'd upon me, glorified
By the deep radiance of the setting sun:
Or him have I descried in distant sky,
A solitary object and sublime,
Above all height! like an aerial Cross,
As it is stationed on some spiry Rock
Of the Chartreuse, for worship. Thus was Man
Ennobled outwardly before mine eyes,
And thus my heart at first was introduc'd
To an unconscious love and reverence
Of human Nature; hence the human form
To me was like an index of delight,
Of grace and honour, power and worthiness.

78 [To Coleridge in Sicily]

THINE be those motions strong and sanative,
A ladder for thy Spirit to reascend
To health and joy and pure contentedness;
To me the grief confined that Thou art gone
From this last spot of earth where Freedom now
Stands single in her only sanctuary,
A lonely wanderer, art gone, by pain
Compell'd and sickness, at this latter day,
This heavy time of change for all mankind;
I feel for Thee, must utter what I feel:

The sympathies, erewhile, in part discharg'd,
Gather afresh, and will have vent again:
My own delights do scarcely seem to me
My own delights; the lordly Alps themselves,
Those rosy Peaks, from which the Morning looks
Abroad on many Nations, are not now
Since thy migration and departure, Friend,
The gladsome image in my memory
Which they were used to be; to kindred scenes,
On errand, at a time how different!
Thou tak'st thy way, carrying a heart more ripe
For all divine enjoyment, with the soul
Which Nature gives to Poets, now by thought
Matur'd, and in the summer of its strength.
Oh! wrap him in your Shades, ye Giant Woods,
On Etna's side, and thou, O flowery Vale
Of Enna! is there not some nook of thine,
From the first playtime of the infant earth
Kept sacred to restorative delight?

79 Imagination, how impaired and restored

YE motions of delight, that through the fields
Stir gently, breezes and soft airs that breathe
The breath of Paradise, and find your way
To the recesses of the soul! Ye Brooks
Muttering along the stones, a busy noise
By day, a quiet one in silent night,
And you, ye Groves, whose ministry it is
To interpose the covert of your shades,
Even as a sleep, betwixt the heart of man
And the uneasy world, 'twixt man himself,
Not seldom, and his own unquiet heart,

Oh! that I had a music and a voice,
Harmonious as your own, that I might tell
What ye have done for me. The morning shines,
Nor heedeth Man's perverseness; Spring returns,
I saw the Spring return, when I was dead
To deeper hope, yet had I joy for her,
And welcomed her benevolence, rejoiced
In common with the Children of her Love,
Plants, insects, beasts in field, and birds in bower.
So neither were complacency nor peace
Nor tender yearnings wanting for my good
Through those distracted times; in Nature still
Glorying, I found a counterpoise in her,
Which, when the spirit of evil was at height
Maintain'd for me a secret happiness;
Her I resorted to, and lov'd so much
I seem'd to love as much as heretofore;
And yet this passion, fervent as it was,
Had suffer'd change; how could there fail to be
Some change, if merely hence, that years of life
Were going on, and with them loss or gain
Inevitable, sure alternative.

*

Oh! soul of Nature, excellent and fair,
That didst rejoice with me, with whom I too
Rejoiced, through early youth before the winds
And powerful waters, and in lights and shades
That march'd and countermarch'd about the hills
In glorious apparition, now all eye
And now all ear; but ever with the heart
Employ'd and the majestic intellect,
Oh! Soul of Nature! that dost overflow
With passion and with life, what feeble men

Walk on this earth! how feeble have I been
When thou wert in thy strength! Nor this through stroke
Of human suffering, such as justifies
Remissness and inaptitude of mind,
But through presumption, even in pleasure pleas'd
Unworthily, disliking here, and there,
Liking, by rules of mimic art transferr'd
To things above all art. But more, for this,
Although a strong infection of the age,
Was never much my habit, giving way
To a comparison of scene with scene,
Bent overmuch on superficial things,
Pampering myself with meagre novelties
Of colour and proportion, to the moods
Of time and season, to the moral power
The affections, and the spirit of the place,
Less sensible. Nor only did the love
Of sitting thus in judgment interrupt
My deeper feelings, but another cause
More subtle and less easily explain'd
That almost seems inherent in the Creature,
Sensuous and intellectual as he is,
A twofold Frame of body and of mind;
The state to which I now allude was one
In which the eye was master of the heart,
When that which is in every stage of life
The most despotic of our senses gain'd
Such strength in me as often held my mind
In absolute dominion. Gladly here,
Entering upon abstruser argument,
Would I endeavour to unfold the means
Which Nature studiously employs to thwart
This tyranny, summons all the senses each
To counteract the other and themselves

And makes them all, and the objects with which all
Are conversant, subservient in their turn
To the great ends of Liberty and Power.

*

There are in our existence spots of time,
Which with distinct pre-eminence retain
A vivifying virtue, whence, depress'd
By false opinion and contentious thought,
Or aught of heavier or more deadly weight,
In trivial occupations, and the round
Of ordinary intercourse, our minds
Are nourished and invisibly repair'd,
A virtue by which pleasure is enhanced
That penetrates, enables us to mount
When high, more high, and lifts us up when fallen.
This efficacious spirit chiefly lurks
Among those passages of life in which
We have had deepest feeling that the mind
Is lord and master, and that outward sense
Is but the obedient servant of her will.
Such moments worthy of all gratitude,
Are scatter'd everywhere, taking their date
From our first childhood: in our childhood even
Perhaps are most conspicuous. Life with me,
As far as memory can look back, is full
Of this beneficent influence. At a time
When scarcely (I was then not six years old)
My hand could hold a bridle, with proud hopes
I mounted, and we rode towards the hills:
We were a pair of horsemen; honest James
Was with me, my encourager and guide.
We had not travell'd long, ere some mischance
Disjoin'd me from my Comrade, and, through fear

Dismounting, down the rough and stony Moor
I led my Horse, and stumbling on, at length
Came to a bottom, where in former times
A Murderer had been hung in iron chains.
The Gibbet-mast was moulder'd down, the bones
And iron case were gone; but on the turf,
Hard by, soon after that fell deed was wrought
Some unknown hand had carved the Murderer's name.
The monumental writing was engraven
In times long past, and still, from year to year,
By superstition of the neighbourhood,
The grass is clear'd away; and to this hour
The letters are all fresh and visible.
Faltering, and ignorant where I was, at length
I chanced to espy those characters inscribed
On the green sod: forthwith I left the spot
And, reascending the bare Common, saw
A naked Pool that lay beneath the hills,
The Beacon on the summit, and more near,
A Girl who bore a Pitcher on her head
And seem'd with difficult steps to force her way
Against the blowing wind. It was, in truth,
An ordinary sight; but I should need
Colours and words that are unknown to man
To paint the visionary dreariness
Which, while I look'd all round for my lost guide,
Did at that time invest the naked Pool,
The Beacon on the lonely Eminence,
The Woman, and her garments vex'd and toss'd
By the strong wind. When, in a blessed season
With those two dear Ones, to my heart so dear,
When in the blessed time of early love,
Long afterwards, I roam'd about
In daily presence of this very scene,

Upon the naked pool and dreary crags,
And on the melancholy Beacon, fell
The spirit of pleasure and youth's golden gleam;
And think ye not with radiance more divine
From these remembrances, and from the power
They left behind? So feeling comes in aid
Of feeling, and diversity of strength
Attends us, if but once we have been strong.
Oh! mystery of Man, from what a depth
Proceed thy honours! I am lost, but see
In simple childhood something of the base
On which thy greatness stands, but this I feel,
That from thyself it is that thou must give,
Else never canst receive. The days gone by
Come back upon me from the dawn almost
Of life: the hiding-places of my power
Seem open; I approach, and then they close;
I see by glimpses now; when age comes on,
May scarcely see at all, and I would give,
While yet we may, as far as words can give,
A substance and a life to what I feel:

*

One Christmas-time,
The day before the holidays began,
Feverish and tired, and restless, I went forth
Into the fields, impatient for the sight
Of those two Horses which should bear us home,
My Brothers and myself. There was a crag,
An Eminence, which from the meeting-point
Of two highways ascending, overlook'd
At least a long half-mile of those two roads
By each of which the expected Steeds might come,
The choice uncertain. Thither I repair'd
Up to the highest summit; 'twas a day

Stormy, and rough, and wild, and on the grass
I sate, half-shelter'd by a naked wall;
Upon my right hand was a single sheep,
A whistling hawthorn on my left, and there,
With those companions at my side, I watch'd,
Straining my eyes intensely, as the mist
Gave intermitting prospect of the wood
And plain beneath. Ere I to School return'd
That dreary time, ere I had been ten days
A dweller in my Father's house, he died,
And I and my two Brothers, Orphans then,
Followed his Body to the Grave. The event
With all the sorrow which it brought appear'd
A chastisement; and when I call'd to mind
That day so lately pass'd, when from the crag
I look'd in such anxiety of hope,
With trite reflections of morality,
Yet in the deepest passion, I bow'd low
To God, who thus corrected my desires;
And afterwards, the wind and sleety rain
And all the business of the elements,
The single sheep, and the one blasted tree,
And the bleak music of that old stone wall,
The noise of wood and water, and the mist
Which on the line of each of those two Roads
Advanced in such indisputable shapes,
All these were spectacles and sounds to which
I often would repair and thence would drink,
As at a fountain; and I do not doubt
That in this later time, when storm and rain
Beat on my roof at midnight, or by day
When I am in the woods, unknown to me
The workings of my spirit thence are brought.

★

From nature doth emotion come, and moods
Of calmness equally are nature's gift,
This is her glory; these two attributes
Are sister horns that constitute her strength;
This twofold influence is the sun and shower
Of all her bounties, both in origin
And end alike benignant. Hence it is,
That Genius which exists by interchange
Of peace and excitation, finds in her
His best and purest Friend, from her receives
That energy by which he seeks the truth,
Is rouz'd, aspires, grasps, struggles, wishes, craves,
From her that happy stillness of the mind
Which fits him to receive it, when unsought.

Such benefit may souls of humblest frame
Partake of, each in their degree; 'tis mine
To speak, what I myself have known and felt
Sweet task! for words find easy way, inspired
By gratitude and confidence in truth.
Long time in search of knowledge desperate,
I was benighted heart and mind; but now
On all sides day began to reappear,
And it was proved indeed that not in vain
I had been taught to reverence a Power
That is the very quality and shape
And image of right reason, that matures
Her processes by steadfast laws, gives birth
To no impatient or fallacious hopes,
No heat of passion or excessive zeal,
No vain conceits, provokes to no quick turns
Of self-applauding intellect, but lifts
The Being into magnanimity;
Holds up before the mind, intoxicate

With present objects and the busy dance
Of things that pass away, a temperate shew
Of objects that endure, and by this course
Disposes her, when over-fondly set
On leaving her incumbrances behind
To seek in Man, and in the frame of life,
Social and individual, what there is
Desirable, affecting, good or fair
Of kindred permanence, the gifts divine
And universal, the pervading grace
That hath been, is, and shall be. Above all
Did Nature bring again that wiser mood
More deeply re-established in my soul,
Which, seeing little worthy or sublime
In what we blazon with the pompous names
Of power and action, early tutor'd me
To look with feelings of fraternal love
Upon those unassuming things, that hold
A silent station in this beauteous world.

80   Conclusion

It was a Summer's night, a close warm night,
Wan, dull and glaring, with a dripping mist
Low-hung and thick that cover'd all the sky,
Half threatening storm and rain; but on we went
Uncheck'd, being full of heart and having faith
In our tried Pilot. Little could we see
Hemm'd round on every side with fog and damp,
And, after ordinary travellers' chat
With our Conductor, silently we sank

Each into commerce with his private thoughts:
Thus did we breast the ascent, and by myself
Was nothing either seen or heard the while
Which took me from my musings, save that once
The Shepherd's Cur did to his own great joy
Unearth a hedgehog in the mountain crags
Round which he made a barking turbulent.
This small adventure, for even such it seemed
In that wild place and at the dead of night,
Being over and forgotten, on we wound
In silence as before. With forehead bent
Earthward, as if in opposition set
Against an enemy, I panted up
With eager pace, and no less eager thoughts.
Thus might we wear perhaps an hour away,
Ascending at loose distance each from each,
And I, as chanced, the foremost of the Band;
When at my feet the ground appear'd to brighten,
And with a step or two seem'd brighter still;
Nor had I time to ask the cause of this,
For instantly a Light upon the turf
Fell like a flash: I looked about, and lo!
The Moon stood naked in the Heavens, at height
Immense above my head, and on the shore
I found myself of a huge sea of mist,
Which, meek and silent, rested at my feet:
A hundred hills their dusky backs upheaved
All over this still Ocean, and beyond,
Far, far beyond, the vapours shot themselves,
In headlands, tongues, and promontory shapes,
Into the Sea, the real Sea, that seem'd
To dwindle, and give up its majesty,
Usurp'd upon as far as sight could reach.
Meanwhile, the Moon look'd down upon this shew

In single glory, and we stood, the mist
Touching our very feet; and from the shore
At distance not the third part of a mile
Was a blue chasm; a fracture in the vapour,
A deep and gloomy breathing-place through which
Mounted the roar of waters, torrents, streams
Innumerable, roaring with one voice.
The universal spectacle throughout
Was shaped for admiration and delight,
Grand in itself alone, but in that breach
Through which the homeless voice of waters rose,
That dark deep thoroughfare had Nature lodg'd
The Soul, the Imagination of the whole.

A meditation rose in me that night
Upon the lonely Mountain when the scene
Had pass'd away, and it appear'd to me
The perfect image of a mighty Mind,
Of one that feeds upon infinity,
That is exalted by an underpresence,
The sense of God, or whatsoe'er is dim
Or vast in its own being, above all
One function of such mind had Nature there
Exhibited by putting forth, and that
With circumstance most awful and sublime,
That domination which she oftentimes
Exerts upon the outward face of things,
So moulds them, and endues, abstracts, combines,
Or by abrupt and unhabitual influence
Doth make one object so impress itself
Upon all others, and pervade them so
That even the grossest minds must see and hear
And cannot chuse but feel. The Power which these
Acknowledge when thus moved, which Nature thus

Thrusts forth upon the senses, is the express
Resemblance, in the fulness of its strength
Made visible, a genuine Counterpart
And Brother of the glorious faculty
Which higher minds bear with them as their own.
That is the very spirit in which they deal
With all the objects of the universe;
They from their native selves can send abroad
Like transformations, for themselves create
A like existence, and, whene'er it is
Created for them, catch it by an instinct;
Them the enduring and the transient both
Serve to exalt; they build up greatest things
From least suggestions, ever on the watch,
Willing to work and to be wrought upon,
They need not extraordinary calls
To rouze them, in a world of life they live,
By sensible impressions not enthrall'd,
But quicken'd, rouz'd, and made thereby more apt
To hold communion with the invisible world.
Such minds are truly from the Deity,
For they are Powers; and hence the highest bliss
That can be known is theirs, the consciousness
Of whom they are habitually infused
Through every image, and through every thought,
And all impressions, hence religion, faith,
And endless occupation for the soul
Whether discursive or intuitive;
Hence sovereignty within and peace at will,
Emotion which best foresight need not fear
Most worthy then of trust when most intense.
Hence chearfulness in every act of life
Hence truth in moral judgements and delight
That fails not in the external universe.

Oh! who is he that hath his whole life long
Preserved, enlarged, this freedom in himself?
For this alone is genuine Liberty:
Witness, ye Solitudes! where I received
My earliest visitations, careless then
Of what was given me, and where now I roam,
A meditative, oft a suffering Man,
And yet, I trust, with undiminish'd powers,
Witness, whatever falls my better mind,
Revolving with the accidents of life,
May have sustain'd, that, howsoe'er misled,
I never, in the quest of right and wrong,
Did tamper with myself from private aims;
Nor was in any of my hopes the dupe
Of selfish passions; nor did wilfully
Yield ever to mean cares and low pursuits;
But rather did with jealousy shrink back
From every combination that might aid
The tendency, too potent in itself,
Of habit to enslave the mind, I mean
Oppress it by the laws of vulgar sense,
And substitute a universe of death,
The falsest of all worlds, in place of that
Which is divine and true. To fear and love,
To love as first and chief, for there fear ends,
Be this ascribed; to early intercourse,
In presence of sublime and lovely forms,
With the adverse principles of pain and joy,
Evil as one is rashly named by those
Who know not what they say. By love, for here
Do we begin and end, all grandeur comes,
All truth and beauty, from pervading love,
That gone, we are as dust. Behold the fields
In balmy spring-time, full of rising flowers

And happy creatures; see that Pair, the Lamb
And the Lamb's Mother, and their tender ways
Shall touch thee to the heart; in some green bower
Rest, and be not alone, but have thou there
The One who is thy choice of all the world,
There linger, lull'd and lost, and rapt away
Be happy to thy fill; thou call'st this love
And so it is, but there is higher love
Than this, a love that comes into the heart
With awe and a diffusive sentiment;
Thy love is human merely; this proceeds
More from the brooding Soul, and is divine.

*

   Oh! yet a few short years of useful life,
And all will be complete, thy race be run,
Thy monument of glory will be raised.
Then, though, too weak to tread the ways of truth,
This Age fall back to old idolatry,
Though men return to servitude as fast
As the tide ebbs, to ignominy and shame
By Nations sink together, we shall still
Find solace in the knowledge which we have,
Bless'd with true happiness if we may be
United helpers forward of a day
Of firmer trust, joint-labourers in a work
(Should Providence such grace to us vouchsafe)
Of their redemption, surely yet to come.
Prophets of Nature, we to them will speak
A lasting inspiration, sanctified
By reason and by truth; what we have loved,
Others will love; and we may teach them how;
Instruct them how the mind of man becomes
A thousand times more beautiful than the earth

On which he dwells, above this Frame of things
(Which, 'mid all revolution in the hopes
And fears of men, doth still remain unchanged)
In beauty exalted, as it is itself
Of substance and of fabric more divine.

SIR WALTER SCOTT

81   [Sir William of Deloraine at the Wizard's
Tomb]

IF thou would'st view fair Melrose aright,
Go visit it by the pale moon-light;
For the gay beams of lightsome day
Gild, but to flout, the ruins gray.
When the broken arches are black in night,
And each shafted oriel glimmers white;
When the cold light's uncertain shower
Streams on the ruined central tower;
When buttress and buttress, alternately,
Seem framed of ebon and ivory;
When silver edges the imagery,
And the scrolls that teach thee to live and die;
When distant Tweed is heard to rave,
And the owlet to hoot o'er the dead man's grave;
Then go—but go alone the while—
Then view St David's ruined pile;
And, home returning, soothly swear,
Was never scene so sad and fair!

Short halt did Deloraine make there;
Little recked he of the scene so fair.

With dagger's hilt, on the wicket strong,
He struck full loud, and struck full long.
The porter hurried to the gate—
'Who knocks so loud, and knocks so late?'
'From Branksome I,' the warrior cried;
And strait the wicket opened wide:
For Branksome's chiefs had in battle stood,
   To fence the rights of fair Melrose;
And lands and livings, many a rood,
   Had gifted the shrine for their souls' repose.

Bold Deloraine his errand said;
The porter bent his humble head;
With torch in hand, and feet unshod,
And noiseless step, the path he trod:
The arched cloisters, far and wide,
Rang to the warrior's clanking stride,
Till, stooping low his lofty crest,
He entered the cell of the ancient priest,
And lifted his barred aventayle,
To hail the Monk of St Mary's aisle.

'The Ladye of Branksome greets thee by me;
   Says, that the fated hour is come,
And that to-night I shall watch with thee,
   To win the treasure of the tomb.'
From sackcloth couch the Monk arose,
   With toil his stiffened limbs he reared;
A hundred years had flung their snows
   On his thin locks and floating beard.

And strangely on the knight looked he,
   And his blue eyes gleamed wild and wide;
'And, darest thou, warrior! seek to see
   What heaven and hell alike would hide?

My breast, in belt of iron pent,
    With shirt of hair and scourge of thorn;
For threescore years, in penance spent,
    My knees those flinty stones have worn:

Yet all too little to atone
For knowing what should ne'er be known.
    Would'st thou thy every future year
        In ceaseless prayer and penance drie,
    Yet wait thy latter end with fear—
        Then, daring warrior, follow me!'

'Penance, father, will I none;
Prayer know I hardly one;
For mass or prayer can I rarely tarry,
Save to patter an Ave Mary,
When I ride on a Border foray:
Other prayer can I none;
So speed me my errand, and let me begone.'

Again on the Knight looked the Churchman old,
And again he sighed heavily:
For he had himself been a warrior bold,
And fought in Spain and Italy.
And he thought on the days that were long since by
When his limbs were strong, and his courage was high:
Now, slow and faint, he led the way,
Where, cloistered round, the garden lay;
The pillared arches were over their head,
And beneath their feet were the bones of the dead.

Spreading herbs and flowerets bright,
Glistened with the dew of night;
Nor herb nor floweret glistened there,
But was carved in the cloister arches as fair.

The Monk gazed long on the lovely moon,
　　Then into the night he looked forth;
And red and bright the streamers light
　　Were dancing in the glowing north.
So had he seen, in fair Castile,
　　The youth in glittering squadrons start,
Sudden the flying jennet wheel,
　　And hurl the unexpected dart.
He knew, by the streamers that shot so bright,
That spirits were riding the northern light.

By a steel-clenched postern door,
　　They entered now the chancel tall;
The darkened roof rose high aloof
　　On pillars lofty, and light, and small;
The keystone, that locked each ribbed aisle,
Was a fleur-de-lys, or a quatre-feuille;
The corbells were carved grotesque and grim;
And the pillars, with clustered shafts so trim,
With plinth and with capital flourished around,
Seemed bundles of lances which garlands had bound.

Full many a scutcheon and banner, riven,
Shook to the cold night-wind of heaven,
　　Around the screened altar's pale;
And there the dying lamps did burn,
Before thy low and lonely urn,
O gallant chief of Otterburne!
　　And thine, dark knight of Liddesdale!
O fading honours of the dead!
O high ambition, lowly laid!

The moon on the east oriel shone,
Through slender shafts of shapely stone,
　　By foliaged tracery combined;

Thou would'st have thought some fairy's hand,
'Twixt poplars straight, the ozier wand,
   In many a freakish knot, had twined;
Then framed a spell, when the work was done,
And changed the willow wreaths to stone.
The silver light, so pale and faint,
Shewed many a prophet and many a saint,
   Whose image on the glass was dyed;
Full in the midst, his cross of red
Triumphant Michael brandished,
   And trampled the apostate's pride.
The moon-beam kissed the holy pane,
And threw on the pavement a bloody stain.

★

'Lo, Warrior! now, the cross of red
Points to the grave of the mighty dead;
Within it burns a wonderous light,
To chase the spirits that love the night:
The lamp shall burn unquenchably,
Until the eternal doom shall be.'
Slow moved the Monk to the broad flag-stone,
Which the bloody cross was traced upon:
He pointed to a secret nook;
A bar from thence the warrior took;
And the Monk made a sign with his withered hand,
The grave's huge portal to expand.

With beating heart, to the task he went;
His sinewy frame o'er the grave-stone bent;
With bar of iron heaved amain,
Till the toil-drops fell from his brows like rain.
It was by dint of passing strength,
That he moved the massy stone at length.

I would you had been there to see
How the light broke forth so gloriously;
Streamed upward to the chancel roof,
And through the galleries far aloof!
No earthly flame blazed e'er so bright:
It shone like heaven's own blessed light;
   And, issuing from the tomb,
Shewed the Monk's cowl, and visage pale;
Danced on the dark-brow'd Warrior's mail,
   And kissed his waving plume.

Before their eyes the wizard lay,
As if he had not been dead a day;
His hoary beard in silver roll'd,
He seemed some seventy winters old;
   A palmer's amice wrapped him round,
   With a wrought Spanish baldric bound,
     Like a pilgrim from beyond the sea;
His left hand held his Book of Might;
A silver cross was in his right;
   The lamp was placed beside his knee:
High and majestic was his look,
At which the fellest fiends had shook;
And all unruffled was his face—
They trusted his soul had gotten grace.

Often had William of Deloraine
Rode through the battle's bloody plain,
And trampled down the warriors slain,
   And neither known remorse nor awe;
Yet now remorse and awe he own'd;
His breath came thick, his head swam round,
   When this strange scene of death he saw.

Bewildered and unnerved, he stood,
And the priest prayed fervently, and loud;
With eyes averted, prayed he,
He might not endure the sight to see,
Of the man he had loved so brotherly.

And when the priest his death-prayer had prayed,
Thus unto Deloraine he said—
'Now speed thee what thou hast to do,
Or, warrior, we may dearly rue;
For those thou mayest not look upon,
Are gathering fast round the yawning stone!'—
Then Deloraine, in terror, took
From the cold hand the mighty book,
With iron clasped, and with iron bound:
He thought, as he took it, the dead man frowned;
But the glare of the sepulchral light,
Perchance, had dazzled the warrior's sight.

When the huge stone sunk o'er the tomb,
The night returned, in double gloom;
For the moon had gone down, and the stars were few;
And, as the knight and priest withdrew,
With wavering steps, and dizzy brain,
They hardly might the postern gain.
'Tis said, as through the aisles they passed,
They heard strange noises on the blast;
And through the cloister-galleries small,
Which at mid-height thread the chancel wall,
Loud sobs, and laughter louder, ran,
And voices unlike the voice of man;
As if the fiends kept holiday,
Because these spells were brought to day.
I cannot tell how the truth may be;
I say the tale as 'twas said to me.

'Now, hie thee hence,' the father said,
'And when we are on death-bed laid,
O may our dear Ladye, and sweet St John,
Forgive our souls for the deed we have done!'
 The Monk returned him to his cell,
  And many a prayer and penance sped;
 When the convent met at the noontide bell—
  The Monk of St Mary's aisle was dead!
Before the cross was the body laid,
With hands clasped fast, as if still he prayed.

82   ['A Father's Notes of Woe']

Sweet Teviot! on thy silver tide
 The glaring bale-fires blaze no more;
No longer steel-clad warriors ride
 Along thy wild and willowed shore;
Where'er thou wind'st by dale or hill,
All, all is peaceful, all is still,
 As if thy waves, since Time was born,
Since first they rolled their way to Tweed,
Had only heard the shepherd's reed,
 Nor started at the bugle-horn.

Unlike the tide of human time,
Which, though it change in ceaseless flow,
Retains each grief, retains each crime,
 Its earliest course was doomed to know;
And, darker as it downward bears,
Is stained with past and present tears.
 Low as that tide has ebbed with me,
It still reflects to memory's eye
The hour my brave, my only boy
 Fell by the side of great Dundee.

Why, when the volleying musket played
Against the bloody Highland blade,
Why was not I beside him laid!—
Enough—he died the death of fame;
Enough—he died with conquering Græme.

83   [The Minstrel Responds to Flattery]

CALL it not vain—they do not err,
  Who say, that when the poet dies,
Mute Nature mourns her worshipper,
  And celebrates his obsequies;
Who say, tall cliff, and cavern lone,
For the departed bard make moan;
That mountains weep in crystal rill;
That flowers in tears of balm distil;
Through his loved groves that breezes sigh,
And oaks, in deeper groan, reply;
And rivers teach their rushing wave
To murmur dirges round his grave.

Not that, in sooth, o'er mortal urn
Those things inanimate can mourn;
But that the stream, the wood, the gale,
Is vocal with the plaintive wail
Of those, who, else forgotten long,
Lived in the poet's faithful song,
And, with the poet's parting breath,
Whose memory feels a second death.
The maid's pale shade, who wails her lot,
That love, true love, should be forgot,
From rose and hawthorn shakes the tear
Upon the gentle minstrel's bier;

The phantom knight, his glory fled,
Mourns o'er the field he heaped with dead;
Mounts the wild blast that sweeps amain,
And shrieks along the battle-plain.
The chief, whose antique crownlet long
Still sparkled in the feudal song,
Now, from the mountain's misty throne,
Sees, in the thanedom once his own,
His ashes undistinguished lie,
His place, his power, his memory die:
His groans the lonely caverns fill,
His tears of rage impel the rill:
All mourn the minstrel's harp unstrung,
Their name unknown, their praise unsung.

84

[The Patriot]

BREATHES there the man, with soul so dead,
Who never to himself hath said,
   This is my own, my native land!
Whose heart hath ne'er within him burned,
As home his footsteps he hath turned,
   From wandering on a foreign strand!
If such there breathe, go, mark him well;
For him no Minstrel raptures swell;
High though his titles, proud his name,
Boundless his wealth as wish can claim;
Despite those titles, power, and pelf,
The wretch, concentred all in self,
Living, shall forfeit fair renown,
And, doubly dying, shall go down
To the vile dust, from whence he sprung,
Unwept, unhonoured, and unsung.

O Caledonia! stern and wild,
Meet nurse for a poetic child!
Land of brown heath and shaggy wood,
Land of the mountain and the flood,
Land of my sires! what mortal hand
Can e'er untie the filial band,
That knits me to thy rugged strand!
Still, as I view each well known scene,
Think what is now, and what hath been,
Seems as, to me, of all bereft,
Sole friends thy woods and streams were left;
And thus I love them better still,
Even in extremity of ill.
By Yarrow's stream still let me stray,
Though none should guide my feeble way;
Still feel the breeze down Ettricke break,
Although it chill my withered cheek;
Still lay my head by Teviot Stone,
Though there, forgotten and alone,
The Bard may draw his parting groan.

85   Lochinvar

LADY HERON'S SONG

O, YOUNG Lochinvar is come out of the west,
Through all the wide Border his steed was the best;
And save his good broad-sword he weapons had none,
He rode all unarmed, and he rode all alone.
So faithful in love, and so dauntless in war,
There never was knight like the young Lochinvar.

He staid not for brake, and he stopped not for stone;
He swam the Eske river where ford there was none;
But, ere he alighted at Netherby gate,
The bride had consented, the gallant came late:
For a laggard in love, and a dastard in war,
Was to wed the fair Ellen of brave Lochinvar.

So boldly he entered the Netherby Hall,
Among bride's-men, and kinsmen, and brothers, and all:
Then spoke the bride's father, his hand on his sword,
(For the poor craven bridegroom said never a word,)
'O come ye in peace here, or come ye in war,
Or to dance at our bridal, young Lord Lochinvar?'

'I long wooed your daughter, my suit you denied;—
Love swells like the Solway, but ebbs like its tide—
And now am I come, with this lost love of mine,
To lead but one measure, drink one cup of wine.
There are maidens in Scotland more lovely by far,
That would gladly be bride to the young Lochinvar.'

The bride kissed the goblet; the knight took it up,
He quaffed off the wine, and he threw down the cup.
She looked down to blush, and she looked up to sigh,
With a smile on her lips, and a tear in her eye.
He took her soft hand, ere her mother could bar,—
'Now tread we a measure!' said young Lochinvar.

So stately his form, and so lovely her face,
That never a hall such a galliard did grace;
While her mother did fret, and her father did fume,
And the bridegroom stood dangling his bonnet and plume;
And the bride-maidens whispered, ' 'Twere better by far
To have matched our fair cousin with young Lochinvar.'

One touch to her hand, and one word in her ear,
When they reached the hall-door, and the charger stood near;
So light to the croupe the fair lady he swung,
So light to the saddle before her he sprung!—
'She is won! we are gone, over bank, bush, and scaur;
They'll have fleet steeds that follow,' quoth young Lochinvar.

There was mounting 'mong Græmes of the Netherby clan;
Forsters, Fenwicks, and Musgraves, they rode and they ran:
There was racing, and chasing, on Cannobie Lee,
But the lost bride of Netherby ne'er did they see.
So daring in love, and so dauntless in war,
Have ye e'er heard of gallant like young Lochinvar?

86   Song

SOLDIER, rest! thy warfare o'er,
Sleep the sleep that knows not breaking;
Dream of battled fields no more,
    Days of danger, nights of waking.
In our isle's enchanted hall,
    Hands unseen thy couch are strewing,
Fairy strains of music fall,
    Every sense in slumber dewing.
Soldier, rest! thy warfare o'er,
Dream of fighting fields no more:
Sleep the sleep that knows not breaking,
    Morn of toil, nor night of waking.

No rude sound shall reach thine ear,
    Armour's clang, or war-steed champing,
Trump nor pibroch summon here
    Mustering clan, or squadron tramping.

Yet the lark's shrill fife may come
   At the day-break from the fallow,
And the bittern sound his drum
   Booming from the sedgy shallow.
Ruder sounds shall none be near,
Guards nor warders challenge here,
Here's no war-steed's neigh and champing,
   Shouting clans or squadrons stamping.

Huntsman, rest! thy chase is done,
   While our slumbrous spells assail ye,
Dream not with the rising sun,
   Bugles here shall sound reveillie.
Sleep! the deer is in his den;
   Sleep! thy hounds are by thee lying;
Sleep! nor dream in yonder glen,
   How thy gallant steed lay dying.
Huntsman, rest! thy chase is done,
Think not of the rising sun,
For at dawning to assail ye,
Here no bugles sound reveillie.

87   The Gathering

Time rolls his ceaseless course. The race of yore
   Who danced our infancy upon their knee,
And told our marvelling boy-hood legends store,
   Of their strange ventures happ'd by land or sea,
How are they blotted from the things that be!
   How few, all weak and wither'd of their force,
Wait, on the verge of dark eternity,
   Like stranded wrecks, the tide returning hoarse,
To sweep them from our sight! Time rolls his ceaseless course.

Yet live there still who can remember well,
  How, when a mountain chief his bugle blew,
Both field and forest, dingle, cliff, and dell,
  And solitary heath, the signal knew;
And fast the faithful clan around him drew,
  What time the warning note was keenly wound,
What time aloft their kindred banner flew,
  While clamorous war-pipes yelled the gathering sound,
And while the Fiery Cross glanced, like a meteor, round.

88   ['Farewell, thou Minstrel Harp']

HARP of the North, farewell! The hills grow dark,
  On purple peaks a deeper shade descending;
In twilight copse the glow-worm lights her spark,
  The deer, half-seen, are to the covert wending.
Resume thy wizard elm! the fountain lending,
  And the wild breeze, thy wilder minstrelsy;
Thy numbers sweet with Nature's vespers blending,
  With distant echo from the fold and lea,
And herd-boy's evening pipe, and hum of housing bee.

Yet, once again, farewell, thou Minstrel Harp!
  Yet, once again, forgive my feeble sway,
And little reck I of the censure sharp
  May idly cavil at an idle lay.
Much have I owed thy strains on life's long way,
  Through secret woes the world has never known,
When on the weary night dawned wearier day,
  And bitterer was the grief devoured alone.
That I o'erlive such woes, Enchantress! is thine own.

Hark! as my lingering footsteps slow retire,
   Some Spirit of the Air has waked thy string!
'Tis now a Seraph bold, with touch of fire,
   'Tis now the brush of Fairy's frolic wing.
Receding now, the dying numbers ring
   Fainter and fainter down the rugged dell,
And now the mountain breezes scarcely bring
   A wandering witch-note of the distant spell—
And now, 'tis silent all!—Enchantress, fare thee well!

89   Song

'A WEARY lot is thine, fair maid,
   A weary lot is thine!
To pull the thorn thy brow to braid,
   And press the rue for wine!
A lightsome eye, a soldier's mien,
   A feather of the blue,
A doublet of the Lincoln green,—
   No more of me you knew,
             My love!
   No more of me you knew.

This morn is merry June, I trow,
   The rose is budding fain;
But she shall bloom in winter snow,
   Ere we two meet again.'—
He turned his charger as he spake,
   Upon the river shore,
He gave his bridle reins a shake,
   Said, 'Adieu for evermore,
             My love!
   And adieu for evermore.'—

90   ## The Dreary Change

THE sun upon the Weirdlaw Hill,
  In Ettrick's vale, is sinking sweet;
The westland wind is hush and still,
  The lake lies sleeping at my feet.
Yet not the landscape to mine eye
  Bears those bright hues that once it bore;
Though evening, with her richest dye,
  Flames o'er the hills of Ettrick's shore.

With listless look along the plain
  I see Tweed's silver current glide,
And coldly mark the holy fane
  Of Melrose rise in ruin'd pride.
The quiet lake, the balmy air,
  The hill, the stream, the tower, the tree,—
Are they still such as once they were,
  Or is the dreary change in me?

Alas, the warp'd and broken board,
  How can it bear the painter's dye!
The harp of strain'd and tuneless chord,
  How to the minstrel's skill reply!
To aching eyes each landscape lowers,
  To feverish pulse each gale blows chill;
And Araby's or Eden's bowers
  Were barren as this moorland hill.

91 ## To an Oak Tree

IN THE CHURCHYARD OF ——, IN THE HIGHLANDS OF
SCOTLAND, SAID TO MARK THE GRAVE OF CAPTAIN
WOGAN, KILLED IN 1649

EMBLEM of England's ancient faith,
　　Full proudly may thy branches wave,
Where loyalty lies low in death,
　　And valour fills a timeless grave.

And thou, brave tenant of the tomb!
　　Repine not if our clime deny,
Above thine honour'd sod to bloom,
　　The flowerets of a milder sky.

These owe their birth to genial May;
　　Beneath a fiercer sun they pine,
Before the winter storm decay—
　　And can their worth be type of thine?

No! for, 'mid storms of Fate opposing,
　　Still higher swell'd thy dauntless heart,
And, while Despair the scene was closing,
　　Commenced thy brief but brilliant part.

'Twas then thou sought'st on Albyn's hill,
　　(When England's sons the strife resign'd)
A rugged race resisting still,
　　And unsubdued though unrefined.

Thy death's-hour heard no kindred wail,
　　No holy knell thy requiem rung;
Thy mourners were the plaided Gael,
　　Thy dirge the clamorous pibroch sung.

Yet who, in Fortune's summer-shine
   To waste life's longest term away,
Would change that glorious dawn of thine,
   Though darken'd ere its noontide day?

Be thine the Tree whose dauntless boughs
   Brave summer's drought and winter's gloom!
Rome bound with oak her patriots' brows,
   As Albyn shadows Wogan's tomb.

92   [Madge Wildfire sings]

Proud Maisie is in the wood,
   Walking so early;
Sweet Robin sits on the bush,
   Singing so rarely.

'Tell me, thou bonny bird,
   When shall I marry me?'—
'When six braw gentlemen
   Kirkward shall carry ye.'

'Who makes the bridal bed,
   Birdie, say truly?'
'The gray-headed sexton
   That delves the grave duly.

'The glow-worm o'er grave and stone
   Shall light thee steady.
The owl from the steeple sing,
   "Welcome, proud lady."'

93   The Song of the Reim-kennar

STERN eagle of the far north-west,
Thou that bearest in thy grasp the thunderbolt,
Thou whose rushing pinions stir ocean to madness,
Thou the destroyer of herds, thou the scatterer of navies,
Amidst the scream of thy rage,
Amidst the rushing of thy onward wings,
Though thy scream be loud as the cry of a perishing nation,
Though the rushing of thy wings be like the roar of ten thousand
        waves,
Yet hear, in thine ire and thy haste,
Hear thou the voice of the Reim-kennar.

Thou hast met the pine-trees of Drontheim,
Their dark-green heads lie prostrate beside their up-rooted stems;
Thou hast met the rider of the ocean,
The tall, the strong bark of the fearless rover,
And she has struck to thee the topsail
That she had not veil'd to a royal armada;
Thou hast met the tower that bears its crest among the clouds,
The battled massive tower of the Jarl of former days,
And the cope-stone of the turret
Is lying upon its hospitable hearth;
But thou too shalt stoop, proud compeller of clouds,
When thou hearest the voice of the Reim-kennar.

There are verses that can stop the stag in the forest,
Ay, and when the dark-coloured dog is opening on his track;
There are verses can make the wild hawk pause on the wing,
Like the falcon that wears the hood and the jesses,
And who knows the shrill whistle of the fowler;

Thou who canst mock at the scream of the drowning mariner,
And the crash of the ravaged forest,
And the groan of the overwhelmed crowds,
When the church hath fallen in the moment of prayer,
There are sounds which thou also must list,
When they are chaunted by the voice of the Reim-kennar.

Enough of woe hast thou wrought on the ocean,
The widows wring their hands on the beach;
Enough of woe hast thou wrought on the land,
The husbandman folds his arms in despair;
Cease thou the waving of thy pinions,
Let the ocean repose in her dark strength;
Cease thou the flashing of thine eye,
Let the thunderbolt sleep in the armoury of Odin;
Be thou still at my bidding, viewless racer of the north-western
    heaven,
Sleep thou at the voice of Norna the Reim-kennar.

Eagle of the far north-western waters,
Thou hast heard the voice of the Reim-kennar,
Thou hast closed thy wide sails at her bidding,
And folded them in peace by thy side.
My blessing be on thy retiring path;
When thou stoopest from thy place on high,
Soft be thy slumbers in the caverns of the unknown ocean,
Rest till destiny shall again awaken thee;
Eagle of the north-west, thou hast heard the voice of the Reim-
    kennar.

94   The Rime of the Ancient Mariner

IN SEVEN PARTS

PART I

An ancient
Mariner meet-
eth three Gal-
lants bidden
to a wedding-
feast, and de-
taineth one.

It is an ancient Mariner
And he stoppeth one of three.
'By thy long grey beard and glittering eye,
Now wherefore stopp'st thou me?

The Bridegroom's doors are opened wide,
And I am next of kin;
The guests are met, the feast is set:
May'st hear the merry din.'

The Wedding-
Guest is spell-
bound by the
eye of the old
seafaring man,
and con-
strained to
hear his tale.

He holds him with his skinny hand,
'There was a ship,' quoth he.
'Hold off! unhand me, grey-beard loon!'
Eftsoons his hand dropt he.

He holds him with his glittering eye—
The Wedding-Guest stood still,
And listens like a three years' child:
The Mariner hath his will.

The Wedding-Guest sat on a stone:
He cannot choose but hear;
And thus spake on that ancient man,
The bright-eyed Mariner.

'The ship was cheered, the harbour cleared,
Merrily did we drop
Below the kirk, below the hill,
Below the lighthouse top.

The Mariner
tells how the
ship sailed
southward
with a good
wind and fair
weather, till it
reached the
line.

The Sun came up upon the left,
Out of the sea came he!
And he shone bright, and on the right
Went down into the sea.

Higher and higher every day,
Till over the mast at noon—'
The Wedding-Guest here beat his breast,
For he heard the loud bassoon.

The Wedding-
Guest heareth
the bridal
music; but
the Mariner
continueth
his tale.

The bride hath paced into the hall,
Red as a rose is she;
Nodding their heads before her goes
The merry minstrelsy.

The Wedding-Guest he beat his breast,
Yet he cannot choose but hear;
And thus spake on that ancient man,
The bright-eyed Mariner.

The ship
driven by a
storm toward
the south pole

'And now the STORM-BLAST came, and he
Was tyrannous and strong:
He struck with his o'ertaking wings,
And chased us south along.

With sloping masts and dipping prow,
As who pursued with yell and blow
Still treads the shadow of his foe,
And forward bends his head,
The ship drove fast, loud roared the blast,
And southward aye we fled.

And now there came both mist and snow,
And it grew wondrous cold:
And ice, mast-high, came floating by,
As green as emerald.

The land of
ice, and of
fearful sounds
where no
living thing
was to be seen.

And through the drifts the snowy clifts
Did send a dismal sheen:
Nor shapes of men nor beasts we ken—
The ice was all between.

The ice was here, the ice was there,
The ice was all around:
It cracked and growled, and roared and howled,
Like noises in a swound!

Till a great
sea-bird,
called the
Albatross,
came through
the snow-fog,
and was
received with
great joy and
hospitality.

At length did cross an Albatross,
Thorough the fog it came;
As if it had been a Christian soul,
We hailed it in God's name.

It ate the food it ne'er had eat,
And round and round it flew.
The ice did split with a thunder-fit;
The helmsman steered us through!

And lo! the
Albatross
proveth a bird
of good omen,
and followeth
the ship as it
returned
northward
through fog
and floating
ice.

And a good south wind sprung up behind;
The Albatross did follow,
And every day, for food or play,
Came to the mariners' hollo!

In mist or cloud, on mast or shroud,
It perched for vespers nine;
While all the night, through fog-smoke white,
Glimmered the white Moon-shine.'

The ancient
Mariner
inhospitably
killeth the
pious bird of
good omen.

'God save thee, ancient Mariner!
From the fiends, that plague thee thus!—
Why look'st thou so?'—'With my cross-bow
I shot the ALBATROSS.

PART II

The Sun now rose upon the right:
Out of the sea came he,
Still hid in mist, and on the left
Went down into the sea.

And the good south wind still blew behind,
But no sweet bird did follow,
Nor any day for food or play
Came to the mariners' hollo!

His shipmates cry out against the ancient Mariner, for killing the bird of good luck.

And I had done a hellish thing,
And it would work 'em woe:
For all averred, I had killed the bird
That made the breeze to blow.
Ah wretch! said they, the bird to slay,
That made the breeze to blow!

But when the fog cleared off, they justify the same, and thus make themselves accomplices in the crime.

Nor dim nor red, like God's own head,
The glorious Sun uprist:
Then all averred, I had killed the bird
That brought the fog and mist.
'Twas right, said they, such birds to slay,
That bring the fog and mist.

The fair breeze continues; the ship enters the Pacific Ocean, and sails northward, even till it reaches the Line.

The fair breeze blew, the white foam flew.
The furrow followed free;
We were the first that ever burst
Into that silent sea.

The ship hath been suddenly becalmed.

Down dropt the breeze, the sails dropt down,
'Twas sad as sad could be;
And we did speak only to break
The silence of the sea!

All in a hot and copper sky,
The bloody Sun, at noon,
Right up above the mast did stand,
No bigger than the Moon.

Day after day, day after day,
We stuck, nor breath nor motion;
As idle as a painted ship
Upon a painted ocean.

And the Alba-
tross begins to
be avenged.

Water, water, every where,
And all the boards did shrink;
Water, water, every where,
Nor any drop to drink.

The very deep did rot: O Christ!
That ever this should be!
Yea, slimy things did crawl with legs
Upon the slimy sea.

About, about, in reel and rout
The death-fires danced at night;
The water, like a witch's oils,
Burnt green, and blue and white.

A Spirit had
followed them;
one of the in-
visible inhabi-
tants of this
planet, neither
departed souls

And some in dreams assuréd were
Of the Spirit that plagued us so;
Nine fathom deep he had followed us
From the land of mist and snow.

nor angels; concerning whom the learned Jew, Josephus, and the Platonic Con-
stantinopolitan, Michael Psellus, may be consulted. They are very numerous,
and there is no climate or element without one or more.

And every tongue, through utter drought,
Was withered at the root;
We could not speak, no more than if
We had been choked with soot.

The shipmates,
in their sore
distress, would
fain throw the
whole guilt on
the ancient
Mariner: in sign whereof they hang the dead sea-bird round his neck.

Ah! well a–day! what evil looks
Had I from old and young!
Instead of the cross, the Albatross
About my neck was hung.

PART III

There passed a weary time. Each throat
Was parched, and glazed each eye.
A weary time! a weary time!
How glazed each weary eye,
When looking westward, I beheld
A something in the sky.

The ancient
Mariner be-
holdeth a sign
in the element
afar off.

At first it seemed a little speck,
And then it seemed a mist;
It moved and moved, and took at last
A certain shape, I wist.

A speck, a mist, a shape, I wist!
And still it neared and neared:
As if it dodged a water-sprite,
It plunged and tacked and veered.

At its nearer
approach, it
seemeth him
to be a ship:
and at a dear
ransom he
freeth his
speech from
the bonds of
thirst.

With throats unslaked, with black lips baked,
We could nor laugh nor wail;
Through utter drought all dumb we stood!
I bit my arm, I sucked the blood,
And cried, A sail! a sail!

A flash of joy;

With throats unslaked, with black lips baked,
Agape they heard me call:
Gramercy! they for joy did grin,
And all at once their breath drew in,
As they were drinking all.

And horror follows. For can it be a ship that comes onward without wind or tide?

See! see! (I cried) she tacks no more!
Hither to work us weal;
Without a breeze, without a tide,
She steadies with upright keel!

The western wave was all a-flame.
The day was well nigh done!
Almost upon the western wave
Rested the broad bright Sun;
When that strange shape drove suddenly
Betwixt us and the Sun.

It seemeth him but the skeleton of a ship.

And straight the Sun was flecked with bars,
(Heaven's Mother send us grace!)
As if through a dungeon-grate he peered
With broad and burning face.

And its ribs are seen as bars on the face of the setting Sun.

Alas! (thought I, and my heart beat loud)
How fast she nears and nears!
Are those *her* sails that glance in the Sun,
Like restless gossameres?

The Spectre-Woman and her Death-mate, and no other on board the skeleton ship.

Are those *her* ribs through which the Sun
Did peer, as through a grate?
And is that Woman all her crew?
Is that a DEATH? and are there two?
Is DEATH that woman's mate?

Like vessel, like crew!

Her lips were red, *her* looks were free,
Her locks were yellow as gold:
Her skin was as white as leprosy,
The Night-mare LIFE-IN-DEATH was she
Who thicks man's blood with cold.

145

Death and
Life-in-Death
have diced for
the ship's crew,
and she (the
latter) winneth
the ancient
Mariner.

The naked hulk alongside came,
And the twain were casting dice;
"The game is done! I've won! I've won!"
Quoth she, and whistles thrice.

No twilight
within the
courts of the
Sun.

The Sun's rim dips; the stars rush out:
At one stride comes the dark;
With far-heard whisper, o'er the sea,
Off shot the spectre-bark.

At the rising
of the Moon,

We listened and looked sideways up!
Fear at my heart, as at a cup,
My life-blood seemed to sip!
The stars were dim, and thick the night,
The steersman's face by his lamp gleamed white;
From the sails the dew did drip—
Till clomb above the eastern bar
The hornéd Moon, with one bright star
Within the nether tip.

One after
another,

One after one, by the star-dogged Moon,
Too quick for groan or sigh,
Each turned his face with a ghastly pang,
And cursed me with his eye.

His shipmates
drop down
dead.

Four times fifty living men,
(And I heard nor sigh nor groan)
With heavy thump, a lifeless lump,
They dropped down one by one.

But Life-in-
Death begins
her work on
the ancient
Mariner.

The souls did from their bodies fly,—
They fled to bliss or woe!
And every soul, it passed me by,
Like the whizz of my cross-bow!'

PART IV

The Wedding-
Guest feareth
that a Spirit
is talking to
him;

'I fear thee, ancient Mariner!
I fear thy skinny hand!
And thou art long, and lank, and brown,
As is the ribbed sea-sand.

I fear thee and thy glittering eye,
And thy skinny hand, so brown.'—

But the
ancient Ma-
riner assureth
him of his
bodily life, and
proceedeth to
relate his hor-
rible penance.

'Fear not, fear not, thou Wedding-Guest!
This body dropt not down.

Alone, alone, all, all alone,
Alone on a wide wide sea!
And never a saint took pity on
My soul in agony.

He despiseth
the creatures
of the calm,

The many men, so beautiful!
And they all dead did lie:
And a thousand thousand slimy things
Lived on; and so did I.

And envieth
that *they*
should live,
and so many
lie dead.

I looked upon the rotting sea,
And drew my eyes away;
I looked upon the rotting deck,
And there the dead men lay.

I looked to heaven, and tried to pray;
But or ever a prayer had gusht,
A wicked whisper came, and made
My heart as dry as dust.

I closed my lids, and kept them close,
And the balls like pulses beat;
For the sky and the sea, and the sea and the sky
Lay like a load on my weary eye,
And the dead were at my feet.

But the curse liveth for him in the eye of the dead men.

The cold sweat melted from their limbs
Nor rot nor reek did they:
The look with which they looked on me
Had never passed away.

An orphan's curse would drag to hell
A spirit from on high;
But oh! more horrible than that
Is the curse in a dead man's eye!
Seven days, seven nights, I saw that curse,
And yet I could not die.

In his loneliness and fixedness he yearneth towards the journeying Moon, and the stars that still sojourn, yet still move onward; and every where the blue sky belongs to them, and is

The moving Moon went up the sky.
And no where did abide:
Softly she was going up,
And a star or two beside—

Her beams bemocked the sultry main,
Like April hoar-frost spread;
But where the ship's huge shadow lay,
The charmèd water burnt alway
A still and awful red.

their appointed rest, and their native country and their own natural homes, which they enter unannounced, as lords that are certainly expected and yet there is a silent joy at their arrival.

By the light of the Moon he beholdeth God's creatures of the great calm.

Beyond the shadow of the ship,
I watched the water-snakes:
They moved in tracks of shining white,
And when they reared, the elfish light
Fell off in hoary flakes.

Within the shadow of the ship
I watched their rich attire:
Blue, glossy green, and velvet black,
They coiled and swam; and every track
Was a flash of golden fire.

Their beauty and their happiness.

O happy living things! no tongue
Their beauty might declare:
A spring of love gushed from my heart,
He blesseth them in his heart.

And I blessed them unaware:
Sure my kind saint took pity on me,
And I blessed them unaware.

The spell begins to break.

The self-same moment I could pray;
And from my neck so free
The Albatross fell off, and sank
Like lead into the sea.

Part V

Oh sleep! it is a gentle thing,
Beloved from pole to pole!
To Mary Queen the praise be given!
She sent the gentle sleep from Heaven,
That slid into my soul.

By grace of the holy Mother, the ancient Mariner is refreshed with rain.

The silly buckets on the deck,
That had so long remained,
I dreamt that they were filled with dew;
And when I awoke, it rained.

My lips were wet, my throat was cold,
My garments all were dank;
Sure I had drunken in my dreams,
And still my body drank.

I moved, and could not feel my limbs:
I was so light—almost
I thought that I had died in sleep,
And was a blessèd ghost.

He heareth
sounds and
seeth strange
sights and
commotions in
the sky and
the element.

And soon I heard a roaring wind:
It did not come anear;
But with its sound it shook the sails,
That were so thin and sere.

The upper air burst into life!
And a hundred fire-flags sheen,
To and fro they were hurried about!
And to and fro, and in and out,
The wan stars danced between.

And the coming wind did roar more loud,
And the sails did sigh like sedge;
And the rain poured down from one black cloud;
The Moon was at its edge.

The thick black cloud was cleft, and still
The Moon was at its side:
Like waters shot from some high crag,
The lightning fell with never a jag,
A river steep and wide.

The bodies of
the ship's crew
are inspired
and the ship
moves on;

The loud wind never reached the ship,
Yet now the ship moved on!
Beneath the lightning and the Moon
The dead men gave a groan.

They groaned, they stirred, they all uprose,
Nor spake, nor moved their eyes;
It had been strange, even in a dream,
To have seen those dead men rise.

The helmsman steered, the ship moved on;
Yet never a breeze up-blew;

The mariners all 'gan work the ropes,
Where they were wont to do;
They raised their limbs like lifeless tools—
We were a ghastly crew.

The body of my brother's son
Stood by me, knee to knee:
The body and I pulled at one rope,
But he said nought to me.'

'I fear thee, ancient Mariner!'
'Be calm, thou Wedding-Guest!
'Twas not those souls that fled in pain,
Which to their corses came again,
But a troop of spirits blest:

But not by the souls of the men, nor by dæmons of earth or middle air, but by a blessed troop of angelic spirits, sent down by the invocation of the guardian saint.

For when it dawned—they dropped their arms,
And clustered round the mast;
Sweet sounds rose slowly through their mouths,
And from their bodies passed.

Around, around, flew each sweet sound,
Then darted to the Sun;
Slowly the sounds came back again,
Now mixed, now one by one.

Sometimes a-dropping from the sky
I heard the sky-lark sing;
Sometimes all little birds that are
How they seemed to fill the sea and air
With their sweet jargoning!

And now 'twas like all instruments,
Now like a lonely flute;
And now it is an angel's song,
That makes the heavens be mute.

It ceased; yet still the sails made on
A pleasant noise till noon,
A noise like of a hidden brook
In the leafy month of June,
That to the sleeping woods all night
Singeth a quiet tune.

Till noon we quietly sailed on,
Yet never a breeze did breathe:
Slowly and smoothly went the ship,
Moved onward from beneath.

The lonesome
Spirit from
the south-pole
carries on the
ship as far as
the Line, in
obedience to
the angelic
troop, but still
requireth
vengeance.

Under the keel nine fathom deep,
From the land of mist and snow,
The spirit slid: and it was he
That made the ship to go.
The sails at noon left off their tune,
And the ship stood still also.

The Sun, right up above the mast,
Had fixed her to the ocean:
But in a minute she 'gan stir,
With a short uneasy motion—
Backwards and forwards half her length
With a short uneasy motion.

Then like a pawing horse let go,
She made a sudden bound:
It flung the blood into my head,
And I fell down in a swound.

The Polar
Spirit's fellow-
dæmons, the
invisible in-
habitants of
the element,
take part in
his wrong;

How long in that same fit I lay,
I have not to declare;
But ere my living life returned,
I heard and in my soul discerned
Two voices in the air.

and two of them relate, one to the other, that penance long and heavy for the ancient Mariner hath been accorded to the Polar Spirit, who returneth southward.

"Is it he?" quoth one, "Is this the man?
By him who died on cross,
With his cruel bow he laid full low
The harmless Albatross.

The spirit who bideth by himself
In the land of mist and snow,
He loved the bird that loved the man
Who shot him with his bow."

The other was a softer voice,
As soft as honey-dew:
Quoth he, "The man hath penance done,
And penance more will do."

PART VI

FIRST VOICE

"But tell me, tell me! speak again,
Thy soft response renewing—
What makes that ship drive on so fast?
What is the ocean doing?"

SECOND VOICE

"Still as a slave before his lord,
The ocean hath no blast;
His great bright eye most silently
Up to the Moon is cast—

If he may know which way to go;
For she guides him smooth or grim.
See, brother, see! how graciously
She looketh down on him."

FIRST VOICE

The Mariner
hath been
cast into a
trance: for the
angelic power
causeth the
vessel to drive
northward
faster than
human life
could endure.

"But why drives on that ship so fast,
Without or wave or wind?"

SECOND VOICE

"The air is cut away before,
And closes from behind.

Fly, brother, fly! more high, more high!
Or we shall be belated:
For slow and slow that ship will go,
When the Mariner's trance is abated."

The super-
natural motion
is retarded;
the Mariner
awakes, and
his penance
begins anew.

I woke, and we were sailing on
As in a gentle weather:
'Twas night, calm night, the moon was high;
The dead men stood together.

All stood together on the deck,
For a charnel-dungeon fitter:
All fixed on me their stony eyes,
That in the Moon did glitter.

The pang, the curse, with which they died,
Had never passed away:
I could not draw my eyes from theirs,
Nor turn them up to pray.

The curse is
finally ex-
piated.

And now this spell was snapt: once more
I viewed the ocean green,
And looked far forth, yet little saw
Of what had else been seen—

Like one, that on a lonesome road
Doth walk in fear and dread,
And having once turned round walks on,
And turns no more his head;
Because he knows, a frightful fiend
Doth close behind him tread.

But soon there breathed a wind on me,
Nor sound nor motion made:
Its path was not upon the sea,
In ripple or in shade.

It raised my hair, it fanned my cheek
Like a meadow-gale of spring—
It mingled strangely with my fears,
Yet it felt like a welcoming.

Swiftly, swiftly flew the ship,
Yet she sailed softly too:
Sweetly, sweetly blew the breeze—
On me alone it blew.

And the
ancient
Mariner be-
holdeth his
native
country.

Oh! dream of joy! is this indeed
The light-house top I see?
Is this the hill? is this the kirk?
Is this mine own countree?

We drifted o'er the harbour-bar,
And I with sobs did pray—
O let me be awake, my God!
Or let me sleep alway.

The harbour-bay was clear as glass.
So smoothly it was strewn!
And on the bay the moonlight lay,
And the shadow of the Moon.

The rock shone bright, the kirk no less,
That stands above the rock:
The moonlight steeped in silentness
The steady weathercock.

And the bay was white with silent light,
Till rising from the same,
Full many shapes, that shadows were,
In crimson colours came.

*The angelic
spirits leave
the dead
bodies,*

*And appear in
their own
forms of light.*

A little distance from the prow
Those crimson shadows were:
I turned my eyes upon the deck—
Oh, Christ! what saw I there!

Each corse lay flat, lifeless and flat,
And, by the holy rood!
A man all light, a seraph-man,
On every corse there stood.

This seraph-band, each waved his hand:
It was a heavenly sight!
They stood as signals to the land,
Each one a lovely light;

This seraph-band, each waved his hand,
No voice did they impart—
No voice; but oh! the silence sank
Like music on my heart.

But soon I heard the dash of oars,
I heard the Pilot's cheer;
My head was turned perforce away,
And I saw a boat appear.

156

The Pilot and the Pilot's boy,
I heard them coming fast:
Dear Lord in Heaven! it was a joy
The dead men could not blast.

I saw a third—I heard his voice:
It is the Hermit good!
He singeth loud his godly hymns
That he makes in the wood.
He'll shrieve my soul, he'll wash away
The Albatross's blood.

Part VII

*The Hermit of
the Wood,*

This Hermit good lives in that wood
Which slopes down to the sea.
How loudly his sweet voice he rears!
He loves to talk with marineres
That come from a far countree.

He kneels at morn, and noon, and eve—
He hath a cushion plump:
It is the moss that wholly hides
The rotted old oak-stump.

The skiff-boat neared: I heard them talk,
"Why, this is strange, I trow!
Where are those lights so many and fair,
That signal made but now?"

*Approacheth
the ship with
wonder.*

"Strange, by my faith!" the Hermit said—
"And they answered not our cheer!
The planks looked warped! and see those sails,
How thin they are and sere!
I never saw aught like to them,
Unless perchance it were

Brown skeletons of leaves that lag
My forest-brook along;
When the ivy-tod is heavy with snow,
And the owlet whoops to the wolf below,
That eats the she-wolf's young."

"Dear Lord! it hath a fiendish look"—
(The Pilot made reply)
"I am a-feared"—"Push on, push on!"
Said the Hermit cheerily.

The boat came closer to the ship,
But I nor spake nor stirred;
The boat came close beneath the ship,
And straight a sound was heard.

The ship
suddenly
sinketh.

Under the water it rumbled on,
Still louder and more dread:
It reached the ship, it split the bay;
The ship went down like lead.

The ancient
Mariner is
saved in the
Pilot's boat.

Stunned by that loud and dreadful sound,
Which sky and ocean smote,
Like one that hath been seven days drowned
My body lay afloat;
But swift as dreams, myself I found
Within the Pilot's boat.

Upon the whirl, where sank the ship,
The boat spun round and round;
And all was still, save that the hill
Was telling of the sound.

I moved my lips—the Pilot shrieked
And fell down in a fit;
The holy Hermit raised his eyes,
And prayed where he did sit.

I took the oars: the Pilot's boy,
Who now doth crazy go,
Laughed loud and long, and all the while
His eyes went to and fro.
"Ha! ha!" quoth he, "full plain I see,
The Devil knows how to row."

And now, all in my own countree,
I stood on the firm land!
The Hermit stepped forth from the boat,
And scarcely he could stand.

The ancient Mariner earnestly entreateth the Hermit to shrieve him; and the penance of life falls on him.

"O shrieve me, shrieve me, holy man!"
The Hermit crossed his brow.
"Say quick," quoth he, "I bid thee say—
What manner of man art thou?"

Forthwith this frame of mine was wrenched
With a woful agony,
Which forced me to begin my tale;
And then it left me free.

And ever and anon throughout his future life an agony constraineth him to travel from land to land;

Since then, at an uncertain hour,
That agony returns:
And till my ghastly tale is told,
This heart within me burns.

I pass, like night, from land to land;
I have strange power of speech;
That moment that his face I see,
I know the man that must hear me:
To him my tale I teach.

What loud uproar bursts from that door!
The wedding-guests are there:
But in the garden-bower the bride
And bride-maids singing are:
And hark the little vesper bell,
Which biddeth me to prayer!

O Wedding-Guest! this soul hath been
Alone on a wide wide sea:
So lonely 'twas, that God himself
Scarce seeméd there to be.

O sweeter than the marriage-feast,
'Tis sweeter far to me,
To walk together to the kirk
With a goodly company!—

To walk together to the kirk,
And all together pray,
While each to his great Father bends,
Old men, and babes, and loving friends
And youths and maidens gay!

And to teach,
by his own
example, love
and reverence
to all things
that God made
and loveth.

Farewell, farewell! but this I tell
To thee, thou Wedding-Guest!
He prayeth well, who loveth well
Both man and bird and beast.

He prayeth best, who loveth best
All things both great and small;
For the dear God who loveth us,
He made and loveth all.'

The Mariner, whose eye is bright,
Whose beard with age is hoar,
Is gone: and now the Wedding-Guest
Turned from the bridegroom's door.

He went like one that hath been stunned,
And is of sense forlorn:
A sadder and a wiser man,
He rose the morrow morn.
    1798–1834.

95   ['The Scars Remaining']

ALAS! they had been friends in youth;
But whispering tongues can poison truth;
And constancy lives in realms above;
And life is thorny; and youth is vain;
And to be wroth with one we love
Doth work like madness in the brain.
And thus it chanced, as I divine,
With Roland and Sir Leoline.
Each spake words of high disdain
And insult to his heart's best brother:
They parted—ne'er to meet again!
But never either found another
To free the hollow heart from paining—
They stood aloof, the scars remaining,
Like cliffs which had been rent asunder;
A dreary sea now flows between;—
But neither heat, nor frost, nor thunder,
Shall wholly do away, I ween,
The marks of that which once hath been.

96 ## Frost at Midnight

THE Frost performs its secret ministry,
Unhelped by any wind. The owlet's cry
Came loud—and hark, again! loud as before.
The inmates of my cottage, all at rest,
Have left me to that solitude, which suits
Abstruser musings: save that at my side
My cradled infant slumbers peacefully.
'Tis calm indeed! so calm, that it disturbs
And vexes meditation, with its strange
And extreme silentness. Sea, hill, and wood,
This populous village! Sea, and hill, and wood,
With all the numberless goings-on of life,
Inaudible as dreams! the thin blue flame
Lies on my low-burnt fire, and quivers not;
Only that film, which fluttered on the grate,
Still flutters there, the sole unquiet thing.
Methinks, its motion in this hush of nature
Gives it dim sympathies with me who live,
Making it a companionable form,
Whose puny flaps and freaks the idling Spirit
By its own moods interprets, every where
Echo or mirror seeking of itself,
And makes a toy of Thought.

But O! how oft,
How oft, at school, with most believing mind,
Presageful, have I gazed upon the bars,
To watch that fluttering *stranger*! and as oft
With unclosed lids, already had I dreamt
Of my sweet birth-place, and the old church-tower,
Whose bells, the poor man's only music, rang
From morn to evening, all the hot Fair-day,
So sweetly, that they stirred and haunted me

With a wild pleasure, falling on mine ear
Most like articulate sounds of things to come!
So gazed I, till the soothing things, I dreamt,
Lulled me to sleep, and sleep prolonged my dreams!
And so I brooded all the following morn,
Awed by the stern preceptor's face, mine eye
Fixed with mock study on my swimming book:
Save if the door half-opened, and I snatched
A hasty glance, and still my heart leaped up,
For still I hoped to see the *stranger's* face,
Townsman, or aunt, or sister more beloved,
My play-mate when we both were clothed alike!

    Dear Babe, that sleepest cradled by my side,
Whose gentle breathings, heard in this deep calm,
Fill up the interspersed vacancies
And momentary pauses of the thought!
My babe so beautiful! it thrills my heart
With tender gladness, thus to look at thee,
And think that thou shalt learn far other lore,
And in far other scenes! For I was reared
In the great city, pent 'mid cloisters dim,
And saw nought lovely but the sky and stars.
But *thou*, my babe! shalt wander like a breeze
By lakes and sandy shores, beneath the crags
Of ancient mountain, and beneath the clouds,
Which image in their bulk both lakes and shores
And mountain crags: so shalt thou see and hear
The lovely shapes and sounds intelligible
Of that eternal language, which thy God
Utters, who from eternity doth teach
Himself in all, and all things in himself.
Great universal Teacher! he shall mould
Thy spirit, and by giving make it ask.

Therefore all seasons shall be sweet to thee,
Whether the summer clothe the general earth
With greenness, or the redbreast sit and sing
Betwixt the tufts of snow on the bare branch
Of mossy apple-tree, while the nigh thatch
Smokes in the sun-thaw; whether the eave-drops fall
Heard only in the trances of the blast,
Or if the secret ministry of frost
Shall hang them up in silent icicles,
Quietly shining to the quiet Moon.

97   from *FEARS IN SOLITUDE*

ON the green sheep-track, up the heathy hill,
Homeward I wind my way; and lo! recalled
From bodings that have well-nigh wearied me,
I find myself upon the brow, and pause
Startled! And after lonely sojourning
In such a quiet and surrounded nook,
This burst of prospect, here the shadowy main,
Dim-tinted, there the mighty majesty
Of that huge amphitheatre of rich
And elmy fields, seems like society—
Conversing with the mind, and giving it
A livelier impulse and a dance of thought!
And now, beloved Stowey! I behold
Thy church-tower, and, methinks, the four huge elms
Clustering, which mark the mansion of my friend;
And close behind them, hidden from my view,
Is my own lowly cottage, where my babe
And my babe's mother dwell in peace! With light
And quickened footsteps thitherward I tend,
Remembering thee, O green and silent dell!

And grateful, that by nature's quietness
And solitary musings, all my heart
Is softened, and made worthy to indulge
Love, and the thoughts that yearn for human kind.

98   Kubla Khan

IN Xanadu did KUBLA KHAN
A stately pleasure-dome decree:
Where ALPH, the sacred river, ran
Through caverns measureless to man
    Down to a sunless sea.
So twice six[1] miles of fertile ground
With walls and towers were girdled round:
And there were gardens bright with sinuous rills,
Where blossomed many an incense-bearing tree;
And here were forests ancient as the hills,
Enfolding sunny spots of greenery.

But oh! that deep romantic chasm which slanted
Down the green hill athwart a cedarn cover!
A savage place! as holy and inchanted
As e'er beneath a waning moon was haunted
By woman wailing for her demon-lover!
And from this chasm, with ceaseless turmoil seething,
As if this earth in fast thick pants were breathing,
A mighty fountain momently was forced:
Amid whose swift half-intermitted Burst
Huge fragments vaulted like rebounding hail,
Or chaffy grain beneath the thresher's flail;

---

[1] l. 6. six] Coleridge's MS. (British Museum); the printed texts read
['five'.]

And 'mid these dancing rocks at once and ever
It flung up momently the sacred river.
Five miles meandering with a mazy motion
Through wood and dale the sacred river ran,
Then reached the caverns measureless to man,
And sank in tumult to a lifeless ocean:
And 'mid this tumult Kubla heard from far
Ancestral voices prophesying war!

    The shadow of the dome of pleasure
    Floated midway on the waves;
    Where was heard the mingled measure
    From the fountain and the caves.
It was a miracle of rare device,
A sunny pleasure-dome with caves of ice!

    A damsel with a dulcimer
    In a vision once I saw:
    It was an Abyssinian maid,
    And on her dulcimer she play'd,
    Singing of Mount Abora.
    Could I revive within me
    Her symphony and song,
    To such a deep delight 'twould win me,
That with music loud and long,
I would build that dome in air,
That sunny dome! those caves of ice!
And all who heard should see them there,
And all should cry, Beware! Beware!
His flashing eyes, his floating hair!
Weave a circle round him thrice,
And close your eyes with holy dread:
For he on honey-dew hath fed,
And drunk the milk of Paradise.

Dejection

AN ODE

> Late, late yestreen I saw the new Moon,
> With the old Moon in her arms;
> And I fear, I fear, my Master dear!
> We shall have a deadly storm.
> *Ballad of Sir* PATRICK SPENCE

WELL! If the Bard was weather-wise, who made
 The grand old ballad of Sir Patrick Spence,
 This night, so tranquil now, will not go hence
Unrous'd by winds, that ply a busier trade
Than those which mould yon clouds in lazy flakes,
Or the dull sobbing draft, that moans and rakes
  Upon the strings of the Æolian lute,
  Which better far were mute.
 For lo! the New-moon winter-bright!
 And overspread with phantom-light,
 (With swimming phantom-light o'erspread
 But rimm'd and circled by a silver thread)
I see the old Moon in her lap, foretelling
 The coming-on of rain and squally blast.
And oh! that even now the gust were swelling,
 And the slant night-shower driving loud and fast!
Those sounds which oft have raised me, whilst they awed,
  And sent my soul abroad,
Might now perhaps their wonted impulse give,
Might startle this dull pain, and make it move and live!

A grief without a pang, void, dark, and drear,
 A stifled, drowsy, unimpassion'd grief,
 Which finds no natural outlet, no relief,
  In word, or sigh, or tear—

O Lady! in this wan and heartless mood,
To other thoughts by yonder throstle woo'd,
   All this long eve, so balmy and serene,
Have I been gazing on the western sky,
   And its peculiar tint of yellow green:
And still I gaze—and with how blank an eye!
And those thin clouds above, in flakes and bars,
That give away their motion to the stars;
Those stars, that glide behind them or between,
Now sparkling, now bedimm'd, but always seen:
Yon crescent Moon, as fix'd as if it grew
In its own cloudless, starless lake of blue;
I see them all so excellently fair,
I see, not feel, how beautiful they are!

    My genial spirits fail,
    And what can these avail,
To lift the smoth'ring weight from off my breast?
    It were a vain endeavour
    Though I should gaze for ever
On that green light that lingers in the west:
I may not hope from outward forms to win
The passion and the life, whose fountains are within.

O Lady! we receive but what we give.
And in our life alone does nature live;
Ours is her wedding garment, ours her shroud!
   And would we aught behold, of higher worth,
Than that inanimate cold world allow'd
To the poor loveless ever-anxious crowd,
   Ah! from the soul itself must issue forth,
A light, a glory, a fair luminous cloud
    Enveloping the Earth—

And from the soul itself must there be sent
  A sweet and potent voice, of its own birth,
Of all sweet sounds the life and element!

O pure of heart! thou need'st not ask of me
What this strong music in the soul may be!
What, and wherein it doth exist,
This light, this glory, this fair luminous mist,
This beautiful and beauty-making power.
  Joy, virtuous Lady! Joy that ne'er was given,
Save to the pure, and in their purest hour,
Life, and life's effluence, cloud at once and shower,
Joy, Lady! is the spirit and the power,
Which wedding Nature to us gives in dow'r
  A new Earth and new Heaven,
Undreamt of by the sensual and the proud—
Joy is the sweet voice, Joy the luminous cloud—
        We in ourselves rejoice!
And thence flows all that charms or ear or sight,
    All melodies the echoes of that voice,
    All colours a suffusion from that light.

There was a time when, though my path was rough,
    This joy within me dallied with distress,
And all misfortunes were but as the stuff
      Whence Fancy made me dreams of happiness:
    For hope grew round me, like the twining vine,
      And fruits, and foliage, not my own, seem'd mine.
    But now afflictions bow me down to earth:
    Nor care I that they rob me of my mirth;
    But oh! each visitation
Suspends what nature gave me at my birth,
    My shaping spirit of Imagination.

For not to think of what I needs must feel,
  But to be still and patient, all I can;
And haply by abstruse research to steal
  From my own nature all the natural Man—
  This was my sole resource, my only plan:
Till that which suits a part infects the whole,
And now is almost grown the habit of my Soul.

Hence, viper thoughts, that coil around my mind,
    Reality's dark dream!
I turn from you, and listen to the wind,
    Which long has rav'd unnotic'd. What a scream
Of agony by torture lengthen'd out
That lute sent forth! Thou Wind, that rav'st without,
    Bare crag, or mountain-tairn, or blasted tree,
Or pine-grove whither woodman never clomb,
Or lonely house, long held the witches' home,
    Methinks were fitter instruments for thee,
Mad Lutanist! who in this month of show'rs,
Of dark-brown gardens, and of peeping flow'rs,
Mak'st Devils' yule, with worse than wintry song,
The blossoms, buds, and tim'rous leaves among.
    Thou Actor, perfect in all tragic sounds!
Thou mighty Poet, e'en to Frenzy bold!
    What tell'st thou now about?
    'Tis of the rushing of an Host in rout,
  With groans of trampled men, with smarting wounds—
At once they groan with pain, and shudder with the cold!
But hush! there is a pause of deepest silence!
  And all that noise, as of a rushing crowd,
With groans, and tremulous shudderings—all is over—
  It tells another tale, with sounds less deep and loud!
    A tale of less affright,
    And temper'd with delight,

As Otway's self had fram'd the tender lay—
 'Tis of a little child
 Upon a lonesome wild,
Not far from home, but she hath lost her way;
And now moans low in bitter grief and fear,
And now screams loud, and hopes to make her mother hear.

'Tis midnight, but small thoughts have I of sleep:
Full seldom may my friend such vigils keep!
Visit her, gentle Sleep! with wings of healing,
 And may this storm be but a mountain-birth,
May all the stars hang bright above her dwelling,
 Silent as though they watch'd the sleeping Earth!
  With light heart may she rise,
  Gay fancy, cheerful eyes,
 Joy lift her spirit, joy attune her voice;
To her may all things live, from Pole to Pole,
Their life the eddying of her living soul!
 O simple spirit, guided from above,
Dear Lady! friend devoutest of my choice,
Thus may'st thou ever, evermore rejoice.

100   The Pains of Sleep

 Ere on my bed my limbs I lay,
 It hath not been my use to pray
 With moving lips or bended knees;
 But silently, by slow degrees,
 My spirit I to Love compose,
 In humble trust mine eye-lids close,
 With reverential resignation,

No wish conceived, no thought exprest,
Only a sense of supplication;
A sense o'er all my soul imprest
That I am weak, yet not unblest,
Since in me, round me, every where
Eternal Strength and Wisdom are.

But yester-night I prayed aloud
In anguish and in agony,
Up-starting from the fiendish crowd
Of shapes and thoughts that tortured me:
A lurid light, a trampling throng,
Sense of intolerable wrong,
And whom I scorned, those only strong!
Thirst of revenge, the powerless will
Still baffled, and yet burning still!
Desire with loathing strangely mixed
On wild or hateful objects fixed.
Fantastic passions! maddening brawl!
And shame and terror over all!
Deeds to be hid which were not hid,
Which all confused I could not know
Whether I suffered, or I did:
For all seemed guilt, remorse or woe,
My own or others still the same
Life-stifling fear, soul-stifling shame.

So two nights passed: the night's dismay
Saddened and stunned the coming day.
Sleep, the wide blessing, seemed to me
Distemper's worst calamity.
The third night, when my own loud scream
Had waked me from the fiendish dream,
O'ercome with sufferings strange and wild,

I wept as I had been a child;
And having thus by tears subdued
My anguish to a milder mood,
Such punishments, I said, were due
To natures deepliest stained with sin,—
For aye entempesting anew
The unfathomable hell within,
The horror of their deeds to view,
To know and loathe, yet wish and do!
Such griefs with such men well agree,
But wherefore, wherefore fall on me?
To be beloved is all I need,
And whom I love, I love indeed.

101 ## Youth and Age

VERSE, a breeze mid blossoms straying,
Where Hope clung feeding, like a bee—
Both were mine! Life went a-maying
      With Nature, Hope, and Poesy,
        When I was young!

When I was young?—Ah, woful When!
Ah! for the change 'twixt Now and Then!
This breathing house not built with hands,
This body that does me grievous wrong,
O'er aery cliffs and glittering sands,
How lightly then it flashed along:—
Like those trim skiffs, unknown of yore,
On winding lakes and rivers wide,
That ask no aid of sail or oar,
That fear no spite of wind or tide!

Nought cared this body for wind or weather
When Youth and I lived in't together.

Flowers are lovely; Love is flower-like;
Friendship is a sheltering tree;
O! the joys, that came down shower-like,
Of Friendship, Love, and Liberty,
          Ere I was old!

Ere I was old? Ah woful Ere,
Which tells me, Youth's no longer here!
O Youth! for years so many and sweet,
'Tis known, that Thou and I were one,
I'll think it but a fond conceit—
It cannot be that Thou art gone!

Thy vesper-bell hath not yet tolled:—
And thou wert aye a masker bold!
What strange disguise hast now put on,
To make believe, that thou art gone?
I see these locks in silvery slips,
This drooping gait, this altered size:
But Spring-tide blossoms on thy lips,
And tears take sunshine from thine eyes!
Life is but thought: so think I will
That Youth and I are house-mates still.

Dew-drops are the gems of morning,
But the tears of mournful eve!
Where no hope is, life's a warning
That only serves to make us grieve,
          When we are old:

That only serves to make us grieve
With oft and tedious taking-leave,
Like some poor nigh-related guest,
That may not rudely be dismist;
Yet hath outstayed his welcome while,
And tells the jest without the smile.

102   A Fragment

ENCINCTURED with a twine of leaves,
That leafy twine his only dress!
A lovely Boy was plucking fruits,
By moonlight, in a wilderness.
The moon was bright, the air was free,
And fruits and flowers together grew
   On many a shrub and many a tree:
And all put on a gentle hue,
Hanging in the shadowy air
Like a picture rich and rare.
It was a climate where, they say,
The night is more belov'd than day.
But who that beauteous Boy beguiled,
That beauteous Boy to linger here?
Alone, by night, a little child,
In place so silent and so wild—
Has he no friend, no loving mother near?

ROBERT SOUTHEY

The Ebb Tide

SLOWLY thy flowing tide
Came in, old Avon! scarcely did mine eyes,
As watchful I roam'd thy green-wood side,
    Perceive its gentle rise.

With many a stroke and strong
The labouring boatmen upward plied their oars,
Yet little way they made, though labouring long
    Between thy winding shores.

Now down thine ebbing tide
The unlaboured boat falls rapidly along;
The solitary helms-man sits to guide,
    And sings an idle song.

Now o'er the rocks, that lay
So silent late, the shallow current roars;
Fast flow thy waters on their sea-ward way
    Thro' wider-spreading shores.

Avon! I gaze and know
The lesson emblemed in thy varying way;
It speaks of human joys that rise so slow,
    So rapidly decay.

Kingdoms that long have stood,
And slow to strength and power attain'd at last,
Thus from the summit of high fortune's flood
    Ebb to their ruin fast.

Thus like thy flow appears
Time's tardy course to manhood's envied stage;
Alas! how hurryingly the ebbing years
Then hasten to old age!

104 ## The Battle of Blenheim

I

IT was a summer evening,
Old Kaspar's work was done,
And he before his cottage door
Was sitting in the sun,
And by him sported on the green
His little grandchild Wilhelmine.

II

She saw her brother Peterkin
Roll something large and round,
Which he beside the rivulet
In playing there had found;
He came to ask what he had found,
That was so large, and smooth, and round.

III

Old Kaspar took it from the boy,
Who stood expectant by;
And then the old man shook his head,
And with a natural sigh,
'Tis some poor fellow's skull, said he,
Who fell in the great victory.

IV

I find them in the garden,
　For there's many here about,
And often when I go to plough,
　The ploughshare turns them out;
For many thousand men, said he,
Were slain in the great victory.

V

Now tell us what 'twas all about,
　Young Peterkin, he cries,
And little Wilhelmine looks up
　With wonder-waiting eyes;
Now tell us all about the war,
And what they kill'd each other for.

VI

It was the English, Kaspar cried,
　That put the French to rout;
But what they kill'd each other for,
　I could not well make out;
But every body said, quoth he,
That 'twas a famous victory.

VII

My father lived at Blenheim then,
　Yon little stream hard by;
They burnt his dwelling to the ground
　And he was forced to fly;
So with his wife and child he fled,
Nor had he where to rest his head.

VIII

With fire and sword the country round
   Was wasted far and wide,
And many a childing mother then,
   And new-born baby died.
But things like that, you know, must be
At every famous victory.

IX

They say it was a shocking sight
   After the field was won,
For many thousand bodies here
   Lay rotting in the sun;
But things like that, you know, must be
After a famous victory.

X

Great praise the Duke of Marlbro' won,
   And our good Prince Eugene.—
Why 'twas a very wicked thing!
   Said little Wilhelmine.
Nay—nay—my little girl, quoth he,
It was a famous victory.

XI

And every body praised the Duke
   Who this great fight did win.
But what good came of it at last?
   Quoth little Peterkin.
Why that I cannot tell, said he,
But 'twas a famous victory.

105   [Kehama's Curse]

I CHARM thy life
From the weapons of strife,
From stone and from wood,
From fire and from flood,
From the serpent's tooth,
And the beasts of blood:
From Sickness I charm thee,
And Time shall not harm thee;
But Earth which is mine,
Its fruits shall deny thee;
And Water shall hear me,
And know thee and fly thee;
And the Winds shall not touch thee
When they pass by thee,
And the Dews shall not wet thee,
When they fall nigh thee:
And thou shalt seek Death
To release thee, in vain;
Thou shalt live in thy pain
While Kehama shall reign,
With a fire in thy heart,
And a fire in thy brain;
And Sleep shall obey me,
And visit thee never,
And the Curse shall be on thee
For ever and ever.

106 ['Love Indestructible']

THEY sin who tell us Love can die.
　With life all other passions fly,
　　All others are but vanity.
　In Heaven Ambition cannot dwell,
　Nor Avarice in the vaults of Hell;
　Earthly these passions of the Earth,
They perish where they have their birth;
　　But Love is indestructible.
　Its holy flame for ever burneth,
From Heaven it came, to Heaven returneth;
　Too oft on Earth a troubled guest,
　At times deceived, at times opprest,
　　It here is tried and purified,
　Then hath in Heaven its perfect rest:
　It soweth here with toil and care,
But the harvest time of Love is there.

107 Epitaph

TIME and the World, whose magnitude and weight
Bear on us in this Now, and hold us here
To earth inthralled,—what are they in the past?
And in the prospect of the immortal soul
How poor a speck! Not here her resting-place,
Her portion is not here: and happiest they
Who, gathering early all that earth can give,
Shake off its mortal coil, and speed for Heaven.
Such fate had he whose relics here repose.
Few were his years, but yet enough to teach
Love, duty, generous feelings, high desires,

Faith, hope, devotion: and what more could length
Of days have brought him? What, but vanity;
Joys, frailer even than health or human life;
Temptation; sin and sorrow, both too sure;
Evils that wound, and cares that fret, the heart!
Repine not, therefore, ye who love the dead.

WALTER SAVAGE LANDOR

108   [The Shepherd and the Nymph]

'Twas evening, though not sun-set, and spring-tide
Level with these green meadows, seem'd yet higher;
'Twas pleasant: and I loosen'd from my neck
The pipe you gave me, and began to play.
O that I ne'er had learnt the tuneful art!
It always brings us enemies or love!
Well, I was playing—when above the waves
Some swimmer's head methought I saw ascend;
I, sitting still, survey'd it, with my pipe
Awkwardly held before my lips half-clos'd.
Gebir! it was a nymph! a nymph divine!
I cannot wait describing how she came,
How I was sitting, how she first assum'd
The sailor: of what happened there remains
Enough to say, and too much to forget.
The sweet deceiver stept upon this bank
Before I was aware; for, with surprize
Moments fly rapid as with love itself.
Stooping to tune afresh the hoarsen'd reed,

I heard a rustling; and where that arose
My glance first lighted on her nimble feet.
Her feet resembled those long shells explored
By him who to befriend his steeds' dim sight
Would blow the pungent powder in their eye.—
Her eyes too! O immortal Gods! her eyes
Resembled—what could they resemble—what
Ever resemble those! E'en her attire
Was not of wonted woof nor vulgar art:
Her mantle shew'd the yellow samphire-pod,
Her girdle, the dove-colour'd wave serene.
'Shepherd,' said she, 'and will you wrestle now,
And with the sailor's hardier race engage?'
I was rejoiced to hear it, and contrived
How to keep up contention;—could I fail
By pressing not too strongly, yet to press?
'Whether a shepherd, as indeed you seem,
Or whether of the hardier race you boast,
I am not daunted, no: I will engage.'
'But first,' said she, 'what wager will you lay?'
'A sheep,' I answered: 'add whate'er you will.'
'I cannot,' she replied, 'make that return:
Our hided vessels, in their pitchy round,
Seldom, unless from rapine, hold a sheep.
But I have sinuous shells, of pearly hue
Within, and they that lustre have imbibed
In the sun's palace porch; where, when unyoked,
His chariot wheel stands midway in the wave.
Shake one, and it awakens; then apply
Its polished lips to your attentive ear,
And it remembers its august abodes,
And murmurs as the ocean murmurs there.
And I have others given me by the nymphs,
Of sweeter sound than any pipe you have.—

But we, by Neptune, for no pipe contend;
This time a sheep I win, a pipe the next.'
Now came she forward, eager to engage;
But, first her dress, her bosom then, survey'd,
And heav'd it, doubting if she could deceive.
Her bosom seem'd, inclos'd in haze like heav'n,
To baffle touch; and rose forth undefined.
Above her knees she drew the robe succinct,
Above her breast, and just below her arms:
'This will preserve my breath, when tightly bound,
If struggle and equal strength should so constrain.'
Thus, pulling hard to fasten it, she spoke,
And, rushing at me, closed. I thrill'd throughout
And seem'd to lessen and shrink up with cold.
Again, with violent impulse gushed my blood;
And hearing nought external, thus absorb'd,
I heard it, rushing through each turbid vein,
Shake my unsteady swimming sight in air.
Yet with unyielding though uncertain arms,
I clung around her neck; the vest beneath
Rustled against our slippery limbs entwined:
Often mine, springing with eluded force,
Started aside, and trembled, till replaced.
And when I most succeeded, as I thought,
My bosom and my throat felt so comprest
That life was almost quivering on my lips,
Yet nothing was there painful! these are signs
Of secret arts, and not of human might,
What arts I can not tell: I only know
My eyes grew dizzy, and my strength decay'd,
I was indeed o'ercome!—with what regret,
And more, with what confusion, when I reached
The fold, and yielding up the sheep, she cried,
'This pays a shepherd to a conquering maid.'

She smil'd, and more of pleasure than disdain
Was in her dimpled chin and liberal lip,
And eyes that languished, lengthening,—just like love.
She went away: I on the wicker gate
Lean'd, and could follow with my eyes alone.
The sheep she carried easy as a cloak.
But when I heard its bleating, as I did,
And saw, she hastening on, its hinder feet
Struggle, and from her snowy shoulder slip,
(One shoulder its poor efforts had unveil'd,)
Then, all my passions mingling fell in tears!
Restless then ran I to the highest ground
To watch her; she was gone; gone down the tide;
And the long moon-beam on the hard wet sand
Lay like a jasper column half uprear'd.

109   On Man

IN his own image the Creator made,
     His own pure sunbeam quicken'd thee, O man!
     Thou breathing dial! since thý day began
The present hour was ever markt with shade!

110   [Rose Aylmer, 1779–1800]

AH what avails the sceptred race,
     Ah what the form divine!
What every virtue, every grace!
     Rose Aylmer, all were thine.
Rose Aylmer, whom these wakeful eyes
     May weep, but never see,
A night of memories and of sighs
     I consecrate to thee.

111 Progress of evening

FROM yonder wood, mark blue-eyed Eve proceed:
First through the deep and warm and secret glens,
Through the pale glimmering privet-scented lane,
And through those alders by the river-side:
Now the soft dust impedes her, which the sheep
Have hollow'd out beneath their hawthorn shade.
But ah! look yonder! see a misty tide
Rise up the hill, lay low the frowning grove,
Enwrap the gay white mansion, sap its sides
Until they sink and melt away like chalk;
Now it comes down against our village-tower,
Covers its base, floats o'er its arches, tears
The clinging ivy from the battlements,
Mingles in broad embrace the obdurate stone,
(All one vast ocean) and goes swelling on
In slow and silent, dim and deepening waves.

['Poems Addressed to Ianthe']

112 [1]

IANTHE! you resolve to cross the sea!
    A path forbidden *me*!
Remember, while the Sun his blessing sheds
    Upon the mountain-heads,
How often we have watcht him laying down
    His brow, and dropt our own
Against each other's, and how faint and short
    And sliding the support!
What will succede it now? Mine is unblest,
    Ianthe! nor will rest

186

But on the very thought that swells with pain.
　　O bid me hope again!
O give me back what Earth, what (without you)
　　Not Heaven itself can do—
One of the golden days that we have past,
　　And let it be my last!
Or else the gift would be, however sweet,
　　Fragile and incomplete.

113　　　　　　　　　[II]

　REMAIN, ah not in youth alone,
　　Tho' youth, where you are, long will stay,
But when my summer days are gone,
　　And my autumnal haste away.
　　'Can I be always by your side?'
　No; but the hours you can, you must,
Nor rise at Death's approaching stride,
　Nor go when dust is gone to dust.

114　　　　　　　　　[III]

PAST ruin'd Ilion Helen lives,
　　Alcestis rises from the shades;
Verse calls them forth; 'tis verse that gives
　　Immortal youth to mortal maids.

Soon shall Oblivion's deepening veil
　　Hide all the peopled hills you see,
The gay, the proud, while lovers hail
　　In distant ages you and me.

The tear for fading beauty check,
For passing glory cease to sigh,
One form shall rise above the wreck,
One name, Ianthe, shall not die.

115   [IV]

My hopes retire; my wishes as before
Struggle to find their resting-place in vain:
The ebbing sea thus beats against the shore;
The shore repels it; it returns again.

116   [V]

From you, Ianthe, little troubles pass
    Like little ripples down a sunny river;
Your pleasures spring like daisies in the grass,
    Cut down, and up again as blithe as ever.

117   [VI]

'Do you remember me? or are you proud?'
Lightly advancing thro' her star-trimm'd crowd,
    Ianthe said, and lookt into my eyes.
'A *yes*, a *yes*, to both: for Memory
Where you but once have been must ever be,
    And at your voice Pride from his throne must rise.'

118

[VII]

WELL I remember how you smiled
　　To see me write your name upon
The soft sea-sand. . . . 'O! *what a child!*
　　You think you're writing upon stone!'
I have since written what no tide
　　Shall ever wash away, what men
Unborn shall read o'er ocean wide
　　And find Ianthe's name agen.

119 ## The Maid's Lament

I LOVED him not; and yet, now he is gone,
　　I feel I am alone.
I check'd him while he spoke; yet, could he speak,
　　Alas! I would not check.
For reasons not to love him once I sought,
　　And wearied all my thought
To vex myself and him: I now would give
　　My love could he but live
Who lately lived for me, and, when he found
　　'Twas vain, in holy ground
He hid his face amid the shades of death!
　　I waste for him my breath
Who wasted his for me! but mine returns,
　　And this lorn bosom burns
With stifling heat, heaving it up in sleep,
　　And waking me to weep
Tears that had melted his soft heart: for years
　　Wept he as bitter tears!
Merciful God! such was his latest prayer,
　　These may she never share!

Quieter is his breath, his breast more cold,
 Than daisies in the mould,
Where children spell, athwart the churchyard gate,
 His name and life's brief date.
Pray for him, gentle souls, whoe'er you be,
 And, oh! pray too for me!

120   Dirce

 STAND close around, ye Stygian set,
  With Dirce in one boat conveyed!
 Or Charon, seeing, may forget
  That he is old and she a shade.

121   Lines to a Dragon Fly

LIFE (priest and poet say) is but a dream;
 I wish no happier one than to be laid
 Beneath some cool syringa's scented shade
Or wavy willow, by the running stream,
 Brimful of Moral, where the Dragon Fly,
 Wanders as careless and content as I.
Thanks for this fancy, insect king,
Of purple crest and filmy wing,
Who with indifference givest up
The water-lily's golden cup,
To come again and overlook
What I am writing in my book.
Believe me, most who read the line
Will read with hornier eyes than thine;
And yet their souls shall live for ever,
And thine drop dead into the river!
God pardon them, O insect king,
Who fancy so unjust a thing!

Corinna to Tanagra

FROM ATHENS

1

TANAGRA! think not I forget
　　Thy beautifully-storied streets;
Be sure my memory bathes yet
　　In clear Thermodon, and yet greets
The blythe and liberal shepherd-boy,
Whose sunny bosom swells with joy
When we accept his matted rushes
Upheav'd with sylvan fruit; away he bounds, and blushes.

2

I promise to bring back with me
　　What thou with transport wilt receive,
The only proper gift for thee,
　　Of which no mortal shall bereave
In later times thy mouldering walls,
Until the last old turret falls;
A crown, a crown from Athens won,
A crown no God can wear, beside Latona's son.

3

There may be cities who refuse
　　To their own child the honours due,
And look ungently on the Muse;
　　But ever shall those cities rue
The dry, unyielding, niggard breast,
Offering no nourishment, no rest,
To that young head which soon shall rise
Disdainfully, in might and glory, to the skies.

4

Sweetly where cavern'd Dirce flows
    Do white-arm'd maidens chaunt my lay,
Flapping the while with laurel-rose
    The honey-gathering tribes away;
And sweetly, sweetly Attick tongues
Lisp your Corinna's early songs;
    To her with feet more graceful come
The verses that have dwelt in kindred breasts at home.

5

O let thy children lean aslant
    Against the tender mother's knee,
And gaze into her face, and want
    To know what magic there can be
In words that urge some eyes to dance,
While others as in holy trance
    Look up to heaven: be such my praise!
Why linger? I must haste, or lose the Delphic bays.

123   Behold, O Aspasia! I send you verses

BEAUTY! thou art a wanderer on the earth,
    And hast no temple in the fairest isle
Or city over-sea, where wealth and Mirth
    And all the Graces, all the Muses, smile.

Yet these have always nurst thee with such fond,
    Such lasting love, that they have followed up
Thy steps thro' every land, and placed beyond
    The reach of thirsty Time thy nectar-cup.

Thou art a wanderer, Beauty! like the rays
   That now upon the platan, now upon
The sleepy lake, glance quick or idly gaze,
   And now are manifold and now are none.

I have call'd, panting, after thee, and thou
   Hast turn'd and lookt and said some pretty word,
Parting the hair, perhaps, upon my brow,
   And telling me none ever was prefer'd.

In more than one bright form hast thou appear'd,
   In more than one sweet dialect hast thou spoken:
Beauty! thy spells the heart within me heard,
   Griev'd that they bound it, grieves that they are broken.

124   ['The Death of Artemidora']

'ARTEMIDORA! Gods invisible,
While thou art lying faint along the couch,
Have tied the sandal to thy veined feet,
And stand beside thee, ready to convey
Thy weary steps where other rivers flow.
Refreshing shades will waft thy weariness
Away, and voices like thine own come nigh,
Soliciting, nor vainly, thy embrace.'
   Artemidora sigh'd, and would have press'd
The hand now pressing hers, but was too weak.
Fate's shears were over her dark hair unseen
While thus Elpenor spake: he look'd into
Eyes that had given light and life erewhile
To those above them, those now dim with tears
And watchfulness. Again he spake of joy
Eternal. At that word, that sad word, *joy*,

Faithful and fond her bosom heav'd once more,
Her head fell back: one sob, one loud deep sob
Swell'd through the darkened chamber; 'twas not hers:
With her that old boat incorruptible,
Unwearied, undiverted in its course,
Had plash'd the water up the farther strand.

125   ['Ternissa']

    TERNISSA! you are fled!
      I say not to the dead,
But to the happy ones who rest below:
      For, surely, surely, where
      Your voice and graces are,
Nothing of death can any feel or know.
      Girls who delight to dwell
      Where grows most asphodel,
Gather to their calm breasts each word you speak:
      The mild Persephone
      Places you on her knee,
And your cool palm smoothes down stern Pluto's cheek.

126   I STROVE with none, for none was worth my strife:
    Nature I loved, and next to Nature, Art:
I warm'd both hands before the fire of Life;
    It sinks; and I am ready to depart.

127   DEATH stands above me, whispering low
      I know not what into my ear:
    Of his strange language all I know
      Is, there is not a word of fear.

128   For an Epitaph at Fiesole

Lo! where the four mimosas blend their shade,
In calm repose at last is Landor laid;
For ere he slept he saw them planted here
By her his soul had ever held most dear,
And he had lived enough when he had dried her tear.

THOMAS CAMPBELL

129   Hohenlinden

On Linden, when the sun was low,
All bloodless lay the untrodden snow,
And dark as winter was the flow
    Of Iser, rolling rapidly.

But Linden saw another sight,
When the drum beat, at dead of night,
Commanding fires of death to light
    The darkness of her scenery.

By torch and trumpet fast array'd,
Each horseman drew his battle blade,
And furious every charger neigh'd
    To join the dreadful revelry.

Then shook the hills, with thunder riven;
Then rushed the steed, to battle driven;
And, louder than the bolt of heaven,
    Far flash'd the red artillery.

But redder yet that light shall glow,
On Linden's hills of stained snow;
And bloodier yet, the torrent flow
    Of Iser, rolling rapidly.

'Tis morn; but scarce yon level sun
Can pierce the war-clouds, rolling dun,
Where furious Frank, and fiery Hun,
    Shout in their sulph'rous canopy.

The combat deepens. On, ye brave,
Who rush to glory, or the grave!
Wave, Munich, all thy banners wave,
    And charge with all thy chivalry!

Few, few, shall part, where many meet!
The snow shall be their winding sheet,
And every turf, beneath their feet,
    Shall be a soldier's sepulchre.

130   Caroline, II

TO THE EVENING STAR

Gem of the crimson-coloured even,
    Companion of retiring day,
Why at the closing gates of heaven,
    Beloved star, dost thou delay?

So fair thy pensile beauty burns,
    When soft the tear of twilight flows,
So due thy plighted step returns
    To chambers brighter than the rose;

To peace, to pleasure, and to love
    So kind a star thou seem'st to be,
Sure some enamour'd orb above
    Descends and burns to meet with thee.

Thine is the breathing, blushing hour,
    When all unheavenly passions fly;
Chased by the soul-subduing power
    Of love's delicious witchery.

Oh! sacred to the fall of day,
    Queen of propitious stars, appear!
And early rise, and long delay,
    When *Caroline* herself is here.

Shine on her chosen green resort,
    Where trees the sunward summit crown;
And wanton flowers, that well may court
    An angel's feet to tread them down.

Shine on her sweetly-scented road,
    Thou star of evening's purple dome!
That lead'st the nightingale abroad,
    And guid'st the pilgrim to his home.

Shine, where my charmer's sweeter breath
    Embalms the soft exhaling dew;
Where dying winds a sigh bequeath
    To kiss her cheek of rosy hue.

Where, winnow'd by the gentle air,
    Her silken tresses darkly flow,
And fall upon her brow so fair,
    Like shadows on the mountain snow.

Thus, ever thus, at day's decline
  In converse sweet to wander far,
Oh! bring with thee my *Caroline*,
  And thou shalt be my ruling star!

131   Lines on leaving a Scene in Bavaria

ADIEU the woods and waters' side,
  Imperial Danube's rich domain!
Adieu the grotto, wild and wide,
  The rocks abrupt and grassy plain!
  For pallid Autumn once again
Hath swelled each torrent of the hill;
  Her clouds collect, her shadows sail,
  And watery winds that sweep the vale
Grow loud and louder still.

But not the storm dethroning fast
  Yon monarch oak of massy pile,
Nor river roaring to the blast
  Around its dark and desert isle,
  Nor church-bell tolling to beguile
The cloud-born thunder passing by—
  Can sound in discord to my soul:
  Roll on, ye mighty waters, roll!
And rage, thou darkened sky!

Thy blossoms now no longer bright,
  Thy withered woods no longer green,
Yet, Eldurn shore, with dark delight
  I visit thy unlovely scene!

For many a sunset hour serene
My steps have trod thy mellow dew,
When his green light the glow-worm gave,
When Cynthia from the distant wave
Her twilight anchor drew,

And ploughed, as with a swelling sail,
The billowy clouds and starry sea:
Then—while thy hermit nightingale
Sang on his fragrant apple-tree—
Romantic, solitary, free,
The visitant of Eldurn's shore
On such a moonlight mountain strayed
As echoed to the music made
By Druid harps of yore.

Around thy savage hills of oak,
Around thy waters bright and blue,
No hunter's horn the silence broke,
No dying shriek thine echo knew;
But safe, sweet Eldurn woods, to you
The wounded wild deer ever ran,
Whose myrtle bound their grassy cave,
Whose very rocks a shelter gave
From blood-pursuing man.

Oh, heart effusions that arose
From nightly wanderings cherished here!
To him who flies from many woes
Even homeless deserts can be dear!
The last and solitary cheer
Of those that own no earthly home,
Say—is it not, ye banished race,
In such a loved and lonely place
Companionless to roam?

Yes, I have loved thy wild abode,
　　Unknown, unploughed, untrodden shore!
Where scarce the woodman finds a road,
　　And scarce the fisher plies an oar;
　　For man's neglect I love thee more,—
That art nor avarice intrude
　　To tame thy torrent's thunder-shock,
　　Or prune thy vintage of the rock,
Magnificently rude.

Unheeded spreads thy blossomed bud
　　Its milky bosom to the bee;
Unheeded falls along the flood
　　Thy desolate and agèd tree.
　　Forsaken scene, how like to thee
The fate of unbefriended Worth!
　　Like thine her fruit dishonoured falls;
　　Like thee in solitude she calls
A thousand treasures forth.

O silent spirit of the place,
　　If, lingering with the ruined year,
Thy hoary form and awful face
　　I yet might watch and worship here—
　　Thy storm were music to mine ear,
Thy wildest walk a shelter given
　　Sublimer thoughts on earth to find,
　　And share with no unhallowed mind
The majesty of heaven.

What though the bosom friends of Fate,
　　Prosperity's unweanèd brood,
Thy consolations cannot rate,
　　O self-dependent solitude!

Yet with a spirit unsubdued,
Though darkened by the clouds of care,
    To worship thy congenial gloom
    A pilgrim to the Prophet's tomb
The Friendless shall repair.

On him the world hath never smiled,
    Or looked but with accusing eye;
All-silent goddess of the wild,
    To thee that misanthrope shall fly!
    I hear his deep soliloquy,
I mark his proud but ravaged form,
    As stern he wraps his mantle round,
    And bids on winter's bleakest ground
Defiance to the storm.

Peace to his banished heart, at last,
    In thy dominions shall descend,
And, strong as beechwood in the blast,
    His spirit shall refuse to bend;
    Enduring life without a friend,
The world and falsehood left behind,
    Thy votary shall bear elate
    (Triumphant o'er opposing Fate)
His dark inspirèd mind.

But dost thou, Folly, mock the muse
    A wanderer's mountain walk to sing,
Who shuns a warring world, nor woos
    The vulture cover of its wing?
    Then fly, thou cowering, shivering thing,
Back to the fostering world beguiled
    To waste in self-consuming strife
    The loveless brotherhood of life,
Reviling and reviled!

Away, thou lover of the race
   That hither chased yon weeping deer!
If Nature's all-majestic face
   More pitiless than man's appear,
   Or if the wild winds seem more drear
Than man's cold charities below,
   Behold around his peopled plains,
   Where'er the social savage reigns,
Exuberance of woe!

His art and honours wouldst thou seek,
   Embossed on grandeur's giant walls?
Or hear his moral thunders speak
   Where senates light their airy halls,
   Where man his brother man enthralls,
Or sends his whirlwind warrant forth
   To rouse the slumbering fiends of war,
   To dye the blood-warm waves afar,
And desolate the earth?

From clime to clime pursue the scene,
   And mark in all thy spacious way
Where'er the tyrant man has been,
   There Peace, the cherub, cannot stay.
   In wilds and woodlands far away
She builds her solitary bower,
   Where only anchorites have trod,
   Or friendless men to worship God
Have wandered for an hour.

In such a far forsaken vale—
   And such, sweet Eldurn vale, is thine—
Afflicted nature shall inhale
   Heaven-borrowed thoughts and joys divine:

No longer wish, no more repine
For man's neglect or woman's scorn;
   Then wed thee to an exile's lot,
   For, if the world hath loved thee not,
Its absence may be borne.

132   A Thought Suggested by the New Year

THE more we live, more brief appear
   Our life's succeeding stages:
A day to childhood seems a year,
   And years like passing ages.

The gladsome current of our youth,
   Ere passion yet disorders,
Steals, lingering like a river smooth,
   Along its grassy borders.

But as the care-worn cheek grows wan,
   And sorrow's shafts fly thicker,
Ye stars, that measure life to man,
   Why seem your courses quicker?

When joys have lost their bloom and breath,
   And life itself is vapid,
Why, as we reach the Falls of death,
   Feel we its tide more rapid?

It may be strange—yet who would change
   Time's course to slower speeding;
When one by one our friends have gone,
   And left our bosoms bleeding?

Heaven gives our years of fading strength
    Indemnifying fleetness;
And those of youth, a *seeming length*,
    Proportioned to their sweetness.

JOHN GALT (*attributed to*)

133   Canadian Boat-song

LISTEN to me, as when ye heard our father
    Sing long ago the song of other shores—
Listen to me, and then in chorus gather
    All your deep voices, as ye pull your oars:

CHORUS

    Fair these broad meads—these hoary woods are grand;
    But we are exiles from our fathers' land.

From the lone shieling of the misty island
    Mountains divide us, and the waste of seas—
Yet still the blood is strong, the heart is Highland,
    And we in dreams behold the Hebrides:
    Fair these broad meads—these hoary woods are grand;
    But we are exiles from our fathers' land.

We ne'er shall tread the fancy-haunted valley,
    Where 'tween the dark hills creeps the small clear stream,
In arms around the patriarch banner rally,
    Nor see the moon on royal tombstones gleam:
    Fair these broad meads—these hoary woods are grand;
    But we are exiles from our fathers' land.

When the bold kindred, in the time long-vanish'd,
  Conquer'd the soil and fortified the keep,—
No seer foretold the children would be banish'd,
  That a degenerate Lord might boast his sheep:
    Fair these broad meads—these hoary woods are grand;
    But we are exiles from our fathers' land.

Come foreign rage—let Discord burst in slaughter!
  O then for clansman true, and stern claymore—
The hearts that would have given their blood like water,
  Beat heavily beyond the Atlantic roar:
    Fair these broad meads—these hoary woods are grand;
    But we are exiles from our fathers' land.

THOMAS MOORE

Odes to Nea

134

WRITTEN AT BERMUDA

[1]

NEA TYPANNEI
Euripides, *Medea*, v. 967

NAY, tempt me not to love again:
  There was a time when love was sweet;
Dear Nea! had I known thee then,
  Our souls had not been slow to meet!
But, oh! this weary heart hath run
  So many a time the rounds of pain,
Not even for thee, thou lovely one!
  Would I endure such pangs again.

If there be climes where never yet
The print of Beauty's foot was set,
Where man may pass his loveless nights
Unfevered by her false delights—
Thither my wounded soul would fly,
Where rosy cheek or radiant eye
Should bring no more their bliss, their pain,
Or fetter me to earth again!
Dear absent girl! whose eyes of light,
    Though little prized when all my own,
Now float before me, soft and bright
    As when they first enamouring shone!
How many hours of idle waste,
Within those witching arms embraced,
Unmindful of the fleeting day,
Have I dissolved life's dream away!
O bloom of time profusely shed!
O moments! simply, vainly fled,
Yet sweetly too—for love perfumed
The flame which thus my life consumed;
And brilliant was the chain of flowers
In which he led my victim hours!

Say, Nea dear! couldst thou, like her,
When warm to feel and quick to err,
Of loving fond, of roving fonder,
My thoughtless soul might wish to wander—
Couldst thou, like her, the wish reclaim,
    Endearing still, reproaching never,
Till all my heart should burn with shame,
    And be thy own more fixed than ever?
No, no—on earth there's only one
    Could bind such faithless folly fast:
And sure on earth 'tis I alone
    Could make such virtue false at last!

Nea! the heart which she forsook,
    For thee were but a worthless shrine—
Go, lovely girl, that angel look
    Must thrill a soul more pure than mine.
Oh! thou shalt be all else to me,
    That heart can feel or tongue can feign;
I'll praise, admire, and worship thee,
    But must not, dare not, love again.

135   [11]

... Tale iter omne cave.
Propert. lib. iv. eleg. 8

I PRAY you, let us roam no more
Along that wild and lonely shore,
    Where late we thoughtless strayed;
'Twas not for us, whom Heaven intends
To be no more than simple friends,
    Such lonely walks were made.

That little bay where, winding in
From Ocean's rude and angry din
    (As lovers steal to bliss),
The billows kiss the shore, and then
Flow calmly to the deep again,
    As though they did not kiss!

Remember, o'er its circling flood
In what a dangerous dream we stood—
    The silent sea before us,
Around us, all the gloom of grove,
That e'er was spread for guilt or love,
    No eye but Nature's o'er us!

I saw you blush, you felt me tremble,
In vain would formal art dissemble
   All that we wished and thought;
'Twas more than tongue could dare reveal,
'Twas more than virtue ought to feel,
   But all that passion ought!

I stooped to cull, with faltering hand,
A shell that, on the golden sand,
   Before us faintly gleamed;
I raised it to your lips of dew,
You kissed the shell, I kissed it too—
   Good Heaven! how sweet it seemed!

Oh! trust me, 'twas a place, an hour,
The worst that e'er temptation's power
   Could tangle me or you in!
Sweet Nea, let us roam no more
Along that wild and lonely shore,
   Such walks will be our ruin!

136   Go where Glory waits Thee

Go where glory waits thee,
But while fame elates thee,
   Oh! still remember me.
When the praise thou meetest
To thine ear is sweetest,
   Oh! then remember me.
Other arms may press thee,
Dearer friends caress thee,
All the joys that bless thee,

Sweeter far may be;
But when friends are nearest,
And when joys are dearest,
　Oh! then remember me.

When, at eve, thou rovest
By the star thou lovest,
　Oh! then remember me.
Think, when home returning,
Bright we've seen it burning,
　Oh! thus remember me.
Oft as summer closes,
When thine eye reposes
On its ling'ring roses,
　Once so lov'd by thee,
Think of her who wove them,
Her, who made thee love them,
　Oh! then remember me.

When, around thee dying,
Autumn leaves are lying,
　Oh! then remember me.
And, at night, when gazing
On the gay hearth blazing,
　Oh! still remember me.
Then should music, stealing
All the soul of feeling,
To thy heart appealing,
　Draw one tear from thee;
Then let memory bring thee
Strains I us'd to sing thee,—
　Oh! then remember me.

137   ['At the mid hour of night']

AT the mid hour of night, when stars are weeping, I fly
To the lone vale we lov'd, when life shone warm in thine eye,
    And I think that, if spirits can steal from the regions of air
    To revisit past scenes of delight, thou wilt come to me there,
And tell me our love is remember'd, even in the sky!

Then I sing the wild song it once was such rapture to hear;
When our voices, commingling breath'd, like one, on the ear;
    And, as Echo far off through the vale my sad orison rolls,
    I think, oh my love! 'tis thy voice from the kingdom of souls,
Faintly answering still the notes that once were so dear.

138   The Harp that once through Tara's Halls

THE harp that once through TARA's halls,
    The soul of music shed,
Now hangs as mute on TARA's walls
    As if that soul were fled.—
So sleeps the pride of former days,
    So glory's thrill is o'er,
And hearts, that once beat high for praise,
    Now feel that pulse no more!

No more to chiefs and ladies bright
    The harp of TARA swells:
The chord, alone, that breaks at night,
    Its tale of ruin tells.
Thus Freedom now so seldom wakes,
    The only throb she gives,
Is when some heart indignant breaks,
    To shew that still she lives!

139

Take Back the Virgin Page

WRITTEN ON RETURNING A BLANK BOOK

TAKE back the virgin page,
  White and unwritten still;
Some hand, more calm and sage,
  The leaf must fill.
Thoughts come, as pure as light,
  Pure as even *you* require;
But oh! each word I write
  Love turns to fire.

Yet let me keep the book;
  Oft shall my heart renew,
When on its leaves I look,
  Dear thoughts of you!
Like you, 'tis fair and bright;
  Like you, too bright and fair
To let wild passion write
  One wrong wish there!

Haply, when from those eyes
  Far, far away I roam,
Should calmer thoughts arise
  Tow'rds you and home;
Fancy may trace some line,
  Worthy those eyes to meet;
Thoughts that not burn, but shine
  Pure, calm and sweet!

And, as the records are,
  Which wandering seamen keep,
Led by their hidden star
  Through the cold deep;

So may the words I write
　　Tell thro' what storms I stray,
　　You still the unseen light,
　　Guiding my way!

140　Believe me, if all those Endearing Young Charms

BELIEVE me, if all those endearing young charms,
　　Which I gaze on so fondly to-day,
Were to change by to-morrow, and fleet in my arms,
　　Like fairy-gifts, fading away!
Thou wouldst still be ador'd, as this moment thou art,
　　Let thy loveliness fade as it will,
And, around the dear ruin, each wish of my heart
　　Would entwine itself verdantly still!

It is not, while beauty and youth are thine own,
　　And thy cheeks unprofan'd by a tear,
That the fervour and faith of a soul can be known,
　　To which time will but make thee more dear!
No, the heart that has truly lov'd, never forgets,
　　But as truly loves on to the close,
As the sun-flower turns on her god, when he sets,
　　The same look which she turn'd when he rose!

141　She is Far from the Land

SHE is far from the land, where her young hero sleeps,
　　And lovers are round her, sighing;
But coldly she turns from their gaze, and weeps,
　　For her heart in his grave is lying!

She sings the wild song of her dear native plains,
　　Every note which he lov'd awaking—
Ah! little they think, who delight in her strains,
　　How the heart of the Minstrel is breaking!

He had liv'd for his love, for his country he died,
　　They were all that to life had entwin'd him,—
Nor soon shall the tears of his country be dried,
　　Nor long will his love stay behind him.

Oh! make her a grave, where the sun-beams rest,
　　When they promise a glorious morrow;
They'll shine o'er her sleep, like a smile from the West,
　　From her own lov'd Island of sorrow!

142   I saw from the Beach

I SAW from the beach, when the morning was shining,
　　A bark o'er the waters move gloriously on;
I came, when the sun o'er that beach was declining,—
　　The bark was still there, but the waters were gone!

Ah! such is the fate of our life's early promise,
　　So passing the spring-tide of joy we have known:
Each wave, that we danc'd on at morning, ebbs from us,
　　And leaves us, at eve, on the bleak shore alone!

Ne'er tell me of glories, serenely adorning
　　The close of our day, the calm eve of our night;—
Give me back, give me back the wild freshness of Morning,
　　Her clouds and her tears are worth Evening's best light.

Oh, who would not welcome that moment's returning,
  When passion first wak'd a new life thro' his frame,
And his soul—like the wood, that grows precious in burning—
  Gave out all its sweets to love's exquisite flame!

143   Thee, Thee, only Thee

THE dawning of morn, the day-light's sinking,
The night's long hours still find me thinking
      Of thee, thee, only thee.
When friends are met, and goblets crown'd,
  And smiles are near, that once enchanted,
Unreach'd by all that sunshine round,
    My soul, like some dark spot, is haunted
      By thee, thee, only thee.

Whatever in fame's high path could waken
My spirit once, is now forsaken
      For thee, thee, only thee.
Like shores, by which some headlong bark
  To the ocean hurries—resting never—
Life's scenes go by me, bright or dark,
    I know not, heed not, hastening ever
      To thee, thee, only thee.

I have not a joy but of thy bringing,
And pain itself seems sweet, when springing
      From thee, thee, only thee.
Like spells, that nought on earth can break,
  Till lips, that know the charm, have spoken,
This heart, howe'er the world may wake
    Its grief, its scorn, can but be broken
      By thee, thee, only thee.

144 Sweet Innisfallen

SWEET Innisfallen, fare thee well,
  May calm and sunshine long be thine!
How fair thou art let others tell,
  While but to *feel* how fair is mine!

Sweet Innisfallen, fare thee well,
  And long may light around thee smile,
As soft as on that evening fell,
  When first I saw thy fairy isle!

Thou wert *too* lovely then for one,
  Who had to turn to paths of care—
Who had through vulgar crowds to run,
  And leave thee bright and silent there;

No more along thy shores to come,
  But, on the world's dim ocean tost,
Dream of thee sometimes, as a home
  Of sunshine he had seen and lost!

Far better in thy weeping hours
  To part from thee, as I do now,
When mist is o'er thy blooming bowers,
  Like sorrow's veil on beauty's brow.

For, though unrivall'd still thy grace,
  Thou dost not look, as then, *too* blest,
But, in thy shadows, seem'st a place
  Where weary man might hope to rest—

Might hope to rest, and find in thee
   A gloom like Eden's, on the day
He left its shade, when every tree,
   Like thine, hung weeping o'er his way!

Weeping or smiling, lovely isle;
   And still the lovelier for thy tears—
For tho' but rare thy sunny smile,
   'Tis Heav'n's own glance, when it appears.

Like feeling hearts, whose joys are few,
   But, when *indeed* they come, divine—
The steadiest light the sun e'er threw
   Is lifeless to one gleam of thine!

from *LALLA ROOKH*

[1]

145   ['The Golden Hour']

How calm, how beautiful, comes on
The stilly hour, when storms are gone;
When warring winds have died away,
And clouds, beneath the glancing ray,
Melt off, and leave the land and sea
Sleeping in bright tranquillity,—
Fresh as if Day again were born,
Again upon the lap of Morn!
When the light blossoms, rudely torn
And scatter'd at the whirlwind's will,
Hang floating in the pure air still,

Filling it all with precious balm,
In gratitude for this sweet calm;—
And every drop the thunder-showers
Have left upon the grass and flowers
Sparkles, as 'twere the lightning-gem
Whose liquid flame is born of them!
    When, 'stead of one unchanging breeze,
There blow a thousand gentle airs,
And each a different perfume bears,—
    As if the loveliest plants and trees
Had vassal breezes of their own
To watch and wait on them alone,
And waft no other breath than theirs!
When the blue waters rise and fall,
In sleepy sunshine mantling all;
And ev'n that swell the tempest leaves
Is like the full and silent heaves
Of lovers' hearts, when newly blest,
Too newly to be quite at rest!

[11]

146   [The Peri's Lament for Hinda]

FAREWELL—farewell to thee, ARABY's daughter!
    (Thus warbled a PERI beneath the dark sea)
No pearl ever lay, under OMAN's green water,
    More pure in its shell than thy Spirit in thee.

Oh! fair as the sea-flower close to thee growing,
    How light was thy heart till love's witchery came,
Like the wind of the south o'er a summer lute blowing,
    And hush'd all its music and wither'd its frame!

But long, upon ARABY's green sunny highlands,
  Shall maids and their lovers remember the doom
Of her, who lies sleeping among the Pearl Islands,
  With nought but the sea-star to light up her tomb.

And still, when the merry date-season is burning,
  And calls to the palm-groves the young and the old,
The happiest there, from their pastime returning,
  At sunset, will weep when thy story is told.

The young village maid, when with flowers she dresses
  Her dark flowing hair for some festival day,
Will think of thy fate, till neglecting her tresses,
  She mournfully turns from the mirror away.

Nor shall IRAN, belov'd of her Hero! forget thee,—
  Though tyrants watch over her tears as they start,
Close, close by the side of that Hero she'll set thee,
  Embalm'd in the innermost shrine of her heart.

Farewell—be it ours to embellish thy pillow
  With every thing beauteous that grows in the deep;
Each flower of the rock and each gem of the billow
  Shall sweeten thy Bed and illumine thy sleep.

Around thee shall glisten the loveliest amber
  That ever the sorrowing sea-bird has wept;
With many a shell, in whose hollow-wreath'd chamber,
  We, Peris of Ocean, by moonlight have slept.

We'll dive where the gardens of coral lie darkling,
  And plant all the rosiest stems at thy head;
We'll seek where the sands of the Caspian are sparkling,
  And gather their gold to strew over thy bed.

Farewell—farewell—until Pity's sweet fountain
  Is lost in the hearts of the fair and the brave,
They'll weep for the Chieftain who died on that mountain,
  They'll weep for the Maiden who sleeps in this wave.

147   Oft in the Stilly Night

SCOTCH AIR

OFT in the stilly night,
  Ere slumber's chain has bound me,
Fond Mem'ry brings the light
  Of other days around me.
    The smiles, the tears,
      Of boyhood's years,
    The words of love then spoken,
      The eyes that shone,
      Now dimm'd and gone,
    The cheerful hearts now broken!
Thus in the stilly night,
  Ere slumber's chain has bound me,
Sad Mem'ry brings the light
  Of other days around me.

When I remember all
  The friends, so linked together,
I've seen around me fall,
  Like leaves in wintry weather;
    I feel like one,
      Who treads alone
    Some banquet-hall, deserted,
      Whose lights are fled,
      Whose garlands dead,
    And all, but he, departed!

Thus in the stilly night,
  Ere slumber's chain has bound me,
Sad Mem'ry brings the light
  Of other days around me.

JAMES LEIGH HUNT

148   To the Grasshopper and the Cricket

GREEN little vaulter in the sunny grass
Catching your heart up at the feel of June,
Sole voice that's heard amidst the lazy noon,
When ev'n the bees lag at the summoning brass;
And you, warm little housekeeper, who class
With those who think the candles come too soon,
Loving the fire, and with your tricksome tune
Nick the glad silent moments as they pass;
Oh sweet and tiny cousins, that belong,
One to the fields, the other to the hearth,
Both have your sunshine; both though small are strong
At your clear hearts; and both were sent on earth
To sing in thoughtful ears this natural song,—
In doors and out, summer and winter, Mirth.

                                30 December 1816

149   The Nile

IT flows through old hushed Ægypt and its sands,
Like some grave mighty thought threading a dream,

And times and things, as in that vision, seem
Keeping along it their eternal stands,—
Caves, pillars, pyramids, the shepherd bands
That roamed through the young world, the glory extreme
Of high Sesostris, and that southern beam,
The laughing queen that caught the world's great hands.
Then comes a mightier silence, stern and strong,
As of a world left empty of its throng,
And the void weighs on us; and then we wake,
And hear the fruitful stream lapsing along
Twixt villages, and think how we shall take
Our own calm journey on for human sake.

150   from 'THE NYMPHS'

THERE are the fair-limbed Nymphs o' the Woods, (Look ye,
Whom kindred Fancies have brought after me!)
There are the fair-limbed Dryads, who love nooks
In the dry depth of oaks;
Or feel the air in groves, or pull green dresses
For their glad heads in rooty wildernesses;
Or on the golden turf, o'er the dark lines,
Which the sun makes when he declines,
Bend their white dances in and out the pines.
They tend all forests old, and meeting trees,
Wood, copse, or queach, or slippery dell o'erhung
With firs, and with their dusty apples strewn;
And let the visiting beams the boughs among,
And bless the trunks from clingings of disease
And wasted hearts that to the night-wind groan.
They screen the cuckoo when he sings; and teach
The mother blackbird how to lead astray
The unformed spirit of the foolish boy

From thick to thick, from hedge to layery beech,
When he would steal the huddled nest away
Of yellow bills, up-gaping for their food,
And spoil the song of the free solitude.
And they, at sound of the brute, insolent horn,
Hurry the deer out of the dewy morn;
And take into their sudden laps with joy
The startled hare that did but peep abroad;
And from the trodden road
Help the bruised hedgehog. But when tired, they love
The back-turned pheasant, hanging from the tree
His sunny drapery;
And handy squirrel, nibbling hastily;
And fragrant-living bee,
So happy, that he will not move, not he,
Without a song; and hidden, amorous dove,
With his deep breath; and bird of wakeful glow,
Whose louder song is like the voice of life,
Triumphant o'er death's image; but whose deep,
Low, lovelier note is like a gentle wife,
A poor, a pensive, yet a happy one,
Stealing, when day-light's common tasks are done,
An hour for mother's work; and singing low,
While her tired husband and her children sleep.

Then, there the Hamadryads are, their sisters,
Simpler crown twisters,
Who of one favourite tree, in some sweet spot,
Make home and leave it not,
Until the ignorant axe downs its fine head,
And then the nymph is fled.

And there are the Napeads,—names till now
Scarce known, I know not how,

To the rich bosom of my mother soil;
For they in meads and little corner bowers
Of hedge-row fields take care of the fresh flowers,
Keeping their innocent wealth from early spoil
Of beasts and blasts, and other blind mishaps,
For little children's laps,
And for the poet when he goes to hide him
From the town's sight, and for the lass beside him.
'Tis they who nurse in the moist dells
The mild primrose, and ring the sky-blue bells
To the bee's ear in a grass-gliding breeze;
'Tis they encourage, and from tearful wet
Dry up the grateful-breathing violet;
And they that set at ease
The sheath-enfolded fans of rosy bushes,
Ready against their blushes;
And for the Water-Nymphs', their cousins', sake,
Lay out the lily on the lake;
And teach the gentle cattle, when they sup,
To leave the daisy and the buttercup;
That when the bright-eyed Sun
Looks out in May to see what has been done,
The laughing meadows may be bold,
And show their bosoms to him, white and gold.

Too far for me to see, the Limniad takes
Her pleasure in the lakes;
She, that with hills about her, loves to be
At once at home and at her liberty.
Far off I fancy, 'twixt their bowery isles,
Her and her sisters playing their sweet wiles
About a boat, which one of them sits in
And will not let them win;
Till comes a sudden gust, and parts them with new smiles.

Nor can I see the lightsome-footed maids,
The Oreads, that frequent the lifted mountains;
Though by the Muses' help I still might shew,
How some go leaping by the laughing fountains
Down the touched crags; and some o'er deep ravines
Sit listening to the talking streams below;
And some in sloping glades
Of pines lie musing, or betwixt high screens
Of fern and flowers; or, like pavilioned queens
Covered from heat of the blue silent skies,
Sit perfumed underneath the cedarn shades,
Feeding the gazel with his lamping eyes.

Elsewhere, from ridge to ridge
They lay the tempest-levelled tree for bridge;
And help down the poor goat
That stands close-footed with his shivering coat
On a lone point; and echo the sweet calls
The herdsman makes, when singing to their stalls
The loitering cows with his home-loving strain,[1]
That sighs, and carols, and then sighs again,—
A song the sweeter for a taste of pain:
And these are the kind terrors, that with sounds
Of groans about the air, or earthly quaking,
Or great gigantic shadows, that stand making
Gestures upon the fog, warn the low grounds
Against the dreadful snow-rocks, that at last
Loos'd by the voiceful blast,
Burst down from their heaped ices; and come raking
O'er the crushed trees and dwellings nestling under,
Into the dash'd-up stream, with loads of misty thunder.
And O ye sweet and coy Ephydriads, you,

---

[1] 'The Ranz-des-Vaches'.

Why are your names so new
To islands which your liquid lips serene
Keep ever green
There, there the Ephydriads haunt;—there, where a gap
Betwixt a heap of tree-tops, hollow and dun,
Shews where the waters run,
And whence the fountain's tongue begins to lap.
There lie they, lulled by little whiffling tones
Of rills among the stones,
Or by the rounder murmur, glib and flush,
Of the escaping gush,
That laughs and tumbles, like a conscious thing,
For joy of all its future travelling.
The lizard circuits them; and his grave will
The frog, with reckoning leap, enjoys apart,
Till now and then the woodcock frights his heart
With brushing down to dip his dainty bill.
Close by, from bank to bank,
A little bridge there is, a one-railed plank;
And all is woody, mossy, and watery.
Sometimes a poet from that bridge might see
A Nymph reach downwards, holding by a bough
With tresses o'er her brow,
And with her white back stoop
The pushing stream to scoop
In a green gourd cup, shining sunnily.

The rills, a little farther onward, leave
The shady hollows; and united, heave
A river forth, that looking out as 'twere
For his fine way, turns, and with widening fair,
Lapses, full-bedded, between lawny brims.
Thence, from the dazzling of the noon, he swims
With darker sides into the woods, and there

Washes the Nymphs, that in sun-sprinkled ease
Haunt the white liquid spots, 'twixt shade reflecting trees.

Those are the Naiads, who keep neat
The banks from sedge, and from the dull-dropp'd feet
Of cattle that break down the fibrous mould.
They snap the selfish nets, that, overbold,
Cross the whole river, and might trip the keels
Of summer boats. Theirs are the kind appeals
And unseen beckoning, holding baits of grass,
That win the sheep into their washing-place;
And they too, in their gentleness, uphold
The sighing nostrils of the stag, when he
Takes to the wrapping water wretchedly;
And tow'rds the amorous noon, when some young poet
Comes there to bathe, and yet half thrills to do it,
Hovering with his ripe locks, and fair light limbs,
And trying with cold foot the banks and brims,
They win him to the water with sweet fancies,
Till in the girdling stream he pants and dances.
There's a whole bevy there in that recess
Rounding from the main stream: some sleep, some dress
Each other's locks, some swim about, some sit
Parting their own moist hair, or fingering it
Lightly, to let the curling air go through:
Some make them green and lilied coronets new;
And one there from her tender instep shakes
The matted sedge; a second, as she swims,
Looks round with pride upon her easy limbs;
A third, just holding by a bough, lets float
Her slumberous body like an anchored boat,
Looking with level eye at the glib flakes
And the strange crooked quivering which it makes,
Seen through the weltering of the watery glass:

Others (which make the rest look at them) pass,
Nodding and smiling, in the middle tide,
And luring swans on, which like fondled things
Eye poutingly their hands; yet following, glide
With unsuperfluous lift of their proud wings.

And far beyond upon another side,
Remembrance almost helps me to discern
Their stouter sisters, the great Nereids, turn
And toss upon the ocean's lifting billows,
Making them banks and pillows,
Upon whose springiness they lean and ride;
Some with an inward back; some upward-eyed,
Feeling the sky; and some with sidelong hips,
O'er which the surface of the water slips.
Sometimes, when morning runs along the sea
In a gold path, they cross it glancingly;
Sometimes they may be seen, going along
By the red sun-set in a silver throng;
And sometimes, when the black clouds send before
Their windy voices, they come past the shore,
Stooping in haste, and driving through the foam
The hunch-backed dolphins home:
But most they love sleek seas and springy sands
Under green rocks, on days of golden weather;
And there, in their free beauty, they'll take hands
And dance about a boat, which to the shore
They helped the night before;
Or dress their locks with myrtles or pearl bands;
Or sit and make them fans of many a feather
Which the gull sheds; or colour, like their own,
The parted lips of shells that are up thrown,
With which, and coral, and the glib sea flowers,
They furnish their faint bowers.

I have not told your loves; I have not told
Your perfect loves, ye Nymphs! Those are among
The perfect virtues only to be sung
By your own glorious lovers, who have passed
Death, and all drear mistake, and sit at last
In the clear thrill of their hoped age of gold.

HENRY KIRKE WHITE

151   from 'CLIFTON GROVE'

Lo! in the West, fast fades the ling'ring light,
And day's last vestige takes its silent flight.
No more, is heard the Woodman's measur'd stroke
Which, with the dawn, from yonder dingle broke;
No more, hoarse clam'ring o'er th' uplifted head,
The Crows assembling, seek their wind-rock'd bed;
Still'd is the Village hum—the Woodland sounds
Have ceas'd to echo o'er the dewy grounds,
And general silence reigns, save when below,
The murmuring Trent is scarcely heard to flow;
And save when, swung by 'nighted Rustic late,
Oft, on its hinge, rebounds the jarring gate.
Or, when the sheep-bell, in the distant vale,
Breathes its wild music on the downy gale.

Now, when the Rustic wears the social smile,
Releas'd from day and its attendant toil,
And draws his Household round their evening fire,
And tells the oft-told tales that never tire:
Or, where the Town's blue turrets dimly rise,

And Manufacture taints the ambient skies,
The pale Mechanic leaves the lab'ring loom,
The air-pent hold, the pestilential room,
And rushes out, impatient to begin
The stated course of customary sin:
Now, now, my solitary way I bend
Where solemn Groves in awful state impend,
And cliffs, that boldly rise above the plain,
Bespeak, blest Clifton! thy sublime domain.
Here, lonely wand'ring o'er the sylvan bow'r,
I come, to pass the meditative hour;
To bid awhile, the strife of passion cease,
And woo the calms of solitude, and peace.
And oh! thou sacred pow'r, who rear'st on high
Thy leafy throne where waving poplars sigh!
Genius of woodland shades! whose mild control
Steals with resistless witch'ry to the soul.
Come with thy wonted ardour, and inspire
My glowing bosom with thy hallow'd fire.
And thou too Fancy! from thy starry sphere,
Where to the hymning orbs thou lend'st thine ear,
Do thou descend, and bless my ravish'd sight,
Veil'd in soft visions of serene delight.
At thy command the gale that passes by
Bears in its whispers mystic harmony.
Thou wav'st thy wand, and lo! what forms appear!
On the dark cloud what giant shapes career!
The ghosts of Ossian skim the misty vale,
And hosts of Sylphids on the Moon-beam sail.

This gloomy Alcove, darkling to the sight,
Where meeting trees create eternal night;
Save, when from yonder stream, the sunny ray,
Reflected gives a dubious gleam of day;

Recalls endearing to my alter'd mind,
Times, when beneath the boxen hedge reclin'd
I watch'd the Lapwing to her clam'rous brood;
Or lur'd the Robin to its scatter'd food;
Or woke with song the woodland echo wild,
And at each gay response delighted, smil'd.
How oft, when Childhood threw its golden ray
Of gay Romance, o'er every happy day;
Here, would I run, a visionary boy,
When the hoarse Tempest shook the vaulted sky,
And fancy led, beheld th'Almighty's form
Sternly careering on the eddying storm;
And heard, while awe congeal'd my inmost soul,
His voice terrific, in the thunders roll.
With secret joy, I view'd with vivid glare,
The volley'd lightnings cleave the sullen air;
And, as the warring winds around revil'd,
With awful pleasure big,—I heard, and smil'd.
Belov'd remembrance!—Mem'ry which endears
This silent spot to my advancing years.
Here, dwells eternal peace, eternal rest,
In shades like these to live, is to be blest.

152   To an Early Primrose

MILD offspring of a dark and sullen sire!
Whose modest form, so delicately fine,
Was nurs'd in whirling storms
And cradled in the winds.

Thee, when young spring first question'd winter's sway,
And dar'd the sturdy Blust'rer to the fight,
  Thee on this bank he threw
  To make his Victory.

In this low vale, the promise of the year,
Serene, thou openest to the nipping gale.
  Unnotic'd, and alone,
  Thy tender elegance.

So Virtue blooms, brought forth amid the storms
Of chill adversity, in some lone walk
  Of life, she rears her head
  Obscure and unobserv'd;

While every bleaching breeze that on her blows,
Chastens her spotless purity of breast,
  And hardens her to bear
  Serene the ills of life.

THOMAS LOVE PEACOCK

153   ## The Sun-Dial

  THE ivy o'er the mouldering wall
 Spreads like a tree, the growth of years:
 The wild wind through the doorless hall
 A melancholy music rears,
 A solitary voice, that sighs
 O'er man's forgotten pageantries.
  Above the central gate, the clock,
 Through clustering ivy dimly seen,

Seems, like the ghost of Time, to mock
The wrecks of power that once has been.
The hands are rusted on its face;
Even where they ceased, in years gone by,
To keep the flying moments' pace;
Fixing, in Fancy's thoughtful eye,
A point of ages passed away,
A speck of time, that owns no tie
With aught that lives and breathes to-day.
   But 'mid the rank and towering grass,
Where breezes wave, in mournful sport,
The weeds that choke the ruined court,
The careless hours, that circling pass,
Still trace upon the dialled brass
The shade of their unvarying way:
And evermore, with every ray
That breaks the clouds and gilds the air,
Time's stealthy steps are imaged there:
Even as the long-revolving years
In self-respecting circles flow,
From the first bud the hedge-row bears,
To wintry Nature's robe of snow.
The changeful forms of mortal things
Decay and pass; and art and power
Oppose in vain the doom that flings
Oblivion on their closing hour:
While still, to every woodland vale,
New blooms, new fruits, the seasons bring,
For other eyes and lips to hail
With looks and sounds of welcoming:
As where some stream light-eddying roves
By sunny meads and shadowy groves,
Wave following wave departs for ever,
But still flows on the eternal river.

232

154 [Song by Mr. Cypress]

THERE is a fever of the spirit,
 The brand of Cain's unresting doom,
Which in the lone dark souls that bear it
 Glows like the lamp in Tullia's tomb:
Unlike that lamp, its subtle fire
 Burns, blasts, consumes its cell, the heart,
Till, one by one, hope, joy, desire,
 Like dreams of shadowy smoke depart.

When hope, love, life itself, are only
 Dust—spectral memories—dead and cold—
The unfed fire burns bright and lonely,
 Like that undying lamp of old:
And by that drear illumination,
 Till time its clay-built home has rent,
Thought broods on feeling's desolation—
 The soul is its own monument.

155 Newark Abbey

AUGUST, 1842

WITH A REMINISCENCE OF [FANNY FALKNER]
AUGUST, 1807

 I GAZE, where August's sunbeam falls
Along these gray and lonely walls,
Till in its light absorbed appears
The lapse of five-and-thirty years.

If change there be, I trace it not
In all this consecrated spot:
No new imprint of Ruin's march
On roofless wall and frameless arch:
The hills, the woods, the fields, the stream,
Are basking in the self-same beam:
The fall, that turns the unseen mill,
As then it murmured, murmurs still:
It seems, as if in one were cast
The present and the imaged past,
Spanning, as with a bridge sublime,
That awful lapse of human time,
That gulph, unfathomably spread
Between the living and the dead.

For all too well my spirit feels
The only change this scene reveals:
The sunbeams play, the breezes stir,
Unseen, unfelt, unheard by her,
Who, on that long-past August day,
First saw with me these ruins gray.

Whatever span the Fates allow,
Ere I shall be as she is now,
Still in my bosom's inmost cell
Shall that deep-treasured memory dwell:
That, more than language can express,
Pure miracle of loveliness,
Whose voice so sweet, whose eyes so bright,
Were my soul's music, and its light,
In those blest days, when life was new,
And hope was false, but love was true.

Love and Age

I PLAYED with you 'mid cowslips blowing,
When I was six and you were four;
When garlands weaving, flower-balls throwing,
Were pleasures soon to please no more.
Through groves and meads, o'er grass and heather,
With little playmates, to and fro,
We wandered hand in hand together;
But that was sixty years ago.

You grew a lovely roseate maiden,
And still our early love was strong;
Still with no care our days were laden,
They glided joyously along;
And I did love you, very dearly,
How dearly words want power to show;
I thought your heart was touched as nearly;
But that was fifty years ago.

Then other lovers came around you,
Your beauty grew from year to year,
And many a splendid circle found you
The centre of its glittering sphere.
I saw you then, first vows forsaking,
On rank and wealth your hand bestow;
Oh, then I thought my heart was breaking,—
But that was forty years ago.

And I lived on, to wed another:
No cause she gave me to repine;
And when I heard you were a mother,
I did not wish the children mine.

My own young flock, in fair progression,
Made up a pleasant Christmas row:
My joy in them was past expression;—
But that was thirty years ago.

You grew a matron plump and comely,
You dwelt in fashion's brightest blaze;
My earthly lot was far more homely;
But I too had my festal days.
No merrier eyes have ever glistened
Around the hearth-stone's wintry glow,
Than when my youngest child was christened:—
But that was twenty years ago.

Time passed. My eldest girl was married,
And I am now a grandsire grey;
One pet of four years old I've carried
Among the wild-flowered meads to play.
In our old fields of childish pleasure,
Where now, as then, the cowslips blow,
She fills her basket's ample measure,—
And that is not ten years ago.

But though first love's impassioned blindness
Has passed away in colder light,
I still have thought of you with kindness,
And shall do, till our last good-night.
The ever-rolling silent hours
Will bring a time we shall not know,
When our young days of gathering flowers
Will be an hundred years ago.

157   Margaret Love Peacock
       for her tombstone, 1826

LONG night succeeds thy little day;
    Oh blighted blossom! can it be,
That this grey stone and grassy clay
    Have closed our anxious care of thee?

The half-form'd speech of artless thought,
    That spoke a mind beyond thy years;
The song, the dance, by nature taught;
    The sunny smiles, the transient tears;

The symmetry of face and form,
    The eye with light and life replete;
The little heart so fondly warm;
    The voice so musically sweet.

These lost to hope, in memory yet
    Around the hearts that lov'd thee cling,
Shadowing, with long and vain regret,
    The too fair promise of thy spring.

GEORGE GORDON NOEL, LORD BYRON

158   I

WHEN we two parted
    In silence and tears,
Half broken-hearted
    To sever for years,

Pale grew thy cheek and cold,
   Colder thy kiss;
Truly that hour foretold
   Sorrow to this.

2

The dew of the morning
   Sunk chill on my brow—
It felt like the warning
   Of what I feel now.
Thy vows are all broken,
   And light is thy fame;
I hear thy name spoken,
   And share in its shame.

3

They name thee before me,
   A knell to mine ear;
A shudder comes o'er me—
   Why wert thou so dear?
They know not I knew thee,
   Who knew thee too well:—
Long, long shall I rue thee,
   Too deeply to tell.

4

In secret we met—
   In silence I grieve,
That thy heart could forget,
   Thy spirit deceive.
If I should meet thee
   After long years,
How should I greet thee!—
   With silence and tears.

1808

159   [William Lisle Bowles]

HAIL, Sympathy! thy soft idea brings
A thousand visions of a thousand things,
And shows, still whimpering thro' three-score of years,
The maudlin prince of mournful sonneteers.
And art thou not their prince? harmonious BOWLES!
Thou first, great oracle of tender souls!
Whether thou sing'st with equal ease, and grief,
The fall of empires, or a yellow leaf;
Whether thy muse most lamentably tells
What merry sounds proceed from Oxford bells,
Or, still in bells delighting, finds a friend,
In every chime that jingled from Ostend?
Ah! how much juster were thy Muse's hap,
If to thy bells thou would'st but add a cap!
Delightful BOWLES! still blessing, and still blest,
All love thy strain, but children like it best.
'Tis thine, with gentle LITTLE's moral song,
To soothe the mania of the amorous throng!
With thee our nursery damsels shed their tears,
Ere Miss, as yet, completes her infant years:
But in her teens thy whining powers are vain;
She quits poor BOWLES for LITTLE's purer strain.
Now to soft themes thou scornest to confine
The lofty numbers of a harp like thine:
'Awake a louder and a loftier strain,'
Such as none heard before, or will again;
Where all discoveries jumbled from the flood,
Since first the leaky ark repos'd in mud,
By more or less, are sung in every book,
From Captain NOAH down to Captain COOK.
Nor this alone, but pausing on the road,
The Bard sighs forth a gentle episode;

And gravely tells—attend, each beauteous Miss!—
When first Madeira trembled to a kiss.
BOWLES! in thy memory let this precept dwell:
Stick to thy Sonnets, man! at least they sell.
But if some new-born whim, or larger bribe,
Prompt thy crude brain, and claim thee for a scribe;
If 'chance some bard, though once by dunces fear'd,
Now, prone in dust, can only be rever'd;
If POPE, whose fame and genius, from the first,
Have foil'd the best of critics, needs the worst,
Do thou essay; each fault, each failing scan;
The first of poets was, alas! but man!
Rake from each ancient dunghill ev'ry pearl,
Consult Lord Fanny, and confide in CURLL;
Let all the scandals of a former age,
Perch on thy pen and flutter o'er thy page;
Affect a candour which thou can'st not feel,
Clothe envy in the garb of honest zeal;
Write, as if St. John's soul could still inspire,
And do from hate what MALLET did for hire.
Oh! had'st thou liv'd in that congenial time,
To rave with DENNIS, and with RALPH to rhyme,
Throng'd with the rest around his living head,
Not rais'd thy hoof against the lion dead,
A meet reward had crown'd thy glorious gains,
And link'd thee to the Dunciad for thy pains.

160   [Sunset over the Ægean]

> SLOW sinks, more lovely ere his race be run,
> Along Morea's hills the setting Sun;
> Not as in Northern climes obscurely bright,
> But one unclouded blaze of living light;

O'er the hush'd deep the yellow beam he throws,
Gilds the green wave that trembles as it glows;
On old Ægina's rock and Hydra's isle,
The God of gladness sheds his parting smile;
O'er his own regions lingering loves to shine,
Though there his altars are no more divine.
Descending fast the mountain-shadows kiss
Thy glorious Gulph, unconquer'd Salamis!
Their azure arches through the long expanse
More deeply purpled meet his mellowing glance,
And tenderest tints, along their summits driven,
Mark his gay course and own the hues of Heaven;
Till darkly shaded from the land and deep,
Behind his Delphian rock he sinks to sleep.

161   [Dedication] To Ianthe

N OT in those climes where I have late been straying,
Though Beauty there hath long been matchless deemed;
Not in those visions to the heart displaying
Forms which it sighs but to have only dreamed,
Hath aught like thee in truth or fancy seemed:
Nor, having seen thee, shall I vainly seek
To paint those charms which varied as they beamed—
To such as see thee not my words were weak;
To those who gaze on thee what language could they speak?

Ah! may'st thou ever be what now thou art,
Nor unbeseem the promise of thy spring,
As fair in form, as warm yet pure in heart,
Love's image upon earth without his wing,

241

And guileless beyond Hope's imagining!
And surely she who now so fondly rears
Thy youth, in thee, thus hourly brightening,
Beholds the rainbow of her future years,
Before whose heavenly hues all sorrow disappears.

Young Peri of the West!—'tis well for me
My years already doubly number thine;
My loveless eye unmoved may gaze on thee,
And safely view thy ripening beauties shine;
Happy, I ne'er shall see them in decline,
Happier that while all younger hearts shall bleed,
Mine shall escape the doom thine eyes assign
To those whose admiration shall succeed,
But mixed with pangs to Love's even loveliest hours decreed.

Oh! let that eye, which, wild as the Gazelle's,
Now brightly bold or beautifully shy,
Wins as it wanders, dazzles where it dwells,
Glance o'er this page; nor to my verse deny
That smile for which my breast might vainly sigh
Could I to thee be ever more than friend:
This much, dear maid, accord; nor question why
To one so young my strain I would commend,
But bid me with my wreath one matchless lily blend.

Such is thy name with this my verse entwined;
And long as kinder eyes a look shall cast
On Harold's page, Ianthe's here enshrined
Shall thus be first beheld, forgotten last:
My days once number'd, should this homage past
Attract thy fairy fingers near the lyre
Of him who hailed thee loveliest as thou wast,
Such is the most my memory may desire;
Though more than Hope can claim, could Friendship less require?

162   [The Eve of Waterloo]

THERE was a sound of revelry by night,
And Belgium's capital had gathered then
Her Beauty and her Chivalry, and bright
The lamps shone o'er fair women and brave men;
A thousand hearts beat happily; and when
Music arose with its voluptuous swell,
Soft eyes look'd love to eyes which spake again,
And all went merry as a marriage-bell;
But hush! hark! a deep sound strikes like a rising knell!

Did ye not hear it?—No; 'twas but the wind,
Or the car rattling o'er the stony street;
On with the dance! let joy be unconfined;
No sleep till morn, when Youth and Pleasure meet
To chase the glowing Hours with flying feet—
But hark!—that heavy sound breaks in once more,
As if the clouds its echo would repeat;
And nearer, clearer, deadlier than before!
Arm! Arm! it is—it is—the cannon's opening roar!

Within a windowed niche of that high hall
Sate Brunswick's fated chieftain; he did hear
That sound the first amidst the festival,
And caught its tone with Death's prophetic ear;
And when they smiled because he deem'd it near,
His heart more truly knew that peal too well
Which stretch'd his father on a bloody bier,
And roused the vengeance blood alone could quell:
He rush'd into the field, and, foremost fighting, fell.

Ah! then and there was hurrying to and fro,
And gathering tears, and tremblings of distress,
And cheeks all pale, which but an hour ago
Blush'd at the praise of their own loveliness;
And there were sudden partings, such as press
The life from out young hearts, and choking sighs
Which ne'er might be repeated; who could guess
If ever more should meet those mutual eyes
Since upon night so sweet such awful morn could rise?

And there was mounting in hot haste: the steed,
The mustering squadron, and the clattering car,
Went pouring forward with impetuous speed,
And swiftly forming in the ranks of war;
And the deep thunder peal on peal afar;
And near, the beat of the alarming drum
Roused up the soldier ere the morning star;
While throng'd the citizens with terror dumb,
Or whispering, with white lips—'The foe! they come! they come!'

And wild and high the 'Cameron's gathering' rose!
The war-note of Lochiel, when Albyn's hills
Have heard, and heard, too, have her Saxon foes:—
How in the noon of night that pibroch thrills,
Savage and shrill! But with the breath which fills
Their mountain-pipe, so fill the mountaineers
With the fierce native daring which instils
The stirring memory of a thousand years,
And Evan's, Donald's fame rings in each clansman's ears!

And Ardennes waves above them her green leaves,
Dewy with nature's tear-drops as they pass,
Grieving, if aught inanimate e'er grieves,
Over the unreturning brave,—alas!

Ere evening to be trodden like the grass
Which now beneath them, but above shall grow
In its next verdure, when this fiery mass
Of living valour, rolling on the foe
And burning with high hope, shall moulder cold and low.

Last noon beheld them full of lusty life,
Last eve in Beauty's circle proudly gay,
The midnight brought the signal-sound of strife,
The morn the marshalling in arms,—the day
Battle's magnificently-stern array!
The thunder-clouds close o'er it, which when rent
The earth is covered thick with other clay,
Which her own clay shall cover, heaped and pent,
Rider and horse,—friend, foe,— in one red burial blent!

163   [Lake Leman]

CLEAR, placid Leman! thy contrasted lake,
With the wide world I dwelt in, is a thing
Which warns me, with its stillness, to forsake
Earth's troubled waters for a purer spring.
This quiet sail is as a noiseless wing
To waft me from distraction; once I loved
Torn ocean's roar, but thy soft murmuring
Sounds sweet as if a sister's voice reproved,
That I with stern delights should e'er have been so moved.

It is the hush of night, and all between
Thy margin and the mountains, dusk, yet clear,
Mellowed and mingling, yet distinctly seen,
Save darken'd Jura, whose capt heights appear

Precipitously steep; and drawing near,
There breathes a living fragrance from the shore,
Of flowers yet fresh with childhood; on the ear
Drops the light drip of the suspended oar,
Or chirps the grasshopper one good-night carol more;

He is an evening reveller, who makes
His life an infancy, and sings his fill;
At intervals, some bird from out the brakes
Starts into voice a moment, then is still.
There seems a floating whisper on the hill,
But that is fancy, for the starlight dews
All silently their tears of love instil,
Weeping themselves away, till they infuse
Deep into Nature's breast the spirit of her hues.

Ye stars! which are the poetry of heaven!
If in your bright leaves we would read the fate
Of men and empires,—'tis to be forgiven,
That in our aspirations to be great,
Our destinies o'erleap their mortal state,
And claim a kindred with you; for ye are
A beauty and a mystery, and create
In us such love and reverence from afar,
That fortune, fame, power, life, have named themselves a star.

All heaven and earth are still—though not in sleep,
But breathless, as we grow when feeling most;
And silent, as we stand in thoughts too deep:—
All heaven and earth are still: From the high host
Of stars, to the lull'd lake and mountain-coast,
All is concentred in a life intense,
Where not a beam, nor air, nor leaf is lost,
But hath a part of being, and a sense
Of that which is of all Creator and defence.

Then stirs the feeling infinite, so felt
In solitude, where we are *least* alone;
A truth, which through our being then doth melt
And purifies from self: it is a tone,
The soul and source of music, which makes known
Eternal harmony, and sheds a charm
Like to the fabled Cytherea's zone,
Blinding all things with beauty; —'twould disarm
The spectre Death, had he substantial power to harm.

164 ['The Fatal Spell']

OH Love! no habitant of earth thou art—
An unseen seraph, we believe in thee,
A faith whose martyrs are the broken heart,
But never yet hath seen, nor e'er shall see
The naked eye, thy form, as it should be;
The mind hath made thee, as it peopled heaven,
Even with its own desiring phantasy,
And to a thought such shape and image given,
As haunts the unquench'd soul—parch'd—wearied—wrung—and
riven.

Of its own beauty is the mind diseased,
And fevers into false creation:—where,
Where are the forms the sculptor's soul hath seiz'd?
In him alone. Can Nature shew so fair?
Where are the charms and virtues which we dare
Conceive in boyhood and pursue as men,
The unreach'd Paradise of our despair,
Which o'er-informs the pencil and the pen,
And overpowers the page where it would bloom again?

Who loves, raves—'tis youth's frenzy—but the cure
Is bitterer still; as charm by charm unwinds
Which robed our idols, and we see too sure
Nor worth nor beauty dwells from out the mind's
Ideal shape of such; yet still it binds
The fatal spell, and still it draws us on,
Reaping the whirlwind from the oft-sown winds;
The stubborn heart, its alchemy begun,
Seems ever near the prize,—wealthiest when most undone.

We wither from our youth, we gasp away—
Sick—sick; unfound the boon—unslaked the thirst,
Though to the last, in verge of our decay,
Some phantom lures, such as we sought at first—
But all too late,—so are we doubly curst.
Love, fame, ambition, avarice—'tis the same,
Each idle—and all ill—and none the worst—
For all are meteors with a different name,
And Death the sable smoke where vanishes the flame.

Few—none—find what they love or could have loved,
Though accident, blind contact, and the strong
Necessity of loving, have removed
Antipathies—but to recur, ere long,
Envenomed with irrevocable wrong;
And Circumstance, that unspiritual god
And miscreator, makes and helps along
Our coming evils with a crutch-like rod,
Whose touch turns Hope to dust,—the dust we all have trod.

Our life is a false nature: 'tis not in
The harmony of things,—this hard decree,
This uneradicable taint of sin,
This boundless upas, this all-blasting tree,

Whose root is earth, whose leaves and branches be
The skies which rain their plagues on men like dew—
Disease, death, bondage—all the woes we see—
And worse, the woes we see not—which throb through
The immediate soul, with heart-aches ever new.

165   ['By the Deep Sea']

OH! that the Desart were my dwelling place,
With one fair Spirit for my minister,
That I might all forget the human race,
And, hating no one, love but only her!
Ye Elements!—in whose ennobling stir
I feel myself exalted—Can ye not
Accord me such a being? Do I err
In deeming such inhabit many a spot?
Though with them to converse can rarely be our lot.

There is a pleasure in the pathless woods,
There is a rapture on the lonely shore,
There is society, where none intrudes,
By the deep Sea, and music in its roar:
I love not Man the less, but Nature more,
From these our interviews, in which I steal
From all I may be, or have been before,
To mingle with the Universe, and feel
What I can ne'er express, yet can not all conceal.

Roll on, thou deep and dark blue ocean—roll!
Ten thousand fleets sweep over thee in vain;
Man marks the earth with ruin—his control
Stops with the shore;—upon the watery plain

The wrecks are all thy deed, nor doth remain
A shadow of man's ravage, save his own,
When, for a moment, like a drop of rain,
He sinks into thy depths with bubbling groan,
Without a grave, unknell'd, uncoffin'd, and unknown.

His steps are not upon thy paths, thy fields
Are not a spoil for him,—thou dost arise
And shake him from thee; the vile strength he wields
For earth's destruction thou dost all despise,
Spurning him from thy bosom to the skies,
And send'st him, shivering in thy playful spray
And howling, to his Gods, where haply lies
His petty hope in some near port or bay,
And dashest him again to earth:—there let him lay.

The armaments which thunderstrike the walls
Of rock-built cities, bidding nations quake,
And monarchs tremble in their capitals,
The oak leviathans, whose huge ribs make
Their clay creator the vain title take
Of lord of thee, and arbiter of war;
These are thy toys, and, as the snowy flake,
They melt into thy yeast of waves, which mar
Alike the Armada's pride, or spoils of Trafalgar.

Thy shores are empires, changed in all save thee—
Assyria, Greece, Rome, Carthage, what are they?
Thy waters wash'd them power while they were free,
And many a tyrant since; their shores obey
The stranger, slave, or savage; their decay
Has dried up realms to desarts:—not so thou,
Unchangeable save to thy wild waves' play—
Time writes no wrinkle on thine azure brow—
Such as creation's dawn beheld, thou rollest now.

166   She Walks in Beauty

SHE walks in beauty, like the night
    Of cloudless climes and starry skies;
And all that's best of dark and bright
    Meet in her aspect and her eyes:
Thus mellow'd to that tender light
    Which heaven to gaudy day denies.

One shade the more, one ray the less,
    Had half impair'd the nameless grace
Which waves in every raven tress,
    Or softly lightens o'er her face;
Where thoughts serenely sweet express
    How pure, how dear their dwelling-place.

And on that cheek, and o'er that brow,
    So soft, so calm, yet eloquent,
The smiles that win, the tints that glow,
    But tell of days in goodness spent,
A mind at peace with all below,
    A heart whose love is innocent!

167   Fare Thee Well!

FARE thee well! and if for ever—
    Still for ever, fare *thee well*—
Even though unforgiving, never
    'Gainst thee shall my heart rebel.—
Would that breast were bared before thee
    Where thy head so oft hath lain,
While that placid sleep came o'er thee
        Which thou ne'er canst know again:

Would that breast by thee glanc'd over,
  Every inmost thought could show!
Then, thou would'st at last discover
  'Twas not well to spurn it so—
Though the world for this commend thee—
  Though it smile upon the blow,
Even its praises must offend thee,
  Founded on another's woe—
Though my many faults defaced me,
  Could no other arm be found
Than the one which once embraced me
  To inflict a cureless wound?
Yet—oh, yet—thyself deceive not—
  Love may sink by slow decay,
But by sudden wrench, believe not
  Hearts can thus be torn away;
Still thine own its life retaineth—
  Still must mine—though bleeding—beat,
And the undying thought which paineth
  Is—that we no more may meet.—
These are words of deeper sorrow
  Than the wail above the dead,
Both shall live—but every morrow
  Wake us from a widowed bed.—
And when thou would'st solace gather—
  When our child's first accents flow—
Wilt thou teach her to say,—'Father!'
  Though his care she must forego?
When her little hands shall press thee—
  When her lip to thine is prest—
Think of him whose prayer shall bless thee—
  Think of him thy love had bless'd.
Should her lineaments resemble
  Those thou never more may'st see—

Then thy heart will softly tremble
  With a pulse yet true to me.—
All my faults—perchance thou knowest—
  All my madness—none can know;
All my hopes—where'er thou goest—
  Wither—yet with *thee* they go.—
Every feeling hath been shaken,
  Pride—which not a world could bow—
Bows to thee—by thee forsaken
  Even my soul forsakes me now.—
But 'tis done—all words are idle—
  Words from me are vainer still;
But the thoughts we cannot bridle
  Force their way without the will.—
Fare thee well!—thus disunited—
  Torn from every nearer tie—
Seared in heart—and lone—and blighted—
  More than this I scarce can die.—

168   A Sketch from Private Life

> Honest—Honest Iago!
> If that thou be'st a devil, I cannot kill thee.
> SHAKESPEARE.

BORN in the garret, in the kitchen bred,
Promoted thence to deck her mistress' head;
Next—for some gracious service unexprest,
And from its wages only to be guess'd—
Rais'd from the toilet to the table,—where
Her wondering betters wait behind her chair.
With eye unmoved, and forehead unabash'd,
She dines from off the plate she lately wash'd,

Quick with the tale, and ready with the lie—
The genial confidante, and general spy—
Who could, ye gods! her next employment guess—
An only infant's earliest governess!
She taught the child to read, and taught so well,
That she herself, by teaching, learn'd to spell.
An adept next in penmanship she grows,
As many a nameless slander deftly shows:
What she had made the pupil of her art,
None know—but that high Soul secur'd the heart,
And panted for the truth it could not hear,
With longing breast and undeluded ear.

Foil'd was perversion by that youthful mind,
Which Flattery fool'd not—Baseness could not blind,
Deceit infect not—near Contagion soil—
Indulgence weaken—nor Example spoil—
Nor master'd Science tempt her to look down
On humbler talents with a pitying frown—
Nor Genius swell—nor Beauty render vain—
Nor Envy ruffle to retaliate pain—
Nor Fortune change—Pride raise—nor Passion bow,
Nor Virtue teach austerity—till now.
Serenely purest of her sex that live,
But wanting one sweet weakness—to forgive,
Too shock'd at faults her soul can never know,
She deems that all could be like her below:
Foe to all Vice, yet hardly Virtue's friend,
For Virtue pardons those she would amend.

But to the theme:—now laid aside too long,
The baleful burthen of this honest song—
Though all her former functions are no more,
She rules the circle which she served before.

If mothers—none know why—before her quake;
If daughters dread her for the mothers' sake;
If early habits—those false links, which bind
At times the loftiest to the meanest mind—
Have given her power too deeply to instil
The angry essence of her deadly will;
If like a snake she steal within your walls,
Till the black slime betray her as she crawls;
If like a viper to the heart she wind,
And leave the venom there she did not find;—
What marvel that this hag of hatred works
Eternal evil latent as she lurks,
To make a Pandemonium where she dwells,
And reign the Hecate of domestic hells?
Skill'd by a touch to deepen scandal's tints
With all the kind mendacity of hints,
While mingling truth with falsehood—sneers with smiles—
A thread of candour with a web of wiles:
A plain blunt show of briefly-spoken seeming,
To hide her bloodless heart's soul-harden'd scheming;
A lip of lies—a face formed to conceal;
And, without feeling, mock at all who feel:
With a vile mask the Gorgon would disown;
A cheek of parchment—and an eye of stone.
Mark, how the channels of her yellow blood
Ooze to her skin, and stagnate there to mud,
Cased like the centipede in saffron mail,
Or darker greenness of the scorpion's scale—
(For drawn from reptiles only may we trace
Congenial colours in that soul or face)—
Look on her features! and behold her mind
As in a mirror of itself defined:
Look on the picture! deem it not o'ercharged—
There is no trait which might not be enlarged:

Yet true to 'Nature's journeymen,' who made
This monster when their mistress left off trade,—
This female dog-star of her little sky,
Where all beneath her influence droop or die.

Oh! wretch without a tear—without a thought,
Save joy above the ruin thou hast wrought—
The time shall come, nor long remote, when thou
Shalt feel far more than thou inflictest now;
Feel for thy vile self-loving self in vain,
And turn thee howling in unpitied pain.
May the strong curse of crush'd affections light
Back on thy bosom with reflected blight!
And make thee in thy leprosy of mind
As loathsome to thyself as to mankind!
Till all thy self-thoughts curdle into hate,
Black—as thy will for others would create:
Till thy hard heart be calcined into dust,
And thy soul welter in its hideous crust.
Oh, may thy grave be sleepless as the bed,—
The widow'd couch of fire, that thou hast spread!
Then, when thou fain would'st weary Heaven with prayer,
Look on thine earthly victims—and despair!
Down to the dust!—and, as thou rott'st away,
Even worms shall perish on thy poisonous clay.
But for the love I bore, and still must bear,
To her thy malice from all ties would tear—
Thy name—thy human name—to every eye
The climax of all scorn should hang on high,
Exalted o'er thy less abhorr'd compeers—
And festering in the infamy of years.

30 March 1816

169   So, we'll go no more a roving
       So late into the night,
  Though the heart be still as loving,
    And the moon be still as bright.

  For the sword outwears its sheath,
    And the soul wears out the breast,
  And the heart must pause to breathe,
    And love itself have rest.

  Though the night was made for loving,
    And the day returns too soon,
  Yet we'll go no more a roving
    By the light of the moon.

170   ['My Days of Love are Over']

No more—no more—Oh! never more on me
  The freshness of the heart can fall like dew,
Which out of all the lovely things we see
  Extracts emotions beautiful and new,
Hived in our bosoms like the bag o'the bee:
  Think'st thou the honey with those objects grew?
Alas! 'twas not in them, but in thy power
To double even the sweetness of a flower.

No more—no more—Oh! never more, my heart,
  Canst thou be my sole world, my universe!
Once all in all, but now a thing apart,
  Thou canst not be my blessing or my curse:
The illusion's gone for ever, and thou art
  Insensible, I trust, but none the worse,
And in thy stead I've got a deal of judgment,
Though heaven knows how it ever found a lodgement.

My days of love are over, me no more
    The charms of maid, wife, and still less of widow,
Can make the fool of which they made before,—
    In short, I must not lead the life I did do;
The credulous hope of mutual minds is o'er,
    The copious use of claret is forbid too,
So for a good old-gentlemanly vice,
I think I must take up with avarice.

Ambition was my idol, which was broken
    Before the shrines of Sorrow, and of Pleasure;
And the two last have left me many a token
    O'er which reflection may be made at leisure:
Now, like Friar Bacon's brazen head, I've spoken,
    'Time is, Time was, Time's past,'—a chymic treasure
Is glittering youth, which I have spent betimes—
My heart in passion, and my head on rhymes.

What is the end of fame? 'tis but to fill
    A certain portion of uncertain paper:
Some liken it to climbing up a hill,
    Whose summit, like all hills, is lost in vapour;
For this men write, speak, preach, and heroes kill,
    And bards burn what they call their 'midnight taper,'
To have, when the original is dust,
A name, a wretched picture, and worse bust.

171   [Haidée and Don Juan]

It was the cooling hour, just when the rounded
    Red sun sinks down behind the azure hill,
Which then seems as if the whole earth it bounded,
    Circling all nature, hush'd, and dim, and still,

With the far mountain-crescent half surrounded
  On one side, and the deep sea calm and chill
Upon the other, and the rosy sky,
With one star sparkling through it like an eye.

And thus they wander'd forth, and hand in hand,
  Over the shining pebbles and the shells,
Glided along the smooth and harden'd sand,
  And in the worn and wild receptacles
Work'd by the storms, yet work'd as it were plann'd,
  In hollow halls, with sparry roofs and cells,
They turn'd to rest; and, each clasp'd by an arm,
Yielded to the deep twilight's purple charm.

They look'd up to the sky, whose floating glow
  Spread like a rosy ocean, vast and bright;
They gazed upon the glittering sea below,
  Whence the broad moon rose circling into sight;
They heard the wave's splash, and the wind so low,
  And saw each other's dark eyes darting light
Into each other—and, beholding this,
Their lips drew near, and clung into a kiss;

A long, long kiss, a kiss of youth, and love,
  And beauty, all concentrating like rays
Into one focus, kindled from above;
  Such kisses as belong to early days,
Where heart, and soul, and sense, in concert move,
  And the blood's lava, and the pulse a blaze,
Each kiss a heart-quake,—for a kiss's strength,
I think, it must be reckon'd by its length.

★

Alas! they were so young, so beautiful,
  So lonely, loving, helpless, and the hour
Was that in which the heart is always full,
  And, having o'er itself no further power,
Prompts deeds eternity cannot annul,
  But pays off moments in an endless shower
Of hell-fire—all prepared for people giving
Pleasure or pain to one another living.

Alas! for Juan and Haidée! they were
  So loving and so lovely—till then never,
Excepting our first parents, such a pair
  Had run the risk of being damn'd for ever;
And Haidée, being devout as well as fair,
  Had, doubtless, heard about the Stygian river,
And hell and purgatory—but forgot
Just in the very crisis she should not.

They look upon each other, and their eyes
  Gleam in the moonlight; and her white arm clasps
Round Juan's head, and his around her lies
  Half buried in the tresses which it grasps;
She sits upon his knee, and drinks his sighs,
  He hers, until they end in broken gasps;
And thus they form a group that's quite antique,
Half naked, loving, natural, and Greek.

And when those deep and burning moments pass'd,
  And Juan sunk to sleep within her arms,
She slept not, but all tenderly, though fast,
  Sustain'd his head upon her bosom's charms;
And now and then her eye to heaven is cast,
  And then on the pale cheek her breast now warms,
Pillow'd on her o'erflowing heart, which pants
With all it granted, and with all it grants.

An infant when it gazes on a light,
  A child the moment when it drains the breast,
A devotee when soars the Host in sight,
  An Arab with a stranger for a guest,
A sailor when the prize has struck in fight,
  A miser filling his most hoarded chest,
Feel rapture; but not such true joy are reaping
As they who watch o'er what they love while sleeping.

For there it lies so tranquil, so beloved,
  All that it hath of life with us is living;
So gentle, stirless, helpless, and unmoved,
  And all unconscious of the joy 'tis giving;
All it hath felt, inflicted, pass'd, and proved,
  Hush'd into depths beyond the watcher's diving;
There lies the thing we love with all its errors
And all its charms, like death without its terrors.

*

Hail, Muse! *et cetera.*—We left Juan sleeping,
  Pillow'd upon a fair and happy breast,
And watch'd by eyes that never yet knew weeping,
  And loved by a young heart, too deeply blest
To feel the poison through her spirit creeping,
  Or know who rested there; a foe to rest
Had soil'd the current of her sinless years,
And turn'd her pure heart's purest blood to tears!

Oh, Love! what is it in this world of ours
  Which makes it fatal to be loved? Ah why
With cypress branches hast thou wreathed thy bowers,
  And made thy best interpreter a sigh?

As those who dote on odours pluck the flowers,
    And place them on their breast—but place to die—
Thus the frail beings we would fondly cherish
Are laid within our bosoms but to perish.

*

Yet they were happy,—happy in the illicit
    Indulgence of their innocent desires;
But more imprudent grown with every visit,
    Haidée forgot the island was her sire's;
When we have what we like, 'tis hard to miss it,
    At least in the beginning, ere one tires;
Thus she came often, not a moment losing,
Whilst her piratical papa was cruising.

*

Haidée and Juan carpeted their feet
    On crimson satin, border'd with pale blue;
Their sofa occupied three parts complete
    Of the apartment—and appear'd quite new;
The velvet cushions—(for a throne more meet)—
    Were scarlet, from whose glowing centre grew
A sun emboss'd in gold, whose rays of tissue,
Meridian-like, were seen all light to issue.

Crystal and marble, plate and porcelain,
    Had done their work of splendour; Indian mats
And Persian carpets, which the heart bled to stain,
    Over the floors were spread; gazelles and cats,
And dwarfs and blacks, and such like things, that gain
    Their bread as ministers and favourites—(that's
To say, by degradation)—mingled there
As plentiful as in a court or fair.

There was no want of lofty mirrors, and
　　The tables, most of ebony inlaid
With mother of pearl or ivory, stood at hand,
　　Or were of tortoise-shell or rare woods made,
Fretted with gold or silver:—by command
　　The greater part of these were ready spread
With viands and sherbets in ice—and wine—
Kept for all comers, at all hours to dine.

★

And now they were diverted by their suite,
　　Dwarfs, dancing girls, black eunuchs, and a poet,
Which made their new establishment complete;
　　The last was of great fame, and liked to show it:
His verses rarely wanted their due feet—
　　And for his theme—he seldom sung below it,
He being paid to satirise or flatter,
As the psalm says, 'inditing a good matter.'

He praised the present, and abused the past,
　　Reversing the good custom of old days,
An eastern antijacobin at last
　　He turn'd, preferring pudding to *no* praise—
For some few years his lot had been o'ercast
　　By his seeming independent in his lays,
But now he sung the Sultan and the Pacha
With truth like Southey and with verse like Crashaw.

He was a man who had seen many changes,
　　And always changed as true as any needle;
His polar star being one which rather ranges,
　　And not the fix'd—he knew the way to wheedle:

So vile he 'scaped the doom which oft avenges;
    And being fluent (save indeed when fee'd ill),
He lied with such a fervour of intention—
There was no doubt he earn'd his laureate pension.

But he had genius,—when a turncoat has it
    The 'Vates irritabilis' takes care
That without notice few full moons shall pass it;
    Even good men like to make the public stare:—
But to my subject—let me see—what was it?—
    Oh!—the third canto—and the pretty pair—
Their loves, and feasts, and house, and dress, and mode
Of living in their insular abode.

Their poet, a sad trimmer, but no less
    In company a very pleasant fellow,
Had been the favourite of full many a mess
    Of men, and made them speeches when half mellow;
And though his meaning they could rarely guess,
    Yet still they deign'd to hiccup or to bellow
The glorious meed of popular applause,
Of which the first ne'er knows the second cause.

But now being lifted into high society,
    And having pick'd up several odds and ends
Of free thoughts in his travels, for variety,
    He deem'd, being in a lone isle, among friends,
That without any danger of a riot, he
    Might for long lying make himself amends;
And singing as he sung in his warm youth,
Agree to a short armistice with truth.

He had travell'd 'mongst the Arabs, Turks, and Franks,
    And knew the self-loves of the different nations;

And having lived with people of all ranks,
    Had something ready upon most occasions—
Which got him a few presents and some thanks.
    He varied with some skill his adulations;
To 'do at Rome as Romans do,' a piece
Of conduct was which he observed in Greece.

Thus, usually, when he was ask'd to sing,
    He gave the different nations something national;
'Twas all the same to him—'God save the king,'
    Or 'Ça ira,' according to the fashion all;
His muse made increment of anything,
    From the high lyrical to the low rational:
If Pindar sang horse-races, what should hinder
Himself from being as pliable as Pindar?

In France, for instance, he would write a chanson;
    In England, a six canto quarto tale;
In Spain, he'd make a ballad or romance on
    The last war—much the same in Portugal;
In Germany, the Pegasus he'd prance on
    Would be old Goëthe's — (see what says De Staël);
In Italy, he'd ape the 'Trecentisti;'
In Greece, he'd sing some sort of hymn like this t'ye:

I

The isles of Greece, the isles of Greece!
    Where burning Sappho loved and sung,
Where grew the arts of war and peace,—
    Where Delos rose, and Phœbus sprung!
Eternal summer gilds them yet,
But all, except their sun, is set.

2

The Scian and the Teian muse,
    The hero's harp, the lover's lute,
Have found the fame your shores refuse;
    Their place of birth alone is mute
To sounds which echo further west
Than your sires' 'Islands of the Blest.'

3

The mountains look on Marathon—
    And Marathon looks on the sea;
And musing there an hour alone,
    I dream'd that Greece might still be free;
And standing on the Persian's grave
I could not deem myself a slave.

4

A king sate on the rocky brow
    Which looks o'er sea-born Salamis;
And ships, by thousands, lay below,
    And men in nations;—all were his!
He counted them at break of day—
And when the sun set where were they?

5

And where are they? and where art thou,
    My country? On thy voiceless shore
The heroic tune is tuneless now—
    The heroic bosom beats no more!
And must thy lyre, so long divine,
Degenerate into hands like mine?

6

'Tis something, in the dearth of fame,
  Though link'd among a fetter'd race,
To feel at least a patriot's shame,
  Even as I sing, suffuse my face;
For what is left the poet here?
For Greeks a blush—for Greece a tear.

7

Must *we* but weep o'er days more blest?
  Must *we* but blush?—Our fathers bled.
Earth! render back from out thy breast
  A remnant of our Spartan dead!
Of the three hundred grant but three,
To make a new Thermopylae!

8

What, silent still? and silent all?
  Ah! no; —the voices of the dead
Sound like a distant torrent's fall,
  And answer, 'Let one living head,
But one arise,—we come, we come!'
'Tis but the living who are dumb.

9

In vain—in vain: strike other chords;
  Fill high the cup with Samian wine!
Leave battles to the Turkish hordes,
  And shed the blood of Scio's vine!
Hark! rising to the ignoble call—
How answers each bold bacchanal!

10

You have the Pyrrhic dance as yet,
  Where is the Pyrrhic phalanx gone?
Of two such lessons, why forget
  The nobler and the manlier one?
You have the letters Cadmus gave—
Think ye he meant them for a slave?

11

Fill high the bowl with Samian wine!
  We will not think of themes like these!
It made Anacreon's song divine:
  He served—but served Polycrates—
A tyrant; but our masters then
Were still, at least, our countrymen.

12

The tyrant of the Chersonese
  Was freedom's best and bravest friend;
That tyrant was Miltiades!
  Oh! that the present hour would lend
Another despot of the kind!
Such chains as his were sure to bind.

13

Fill high the bowl with Samian wine!
  On Suli's rock, and Parga's shore,
Exists the remnant of a line
  Such as the Doric mothers bore;
And there, perhaps, some seed is sown,
The Heracleidan blood might own.

14

Trust not for freedom to the Franks—
　　They have a king who buys and sells;
In native swords, and native ranks,
　　The only hope of courage dwells;
But Turkish force, and Latin fraud,
Would break your shield, however broad.

15

Fill high the bowl with Samian wine!
　　Our virgins dance beneath the shade—
I see their glorious black eyes shine;
　　But gazing on each glowing maid,
My own the burning tear-drop laves,
To think such breasts must suckle slaves.

16

Place me on Sunium's marbled steep,
　　Where nothing, save the waves and I,
May hear our mutual murmurs sweep;
　　There, swan-like, let me sing and die:
A land of slaves shall ne'er be mine—
Dash down yon cup of Samian wine!

★

They were alone once more; for them to be
　　Thus was another Eden; they were never
Weary, unless when separate: the tree
　　Cut from its forest root of years—the river
Damm'd from its fountain—the child from the knee
　　And breast maternal wean'd at once for ever,—
Would wither less than these two torn apart;
Alas! there is no instinct like the heart—

The heart—which may be broken: happy they!
 Thrice fortunate! who of that fragile mould,
The precious porcelain of human clay,
 Break with the first fall: they can ne'er behold
The long year link'd with heavy day on day,
 And all which must be borne, and never told;
While life's strange principle will often lie
Deepest in those who long the most to die.

'Whom the gods love die young' was said of yore,
 And many deaths do they escape by this:
The death of friends, and that which slays even more—
 The death of friendship, love, youth, all that is,
Except mere breath; and since the silent shore
 Awaits at last even those who longest miss
The old archer's shafts, perhaps the early grave
Which men weep over may be meant to save.

Haidée and Juan thought not of the dead.
 The heavens and earth, and air, seem'd made for them:
They found no fault with Time, save that he fled;
 They saw not in themselves aught to condemn:
Each was the other's mirror, and but read
 Joy sparkling in their dark eyes like a gem,
And knew such brightness was but the reflection
Of their exchanging glances of affection.

The gentle pressure, and the thrilling touch,
 The least glance better understood than words,
Which still said all, and ne'er could say too much;
 A language, too, but like to that of birds,
Known but to them, at least appearing such
 As but to lovers a true sense affords;
Sweet playful phrases, which would seem absurd
To those who have ceased to hear such, or ne'er heard.

All these were theirs, for they were children still,
    And children still they should have ever been;
They were not made in the real world to fill
    A busy character in the dull scene,
But like two beings born from out a rill,
    A nymph and her beloved, all unseen
To pass their lives in fountains and on flowers,
And never know the weight of human hours.

Moons changing had roll'd on, and changeless found
    Those their bright rise had lighted to such joys
As rarely they beheld throughout their round;
    And these were not of the vain kind which cloys,
For theirs were buoyant spirits, never bound
    By the mere senses; and that which destroys
Most love, possession, unto them appear'd
A thing which each endearment more endear'd.

Oh beautiful! and rare as beautiful!
    But theirs was love in which the mind delights
To lose itself, when the old world grows dull,
    And we are sick of its hack sounds and sights,
Intrigues, adventures of the common school,
    Its petty passions, marriages, and flights,
Where Hymen's torch but brands one strumpet more,
Whose husband only knows her not a wh-re.

Hard words; harsh truth; a truth which many know.
    Enough.—The faithful and the fairy pair,
Who never found a single hour too slow,
    What was it made them thus exempt from care?
Young innate feelings all have felt below
    Which perish in the rest, but in them were
Inherent; what we mortals call romantic,
And always envy, though we deem it frantic.

This is in others a factitious state,
   An opium dream of too much youth and reading,
But was in them their nature, or their fate:
   No novels e'er had set their young hearts bleeding,
For Haidée's knowledge was by no means great,
   And Juan was a boy of saintly breeding;
So that there was no reason for their loves
More than for those of nightingales or doves.

They gazed upon the sunset; 'tis an hour
   Dear unto all, but dearest to *their* eyes,
For it had made them what they were: the power
   Of love had first o'erwhelm'd them from such skies,
When happiness had been their only dower,
   And twilight saw them link'd in passion's ties;
Charm'd with each other, all things charm'd that brought
The past still welcome as the present thought.

I know not why, but in that hour to-night,
   Even as they gazed, a sudden tremor came,
And swept, as 'twere, across their hearts' delight,
   Like the wind o'er a harp-string, or a flame,
When one is shook in sound, and one in sight;
   And thus some boding flash'd through either frame,
And called from Juan's breast a faint low sigh,
While one new tear arose in Haidée's eye.

That large black prophet eye seem'd to dilate
   And follow far the disappearing sun,
As if their last day of a happy date
   With his broad, bright, and dropping orb were gone;
Juan gazed on her as to ask his fate—
   He felt a grief, but knowing cause for none,
His glance inquired of hers for some excuse
For feelings causeless, or at least abstruse.

She turn'd to him, and smiled, but in that sort
  Which makes not others smile; then turn'd aside:
Whatever feeling shook her, it seem'd short,
  And master'd by her wisdom or her pride;
When Juan spoke, too—it might be in sport—
  Of this their mutual feeling, she replied—
'If it should be so,—but—it cannot be—
Or I at least shall not survive to see.'

Juan would question further, but she press'd
  His lips to hers, and silenced him with this,
And then dismiss'd the omen from her breast,
  Defying augury with that fond kiss;
And no doubt of all methods 'tis the best:
  Some people prefer wine—'tis not amiss;
I have tried both; so those who would a part take
May choose between the headache and the heartache.

One of the two according to your choice,
  Woman or wine, you'll have to undergo;
Both maladies are taxes on our joys:
  But which to choose, I really hardly know;
And if I had to give a casting voice,
  For both sides I could many reasons show,
And then decide, without great wrong to either,
It were much better to have both than neither.

Juan and Haidée gazed upon each other
  With swimming looks of speechless tenderness,
Which mix'd all feelings, friend, child, lover, brother,
  All that the best can mingle and express
When two pure hearts are pour'd in one another,
  And love too much, and yet can not love less;
But almost sanctify the sweet excess
By the immortal wish and power to bless.

Mix'd in each other's arms, and heart in heart,
　　Why did they not then die?—they had lived too long
Should an hour come to bid them breathe apart;
　　Years could but bring them cruel things or wrong,
The world was not for them, nor the world's art
　　For beings passionate as Sappho's song;
Love was born *with* them, *in* them, so intense,
It was their very spirit—not a sense.

They should have lived together deep in woods,
　　Unseen as sings the nightingale; they were
Unfit to mix in these thick solitudes
　　Call'd social, haunts of Hate and Vice, and Care;
How lonely every freeborn creature broods!
　　The sweetest song-birds nestle in a pair;
The eagle soars alone; the gull and crow
Flock o'er their carrion, just like men below.

Now pillow'd cheek to cheek, in loving sleep,
　　Haidée and Juan their siesta took,
A gentle slumber, but it was not deep,
　　For ever and anon a something shook
Juan, and shuddering o'er his frame would creep;
　　And Haidée's sweet lips murmur'd like a brook
A wordless music, and her face so fair
Stirr'd with her dream as rose-leaves with the air;

Or as the stirring of a deep clear stream
　　Within an Alpine hollow, when the wind
Walks over it, was she shaken by the dream,
　　The mystical usurper of the mind—
O'erpowering us to be whate'er may seem
　　Good to the soul which we no more can bind;
Strange state of being! (for 'tis still to be),
Senseless to feel, and with seal'd eyes to see.

Stanzas—April, 1814

Away! the moor is dark beneath the moon,
  Rapid clouds have drank the last pale beam of even:
Away! the gathering winds will call the darkness soon,
  And profoundest midnight shroud the serene lights of heaven.

Pause not! The time is past! Every voice cries, Away!
  Tempt not with one last tear thy friend's ungentle mood:
Thy lover's eye, so glazed and cold, dares not entreat thy stay:
  Duty and dereliction guide thee back to solitude.

Away, away! to thy sad and silent home;
  Pour bitter tears on its desolated hearth;
Watch the dim shades as like ghosts they go and come,
  And complicate strange webs of melancholy mirth.

The leaves of wasted autumn woods shall float around thine head:
  The blooms of dewy spring shall gleam beneath thy feet:
But thy soul or this world must fade in the frost that binds the
    dead,
  Ere midnight's frown and morning's smile, ere thou and peace
    may meet.

The cloud shadows of midnight possess their own repose,
  For the weary winds are silent, or the moon is in the deep:
Some respite to its turbulence unresting ocean knows;
  Whatever moves, or toils, or grieves, hath its appointed sleep.

Thou in the grave shalt rest—yet till the phantoms flee
  Which that house and heath and garden made dear to thee
    erewhile,
Thy remembrance, and repentance, and deep musings are not free
From the music of two voices and the light of one sweet smile.

173   Hymn to Intellectual Beauty

THE awful shadow of some unseen Power
     Floats tho' unseen among us; visiting
     This various world with as inconstant wing
As summer winds that creep from flower to flower;
Like moonbeams that behind some piny mountain shower,
          It visits with inconstant glance
          Each human heart and countenance;
Like hues and harmonies of evening,
          Like clouds in starlight widely spread,
          Like memory of music fled,
          Like aught that for its grace may be
Dear, and yet dearer for its mystery.

Spirit of BEAUTY, that dost consecrate
     With thine own hues all thou dost shine upon
     Of human thought or form, where art thou gone?
Why dost thou pass away and leave our state,
This dim vast vale of tears, vacant and desolate?
          Ask why the sunlight not forever
          Weaves rainbows o'er yon mountain river,
Why aught should fail and fade that once is shewn,
          Why fear and dream and death and birth
          Cast on the daylight of this earth
          Such gloom, why man has such a scope
For love and hate, despondency and hope?

No voice from some sublimer world hath ever
     To sage or poet these responses given:
     Therefore the names of Demon, Ghost, and Heaven,
Remain the records of their vain endeavour:
Frail spells, whose uttered charm might not avail to sever,

From all we hear and all we see,
  Doubt, chance, and mutability.
Thy light alone, like mist o'er mountains driven,
    Or music by the night wind sent
    Thro' strings of some still instrument,
    Or moonlight on a midnight stream,
Gives grace and truth to life's unquiet dream.

Love, Hope, and Self-esteem, like clouds, depart
  And come, for some uncertain moments lent.
  Man were immortal, and omnipotent,
Didst thou, unknown and awful as thou art,
Keep with thy glorious train firm state within his heart.
    Thou messenger of sympathies,
    That wax and wane in lovers' eyes—
Thou, that to human thought art nourishment,
    Like darkness to a dying flame!
    Depart not as thy shadow came:
    Depart not, lest the grave should be,
Like life and fear, a dark reality.

While yet a boy I sought for ghosts, and sped
  Thro' many a listening chamber, cave and ruin,
  And starlight wood, with fearful steps pursuing
Hopes of high talk with the departed dead.
I called on poisonous names with which our youth is fed:
    I was not heard: I saw them not:
    When musing deeply on the lot
Of life, at that sweet time when winds are wooing
    All vital things that wake to bring
    News of birds and blossoming,
    Sudden, thy shadow fell on me:
I shrieked, and clasped my hands in ecstacy!

I vowed that I would dedicate my powers
　　To thee and thine: have I not kept the vow?
　　With beating heart and streaming eyes, even now
I call the phantoms of a thousand hours
Each from his voiceless grave: they have in visioned bowers
　　　　Of studious zeal or love's delight
　　　　Outwatched with me the envious night:
They know that never joy illumed my brow,
　　　　Unlinked with hope that thou wouldst free
　　　　This world from its dark slavery,
　　　　That thou O awful LOVELINESS,
Wouldst give whate'er these words cannot express.

The day becomes more solemn and serene
　　When noon is past: there is a harmony
　　In autumn, and a lustre in its sky,
Which thro' the summer is not heard or seen,
As if it could not be, as if it had not been!
　　　　Thus let thy power, which like the truth
　　　　Of nature on my passive youth
　　Descended, to my onward life supply
　　　　Its calm, to one who worships thee,
　　　　And every form containing thee,
　　　　Whom, SPIRIT fair, thy spells did bind
To fear himself, and love all human kind.

174　　　　　On Fanny Godwin

　　HER voice did quiver as we parted,
　　　　Yet knew I not that heart was broken
　　From which it came, and I departed
　　　　Heeding not the words then spoken.
　　　　　Misery—O Misery,
　　　　　This world is all too wide for thee.

175   Ozymandias

I MET a traveller from an antique land
Who said: Two vast and trunkless legs of stone
Stand in the desert. Near them, on the sand,
Half sunk, a shattered visage lies, whose frown,
And wrinkled lip, and sneer of cold command,
Tell that its sculptor well those passions read
Which yet survive, stamped on these lifeless things,
The hand that mocked them, and the heart that fed:
And on the pedestal these words appear:
'My name is Ozymandias, king of kings:
Look on my works, ye Mighty, and despair!'
Nothing beside remains. Round the decay
Of that colossal wreck, boundless and bare
The lone and level sands stretch far away.

176   Sonnet

LIFT not the painted veil which those who live
Call Life: though unreal shapes be pictured there,
And it but mimic all we would believe
With colours idly spread:—behind, lurk Fear
And Hope, twin destinies; who ever weave
The shadows, which the world calls substance, there.
I knew one who had lifted it—he sought,
For his lost heart was tender, things to love
But found them not, alas! nor was there aught
The world contains, the which he could approve.
Through the unheeding many he did move,
A splendour among shadows, a bright blot
Upon this gloomy scene, a Spirit that strove
For truth, and like the Preacher found it not.

177　　　　　Ode to the West Wind

I

O WILD West Wind, thou breath of Autumn's being,
Thou, from whose unseen presence the leaves dead
Are driven, like ghosts from an enchanter fleeing,

Yellow, and black, and pale, and hectic red,
Pestilence-stricken multitudes: O, thou,
Who chariotest to their dark wintry bed

The winged seeds, where they lie cold and low,
Each like a corpse within its grave, until
Thine azure sister of the Spring shall blow

Her clarion o'er the dreaming earth, and fill
(Driving sweet buds like flocks to feed in air)
With living hues and odours plain and hill:

Wild Spirit, which art moving every where;
Destroyer and preserver; hear, O, hear!

II

Thou on whose streams, 'mid the steep sky's commotion
Loose clouds like earth's decaying leaves are shed,
Shook from the tangled boughs of Heaven and Ocean,

Angels of rain and lightning: there are spread
On the blue surface of thine airy surge,
Like the bright hair uplifted from the head

Of some fierce Mænad, even from the dim verge
Of the horizon to the zenith's height,
The locks of the approaching storm. Thou dirge

Of the dying year, to which this closing night
Will be the dome of a vast sepulchre,
Vaulted with all thy congregated might

Of vapours, from whose solid atmosphere
Black rain, and fire, and hail will burst: O, hear!

III

Thou who didst waken from his summer dreams
The blue Mediterranean, where he lay,
Lulled by the coil of his crystalline streams,

Beside a pumice isle in Baiæ's bay,
And saw in sleep old palaces and towers
Quivering within the wave's intenser day,

All overgrown with azure moss and flowers
So sweet, the sense faints picturing them! Thou
For whose path the Atlantic's level powers

Cleave themselves into chasms, while far below
The sea-blooms and the oozy woods which wear
The sapless foliage of the ocean, know

Thy voice, and suddenly grow grey with fear,
And tremble and despoil themselves: O, hear!

IV

If I were a dead leaf thou mightest bear;
If I were a swift cloud to fly with thee;
A wave to pant beneath thy power, and share

The impulse of thy strength, only less free
Than thou, O, uncontroulable! If even
I were as in my boyhood, and could be

The comrade of thy wanderings over heaven,
As then, when to outstrip thy skiey speed
Scarce seemed a vision; I would ne'er have striven

As thus with thee in prayer in my sore need.
Oh! lift me as a wave, a leaf, a cloud!
I fall upon the thorns of life! I bleed!

A heavy weight of hours has chained and bowed
One too like thee; tameless, and swift, and proud.

v

Make me thy lyre, even as the forest is:
What if my leaves are falling like its own!
The tumult of thy mighty harmonies

Will take from both a deep, autumnal tone,
Sweet though in sadness. Be thou, spirit fierce,
My spirit! Be thou me, impetuous one!

Drive my dead thoughts over the universe
Like withered leaves to quicken a new birth!
And, by the incantation of this verse,

Scatter, as from an unextinguished hearth
Ashes and sparks, my words among mankind!
Be through my lips to unawakened earth

The trumpet of a prophecy! O, wind,
If Winter comes, can Spring be far behind?

178   # To a Skylark

HAIL to thee, blithe spirit!
    Bird thou never wert,
That from heaven, or near it,
    Pourest thy full heart
In profuse strains of unpremeditated art.

Higher still and higher
    From the earth thou springest
Like a cloud of fire;
    The blue deep thou wingest,
And singing still dost soar, and soaring ever singest.

In the golden lightning
    Of the sunken sun,
O'er which clouds are bright'ning,
    Thou dost float and run;
Like an unbodied joy whose race is just begun.

The pale purple even
    Melts around thy flight;
Like a star of heaven
    In the broad day-light
Thou art unseen, but yet I hear thy shrill delight,

Keen as are the arrows
    Of that silver sphere,
Whose intense lamp narrows
    In the white dawn clear
Until we hardly see, we feel that it is there.

All the earth and air
    With thy voice is loud,
As, when night is bare,
    From one lonely cloud
The moon rains out her beams, and heaven is overflowed.

What thou art we know not;
    What is most like thee?
From rainbow clouds there flow not
    Drops so bright to see
As from thy presence showers a rain of melody.

Like a poet hidden
    In the light of thought,
Singing hymns unbidden,
    Till the world is wrought
To sympathy with hopes and fears it heeded not:

Like a high-born maiden
    In a palace tower,
Soothing her love-laden
    Soul in secret hour
With music sweet as love, which overflows her bower:

Like a glow-worm golden
    In a dell of dew,
Scattering unbeholden
    Its aerial hue
Among the flowers and grass, which screen it from the view:

Like a rose embowered
    In its own green leaves,
By warm winds deflowered,
    Till the scent it gives
Makes faint with too much sweet these heavy-winged thieves:

Sound of vernal showers
  On the twinkling grass,
Rain-awakened flowers,
  All that ever was
Joyous, and clear, and fresh, thy music doth surpass:

Teach us, sprite or bird,
  What sweet thoughts are thine:
I have never heard
  Praise of love or wine
That panted forth a flood of rapture so divine.

Chorus Hymenæal,
  Or triumphal chaunt,
Matched with thine would be all
  But an empty vaunt,
A thing wherein we feel there is some hidden want.

What objects are the fountains
  Of thy happy strain?
What fields, or waves, or mountains?
  What shapes of sky or plain?
What love of thine own kind? what ignorance of pain?

With thy clear keen joyance
  Languor cannot be:
Shadow of annoyance
  Never came near thee:
Thou lovest; but ne'er knew love's sad satiety.

Waking or asleep,
  Thou of death must deem
Things more true and deep
  Than we mortals dream,
Or how could thy notes flow in such a crystal stream?

We look before and after,
  And pine for what is not:
Our sincerest laughter
  With some pain is fraught;
Our sweetest songs are those that tell of saddest thought.

Yet if we could scorn
  Hate, and pride, and fear;
If we were things born
  Not to shed a tear,
I know not how thy joy we ever should come near.

Better than all measures
  Of delightful sound,
Better than all treasures
  That in books are found,
Thy skill to poet were, thou scorner of the ground!

Teach me half the gladness
  That thy brain must know,
Such harmonious madness
  From my lips would flow,
The world should listen then, as I am listening now.

179   from *EPIPSYCHIDION*

TRUE Love in this differs from gold and clay,
That to divide is not to take away.
Love is like understanding, that grows bright,
Gazing on many truths; 'tis like thy light,
Imagination! which from earth and sky,
And from the depths of human phantasy,
As from a thousand prisms and mirrors, fills
The Universe with glorious beams, and kills

Error, the worm, with many a sun-like arrow
Of its reverberated lightning. Narrow
The heart that loves, the brain that contemplates,
The life that wears, the spirit that creates
One object, and one form, and builds thereby
A sepulchre for its eternity.

Mind from its object differs most in this:
Evil from good; misery from happiness;
The baser from the nobler; the impure
And frail, from what is clear and must endure.
If you divide suffering and dross, you may
Diminish till it is consumed away;
If you divide pleasure and love and thought,
Each part exceeds the whole; and we know not
How much, while any yet remains unshared,
Of pleasure may be gained, of sorrow spared:
The truth is that deep well, whence sages draw
The unenvied light of hope; the eternal law
By which those live, to whom this world of life
Is as a garden ravaged, and whose strife
Tills for the promise of a later birth
The wilderness of this Elysian earth.

from *ADONAIS*

180   An Elegy on the Death of John Keats

PEACE, peace! he is not dead, he doth not sleep—
He hath awakened from the dream of life—
'Tis we, who lost in stormy visions, keep
With phantoms an unprofitable strife,
And in mad trance, strike with our spirit's knife

Invulnerable nothings.—*We* decay
Like corpses in a charnel; fear and grief
Convulse us and consume us day by day,
And cold hopes swarm like worms within our living clay.

He has outsoared the shadow of our night;
Envy and calumny and hate and pain,
And that unrest which men miscall delight,
Can touch him not and torture not again;
From the contagion of the world's slow stain
He is secure, and now can never mourn
A heart grown cold, a head grown grey in vain;
Nor, when the spirit's self has ceased to burn,
With sparkless ashes load an unlamented urn.

He lives, he wakes—tis Death is dead, not he;
Mourn not for Adonais.—Thou young Dawn
Turn all thy dew to splendour, for from thee
The spirit thou lamentest is not gone;
Ye caverns and ye forests, cease to moan!
Cease ye faint flowers and fountains, and thou Air
Which like a mourning veil thy scarf hadst thrown
O'er the abandoned Earth, now leave it bare
Even to the joyous stars which smile on its despair!

He is made one with Nature: there is heard
His voice in all her music, from the moan
Of thunder, to the song of night's sweet bird;
He is a presence to be felt and known
In darkness and in light, from herb and stone,
Spreading itself where'er that Power may move
Which has withdrawn his being to its own;
Which wields the world with never wearied love,
Sustains it from beneath, and kindles it above.

He is a portion of the loveliness
Which once he made more lovely: he doth bear
His part, while the one Spirit's plastic stress
Sweeps through the dull dense world, compelling there,
All new successions to the forms they wear;
Torturing th' unwilling dross that checks its flight
To its own likeness, as each mass may bear;
And bursting in its beauty and its might
From trees and beasts and men into the Heaven's light.

The splendours of the firmament of time
May be eclipsed, but are extinguished not;
Like stars to their appointed height they climb,
And death is a low mist which cannot blot
The brightness it may veil. When lofty thought
Lifts a young heart above its mortal lair,
And love and life contend in it, for what
Shall be its earthly doom, the dead live there
And move like winds of light on dark and stormy air.

The inheritors of unfulfilled renown
Rose from their thrones, built beyond mortal thought,
Far in the Unapparent. Chatterton
Rose pale, his solemn agony had not
Yet faded from him; Sidney, as he fought
And as he fell and as he lived and loved
Sublimely mild, a Spirit without spot,
Arose; and Lucan, by his death approved:
Oblivion as they rose shrank like a thing reproved.

And many more, whose names on Earth are dark
But whose transmitted effluence cannot die
So long as fire outlives the parent spark,
Rose, robed in dazzling immortality.

'Thou art become as one of us,' they cry,
'It was for thee yon kingless sphere has long
Swung blind in unascended majesty,
Silent alone amid an Heaven of Song.
Assume thy winged throne, thou Vesper of our throng!'

Who mourns for Adonais? oh, come forth
Fond wretch! and know thyself and him aright.
Clasp with thy panting soul the pendulous Earth;
As from a centre, dart thy spirit's light
Beyond all worlds, until its spacious might
Satiate the void circumference: then shrink
Even to a point within our day and night;
And keep thy heart light lest it make thee sink
When hope has kindled hope, and lured thee to the brink.

Or go to Rome, which is the sepulchre,
O, not of him, but of our joy: 'tis nought
That ages, empires, and religions there
Lie buried in the ravage they have wrought;
For such as he can lend,—they borrow not
Glory from those who made the world their prey;
And he is gathered to the kings of thought
Who waged contention with their time's decay,
And of the past are all that cannot pass away.

Go thou to Rome,—at once the Paradise,
The grave, the city, and the wilderness;
And where its wrecks like shattered mountains rise,
And flowering weeds, and fragrant copses dress
The bones of Desolation's nakedness
Pass, till the Spirit of the spot shall lead
Thy footsteps to a slope of green access
Where, like an infant's smile, over the dead,
A light of laughing flowers along the grass is spread.

And gray walls moulder round, on which dull Time
Feeds, like slow fire upon a hoary brand;
And one keen pyramid with wedge sublime,
Pavilioning the dust of him who planned
This refuge for his memory, doth stand
Like flame transformed to marble; and beneath,
A field is spread, on which a newer band
Have pitched in Heaven's smile their camp of death,
Welcoming him we lose with scarce extinguished breath.

Here pause: these graves are all too young as yet
To have outgrown the sorrow which consigned
Its charge to each; and if the seal is set,
Here, on one fountain of a mourning mind,
Break it not thou! too surely shalt thou find
Thine own well full, if thou returnest home,
Of tears and gall. From the world's bitter wind
Seek shelter in the shadow of the tomb.
What Adonais is, why fear we to become?

The One remains, the many change and pass;
Heaven's light forever shines, Earth's shadows fly;
Life, like a dome of many-coloured glass,
Stains the white radiance of Eternity,
Until Death tramples it to fragments.—Die,
If thou wouldst be with that which thou dost seek!
Follow where all is fled!—Rome's azure sky,
Flowers, ruins, statues, music, words, are weak
The glory they transfuse with fitting truth to speak.

Why linger, why turn back, why shrink, my Heart?
Thy hopes are gone before: from all things here
They have departed; thou shouldst now depart!
A light is past from the revolving year,

And man, and woman; and what still is dear
Attracts to crush, repels to make thee wither.
The soft sky smiles,—the low wind whispers near:
'Tis Adonais calls! oh, hasten thither,
No more let Life divide what Death can join together.

That Light whose smile kindles the Universe,
That Beauty in which all things work and move,
That Benediction which the eclipsing Curse
Of birth can quench not, that sustaining Love
Which through the web of being blindly wove
By man and beast and earth and air and sea,
Burns bright or dim, as each are mirrors of
The fire for which all thirst; now beams on me,
Consuming the last clouds of cold mortality.

The breath whose might I have invoked in song
Descends on me; my spirit's bark is driven,
Far from the shore, far from the trembling throng
Whose sails were never to the tempest given;
The massy earth and sphered skies are riven!
I am borne darkly, fearfully, afar;
Whilst burning through the inmost veil of Heaven,
The soul of Adonais, like a star,
Beacons from the abode where the Eternal are.

181   To Night

Swiftly walk over the western wave,
    Spirit of Night!
Out of the misty eastern cave,
Where, all the long and lone daylight,
Thou wovest dreams of joy and fear,
Which make thee terrible and dear,—
    Swift be thy flight!

Wrap thy form in a mantle grey,
    Star-inwrought!
Blind with thine hair the eyes of day,
Kiss her until she be wearied out,
Then wander o'er city, and sea, and land,
Touching all with thine opiate wand—
    Come, long sought!

When I arose and saw the dawn,
    I sighed for thee;
When light rode high, and the dew was gone,
And noon lay heavy on flower and tree,
And the weary Day turned to his rest,
Lingering like an unloved guest,
    I sighed for thee.

Thy brother Death came, and cried,
    Wouldst thou me?
Thy sweet child Sleep, the filmy-eyed,
Murmured like a noon-tide bee,
Shall I nestle near thy side?
Wouldst thou me?—And I replied,
    No, not thee!

Death will come when thou art dead,
    Soon, too soon—
Sleep will come when thou art fled;
Of neither would I ask the boon
I ask of thee, beloved Night—
Swift be thine approaching flight,
    Come soon, soon!

182   To ——— [? Emilia Viviani]

MUSIC, when soft voices die,
Vibrates in the memory—
Odours, when sweet violets sicken,
Live within the sense they quicken.

Rose leaves, when the rose is dead,
Are heaped for the beloved's bed;
And so thy thoughts, when thou art gone,
Love itself shall slumber on.

183   Song

RARELY, rarely, comest thou,
    Spirit of Delight!
Wherefore hast thou left me now
    Many a day and night?
Many a weary night and day
'Tis since thou art fled away.

How shall ever one like me
    Win thee back again?
With the joyous and the free
    Thou wilt scoff at pain.
Spirit false! thou hast forgot
All but those who need thee not.

As a lizard with the shade
    Of a trembling leaf,
Thou with sorrow art dismayed;
    Even the sighs of grief
Reproach thee, that thou art not near,
And reproach thou wilt not hear.

Let me set my mournful ditty
   To a merry measure,
Thou wilt never come for pity,
   Thou wilt come for pleasure,
Pity then will cut away
Those cruel wings, and thou wilt stay.

I love all that thou lovest,
   Spirit of Delight!
The fresh Earth in new leaves drest,
   And the starry night;
Autumn evening, and the morn
When the golden mists are born.

I love snow, and all the forms
   Of the radiant frost;
I love waves, and winds, and storms,
   Every thing almost
Which is Nature's, and may be
Untainted by man's misery.

I love tranquil solitude,
   And such society
As is quiet, wise and good;
   Between thee and me
What difference? but thou dost possess
The things I seek, not love them less.

I love Love—though he has wings,
   And like light can flee,
But above all other things,
   Spirit, I love thee—
Thou art love and life! Oh, come,
Make once more my heart thy home.

184 Mutability

THE flower that smiles to-day
  To-morrow dies;
All that we wish to stay,
  Tempts and then flies;
What is this world's delight?
Lightning that mocks the night,
  Brief even as bright.

Virtue, how frail it is!
  Friendship how rare!
Love, how it sells poor bliss
  For proud despair!
But we, though soon they fall,
Survive their joy and all
  Which ours we call.

Whilst skies are blue and bright,
  Whilst flowers are gay,
Whilst eyes that change ere night
  Make glad the day;
Whilst yet the calm hours creep,
Dream thou—and from thy sleep
  Then wake to weep.

185 Stanzas to [Edward Williams]

I

THE serpent is shut out from paradise.
  The wounded deer must seek the herb no more
    In which its heart-cure lies:
  The widowed dove must cease to haunt a bower,

Like that from which its mate with feignèd sighs
    Fled in the April hour.
  I too must seldom seek again
Near happy friends a mitigated pain.

II

Of hatred I am proud,—with scorn content;
  Indifference, that once hurt me, now is grown
    Itself indifferent.
  But, not to speak of love, pity alone
Can break a spirit already more than bent.
    The miserable one
  Turns the mind's poison into food,—
Its medicine is tears,—its evil good.

III

Therefore if now I see you seldomer,
  Dear friends, dear *friend*! know that I only fly
    Your looks, because they stir
  Griefs that should sleep, and hopes that cannot die:
The very comfort that they minister
    I scarce can bear, yet I,
  So deeply is the arrow gone,
Should quickly perish if it were withdrawn.

IV

When I return to my cold home, you ask
  Why I am not as I have ever been.
    You spoil me for the task
  Of acting a forced part on life's dull scene,—
Of wearing on my brow the idle mask
    Of author, great or mean,
  In the world's Carnival. I sought
Peace thus, and but in you I found it not.

V

Full half an hour, to-day, I tried my lot
  With various flowers, and every one still said,
    'She loves me—loves me not.'
  And if this meant a vision long since fled—
If it meant fortune, fame, or peace of thought—
    If it meant,—but I dread
  To speak what you may know too well:
Still there was truth in the sad oracle.

VI

The crane o'er seas and forests seeks her home;
  No bird so wild but has its quiet nest,
    When it no more would roam;
  The sleepless billows on the ocean's breast
Break like a bursting heart, and die in foam,
    And thus at length find rest:
  Doubtless there is a place of peace
Where my weak heart and all its throbs shall cease.

VII

I asked her, yesterday, if she believed
  That I had resolution. One who had
    Would ne'er have thus relieved
  His heart with words,—but what his judgment bade
Would do, and leave the scorner unrelieved.
    These verses are too sad
  To send to you, but that I know,
Happy yourself, you feel another's woe.

186   To —— [? Emilia Viviani]

ONE word is too often profaned
    For me to profane it,
One feeling too falsely disdained
    For thee to disdain it.
One hope is too like despair
    For prudence to smother,
And Pity from thee more dear,
    Than that from another.

I can give not what men call love,
    But wilt thou accept not
The worship the heart lifts above
    And the Heavens reject not,
The desire of the moth for the star,
    Of the night for the morrow,
The devotion to something afar
    From the sphere of our sorrow?

187   Lines

WHEN the lamp is shattered
The light in the dust lies dead—
    When the cloud is scattered
The rainbow's glory is shed.
    When the lute is broken,
Sweet tones are remembered not;
    When the lips have spoken,
Loved accents are soon forgot.

As music and splendour
Survive not the lamp and the lute,
  The heart's echoes render
No song when the spirit is mute:—
  No song but sad dirges,
Like the wind through a ruined cell,
  Or the mournful surges
That ring the dead seaman's knell.

  When hearts have once mingled
Love first leaves the well-built nest,
  The weak one is singled
To endure what it once possest.
  O, Love! who bewailest
The frailty of all things here,
  Why choose you the frailest
For your cradle, your home and your bier?

  Its passions will rock thee
As the storms rock the ravens on high:
  Bright reason will mock thee,
Like the sun from a wintry sky.
  From thy nest every rafter
Will rot, and thine eagle home
  Leave thee naked to laughter,
When leaves fall and cold winds come.

188   To Jane: The Recollection

I

Now the last day of many days,
  All beautiful and bright as thou,
    The loveliest and the last, is dead,

Rise, Memory, and write its praise!
   Up,—to thy wonted work! come, trace
    The epitaph of glory fled,—
For now the Earth has changed its face,
   A frown is on the Heaven's brow.

II

We wandered to the Pine Forest
   That skirts the Ocean's foam,
The lightest wind was in its nest,
   The tempest in its home.
The whispering waves were half asleep,
   The clouds were gone to play,
And on the bosom of the deep
   The smile of Heaven lay;
It seemed as if the hour were one
   Sent from beyond the skies,
Which scattered from above the sun
   A light of Paradise.

III

We paused amid the pines that stood
   The giants of the waste,
Tortured by storms to shapes as rude
   As serpents interlaced,
And soothed by every azure breath,
   That under Heaven is blown,
To harmonies and hues beneath,
   As tender as its own;
Now all the tree-tops lay asleep,
   Like green waves on the sea,
As still as in the silent deep
   The ocean woods may be.

IV

How calm it was!—the silence there
  By such a chain was bound
That even the busy woodpecker
  Made stiller by her sound
The inviolable quietness;
  The breath of peace we drew
With its soft motion made not less
  The calm that round us grew.
There seemed from the remotest seat
  Of the white mountain waste,
To the soft flower beneath our feet,
  A magic circle traced,—
A spirit interfused around,
  A thrilling, silent life,—
To momentary peace it bound
  Our mortal nature's strife;
And still I felt the centre of
  The magic circle there
Was one fair form that filled with love
  The lifeless atmosphere.

V

We paused beside the pools that lie
  Under the forest bough,—
Each seemed as 'twere a little sky
  Gulfed in a world below;
A firmament of purple light
  Which in the dark earth lay,
More boundless than the depth of night,
  And purer than the day—
In which the lovely forests grew,
  As in the upper air,

More perfect both in shape and hue
   Than any spreading there.
There lay the glade and neighbouring lawn,
   And through the dark green wood
The white sun twinkling like the dawn
   Out of a speckled cloud.
Sweet views which in our world above
   Can never well be seen,
Were imaged by the water's love
   Of that fair forest green.
And all was interfused beneath
   With an Elysian glow,
An atmosphere without a breath,
   A softer day below.
Like one beloved the scene had lent
   To the dark water's breast,
Its every leaf and lineament
   With more than truth expressed;
Until an envious wind crept by,
   Like an unwelcome thought,
Which from the mind's too faithful eye
   Blots one dear image out.
Though thou art ever fair and kind,
   The forests ever green,
Less oft is peace in S[helley]'s mind,
   Than calm in waters, seen.

189   A Song

A WIDOW bird sate mourning for her love
   Upon a wintry bough;
The frozen wind kept on above,
   The freezing stream below.

There was no leaf upon the forest bare,
  No flower upon the ground,
And little motion in the air
  Except the mill-wheel's sound.

JOHN KEBLE

190   Balaam

O FOR a sculptor's hand,
  That thou might'st take thy stand,
Thy wild hair floating on the eastern breeze,
  Thy tranc'd yet open gaze
  Fix'd on the desert haze,
As one who deep in heaven some airy pageant sees.

In outline dim and vast
  Their fearful shadows cast
The giant forms of empires on their way
  To ruin: one by one
  They tower and they are gone,
Yet in the Prophet's soul the dreams of avarice stay.

No sun or star so bright
  In all the world of light
That they should draw to heaven his downward eye,
  He hears th' Almighty's word,
  He sees the angel's sword,
Yet low upon the earth his heart and treasure lie.

Lo from yon argent field,
  To him and us reveal'd
One gentle star glides down, on earth to dwell.

Chain'd as they are below
Our eyes may see it glow,
And as it mounts again, may track its brightness well.

To him it glar'd afar,
A token of wild war,
The banner of his Lord's victorious wrath:
  But close to us it gleams,
  Its soothing lustre streams
Around our home's green walls, and on our churchway path.

We in the tents abide
Which he at distance eyed
Like goodly cedars by the waters spread,
  While seven red altar-fires
  Rose up in wavy spires,
Where on the mount he watch'd his sorceries dark and dread.

He watch'd till morning's ray
On lake and meadow lay,
And willow-shaded streams, that silent sweep
  Around the banner'd lines,
  Where by their several signs
The desert-wearied tribes in sight of Canaan sleep.

He watch'd till knowledge came
Upon his soul like flame,
Not of those magic fires at random caught:
  But true prophetic light
  Flash'd o'er him, high and bright,
Flash'd once, and died away, and left his darken'd thought.

And can he choose but fear,
  Who feels his GOD so near,
That when he fain would curse, his powerless tongue
  In blessing only moves?—
  Alas! the world he loves
Too close around his heart her tangling veil hath flung.

  Sceptre and Star divine,
  Who in thine inmost shrine
Hast made us worshippers, O claim thine own;
  More than thy seers we know—
  O teach our love to grow
Up to thy heavenly light, and reap what Thou hast sown.

191   from 'FOREST LEAVES IN AUTUMN'

  RED o'er the forest glows the setting sun,
    The line of yellow light dies fast away
  That crown'd the eastern copse: and chill and dun
    Falls on the moor the brief November day.

  Now the tir'd hunter winds a parting note,
    And Echo bids good-night from every glade;
  Yet wait awhile, and see the calm leaves float
    Each to his rest beneath their parent shade.

  How like decaying life they seem to glide!
    And yet no second spring have they in store,
  But where they fall forgotten to abide,
    Is all their portion, and they ask no more.

  Soon o'er their heads blithe April airs shall sing,
    A thousand wild-flowers round them shall unfold,
  The green buds glisten in the dews of Spring,
    And all be vernal rapture as of old.

Unconscious they in waste oblivion lie,
   In all the world of busy life around
No thought of them; in all the bounteous sky
   No drop, for them, of kindly influence found.

Man's portion is to die and rise again—
   Yet he complains, while these unmurmuring part
With their sweet lives, as pure from sin and stain,
   As his when Eden held his virgin heart.

FELICIA HEMANS

192   The Hour of Death

*Il est dans la Nature d'aimer à se livrer à l'idée même qu'on
redoute.—Corinne*

LEAVES have their time to fall,
And flowers to wither at the north-wind's breath,
   And stars to set—but all,
Thou hast *all* seasons for thine own, oh! Death.

Day is for mortal care,
Eve, for glad meetings round the joyous hearth,
   Night, for the dreams of sleep, the voice of prayer—
But all for thee, thou Mightiest of the earth.

The banquet hath its hour,
Its feverish hour, of mirth, and song, and wine;
   There comes a day for grief's o'erwhelming power,
A time for softer tears—but all are thine.

Youth and the opening rose
May look like things too glorious for decay,
 And smile at thee—but thou art not of those
That wait the ripen'd bloom to seize their prey.

 Leaves have their time to fall,
And flowers to wither at the north-wind's breath,
 And stars to set—but all,
Thou hast *all* seasons for thine own, oh! Death.

 We know when moons shall wane,
When summer birds from far shall cross the sea,
 When autumn's hue shall tinge the golden grain—
But who shall teach us when to look for thee?

 Is it when spring's first gale
Comes forth to whisper where the violets lie?
 Is it when roses in our paths grow pale?—
They have *one* season—*all* are ours to die!

 Thou art where billows foam,
Thou art where music melts upon the air;
 Thou art around us in our peaceful home,
And the world calls us forth—and thou art there.

 Thou art where friend meets friend,
Beneath the shadow of the elm to rest—
 Thou art where foe meets foe, and trumpets rend
The skies, and swords beat down the princely crest.

 Leaves have their time to fall,
And flowers to wither at the north-wind's breath,
 And stars to set—but all,
Thou hast *all* seasons for thine own, oh! Death.

JOHN CLARE

February

I

THE snow has left the cottage top;
   The thatch-moss grows in brighter green;
And eaves in quick succession drop,
   Where grinning icicles have been;
Pit-patting with a pleasant noise
   In tubs set by the cottage-door;
While ducks and geese, with happy joys,
   Plunge in the yard-pond brimming o'er.

II

The sun peeps through the window-pane;
   Which children mark with laughing eye,
And in the wet street steal again
   To tell each other Spring is nigh:
Then, as young hope the past recalls,
   In playing groups they often draw,
To build beside the sunny walls
   Their spring-time huts of sticks or straw.

III

And oft in pleasure's dreams they hie
   Round homesteads by the village side,
Scratching the hedgerow mosses by,
   Where painted pooty shells abide;
Mistaking oft the ivy spray
   For leaves that come with budding Spring,
And wond'ring, in their search for play,
   Why birds delay to build and sing.

IV

The milkmaid singing leaves her bed,
    As glad as happy thoughts can be,
While magpies chatter o'er her head
    As jocund in the change as she:
Her cows around the closes stray,
    Nor ling'ring wait the foddering-boy;
Tossing the mole-hills in their play,
    And staring round with frolic joy.

V

The shepherd now is often seen
    Near warm banks o'er his hook to bend;
Or o'er a gate or stile to lean,
    Chattering to a passing friend:
Ploughmen go whistling to their toils,
    And yoke again the rested plough;
And, mingling o'er the mellow soils,
    Boys shout, and whips are noising now.

VI

The barking dogs, by lane and wood,
    Drive sheep a-field from foddering ground;
And Echo, in her summer mood,
    Briskly mocks the cheering sound.
The flocks, as from a prison broke,
    Shake their wet fleeces in the sun,
While, following fast, a misty smoke
    Reeks from the moist grass as they run.

VII

No more behind his master's heels
    The dog creeps on his winter-pace;
But cocks his tail, and o'er the fields
    Runs many a wild and random chase,

Following, in spite of chiding calls,
  The startled cat with harmless glee,
Scaring her up the weed-green walls,
  Or mossy mottled apple-tree.

VIII

As crows from morning perches fly,
  He barks and follows them in vain;
E'en larks will catch his nimble eye,
  And off he starts and barks again,
With breathless haste and blinded guess,
  Oft following where the hare hath gone;
Forgetting, in his joy's excess,
  His frolic puppy-days are done!

IX

The hedgehog, from his hollow root,
  Sees the wood-moss clear of snow,
And hunts the hedge for fallen fruit—
  Crab, hip, and winter-bitten sloe;
But often check'd by sudden fears,
  As shepherd-dog his haunt espies,
He rolls up in a ball of spears,
  And all his barking rage defies.

X

The gladden'd swine bolt from the sty,
  And round the yard in freedom run,
Or stretching in their slumbers lie
  Beside the cottage in the sun.
The young horse whinneys to his mate,
  And, sickening from the thresher's door,
Rubs at the straw-yard's banded gate,
  Longing for freedom on the moor.

XI

The small birds think their wants are o'er,
  To see the snow-hills fret again,
And, from the barn's chaff-litter'd door,
  Betake them to the greening plain.
The woodman's robin startles coy,
  Nor longer to his elbow comes,
To peck, with hunger's eager joy,
  'Mong mossy stulps the litter'd crumbs.

XII

'Neath hedge and walls that screen the wind,
  The gnats for play will flock together;
And e'en poor flies some hope will find
  To venture in the mocking weather;
From out their hiding-holes again,
  With feeble pace, they often creep
Along the sun-warm'd window-pane,
  Like dreaming things that walk in sleep.

XIII

The mavis thrush with wild delight,
  Upon the orchard's dripping tree,
Mutters, to see the day so bright,
  Fragments of young Hope's poesy:
And oft Dame stops her buzzing wheel
  To hear the robin's note once more,
Who tootles while he pecks his meal
  From sweet-briar hips beside the door.

XIV

The sunbeams on the hedges lie,
  The south wind murmurs summer-soft;
The maids hang out white clothes to dry
  Around the elder-skirted croft:

A calm of pleasure listens round,
    And almost whispers Winter by;
While Fancy dreams of Summer's sound,
    And quiet rapture fills the eye.

XV

Thus Nature of the Spring will dream
    While south winds thaw; but soon again
Frost breathes upon the stiff'ning stream,
    And numbs it into ice: the plain
Soon wears its mourning garb of white;
    And icicles, that fret at noon,
Will eke their icy tails at night
Beneath the chilly stars and moon.

XVI

Nature soon sickens of her joys,
    And all is sad and dumb again.
Save merry shouts of sliding boys
    About the frozen furrow'd plain.
The foddering-boy forgets his song,
    And silent goes with folded arms;
And croodling shepherds bend along,
    Crouching to the whizzing storms.

194   ## To the Snipe

LOVER of swamps
    And quagmire overgrown
With hassock-tufts of sedge, where fear encamps
    Around thy home alone,

JOHN CLARE

The trembling grass
Quakes from the human foot,
Nor bears the weight of man to let him pass
Where thou, alone and mute,

Sittest at rest
In safety, near the clump
Of huge flag-forest that thy haunts invest
Or some old sallow stump,

Thriving on seams
That tiny islands swell,
Just hilling from the mud and rancid streams,
Suiting thy nature well;

For here thy bill,
Suited by wisdom good,
Of rude unseemly length, doth delve and drill
The jellied mass for food;

And here, mayhap,
When summer suns have drest
The moor's rude, desolate and spongy lap,
May hide thy mystic nest—

Mystic indeed;
For isles that oceans make
Are scarcely more secure for birds to build
Than this flag-hidden lake.

Boys thread the woods
To their remotest shades;
But in these marshy flats, these stagnant floods,
Security pervades.

From year to year
Places untrodden lie,
Where man nor boy nor stock hath ventured near,
Naught gazed on but the sky

And fowl that dread
The very breath of man,
Hiding in spots that never knew his tread,
A wild and timid clan,

Widgeon and teal
And wild duck—restless lot,
That from man's dread sight will ever steal
To the most dreary spot.

Here tempests howl
Around each flaggy plot,
Where they who dread man's sight, the water fowl,
Hide and are frightened not.

'Tis power divine
That heartens them to brave
The roughest tempest and at ease recline
On marshes or the wave.

Yet instinct knows
Not safety's bounds:—to shun
The firmer ground where skulking fowler goes
With searching dogs and gun,

By tepid springs
Scarcely one stride across
(Though bramble from its edge a shelter flings
Thy safety is at loss)

—And never choose
The little sinky foss,
Streaking the moors whence spa-red water spews
From pudges fringed with moss;

Freebooters there,
Intent to kill or slay,
Startle with cracking guns the trepid air,
And dogs thy haunts betray.

From danger's reach
Here thou art safe to roam,
Far as these washy flag-sown marshes stretch
A still and quiet home.

In these thy haunts
I've gleaned habitual love;
From the vague world where pride and folly taunts
I muse and look above.

Thy solitudes
The unbounded heaven esteems,
And here my heart warms into higher moods
And dignifying dreams.

I see the sky
Smile on the meanest spot,
Giving to all that creep or walk or fly
A calm and cordial lot.

Thine teaches me
Right feelings to employ—
That in the dreariest places peace will be
A dweller and a joy.

195

WINTER winds cold and blea
Chilly blows o'er the lea:
Wander not out to me,
    Jenny so fair,
Wait in thy cottage free.
    I will be there.

Wait in thy cushioned chair
Wi' thy white bosom bare.
Kisses are sweetest there:
    Leave it for me.
Free from the chilly air
    I will meet thee.

How sweet can courting prove,
How can I kiss my love
Muffled in hat and glove
    From the chill air?
Quaking beneath the grove,
    What love is there!

Lay by thy woollen vest,
Drape no cloak o'er thy breast:
Where my hand oft hath pressed,
    Pin nothing there:
Where my head droops to rest,
    Leave its bed bare.

196 Summer Images

Now swarthy Summer, by rude health embrowned,
   Precedence takes of rosy-fingered Spring;
And laughing Joy, with wild flowers prank'd and crown'd,
   A wild and giddy thing,
And Health robust, from every care unbound,
   Come on the zephyr's wing,
      And cheer the toiling clown.

Happy as holiday-enjoying face,
   Loud tongued, and 'merry as a marriage-bell',
Thy lightsome step sheds joy in every place;
   And where the troubled dwell,
Thy witching charms wean them of half their cares;
   And from thy sunny spell,
      They greet joy unawares.

Then with thy sultry locks all loose and rude,
   And mantle laced with gems of garish light,
Come as of wont; for I would fain intrude,
   And in the world's despite,
Share the rude mirth that thy own heart beguiles;
   If haply so I might
      Win pleasure from thy smiles.

Me not the noise of brawling pleasure cheers,
   In nightly revels or in city streets;
But joys which soothe, and not distract the ears,
   That one at leisure meets
In the green woods, and meadows summer-shorn,
   Or fields, where bee-fly greets
      The ears with mellow horn.

The green-swathed grasshopper, on treble pipe,
   Sings there, and dances, in mad-hearted pranks;
There bees go courting every flower that's ripe,
   On baulks and sunny banks;
And droning dragon-fly, on rude bassoon,
   Attempts to give God thanks
      In no discordant tune.

The speckled thrush, by self-delight imbued,
   There sings unto himself for joy's amends,
And drinks the honey-dew of solitude.
   There Happiness attends
With inbred Joy until the heart o'erflow,
   Of which the world's rude friends,
      Naught heeding, nothing know.

There the gay river, laughing as it goes,
   Plashes with easy wave its flaggy sides,
And to the calm of heart, in calmness shows
   What pleasure there abides,
To trace its sedgy banks, from trouble free:
   Spots, Solitude provides
      To muse, and happy be.

There ruminating 'neath some pleasant bush,
   On sweet silk grass I stretch me at mine ease,
Where I can pillow on the yielding rush;
   And, acting as I please,
Drop into pleasant dreams; or musing lie,
   Mark the wind-shaken trees,
      And cloud-betravelled sky,

There think me how some barter joy for care,
   And waste life's summer-health in riot rude,
Of nature, nor of nature's sweets aware.

Where passions vain and rude
By calm reflection softened are and still;
   And the heart's better mood
      Feels sick of doing ill.

There I can live, and at my leisure seek
   Joys far from cold restraints—not fearing pride—
Free as the winds, that breathe upon my cheek
   Rude health, so long denied.
Here poor Integrity can sit at ease,
   And list self-satisfied
      The song of honey-bees;

And green lane traverse, heedless where it goes,
   Naught guessing, till some sudden turn espies
Rude batter'd finger-post, that stooping shows
   Where the snug mystery lies;
And then a mossy spire, with ivy crown,
   Clears up the short surprise,
      And shows a peeping town.

I see the wild flowers, in their summer morn
   Of beauty, feeding on joy's luscious hours;
The gay convolvulus, wreathing round the thorn,
   Agape for honey showers;
And slender kingcup, burnished with the dew
   Of morning's early hours,
      Like gold yminted new.

And mark by rustic bridge, o'er shallow stream,
   Cow-tending boy, to toil unreconciled,
Absorbed as in some vagrant summer dream;
   Who now, in gestures wild,

Starts dancing to his shadow on the wall,
   Feeling self-gratified,
      Nor fearing human thrall:

Or thread the sunny valley laced with streams,
   Of forests rude, and the o'ershadow'd brims
Of simple ponds, where idle shepherd dreams,
   And streaks his listless limbs;
Or trace hay-scented meadows, smooth and long,
   Where joy's wild impulse swims
      In one continued song.

I love at early morn, from new-mown swath,
   To see the startled frog his route pursue;
To mark while, leaping o'er the dripping path,
   His bright sides scatter dew;
The early lark that from its bustle flies
   To hail his matin new;
      And watch him to the skies:

And note on hedgerow baulks, in moisture sprent,
   The jetty snail creep from the mossy thorn,
With earnest heed, and tremulous intent,
   Frail brother of the morn,
That from the tiny bent's dew-misted leaves
   Withdraws his timid horn,
      And fearful vision weaves:

Or swallow heed on smoke-tanned chimney-top,
   Wont to be first unsealing Morning's eye,
Ere yet the bee hath gleaned one wayward drop
   Of honey on his thigh;
To see him seek morn's airy couch to sing,
   Until the golden sky
      Bepaint his russet wing:

Or sawning boy by tanning corn to spy,
　With clapping noise to startle birds away,
And hear him bawl to every passer-by
　To know the hour of day;
And see the uncradled breezes, fresh and strong,
　With waking blossoms play,
　　And breathe Æolian song.

I love the south-west wind, or low or loud,
　And not the less when sudden drops of rain
Moisten my pallid cheeks from ebon cloud,
　Threatening soft showers again,
That over lands new ploughed and meadow grounds,
　Summer's sweet breath unchain,
　　And wake harmonious sounds.

Rich music breathes in Summer's every sound;
　And in her harmony of varied greens,
Woods, meadows, hedge-rows, corn-fields, all around
　Much beauty intervenes,
Filling with harmony the ear and eye;
　While o'er the mingling scenes
　　Far spreads the laughing sky.

See, how the wind-enamoured aspin leaves
　Turn up their silver lining to the sun!
And list! the brustling noise, that oft deceives,
　And makes the sheep-boy run:
The sound so mimics fast-approaching showers,
　He thinks the rain's begun,
　　And hastes to sheltering bowers.

But now the Evening curdles dank and grey,
　Changing her watchet hue for sombre weed;
And moping owls, to close the lids of day,
　On drowsy wing proceed;

While chickering crickets, tremulous and long,
  Light's farewell inly heed,
    And give it parting song.

The pranking bat its flighty circlet makes;
  The glow-worm burnishes its lamp anew,
O'er meadows dew-besprent; the beetle wakes
  Inquiries ever new,
Teazing each passing ear with murmurs vain,
  As wanting to pursue
    His homeward path again.

Hark! 'tis the melody of distant bells
  That on the wind with pleasing hum rebounds
By fitful starts, then musically swells
  O'er the dun stilly grounds;
While on the meadow-bridge the pausing boy
  Listens the mellow sounds,
    And hums in vacant joy.

Now homeward-bound, the hedger bundles round
  His evening faggot, and with every stride
His leathern doublet leaves a rustling sound.
  Till silly sheep beside
His path start tremulous, and once again
  Look back dissatisfied,
    Then scour the dewy plain.

How sweet the soothing calmness that distills
  O'er the heart's every sense its opiate dews,
In meek-eyed moods and ever balmy trills!
  That softens and subdues,
With gentle Quiet's bland and sober train,
  Which dreamy eve renews
    In many a mellow strain.

I love to walk the fields; they are to me
   A legacy no evil can destroy;
They, like a spell, set every rapture free
   That cheer'd me when a boy.
Play—pastime—all Time's blotting pen conceal'd,
   Comes like a new-born joy,
      To greet me in the field.

For Nature's objects ever harmonize
   With emulous Taste, that vulgar deed annoys;
It loves in pensive moods to sympathize,
   And meet vibrating joys
O'er Nature's pleasing things; nor slighting, deems
   Pastimes, the Muse employs,
      Vain and obtrusive themes.

197   Clock-a-Clay

In the cowslip pips I lie,
Hidden from the buzzing fly,
While green grass beneath me lies,
Pearled with dew like fishes' eyes,
Here I lie, a clock-a-clay,
Waiting for the time o' day.

While grassy forest quakes surprise,
And the wild wind sobs and sighs,
My gold home rocks as like to fall,
On its pillar green and tall;
When the pattering rain drives by
Clock-a-clay keeps warm and dry.

Day by day and night by night,
All the week I hide from sight;
In the cowslip pips I lie,
In rain and dew still warm and dry;
Day and night, and night and day,
Red, black-spotted clock-a-clay.

My home shakes in wind and showers,
Pale green pillar topped with flowers,
Bending at the wild wind's breath,
Till I touch the grass beneath;
Here I live, lone clock-a-clay,
Watching for the time of day.

198   [Stanzas from 'Child Harold']

How beautiful this hill of fern swells on!
So beautiful the chapel peeps between
The hornbeams—with its simple bell. Alone
I wander here, hid in a palace green.
Mary is absent—but the forest queen,
Nature, is with me. Morning, noon and gloaming,
I write my poems in these paths unseen;
And when among these brakes and beeches roaming,
I sigh for truth, and home, and love and woman.

I sigh for one and two—and still I sigh,
For many are the whispers I have heard
From beauty's lips. Love's soul on many an eye
Hath pierced my heart with such intense regard,
I looked for joy and pain was the reward.

I think of them I love, each girl and boy,
Babes of two mothers,—on this velvet sward,
And Nature thinks—in her so sweet employ,
While dews fall on each blossom, weeping joy.

Here is the chapel-yard enclosed with pales,
And oak trees nearly top its little bell.
Here is the little bridge with guiding rail
That leads me on to many a pleasant dell.
The fern-owl chatters like a startled knell
To Nature—yet 'tis sweet at evening still.
A pleasant road curves round the gentle swell,
Where Nature seems to have her own sweet will,
Planting her beech and thorn about the sweet fern hill.

I have had many loves—and seek no more.
These solitudes my last delights shall be,
The leaf hid forest, and the lonely shore,
Seem to my mind like beings that are free.
Yet would I had some eye to smile on me,
Some heart where I could make a happy home in,
Sweet Susan that was wont my love to be
And Bessy of the glen—for I've been roaming
With both at morn and noon and dusky gloaming.

Cares gather round: I snap their chains in two
And smile in agony and laugh in tears,
Like playing with a deadly serpent, who
Stings to the death—there is no room for fears
Where death would bring me happiness. His sheers
Kill cares that hiss to poison many a vein.
The thought to be extinct my fate endears.
Pale Death, the grand physician, cures all pain:
The dead rest well—who lived for joys in vain.

This twilight seems a veil of gauze and mist,
Trees seem dark hills between the earth and sky,
Winds sob awake, and then a gusty hist
Fans through the wheat like serpents gliding by.
I love to stretch my length 'twixt earth and sky,
And see the inky foliage o'er me wave,
Though shades are still my prison where I lie.
Long use grows nature which I easy brave,
And think how sweet cares rest within the grave.

Remind me not of other years, or tell
My broken hopes of joys they are to meet,
While thy own falsehoods ring the loudest knell
To one fond heart that aches too cold to beat.
Mary, how oft with fondness I repeat
That name alone to give my troubles rest.
The very sound, though bitter, seemeth sweet—
In my love's home and thy own faithless breast
Truth's bonds are broke and every nerve distrest.

Life is to me a dream that never wakes:
Night finds me on this lengthening road alone.
Love is to me a thought that ever aches,
A frost-bound thought that freezes life to stone.
Mary, in truth and nature still my own,
That warms the winter of my aching breast,
Thy name is joy, nor will I life bemoan.
Midnight, when sleep takes charge of Nature's rest,
Finds me awake and friendless—not distrest.

Tie all my cares up in thy arms, o Sleep,
And give my weary spirits peace and rest.
I'm not an outlaw in this midnight deep,
If prayers are offered from sweet woman's breast.

One, and one only, made my being blest,
And fancy shapes her form in every dell.
On that sweet bosom I've had hours of rest,
Though now, through years of absence doomed to dwell,
Day seems my night, and Night seems blackest hell.

199 No single hour can stand for naught,
  No moment-hand can move
  But calendars an aching thought
  Of my first lonely love.

  Where silence doth the loudest call
  My secrets to betray,
  As moonlight holds the night in thrall,
  As suns reveal the day,

  I hide it in the silent shades
  Till silence finds a tongue,
  I make its grave where time invades
  Till time becomes a song.

  I bid my foolish heart be still,
  But hopes will not be chid.
  My heart will beat—and burn—and chill,
  First love will not be hid.

  When summer ceases to be green
  And winter bare and blea—
  Death may forget what I have been,
  But I must cease to be.

When words refuse before the crowd
My Mary's name to give,
The muse in silence sings aloud:
And there my love will live.

200   LOVE lives beyond
The tomb, the earth, which fades like dew—
      I love the fond,
The faithful, and the true.

      Love lies in sleep,
'Tis happiness of healthy dreams,
      Eve's dews may weep,
But love delightful seems.

      'Tis seen in flowers,
And in the even's pearly dew,
      On earth's green hours,
And in the heaven's eternal blue.

      'Tis heard in Spring
When light and sunbeams, warm and kind,
      On angel's wing
Bring love and music to the mind.

      And where's the voice,
So young, so beautiful, and sweet
      As Nature's choice,
Where Spring and lovers meet?

      Love lives beyond
The tomb, the earth, the flowers, and dew.
      I love the fond,
The faithful, young, and true.

201 ## An Invite to Eternity

WILT thou go with me, sweet maid
Say, maiden, wilt thou go with me
Through the valley depths of shade,
Of night and dark obscurity,
Where the path hath lost its way,
Where the sun forgets the day,—
Where there's nor light nor life to see,
Sweet maiden, wilt thou go with me?

Where stones will turn to flooding streams,
Where plains will rise like ocean waves,
Where life will fade like visioned dreams
And mountains darken into caves,
Say, maiden, wilt thou go with me
Through this sad non-identity,
Where parents live and are forgot,
And sisters live and know us not?

Say, maiden, wilt thou go with me
In this strange death of life to be,
To live in death and be the same,
Without this life, or home, or name,
At once to be and not to be—
That was and is not—yet to see
Things pass like shadows, and the sky
Above, below, around us lie?

The land of shadows wilt thou trace,
And look—nor know each other's face;
The present mixed with reason gone,
And past and present all as one?

Say, maiden, can thy life be led
To join the living with the dead?
Then trace thy footsteps on with me:
We're wed to one eternity.

202   I am

I AM: yet what I am none cares or knows,
    My friends forsake me like a memory lost,
I am the self-consumer of my woes—
    They rise and vanish in oblivious host,
Like shadows in love's frenzied, stifled throes:—
And yet I am, and live—like vapours tost

Into the nothingness of scorn and noise,
    Into the living sea of waking dreams,
Where there is neither sense of life or joys,
    But the vast shipwreck of my life's esteems;
Even the dearest, that I love the best,
Are strange—nay, rather stranger than the rest.

I long for scenes, where man has never trod,
    A place where woman never smiled or wept—
There to abide with my Creator, GOD,
    And sleep as I in childhood sweetly slept,
Untroubling, and untroubled where I lie,
The grass below—above the vaulted sky.

203   A Vision

I LOST the love of heaven above,
    I spurned the lust of earth below,
I felt the sweets of fancied love,
    And hell itself my only foe.

I lost earth's joys, but felt the glow
   Of heaven's flame abound in me,
Till loveliness and I did grow
   The bard of immortality.

I loved, but woman fell away,
   I hid me from her faded fame,
I snatch'd the sun's eternal ray
   And wrote till earth was but a name.

In every language upon earth,
   On every shore, o'er every sea,
I gave my name immortal birth
   And kept my spirit with the free.

2 August 1844

204   The Peasant Poet

H<small>E</small> loved the brook's soft sound,
   The swallow swimming by.
He loved the daisy-covered ground,
   The cloud-bedappled sky.
To him the dismal storm appeared
   The very voice of God;
And when the evening rack was reared
   Stood Moses with his rod.
And everything his eyes surveyed,
   The insects in the brake,
Were creatures God Almighty made,
   He loved them for His sake—
A silent man in life's affairs,
   A thinker from a boy,
A peasant in his daily cares,
   A poet in his joy.

205 ['Secret Love']

I HID my love when young till I
Couldn't bear the buzzing of a fly;
I hid my love to my despite
Till I could not bear to look at light:
I dare not gaze upon her face
But left her memory in each place;
Where'er I saw a wild flower lie
I kissed and bade my love good bye.

I met her in the greenest dells
Where dewdrops pearl the wood blue bells;
The lost breeze kissed her bright blue eye,
The bee kissed and went singing by,
A sunbeam found a passage there,
A gold chain round her neck so fair;
As secret as the wild bee's song
She lay there all the summer long.

I hid my love in field and town
Till een the breeze would knock me down;
The bees seemed singing ballads oer,
The fly's bass turned a lion's roar;
And even silence found a tongue,
To haunt me all the summer long;
The riddle Nature could not prove
Was nothing else but secret love.

206 Language has not the power to speak what love indites:
The Soul lies buried in the ink that writes.

JOHN KEATS

207 ## Dedication

TO LEIGH HUNT, ESQ.

GLORY and Loveliness have passed away;
  For if we wander out in early morn,
  No wreathed incense do we see upborne
Into the east, to meet the smiling day:
No crowd of nymphs soft voic'd and young, and gay,
  In woven baskets bringing ears of corn,
  Roses, and pinks, and violets, to adorn
The shrine of Flora in her early May.
But there are left delights as high as these,
  And I shall ever bless my destiny,
That in a time, when under pleasant trees
  Pan is no longer sought, I feel a free,
A leafy luxury, seeing I could please,
  With these poor offerings, a man like thee.

208 ## On First Looking into Chapman's Homer

MUCH have I travell'd in the realms of gold,
  And many goodly states and kingdoms seen;
  Round many western islands have I been
Which bards in fealty to Apollo hold.
Oft of one wide expanse had I been told
  That deep-brow'd Homer ruled as his demesne;
  Yet did I never breathe its pure serene
Till I heard Chapman speak out loud and bold:

Then felt I like some watcher of the skies
   When a new planet swims into his ken;
Or like stout Cortez when with eagle eyes
   He star'd at the Pacific—and all his men
Look'd at each other with a wild surmise—
   Silent, upon a peak in Darien.

209   Addressed to [Haydon]

GREAT spirits now on earth are sojourning;
   He of the cloud, the cataract, the lake,
   Who on Helvellyn's summit, wide awake,
Catches his freshness from Archangel's wing:
He of the rose, the violet, the spring,
   The social smile, the chain for Freedom's sake:
   And lo!—whose stedfastness would never take
A meaner sound than Raphael's whispering.
And other spirits there are standing apart
   Upon the forehead of the age to come;
These, these will give the world another heart,
   And other pulses. Hear ye not the hum
Of mighty workings?——
   Listen awhile ye nations, and be dumb.

210   *ENDYMION*

from BOOK I

A THING of beauty is a joy for ever:
Its loveliness increases; it will never
Pass into nothingness; but still will keep
A bower quiet for us, and a sleep

Full of sweet dreams, and health, and quiet breathing.
Therefore, on every morrow, are we wreathing
A flowery band to bind us to the earth,
Spite of despondence, of the inhuman dearth
Of noble natures, of the gloomy days,
Of all the unhealthy and o'er-darkened ways
Made for our searching: yes, in spite of all,
Some shape of beauty moves away the pall
From our dark spirits. Such the sun, the moon,
Trees old and young, sprouting a shady boon
For simple sheep; and such are daffodils
With the green world they live in; and clear rills
That for themselves a cooling covert make
'Gainst the hot season; the mid-forest brake,
Rich with a sprinkling of fair musk-rose blooms:
And such too is the grandeur of the dooms
We have imagined for the mighty dead;
All lovely tales that we have heard or read:
An endless fountain of immortal drink,
Pouring unto us from the heaven's brink.

Nor do we merely feel these essences
For one short hour; no, even as the trees
That whisper round a temple become soon
Dear as the temple's self, so does the moon,
The passion poesy, glories infinite,
Haunt us till they become a cheering light
Unto our souls, and bound to us so fast,
That, whether there be shine, or gloom o'ercast,
They always must be with us, or we die.

*

from BOOK II

211 O SOVEREIGN power of love! O grief! O balm!
All records, saving thine, come cool; and calm,
And shadowy, through the mist of passed years:
For others, good or bad, hatred and tears
Have become indolent; but touching thine,
One sigh doth echo, one poor sob doth pine,
One kiss brings honey-dew from buried days.
The woes of Troy, towers smothering o'er their blaze,
Stiff-holden shields, far-piercing spears, keen blades,
Struggling, and blood, and shrieks—all dimly fades
Into some backward corner of the brain;
Yet, in our very souls, we feel amain
The close of Troilus and Cressid sweet.
Hence, pageant history! hence, gilded cheat!
Swart planet in the universe of deeds!
Wide sea, that one continuous murmur breeds
Along the pebbled shore of memory!
Many old rotten-timber'd boats there be
Upon thy vaporous bosom, magnified
To goodly vessels; many a sail of pride,
And golden-keel'd, is left unlaunch'd and dry.
But wherefore this? What care, though owl did fly
About the great Athenian admiral's mast?
What care, though striding Alexander past
The Indus with his Macedonian numbers?
Though old Ulysses tortured from his slumbers
The glutted Cyclops, what care?—Juliet leaning
Amid her window-flowers,—sighing,—weaning
Tenderly her fancy from its maiden snow,
Doth more avail than these: the silver flow
Of Hero's tears, the swoon of Imogen,
Fair Pastorella in the bandit's den,

Are things to brood on with more ardency
Than the death-day of empires. Fearfully
Must such conviction come upon his head,
Who, thus far, discontent, has dared to tread,
Without one muse's smile, or kind behest,
The path of love and poesy. But rest,
In chafing restlessness, is yet more drear
Than to be crush'd, in striving to uprear
Love's standard on the battlements of song.

212   The Eve of St. Agnes

I

St. Agnes' Eve—Ah, bitter chill it was!
The owl, for all his feathers, was a-cold;
The hare limp'd trembling through the frozen grass,
And silent was the flock in woolly fold:
Numb were the Beadsman's fingers, while he told
His rosary, and while his frosted breath,
Like pious incense from a censer old,
Seem'd taking flight for heaven, without a death,
Past the sweet Virgin's picture, while his prayer he saith.

II

His prayer he saith, this patient, holy man;
Then takes his lamp, and riseth from his knees,
And back returneth, meagre, barefoot, wan,
Along the chapel aisle by slow degrees:
The sculptur'd dead, on each side, seem to freeze,
Emprison'd in black, purgatorial rails:
Knights, ladies, praying in dumb orat'ries,
He passeth by; and his weak spirit fails
To think how they may ache in icy hoods and mails.

III

Northward he turneth through a little door,
And scarce three steps, ere Music's golden tongue
Flatter'd to tears this aged man and poor;
But no—already had his deathbell rung;
The joys of all his life were said and sung:
His was harsh penance on St. Agnes' Eve:
Another way he went, and soon among
Rough ashes sat he for his soul's reprieve,
And all night kept awake, for sinners' sake to grieve.

IV

That ancient Beadsman heard the prelude soft;
And so it chanc'd, for many a door was wide,
From hurry to and fro. Soon, up aloft,
The silver, snarling trumpets 'gan to chide:
The level chambers, ready with their pride,
Were glowing to receive a thousand guests:
The carved angels, ever eager-eyed,
Star'd, where upon their heads the cornice rests,
With hair blown back, and wings put cross-wise on their breasts.

V

At length burst in the argent revelry,
With plume, tiara, and all rich array,
Numerous as shadows haunting fairily
The brain, new-stuff'd, in youth, with triumphs gay
Of old romance. These let us wish away,
And turn, sole-thoughted, to one Lady there,
Whose heart had brooded, all that wintry day,
On love, and wing'd St. Agnes' saintly care,
As she had heard old dames full many times declare.

VI

They told her how, upon St. Agnes' Eve,
Young virgins might have visions of delight,
And soft adorings from their loves receive
Upon the honey'd middle of the night,
If ceremonies due they did aright;
As, supperless to bed they must retire,
And couch supine their beauties, lily white;
Nor look behind, nor sideways, but require
Of Heaven with upward eyes for all that they desire.

VII

Full of this whim was thoughtful Madeline:
The music, yearning like a God in pain,
She scarcely heard: her maiden eyes divine,
Fix'd on the floor, saw many a sweeping train
Pass by—she heeded not at all: in vain
Came many a tiptoe, amorous cavalier,
And back retir'd; not cool'd by high disdain,
But she saw not: her heart was otherwhere:
She sigh'd for Agnes' dreams, the sweetest of the year.

VIII

She danc'd along with vague, regardless eyes,
Anxious her lips, her breathing quick and short:
The hallow'd hour was near at hand: she sighs
Amid the timbrels, and the throng'd resort
Of whisperers in anger, or in sport;
'Mid looks of love, defiance, hate, and scorn,
Hoodwink'd with faery fancy; all amort,
Save to St. Agnes and her lambs unshorn,
And all the bliss to be before to-morrow morn.

IX

So, purposing each moment to retire,
She linger'd still. Meantime, across the moors,
Had come young Porphyro, with heart on fire
For Madeline. Beside the portal doors,
Buttress'd from moonlight, stands he, and implores
All saints to give him sight of Madeline,
But for one moment in the tedious hours,
That he might gaze and worship all unseen;
Perchance speak, kneel, touch, kiss—in sooth such things have
    been.

X

He ventures in: let no buzz'd whisper tell:
All eyes be muffled, or a hundred swords
Will storm his heart, Love's fev'rous citadel:
For him, those chambers held barbarian hordes,
Hyena foemen, and hot-blooded lords,
Whose very dogs would execrations howl
Against his lineage: not one breast affords
Him any mercy, in that mansion foul,
Save one old beldame, weak in body and in soul.

XI

Ah, happy chance! the aged creature came,
Shuffling along with ivory-headed wand,
To where he stood, hid from the torch's flame,
Behind a broad hall-pillar, far beyond
The sound of merriment and chorus bland:
He startled her; but soon she knew his face,
And grasp'd his fingers in her palsied hand,
Saying, 'Mercy, Porphyro! hie thee from this place;
They are all here to-night, the whole blood-thirsty race!

XII

'Get hence! get hence! there's dwarfish Hildebrand;
He had a fever late, and in the fit
He cursed thee and thine, both house and land:
Then there's that old Lord Maurice, not a whit
More tame for his gray hairs—Alas me! flit!
Flit like a ghost away.'—'Ah, Gossip dear,
We're safe enough; here in this arm-chair sit,
And tell me how'—'Good saints! not here, not here;
Follow me, child, or else these stones will be thy bier.'

XIII

He follow'd through a lowly arched way,
Brushing the cobwebs with his lofty plume,
And as she mutter'd 'Well-a—well-a-day!'
He found him in a little moonlight room,
Pale, lattic'd, chill, and silent as a tomb.
'Now tell me where is Madeline,' said he,
'O tell me, Angela, by the holy loom
Which none but secret sisterhood may see,
When they St. Agnes' wool are weaving piously.'

XIV

'St. Agnes! Ah! it is St. Agnes' Eve—
Yet men will murder upon holy days:
Thou must hold water in a witch's sieve,
And be liege-lord of all the Elves and Fays,
To venture so: it fills me with amaze
To see thee, Porphyro!—St. Agnes' Eve!
God's help! my lady fair the conjuror plays
This very night: good angels her deceive!
But let me laugh awhile, I've mickle time to grieve.'

XV

Feebly she laugheth in the languid moon,
While Porphyro upon her face doth look,
Like puzzled urchin on an aged crone
Who keepeth clos'd a wond'rous riddle-book,
As spectacled she sits in chimney nook.
But soon his eyes grew brilliant, when she told
His lady's purpose; and he scarce could brook
Tears, at the thought of those enchantments cold,
And Madeline asleep in lap of legends old.

XVI

Sudden a thought came like a full-blown rose,
Flushing his brow, and in his pained heart
Made purple riot: then doth he propose
A stratagem, that makes the beldame start:
'A cruel man and impious thou art:
Sweet lady, let her pray, and sleep, and dream
Alone with her good angels, far apart
From wicked men like thee. Go, go!—I deem
Thou canst not surely be the same that thou didst seem.'

XVII

'I will not harm her, by all saints I swear,'
Quoth Porphyro: 'O may I ne'er find grace
When my weak voice shall whisper its last prayer,
If one of her soft ringlets I displace,
Or look with ruffian passion in her face:
Good Angela, believe me by these tears;
Or I will, even in a moment's space,
Awake, with horrid shout, my foemen's ears,
And beard them, though they be more fang'd than wolves and
        bears.'

XVIII

'Ah! why wilt thou affright a feeble soul?
A poor, weak, palsy-stricken, churchyard thing,
Whose passing-bell may ere the midnight toll;
Whose prayers for thee, each morn and evening,
Were never miss'd.'—Thus plaining, doth she bring
A gentler speech from burning Porphyro;
So woful, and of such deep sorrowing,
That Angela gives promise she will do
Whatever he shall wish, betide her weal or woe.

XIX

Which was, to lead him, in close secrecy,
Even to Madeline's chamber, and there hide
Him in a closet, of such privacy
That he might see her beauty unespied,
And win perhaps that night a peerless bride,
While legion'd fairies pac'd the coverlet,
And pale enchantment held her sleepy-eyed.
Never on such a night have lovers met,
Since Merlin paid his Demon all the monstrous debt.

XX

'It shall be as thou wishest,' said the Dame:
'All cates and dainties shall be stored there
Quickly on this feast-night: by the tambour frame
Her own lute thou wilt see: no time to spare,
For I am slow and feeble, and scarce dare
On such a catering trust my dizzy head.
Wait here, my child, with patience; kneel in prayer
The while: Ah! thou must needs the lady wed,
Or may I never leave my grave among the dead.'

XXI

So saying, she hobbled off with busy fear.
The lover's endless minutes slowly pass'd;
The dame return'd, and whisper'd in his ear
To follow her; with aged eyes aghast
From fright of dim espial. Safe at last,
Through many a dusky gallery, they gain
The maiden's chamber, silken, hush'd, and chaste;
Where Porphyro took covert, pleas'd amain.
His poor guide hurried back with agues in her brain.

XXII

Her falt'ring hand upon the balustrade,
Old Angela was feeling for the stair,
When Madeline, St. Agnes' charmed maid,
Rose, like a mission'd spirit, unaware:
With silver taper's light, and pious care,
She turn'd, and down the aged gossip led
To a safe level matting. Now prepare,
Young Porphyro, for gazing on that bed;
She comes, she comes again, like ring-dove fray'd and fled.

XXIII

Out went the taper as she hurried in;
Its little smoke, in pallid moonshine, died:
She clos'd the door, she panted, all akin
To spirits of the air, and visions wide:
No uttered syllable, or, woe betide!
But to her heart, her heart was voluble,
Paining with eloquence her balmy side;
As though a tongueless nightingale should swell
Her throat in vain, and die, heart-stifled, in her dell.

XXIV

A casement high and triple-arch'd there was,
All garlanded with carven imag'ries,
Of fruits, and flowers, and bunches of knot-grass,
And diamonded with panes of quaint device,
Innumerable of stains and splendid dyes,
As are the tiger-moth's deep-damask'd wings;
And in the midst, 'mong thousand heraldries,
And twilight saints, and dim emblazonings,
A shielded scutcheon blush'd with blood of queens and kings.

XXV

Full on this casement shone the wintry moon,
And threw warm gules on Madeline's fair breast,
As down she knelt for heaven's grace and boon;
Rose-bloom fell on her hands, together prest,
And on her silver cross soft amethyst,
And on her hair a glory, like a saint:
She seem'd a splendid angel, newly drest,
Save wings, for heaven:—Porphyro grew faint:
She knelt, so pure a thing, so free from mortal taint.

XXVI

Anon his heart revives: her vespers done,
Of all its wreathed pearls her hair she frees;
Unclasps her warmed jewels one by one;
Loosens her fragrant boddice; by degrees
Her rich attire creeps rustling to her knees:
Half-hidden, like a mermaid in sea-weed,
Pensive awhile she dreams awake, and sees,
In fancy, fair St. Agnes in her bed,
But dares not look behind, or all the charm is fled.

XXVII

Soon, trembling in her soft and chilly nest,
In sort of wakeful swoon, perplex'd she lay,
Until the poppied warmth of sleep oppress'd
Her soothed limbs, and soul fatigued away;
Flown, like a thought, until the morrow-day;
Blissfully haven'd both from joy and pain;
Clasp'd like a missal where swart Paynims pray;
Blinded alike from sunshine and from rain,
As though a rose should shut, and be a bud again.

XXVIII

Stol'n to this paradise, and so entranced,
Porphyro gazed upon her empty dress,
And listen'd to her breathing, if it chanced
To wake into a slumberous tenderness;
Which when he heard, that minute did he bless,
And breath'd himself: then from the closet crept,
Noiseless as fear in a wide wilderness,
And over the hush'd carpet, silent, stept,
And 'tween the curtains peep'd, where, lo!—how fast she slept.

XXIX

Then by the bed-side, where the faded moon
Made a dim, silver twilight, soft he set
A table, and, half anguish'd, threw thereon
A cloth of woven crimson, gold, and jet:—
O for some drowsy Morphean amulet!
The boisterous, midnight, festive clarion,
The kettle-drum, and far-heard clarionet,
Affray his ears, though but in dying tone:—
The hall door shuts again, and all the noise is gone.

XXX

And still she slept an azure-lidded sleep,
  In blanched linen, smooth, and lavender'd,
While he from forth the closet brought a heap
  Of candied apple, quince, and plum, and gourd;
With jellies soother than the creamy curd,
  And lucent syrops, tinct with cinnamon;
Manna and dates, in argosy transferr'd
  From Fez; and spiced dainties, every one,
From silken Samarcand to cedar'd Lebanon.

XXXI

These delicates he heap'd with glowing hand
  On golden dishes and in baskets bright
Of wreathed silver: sumptuous they stand
  In the retired quiet of the night,
Filling the chilly room with perfume light.—
  'And now, my love, my seraph fair, awake!
Thou art my heaven, and I thine eremite:
  Open thine eyes, for meek St. Agnes' sake,
Or I shall drowse beside thee, so my soul doth ache.'

XXXII

Thus whispering, his warm, unnerved arm
  Sank in her pillow. Shaded was her dream
By the dusk curtains:—'twas a midnight charm
  Impossible to melt as iced stream:
The lustrous salvers in the moonlight gleam;
  Broad golden fringe upon the carpet lies:
It seem'd he never, never could redeem
  From such a stedfast spell his lady's eyes;
So mus'd awhile, entoil'd in woofed phantasies.

XXXIII

Awakening up, he took her hollow lute,—
Tumultuous,—and, in chords that tenderest be,
He play'd an ancient ditty, long since mute,
In Provence call'd, 'La belle dame sans mercy':
Close to her ear touching the melody;—
Wherewith disturb'd, she utter'd a soft moan:
He ceased—she panted quick—and suddenly
Her blue affrayed eyes wide open shone:
Upon his knees he sank, pale as smooth-sculptured stone.

XXXIV

Her eyes were open, but she still beheld,
Now wide awake, the vision of her sleep:
There was a painful change, that nigh expell'd
The blisses of her dream so pure and deep
At which fair Madeline began to weep,
And moan forth witless words with many a sigh;
While still her gaze on Porphyro would keep;
Who knelt, with joined hands and piteous eye,
Fearing to move or speak, she look'd so dreamingly.

XXXV

'Ah, Porphyro!' said she, 'but even now
Thy voice was at sweet tremble in mine ear,
Made tuneable with every sweetest vow;
And those sad eyes were spiritual and clear:
How chang'd thou art! how pallid, chill, and drear!
Give me that voice again, my Porphyro,
Those looks immortal, those complainings dear!
Oh leave me not in this eternal woe,
For if thou diest, my Love, I know not where to go.'

XXXVI

Beyond a mortal man impassion'd far
At these voluptuous accents, he arose,
Ethereal, flush'd, and like a throbbing star
Seen mid the sapphire heaven's deep repose;
Into her dream he melted, as the rose
Blendeth its odour with the violet,—
Solution sweet: meantime the frost-wind blows
Like Love's alarum pattering the sharp sleet
Against the window-panes; St. Agnes' moon hath set.

XXXVII

'Tis dark: quick pattereth the flaw-blown sleet:
'This is no dream, my bride, my Madeline!'
'Tis dark: the iced gusts still rave and beat:
'No dream, alas! alas! and woe is mine!
Porphyro will leave me here to fade and pine.—
Cruel! what traitor could thee hither bring?
I curse not, for my heart is lost in thine,
Though thou forsakest a deceived thing;—
A dove forlorn and lost with sick unpruned wing.'

XXXVIII

'My Madeline! sweet dreamer! lovely bride!
Say, may I be for aye thy vassal blest?
Thy beauty's shield, heart-shap'd and vermeil dyed?
Ah, silver shrine, here will I take my rest
After so many hours of toil and quest,
A famish'd pilgrim,—saved by miracle.
Though I have found, I will not rob thy nest
Saving of thy sweet self; if thou think'st well
To trust, fair Madeline, to no rude infidel.

XXXIX

'Hark! 'tis an elfin-storm from faery land,
Of haggard seeming, but a boon indeed:
Arise—arise! the morning is at hand;—
The bloated wassaillers will never heed:—
Let us away, my love, with happy speed;
There are no ears to hear, or eyes to see,—
Drown'd all in Rhenish and the sleepy mead:
Awake! arise! my love, and fearless be,
For o'er the southern moors I have a home for thee.'

XL

She hurried at his words, beset with fears,
For there were sleeping dragons all around,
At glaring watch, perhaps, with ready spears—
Down the wide stairs a darkling way they found.—
In all the house was heard no human sound.
A chain-droop'd lamp was flickering by each door;
The arras, rich with horseman, hawk, and hound,
Flutter'd in the besieging wind's uproar;
And the long carpets rose along the gusty floor.

XLI

They glide, like phantoms, into the wide hall;
Like phantoms, to the iron porch, they glide;
Where lay the Porter, in uneasy sprawl,
With a huge empty flaggon by his side:
The wakeful bloodhound rose, and shook his hide,
But his sagacious eye an inmate owns:
By one, and one, the bolts full easy slide:—
The chains lie silent on the footworn stones;—
The key turns, and the door upon its hinges groans.

XLII

And they are gone: ay, ages long ago
These lovers fled away into the storm.
That night the Baron dreamt of many a woe,
And all his warrior-guests, with shade and form
Of witch, and demon, and large coffin-worm,
Were long be-nightmar'd. Angela the old
Died palsy-twich'd, with meagre face deform;
The Beadsman, after thousand aves told,
For aye unsought for slept among his ashes cold.

213   Ode to a Nightingale

1

My heart aches, and a drowsy numbness pains
    My sense, as though of hemlock I had drunk,
Or emptied some dull opiate to the drains
    One minute past, and Lethe-wards had sunk:
'Tis not through envy of thy happy lot,
    But being too happy in thy happiness,—
        That thou, light-winged Dryad of the trees,
            In some melodious plot
    Of beechen green, and shadows numberless,
        Singest of summer in full-throated ease.

2

O for a draught of vintage! that hath been
    Cool'd a long age in the deep-delved earth,
Tasting of Flora and the country green,
    Dance, and Provençal song, and sunburnt mirth!

O for a beaker full of the warm South,
  Full of the true, the blushful Hippocrene,
    With beaded bubbles winking at the brim,
      And purple-stained mouth;
  That I might drink, and leave the world unseen,
    And with thee fade away into the forest dim:

3

Fade far away, dissolve, and quite forget
  What thou among the leaves hast never known,
The weariness, the fever, and the fret
  Here, where men sit and hear each other groan;
Where palsy shakes a few, sad, last gray hairs,
    Where youth grows pale, and spectre-thin, and dies;
      Where but to think is to be full of sorrow
        And leaden-eyed despairs,
  Where Beauty cannot keep her lustrous eyes,
    Or new Love pine at them beyond to-morrow.

4

Away! away! for I will fly to thee,
  Not charioted by Bacchus and his pards,
But on the viewless wings of Poesy,
  Though the dull brain perplexes and retards:
Already with thee! tender is the night,
    And haply the Queen-Moon is on her throne,
      Cluster'd around by all her starry Fays;
        But here there is no light,
Save what from heaven is with the breezes blown
    Through verdurous glooms and winding mossy ways.

5

I cannot see what flowers are at my feet,
   Nor what soft incense hangs upon the boughs,
But, in embalmed darkness, guess each sweet
   Wherewith the seasonable month endows
The grass, the thicket, and the fruit-tree wild;
   White hawthorn, and the pastoral eglantine;
     Fast fading violets cover'd up in leaves;
       And mid-May's eldest child,
The coming musk-rose, full of dewy wine,
     The murmurous haunt of flies on summer eves.

6

Darkling I listen; and, for many a time
   I have been half in love with easeful Death,
Call'd him soft names in many a mused rhyme,
   To take into the air my quiet breath;
Now more than ever seems it rich to die,
   To cease upon the midnight with no pain,
     While thou art pouring forth thy soul abroad
       In such an ecstasy!
Still wouldst thou sing, and I have ears in vain—
   To thy high requiem become a sod.

7

Thou wast not born for death, immortal Bird!
   No hungry generations tread thee down;
The voice I hear this passing night was heard
   In ancient days by emperor and clown:
Perhaps the self-same song that found a path
   Through the sad heart of Ruth, when, sick for home,
     She stood in tears amid the alien corn;
       The same that oft-times hath
Charm'd magic casements, opening on the foam
   Of perilous seas, in faery lands forlorn.

8

Forlorn! the very word is like a bell
　　To toll me back from thee to my sole self!
Adieu! the fancy cannot cheat so well
　　As she is fam'd to do, deceiving elf.
Adieu! adieu! thy plaintive anthem fades
　　Past the near meadows, over the still stream,
　　　Up the hill-side; and now 'tis buried deep
　　　　In the next valley-glades:
　　Was it a vision, or a waking dream?
　　Fled is that music:—Do I wake or sleep?

214　　　　　　Ode on a Grecian Urn

1

THOU still unravish'd bride of quietness,
　　Thou foster-child of silence and slow time,
Sylvan historian, who canst thus express
　　A flowery tale more sweetly than our rhyme:
What leaf-fring'd legend haunts about thy shape
　　Of deities or mortals, or of both,
　　　In Tempe or the dales of Arcady?
　　What men or gods are these? What maidens loath?
What mad pursuit? What struggle to escape?
　　　What pipes and timbrels? What wild ecstasy?

2

Heard melodies are sweet, but those unheard
　　Are sweeter; therefore, ye soft pipes, play on;
Not to the sensual ear, but, more endear'd,
　　Pipe to the spirit ditties of no tone:

Fair youth, beneath the trees, thou canst not leave
  Thy song, nor ever can those trees be bare;
    Bold Lover, never, never canst thou kiss,
Though winning near the goal—yet, do not grieve;
  She cannot fade, though thou hast not thy bliss,
    For ever wilt thou love, and she be fair!

3

Ah, happy, happy boughs! that cannot shed
  Your leaves, nor ever bid the Spring adieu;
And, happy melodist, unwearied,
  For ever piping songs for ever new;
More happy love! more happy, happy love!
  For ever warm and still to be enjoy'd,
    For ever panting, and for ever young;
All breathing human passion far above,
  That leaves a heart high-sorrowful and cloy'd,
    A burning forehead, and a parching tongue.

4

Who are these coming to the sacrifice?
  To what green altar, O mysterious priest,
Lead'st thou that heifer lowing at the skies,
  And all her silken flanks with garlands drest?
What little town by river or sea shore,
  Or mountain-built with peaceful citadel,
  Is emptied of this folk, this pious morn?
And, little town, thy streets for evermore
  Will silent be; and not a soul to tell
    Why thou art desolate, can e'er return.

5

O Attic shape! Fair attitude! with brede
　　Of marble men and maidens overwrought,
With forest branches and the trodden weed;
　　Thou, silent form, dost tease us out of thought
As doth eternity: Cold Pastoral!
　　When old age shall this generation waste,
　　　　Thou shalt remain, in midst of other woe
Than ours, a friend to man, to whom thou say'st,
　　'Beauty is truth, truth beauty,'—that is all
　　　　Ye know on earth, and all ye need to know.

215　　　　　　　　Ode to Psyche

O GODDESS! hear these tuneless numbers, wrung
　　By sweet enforcement and remembrance dear,
And pardon that thy secrets should be sung
　　Even into thine own soft-conched ear:
Surely I dreamt to-day, or did I see
　　The winged Psyche with awaken'd eyes?
I wander'd in a forest thoughtlessly,
　　And, on the sudden, fainting with surprise,
Saw two fair creatures, couched side by side
　　In deepest grass, beneath the whisp'ring roof
　　Of leaves and trembled blossoms, where there ran
　　　　　　A brooklet, scarce espied:

'Mid hush'd, cool-rooted flowers, fragrant-eyed,
　　Blue, silver-white, and budded Tyrian,
They lay calm-breathing on the bedded grass;
　　Their arms embraced, and their pinions too;
　　Their lips touch'd not, but had not bade adieu,

As if disjoined by soft-handed slumber,
And ready still past kisses to outnumber
   At tender eye-dawn of aurorean love:
      The winged boy I knew;
   But who wast thou, O happy, happy dove?
      His Psyche true!

O latest born and loveliest vision far
   Of all Olympus' faded hierarchy!
Fairer than Phœbe's sapphire-region'd star,
   Or Vesper, amorous glow-worm of the sky;
Fairer than these, though temple thou hast none,
      Nor altar heap'd with flowers;
Nor virgin-choir to make delicious moan
      Upon the midnight hours;
No voice, no lute, no pipe, no incense sweet
   From chain-swung censer teeming;
No shrine, no grove, no oracle, no heat
   Of pale-mouth'd prophet dreaming.

O brightest! though too late for antique vows,
   Too, too late for the fond believing lyre,
When holy were the haunted forest boughs,
   Holy the air, the water, and the fire;
Yet even in these days so far retir'd
   From happy pieties, thy lucent fans,
      Fluttering among the faint Olympians,
I see, and sing, by my own eyes inspir'd.
So let me be thy choir, and make a moan
      Upon the midnight hours;
Thy voice, thy lute, thy pipe, thy incense sweet
   From swinged censer teeming;
Thy shrine, thy grove, thy oracle, thy heat
   Of pale-mouth'd prophet dreaming.

Yes, I will be thy priest, and build a fane
  In some untrodden region of my mind,
Where branched thoughts, new grown with pleasant pain,
  Instead of pines shall murmur in the wind:
Far, far around shall those dark-cluster'd trees
  Fledge the wild-ridged mountains steep by steep;
And there by zephyrs, streams, and birds, and bees,
  The moss-lain Dryads shall be lull'd to sleep;
And in the midst of this wide quietness
A rosy sanctuary will I dress
With the wreath'd trellis of a working brain,
  With buds, and bells, and stars without a name,
With all the gardener Fancy e'er could feign,
  Who breeding flowers, will never breed the same:
And there shall be for thee all soft delight
  That shadowy thought can win,
A bright torch, and a casement ope at night,
  To let the warm Love in!

216   To Autumn

I

SEASON of mists and mellow fruitfulness,
  Close bosom-friend of the maturing sun;
Conspiring with him how to load and bless
  With fruit the vines that round the thatch-eves run;
To bend with apples the moss'd cottage-trees,
  And fill all fruit with ripeness to the core;
    To swell the gourd, and plump the hazel shells
  With a sweet kernel; to set budding more,
And still more, later flowers for the bees,
Until they think warm days will never cease,
    For Summer has o'er-brimm'd their clammy cells.

2

Who hath not seen thee oft amid thy store?
　　Sometimes whoever seeks abroad may find
Thee sitting careless on a granary floor,
　　Thy hair soft-lifted by the winnowing wind;
Or on a half-reap'd furrow sound asleep,
　　Drows'd with the fume of poppies, while thy hook
　　　　Spares the next swath and all its twined flowers:
And sometimes like a gleaner thou dost keep
　　Steady thy laden head across a brook;
　　Or by a cyder-press, with patient look,
　　　　Thou watchest the last oozings hours by hours.

3

Where are the songs of Spring? Ay, where are they?
　　Think not of them, thou hast thy music too,—
While barred clouds bloom the soft-dying day,
　　And touch the stubble-plains with rosy hue;
Then in a wailful choir the small gnats mourn
　　Among the river sallows, borne aloft
　　　　Or sinking as the light wind lives or dies;
And full-grown lambs loud bleat from hilly bourn;
　　Hedge-crickets sing; and now with treble soft
　　The red-breast whistles from a garden croft;
　　　　And gathering swallows twitter in the skies.

217　　　　　　Ode on Melancholy

1

No, no, go not to Lethe, neither twist
　　Wolf's-bane, tight-rooted, for its poisonous wine;
Nor suffer thy pale forehead to be kiss'd
　　By nightshade, ruby grape of Proserpine;

Make not your rosary of yew-berries,
  Nor let the beetle, nor the death-moth be
    Your mournful Psyche, nor the downy owl
A partner in your sorrow's mysteries;
  For shade to shade will come too drowsily,
    And drown the wakeful anguish of the soul.

2

But when the melancholy fit shall fall
  Sudden from heaven like a weeping cloud,
That fosters the droop-headed flowers all,
  And hides the green hill in an April shroud;
Then glut thy sorrow on a morning rose,
  Or on the rainbow of the salt sand-wave,
    Or on the wealth of globed peonies;
Or if thy mistress some rich anger shows,
  Emprison her soft hand, and let her rave,
    And feed deep, deep upon her peerless eyes.

3

She dwells with Beauty—Beauty that must die;
  And Joy, whose hand is ever at his lips
Bidding adieu; and aching Pleasure nigh,
  Turning to poison while the bee-mouth sips:
Ay, in the very temple of Delight
  Veil'd Melancholy has her sovran shrine,
    Though seen of none save him whose strenuous tongue
  Can burst Joy's grape against his palate fine;
His soul shall taste the sadness of her might,
    And be among her cloudy trophies hung.

'HYPERION'

A FRAGMENT

from BOOK I

[SATURN]

DEEP in the shady sadness of a vale
Far sunken from the healthy breath of morn,
Far from the fiery noon, and eve's one star,
Sat gray-hair'd Saturn, quiet as a stone,
Still as the silence round about his lair;
Forest on forest hung about his head
Like cloud on cloud. No stir of air was there,
Not so much life as on a summer's day
Robs not one light seed from the feather'd grass,
But where the dead leaf fell, there did it rest.
A stream went voiceless by, still deadened more
By reason of his fallen divinity
Spreading a shade: the Naiad 'mid her reeds
Press'd her cold finger closer to her lips.

Along the margin-sand large foot-marks went,
No further than to where his feet had stray'd,
And slept there since. Upon the sodden ground
His old right hand lay nerveless, listless, dead,
Unsceptred; and his realmless eyes were closed;
While his bow'd head seem'd list'ning to the Earth,
His ancient mother, for some comfort yet.

It seem'd no force could wake him from his place;
But there came one, who with a kindred hand
Touch'd his wide shoulders, after bending low
With reverence, though to one who knew it not.

She was a Goddess of the infant world;
By her in stature the tall Amazon
Had stood a pigmy's height: she would have ta'en
Achilles by the hair and bent his neck;
Or with a finger stay'd Ixion's wheel.
Her face was large as that of Memphian sphinx,
Pedestal'd haply in a palace court,
When sages look'd to Egypt for their lore.
But oh! how unlike marble was that face:
How beautiful, if sorrow had not made
Sorrow more beautiful than Beauty's self.
There was a listening fear in her regard,
As if calamity had but begun;
As if the vanward clouds of evil days
Had spent their malice, and the sullen rear
Was with its stored thunder labouring up.
One hand she press'd upon that aching spot
Where beats the human heart, as if just there,
Though an immortal, she felt cruel pain:
The other upon Saturn's bended neck
She laid, and to the level of his ear
Leaning with parted lips, some words she spake
In solemn tenour and deep organ tone:
Some mourning words, which in our feeble tongue
Would come in these like accents; O how frail
To that large utterance of the early Gods!
'Saturn, look up!—though wherefore, poor old King?
I have no comfort for thee, no not one:
I cannot say, "O wherefore sleepest thou?"
For heaven is parted from thee, and the earth
Knows thee not, thus afflicted, for a God;
And ocean too, with all its solemn noise,
Has from thy sceptre pass'd; and all the air
Is emptied of thine hoary majesty.

Thy thunder, conscious of the new command,
Rumbles reluctant o'er our fallen house;
And thy sharp lightning in unpractised hands
Scorches and burns our once serene domain.
O aching time! O moments big as years!
All as ye pass swell out the monstrous truth,
And press it so upon our weary griefs
That unbelief has not a space to breathe.
Saturn, sleep on:—O thoughtless, why did I
Thus violate thy slumbrous solitude?
Why should I ope thy melancholy eyes?
Saturn, sleep on! while at thy feet I weep.'

As when, upon a tranced summer-night,
Those green-rob'd senators of mighty woods,
Tall oaks, branch-charmed by the earnest stars,
Dream, and so dream all night without a stir,
Save from one gradual solitary gust
Which comes upon the silence, and dies off,
As if the ebbing air had but one wave;
So came these words and went; the while in tears
She touch'd her fair large forehead to the ground,
Just where her falling hair might be outspread
A soft and silken mat for Saturn's feet.
One moon, with alteration slow, had shed
Her silver seasons four upon the night,
And still these two were postured motionless,
Like natural sculpture in cathedral cavern;
The frozen God still couchant on the earth,
And the sad Goddess weeping at his feet:
Until at length old Saturn lifted up
His faded eyes, and saw his kingdom gone,
And all the gloom and sorrow of the place,
And that fair kneeling Goddess . . .

from BOOK II

['THE BRUISED TITANS']

JUST at the self-same beat of Time's wide wings
Hyperion slid into the rustled air,
And Saturn gain'd with Thea that sad place
Where Cybele and the bruised Titans mourn'd.
It was a den where no insulting light
Could glimmer on their tears; where their own groans
They felt, but heard not, for the solid roar
Of thunderous waterfalls and torrents hoarse,
Pouring a constant bulk, uncertain where.
Crag jutting forth to crag, and rocks that seem'd
Ever as if just rising from a sleep,
Forehead to forehead held their monstrous horns;
And thus in thousand hugest phantasies
Made a fit roofing to this nest of woe.
Instead of thrones, hard flint they sat upon,
Couches of rugged stone, and slaty ridge
Stubborn'd with iron. All were not assembled:
Some chain'd in torture, and some wandering.
Coeus, and Gyges, and Briareüs,
Typhon, and Dolor, and Porphyrion,
With many more, the brawniest in assault,
Were pent in regions of laborious breath;
Dungeon'd in opaque element, to keep
Their clenched teeth still clench'd, and all their limbs
Lock'd up like veins of metal, crampt and screw'd;
Without a motion, save of their big hearts
Heaving in pain, and horribly convuls'd
With sanguine feverous boiling gurge of pulse.
Mnemosyne was straying in the world;
Far from her moon had Phœbe wandered;

And many else were free to roam abroad,
But for the main, here found they covert drear.

Scarce images of life, one here, one there,
Lay vast and edgeways; like a dismal cirque
Of Druid stones, upon a forlorn moor,
When the chill rain begins at shut of eve,
In dull November, and their chancel vault,
The Heaven itself, is blinded throughout night.
Each one kept shroud, nor to his neighbour gave
Or word, or look, or action of despair.
Creüs was one; his ponderous iron mace
Lay by him, and a shatter'd rib of rock
Told of his rage, ere he thus sank and pined.
Iäpetus another; in his grasp,
A serpent's plashy neck, its barbed tongue
Squeez'd from the gorge, and all its uncurl'd length
Dead; and because the creature could not spit
Its poison in the eyes of conquering Jove.
Next Cottus: prone he lay, chin uppermost,
As though in pain; for still upon the flint
He ground severe his skull, with open mouth
And eyes at horrid working. Nearest him
Asia, born of most enormous Caf,
Who cost her mother Tellus keener pangs,
Though feminine, than any of her sons:
More thought than woe was in her dusky face,
For she was prophesying of her glory;
And in her wide imagination stood
Palm-shaded temples, and high rival fanes,
By Oxus or in Ganges' sacred isles.
Even as Hope upon her anchor leans,
So leant she, not so fair, upon a tusk

Shed from the broadest of her elephants.
Above her, on a crag's uneasy shelve,
Upon his elbow rais'd, all prostrate else,
Shadow'd Enceladus; once tame and mild
As grazing ox unworried in the meads;
Now tiger-passion'd, lion-thoughted, wroth,
He meditated, plotted, and even now
Was hurling mountains in that second war,
Not long delay'd, that scar'd the younger Gods
To hide themselves in forms of beast and bird.
Nor far hence Atlas; and beside him prone
Phorcus, the sire of Gorgons. Neighbour'd close
Oceanus, and Tethys, in whose lap
Sobb'd Clymene among her tangled hair.
In midst of all lay Themis, at the feet
Of Ops the queen all clouded round from sight;
No shape distinguishable, more than when
Thick night confounds the pine-tops with the clouds:
And many else whose names may not be told.

220   [Sonnet]

Jan. 1817

AFTER dark vapours have oppress'd our plains
   For a long dreary season, comes a day
   Born of the gentle South, and clears away
From the sick heavens all unseemly stains.
The anxious month, relieved from its pains,
   Takes as a long-lost right the feel of May;
   The eyelids with the passing coolness play
Like rose leaves with the drip of summer rains.

And calmest thoughts come round us; as, of leaves
 Budding,—fruit ripening in stillness,—autumn suns
Smiling at eve upon the quiet sheaves,—
Sweet Sappho's cheek,—a smiling infant's breath,—
 The gradual sand that through an hour-glass runs,—
A woodland rivulet,—a Poet's death.

221   Modern Love

AND what is love? It is a doll dress'd up
For idleness to cosset, nurse, and dandle;
A thing of soft misnomers, so divine
That silly youth doth think to make itself
Divine by loving, and so goes on
Yawning and doting a whole summer long,
Till Miss's comb is made a pearl tiara,
And common Wellingtons turn Romeo boots;
Then Cleopatra lives at number seven,
And Antony resides in Brunswick Square.
Fools! if some passions high have warm'd the world,
If Queens and Soldiers have play'd deep for hearts,
It is no reason why such agonies
Should be more common than the growth of weeds.
Fools! make me whole again that weighty pearl
The Queen of Egypt melted, and I'll say
That ye may love in spite of beaver hats.

222   [Sonnet]

             1817

WHEN I have fears that I may cease to be
 Before my pen has glean'd my teeming brain,
Before high-piled books, in charact'ry,
 Hold like rich garners the full-ripen'd grain;

When I behold, upon the night's starr'd face,
  Huge cloudy symbols of a high romance,
And think that I may never live to trace
  Their shadows, with the magic hand of chance;
And when I feel, fair creature of an hour!
  That I shall never look upon thee more,
Never have relish in the faery power
  Of unreflecting love!—then on the shore
Of the wide world I stand alone, and think
Till Love and Fame to nothingness do sink.

223   [Epistle to John Hamilton Reynolds]

Teignmouth
25 March 1818

DEAR Reynolds! as last night I lay in bed,
There came before my eyes that wonted thread
Of shapes, and shadows, and remembrances,
That every other minute vex and please:
Things all disjointed come from north and south,—
Two Witch's eyes above a Cherub's mouth,
Voltaire with casque and shield and havergeon,
And Alexander with his nightcap on;
Old Socrates a-tying his cravat,
And Hazlitt playing with Miss Edgeworth's Cat;
And Junius Brutus, pretty well, so so,
Making the best of 's way towards Soho.

Few are there who escape these visitings,—
Perhaps one or two whose lives have patent wings,
And thro' whose curtains peeps no hellish nose,
No wild-boar tushes, and no Mermaid's toes;

But flowers bursting out with lusty pride,
And young Æolian harps personified;
Some Titian colours touch'd into real life,—
The sacrifice goes on; the pontiff knife
Gleams in the Sun, the milk-white heifer lows,
The pipes go shrilly, the libation flows:
A white sail shows above the green-head cliff,
Moves round the point, and throws her anchor stiff;
The mariners join hymn with those on land.

You know the enchanted Castle,—it doth stand
Upon a rock, on the border of a Lake,
Nested in trees, which all do seem to shake
From some old magic-like Urganda's Sword.
O Phœbus! that I had thy sacred word
To show this Castle, in fair dreaming wise,
Unto my friend, while sick and ill he lies!

You know it well enough, where it doth seem
A mossy place, a Merlin's Hall, a dream;
You know the clear Lake, and the little Isles,
The mountains blue, and cold near neighbour rills,
All which elsewhere are but half animate;
There do they look alive to love and hate,
To smiles and frowns; they seem a lifted mound
Above some giant, pulsing underground.

Part of the Building was a chosen See,
Built by a banished Santon of Chaldee;
The other part, two thousand years from him,
Was built by Cuthbert de Saint Aldebrim;
Then there's a little wing, far from the Sun,
Built by a Lapland Witch turn'd maudlin Nun;
And many other juts of aged stone
Founded with many a mason-devil's groan.

The doors all look as if they oped themselves,
The windows as if latched by Fays and Elves,
And from them comes a silver flash of light,
As from the westward of a Summer's night;
Or like a beauteous woman's large blue eyes
Gone mad thro' olden songs and poesies.

See! what is coming from the distance dim!
A golden Galley all in silken trim!
Three rows of oars are lightening, moment whiles,
Into the verd'rous bosoms of those isles;
Towards the shade, under the Castle wall,
It comes in silence,—now 'tis hidden all.

The Clarion sounds, and from a Postern-gate
An echo of sweet music doth create
A fear in the poor Herdsman, who doth bring
His beasts to trouble the enchanted spring,—
He tells of the sweet music, and the spot,
To all his friends, and they believe him not.

O, that our dreamings all, of sleep or wake,
Would all their colours from the sunset take:
From something of material sublime,
Rather than shadow our own soul's day-time
In the dark void of night. For in the world
We jostle,—but my flag is not unfurl'd
On the Admiral-staff,—and so philosophise
I dare not yet! Oh, never will the prize,
High reason, and the love of good and ill,
Be my award! Things cannot to the will
Be settled, but they tease us out of thought;
Or is it that imagination brought

Beyond its proper bound, yet still confin'd,
Lost in a sort of Purgatory blind,
Cannot refer to any standard law
Of either earth or heaven? It is a flaw
In happiness, to see beyond our bourn,—
It forces us in summer skies to mourn,
It spoils the singing of the Nightingale.

Dear Reynolds! I have a mysterious tale,—
And cannot speak it: the first page I read
Upon a Lampit-rock of green sea-weed
Among the breakers; 'twas a quiet eve,
The rocks were silent, the wide sea did wave
An untumultuous fringe of silver foam
Along the flat brown sand; I was at home
And should have been most happy,—but I saw
Too far into the sea, where every maw
The greater on the less feeds evermore;—
But I saw too distinct into the core
Of an eternal fierce destruction,—
And so from happiness I far was gone.
Still am I sick of it, and tho', to-day,
I've gather'd young spring-leaves, and flowers gay
Of periwinkle and wild strawberry,
Still do I that most fierce destruction see,—
The Shark at savage prey,—the Hawk at pounce,—
The gentle Robin, like a Pard or Ounce,
Ravening a Worm,—Away, ye horrid moods!
Moods of one's mind! You know I hate them well,
You know I'd sooner be a clapping Bell
To some Kamtschatkan Missionary Church,
Than with these horrid moods be left i' the lurch.

224   ## To Ailsa Rock

HEARKEN, thou craggy ocean pyramid!
  Give answer from thy voice, the sea-fowl's screams!
  When were thy shoulders mantled in huge streams?
When, from the sun, was thy broad forehead hid?
How long is't since the mighty power bid
  Thee heave to airy sleep from fathom dreams?
  Sleep in the lap of thunder or sun-beams,
Or when grey clouds are thy cold cover-lid?
Thou answer'st not, for thou art dead asleep;
  Thy life is but two dead eternities—
The last in air, the former in the deep;
  First with the whales, last with the eagle-skies—
Drown'd wast thou till an earthquake made thee steep,
  Another cannot wake thy giant size.

225   ## Stanzas

IN a drear-nighted December,
Too happy, happy tree,
Thy branches ne'er remember
Their green felicity:
The north cannot undo them,
With a sleety whistle through them;
Nor frozen thawings glue them
From budding at the prime.

In a drear-nighted December,
Too happy, happy brook,
Thy bubblings ne'er remember
Apollo's summer look;

But with a sweet forgetting,
They stay their crystal fretting,
Never, never petting
About the frozen time.

Ah! would 'twere so with many
A gentle girl and boy!
But were there ever any
Writhed not at passed joy?
To know the change and feel it,
When there is none to heal it,
Nor numbed sense to steel it,
Was never said in rhyme.

226

Ode on Indolence

1819

'They toil not, neither do they spin'.

I

ONE morn before me were three figures seen,
   With bowed necks, and joined hands, side-faced;
And one behind the other stepp'd serene,
   In placid sandals, and in white robes graced;
     They pass'd, like figures on a marble urn,
   When shifted round to see the other side;
They came again; as when the urn once more
     Is shifted round, the first seen shades return;
   And they were strange to me, as may betide
With vases, to one deep in Phidian lore.

II

How is it, Shadows! that I knew ye not?
  How came ye muffled in so hush a mask?
Was it a silent deep-disguised plot
  To steal away, and leave without a task
    My idle days? Ripe was the drowsy hour;
  The blissful cloud of summer-indolence
Benumb'd my eyes; my pulse grew less and less;
    Pain had no sting, and pleasure's wreath no flower:
  O, why did ye not melt, and leave my sense
Unhaunted quite of all but—nothingness?

III

A third time pass'd they by, and, passing, turn'd
  Each one the face a moment whiles to me;
Then faded, and to follow them I burn'd
  And ached for wings, because I knew the three;
    The first was a fair Maid, and Love her name;
  The second was Ambition, pale of cheek,
And ever watchful with fatigued eye;
    The last, whom I love more, the more of blame
  Is heap'd upon her, maiden most unmeek,—
I knew to be my demon Poesy.

IV

They faded, and, forsooth! I wanted wings:
  O folly! What is Love? and where is it?
And for that poor Ambition! it springs
  From a man's little heart's short fever-fit;
    For Poesy!—no,—she has not a joy,—
  At least for me,—so sweet as drowsy noons,
And evenings steep'd in honied indolence;
    O, for an age so shelter'd from annoy,
  That I may never know how change the moons,
Or hear the voice of busy common-sense!

V

And once more came they by;—alas! wherefore?
  My sleep had been embroider'd with dim dreams;
My soul had been a lawn besprinkled o'er
    With flowers, and stirring shades, and baffled beams:
      The morn was clouded, but no shower fell,
      Tho' in her lids hung the sweet tears of May;
The open casement press'd a new-leaved vine,
    Let in the budding warmth and throstle's lay;
      O Shadows! 'twas a time to bid farewell!
Upon your skirts had fallen no tears of mine.

VI

So, ye three Ghosts, adieu! Ye cannot raise
  My head cool-bedded in the flowery grass;
For I would not be dieted with praise,
    A pet-lamb in a sentimental farce!
      Fade softly from my eyes, and be once more
In masque-like figures on the dreamy urn;
Farewell! I yet have visions for the night,
    And for the day faint visions there is store;
Vanish, ye Phantoms! from my idle spright,
    Into the clouds, and never more return!

227   La Belle Dame Sans Merci

I

O WHAT can ail thee, knight-at-arms,
  Alone and palely loitering?
The sedge has wither'd from the lake,
  And no birds sing.

II

O what can ail thee, knight-at-arms,
  So haggard and so woe-begone?
The squirrel's granary is full,
  And the harvest's done.

III

I see a lily on thy brow
  With anguish moist and fever dew,
And on thy cheek a fading rose
  Fast withereth too.

IV

I met a lady in the meads,
  Full beautiful, a faery's child,
Her hair was long, her foot was light,
  And her eyes were wild.

V

I made a garland for her head,
  And bracelets too, and fragrant zone;
She look'd at me as she did love,
  And made sweet moan.

VI

I set her on my pacing steed,
  And nothing else saw all day long,
For sideways would she bend, and sing
  A faery's song.

VII

She found me roots of relish sweet,
  And honey wild, and manna dew,
And sure in language strange she said—
  'I love thee true!'

VIII

She took me to her elfin grot,
 And there she wept and sigh'd full sore,
And there I shut her wild wild eyes
 With kisses four.

IX

And there she lulled me asleep,
 And there I dream'd—Ah! woe betide!
The latest dream I ever dream'd
 On the cold hill's side.

X

I saw pale kings and princes too,
 Pale warriors, death-pale were they all;
Who cried—'La Belle Dame sans Merci
 Hath thee in thrall!'

XI

I saw their starved lips in the gloam,
 With horrid warning gaped wide,
And I awoke and found me here,
 On the cold hill's side.

XII

And this is why I sojourn here,
 Alone and palely loitering,
Though the sedge is wither'd from the lake,
 And no birds sing.

from 'THE FALL OF HYPERION'

A Dream

METHOUGHT I stood where trees of every clime,
Palm, myrtle, oak, and sycamore, and beech,
With plantain and spice-blossoms, made a screen,
In neighbourhood of fountains (by the noise
Soft-showering in my ears,) and (by the touch
Of scent) not far from roses. Twining round
I saw an arbour with a drooping roof
Of trellis vines, and bells, and larger blooms,
Like floral censers, swinging light in air;
Before its wreathed doorway, on a mound
Of moss, was spread a feast of summer fruits,
Which, nearer seen, seem'd refuse of a meal
By angel tasted or our Mother Eve;
For empty shells were scattered on the grass,
And grape-stalks but half-bare, and remnants more
Sweet-smelling, whose pure kinds I could not know.
Still was more plenty than the fabled horn
Thrice emptied could pour forth, at banqueting
For Proserpine return'd to her own fields,
Where the white heifers low. And appetite
More yearning than on Earth I ever felt
Growing within, I ate deliciously;
And, after not long, thirsted, for thereby
Stood a cool vessel of transparent juice
Sipp'd by the wander'd bee, the which I took,
And pledging all the mortals of the world,
And all the dead whose names are in our lips,
Drank. That full draught is parent of my theme.
No Asian poppy nor elixir fine

Of the soon-fading jealous Caliphat;
No poison gender'd in close monkish cell,
To thin the scarlet conclave of old men,
Could so have rapt unwilling life away.
Among the fragrant husks and berries crush'd
Upon the grass I struggled hard against
The domineering potion; but in vain:
The cloudy swoon came on, and down I sank,
Like a Silenus on an antique vase.
How long I slumber'd 'tis a chance to guess.
When sense of life return'd, I started up
As if with wings; but the fair trees were gone,
The mossy mound and arbour were no more:
I look'd around upon the carved sides
Of an old sanctuary with roof august,
Builded so high, it seem'd that filmed clouds
Might spread beneath, as o'er the stars of heaven;
So old the place was, I remember'd none
The like upon the Earth: what I had seen
Of grey cathedrals, buttress'd walls, rent towers,
The superannuations of sunk realms,
Or Nature's rocks toil'd hard in waves and winds,
Seem'd but the faulture of decrepit things
To that eternal domed Monument.
Upon the marble at my feet there lay
Store of strange vessels and large draperies,
Which needs had been of dyed asbestos wove,
Or in that place the moth could not corrupt,
So white the linen, so, in some, distinct
Ran imageries from a sombre loom.
All in a mingled heap confus'd there lay
Robes, golden tongs, censer and chafing-dish,
Girdles, and chains, and holy jewelries.

Turning from these with awe, once more I rais'd
My eyes to fathom the space every way;
The embossed roof, the silent massy range
Of columns north and south, ending in mist
Of nothing, then to eastward, where black gates
Were shut against the sunrise evermore.—
Then to the west I look'd, and saw far off
An image, huge of feature as a cloud,
At level of whose feet an altar slept,
To be approach'd on either side by steps
And marble balustrade, and patient travail
To count with toil the innumerable degrees.
Towards the altar sober-paced I went,
Repressing haste, as too unholy there;
And, coming nearer, saw beside the shrine
One minist'ring; and there arose a flame.—
When in mid-way the sickening east-wind
Shifts sudden to the south, the small warm rain
Melts out the frozen incense from all flowers,
And fills the air with so much pleasant health
That even the dying man forgets his shroud;—
Even so that lofty sacrificial fire,
Sending forth Maian incense, spread around
Forgetfulness of everything but bliss,
And clouded all the altar with soft smoke;
From whose white fragrant curtains thus I heard
Language pronounc'd: 'If thou canst not ascend
These steps, die on that marble where thou art.
Thy flesh, near cousin to the common dust,
Will parch for lack of nutriment—thy bones
Will wither in few years, and vanish so
That not the quickest eye could find a grain
Of what thou now art on that pavement cold.
The sands of thy short life are spent this hour,

And no hand in the universe can turn
Thy hourglass, if these gummed leaves be burnt
Ere thou canst mount up these immortal steps.'
I heard, I look'd: two senses both at once,
So fine, so subtle, felt the tyranny
Of that fierce threat and the hard task proposed.
Prodigious seem'd the toil; the leaves were yet
Burning—when suddenly a palsied chill
Struck from the paved level up my limbs,
And was ascending quick to put cold grasp
Upon those streams that pulse beside the throat . . .

229 [Lines supposed to have been addressed to
Fanny Brawne]

THIS living hand, now warm and capable
Of earnest grasping, would, if it were cold
And in the icy silence of the tomb,
So haunt thy days and chill thy dreaming nights
That thou would[st] wish thine own heart dry of blood
So in my veins red life might stream again,
And thou be conscience-calm'd—see here it is—
I hold it towards you.

230 Sonnet

[Written on a blank page in Shakespeare's *Poems* facing
'A Lover's Complaint']

BRIGHT star! would I were steadfast as thou art—
    Not in lone splendour hung aloft the night,
And watching, with eternal lids apart,
    Like Nature's patient, sleepless Eremite,

The moving waters at their priestlike task
　　Of pure ablution round earth's human shores,
Or gazing on the new soft fallen mask
　　Of snow upon the mountains and the moors—
No—yet still steadfast, still unchangeable,
　　Pillow'd upon my fair love's ripening breast,
To feel for ever its soft fall and swell,
　　Awake for ever in a sweet unrest,
Still, still to hear her tender-taken breath,
And so live ever—or else swoon to death.

GEORGE DARLEY

231　　['The Enchanted Lyre']

WHEREFORE, unlaurelled Boy!
　　Whom the contemptuous Muse will not inspire,
With a sad kind of joy,
　　Still sing'st thou to thy solitary lyre?

The melancholy winds
　　Pour through unnumber'd reeds their idle woes:
And every Naiad finds
　　A stream to weep her sorrow as it flows.

Her sighs unto the air
　　The wood-maid's native oak doth broadly tell:
And Echo's fond despair
　　Intelligible rocks re-syllable.

Wherefore then should not I,
　　Albeit no haughty Muse my breast inspire,
Fated of grief to die,
　　Impart it to a solitary lyre?

232 The Dove's Loneliness

BREAK not my loneliness, O Wanderer!
There's nothing sweet but Melancholy, here.—
'Mid these dim walks and grassy wynds are seen
No gaudy flowers, undarkening the green:
No wanton bird chirrups from tree to tree,
Not a disturber of the woods but me!
Scarce in a summer doth a wild bee come
To wake my sylvan echo with his hum:
But for my weeping lullaby I have
The everlasting cadence of the wave
That falls in little breakers on the shore,
And rather seems to strive to roar—than roar;
Light Zephyr, too, spreads out his silver wings
On each green leaf, and in a whisper sings
His love to every blossom in her ear,
Too low, too soft, too sweet, for me to hear!
The soul of Peace breathes a wide calm around,
And hallows for her shrine this sacred spot of ground.
   Her bird am I!—and rule the shade for her,
A timid guard, and trembling minister!
My cradling palace hung amid the leaves
Of a wide-swaying beech: a woodbine weaves,
Fine spinster of the groves! my canopy
Of purpling trellis and embroidery:
My pendant chair, lined with the velvet green
That nature clothes her russet children in,
Moss of the silkiest thread: This is my throne,
Here I do sit, queen of the woods, alone!
And as the winds come swooning through the trees,
I join my murmurs to their melodies;
Murmurs of joy,—for I am pleased to find
No visitors more constant than the wind:

My heart beats high at every step you come
Nearer the bosom of my woodland home;
And blame me not, if when you turn away
I wish that to some other scenes you'd stray,
Some brighter, lovelier scenes; these are too sad,
Too still, and deepen into deeper shade.—
See! the gay hillocks on the neighbouring shore,
Nodding their tufted crowns, invite thee o'er;
The daisy winks, and the pale cowslip throws
Her jealous looks ascant—red burns the rose—
Spare hawthorn all her glittering wealth displays,
Stars, blossoms, buds, and hangs them in the blaze,
To lure thine eye—the slope as fresh and sweet,
Spreads her lush carpet to entice thy feet.
Here are but weeds, and a few sorry gems
Scattered upon the straggling woodbine's stems,
Hoar trees and withered fern—Ah, stranger, go:
I would not stay to make thee tremble so!
Were I a man, and thou a little dove,
I would, at thy least prayer, at once remove.
Then, stranger, turn!—and should'st thou hear me coo,
From this deep-bosomed wood, a hoarse adieu—
The secret satisfaction of my mind,
That thou art gone, and I am left behind—
Smile thou, and say Farewell!—The bird of Peace,
Hope, Innocence, and Love, and Loveliness,
Thy sweet Egeria's bird of birds! doth pray
By the name best-beloved, thou'lt wend thy way,
In pity of her pain!—Though I know well
Thou would'st not harm me, I must tremble still:
My heart's the home of fear—Ah! turn thee then,
And leave me to my loneliness again!

233   [Lilian's Song]

HEAR! hear!
How the vale-bells tinkle all around
As the sweet wind shakes them—hear!
   What a wild and sylvan sound!

Hear! hear!
How the soft waves talk beneath the bank!
And rush sighs to willow—hear!
   The reed to the osier dank.

Hear! hear!
How the blue fly hizzes in the air
With his voice in his tiny wings—hear!
   He sings at his flowery fare.

Hear! hear!
How the wood-bird murmurs in the dark,
And the distant cuckoo chimes—hear!
   From the sun-cloud trills the lark.

234   A Song[1]

IT is not Beauty I demand,
   A crystal brow, the moon's despair
Nor the snow's daughter, a white hand,
   Nor mermaid's yellow pride of hair.

[1] [Disguised in archaistic spelling, this song was first printed in *The Literary Gazette* of 12 April 1828 as 'A ryghte pythie Songe by T[homas]. C[arew].' and later included in *The Golden Treasury* (1861) as an anonymous Caroline lyric. Darley's authorship was disclosed posthumously in 1868 by Archbishop Trench.]

Tell me not of your starry eyes,
   Your lips that seem on roses fed,
Your breasts where Cupid tumbling lies,
   Nor sleeps for kissing of his bed.

A bloomy pair of vermeil cheeks,
   Like Hebe's in her ruddiest hours,
A breath that softer music speaks
   Than summer winds a-wooing flowers.

These are but gauds; nay, what are lips?
   Coral beneath the ocean-stream,
Whose brink when your adventurer [s]ips
   Full oft he perisheth on them.

And what are cheeks but ensigns oft
   That wave hot youth to fields of blood?
Did Helen's breast, though ne'er so soft,
   Do Greece or Ilium any good?

Eyes can with baleful ardour burn,
   Poison can breath that erst perfumed,
There's many a white hand holds an urn
   With lovers' hearts to dust consumed.

For crystal brows, there's naught within,
   They are but empty cells for pride;
He who the syren's hair would win
   Is mostly strangled in the tide.

Give me, instead of beauty's bust,
   A tender heart, a loyal mind,
Which with temptation I could trust,
   Yet never linked with error find.

One in whose gentle bosom, I
    Could pour my secret heart of woes,
Like the care-burthened honey-fly
    That hides his murmurs in the rose.

My earthly comforter! whose love
    So indefeasible might be,
That when my spirit won above
    Hers could not stay for sympathy.

from *NEPENTHE*

[1]

235   ['In Dreamy Swoon']

OVER a bloomy land untrod
By heavier foot than bird or bee
Lays on the grassy-bosomed sod,
    I past one day in reverie:
High on his un-pavilioned throne
The heaven's hot tyrant sat alone,
And like the fabled king of old
Was turning all he touched to gold:
The glittering fountains seemed to pour
Steep downward rills of molten ore,
Glassily tinkling smooth between
Broom-shaded banks of golden green,
And o'er the yellow pasture straying
Dallying still yet undelaying,
In hasty trips from side to side
Footing adown their steepy slide

Headlong, impetuously playing
With the flowery border pied,
That edged the rocky mountain stair
They pattered down incessant there,
To lowlands sweet and calm and wide.
With golden lip and glistening bell
Burned every bee-cup on the fell
Whate'er its native un-sunned hue,
Snow white or crimson or cold blue;
Even the black lustres of the sloe
Glanced as they sided to the glow,
And furze in russet frock arrayed
With saffron knots, like shepherd maid,
Broadly tricked out her rough brocade.
The singed mosses curling here,
A golden fleece too short to shear!
Crumbled to sparkling dust beneath
My light step on that sunny heath.

Light!—for the ardor of the clime
Made rare my spirit, that sublime
Bore me as buoyant as young Time
Over the green Earth's grassy prime,
Ere his slouch'd wing caught up her slime;
And sprang I not from clay and crime,
Had from those humming beds of thyme
Lifted me near the starry chime
To learn an empyrean rhyme.

No melody beneath the moon
Sweeter than this deep runnel tune!
Here on the greensward grown hot gray,
Crisp as the unshorn desert hay,

Where his moist pipe the dulcet rill
For humorous grasshopper doth fill,
That spits himself from blade to blade
By long o'er-rest uneasy made;
Here, ere the stream by fountain pushes
Lose himself brightly in the rushes
With butterfly path among the bushes,
I'll lay me, on these mosses brown,
Murmuring beside his murmurs down,
And from the liquid tale he tells
Glean out some broken syllables,
Or close mine eyes in dreamy swoon,
As by hoarse-winding deep Gihoon
Soothes with the hum his idle pain
The melancholy Tartar swain,
Sole mark on that huge-meadowed plain!

[11]

236   ['Hundred-sunned Phenix']

O BLEST unfabled Incense Tree
That burns in glorious Araby,
With red scent chalicing the air
Till earth-life grow Elysian there!

Half buried to her flaming breast
In this bright tree, she makes her nest,
Hundred-sunned Phenix! when she must
Crumble at length to hoary dust!

Her gorgeous death-bed! her rich pyre
Burnt up with aromatic fire!

Her urn, sight high from spoiler men!
Her birthplace when self-born again!

The mountainless green wilds among
Here ends she her unechoing song!
With amber tears and odorous sighs
Mourned by the desert where she dies!

Laid like the young fawn mossily
In sun-green vales of Araby,
I woke, hard by the Phenix tree
That with shadeless boughs flamed over me;
And upward called by a dumb cry
With moonbroad orbs of wonder, I
Beheld the immortal Bird on high
Glassing the great sun in her eye;
Steadfast she gazed upon his fire,
Still her destroyer and her sire!
As if to his her soul of flame
Had flown already, whence it came;
Like those that sit and glare so still,
Intense with their death struggle, till
We touch, and curdle at their chill!—
But breathing yet while she doth burn,
  The deathless Daughter of the sun!
Slowly to crimson embers turn
  The beauties of the brightsome one;
O'er the broad nest her silver wings
Shook down their wasteful glitterings;
Her brinded neck high-arched in air
Like a small rainbow faded there;
But brighter glowed her plumy crown
Mouldering to golden ashes down;

With fume of sweet woods, to the skies,
Pure as a Saint's adoring sighs,
Warm as a prayer in Paradise,
Her life-breath rose in sacrifice!
The while with shrill triumphant tone
Sounding aloud, aloft, alone,
Ceaseless her joyful deathwail she
Sang to departing Araby!

[III]

237   ['Onward to Far Ida']

BRIGHT-haired Spirit! Golden Brow!
Onward to far Ida now!
Leaving these garden lands below
In sea-born dews to steep their glow:
Caria and Lycia, dulcet climes!
Beds of flowers whose odor limes
The o'erflying fast far bird, their thrall
Hovering entranced till he fall;
Broad Meonia's streamy vales
Winding beneath us, white with swans
Borne by their downy-swelling sails;
Each her lucid beauty scans,
Bending her slow beak round, and sees
Her grandeur as she floats along
Gracefully ruffled by the breeze,
And troats for joy, too proud for song:
Leave we the downlands, tho' be there
Joy a lifelong sojourner;
There for ever wildwood numbers

Poured in Doric strains dilute
Thro' the unlaborious flute,
Soothe Disquiet to his slumbers;
In his rosebed sleeps the bee
Lulled by Lydian melody,
Half the honied morn in vain!
Idler still than Doric swain,
Steept in double sweetness he
Hums, as he dreams, his wildwood strain;
The Mysian vineplucker sings i' the tree;
And Ionia's echoing train
Of reapers, bending down the lea,
Make rich the winds with minstrelsy.

[IV]

238

['Hoopoe']

SOLITARY wayfarer!
Minstrel winged of the green wild!
What dost thou delaying here,
Like a wood-bewildered child
Weeping to his far-flown troop,
Whoop! and plaintive whoop! and whoop!
Now from rock and now from tree,
Bird! methinks thou whoop'st to me,
Flitting before me upward still
With clear warble, as I've heard
Oft on my native Northern hill
No less wild and lone a bird,
Luring me with his sweet chee-chee
Up the mountain crags which he
Tript as lightly as a bee,

O'er steep pastures, far among
Thickets, and briary lanes along,
Following still a fleeting song!—
If such my errant nature, I
Vainly to curb or coop it try,
Now that the sundrop thro' my frame,
Kindles another soul of flame!
Whoop on, whoop on, thou canst not wing
Too fast or far, thou well-named thing,
Hoopoe, if of that tribe which sing
Articulate in the desert ring!

[v]

['The Unicorn']

239

Lo! in the mute, mid wilderness,
What wondrous Creature?—of no kind!—
His burning lair doth largely press—
Gaze fixt—and feeding on the wind?
His fell is of the desert dye,
And tissue adust, dun-yellow and dry,
Compact of living sands; his eye
Black luminary, soft and mild,
With its dark lustre cools the wild;
From his stately forehead springs
Piercing to heaven, a radiant horn,—
Lo! the compeer of lion-kings!
The steed self-armed, the Unicorn!
Ever heard of, never seen,
With a main of sands between
Him and approach; his lonely pride
To course his arid arena wide,

Free as the hurricane, or lie here
Lord of his couch as his career!—
Wherefore should this foot profane
His sanctuary, still domain?
Let me turn, ere eye so bland
Perchance be fire-shot, like heaven's brand,
To wither my boldness! Northward now,
Behind the white star on his brow
Glittering straight against the sun,
Far athwart his lair I run.

240   Serenade of a Loyal Martyr

SWEET in her green cell the Flower of Beauty slumbers,
    Lulled by the faint breezes sighing thro' her hair;
Sleeps she, and hears not the melancholy numbers
    Breathed to my sad lute amid the lonely air?

Down from the high cliffs the rivulet is teeming
    To wind round the willow banks that lure him from above:
O that in tears from my rocky prison streaming,
    I too could glide to the bower of my love!

Ah! where the woodbines with sleepy arms have wound her
    Opes she her eyelids at the dream of my lay,
Listening like the dove, while the fountains echo round her,
    To her lost mate's call in the forests far away?

Come, then, my Bird!—for the peace thou ever bearest,
    Still heaven's messenger of comfort to me,
Come!—this fond bosom, my faithfullest! my fairest!
    Bleeds with its death-wound, but deeper yet for thee.

241   The Sea-Ritual

PRAYER unsaid and mass unsung,
Deadman's dirge must still be rung:
    Dingle-dong, the dead-bells sound;
    Mermen chant his dirge around.

Wash him bloodless, smoothe him fair,
Stretch his limbs and sleek his hair:
    Dingle-dong, the dead-bells go;
    Mermen swing them to and fro!

In the wormless sands shall he
Feast for no foul gluttons be:
    Dingle-dong, the dead-bells toll;
    Mermen ring his requiem-knoll!

We must with a tombstone brave
Shut the shark out of his grave:
    Dingle-dong, the dead-bells chime;
    Mermen keep the tune and time!

Such a slab will we lay o'er him,
All the dead shall rise before him:
    Dingle-dong, the dead-bells boom;
    Mermen lay him in his tomb!

242   The Mermaiden's Vesper Hymn

TROOP home to silent grots and caves!
Troop home, and mimic as you go
The mournful winding of the waves,
    Which to their dark abysses flow!

At this sweet hour all things beside
  In amorous pairs to covert creep:
The swans that brush the evening tide,
  Homeward in snowy couples keep.

In his green den the murmuring seal
  Close by his sleek companion lies;
While singly we to bedward steal,
  And close in fruitless sleep our eyes.

In bowers of love men take their rest,
  In loveless bowers we sigh alone,—
With bosom-friends are others blest,
  But we have none! but we have none!

HARTLEY COLERIDGE

243   Sonnet: To a Friend

WHEN we were idlers with the loitering rills,
The need of human love we little noted:
Our love was nature; and the peace that floated
On the white mist, and dwelt upon the hills,
To sweet accord subdued our wayward wills:
One soul was ours, one mind, one heart devoted,
That, wisely doating, ask'd not why it doated,
And ours the unknown joy, which knowing kills.
But now I find, how dear thou wert to me;
That man is more than half of nature's treasure,
Of that fair Beauty which no eye can see,
Of that sweet music which no ear can measure;
And now the streams may sing for others' pleasure,
The hills sleep on in their eternity.

244 ## Sonnet

LONG time a child, and still a child, when years
Had painted manhood on my cheek, was I;
For yet I lived like one not born to die;
A thriftless prodigal of smiles and tears,
No hope I needed, and I knew no fears.
But sleep, though sweet, is only sleep, and waking,
I waked to sleep no more, at once o'ertaking
The vanguard of my age, with all arrears
Of duty on my back. Nor child, nor man,
Nor youth, nor sage, I find my head is grey,
For I have lost the race I never ran,
A rathe December blights my lagging May;
And still I am a child, tho' I be old,
Time is my debtor for my years untold.

245 ## Sonnet: November

THE mellow year is hasting to its close;
The little birds have almost sung their last,
Their small notes twitter in the dreary blast—
That shrill-piped harbinger of early snows:
The patient beauty of the scentless rose,
Oft with the Morn's hoar chrystal quaintly glass'd,
Hangs, a pale mourner for the summer past,
And makes a little summer where it grows:
In the chill sunbeam of the faint brief day
The dusky waters shudder as they shine,
The russet leaves obstruct the straggling way
Of oozy brooks, which no deep banks define,
And the gaunt woods, in ragged, scant array,
Wrap their old limbs with sombre ivy twine.

Poietes Apoietes

No hope have I to live a deathless name,
   A power immortal in the world of mind,
A sun to light with intellectual flame,
   The universal soul of human kind.

Not mine the skill in memorable phrase,
   The hidden truths of passion to reveal,
To bring to light the intermingling ways,
   By which unconscious motives darkling steal.

To show how forms the sentient heart affect,
   How thoughts and feelings mutually combine,
How oft the pure, impassive intellect
   Shares the mischances of his mortal shrine.

Nor can I summons from the dark abyss
   Of time, the spirit of forgotten things,
Bestow unfading life on transient bliss—
   Bid memory live with 'healing on its wings.'

Or give a substance to the haunting shades,
   Whose visitation shames the vulgar earth,
Before whose light the ray of morning fades,
   And hollow yearning chills the soul of mirth.

I have no charm to renovate the youth
   Of old authentic dictates of the heart,—
To wash the wrinkles from the face of Truth,
   And out of Nature form creative Art.

Divinest Poesy!—'tis thine to make
   Age young—youth old—to baffle tyrant Time,
From antique strains the hoary dust to shake,
   And with familiar grace to crown new rhyme.

Long have I loved thee—long have loved in vain,
  Yet large the debt my spirit owes to thee,
Thou wreath'd'st my first hours in a rosy chain,
  Rocking the cradle of my infancy.

The lovely images of earth and sky
  From thee I learn'd within my soul to treasure;
And the strong magic of thy minstrelsy
  Charms the world's tempest to a sweet, sad measure.

Nor Fortune's spite—nor hopes that once have been—
  Hopes which no power of Fate can give again,—
Not the sad sentence—that my life must wean
  From dear domestic joys—nor all the train

Of pregnant ills—and penitential harms
  That dog the rear of youth unwisely wasted,
Can dim the lustre of thy stainless charms,
  Or sour the sweetness that in thee I tasted.

JOHN HAMILTON REYNOLDS

247   *PETER BELL*

PREFACE

IT is now a period of one-and-twenty years since I first wrote
some of the most perfect compositions (except certain pieces I
have written in my later days) that ever dropped from poetical
pen. My heart hath been right and powerful all its years. I never
thought an evil or a weak thought in my life. It has been my aim
and my achievement to deduce moral thunder from buttercups,

daisies,[1] celandines, and (as a poet, scarcely inferior to myself, hath it) 'such small deer.' Out of sparrows' eggs I have hatched great truths, and with sextons' barrows have I wheeled into human hearts, piles of the weightiest philosophy. I have persevered with a perseverance truly astonishing, in persons of not the most pursy purses;—but to a man of my inveterate morality and independent stamp, (of which Stamps I am proud to be a Distributor) the sneers and scoffings of impious Scotchmen, and the neglect of my poor uninspired countrymen, fall as the dew upon the thorn, (on which plant I have written an immortal stanza or two) and are as fleeting as the spray of the waterfall, (concerning which water-fall I have composed some great lines which the world will not let die.)—Accustomed to mountain solitudes, I can look with a calm and dispassionate eye upon that fiend-like, vulture-souled, adder-fanged critic, whom I have not patience to name, and of whose Review I loathe the title, and detest the contents.—Philosophy has taught me to forgive the misguided miscreant, and to speak of him only in terms of patience and pity. I love my venerable Monarch and the Prince Regent.[2] My Ballads are the noblest pieces of verse in the whole range of English poetry: and I take this opportunity of telling the world I am a great man. Milton was also a great man. Ossian was a blind old fool. Copies of my previous works may be had in any numbers, by application at my publisher.

Of PETER BELL I have only thus much to say: it completes the simple system of natural narrative, which I began so early as 1798. It is written in that pure unlaboured style, which can only be met with among labourers;—and I can safely say, that while its

[1] A favourite flower of mine. It was a favourite with Chaucer, but he did not understand its moral mystery as I do.

'Little Cyclops, with one eye.'

Poems by ME.

[2] Mr. Vansittart, the great Chancellor of the Exchequer, is a noble character:—and I consecrate this note to that illustrious financier.

imaginations spring beyond the reach of the most imaginative, its occasional meaning occasionally falls far below the meanest capacity. As these are the days of counterfeits, I am compelled to caution my readers against them, 'for such are abroad.' However, I here declare this to be the true Peter; this to be the old original Bell. I commit my Ballad confidently to posterity. I love to read my own poetry: it does my heart good.

W. W.

N.B. The novel of Rob Roy is not so good as my Poem on the same subject.

PETER BELL

I

It is the thirty-first of March,
A gusty evening—half past seven;
The moon is shining o'er the larch,
A simple shape—a cock'd-up arch,
Rising bigger than a star,
Though the stars are thick in Heaven.

2

Gentle moon! how canst thou shine
Over graves and over trees,
With as innocent a look
As my own grey eye-ball sees,
When I gaze upon a brook?

3

Od's me! how the moon doth shine:
It doth make a pretty glitter,
Playing in the waterfall;
As when Lucy Gray doth litter
Her baby-house with bugles small.

4

Beneath the ever blessed moon
An old man o'er an old grave stares,
You never look'd upon his fellow;
His brow is covered with grey hairs,
As though they were an umbrella.

5

He hath a noticeable look,[1]
This old man hath—this grey old man;
He gazes at the graves, and seems,
With over waiting, over wan,
Like Susan Harvey's[2] pan of creams.

6

'Tis Peter Bell—'tis Peter Bell,
Who never stirreth in the day;
His hand is wither'd—he is old!
On Sundays he is us'd to pray,
In winter he is very cold.[3]

7

I've seen him in the month of August,
At the wheat-field, hour by hour,
Picking ear,—by ear,—by ear,—
Through wind,—and rain,—and sun,—and shower,
From year,—to year,—to year,—to year.

[1] 'A noticeable man with large grey eyes.'

Lyrical Ballads.

[2] Dairy-maid to Mr. Gill.

[3] Peter Bell resembleth Harry Gill in this particular:
'His teeth they chatter, chatter, chatter.'
I should have introduced this fact in the text, but that Harry Gill would not rhyme. I reserve this for my blank verse.

8

You never saw a wiser man,
He knows his Numeration Table;
He counts the sheep of Harry Gill,[1]
Every night that he is able,
When the sheep are on the hill.

9

Betty Foy—*My* Betty Foy,
Is the aunt of Peter Bell;
And credit me, as I would have you,
Simon Lee was once his nephew,
And his niece is Alice Fell.[2]

10

He is rurally related;
Peter Bell hath country cousins,
(He had once a worthy mother)
Bells and Peters by the dozens,
But Peter Bell he hath no brother.

11

Not a brother owneth he,
Peter Bell he hath no brother;
His mother had no other son,
No other son e'er call'd her mother;
Peter Bell hath brother none.

[1] Harry Gill was the original proprietor of Barbara Lewthwaite's pet-lamb; and he also bred Betty Foy's celebrated poney, got originally out of a Night-mare, by a descendant of the great Trojan horse.

[2] Mr. Sheridan, in his sweet poem of the Critic, supplies one of his heroes with as singularly clustering a relationship.

12

Hark! the church-yard brook is singing
Its evening song amid the leaves;
And the peering moon doth look
Sweetly on the singing brook,
Round[1] and sad as though it grieves.

13

Peter Bell doth lift his hand,
That thin hand, which in the light
Looketh like to oiled paper;
Paper oiled,—oily bright,—
And held up to a waxen taper.

14

The hand of Peter Bell is busy,
Under the pent-house of his hairs;
His eye is like a solemn sermon;
The little flea severely fares.
'Tis a sad day for the vermin.

15

He is thinking of the Bible—
Peter Bell is old and blest;
He doth pray and scratch away,
He doth scratch, and bitten, pray
To *flee* away, and be at rest.

[1] I have here changed the shape of the moon, not from any poetical heedlessness, or human perversity, but because man is fond of change, and in this I have studied the metaphysical varieties of our being.

16

At home his foster child is cradled—
Four brown bugs are feeding there:[1]
Catch as many, sister Ann,
Catch as many as you can[2]
And yet the little insects spare.

17

Why should blessed insects die?
The flea doth skip o'er Betty Foy,
Like a little living thing:
Though it hath not fin or wing,
Hath it not a moral joy?

18

I the poet of the mountain,
Of the waterfall and fell,
I the mighty mental medlar,
I the lonely lyric pedlar,
I the Jove of Alice Fell.

19

I the Recluse—a gentle man,[3]
A gentle man—a simple creature,
Who would not hurt, God shield the thing,
The merest, meanest May-bug's wing,
Am tender in my tender nature.

---

[1] I have a similar idea in my Poem on finding a Bird's Nest:—
'Look! *five* blue eggs are gleaming there.'
But the numbers are different, so I trust no one will differ with the numbers.

[2] I have also given these lines before; but in thus printing them again, I neither tarnish their value, nor injure their novelty.

[3] See my Sonnet to Sleep:—
'I surely not a man ungently made.'

20

I do doat on my dear wife,
On the linnet, on the worm,
I can see sweet written salads
Growing in the Lyric Ballads,
And always find them green and firm.

21

Peter Bell is laughing now,
Like a dead man making faces;
Never saw I smile so old,
On face so wrinkled and so cold,
Since the Idiot Boy's grimaces.

22

He is thinking of the moors,
Where I saw him in his breeches;
Ragged though they were, a pair
Fit for a grey old man to wear;
Saw him poking,—gathering leeches.[1]

23

And gather'd leeches are to him,
To Peter Bell, like gather'd flowers;
They do yield him such delight,
As roses poach'd from porch at night,
Or pluck'd from oratoric[2] bowers.

---

[1] See my story of the Leech-gatherer, the finest poem in the world,—
except this.

[2] 'Ah!' said the Briar, 'blame me not.'

Waterfall and Eglantine.

Also,—

'The Oak a Giant and a Sage,
His neighbour thus address'd.'

24

How that busy smile doth hurry
O'er the cheek of Peter Bell;
He is surely in a flurry,
Hurry skurry—hurry skurry,
Such delight I may not tell.

25

His stick is made of wilding wood,
His hat was formerly of felt,
His duffel cloak of wool is made,
His stockings are from stock in trade,
His belly's belted with a belt.

26

His father was a bellman once,
His mother was a beldame old;
They kept a shop at Keswick Town,
Close by the Bell, (beyond the Crown),
And pins and peppermint they sold.

27

He is stooping now about
O'er the grave-stones one and two;
The clock is now a striking eight,
Four more hours and 'twill be late,
And Peter Bell hath much to do.

28

O'er the grave-stones three and four,
Peter stoopeth old and wise;
He counteth with a wizard glee
The graves of all his family,
While the hooting owlet cries.

29

Peter Bell he readeth ably,
All his letters he can tell;
Roman W,—Roman S,
In a minute he can guess,
Without the aid of Dr. Bell.

30

Peter keeps a gentle poney,
But the poney is not here;
Susan who is very tall,[1]
And very sick and sad withal,
Rides it slowly far and near.

31

Hark! the voice of Peter Bell,
And the belfry bell is knelling;
It soundeth drowsily and dead,
As though a corse th' 'Excursion' read;
Or Martha Ray her tale was telling.

32

Do listen unto Peter Bell,
While your eyes with tears do glisten:
Silence! his old eyes do read
All, on which the boys do tread
When holidays do come—Do listen!

33

The ancient Marinere lieth here,
Never to rise, although he pray'd,—

[1] '*Long Susan* lay deep lost in thought.'
                                    The Idiot Boy.

But all men, all, must have their fallings;
And, like the Fear of Mr. Collins,[1]
He died 'of sounds himself had made.'

34

Dead ma d mother,—Martha Ray,
Old Matthew too, and Betty Foy,
Lack-a-daisy! here's a rout full;
Simon Lee whose age was doubtful,[2]
Simon even the Fates destroy.

35

Harry Gill is gone to rest,
Goody Blake is food for maggot;
They lie sweetly side by side,
Beautiful as when they died;
Never more shall she pick faggot.

---

[1] See what I have said of this man in my excellent supplementary *Preface*.
[2] I cannot resist quoting the following lines, to shew how I preserve my system from youth to age. As Simon was, so he is. And one and twenty years have scarcely altered (except by death) that cheerful and cherry-cheeked Old Huntsman. This is the truth of Poetry.

> 'In the sweet shire of Cardigan,
>   Not far from pleasant Ivor-hall;
> An old man dwells—a little man—
>   I've heard he once was tall;
> Of years he has upon his back,
>   No doubt, a burthen weighty;
> He says he is threescore and ten,
>   But others say he's eighty.'

These lines were written in the summer of 1798, and I bestowed great labour upon them.

36

Still he reads, and still the moon
On the church-yard's mounds doth shine;
The brook is still demurely singing,
Again the belfry bell is ringing,
'Tis nine o'clock, six, seven, eight, nine!

37

Patient Peter pores and proses
On, from simple grave to grave;
Here marks the children snatch'd to heaven,
None left to blunder 'we are seven;'—
Even Andrew Jones[1] no power could save.

38

What a Sexton's work[2] is here,
Lord! the Idiot Boy is gone;
And Barbara Lewthwaite's fate the same,
And cold as mutton is her lamb;
And Alice Fell is bone by bone.

39

And tears are thick with Peter Bell,
Yet still he sees one blessed tomb;
Tow'rds it he creeps with spectacles,
And bending on his leather knees,
He reads the *Lake*iest Poet's doom.

---

[1] Andrew Jones was a very singular old man.—See my Poem,
　　'I hate that Andrew Jones—he'll breed,' &c.
[2] 'Let thy wheelbarrow alone, &c.' See my poem to a Sexton.

40

The letters printed are by fate,
The death they say was suicide;
He reads—'Here lieth W. W.
Who never more will trouble you, trouble you:'
The old man smokes who 'tis that died.

41

Go home, go home—old Man, go home;
Peter, lay thee down at night,
Thou art happy, Peter Bell,
Say thy prayers for Alice Fell,
Thou hast seen a blessed sight.

42

He quits that moon-light yard of skulls,
And still he feels right glad, and smiles
With moral joy at that old tomb;
Peter's cheek recals its bloom,
And as he creepeth by the tiles,
He mutters ever—'W. W.
Never more will trouble you, trouble you.'

HERE ENDETH THE BALLAD OF PETER BELL

SUPPLEMENTARY ESSAY

I BEG leave, once for all, to refer the Reader to my previous
Poems, for illustrations of the names of the characters, and the
severe simplicity contained in this affecting Ballad. I purpose, in
the course of a few years, to write laborious lives of all the old
people who enjoy sinecures in the text, or are pensioned off in the
notes, of my Poetry. The Cumberland Beggar is dead. He could

not crawl out of the way of a fierce and fatal post chaise, and so fell a sacrifice to the Philosophy of Nature. I shall commence the work in heavy quarto, like the Excursion, with that 'old, old Man,' (as the too joyous Spenser saith.)—If ever I should be surprised into a second edition, I shall write an extra-supplementary Essay on the principles of simple Poetry. I now conclude, with merely extracting (from my own works) the following eloquent and just passage (my Prose is extremely good) contained in the two volumes lately published, and not yet wholly disposed of:—

'A sketch of my own notion of the Constitution of Fame has been given; and as far as concerns myself, I have cause to be satisfied.—The love, the admiration, the indifference, the slight, the aversion, and even the contempt, with which these Poems have been received, knowing, as I do, the source within my own mind, from which they have proceeded; and the labour and pains, when labour and pains appeared needful, have been bestowed upon them,—must all, if I think consistently, be received as pledges and tokens, bearing the same general impression though widely different in value;—they are all proofs that for the present time I have not laboured in vain; and afford assurances, more or less authentic, that the products of my industry will endure.' *Lyrical Ballads, Vol. i, p. 368.*

THOMAS HOOD

from 'THE PLEA OF THE MIDSUMMER FAIRIES'

[1]

248   ['The Melodies of Time']

THEN Saturn thus:—'Sweet is the merry lark,
That carols in man's ear so clear and strong;
And youth must love to listen in the dark
That tuneful elegy of Tereus' wrong;

But I have heard that ancient strain too long,
For sweet is sweet but when a little strange,
And I grow weary for some newer song;
For wherefore had I wings, unless to range
Through all things mutable from change to change?

'But wouldst thou hear the melodies of Time,
Listen when sleep and drowsy darkness roll
Over hush'd cities, and the midnight chime
Sounds from their hundred clocks, and deep bells toll
Like a last knell over the dead world's soul,
Saying, Time shall be final of all things,
Whose late, last voice must elegise the whole,—
O then I clap aloft my brave broad wings,
And make the wide air tremble while it rings!'

[11]

249   [The Green Dryad's Plea]

THEN next a merry Woodsman, clad in green,
Stept vanward from his mates, that idly stood
Each at his proper ease, as they had been
Nursed in the liberty of old Shérwood,
And wore the livery of Robin Hood,
Who wont in forest shades to dine and sup,—
So came this chief right frankly, and made good
His haunch against his axe, and thus spoke up,
Doffing his cap, which was an acorn's cup:—

'We be small foresters and gay, who tend
On trees, and all their furniture of green,
Training the young boughs airily to bend,
And show blue snatches of the sky between;—

Or knit more close intricacies, to screen
Birds' crafty dwellings as may hide them best,
But most the timid blackbird's—she, that seen,
Will bear black poisonous berries to her nest,
Lest man should cage the darlings of her breast.

'We bend each tree in proper attitude,
And founting willows train in silvery falls;
We frame all shady roofs and arches rude,
And verdant aisles leading to Dryads' halls,
Or deep recesses where the Echo calls;—
We shape all plumy trees against the sky,
And carve tall elms' Corinthian capitals,—
When sometimes, as our tiny hatchets ply,
Men say, the tapping woodpecker is nigh.

'Sometimes we scoop the squirrel's hollow cell,
And sometimes carve quaint letters on trees' rind,
That haply some lone musing wight may spell
Dainty Aminta,—Gentle Rosalind,—
Or chastest Laura,—sweetly call'd to mind
In sylvan solitudes, ere he lies down;—
And sometimes we enrich gray stems, with twined
And vagrant ivy,—or rich moss, whose brown
Burns into gold as the warm sun goes down.

'And lastly, for mirth's sake and Christmas cheer,
We bear the seedling berries, for increase,
To graft the Druid oaks, from year to year,
Careful that mistletoe may never cease;—
Wherefore, if thou dost prize the shady peace
Of sombre forests, or to see light break
Through sylvan cloisters, and in spring release
Thy spirit amongst leaves from careful ake,
Spare us our lives for the Green Dryad's sake.'

Then Saturn, with a frown:—'Go forth, and fell
Oak for your coffins, and thenceforth lay by
Your axes for the rust, and bid farewell
To all sweet birds, and the blue peeps of sky
Through tangled branches, for ye shall not spy
The next green generation of the tree;
But hence with the dead leaves, whene'er they fly,—
Which in the bleak air I would rather see,
Than flights of the most tuneful birds that be.

'For I dislike all prime and verdant pets,
Ivy except, that on the aged wall
Preys with its worm-like roots, and daily frets
The crumbled tower it seems to league withal,
King-like, worn down by its own coronal:—
Neither in forest haunts love I to won,
Before the golden plumage 'gins to fall,
And leaves the brown bleak limbs with few leaves on,
Or bare—like Nature in her skeleton.

'For then sit I amongst the crooked boughs,
Wooing dull Memory with kindred sighs;
And there in rustling nuptials we espouse,
Smit by the sadness in each other's eyes;—
But Hope must have green bowers and blue skies,
And must be courted with the gauds of spring;
Whilst Youth leans god-like on her lap, and cries,
What shall we always do, but love and sing?—
And Time is reckon'd a discarded thing.'

[III]

250 [The Fairy's Reply to Saturn]

THEN saith the timid Fay—'Oh, mighty Time!
Well hast thou wrought the cruel Titans' fall,
For they were stain'd with many a bloody crime:
Great giants work great wrongs,—but we are small,
For love goes lowly;—but Oppression's tall,
And with surpassing strides goes foremost still
Where love indeed can hardly reach at all;
Like a poor dwarf o'erburthen'd with good will,
That labours to efface the tracks of ill.—

'Man even strives with Man, but we eschew
The guilty feud, and all fierce strifes abhor;
Nay, we are gentle as sweet heaven's dew,
Beside the red and horrid drops of war,
Weeping the cruel hates men battle for,
Which worldly bosoms nourish in our spite:
For in the gentle breast we ne'er withdraw,
But only when all love hath taken flight,
And youth's warm gracious heart is harden'd quite.

[IV]

251 [Shakespeare: the Fairies' Advocate]

''TIS these that free the small entangled fly,
Caught in the venom'd spider's crafty snare;—
These be the petty surgeons that apply
The healing balsams to the wounded hare,
Bedded in bloody fern, no creature's care!—

These be providers for the orphan brood,
Whose tender mother hath been slain in air,
Quitting with gaping bill her darling's food,
Hard by the verge of her domestic wood.

''Tis these befriend the timid trembling stag,
When, with a bursting heart beset with fears,
He feels his saving speed begin to flag;
For then they quench the fatal taint with tears,
And prompt fresh shifts in his alarum'd ears,
So piteously they view all bloody morts;
Or if the gunner, with his arm, appears,
Like noisy pyes and jays, with harsh reports,
They warn the wild fowl of his deadly sports.

'For these are kindly ministers of nature,
To soothe all covert hurts and dumb distress;
Pretty they be, and very small of stature,—
For mercy still consorts with littleness;—
Wherefore the sum of good is still the less,
And mischief grossest in this world of wrong;—
So do these charitable dwarfs redress
The tenfold ravages of giants strong,
To whom great malice and great might belong.

'Likewise to them are Poets much beholden
For secret favours in the midnight glooms;
Brave Spenser quaff'd out of their goblets golden,
And saw their tables spread of prompt mushrooms,
And heard their horns of honeysuckle blooms
Sounding upon the air most soothing soft,
Like humming bees busy about the brooms,—
And glanc'd this fair queen's witchery full oft,
And in her magic wain soared far aloft.

'Nay I myself, though mortal, once was nurs'd
By fairy gossips, friendly at my birth,
And in my childish ear glib Mab rehears'd
Her breezy travels round our planet's girth,
Telling me wonders of the moon and earth;
My gramarye at her grave lap I conn'd,
Where Puck hath been conven'd to make me mirth;
I have had from Queen Titania tokens fond,
And toy'd with Oberon's permitted wand.

'With figs and plums and Persian dates they fed me,
And delicate cates after my sunset meal,
And took me by my childish hand, and led me
By craggy rocks crested with keeps of steel,
Whose awful bases deep dark woods conceal,
Staining some dead lake with their verdant dyes:
And when the West sparkled at Phœbus' wheel,
With fairy euphrasy they purg'd mine eyes,
To let me see their cities in the skies.

''Twas they first school'd my young imagination
To take its flights like any new-fledg'd bird,
And show'd the span of winged meditation
Stretch'd wider than things grossly seen or heard.
With sweet swift Ariel how I soar'd and stirr'd
The fragrant blooms of spiritual bow'rs!
'Twas they endear'd what I have still preferr'd,
Nature's blest attributes and balmy pow'rs,
Her hills and vales and brooks, sweet birds and flow'rs!

'Wherefore with all true loyalty and duty
Will I regard them in my honouring rhyme,
With love for love, and homages to beauty,
And magic thoughts gather'd in night's cool clime,

With studious verse trancing the dragon Time,
Strong as old Merlin's necromantic spells;
So these dear monarchs of the summer's prime
Shall live unstartled by his dreadful yells,
Till shrill larks warn them to their flowery cells.'

252   Ode: Autumn

I

I SAW old Autumn in the misty morn
Stand shadowless like Silence, listening
To silence, for no lonely bird would sing
Into his hollow ear from woods forlorn,
Nor lowly hedge nor solitary thorn;—
Shaking his languid locks all dewy bright
With tangled gossamer that fell by night,
    Pearling his coronet of golden corn.

II

Where are the songs of Summer?—With the sun,
Oping the dusky eyelids of the south,
Till shade and silence waken up as one,
And Morning sings with a warm odorous mouth.
Where are the merry birds?—Away, away,
On panting wings through the inclement skies,
    Lest owls should prey
    Undazzled at noon-day
And tear with horny beak their lustrous eyes.

III

Where are the blooms of Summer?—in the west,
Blushing their last to the last sunny hours,
When the mild Eve by sudden Night is prest
Like tearful Proserpine, snatch'd from her flow'rs
    To a most gloomy breast.
Where is the pride of Summer,—the green prime,—
The many, many leaves all twinkling?—Three
On the moss'd elm; three on the naked lime
Trembling,—and one upon the old oak tree!
    Where is the Dryad's immortality?—
Gone into mournful cypress and dark yew,
Or wearing the long gloomy Winter through
    In the smooth holly's green eternity.

IV

The squirrel gloats on his accomplish'd hoard,
The ants have brimm'd their garners with ripe grain,
    And honey bees have stor'd
The sweets of Summer in their luscious cells;
The swallows all have wing'd across the main;
But here the Autumn melancholy dwells,
    And sighs her tearful spells
Amongst the sunless shadows of the plain.
      Alone, alone,
      Upon a mossy stone,
She sits and reckons up the dead and gone
With the last leaves for a love-rosary,
Whilst all the wither'd world looks drearily,
Like a dim picture of the drowned past
In the hush'd mind's mysterious far away,
Doubtful what ghostly thing will steal the last
Into that distance, grey upon the grey.

V

O go and sit with her, and be o'ershaded
Under the languid downfall of her hair:
She wears a coronal of flowers faded
Upon her forehead, and a face of care;—
There is enough of wither'd every where
To make her bower,—and enough of gloom;
There is enough of sadness to invite,
If only for the rose that died,—whose doom
Is Beauty's,—she that with the living bloom
Of conscious cheeks most beautifies the light;—
There is enough of sorrowing, and quite
Enough of bitter fruits the earth doth bear,—
Enough of chilly droppings for her bowl;
Enough of fear and shadowy despair,
To frame her cloudy prison for the soul!

253   Ruth

She stood breast high amid the corn,
Clasp'd by the golden light of morn,
Like the sweetheart of the sun,
Who many a glowing kiss had won.

On her cheek an autumn flush,
Deeply ripened;—such a blush
In the midst of brown was born,
Like red poppies grown with corn.

Round her eyes her tresses fell,
Which were blackest none could tell,
But long lashes veil'd a light,
That had else been all too bright.

And her hat, with shady brim,
Made her tressy forehead dim;—
Thus she stood amid the stooks,
Praising God with sweetest looks:—

Sure, I said, heav'n did not mean,
Where I reap thou shouldst but glean,
Lay thy sheaf adown and come,
Share my harvest and my home.

254   The Sea of Death

A FRAGMENT

METHOUGHT I saw
Life swiftly treading over endless space;
And, at her foot-print, but a bygone pace,
The ocean-past, which, with increasing wave,
Swallow'd her steps like a pursuing grave.

Sad were my thoughts that anchor'd silently
On the dead waters of that passionless sea,
Unstirr'd by any touch of living breath:
Silence hung over it, and drowsy Death,
Like a gorged sea-bird, slept with folded wings
On crowded carcases—sad passive things
That wore the thin grey surface, like a veil
Over the calmness of their features pale.

And there were spring-faced cherubs that did sleep
Like water-lilies on that motionless deep,
How beautiful! with bright unruffled hair
On sleek unfretted brows, and eyes that were

Buried in marble tombs, a pale eclipse!
And smile-bedimpled cheeks, and pleasant lips,
Meekly apart, as if the soul intense
Spake out in dreams of its own innocence:
And so they lay in loveliness, and kept
The birth-night of their peace, that Life e'en wept
With very envy of their happy fronts;
For there were neighbour brows scarr'd by the brunts
Of strife and sorrowing—where Care had set
His crooked autograph, and marr'd the jet
Of glossy locks with hollow eyes forlorn,
And lips that curl'd in bitterness and scorn—
Wretched,—as they had breath'd of this world's pain,
And so bequeath'd it to the world again
Through the beholder's heart in heavy sighs.

So lay they garmented in torpid light,
Under the pall of a transparent night,
Like solemn apparitions lull'd sublime
To everlasting rest,—and with them Time
Slept, as he sleeps upon the silent face
Of a dark dial in a sunless place.

255   Sonnet

It is not death, that sometime in a sigh
This eloquent breath shall take its speechless flight;
That sometime these bright stars, that now reply
In sunlight to the sun, shall set in night;
That this warm conscious flesh shall perish quite,
And all life's ruddy springs forget to flow;
That thoughts shall cease, and the immortal spright
Be lapp'd in alien clay and laid below;
It is not death to know this,—but to know

That pious thoughts, which visit at new graves
In tender pilgrimage, will cease to go
So duly and so oft,—and when grass waves
Over the past-away, there may be then
No resurrection in the minds of men.

256   Sonnet: Silence

THERE is a silence where hath been no sound,
     There is a silence where no sound may be,
     In the cold grave—under the deep deep sea,
Or in wide desert where no life is found,
Which hath been mute, and still must sleep profound;
     No voice is hush'd—no life treads silently,
     But clouds and cloudy shadows wander free,
That never spoke, over the idle ground:
But in green ruins, in the desolate walls
     Of antique palaces, where Man hath been,
Though the dun fox, or wild hyena, calls,
     And owls, that flit continually between,
Shriek to the echo, and the low winds moan,
There the true Silence is, self-conscious and alone.

257   The Death-Bed

WE watch'd her breathing thro' the night,
     Her breathing soft and low,
As in her breast the wave of life
     Kept heaving to and fro!

So silently we seemed to speak—
     So slowly moved about!
As we had lent her half our powers
     To eke her living out!

Our very hopes belied our fears,
Our fears our hopes belied—
We thought her dying when she slept,
And sleeping when she died!

For when the morn came dim and sad—
And chill with early showers,
Her quiet eyelids closed—she had
Another morn than ours!

THOMAS BABINGTON,
LORD MACAULAY

258   from 'THE ARMADA'

NIGHT sank upon the dusky beach, and on the purple sea,
Such night in England ne'er had been, nor e'er again shall be.
From Eddystone to Berwick bounds, from Lynn to Milford Bay,
That time of slumber was as bright and busy as the day;
For swift to east and swift to west the ghastly war-flame spread,
High on St. Michael's Mount it shone: it shone on Beachy Head.
Far on the deep the Spaniard saw, along each southern shire,
Cape beyond cape, in endless range, those twinkling points of fire.
The fisher left his skiff to rock on Tamar's glittering waves:
The rugged miners poured to war from Mendip's sunless caves:
O'er Longleat's towers, o'er Cranbourne's oaks, the fiery herald
    flew:
He roused the shepherds of Stonehenge, the rangers of Beaulieu.
Right sharp and quick the bells all night rang out from Bristol
    town,
And ere the day three hundred horse had met on Clifton down;

The sentinel on Whitehall gate looked forth into the night,
And saw o'erhanging Richmond Hill the streak of blood-red light.
Then bugle's note and cannon's roar the deathlike silence broke,
And with one start, and with one cry, the royal city woke.
At once on all her stately gates arose the answering fires;
At once the wild alarum clashed from all her reeling spires;
From all the batteries of the Tower pealed loud the voice of fear;
And all the thousand masts of Thames sent back a louder cheer:
And from the furthest wards was heard the rush of hurrying feet,
And the broad streams of pikes and flags rushed down each roaring
    street;
And broader still became the blaze, and louder still the din,
As fast from every village round the horse came spurring in:
And eastward straight from wild Blackheath the warlike errand
    went,
And roused in many an ancient hall the gallant squires of Kent.
Southward from Surrey's pleasant hills flew those bright couriers
    forth;
High on bleak Hampstead's swarthy moor they started for the
    north;
And on, and on, without a pause, untired they bounded still:
All night from tower to tower they sprang; they sprang from hill
    to hill:
Till the proud peak unfurled the flag o'er Darwin's rocky dales,
Till like volcanoes flared to heaven the stormy hills of Wales,
Till twelve fair counties saw the blaze on Malvern's lonely height,
Till streamed in crimson on the wind the Wrekin's crest of light,
Till broad and fierce the star came forth on Ely's stately fane,
And tower and hamlet rose in arms o'er all the boundless plain;
Till Belvoir's lordly terraces the sign to Lincoln sent,
And Lincoln sped the message on o'er the wide vale of Trent;
Till Skiddaw saw the fire that burned on Gaunt's embattled pile,
And the red glare on Skiddaw roused the burghers of Carlisle.

1832

259 ## A Jacobite's Epitaph

To my true king I offered free from stain
Courage and faith; vain faith, and courage vain.
For him I threw lands, honours, wealth, away,
And one dear hope, that was more prized than they.
For him I languished in a foreign clime,
Grey-haired with sorrow in my manhood's prime;
Heard on Lavernia Scargill's whispering trees,
And pined by Arno for my lovelier Tees;
Beheld each night my home in fevered sleep,
Each morning started from the dream to weep;
Till God, who saw me tried too sorely, gave
The resting-place I asked, an early grave.
O thou, whom chance leads to this nameless stone,
From that proud country which was once mine own,
By those white cliffs I never more must see,
By that dear language which I spake like thee,
Forget all feuds, and shed one English tear
O'er English dust. A broken heart lies here.

WILLIAM BARNES

260 ## Rustic Childhood

No city primness train'd my feet
To strut in childhood through the street,
But freedom let them loose to tread
The yellow cowslip's downcast head;
Or climb, above the twining hop
And ivy, to the elm-tree's top;

Where southern airs of blue-sky'd day
Breath'd o'er the daisy and the may.
   I knew you young, and love you now,
    O shining grass, and shady bough.

Far off from town, where splendour tries
To draw the looks of gather'd eyes,
And clocks, unheeded, fail to warn
The loud-tongued party of the morn,
I spent in woodland shades my day
In cheerful work or happy play,
And slept at night where rustling leaves
Threw moonlight shadows o'er my eaves.
   I knew you young, and love you now,
    O shining grass, and shady bough.

Or in the grassy drove by ranks
Of white-stemm'd ashes or by banks
Of narrow lanes, in-winding round
The hedgy sides of shelving ground;
Where low-shot light struck in to end
Again at some cool-shaded bend,
Where we might see through dark leav'd boughs
The evening light on green hill-brows.
   I knew you young, and love you now,
    O shining grass, and shady bough.

Or on the hillock where I lay
At rest on some bright holyday;
When short noon-shadows lay below
The thorn in blossom white as snow;
And warm air bent the glist'ning tops
Of bushes in the lowland copse,

Before the blue hills swelling high
And far against the southern sky.
  I knew you young, and love you now,
  O shining grass, and shady bough.

261   Sonnet: Leaves

LEAVES of the summer, lovely summer's pride,
  Sweet is the shade below your silent tree,
Whether in waving copses, where ye hide
  My roamings, or in fields that let me see
  The open sky; and whether ye may be
Around the low-stemm'd oak, robust and wide;
Or taper ash upon the mountain side;
  Or lowland elm; your shade is sweet to me.

Whether ye wave above the early flow'rs
  In lively green; or whether, rustling sere,
Ye fly on playful winds, around my feet,

In dying autumn; lovely are your bow'rs,
  Ye early-dying children of the year;
    Holy the silence of your calm retreat.

262   A Winter Night

IT was a chilly winter's night;
  And frost was glitt'ring on the ground,
And evening stars were twinkling bright;
  And from the gloomy plain around
    Came no sound,
But where, within the wood-girt tow'r,
The churchbell slowly struck the hour;

As if that all of human birth
    Had risen to the final day,
And soaring from the wornout earth
    Were called in hurry and dismay,
        Far away;
And I alone of all mankind
    Were left in loneliness behind.

263   Burncombe Hollow

WHILE snowy nightwinds, blowing bleak
Up hill, made rock-borne fir-trees creak,
And drove the snow-flakes, feather-light,
O'er icy streams in playsome flight,
And while the roof was snowy white,
    There blazing cleftwood threw its heat
    With ruddy light, to chilly feet,
        In lonely Burncombe hollow.

And Jenny, that had just put down
Her load of errands brought from town,
Sat leaning backward in her chair,
Cheek-warm, with weather-loosen'd hair;
And told, with smiles 'twas bliss to share,
    Her news; while putting out for heat,
    Down side by side, her comely feet,
        At home in Burncombe hollow.

And while the children ran to pull
Her errands from her basket full,
Her friends and I, all wordless, hung
Upon the words of her gay tongue;

But they with old love, I with young,
    For all my soul, with all my sight,
    Were given up that happy night,
        To Jane of Burncombe hollow.

And where did first her sweet voice own
    Her love for me and me alone,
    But climbing up the eastern side
    Of Burncombe hollow, that did hide
    The western sunset, crimson-dyed,
      O'er leaves that rustled on the ground,
      Below the ivy twining round
        The trees of Burncombe hollow.

And now her careful friends, that bred
    Her up so fair and good, are dead;
    And she, a woman mild and staid,
    Is keeping house where once she play'd
    And won my love, a blooming maid;
      And all the joy my soul can know
      With her will stay, with her must go
        From me in Burncombe hollow.

And so 'tis sweet with her my wife
    To look back o'er our wedded life,
    Which she, e'er smiling in my sight,
    Has made a cloudless day, still bright,
    But waning slowly into night;
      And if I had my time once more
      To choose, I'd choose no maid before
        The maid of Burncombe hollow.

So winter darkness come to brood
O'er sullen moans of waving wood,
Come hov'ring snow, so lightly cast
Upon the ground where ice seals fast
The water from the cutting blast.
    I heed you not, while shelter'd where
    Love lights me up the ruddy glare
      Of fire in Burncombe hollow.

264   Melhill Feast

AYE up at the feast, by Melhill's brow,
So softly below the clouds in flight,
There swept on the wood, the shade and light,
Tree after tree, and bough by bough.

And there, as among the crowd, I took
My wandering way, both to and fro,
Full comely were shapes that day could show,
Face upon face, and look by look.

And there, among girls on left and right,
On one with a winsome smile, I set
My looks; and the more, the more we met
Glance upon glance, and sight by sight.

The road she had come by then was soon
The one of my paths that best I knew,
By glittering gossamer and dew,
Evening by evening, moon by moon.

First by the door of maidens fair,
As fair as the best till she is nigh,
Though now I can heedless pass them by,
One after one, or pair by pair.

Then by the orchards dim and cool,
And then along Woodcombe's timber'd side,
And then by the meads, where waters glide
Shallow by shallow, pool by pool.

And then to the house that stands alone
With roses around the porch and wall,
Where, up by the bridge, the waters fall
Rock under rock, and stone by stone.

Sweet were the hopes I found to cheer
My heart as I thought on time to come,
With one that would bless my happy home,
Moon upon moon, and year by year.

265   Shellbrook

WHEN out by Shellbrook, round by stile and tree,
With longer days and sunny hours come on,
With spring and all its sunny showers come on,
With May and all its shining flowers come on,
How merry, young with young would meet in glee.

And there, how we in merry talk went by
The foam below the river bay, all white,
And blossom on the green-leav'd may, all white,
And chalk beside the dusty way, all white,
Where glitt'ring water match'd with blue the sky.

Or else in winding paths and lanes, along
The timb'ry hillocks, sloping steep, we roam'd;
Or down the dells and dingles deep we roam'd;
Or by the bending brook's wide sweep we roam'd
On holidays, with merry laugh or song.

But now, the frozen churchyard wallings keep
The patch of tower-shaded ground, all white,
Where friends can find the frosted mound, all white
With turfy sides upswelling round, all white
With young offsunder'd from the young in sleep.

266   Musings

BEFORE the falling summer sun
    The boughs are shining all as gold,
And down below them waters run,
    As there in former years they roll'd;
The poolside wall is glowing hot,
    The pool is in a dazzling glare,
And makes it seem as, ah! 'tis not,
    A summer when my life was fair.

The evening, gliding slowly by,
    Seems one of those that long have fled;
The night comes on to star the sky
    As then it darken'd round my head.
A girl is standing by yon door,
    As one in happy times was there,
And this day seems, but is no more,
    A day when all my life was fair.

We hear from yonder feast the hum
    Of voices, as in summers past;
And hear the beatings of the drum
    Again come throbbing on the blast.
There neighs a horse in yonder plot,
    As once there neigh'd our petted mare,
And summer seems, but ah! is not
    The summer when our life was fair.

JOHN HENRY NEWMAN

267   The Pillar of Cloud

LEAD, Kindly Light, amid the encircling gloom,
          Lead Thou me on!
The night is dark, and I am far from home—
          Lead Thou me on!
Keep Thou my feet; I do not ask to see
The distant scene,—one step enough for me.

I was not ever thus, nor pray'd that Thou
          Shouldst lead me on.
I loved to choose and see my path; but now
          Lead Thou me on!
I loved the garish day, and, spite of fears,
Pride ruled my will: remember not past years.

So long Thy power hath blest me, sure it still
          Will lead me on,
O'er moor and fen, o'er crag and torrent, till
          The night is gone;
And with the morn those angel faces smile
Which I have loved long since, and lost awhile.

                                        At Sea. 16 June 1833

268   Refrigerium

THEY are at rest,
We may not stir the heaven of their repose
By rude invoking voice, or prayer addrest
          In waywardness to those
Who in the mountain grots of Eden lie,
And hear the fourfold river as it murmurs by.

They hear it sweep
In distance down the dark and savage vale;
But they at rocky bed or current deep
    Shall never more grow pale.
They hear, and meekly muse, as fain to know
How long untired, unspent, that giant stream shall flow

    And soothing sounds
Blend with the neighb'ring waters as they glide;
Posted along the haunted garden's bounds,
    Angelic forms abide,
Echoing, as words of watch, o'er lawn and grove,
The verses of that hymn which seraphs chant above.

                                            Oxford 1835

WINTHROP MACKWORTH PRAED

from 'THE COUNTY BALL'

269   [The County Member]

SKILL'D to deceive our ears and eyes
By civil looks and civil lies,
Skill'd from the search of men to hide
His narrow bosom's inward pride,
And charm the blockheads he beguiles
By uniformity of smiles,
The County Member, bright Sir Paul,
Is Primo Buffo at the Ball.

Since first he long'd to represent
His fellow-men in Parliament,
Courted the cobblers and their spouses,
And sought his honours in mud-houses,

Full thirty springs have come and fled;
And though from off his shining head
The twin destroyers, Time and Care,
Begin to pluck its fading hair,
Yet where it grew, and where it grows,
Lie powder's never-varying snows,
And hide the havoc years have made
In kind monotony of shade.

Sir Paul is young in all but years;
And when his courteous face appears,
The maiden wall-flowers of the room
Admire the freshness of his bloom,
Hint that his face has made him vain,
And vow 'he grows a boy again';
And giddy girls of gay fifteen
Mimic his manner and his mien,
And when the supple Politician
Bestows his bow of recognition,
Or forces on th' averted ear
The flattery it affects to fear;
They look, and laugh behind the fan,
And dub Sir Paul 'the young old man.'

Look! as he paces round, he greets
With nod and simper all he meets:—
'Ah! ha! your Lordship! is it you
Still slave to beauty and *beaux yeux*?
Well! well!—and how's the gout, my Lord?—
My dear Sir Charles, upon my word
L'air de Paris, since last I knew you
Has been Medea's cauldron to you:

William! my boy! how fast you grow!
Yours is a light fantastic toe,
Wing'd with the wings of Mercury!
I was a scholar once, you see!
And how's the mare you used to ride?
And who's the Hebe by your side?—
Doctor! I thought I heard you sneeze!
How is my dear Hippocrates?
What have you done for old John Oates,
The gouty merchant with five votes?
What! dead! well! well! no fault of yours!
There is no drug that always cures!
Ah! doctor! I begin to break!
And I'm glad of it, for *your* sake—'

As thus the spruce M.P. runs on,
Some quiet dame, who dotes upon
His speeches, buckles, and grimace,
Grows very eloquent in praise.
'How can they say Sir Paul is proud?
I'm sure, in all the evening's crowd,
There's not a man who bows so low;
His words come out so soft and slow;
And, when he begg'd me "keep my seat,"
He look'd so civil and so sweet.'—
'Ma'am,' says her spouse, in harsher tone,
'He only wants to keep his own.'
Her Ladyship is in a huff,
And Miss, enraged at *Ma's* rebuff,
Rings the alarm in t'other ear:
'Lord! now, Papa, you're too severe;
Where in the country will you see
Manners so taking and so free?'
'His manners free? I only know

Our votes have made his letters so!'
'And then he talks with so much ease,
And then he gives such promises!'
'Gives promises? and well he may!
You know they're all he gives away!'
'How folks misrepresent Sir Paul!'
''Tis he misrepresents us all!'
'How very stale! but you'll confess
He has a charming taste in dress;
And uses such delightful scent!
And when he pays a compliment—'
'Eh! and what then, my pretty pet?
What then?—he never pays a debt!'

Sir Paul is skill'd in all the tricks
Of politesse and politics;
Long hath he learn'd to wear a mien
So still, so open, so serene,
That strangers in those features grave
Would strive in vain to read a knave.
Alas! it is believed by all
There is more 'Sir' than 'Saint' in Paul;
He knows the value of a place;
Can give a promise with a grace;
Is quite an adept at excuse;
Sees when a vote will be of use;
And, if the Independents flinch,
Can help his Lordship at a pinch.
Acutely doth he read the fate
Of deep intrigues and plans of state;
And if perchance some powder'd peer
Hath gain'd or lost the Monarch's ear,
Foretells, without a shade of doubt,
The comings in and goings out.

When placemen of distinguish'd note
Mistake, mislead, misname, misquote;
Confound the Papist and the Turk,
Or murder Sheridan and Burke,
Or make a riddle of the Laws,
Sir Paul grows hoarse in his applause:
And when in words of equal size
Some Oppositionist replies,
And talks of taxes and starvation,
And Catholic Emancipation,
The Knight, in indolent repose,
Looks only to the Ayes and Noes.
Let youth say 'Grand!' Sir Paul says 'Stuff!'
Let youth take fire!—Sir Paul takes snuff.

270   Good-night to the Season

> Thus runs the world away.
> *Hamlet*

GOOD-NIGHT to the Season! 'tis over!
    Gay dwellings no longer are gay;
The courtier, the gambler, the lover,
    Are scatter'd like swallows away:
There's nobody left to invite one,
    Except my good uncle and spouse;
My mistress is bathing at Brighton,
    My patron is sailing at Cowes:
For want of a better employment,
    Till Ponto and Don can get out,
I'll cultivate rural enjoyment,
    And angle immensely for trout.

Good-night to the Season!—the lobbies,
    Their changes, and rumours of change,
Which startled the rustic Sir Bobbies,
    And made all the Bishops look strange:
The breaches, and battles, and blunders,
    Perform'd by the Commons and Peers;
The Marquis's eloquent thunders,
    The Baronet's eloquent ears:
Denouncings of Papists and treasons,
    Of foreign dominion and oats;
Misrepresentations of reasons,
    And misunderstandings of notes.

Good-night to the Season!—the buildings
    Enough to make Inigo sick;
The paintings, and plasterings, and gildings
    Of stucco, and marble, and brick;
The orders deliciously blended,
    From love of effect, into one;
The club-houses only intended,
    The palaces only begun;
The hell where the fiend, in his glory,
    Sits staring at putty and stones,
And scrambles from story to story,
    To rattle at midnight his bones.

Good-night to the Season!—the dances,
    The fillings of hot little rooms,
The glancings of rapturous glances,
    The fancyings of fancy costumes;
The pleasures which Fashion makes duties,
    The praisings of fiddles and flutes,
The luxury of looking at beauties,
    The tedium of talking to mutes;

The female diplomatists, planners
   Of matches for Laura and Jane,
The ice of her Ladyship's manners,
   The ice of his Lordship's champagne.

Good-night to the Season!—the rages
   Led off by the chiefs of the throng,
The Lady Matilda's new pages,
   The Lady Eliza's new song;
Miss Fennel's macaw, which at Boodle's
   Is held to have something to say;
Mrs. Splenetic's musical poodles,
   Which bark 'Batti Batti' all day;
The pony Sir Araby sported,
   As hot and as black as a coal,
And the Lion his mother imported,
   In bearskins and grease, from the Pole.

Good-night to the Season!—the Toso,
   So very majestic and tall;
Miss Ayton, whose singing was so-so,
   And Pasta, divinest of all;
The labour in vain of the Ballet,
   So sadly deficient in stars;
The foreigners thronging the Alley,
   Exhaling the breath of cigars;
The 'loge' where some heiress, how killing,
   Environ'd with Exquisites sits,
The lovely one out of her drilling,
   The silly ones out of their wits.

Good-night to the Season!—the splendour
   That beam'd in the Spanish Bazaar;
Where I purchased—my heart was so tender—
   A card-case,—a pasteboard guitar,—

A bottle of perfume,— a girdle,—
  A lithograph'd Riego full-grown,
Whom Bigotry drew on a hurdle
  That artists might draw him on stone,—
A small panorama of Seville,—
  A trap for demolishing flies,—
A caricature of the Devil,—
  And a look from Miss Sheridan's eyes.

Good-night to the Season!—the flowers
  Of the grand horticultural fête,
When boudoirs were quitted for bowers,
  And the fashion was not to be late;
When all who had money and leisure
  Grew rural o'er ices and wines,
All pleasantly toiling for pleasure,
  All hungrily pining for pines,
And making of beautiful speeches,
  And marring of beautiful shows,
And feeding on delicate peaches,
  And treading on delicate toes.

Good-night to the Season!—another
  Will come with its trifles and toys,
And hurry away, like its brother,
  In sunshine, and odour, and noise.
Will it come with a rose or a briar?
  Will it come with a blessing or curse?
Will its bonnets be lower or higher?
  Will its morals be better or worse?
Will it find me grown thinner or fatter,
  Or fonder of wrong or of right,
Or married,—or buried?—no matter,
  Good-night to the Season, Good-night!

271   ## The Vicar

A SECOND EVERY-DAY CHARACTER

SOME years ago, ere Time and Taste
  Had turn'd our parish topsy-turvy,
When Darnel Park was Darnel Waste,
  And roads as little known as scurvy,
The man who lost his way between
  St. Mary's Hill and Sandy Thicket,
Was always shown across the Green,
  And guided to the Parson's wicket.

Back flew the bolt of lissom lath;
  Fair Margaret, in her tidy kirtle,
Led the lorn traveller up the path,
  Through clean-clipt rows of box and myrtle:
And Don and Sancho, Tramp and Tray,
  Upon the parlour steps collected,
Wagg'd all their tails, and seem'd to say,
  'Our master knows you; you're expected.'

Uprose the Reverend Dr. Brown,
  Uprose the Doctor's 'winsome marrow';
The Lady laid her knitting down,
  Her husband clasp'd his ponderous Barrow:
Whate'er the stranger's caste or creed,
  Pundit or Papist, saint or sinner,
He found a stable for his steed,
  And welcome for himself, and dinner.

If, when he reach'd his journey's end,
  And warm'd himself in court or college

He had not gain'd an honest friend,
    And twenty curious scraps of knowledge;—
If he departed as he came,
    With no new light on love or liquor,—
Good sooth, the traveller was to blame,
    And not the Vicarage, nor the Vicar.

His talk was like a stream which runs
    With rapid change from rocks to roses:
It slipp'd from politics to puns;
    It pass'd from Mahomet to Moses:
Beginning with the laws which keep
    The planets in their radiant courses,
And ending with some precept deep
    For dressing eels, or shoeing horses.

He was a shrewd and sound divine,
    Of loud Dissent the mortal terror;
And when, by dint of page and line,
    He 'stablish'd Truth, or startled Error,
The Baptist found him far too deep;
    The Deist sigh'd with saving sorrow;
And the lean Levite went to sleep,
    And dream'd of tasting pork to-morrow.

His sermon never said or show'd
    That Earth is foul, that Heaven is gracious,
Without refreshment on the road
    From Jerome, or from Athanasius:
And sure a righteous zeal inspired
    The hand and head that penn'd and plann'd them;
For all who understood admired,
    And some who did not understand them.

He wrote too, in a quiet way,
  Small treatises, and smaller verses;
And sage remarks on chalk and clay,
  And hints to noble Lords and nurses:
True histories of last year's ghost,
  Lines to a ringlet, or a turban,
And trifles for the Morning Post,
  And nothings for Sylvanus Urban.

He did not think all mischief fair,
  Although he had a knack of joking;
He did not make himself a bear,
  Although he had a taste for smoking:
And when religious sects ran mad,
  He held, in spite of all his learning,
That if a man's belief is bad,
  It will not be improved by burning.

And he was kind, and loved to sit
  In the low hut or garnish'd cottage,
And praise the farmer's homely wit,
  And share the widow's homelier pottage:
At his approach complaint grew mild;
  And when his hand unbarr'd the shutter,
The clammy lips of Fever smiled
  The welcome, which they could not utter.

He always had a tale for me
  Of Julius Caesar, or of Venus;
From him I learn'd the rule of three,
  Cat's cradle, leap-frog, and Quae genus:
I used to singe his powder'd wig,
  To steal the staff he put such trust in;
And make the puppy dance a jig,
  When he began to quote Augustin.

Alack the change! in vain I look
   For haunts in which my boyhood trifled;
The level lawn, the trickling brook,
   The trees I climb'd, the beds I rifled:
The church is larger than before;
   You reach it by a carriage entry;
It holds three hundred people more;
   And pews are fitted up for gentry.

Sit in the Vicar's seat: you'll hear
   The doctrine of a gentle Johnian,
Whose hand is white, whose tone is clear,
   Whose phrase is very Ciceronian.
Where is the old man laid?—look down,
   And construe on the slab before you,
'*Hic jacet GVLIELMVS BROWN,*
   Vir nullâ non donandus lauru.'

SARA COLERIDGE

272 O SLEEP, my babe, hear not the rippling wave,
   Nor feel the breeze that round thee lingering strays,
     To drink thy balmy breath,
     And sigh one long farewell.

Soon shall it mourn above thy wat'ry bed,
And whisper to me on the wave-beat shore,
     Deep murm'ring in reproach,
     Thy sad untimely fate.

Ere those dear eyes had open'd on the light,
In vain to plead, thy coming life was sold,
    O! wakened but to sleep,
    Whence it can wake no more!

A thousand and a thousand silken leaves
The tufted beech unfolds in early spring,
    All clad in tenderest green,
    All of the self-same shape:

A thousand infant faces, soft and sweet,
Each year sends forth, yet every mother views
    Her last not least beloved
    Like its dear self alone.

No musing mind hath ever yet foreshaped
The face to-morrow's sun shall first reveal,
    No heart hath e'er conceived
    What love that face will bring.

O sleep, my babe, nor heed how mourns the gale
To part with thy soft locks and fragrant breath,
    As when it deeply sighs
    O'er autumn's latest bloom.

THOMAS LOVELL BEDDOES

273   A Voice from The Waters

THE swallow leaves her nest,
The soul my weary breast;
But therefore let the rain
   On my grave
Fall pure; for why complain?
Since both will come again
   O'er the wave.

The wind dead leaves and snow
Doth hurry to and fro;
And, once, a day shall break
    O'er the wave,
When a storm of ghosts shall shake
The dead, until they wake
    In the grave.

274   Dirge

If thou wilt ease thine heart
Of love and all its smart,
    Then sleep, dear, sleep;
And not a sorrow
    Hang any tear on your eyelashes;
    Lie still and deep,
    Sad soul, until the sea-wave washes
The rim o' the sun to-morrow,
    In eastern sky.

But wilt thou cure thine heart
Of love and all its smart,
    Then die, dear, die;
'Tis deeper, sweeter,
    Than on a rose bank to lie dreaming
    With folded eye;
    And then alone, amid the beaming
Of love's stars, thou'lt meet her
    In eastern sky.

275   Song by Isbrand

SQUATS on a toad-stool under a tree
    A bodiless childfull of life in the gloom,
Crying with frog voice, 'What shall I be?
Poor unborn ghost, for my mother killed me
    Scarcely alive in her wicked womb.
What shall I be? shall I creep to the egg
    That's cracking asunder yonder by Nile,
            And with eighteen toes
            And a snuff-taking nose,
    Make an Egyptian crocodile?
Sing, "Catch a mummy by the leg
        And crunch him with an upper jaw,
        Wagging tail and clenching claw;
        Take a bill-full from my craw,
        Neighbour raven, caw, O caw,
        Grunt, my crocky, pretty maw!"

'Swine, shall I be you? Thou'rt a dear dog;
    But for a smile, and kiss, and pout,
    I much prefer *your* black-lipped snout,
        Little, gruntless, fairy hog,
        Godson of the hawthorn hedge.
For, when Ringwood snuffs me out,
    And 'gins my tender paunch to grapple,
    Sing, "Twixt your ancles visage wedge,
        And roll up like an apple."

'Serpent Lucifer, how do you do?
Of your worms and your snakes I'd be one or two;
    For in this dear planet of wool and of leather
'Tis pleasant to need neither shirt, sleeve, nor shoe,
    And have arm, leg, and belly together.

Then aches your head, or are you lazy?
Sing, "Round your neck your belly wrap,
Tail-a-top, and make your cap
  Any bee and daisy."

'I'll not be a fool, like the nightingale
Who sits up all midnight without any ale,
  Making a noise with his nose;
Nor a camel, although 'tis a beautiful back;
Nor a duck, notwithstanding the music of quack,
  And the webby, mud-patting toes.
I'll be a new bird with the head of an ass,
  Two pigs' feet, two men's feet, and two of a hen;
Devil-winged; dragon-bellied; grave-jawed, because grass
  Is a beard that's soon shaved, and grows seldom again
    Before it is summer; so cow all the rest;
    The new Dodo is finished. O! come to my nest.'

276   Song

BY FEMALE VOICES

WE have bathed, where none have seen us,
  In the lake and in the fountain,
    Underneath the charmed statue
Of the timid, bending Venus,
  When the water-nymphs were counting
In the waves the stars of night,
  And those maidens started at you,
Your limbs shone through so soft and bright.
    But no secrets dare we tell,
      For thy slaves unlace thee,
      And he, who shall embrace thee,
    Waits to try thy beauty's spell.

BY MALE VOICES

We have crowned thee queen of women,
 Since love's love, the rose, hath kept her
  Court within thy lips and blushes,
And thine eye, in beauty swimming,
 Kissing, we rendered up the sceptre,
At whose touch the startled soul
  Like an ocean bounds and gushes,
And spirits bend at thy controul.
  But no secrets dare we tell,
   For thy slaves unlace thee,
   And he, who shall embrace thee,
  Is at hand, and so farewell.

277   Dirge

WE do lie beneath the grass
 In the moonlight, in the shade
Of the yew-tree. They that pass
 Hear us not. We are afraid
  They would envy our delight,
  In our graves by glow-worm night.
Come follow us, and smile as we;
 We sail to the rock in the ancient waves,
Where the snow falls by thousands into the sea,
 And the drowned and the shipwrecked have
  happy graves.

278   L'Envoi

WHO findeth comfort in the stars and flowers
Apparelling the earth and evening sky,
That moralize throughout their silent hours,
And woo us heaven-wards till we wish to die;

Oft hath he singled from the soothing quire,
For its calm influence, one of softest charm
To still his bosom's pangs, when they desire
A solace for the world's remorseless harm.
Yet they, since to be beautiful and bless
Is but their way of life, will still remain
Cupbearers to the bee in humbleness,
Or look untouched down through the moony rain,
Living and being worlds in bright content,
Ignorant, not in scorn, of his affection's bent.

So thou, whom I have gazed on, seldom seen,
Perchance forgotten to the very name,
Hast in my thoughts the living glory been,
In beauty various, but in grace the same.
At eventide, if planets were above,
Crowning anew the sea of day bereft,
Swayed by the dewy heaviness of love,
My heart felt pleasure in the track thou'dst left:
And so all sights, all musings, pure and fair,
Touching me, raised thy memory to sight,
As the sea-suns awakes the sun in air,—
If they were not reflections, thou the light.
Therefore bend hitherwards, and let thy mildness
Be glassed in fragments through this storm and wildness.

And pardon, if the sick light of despair
Usurp thy semblance oft, with tearful gleam
Displaying haunted shades of tangled care
In my sad scenes: soon shall a pearly beam,
Shed from the forehead of my heaven's queen,—
That front thy hand is pressed on,—bring delight.
Nor frown, nor blame me, if, such charms between,
Spring mockery, or thoughts of dreadest night.

Death's darts are sometimes Love's. So Nature tells,
When laughing waters close o'er drowning men;
When in flowers' honied corners poison dwells;
When Beauty dies; and the unwearied ken,
Of those who seek a cure for long despair,
Will learn. Death hath his dimples everywhere;
Love only on the cheek, which is to me most fair.

279   Sonnet: To Tartar, A Terrier Beauty

SNOW-DROP of dogs, with ear of brownest dye,
Like the last orphan leaf of naked tree
Which shudders in bleak autumn; though by thee,
Of hearing careless and untutored eye,
Not understood articulate speech of men,
Nor marked the artificial mind of books,
—The mortal's voice eternized by the pen,—
Yet hast thou thought and language all unknown
To Babel's scholars; oft intensest looks,
Long scrutiny o'er some dark-veined stone
Dost thou bestow, learning dead mysteries
Of the world's birth-day, oft in eager tone
With quick-tailed fellows bandiest prompt replies,
Solicitudes canine, four-footed amities.

280   Dream-Pedlary

I

IF there were dreams to sell,
    What would you buy?
Some cost a passing bell;
    Some a light sigh,
That shakes from Life's fresh crown
Only a rose-leaf down.

If there were dreams to sell,
Merry and sad to tell,
And the crier rung the bell,
　　What would you buy?

II

A cottage lone and still,
　　With bowers nigh,
Shadowy, my woes to still,
　　Until I die.
Such pearl from Life's fresh crown
Fain would I shake me down.
Were dreams to have at will,
This would best heal my ill,
　　This would I buy.

III

But there were dreams to sell
　　Ill didst thou buy;
Life is a dream, they tell,
　　Waking, to die.
Dreaming a dream to prize,
Is wishing ghosts to rise;
　　And if I had the spell
　　To call the buried well,
　　　Which one would I?

IV

If there are ghosts to raise,
　　What shall I call,
Out of hell's murky haze,
　　Heaven's blue pall?

Raise my loved long-lost boy
To lead me to his joy.—
    There are no ghosts to raise;
    Out of death lead no ways;
      Vain is the call.

V

Know'st thou not ghosts to sue?
    No love thou hast.
Else lie, as I will do,
    And breathe thy last.
So out of Life's fresh crown
Fall like a rose-leaf down.
    Thus are the ghosts to wooe;
    Thus are all dreams made true,
      Ever to last!

281   Alpine Spirit's Song

I

O'ER the snow, through the air, to the mountain,
    With the antelope, with the eagle, ho!
    With a bound, with a feathery row,
To the side of the icy fountain,
    Where the gentians blue-belled blow.
Where the storm-sprite, the rain-drops counting,
    Cowers under the bright rainbow,
      Like a burst of midnight fire,
      Singing shoots my fleet desire,
      Winged with the wing of love,
      Earth below and stars above.

II

Let me rest on the snow, never pressed
   But by chamois light and by eagle fleet,
   Where the hearts of the antelope beat
'Neath the light of the moony cresset,
   Where the wild cloud rests his feet,
And the scented airs caress it
   From the alpine orchis sweet:
      And about the Sandalp lone
      Voices airy breathe a tone,
      Charming, with the sense of love,
      Earth below and stars above.

III

Through the night, like a dragon from Pilate
   Out of murky cave, let us cloudy sail
   Over lake, over bowery vale,
As a chime of bells, at twilight
   In the downy evening gale,
Passes swimming tremulously light;
   Till we reach yon rocky pale
      Of the mountain crowning all,
      Slumber there by waterfall,
      Lonely like a spectre's love,
      Earth beneath, and stars above.

282   The Song of the Western Men

I

A GOOD sword and a trusty hand!
  A merry heart and true!
King James's men shall understand
  What Cornish lads can do!

II

And have they fix'd the where and when?
  And shall Trelawny die?
Here's twenty thousand Cornish men
  Will see the reason why!

III

Out spake their Captain brave and bold,
  A merry wight was he:
'If London Tower were Michael's hold,
  We'll set Trelawny free!

IV

'We'll cross the Tamar, land to land,
  The Severn is no stay—
All side by side, and hand to hand,
  And who shall bid us nay?

V

'And when we come to London Wall,
  A pleasant sight to view,
Come forth! Come forth, ye cowards all,
  To better men than you!

459

VI

'Trelawny he's in keep and hold,
　　Trelawny he may die;
But here's twenty thousand Cornish bold
　　Will see the reason why!'

283　　　　　　Featherstone's Doom

I

TWIST thou and twine! in light and gloom
　　A spell is on thine hand;
The wind shall be thy changeful loom,
　　Thy web, the shifting sand!

II

Twine from this hour in ceaseless toil
　　On Blackrock's sullen shore;—
Till cordage of the sand shall coil
　　Where crested surges roar.

III

'Tis for that hour when from the wave
　　Near voices wildly cried,
When thy stern hand no succour gave
　　The cable at thy side.

NOTE [1869]

The Blackrock is a bold, dark, pillared mass of schist, which rises mid-
way on the shore of Widemouth Bay, near Bude, and is held to be the lair
of the troubled spirit of Featherstone the wrecker, imprisoned therein until
he shall have accomplished his doom.

IV

Twist thou and twine! in light and gloom
　　The spell is on thine hand;
The wind shall be thy changeful loom,
　　Thy web, the shifting sand!

284　　　　　Aishah-Schĕchĭnăh

I

A Shape like folded light: embodied air:
　　Yet wreath'd with flesh, and warm:—
All, that of heaven, is feminine and fair,
　　Moulded, in visible form!

II

She stood—the Lady Schĕchĭnăh of earth,
　　A Chancel for the sky:—
Where woke, to breath and beauty, God's own birth,
　　For men to see Him by!

III

Round her—too pure to mingle with the Day—
　　Light, that was Life, abode:
Folded within her fibres, meekly lay,
　　The link of boundless God.

IV

So linked: so blent: that when, with pulse fulfill'd,
　　Moved, but that infant hand,—
Far, far away, His conscious Godhead thrill'd,
　　And stars might understand!

¹ [The Hebrew title comprises the Talmudic terms signifying respectively Woman and the Presence of God.]

V

Lo! where they pause, with intergathering rest,
  The Threefold, and, the One!
And lo! He binds them to her Orient breast,
  His Manhood girded on!

VI

The Zone, where two glad worlds for ever meet,
  Beneath that bosom, ran:—
Deep in that womb, the conquering Paraclete,
  Smote Godhead on to man!

VII

Sole scene among the stars; where, yearning, glide,
  The Threefold and the One:—
Her God upon her lap: the Virgin-Bride,
  Her awful Child: her Son!

BREACHAN [*pseud.*]

May 1860

285   Death Song

THERE lies a cold corpse upon the sands
  Down by the rolling sea;
Close up the eyes and straighten the hands,
  As a Christian man's should be.

Bury it deep, for the good of thy soul,
  Six feet below the ground;
Let the sexton come and the death-bell toll,
  And good men stand around.

Lay it among the churchyard stones,
 Where the priest hath blessed the clay;
I cannot leave the unburied bones,
 And I fain would go my way.

ELIZABETH BARRETT BROWNING

286   Grief

I TELL you, hopeless grief is passionless—
That only men incredulous of despair,
Half-taught in anguish, through the midnight air,
Beat upward to God's throne in loud access
Of shrieking and reproach. Full desertness
In souls, as countries, lieth silent—bare
Under the blenching, vertical eye-glare
Of the absolute Heavens. Deep-hearted man, express
Grief for thy Dead in silence like to death;
Most like a monumental statue set
In everlasting watch and moveless woe,
Till itself crumble to the dust beneath.
Touch it: the marble eyelids are not wet—
If it could weep, it could arise and go.

287   The Mask

I

I HAVE a smiling face, she said,
 I have a jest for all I meet;
I have a garland for my head,
 And all its flowers are sweet,—
And so you call me gay, she said.

II

Grief taught to me this smile, she said,
  And Wrong did teach this jesting bold;
These flowers were plucked from garden-bed
  While a death-chime was tolled—
And what now will you say?—she said.

III

Behind no prison-grate, she said,
  Which slurs the sunshine half a mile,
Live captives so uncomforted,
  As souls behind a smile.
God's pity let us pray, she said.

IV

I know my face is bright, she said,—
  Such brightness, dying suns diffuse;
I bear upon my forehead shed,
  The sign of what I lose,—
The ending of my day, she said.

V

If I dared leave this smile, she said,
  And take a moan upon my mouth,
And tie a cypress round my head,
  And let my tears run smooth,—
It were the happier way, she said.

VI

And since that must not be, she said,
  I fain your bitter world would leave.
How calmly, calmly, smile the Dead,
  Who do not, therefore, grieve!
The yea of Heaven is yea, she said.

VII

But in your bitter world, she said,
    Face-joy's a costly mask to wear,
And bought with pangs long nourished
    And rounded to despair.
Grief's earnest makes life's play, she said.

VIII

Ye weep for those who weep?—she said—
    Ah fools!—I bid you pass them by;
Go, weep for those whose hearts have bled
    What time their eyes were dry.
Whom sadder can I say?—she said.

288   Sonnets from the Portuguese

I THOUGHT once how Theocritus had sung
Of the sweet years, the dear and wished-for years,
Who each one in a gracious hand appears
To bear a gift for mortals, old or young:
And, as I mused it in his antique tongue,
I saw, in gradual vision through my tears,
The sweet, sad years, the melancholy years, . . .
Those of my own life, who by turns had flung
A shadow across me. Straightway I was 'ware,
So weeping, how a mystic Shape did move
Behind me, and drew me backward by the hair;
And a voice said in mastery while I strove, . . .
'Guess now who holds thee?'—'Death,' I said. But, there,
The silver answer rang, . . . 'Not Death, but Love.'

★

289   IF thou must love me, let it be for nought
Except for love's sake only. Do not say
'I love her for her smile . . her look . . her way
Of speaking gently, . . for a trick of thought
That falls in well with mine, and certes brought
A sense of pleasant ease on such a day—
For these things in themselves, Beloved, may
Be changed, or change for thee,—and love, so wrought,
May be unwrought so. Neither love me for
Thine own dear pity's wiping my cheeks dry,
Since one might well forget to weep, who bore
Thy comfort long, and lose thy love thereby.
But love me for love's sake, that evermore
Thou may'st love on through love's eternity.

*

290   BELOVED, thou hast brought me many flowers
Plucked in the garden, all the summer through
And winter, and it seemed as if they grew
In this close room, nor missed the sun and showers.
So, in the like name of that love of ours,
Take back these thoughts, which here unfolded too,
And which on warm and cold days I withdrew
From my heart's ground. Indeed, those beds and bowers
Be overgrown with bitter weeds and rue,
And wait thy weeding: yet here's eglantine,
Here's ivy!—take them, as I used to do
Thy flowers, and keep them where they shall not pine:
Instruct thine eyes to keep their colours true,
And tell thy soul, their roots are left in mine.

A Denial

I

We have met late—it is too late to meet,
  O friend, not more than friend!
Death's forecome shroud is tangled round my feet,
And if I step or stir, I touch the end.
  In this last jeopardy
Can I approach thee, I, who cannot move?
How shall I answer thy request for love?
  Look in my face and see.

II

I love thee not, I dare not love thee! go
  In silence; drop my hand.
If thou seek roses, seek them where they blow
In garden-alleys, not in desert-sand.
  Can life and death agree,
That thou shouldst stoop thy song to my complaint?
I cannot love thee. If the word is faint,
  Look in my face and see.

III

I might have loved thee in some former days,
  Oh, then, my spirits had leapt
As now they sink, at hearing thy love-praise.
Before these faded cheeks were overwept,
  Had this been asked of me,
To love thee with my whole strong heart and head,—
I should have said still . . . yes, but *smiled* and said,
  'Look in my face and see!'

IV

But now . . God sees me, God, who took my heart
   And drowned it in life's surge.
In all your wide warm earth I have no part—
A light song overcomes me like a dirge.
   Could Love's great harmony
The saints keep step to when their bonds are loose,
Not weigh me down? am *I* a wife to choose?
   Look in my face and see.

V

While I behold, as plain as one who dreams,
   Some woman of full worth,
Whose voice, as cadenced as a silver stream's,
Shall prove the fountain-soul which sends it forth;
   One younger, more thought-free
And fair and gay, than I, thou must forget,
With brighter eyes than these . . which are not wet . .
   Look in my face and see!

VI

So farewell thou, whom I have known too late
   To let thee come so near.
Be counted happy while men call thee great,
And one belovèd woman feels thee dear!—
   Not I!—that cannot be.
I am lost, I am changed,—I must go farther, where
The change shall take me worse, and no one dare
   Look in my face to see.

VII

Meantime I bless thee. By these thoughts of mine
   I bless thee from all such!
I bless thy lamp to oil, thy cup to wine,
Thy hearth to joy, thy hand to an equal touch
   Of loyal troth. For me,
I love thee not, I love thee not!—away!
Here's no more courage in my soul to say
   'Look in my face and see.'

FREDERICK TENNYSON

292   The Glory of Nature

IF only once the chariot of the Morn
   Had scatter'd from its wheels the twilight dun,
   But once the unimaginable Sun
Flash'd godlike thro' perennial clouds forlorn,
And shown us Beauty for a moment born;

If only once blind eyes had seen the Spring,
   Waking amid the triumphs of midnoon;
   But once had seen the lovely Summer boon
Pass by in state like a full-robed King,
The waters dance, the woodlands laugh and sing;

If only once deaf ears had heard the joy
   Of the wild birds, or morning breezes blowing,
   Or silver fountains from their caverns flowing,
Or the deep-voiced rivers rolling by;
Then Night eternal fallen from the sky;

If only once weird Time had rent asunder
   The curtain of the Clouds, and shown us Night
   Climbing into the awful Infinite
Those stairs whose steps are worlds, above and under,
Glory on glory, wonder upon wonder!

The Lightnings lit the Earthquake on his way;
   The sovran Thunder spoken to the World;
   The realm-wide banners of the Wind unfurl'd;
Earth-prison'd Fires broke loose into the day;
Or the great Seas awoke—then slept for aye!

Ah! sure the heart of Man, too strongly tried
   By Godlike Presences so vast and fair,
   Withering with dread, or sick with love's despair,
Had wept for ever, and to Heaven cried,
Or struck with lightnings of delight had died.

But He, though heir of Immortality,
   With mortal dust too feeble for the sight,
   Draws thro' a veil God's overwhelming light;
Use arms the Soul—anon there moveth by
A more majestic Angel—and we die!

CHARLES TENNYSON-TURNER

293   The Steam Threshing-Machine

With the Straw Carrier

FLUSH with the pond the lurid furnace burned
At eve, while smoke and vapour filled the yard;
The gloomy winter sky was dimly starred,
The fly-wheel with a mellow murmur turned;

While, ever rising on its mystic stair
In the dim light, from secret chambers borne,
The straw of harvest, severed from the corn,
Climbed, and fell over, in the murky air.
I thought of mind and matter, will and law,
And then of him, who set his stately seal
Of Roman words on all the forms he saw
Of old-world husbandry: *I* could but feel
With what a rich precision *he* would draw
The endless ladder, and the booming wheel!

294   On the Eclipse of the Moon of
                    October 1865

ONE little noise of life remained—I heard
The train pause in the distance, then rush by,
Brawling and hushing, like some busy fly
That murmurs and then settles; nothing stirred
Beside. The shadow of our travelling earth
Hung on the silver moon, which mutely went
Through that grand process, without token sent,
Or any sign to call a gazer forth,
Had I not chanced to see; dumb was the vault
Of heaven, and dumb the fields—no zephyr swept
The forest walks, or through the coppice crept;
Nor other sound the stillness did assault,
Save that faint-brawling railway's move and halt;
So perfect was the silence Nature kept.

295   The Artist on Penmaenmawr

THE first September day was blue and warm,
Flushing the shaly flanks of Penmaenmawr;

While youths and maidens, in the lucid calm
Exulting, bath'd or bask'd from hour to hour;
What colour-passion did the artist feel!
While evermore the jarring trains went by,
Now, as for evermore, in fancy's eye,
Smutch'd with the cruel fires of Abergele;
Then fell the dark o'er the great crags and downs,
And all the night-struck mountain seem'd to say,
'Farewell! these happy skies, this peerless day!
And these fair seas—and, fairer still than they,
The white-arm'd girls in dark blue bathing-gowns,
Among the snowy gulls and summer spray.'

296   To a 'Tenting' Boy

EARLY thou goest forth, to put to rout
The thievish rooks, that all about thee sail;
While thy tin tube, and monitory shout
Report thy lonely function to the vale;
From spot to spot thou rovest far and near,
While the sick ewe in the next pasture ground
Lifts her white eyelash, points her languid ear,
And turns her pensive face towards the sound;
All day thy little trumpet wails about
The great brown field, and, whilst I slowly climb
The grassy slope, with ready watch drawn out,
To meet thy constant question of the time,
Methinks I owe thee much, my little boy,
For this new duty, and its quiet joy.

ALFRED, LORD TENNYSON

297

The Kraken

BELOW the thunders of the upper deep,
Far, far beneath in the abysmal sea,
His ancient, dreamless, uninvaded sleep
The Kraken sleepeth; faintest sunlights flee
About his shadowy sides: above him swell
Huge sponges of millennial growth and height;
And far away into the sickly light,
From many a wondrous grot and secret cell
Unnumber'd and enormous polypi
Winnow with giant arms the slumbering green.
There hath he lain for ages and will lie
Battening upon huge seaworms in his sleep,
Until the latter fire shall heat the deep;
Then once by man and angels to be seen,
In roaring he shall rise and on the surface die.

298

Mariana

Mariana in the moated grange.
Measure for Measure

WITH blackest moss the flower-plots
    Were thickly crusted, one and all:
The rusted nails fell from the knots
    That held the pear to the gable-wall.
The broken sheds look'd sad and strange:
    Unlifted was the clinking latch;
    Weeded and worn the ancient thatch
Upon the lonely moated grange.

She only said, 'My life is dreary,
    He cometh not,' she said;
She said, 'I am aweary, aweary,
    I would that I were dead!'

Her tears fell with the dews at even;
    Her tears fell ere the dews were dried;
She could not look on the sweet heaven,
    Either at morn or eventide.
After the flitting of the bats,
    When thickest dark did trance the sky,
    She drew her casement-curtain by,
And glanced athwart the glooming flats.
        She only said, 'The night is dreary,
            He cometh not,' she said;
        She said, 'I am aweary, aweary,
            I would that I were dead!'

Upon the middle of the night,
    Waking she heard the night-fowl crow:
The cock sung out an hour ere light:
    From the dark fen the oxen's low
Came to her: without hope of change,
    In sleep she seem'd to walk forlorn,
    Till cold winds woke the grey-eyed morn
About the lonely moated grange.
        She only said, 'The day is dreary,
            He cometh not,' she said;
        She said, 'I am aweary, aweary,
            I would that I were dead!'

About a stone-cast from the wall
    A sluice with blacken'd waters slept,
And o'er it many, round and small,
    The cluster'd marish-mosses crept.

Hard by a poplar shook alway,
  All silver-green with gnarled bark:
  For leagues no other tree did mark
The level waste, the rounding gray.
    She only said, 'My life is dreary,
      He cometh not,' she said;
    She said, 'I am aweary, aweary,
      I would that I were dead!'

And ever when the moon was low,
  And the shrill winds were up and away,
In the white curtain, to and fro,
  She saw the gusty shadow sway.
But when the moon was very low,
  And wild winds bound within their cell,
  The shadow of the poplar fell
Upon her bed, across her brow.
    She only said, 'The night is dreary,
      He cometh not', she said;
    She said, 'I am aweary, aweary,
      I would that I were dead!'

All day within the dreamy house,
  The doors upon their hinges creak'd;
The blue fly sung in the pane; the mouse
  Behind the mouldering wainscot shriek'd,
Or from the crevice peer'd about.
  Old faces glimmer'd thro' the doors,
  Old footsteps trod the upper floors,
Old voices called her from without.
    She only said, 'My life is dreary,
      He cometh not,' she said;
    She said, 'I am aweary, aweary,
      I would that I were dead!'

The sparrow's chirrup on the roof,
    The slow clock ticking, and the sound
Which to the wooing wind aloof
    The poplar made, did all confound
Her sense; but most she loathed the hour
    When the thick-moted sunbeam lay
    Athwart the chambers, and the day
Was sloping toward his western bower.
        Then, said she, 'I am very dreary,
            He will not come,' she said;
        She wept, 'I am aweary, aweary,
            Oh God, that I were dead!'

299   Song

I

A SPIRIT haunts the year's last hours
Dwelling amid these yellowing bowers:
        To himself he talks;
For at eventide, listening earnestly,
At his work you may hear him sob and sigh
        In the walks;
        Earthward he boweth the heavy stalks
Of the mouldering flowers:
    Heavily hangs the broad sunflower
        Over its grave i' the earth so chilly;
    Heavily hangs the hollyhock,
        Heavily hangs the tiger-lily.

II

The air is damp, and hush'd, and close,
As a sick man's room when he taketh repose
    An hour before death;
My very heart faints and my whole soul grieves
At the moist rich smell of the rotting leaves,
    And the breath
    Of the fading edges of box beneath,
And the year's last rose.
    Heavily hangs the broad sunflower
      Over its grave i' the earth so chilly;
    Heavily hangs the hollyhock,
      Heavily hangs the tiger-lily.

from 'THE LOTOS-EATERS'

300   Choric Song

I

THERE is sweet music here that softer falls
Than petals from blown roses on the grass,
Or night-dews on still waters between walls
Of shadowy granite, in a gleaming pass;
Music that gentlier on the spirit lies,
Than tir'd eyelids upon tir'd eyes;
Music that brings sweet sleep down from the blissful skies.
Here are cool mosses deep,
And thro' the moss the ivies creep,
And in the stream the long-leaved flowers weep,
And from the craggy ledge the poppy hangs in sleep.

II

Why are we weigh'd upon with heaviness,
And utterly consumed with sharp distress,
While all things else have rest from weariness?
All things have rest: why should we toil alone,
We only toil, who are the first of things,
And make perpetual moan,
Still from one sorrow to another thrown:
Nor ever fold our wings,
And cease from wanderings,
Nor steep our brows in slumber's holy balm;
Nor hearken what the inner spirit sings,
'There is no joy but calm!'
Why should we only toil, the roof and crown of things?

III

Lo! in the middle of the wood,
The folded leaf is woo'd from out the bud
With winds upon the branch, and there
Grows green and broad, and takes no care,
Sun-steep'd at noon, and in the moon
Nightly dew-fed: and turning yellow
Falls, and floats adown the air.
Lo! sweeten'd with the summer light,
The full-juiced apple, waxing over-mellow,
Drops in a silent autumn night.
All its allotted length of days,
The flower ripens in its place,
Ripens and fades, and falls, and hath no toil,
    Fast-rooted in the fruitful soil.

IV

Hateful is the dark-blue sky,
Vaulted o'er the dark-blue sea.
Death is the end of life; ah, why
Should life all labour be?
Let us alone. Time driveth onward fast,
And in a little while our lips are dumb.
Let us alone. What is it that will last?
All things are taken from us, and become
Portions and parcels of the dreadful Past.
Let us alone. What pleasure can we have
To war with evil? Is there any peace
In ever climbing up the climbing wave?
All things have rest, and ripen toward the grave
In silence; ripen, fall and cease:
Give us long rest or death, dark death, or dreamful ease.

V

How sweet it were, hearing the downward stream,
With half-shut eyes ever to seem
Falling asleep in a half-dream!
To dream and dream, like yonder amber light,
Which will not leave the myrrh-bush on the height;
To hear each other's whisper'd speech;
Eating the Lotos day by day,
To watch the crisping ripples on the beach,
And tender curving lines of creamy spray;
To lend our hearts and spirits wholly
To the influence of mild-minded melancholy;
To muse and brood and live again in memory,
With those old faces of our infancy
Heap'd over with a mound of grass,
Two handfuls of white dust, shut in an urn of brass!

VI

Dear is the memory of our wedded lives,
And dear the last embraces of our wives
And their warm tears: but all hath suffer'd change;
For surely now our household hearths are cold:
Our sons inherit us: our looks are strange:
And we should come like ghosts to trouble joy.
Or else the island princes over-bold
Have eat our substance, and the minstrel sings
Before them of the ten-years' war in Troy,
And our great deeds, as half-forgotten things.
Is there confusion in the little isle?
Let what is broken so remain.
The Gods are hard to reconcile:
'Tis hard to settle order once again.
There *is* confusion worse than death,
Trouble on trouble, pain on pain,
Long labour unto aged breath,
Sore task to hearts worn out with many wars
And eyes grown dim with gazing on the pilot-stars.

VII

But, propt on beds of amaranth and moly,
How sweet (while warm airs lull us, blowing lowly)
With half-dropt eyelid still,
Beneath a heaven dark and holy,
To watch the long bright river drawing slowly
His waters from the purple hill—
To hear the dewy echoes calling
From cave to cave thro' the thick-twined vine—
To watch the emerald-colour'd water falling
Thro' many a wov'n acanthus-wreath divine!
Only to hear and see the far-off sparkling brine,
Only to hear were sweet, stretch'd out beneath the pine.

VIII

The Lotos blooms below the barren peak:
The Lotos blows by every winding creek:
All day the wind breathes low with mellower tone:
Thro' every hollow cave and alley lone
Round and round the spicy downs the yellow Lotos-dust is blown.
We have had enough of action, and of motion we,
Roll'd to starboard, roll'd to larboard, when the surge was seething free,
Where the wallowing monster spouted his foam-fountains in the sea.
Let us swear an oath, and keep it with an equal mind,
In the hollow Lotos-land to live and lie reclined
On the hills like Gods together, careless of mankind.
For they lie beside their nectar, and the bolts are hurl'd
Far below them in the valleys, and the clouds are lightly curl'd
Round their golden houses, girdled with the gleaming world:
Where they smile in secret, looking over wasted lands,
Blight and famine, plague and earthquake, roaring deeps and fiery sands,
Clanging fights, and flaming towns, and sinking ships, and praying hands.
But they smile, they find a music centred in a doleful song
Steaming up, a lamentation and an ancient tale of wrong,
Like a tale of little meaning tho' the words are strong;
Chanted from an ill-used race of men that cleave the soil,
Sow the seed, and reap the harvest with enduring toil,
Storing yearly little dues of wheat, and wine and oil;
Till they perish and they suffer—some, 'tis whisper'd—down in hell
Suffer endless anguish, others in Elysian valleys dwell,
Resting weary limbs at last on beds of asphodel.
Surely, surely, slumber is more sweet than toil, the shore
Than labour in the deep mid-ocean, wind and wave and oar;
Oh rest ye, brother mariners, we will not wander more.

301   ## Tithonus

THE woods decay, the woods decay and fall,
The vapours weep their burthen to the ground,
Man comes and tills the field and lies beneath,
And after many a summer dies the swan.
Me only cruel immortality
Consumes: I wither slowly in thine arms,
Here at the quiet limit of the world,
A white-hair'd shadow roaming like a dream
The ever silent spaces of the East,
Far-folded mists, and gleaming halls of morn.

Alas! for this grey shadow, once a man—
So glorious in his beauty and thy choice,
Who madest him thy chosen, that he seem'd
To his great heart none other than a God!
I ask'd thee, 'Give me immortality.'
Then didst thou grant mine asking with a smile,
Like wealthy men who care not how they give.
But thy strong Hours indignant work'd their wills,
And beat me down and marr'd and wasted me,
And tho' they could not end me, left me maim'd
To dwell in presence of immortal youth,
Immortal age beside immortal youth,
And all I was, in ashes. Can thy love,
Thy beauty, make amends, tho' even now,
Close over us, the silver star, thy guide,
Shines in those tremulous eyes that fill with tears
To hear me? Let me go: take back thy gift:
Why should a man desire in any way
To vary from the kindly race of men,
Or pass beyond the goal of ordinance
Where all should pause, as is most meet for all?

A soft air fans the cloud apart; there comes
A glimpse of that dark world where I was born.
Once more the old mysterious glimmer steals
From thy pure brows, and from thy shoulders pure,
And bosom beating with a heart renew'd.
Thy cheek begins to redden thro' the gloom,
Thy sweet eyes brighten slowly close to mine,
Ere yet they blind the stars, and the wild team
Which love thee, yearning for thy yoke, arise,
And shake the darkness from their loosen'd manes,
And beat the twilight into flakes of fire.

Lo! ever thus thou growest beautiful
In silence, then before thine answer given
Departest, and thy tears are on my cheek.

Why wilt thou ever scare me with thy tears,
And make me tremble lest a saying learnt
In days far-off, on that dark earth, be true?
'The Gods themselves cannot recall their gifts.'

Ay me! ay me! with what another heart
In days far-off, and with what other eyes
I used to watch—if I be he that watch'd—
The lucid outline forming round thee; saw
The dim curls kindle into sunny rings;
Changed with thy mystic change, and felt my blood
Glow with the glow that slowly crimson'd all
Thy presence and thy portals, while I lay,
Mouth, forehead, eyelids, growing dewy-warm
With kisses balmier than half-opening buds
Of April, and could hear the lips that kiss'd
Whispering I knew not what of wild and sweet,
Like that strange song I heard Apollo sing,
While Ilion like a mist rose into towers.

Yet hold me not for ever in thine East:
How can my nature longer mix with thine?
Coldly thy rosy shadows bathe me, cold
Are all thy lights, and cold my wrinkled feet
Upon thy glimmering thresholds, when the steam
Floats up from those dim fields about the homes
Of happy men that have the power to die,
And grassy barrows of the happier dead.
Release me, and restore me to the ground;
Thou seëst all things, thou wilt see my grave:
Thou wilt renew thy beauty morn by morn!
I earth in earth forget these empty courts,
And thee returning on thy silver wheels.

302 ['Go by']

COME not, when I am dead,
    To drop thy foolish tears upon my grave,
To trample round my fallen head,
    And vex the unhappy dust thou wouldst not save.
There let the wind sweep and the plover cry;
        But thou, go by.

Child, if it were thine error or thy crime
    I care no longer, being all unblest:
Wed whom thou wilt, but I am sick of Time,
    And I desire to rest.
Pass on, weak heart, and leave me where I lie:
        Go by, go by.

303   BREAK, break, break
         On thy cold gray stones, O Sea!
      And I would that my tongue could utter
         The thoughts that arise in me.

      O well for the fisherman's boy,
         That he shouts with his sister at play!
      O well for the sailor lad,
         That he sings in his boat on the bay!

      And the stately ships go on
         To their haven under the hill;
      But O for the touch of a vanish'd hand,
         And the sound of a voice that is still!

      Break, break, break
         At the foot of thy crags, O Sea!
      But the tender grace of a day that is dead
         Will never come back to me.

304   from *THE PRINCESS*

      THE splendour falls on castle walls
         And snowy summits old in story:
      The long light shakes across the lakes,
         And the wild cataract leaps in glory.
  Blow, bugle, blow, set the wild echoes flying,
  Blow, bugle; answer, echoes, dying, dying, dying.

      O hark, O hear! how thin and clear,
         And thinner, clearer, farther going!
      O sweet and far from cliff and scar
         The horns of Elfland faintly blowing!
  Blow, let us hear the purple glens replying:
  Blow, bugle; answer, echoes, dying, dying, dying.

O love, they die in yon rich sky,
   They faint on hill or field or river:
Our echoes roll from soul to soul,
   And grow for ever and for ever.
Blow, bugle, blow, set the wild echoes flying,
And answer, echoes, answer, dying, dying, dying.

*

305   TEARS, idle tears, I know not what they mean,
Tears from the depth of some divine despair
Rise in the heart, and gather to the eyes,
In looking on the happy Autumn-fields,
And thinking of the days that are no more.

Fresh as the first beam glittering on a sail,
That brings our friends up from the underworld,
Sad as the last which reddens over one
That sinks with all we love below the verge;
So sad, so fresh, the days that are no more.

Ah, sad and strange as in dark summer dawns
The earliest pipe of half-awaken'd birds
To dying ears, when unto dying eyes
The casement slowly grows a glimmering square;
So sad, so strange, the days that are no more.

Dear as remember'd kisses after death,
And sweet as those by hopeless fancy feign'd
On lips that are for others; deep as love,
Deep as first love, and wild with all regret;
O Death in Life, the days that are no more.

*

306 Ask me no more: the moon may draw the sea;
      The cloud may stoop from heaven and take the shape
      With fold to fold, of mountain or of cape;
But O too fond, when have I answer'd thee?
              Ask me no more.

Ask me no more: what answer should I give?
   I love not hollow cheek or faded eye:
   Yet, O my friend, I will not have thee die!
Ask me no more, lest I should bid thee live;
              Ask me no more.

Ask me no more: thy fate and mine are seal'd:
   I strove against the stream and all in vain:
   Let the great river take me to the main:
No more, dear love, for at a touch I yield;
              Ask me no more.

★

307   Now sleeps the crimson petal, now the white;
      Nor waves the cypress in the palace walk;
      Nor winks the gold fin in the porphyry font:
The fire-fly wakens: waken thou with me.

   Now droops the milkwhite peacock like a ghost,
   And like a ghost she glimmers on to me.

   Now lies the Earth all Danaë to the stars,
   And all thy heart lies open unto me.

   Now slides the silent meteor on, and leaves
   A shining furrow, as thy thoughts in me.

487

Now folds the lily all her sweetness up,
And slips into the bosom of the lake:
So fold thyself, my dearest, thou, and slip
Into my bosom and be lost in me.

★

308   COME down, O maid, from yonder mountain height:
What pleasure lives in height (the shepherd sang),
In height and cold, the splendour of the hills?
But cease to move so near the Heavens, and cease
To glide a sunbeam by the blasted Pine,
To sit a star upon the sparkling spire;
And come, for Love is of the valley, come,
For Love is of the valley, come thou down
And find him; by the happy threshold, he,
Or hand in hand with Plenty in the maize,
Or red with spirted purple of the vats,
Or foxlike in the vine; nor cares to walk
With Death and Morning on the silver horns,
Nor wilt thou snare him in the white ravine,
Nor find him dropt upon the firths of ice,
That huddling slant in furrow-cloven falls
To roll the torrent out of dusky doors:
But follow; let the torrent dance thee down
To find him in the valley; let the wild
Lean-headed Eagles yelp alone, and leave
The monstrous ledges there to slope, and spill
Their thousand wreaths of dangling water-smoke,
That like a broken purpose waste in air:
So waste not thou; but come; for all the vales
Await thee; azure pillars of the hearth
Arise to thee; the children call, and I
Thy shepherd pipe, and sweet is every sound,

Sweeter thy voice, but every sound is sweet;
Myriads of rivulets hurrying thro' the lawn,
The moan of doves in immemorial elms,
And murmuring of innumerable bees.

309   The Daisy

WRITTEN AT EDINBURGH

O LOVE, what hours were thine and mine,
In lands of palm and southern pine;
    In lands of palm, of orange-blossom,
Of olive, aloe, and maize and vine.

What Roman strength Turbià show'd
In ruin, by the mountain road;
    How like a gem, beneath, the city
Of little Monaco, basking, glow'd.

How richly down the rocky dell
The torrent vineyard streaming fell
    To meet the sun and sunny waters,
That only heaved with a summer swell.

What slender campanili grew
By bays, the peacock's neck in hue;
    Where, here and there, on sandy beaches
A milky-bell'd amaryllis blew.

How young Columbus seem'd to rove,
Yet present in his natal grove,
    Now watching high on mountain cornice,
And steering, now, from a purple cove,

Now pacing mute by ocean's rim;
Till, in a narrow street and dim,
  I stay'd the wheels at Cogoletto,
And drank, and loyally drank to him.

Nor knew we well what pleased us most,
Not the clipt palm of which they boast;
  But distant colour, happy hamlet,
A moulder'd citadel on the coast,

Or tower, or high hill-convent, seen
A light amid its olives green;
  Or olive-hoary cape in ocean;
Or rosy blossom in hot ravine,

Where oleanders flush'd the bed
Of silent torrents, gravel-spread;
  And, crossing, oft we saw the glisten
Of ice, far up on a mountain head.

We loved that hall, tho' white and cold,
Those niched shapes of noble mould,
  A princely people's awful princes,
The grave, severe Genovese of old.

At Florence too what golden hours,
In those long galleries, were ours;
  What drives about the fresh Cascinè,
Or walks in Boboli's ducal bowers.

In bright vignettes, and each complete,
Of tower or duomo, sunny-sweet,
  Or palace, how the city glitter'd,
Thro' cypress avenues, at our feet.

But when we crost the Lombard plain
Remember what a plague of rain;
    Of rain at Reggio, rain at Parma;
At Lodi, rain, Piacenza, rain.

And stern and sad (so rare the smiles
Of sunlight) look'd the Lombard piles;
    Porch-pillars on the lion resting,
And sombre, old, colonnaded aisles.

O Milan, O the chanting quires,
The giant windows' blazon'd fires,
    The height, the space, the gloom, the glory!
A mount of marble, a hundred spires!

I climb'd the roofs at break of day;
Sun-smitten Alps before me lay.
    I stood among the silent statues,
And statued pinnacles, mute as they.

How faintly-flush'd, how phantom-fair,
Was Monte Rosa, hanging there
    A thousand shadowy-pencill'd valleys
And snowy dells in a golden air.

Remember how we came at last
To Como; shower and storm and blast
    Had blown the lake beyond his limit,
And all was flooded; and how we past

From Como, when the light was gray,
And in my head, for half the day,
    The rich Virgilian rustic measure
Of Lari Maxume, all the way,

Like ballad-burthen music, kept,
As on The Lariano crept
   To that fair port below the castle
Of Queen Theodolind, where we slept;

Or hardly slept, but watch'd awake
A cypress in the moonlight shake,
   The moonlight touching o'er a terrace
One tall Agavè above the lake.

What more? we took our last adieu,
And up the snowy Splugen drew,
   But ere we reach'd the highest summit
I pluck'd a daisy, I gave it you.

It told of England then to me,
And now it tells of Italy.
   O love, we two shall go no longer
To lands of summer across the sea;

So dear a life your arms enfold
Whose crying is a cry for gold:
   Yet here to-night in this dark city,
When ill and weary, alone and cold,

I found, tho' crush'd to hard and dry,
This nurseling of another sky
   Still in the little book you lent me,
And where you tenderly laid it by:

And I forgot the clouded Forth,
The gloom that saddens Heaven and Earth,
   The bitter east, the misty summer
And gray metropolis of the North.

Perchance, to lull the throbs of pain,
Perchance, to charm a vacant brain,
   Perchance, to dream you still beside me,
My fancy fled to the South again.

310   In the Garden at Swainston

NIGHTINGALES warbled without,
   Within was weeping for thee:
Shadows of three dead men
   Walk'd in the walks with me,
   Shadows of three dead men and thou wast one of the three.

Nightingales sang in his woods:
   The Master was far away:
Nightingales warbled and sang
   Of a passion that lasts but a day;
   Still in the house in his coffin the Prince of courtesy lay.

Two dead men have I known
   In courtesy like to thee:
Two dead men have I loved
   With a love that ever will be:
   Three dead men have I loved and thou art last of the three.

from *IN MEMORIAM*

A[RTHUR]. H[ENRY]. H[ALLAM].

OBIIT MDCCCXXXIII

311   I HELD it truth, with him who sings
     To one clear harp in divers tones,
     That men may rise on stepping-stones
    Of their dead selves to higher things.

But who shall so forecast the years
    And find in loss a gain to match?
    Or reach a hand thro' time to catch
The far-off interest of tears?

Let Love clasp Grief lest both be drown'd,
    Let darkness keep her raven gloss:
    Ah, sweeter to be drunk with loss,
To dance with death, to beat the ground,

Than that the victor Hours should scorn
    The long result of love, and boast,
    'Behold the man that loved and lost,
But all he was is overworn.'

★

312   OLD Yew, which graspest at the stones
    That name the under-lying dead,
    Thy fibres net the dreamless head,
Thy roots are wrapt about the bones.

The seasons bring the flower again,
    And bring the firstling to the flock;
    And in the dusk of thee, the clock
Beats out the little lives of men.

O not for thee the glow, the bloom,
    Who changest not in any gale,
    Nor branding summer suns avail
To touch thy thousand years of gloom:

And gazing on thee, sullen tree,
    Sick for thy stubborn hardihood,
    I seem to fail from out my blood
And grow incorporate into thee.

★

313   DARK house, by which once more I stand
      Here in the long unlovely street,
      Doors, where my heart was used to beat
    So quickly, waiting for a hand,

    A hand that can be clasp'd no more—
      Behold me, for I cannot sleep,
      And like a guilty thing I creep
    At earliest morning to the door.

    He is not here; but far away
      The noise of life begins again,
      And ghastly thro' the drizzling rain
    On the bald street breaks the blank day.

*

314   CALM is the morn without a sound,
      Calm as to suit a calmer grief,
      And only thro' the faded leaf
    The chesnut pattering to the ground:

    Calm and deep peace on this high wold,
      And on these dews that drench the furze,
      And all the silvery gossamers
    That twinkle into green and gold:

    Calm and still light on yon great plain
      That sweeps with all its autumn bowers,
      And crowded farms and lessening towers,
    To mingle with the bounding main:

    Calm and deep peace in this wide air,
      These leaves that redden to the fall;
      And in my heart, if calm at all,
    If any calm, a calm despair:

Calm on the seas, and silver sleep,
  And waves that sway themselves in rest,
  And dead calm in that noble breast
Which heaves but with the heaving deep.

★

315   TO-NIGHT the winds begin to rise
  And roar from yonder dropping day:
  The last red leaf is whirl'd away,
The rooks are blown about the skies;

The forest crack'd, the waters curl'd,
  The cattle huddled on the lea;
  And wildly dash'd on tower and tree
The sunbeam strikes along the world:

And but for fancies, which aver
  That all thy motions gently pass
  Athwart a plane of molten glass,
I scarce could brook the strain and stir

That makes the barren branches loud;
  And but for fear it is not so,
  The wild unrest that lives in woe
Would dote and pore on yonder cloud

That rises upward always higher,
  And onward drags a labouring breast,
  And topples round the dreary west,
A looming bastion fringed with fire.

★

316   I ENVY not in any moods
           The captive void of noble rage,
           The linnet born within the cage,
        That never knew the summer woods:

        I envy not the beast that takes
           His licence in the field of time,
           Unfetter'd by the sense of crime,
        To whom a conscience never wakes;

        Nor, what may count itself as blest,
           The heart that never plighted troth
           But stagnates in the weeds of cloth;
        Nor any want-begotten rest.

        I hold it true, whate'er befall;
           I feel it, when I sorrow most;
           'Tis better to have loved and lost
        Than never to have loved at all.

                ★

317   IF Sleep and Death be truly one,
           And every spirit's folded bloom
           Thro' all its intervital gloom
        In some long trance should slumber on:

        Unconscious of the sliding hour,
           Bare of the body, might it last,
           And silent traces of the past
         Be all the colour of the flower:

        So then were nothing lost to man;
           So that still garden of the souls
           In many a figured leaf enrolls
        The total world since life began;

And love will last as pure and whole
   As when he loved me here in Time,
   And at the spiritual prime
Rewaken with the dawning soul.

★

318   OH yet we trust that somehow good
   Will be the final goal of ill,
   To pangs of nature, sins of will,
Defects of doubt, and taints of blood;

That nothing walks with aimless feet;
   That not one life shall be destroy'd,
   Or cast as rubbish to the void,
When God hath made the pile complete;

That not a worm is cloven in vain;
   That not a moth with vain desire
   Is shrivell'd in a fruitless fire,
Or but subserves another's gain.

Behold, we know not anything;
   I can but trust that good shall fall
   At last—far off—at last, to all,
And every winter change to spring.

So runs my dream: but what am I?
   An infant crying in the night:
   An infant crying for the light:
And with no language but a cry.

★

319   THE wish, that of the living whole
   No life may fail beyond the grave,
   Derives it not from what we have
The likest God within the soul?

Are God and Nature then at strife,
   That Nature lends such evil dreams?
   So careful of the type she seems,
So careless of the single life;

That I, considering everywhere
   Her secret meaning in her deeds,
   And finding that of fifty seeds
She often brings but one to bear,

I falter where I firmly trod,
   And falling with my weight of cares
   Upon the great world's altar-stairs
That slope thro' darkness up to God,

I stretch lame hands of faith, and grope,
   And gather dust and chaff, and call
   To what I feel is Lord of all,
And faintly trust the larger hope.

*

320   'So careful of the type?' but no.
   From scarped cliff and quarried stone
   She cries, 'A thousand types are gone:
I care for nothing, all shall go.

'Thou makest thine appeal to me:
   I bring to life, I bring to death:
   The spirit does but mean the breath:
I know no more.' And he, shall he,

Man, her last work, who seem'd so fair,
   Such splendid purpose in his eyes,
   Who roll'd the psalm to wintry skies,
Who built him fanes of fruitless prayer,

Who trusted God was love indeed
 And love Creation's final law—
 Tho' Nature, red in tooth and claw
With ravine, shriek'd against his creed—

Who loved, who suffer'd countless ills,
 Who battled for the True, the Just,
 Be blown about the desert dust,
Or seal'd within the iron hills?

No more? A monster then, a dream,
 A discord. Dragons of the prime,
 That tare each other in their slime,
Were mellow music match'd with him.

O life as futile, then, as frail!
 O for thy voice to soothe and bless!
 What hope of answer, or redress?
Behind the veil, behind the veil.

*

RISEST thou thus, dim dawn, again,
 And howlest, issuing out of night,
 With blasts that blow the poplar white,
And lash with storm the streaming pane?

Day, when my crown'd estate begun
 To pine in that reverse of doom,
 Which sicken'd every living bloom,
And blurr'd the splendour of the sun;

Who usherest in the dolorous hour
 With thy quick tears that make the rose
 Pull sideways, and the daisy close
Her crimson fringes to the shower;

Who might'st have heaved a windless flame
   Up the deep East, or, whispering, play'd
   A chequer-work of beam and shade
Along the hills, yet look'd the same.

As wan, as chill, as wild as now;
   Day, mark'd as with some hideous crime,
   When the dark hand struck down thro' time,
And cancell'd nature's best: but thou,

Lift as thou may'st thy burthen'd brows
   Thro' clouds that drench the morning star,
   And whirl the ungarner'd sheaf afar,
And sow the sky with flying boughs,

And up thy vault with roaring sound
   Climb thy thick noon, disastrous day;
   Touch thy dull goal of joyless gray,
And hide thy shame beneath the ground.

★

322   WITCH-elms that counterchange the floor
   Of this flat lawn with dusk and bright;
   And thou, with all thy breadth and height
Of foliage, towering sycamore;

How often, hither wandering down,
   My Arthur found your shadows fair,
   And shook to all the liberal air
The dust and din and steam of town:

He brought an eye for all he saw;
   He mixt in all our simple sports;
   They pleased him, fresh from brawling courts
And dusty purlieus of the law.

O joy to him in this retreat,
　　Immantled in ambrosial dark,
　　To drink the cooler air, and mark
The landscape winking thro' the heat:

O sound to rout the brood of cares,
　　The sweep of scythe in morning dew,
　　The gust that round the garden flew,
And tumbled half the mellowing pears!

O bliss, when all in circle drawn
　　About him, heart and ear were fed
　　To hear him, as he lay and read
The Tuscan poets on the lawn:

Or in the all-golden afternoon
　　A guest, or happy sister, sung,
　　Or here she brought the harp and flung
A ballad to the brightening moon:

Nor less it pleased in livelier moods,
　　Beyond the bounding hill to stray,
　　And break the livelong summer day
With banquet in the distant woods;

Whereat we glanced from theme to theme,
　　Discuss'd the books to love or hate,
　　Or touch'd the changes of the state,
Or threaded some Socratic dream;

But if I praised the busy town,
　　He loved to rail against it still,
　　For 'ground in yonder social mill
We rub each other's angles down,

'And merge' he said 'in form and gloss
　　The picturesque of man and man.'
　　We talk'd: the stream beneath us ran,
The wine-flask lying couch'd in moss,

Or cool'd within the glooming wave;
　　And last, returning from afar,
　　Before the crimson-circled star
Had fall'n into her father's grave,

And brushing ankle-deep in flowers,
　　We heard behind the woodbine veil
　　The milk that bubbled in the pail,
And buzzings of the honied hours.

★

323　　When rosy plumelets tuft the larch,
　　And rarely pipes the mounted thrush;
　　Or underneath the barren bush
Flits by the sea-blue bird of March;

Come, wear the form by which I know
　　Thy spirit in time among thy peers;
　　The hope of unaccomplish'd years
Be large and lucid round thy brow.

When summer's hourly-mellowing change
　　May breathe, with many roses sweet,
　　Upon the thousand waves of wheat,
That ripple round the lonely grange;

Come: not in watches of the night,
　　But where the sunbeam broodeth warm,
　　Come, beauteous in thine after form,
And like a finer light in light.

★

324   By night we linger'd on the lawn,
      For underfoot the herb was dry;
      And genial warmth; and o'er the sky
The silvery haze of summer drawn;

And calm that let the tapers burn
      Unwavering: not a cricket chirr'd:
      The brook alone far-off was heard,
And on the board the fluttering urn:

And bats went round in fragrant skies,
      And wheel'd or lit the filmy shapes
      That haunt the dusk, with ermine capes
And woolly breasts and beaded eyes;

While now we sang old songs that peal'd
      From knoll to knoll, where, couch'd at ease,
      The white kine glimmer'd, and the trees
Laid their dark arms about the field.

But when those others, one by one,
      Withdrew themselves from me and night,
      And in the house light after light
Went out, and I was all alone,

A hunger seized my heart; I read
      Of that glad year which once had been,
      In those fall'n leaves which kept their green,
The noble letters of the dead:

And strangely on the silence broke
      The silent-speaking words, and strange
      Was love's dumb cry defying change
To test his worth; and strangely spoke

The faith, the vigour, bold to dwell
   On doubts that drive the coward back,
   And keen thro' wordy snares to track
Suggestion to her inmost cell.

So word by word, and line by line,
   The dead man touch'd me from the past,
   And all at once it seem'd at last
The living soul was flash'd on mine,

And mine in this was wound, and whirl'd
   About empyreal heights of thought,
   And came on that which is, and caught
The deep pulsations of the world,

Æonian music measuring out
   The steps of Time—the shocks of Chance—
   The blows of Death. At length my trance
Was cancell'd, stricken thro' with doubt.

Vague words! but ah, how hard to frame
   In matter-moulded forms of speech,
   Or ev'n for intellect to reach
Thro' memory that which I became:

Till now the doubtful dusk reveal'd
   The knolls once more where, couch'd at ease,
   The white kine glimmer'd, and the trees
Laid their dark arms about the field:

And suck'd from out the distant gloom
   A breeze began to tremble o'er
   The large leaves of the sycamore,
And fluctuate all the still perfume,

And gathering freshlier overhead,
   Rock'd the full-foliaged elms, and swung
   The heavy-folded rose, and flung
The lilies to and fro, and said

'The dawn, the dawn,' and died away;
   And East and West, without a breath,
   Mixt their dim lights, like life and death,
To broaden into boundless day.

★

325   UNWATCH'D, the garden bough shall sway,
   The tender blossom flutter down,
   Unloved, that beech will gather brown,
This maple burn itself away;

Unloved, the sun-flower, shining fair,
   Ray round with flames her disk of seed,
   And many a rose-carnation feed
With summer spice the humming air;

Unloved, by many a sandy bar,
   The brook shall babble down the plain,
   At noon or when the lesser wain
Is twisting round the polar star;

Uncared for, gird the windy grove,
   And flood the haunts of hern and crake;
   Or into silver arrows break
The sailing moon in creek and cove;

Till from the garden and the wild
   A fresh association blow,
   And year by year the landscape grow
Familiar to the stranger's child;

As year by year the labourer tills
　His wonted glebe, or lops the glades;
　And year by year our memory fades
From all the circles of the hills.

*

326　Now fades the last long streak of snow,
　　Now burgeons every maze of quick
　　About the flowering squares, and thick
By ashen roots the violets blow.

Now rings the woodland loud and long,
　The distance takes a lovelier hue,
　And drown'd in yonder living blue
The lark becomes a sightless song.

Now dance the lights on lawn and lea,
　The flocks are whiter down the vale,
　And milkier every milky sail
On winding stream or distant sea:

Where now the seamew pipes, or dives
　In yonder greening gleam, and fly
　The happy birds, that change their sky
To build and brood; that live their lives

From land to land; and in my breast
　Spring wakens too; and my regret
　Becomes an April violet,
And buds and blossoms like the rest.

*

327　Doors, where my heart was used to beat
　　So quickly, not as one that weeps
　　I come once more; the city sleeps;
I smell the meadow in the street;

I hear a chirp of birds; I see
   Betwixt the black fronts long-withdrawn
   A light-blue lane of early dawn,
And think of early days and thee,

And bless thee, for thy lips are bland,
   And bright the friendship of thine eye;
   And in my thoughts with scarce a sigh
I take the pressure of thine hand.

★

328   Love is and was my Lord and King,
   And in his presence I attend
   To hear the tidings of my friend,
Which every hour his couriers bring.

Love is and was my King and Lord,
   And will be, tho' as yet I keep
   Within his court on earth, and sleep
Encompass'd by his faithful guard,

And hear at times a sentinel
   Who moves about from place to place,
   And whispers to the worlds of space,
In the deep night, that all is well.

329   [The Sleeping House]

I heard no sound where I stood
But the rivulet on from the lawn
Running down to my own dark wood;
Or the voice of the long sea-wave as it swell'd
Now and then in the dim-gray dawn;

But I look'd, and round, all round the house I beheld
The death-white curtain drawn;
Felt a horror over me creep,
Prickle my skin and catch my breath,
Knew that the death-white curtain meant but sleep,
Yet I shudder'd and thought like a fool of the sleep of death.

330   ['There is none like her']

THERE is none like her, none.
Nor will be when our summers have deceased.
O, art thou sighing for Lebanon
In the long breeze that streams to thy delicious East,
Sighing for Lebanon,
Dark cedar, tho' thy limbs have here increased,
Upon a pastoral slope as fair,
And looking to the South, and fed
With honey'd rain and delicate air,
And haunted by the starry head
Of her whose gentle will has changed my fate,
And made my life a perfumed altar-flame;
And over whom thy darkness must have spread
With such delight as theirs of old, thy great
Forefathers of the thornless garden, there
Shadowing the snow-limb'd Eve from whom she came.

331   [Vivien's Song]

IN Love, if Love be Love, if Love be ours,
Faith and unfaith can ne'er be equal powers:
Unfaith in aught is want of faith in all.

It is the little rift within the lute,
That by and by will make the music mute,
And ever widening slowly silence all.

The little rift within the lover's lute,
Or little pitted speck in garner'd fruit,
That rotting inward slowly moulders all.

It is not worth the keeping: let it go:
But shall it? answer, darling, answer, no.
And trust me not at all or all in all.

332   ['The Song of Love and Death']

SWEET is true love tho' given in vain, in vain;
And sweet is death who puts an end to pain:
I know not which is sweeter, no, not I.

Love, art thou sweet? then bitter death must be:
Love, thou art bitter; sweet is death to me.
O Love, if death be sweeter, let me die.

Sweet love, that seems not made to fade away,
Sweet death, that seems to make us loveless clay,
I know not which is sweeter, no, not I.

I fain would follow love, if that could be;
I needs must follow death, who calls for me;
Call and I follow, I follow! Let me die.

333

The Passing of Arthur

THAT story which the bold Sir Bedivere,
First made and latest left of all the knights,
Told, when the man was no more than a voice
In the white winter of his age, to those
With whom he dwelt, new faces, other minds.

For on their march to westward, Bedivere,
Who slowly paced among the slumbering host,
Heard in his tent the moanings of the King:

'I found Him in the shining of the stars,
I mark'd Him in the flowering of His fields,
But in His ways with men I find Him not.
I waged His wars, and now I pass and die.
O me! for why is all around us here
As if some lesser god had made the world,
But had not force to shape it as he would,
Till the High God behold it from beyond,
And enter it, and make it beautiful?
Or else as if the world were wholly fair,
But that these eyes of men are dense and dim,
    And have not power to see it as it is:
Perchance, because we see not to the close;—
For I, being simple, thought to work His will,
And have but stricken with the sword in vain;
And all whereon I lean'd in wife and friend
Is traitor to my peace, and all my realm
Reels back into the beast, and is no more.
My God, thou hast forgotten me in my death:
Nay—God my Christ—I pass but shall not die.'

Then, ere that last weird battle in the west,
There came on Arthur sleeping, Gawain kill'd
In Lancelot's war, the ghost of Gawain blown
Along a wandering wind, and past his ear
Went shrilling, 'Hollow, hollow all delight!
Hail, King! to-morrow thou shalt pass away.
Farewell! there is an isle of rest for thee.
And I am blown along a wandering wind,
And hollow, hollow, hollow all delight.'
And fainter onward, like wild birds that change
Their season in the night and wail their way
From cloud to cloud, down the long wind the dream
Shrill'd; but in going mingled with dim cries
Far in the moonlit haze among the hills,
As of some lonely city sack'd by night,
When all is lost, and wife and child with wail
Pass to new lords; and Arthur woke and call'd,
'Who spake? A dream. O light upon the wind,
Thine, Gawain, was the voice—are these dim cries
Thine? or doth all that haunts the waste and wild
Mourn, knowing it will go along with me?'

This heard the bold Sir Bedivere and spake:
'O me, my King, let pass whatever will,
Elves, and the harmless glamour of the field;
But in their stead thy name and glory cling
To all high places like a golden cloud
For ever: but as yet thou shalt not pass.
Light was Gawain in life, and light in death
Is Gawain, for the ghost is as the man;
And care not thou for dreams from him, but rise—
I hear the steps of Modred in the west,
And with him many of thy people, and knights
Once thine, whom thou hast loved, but grosser grown

Than heathen, spitting at their vows and thee.
Right well in heart they know thee for the King.
Arise, go forth and conquer as of old.'

  Then spake King Arthur to Sir Bedivere:
'Far other is this battle in the west
Whereto we move, than when we strove in youth,
And brake the petty kings, and fought with Rome,
Or thrust the heathen from the Roman wall,
And shook him thro' the north. Ill doom is mine
To war against my people and my knights.
The king who fights his people fights himself.
And they my knights, who loved me once, the stroke
That strikes them dead is as my death to me.
Yet let us hence, and find or feel a way
Thro' this blind haze, which ever since I saw
One lying in the dust at Almesbury,
Hath folded in the passes of the world.'

  Then rose the King and moved his host by night,
And ever push'd Sir Modred, league by league,
Back to the sunset bound of Lyonnesse—
A land of old upheaven from the abyss
By fire, to sink into the abyss again;
Where fragments of forgotten peoples dwelt,
And the long mountains ended in a coast
Of ever-shifting sand, and far away
The phantom circle of a moaning sea.
There the pursuer could pursue no more,
And he that fled no further fly the King;
And there, that day when the great light of heaven
Burn'd at his lowest in the rolling year,
On the waste sand by the waste sea they closed.
Nor ever yet had Arthur fought a fight

Like this last, dim, weird battle of the west.
A deathwhite mist slept over sand and sea:
Whereof the chill, to him who breathed it, drew
Down with his blood, till all his heart was cold
With formless fear; and ev'n on Arthur fell
Confusion, since he saw not whom he fought.
For friend and foe were shadows in the mist,
And friend slew friend not knowing whom he slew;
And some had visions out of golden youth,
And some beheld the faces of old ghosts
Look in upon the battle; and in the mist
Was many a noble deed, many a base,
And chance and craft and strength in single fights,
And ever and anon with host to host
Shocks, and the splintering spear, the hard mail hewn,
Shield-breakings, and the clash of brands, the crash
Of battleaxes on shatter'd helms, and shrieks
After the Christ, of those who falling down
Look'd up for heaven, and only saw the mist;
And shouts of heathen and the traitor knights,
Oaths, insult, filth, and monstrous blasphemies,
Sweat, writhings, anguish, labouring of the lungs
In the close mist, and cryings for the light,
Moans of the dying, and voices of the dead.

    Last, as by some one deathbed after wail
Of suffering, silence follows, or thro' death
Or deathlike swoon, thus over all that shore,
Save for some whisper of the seething seas,
A dead hush fell; but when the dolorous day
Grew drearier toward twilight falling, came
A bitter wind, clear from the North, and blew
The mist aside, and with that wind the tide
Rose, and the pale King glanced across the field

Of battle: but no man was moving there;
Nor any cry of Christian heard thereon,
Nor yet of heathen; only the wan wave
Brake in among dead faces, to and fro
Swaying the helpless hands, and up and down
Tumbling the hollow helmets of the fallen,
And shiver'd brands that once had fought with Rome,
And rolling far along the gloomy shores
The voice of days of old and days to be.

Then spake King Arthur to Sir Bedivere,
And whiter than the mist that all day long
Had held the field of battle was the King:

'Hearest thou this great voice that shakes the world,
And wastes the narrow realm whereon we move,
And beats upon the faces of the dead,
My dead, as tho' they had not died for me?—
O Bedivere, for on my heart has fall'n
Confusion, till I know not what I am,
Nor whence I am, nor whether I be King.
Behold, I seem but King among the dead.'

Then spake the bold Sir Bedivere: 'My King,
King everywhere! and so the dead have kings,
There also will I worship thee as King.
Yet still thy life is whole, and still I live
Who love thee; but who hates thee, he that brought
The heathen back among us, yonder stands,
Modred, unharm'd, the traitor of thine house.'

Then spake the King: 'My house hath been my doom.
But call not thou this traitor of my house
Who hath but dwelt beneath one roof with me.
My house are rather they who sware my vows,

Yea, even while they brake them, own'd me King.
And well for thee, saying in my dark hour,
When all the purport of my throne hath fail'd,
That quick or dead thou holdest me for King.
King am I, whatsoever be their cry:
And one last act of kinghood shalt thou see
Yet, ere I pass.' And uttering this the King
Made at the man: then Modred smote his liege
Hard on that helm which many a heathen sword
Had beaten thin; while Arthur at one blow,
Striking the last stroke with Excalibur,
Slew him, and all but slain himself, he fell.

So all day long the noise of battle roll'd
Among the mountains by the winter sea;
Until King Arthur's Table, man by man,
Had fall'n in Lyonnesse about their lord,
King Arthur. Then, because his wound was deep,
The bold Sir Bedivere uplifted him,
And bore him to a chapel nigh the field,
A broken chancel with a broken cross,
That stood on a dark strait of barren land:
On one side lay the Ocean, and on one
Lay a great water, and the moon was full.

Then spake King Arthur to Sir Bedivere:
'The sequel of to-day unsolders all
The goodliest fellowship of famous knights
Whereof this world holds record. Such a sleep
They sleep—the men I loved. I think that we
Shall never more, at any future time,
Delight our souls with talk of knightly deeds,
Walking about the gardens and the halls
Of Camelot, as in the days that were.

I perish by this people which I made,—
Tho' Merlin sware that I should come again
To rule once more; but, let what will be, be,
I am so deeply smitten thro' the helm
That without help I cannot last till morn.
Thou therefore take my brand Excalibur,
Which was my pride; for thou rememberest how
In those old days, one summer noon, an arm
Rose up from out the bosom of the lake,
Clothed in white samite, mystic, wonderful,
Holding the sword—and how I row'd across
And took it, and have worn it, like a king;
And, wheresoever I am sung or told
In aftertime, this also shall be known:
But now delay not: take Excalibur,
And fling him far into the middle mere:
Watch what thou seëst, and lightly bring me word.'

   To him replied the bold Sir Bedivere:
'It is not meet, Sir King, to leave thee thus,
Aidless, alone, and smitten thro' the helm—
A little thing may harm a wounded man;
Yet I thy hest will all perform at full,
Watch what I see, and lightly bring thee word.'

   So saying, from the ruin'd shrine he stept,
And in the moon athwart the place of tombs,
Where lay the mighty bones of ancient men,
Old knights, and over them the sea-wind sang
Shrill, chill, with flakes of foam. He, stepping down
By zigzag paths, and juts of pointed rock,
Came on the shining levels of the lake.

   There drew he forth the brand Excalibur,
And o'er him, drawing it, the winter moon,

Brightening the skirts of a long cloud, ran forth
And sparkled keen with frost against the hilt:
For all the haft twinkled with diamond sparks,
Myriads of topaz-lights, and jacinth-work
Of subtlest jewelry. He gazed so long
That both his eyes were dazzled as he stood,
This way and that dividing the swift mind,
In act to throw: but at the last it seem'd
Better to leave Excalibur conceal'd
There in the many-knotted waterflags,
That whistled stiff and dry about the marge.
So strode he back slow to the wounded King.

Then spake King Arthur to Sir Bedivere:
'Hast thou perform'd my mission which I gave?
What is it thou hast seen? or what hast heard?'

And answer made the bold Sir Bedivere:
'I heard the ripple washing in the reeds,
And the wild water lapping on the crag.'

To whom replied King Arthur, faint and pale:
'Thou hast betray'd thy nature and thy name,
Not rendering true answer, as beseem'd
Thy fëalty, nor like a noble knight:
For surer sign had follow'd, either hand,
Or voice, or else a motion of the mere.
This is a shameful thing for men to lie.
Yet now, I charge thee, quickly go again,
As thou art lief and dear, and do the thing
I bade thee, watch, and lightly bring me word.'

Then went Sir Bedivere the second time
Across the ridge, and paced beside the mere,

Counting the dewy pebbles, fix'd in thought;
But when he saw the wonder of the hilt,
How curiously and strangely chased, he smote
His palms together, and he cried aloud:

'And if indeed I cast the brand away,
Surely a precious thing, one worthy note,
Should thus be lost for ever from the earth,
Which might have pleased the eyes of many men.
What good should follow this, if this were done?
What harm, undone? Deep harm to disobey,
Seeing obedience is the bond of rule.
Were it well to obey then, if a king demand
An act unprofitable, against himself?
The King is sick, and knows not what he does.
What record, or what relic of my lord
Should be to aftertime, but empty breath
And rumours of a doubt? But were this kept,
Stored in some treasure-house of mighty kings,
Some one might show it at a joust of arms,
Saying, "King Arthur's sword, Excalibur,
Wrought by the lonely maiden of the Lake.
Nine years she wrought it, sitting in the deeps
Upon the hidden bases of the hills."
So might some old man speak in the aftertime
To all the people, winning reverence.
But now much honour and much fame were lost.'

So spake he, clouded with his own conceit,
And hid Excalibur the second time,
And so strode back slow to the wounded King.

Then spoke King Arthur, breathing heavily:
'What is it thou hast seen? or what hast heard?'

And answer made the bold Sir Bedivere:
'I heard the water lapping on the crag,
And the long ripple washing in the reeds.'

To whom replied King Arthur, much in wrath:
'Ah, miserable and unkind, untrue,
Unknightly, traitor-hearted! Woe is me!
Authority forgets a dying king,
Laid widow'd of the power in his eye
That bow'd the will. I see thee what thou art,
For thou, the latest-left of all my knights,
In whom should meet the offices of all,
Thou wouldst betray me for the precious hilt;
Either from lust of gold, or like a girl
Valuing the giddy pleasure of the eyes.
Yet, for a man may fail in duty twice,
And the third time may prosper, get thee hence:
But if thou spare to fling Excalibur,
I will arise and slay thee with my hands.'

Then quickly rose Sir Bedivere, and ran,
And, leaping down the ridges lightly, plunged
Among the bulrush beds, and clutch'd the sword,
And strongly wheel'd and threw it. The great brand
Made lightnings in the splendour of the moon,
And flashing round and round, and whirl'd in an arch,
Shot like a streamer of the northern morn,
Seen where the moving isles of winter shock
By night, with noises of the Northern Sea.
So flash'd and fell the brand Excalibur:
But ere he dipt the surface, rose an arm
Clothed in white samite, mystic, wonderful,
And caught him by the hilt, and brandish'd him
Three times, and drew him under in the mere.
And lightly went the other to the King.

Then spoke King Arthur, drawing thicker breath:
'Now see I by thine eyes that this is done.
Speak out: what is it thou hast heard, or seen?'

And answer made the bold Sir Bedivere:
'Sir King, I closed mine eyelids, lest the gems
Should blind my purpose, for I never saw,
Nor shall see, here or elsewhere, till I die,
Not tho' I live three lives of mortal men,
So great a miracle as yonder hilt.
Then with both hands I flung him, wheeling him;
But when I look'd again, behold an arm,
Clothed in white samite, mystic, wonderful,
That caught him by the hilt, and brandish'd him
Three times, and drew him under in the mere.'

And answer made King Arthur, breathing hard:
'My end draws nigh; 'tis time that I were gone.
Make broad thy shoulders to receive my weight,
And bear me to the margin; yet I fear
My wound hath taken cold, and I shall die.'

So saying, from the pavement he half rose,
Slowly, with pain, reclining on his arm,
And looking wistfully with wide blue eyes
As in a picture. Him Sir Bedivere
Remorsefully regarded thro' his tears,
And would have spoken, but he found not words;
Then took with care, and kneeling on one knee,
O'er both his shoulders drew the languid hands,
And rising bore him thro' the place of tombs.

But, as he walk'd, King Arthur panted hard,
Like one that feels a nightmare on his bed

When all the house is mute. So sigh'd the King,
Muttering and murmuring at his ear, 'Quick, quick!
I fear it is too late, and I shall die.'
But the other swiftly strode from ridge to ridge,
Clothed with his breath, and looking, as he walk'd,
Larger than human on the frozen hills.
He heard the deep behind him, and a cry
Before. His own thought drove him like a goad.
Dry clash'd his harness in the icy caves
And barren chasms, and all to left and right
The bare black cliff clang'd round him, as he based
His feet on juts of slippery crag that rang
Sharp-smitten with the dint of armed heels—
And on a sudden, lo! the level lake,
And the long glories of the winter moon.

Then saw they how there hove a dusky barge,
Dark as a funeral scarf from stem to stern,
Beneath them; and descending they were ware
That all the decks were dense with stately forms,
Black-stoled, black-hooded, like a dream—by these
Three Queens with crowns of gold: and from them rose
A cry that shiver'd to the tingling stars,
And, as it were one voice, an agony
Of lamentation, like a wind that shrills
All night in a waste land, where no one comes,
Or hath come, since the making of the world.

Then murmur'd Arthur, 'Place me in the barge.'
So to the barge they came. There those three Queens
Put forth their hands, and took the King, and wept.
But she, that rose the tallest of them all
And fairest, laid his head upon her lap,
And loosed the shatter'd casque, and chafed his hands,

And call'd him by his name, complaining loud,
And dropping bitter tears against a brow
Striped with dark blood: for all his face was white
And colourless, and like the wither'd moon
Smote by the fresh beam of the springing east;
And all his greaves and cuisses dash'd with drops
Of onset; and the light and lustrous curls—
That made his forehead like a rising sun
High from the daïs-throne—were parch'd with dust;
Or, clotted into points and hanging loose,
Mix'd with the knightly growth that fringed his lips.
So like a shatter'd column lay the King;
Not like that Arthur who, with lance in rest,
From spur to plume a star of tournament,
Shot thro' the lists at Camelot, and charged
Before the eyes of ladies and of kings.

Then loudly cried the bold Sir Bedivere:
'Ah! my Lord Arthur, whither shall I go?
Where shall I hide my forehead and my eyes?
For now I see the true old times are dead,
When every morning brought a noble chance,
And every chance brought out a noble knight.
Such times have been not since the light that led
The holy Elders with the gift of myrrh.
But now the whole Round Table is dissolved
Which was an image of the mighty world,
And I, the last, go forth companionless,
And the days darken round me, and the years,
Among new men, strange faces, other minds.'

And slowly answer'd Arthur from the barge:
'The old order changeth, yielding place to new,
And God fulfils himself in many ways,

Lest one good custom should corrupt the world.
Comfort thyself: what comfort is in me?
I have lived my life, and that which I have done
May He within himself make pure! but thou
If thou shouldst never see my face again,
Pray for my soul. More things are wrought by prayer
Than this world dreams of. Wherefore, let thy voice
Rise like a fountain for me night and day.
For what are men better than sheep or goats
That nourish a blind life within the brain,
If, knowing God, they lift not hands of prayer
Both for themselves and those who call them friend?
For so the whole round earth is every way
Bound by gold chains about the feet of God.
But now farewell. I am going a long way
With these thou seëst—if indeed I go
(For all my mind is clouded with a doubt)—
To the island-valley of Avilion;
Where falls not hail, or rain, or any snow,
Nor ever wind blows loudly; but it lies
Deep-meadow'd, happy, fair with orchard lawns
And bowery hollows crown'd with summer sea,
Where I will heal me of my grievous wound.'

   So said he, and the barge with oar and sail
Moved from the brink, like some full-breasted swan
That, fluting a wild carol ere her death,
Ruffles her pure cold plume, and takes the flood
With swarthy webs. Long stood Sir Bedivere
Revolving many memories, till the hull
Look'd one black dot against the verge of dawn,
And on the mere the wailing died away.

   But when that moan had past for evermore,
The stillness of the dead world's winter dawn

Amazed him, and he groan'd, 'The King is gone.'
And therewithal came on him the weird rhyme,
'From the great deep to the great deep he goes.'

Whereat he slowly turn'd and slowly clomb
The last hard footstep of that iron crag;
Thence mark'd the black hull moving yet, and cried,
'He passes to be King among the dead,
And after healing of his grievous wound
He comes again; but—if he come no more—
O me, be yon dark Queens in yon black boat,
Who shriek'd and wail'd, the three whereat we gazed
On that high day, when, clothed with living light,
They stood before his throne in silence, friends
Of Arthur, who should help him at his need?'

Then from the dawn it seem'd there came, but faint
As from beyond the limit of the world,
Like the last echo born of a great cry,
Sounds, as if some fair city were one voice
Around a king returning from his wars.

Thereat once more he moved about, and clomb
Ev'n to the highest he could climb, and saw,
Straining his eyes beneath an arch of hand,
Or thought he saw, the speck that bare the King,
Down that long water opening on the deep
Somewhere far off, pass on and on, and go
From less to less and vanish into light.
And the new sun rose bringing the new year.

334　　　　　Crossing the Bar

SUNSET and evening star,
　　And one clear call for me!
And may there be no moaning of the bar,
　　When I put out to sea,

But such a tide as moving seems asleep,
　　Too full for sound and foam
When that which drew from out the boundless deep
　　Turns again home.

Twilight and evening bell,
　　And after that the dark!
And may there be no sadness of farewell,
　　When I embark;

For tho' from out our bourne of Time and Place
　　The flood may bear me far,
I hope to see my Pilot face to face
　　When I have crost the bar.

EDWARD FITZGERALD

335　　　from *THE RUBÁIYÁT OF*
OMAR KHAYYÁM

WAKE! For the Sun, who scatter'd into flight
The Stars before him from the Field of Night,
　　Drives Night along with them from Heav'n, and strikes
The Sultán's Turret with a Shaft of Light.

Before the phantom of False morning died,
Methought a Voice within the Tavern cried,
  'When all the Temple is prepared within,
Why nods the drowsy Worshipper outside?'

And, as the Cock crew, those who stood before
The Tavern shouted—'Open then the Door!
  You know how little while we have to stay,
And, once departed, may return no more.'

Now the New Year reviving old Desires,
The thoughtful Soul to Solitude retires,
  Where the WHITE HAND OF MOSES on the Bough
Puts out, and Jesus from the Ground suspires.

Iram indeed is gone with all his Rose,
And Jamshýd's Sev'n-ring'd Cup where no one knows;
  But still a Ruby kindles in the Vine,
And many a Garden by the Water blows.

And David's lips are lockt; but in divine
High-piping Pehleví, with 'Wine! Wine! Wine!
  Red Wine!'—the Nightingale cries to the Rose
That sallow cheek of hers to incarnadine.

Come, fill the Cup, and in the fire of Spring
Your Winter-garment of Repentance fling:
  The Bird of Time has but a little way
To flutter—and the Bird is on the Wing.

Whether at Naishápúr or Babylon,
Whether the Cup with sweet or bitter run,
  The Wine of Life keeps oozing drop by drop,
The Leaves of Life keep falling one by one.

Each Morn a thousand Roses brings, you say;
Yes, but where leaves the Rose of Yesterday?
    And this first Summer month that brings the Rose
Shall take Jamshýd and Kaikobád away.

Well, let it take them! What have we to do
With Kaikobád the Great, or Kaikhosrú?
    Let Zál and Rustum bluster as they will,
Or Hátim call to Supper—heed not you.

With me along the strip of Herbage strown
That just divides the desert from the sown,
    Where name of Slave and Sultán is forgot—
And Peace to Mahmúd on his golden Throne?

A Book of Verses underneath the Bough,
A Jug of Wine, a Loaf of Bread—and Thou
    Beside me singing in the Wilderness—
Oh, Wilderness were Paradise enow!

Some for the Glories of This World; and some
Sigh for the Prophet's Paradise to come;
    Ah, take the Cash, and let the Credit go,
Nor heed the rumble of a distant Drum!

Look to the blowing Rose about us—'Lo,
Laughing,' she says, 'into the world I blow.
    At once the silken tassel of my Purse
Tear, and its Treasure on the Garden throw.'

And those who husbanded the Golden grain,
And those who flung it to the winds like Rain,
    Alike to no such aureate Earth are turn'd
As, buried once, Men want dug up again.

The Worldly Hope men set their Hearts upon
Turns Ashes—or it prospers; and anon,
    Like Snow upon the Desert's dusty Face,
Lighting a little hour or two—is gone.

Think, in this batter'd Caravanserai
Whose Portals are alternate Night and Day
    How Sultán after Sultán with his Pomp
Abode his destined Hour, and went his way.

They say the Lion and the Lizard keep
The Courts where Jamshýd gloried and drank deep:
    And Bahrám, that great Hunter—the Wild Ass
Stamps o'er his Head, but cannot break his Sleep.

I sometimes think that never blows so red
The Rose as where some buried Cæsar bled;
    That every Hyacinth the Garden wears
Dropt in her Lap from some once lovely Head.

And this reviving Herb whose tender Green
Fledges the River-Lip on which we lean—
    Ah, lean upon it lightly! for who knows
From what once lovely Lip it springs unseen!

Ah, my Belovéd, fill the Cup that clears
To-DAY of past Regrets and Future Fears:
    To-morrow!—Why, To-morrow I may be
Myself with Yesterday's Sev'n thousand Years.

For some we loved, the loveliest and the best
That from his Vintage rolling Time hath prest,
    Have drunk their Cup a Round or two before,
And one by one crept silently to rest.

And we, that now make merry in the Room
They left, and Summer dresses in new bloom,
   Ourselves must we beneath the Couch of Earth
Descend—ourselves to make a Couch—for whom?

Ah, make the most of what we yet may spend,
Before we too into the Dust descend;
   Dust into Dust, and under Dust to lie
Sans Wine, sans Song, sans Singer, and—sans End!

THOMAS STODDART

336   ['Mirthful Lunacy']

FAIR Lunacy! I see thee, with a crown
Of hawthorn and sweet daisies, bending down
To mirror thy young image in a spring;
And thou wilt kiss that shadow of a thing
As soul-less as thyself. 'Tis tender, too,
The smile that meeteth thine! the holy hue
Of health! the pearly radiance of the brow!
All, all as tender—beautiful as thou!

And wilt thou say, my sister, there is none
Will answer thee? Thou art—thou art alone,
A pure, pure being! but the God on high
Is with thee ever, as thou goest by.

Thou poetess! that harpest to the moon,
And, in soft concert to the silver tune
Of waters, play'd on by the magic wind,
As he comes streaming, with his hair untwined,
Dost sing light strains of melody and mirth,—
I hear thee, hymning on thy holy birth,

How thou wert moulded of thy mother Love,
That came, like seraph, from the stars above,
And was so sadly wedded unto Sin,
That thou wert born, and Sorrow was thy twin.
Sorrow and mirthful Lunacy! that be
Together link'd for time, I deem of ye
That ye are worshipp'd as none others are,—
One as a lonely shadow, one a star!

337

Her, A Statue

HER life is in the marble! yet a fall
Of sleep lies on the heart's fair arsenal,
Like new shower'd snow. You hear no whisper through
Those love-divided lips; no pearly dew
Trembles on her pale orbs, that seem to be
Bent on a dream of immortality!

She sleeps: her life is sleep,—a holy rest!
Like that of wing-borne cloud, that, in the west,
Laves his aerial image, till afar
The sunlight leaves him, melting into star.
Did Phidias from her brow the veil remove,
Uncurtaining the peerless queen of love?
The fluent stone in marble waves recoil'd,
Touch'd by his hand, and left the wondrous child,
A Venus of the foam! How softly fair
The dove-like passion on the sacred air
Floats round her, nesting in her wreathed hair,
That tells, though shadeless, of its auburn hue,
Bathed in a hoar of diamond-dropping dew!

How beautiful!—Was this not one of eld,
That Chaos on his boundless bosom held,

Till Earth came forward in a rush of storm,
Closing his ribs upon her wingless form?
How beautiful!—The very lips do speak
Of love, and bid us worship: the pale cheek
Seems blushing through the marble—through the snow!
And the undrap'ried bosom feels a flow
Of fever on its brightness; every vein
At the blue pulse swells softly, like a chain
Of gentle hills. I would not fling a wreath
Of jewels on the brow, to flash beneath
Those queenly tresses; for itself is more
Than sea-born pearl of some Elysian shore!

Such, with a heart like woman! I would cast
Life at her foot, and, as she glided past,
Would bid her trample on the slavish thing—
Tell her, I'd rather feel me withering
Under her step, than be unknown for aye:
  And, when her pride had crush'd me, she might see
A love-wing'd spirit glide in glory by,
  Striking the tent of its mortality!

ROBERT BROWNING

338   The Lost Mistress

I

ALL's over, then—does truth sound bitter
    As one at first believes?
Hark, 'tis the sparrows' good-night twitter
    About your cottage eaves!

II

And the leaf-buds on the vine are woolly,
    I noticed that to-day;
One day more bursts them open fully
    —You know the red turns gray.

III

To-morrow we meet the same then, dearest?
    May I take your hand in mine?
Mere friends are we,—well, friends the merest
    Keep much that I resign:

IV

For each glance of the eye so bright and black,
    Though I keep with heart's endeavour,—
Your voice, when you wish the snowdrops back,
    Though it stay in my soul for ever!—

V

Yet I will but say what mere friends say,
    Or only a thought stronger;
I will hold your hand but as long as all may,
    Or so very little longer!

339   Meeting at Night

I

THE grey sea and the long black land;
And the yellow half-moon large and low;
And the startled little waves that leap
In fiery ringlets from their sleep,
As I gain the cove with pushing prow,
And quench its speed in the slushy sand.

II

Then a mile of warm sea-scented beach;
Three fields to cross till a farm appears;
A tap at the pane, the quick sharp scratch
And blue spurt of a lighted match,
And a voice less loud, thro' its joys and fears,
Than the two hearts beating each to each!

340   Parting at Morning

Round the cape of a sudden came the sea,
And the sun looked over the mountain's rim—
And straight was a path of gold for him,
And the need of a world of men for me.

341   Home-Thoughts, from Abroad

I

Oh, to be in England
Now that April's there,
And whoever wakes in England
Sees, some morning, unaware,
That the lowest boughs and the brush-wood sheaf
Round the elm-tree bole are in tiny leaf,
While the chaffinch sings on the orchard bough
In England—now!

II

And after April, when May follows,
And the whitethroat builds, and all the swallows—
Hark! where my blossomed pear-tree in the hedge
Leans to the field and scatters on the clover
Blossoms and dewdrops—at the bent spray's edge—

That's the wise thrush; he sings each song twice over
Lest you should think he never could recapture
The first fine careless rapture!
And though the fields look rough with hoary dew,
All will be gay when noontide wakes anew
The buttercups, the little children's dower
—Far brighter than this gaudy melon-flower!

342   ## Any Wife to any Husband

1

My love, this is the bitterest, that thou—
Who art all truth, and who dost love me now
    As thine eyes say, as thy voice breaks to say—
Should'st love so truly, and could'st love me still
A whole long life through, had but love its will,
    Would death that leads me from thee brook delay!

2

I have but to be by thee, and thy hand
Will never let mine go, nor heart withstand
    The beating of my heart to reach its place.
When shall I look for thee and feel thee gone?
When cry for the old comfort and find none?
    Never, I know! Thy soul is in thy face.

3

Oh, I should fade—'tis willed so! Might I save,
Gladly I would, whatever beauty gave
    Joy to thy sense, for that was precious too.
It is not to be granted. But the soul
Whence the love comes, all ravage leaves that whole;
    Vainly the flesh fades—soul makes all things new.

4

It would not be because my eye grew dim
Thou could'st not find the love there, thanks to Him
    Who never is dishonoured in the spark
He gave us from his fire of fires, and bade
Remember whence it sprang, nor be afraid
    While that burns on, though all the rest grow dark.

5

So, how thou would'st be perfect, white and clean
Outside as inside, soul and soul's demesne
    Alike, this body given to show it by!
Oh, three-parts through the worst of life's abyss,
What plaudits from the next world after this,
    Could'st thou repeat a stroke and gain the sky!

6

And is it not the bitterer to think
That, disengage our hands and thou wilt sink
    Although thy love was love in very deed?
I know that nature! Pass a festive day,
Thou dost not throw its relic-flower away
    Nor bid its music's loitering echo speed.

7

Thou let'st the stranger's glove lie where it fell;
If old things remain old things all is well,
    For thou art grateful as becomes man best:
And hadst thou only heard me play one tune,
Or viewed me from a window, not so soon
    With thee would such things fade as with the rest.

8

I seem to see! We meet and part; 'tis brief:
The book I opened keeps a folded leaf,
   The very chair I sat on, breaks the rank;
That is a portrait of me on the wall—
Three lines, my face comes at so slight a call;
   And for all this, one little hour to thank.

9

But now, because the hour through years was fixed,
Because our inmost beings met and mixed,
   Because thou once hast loved me—wilt thou dare
Say to thy soul and Who may list beside,
'Therefore she is immortally my bride,
   Chance cannot change my love, nor time impair.

10

'So, what if in the dusk of life that's left,
I, a tired traveller of my sun bereft,
   Look from my path when, mimicking the same,
The fire-fly glimpses past me, come and gone?
—Where was it till the sunset? where anon
   It will be at the sunrise! What's to blame?'

11

Is it so helpful to thee? Canst thou take
The mimic up, nor, for the true thing's sake,
   Put gently by such efforts at a beam?
Is the remainder of the way so long,
Thou need'st the little solace, thou the strong?
   Watch out thy watch, let weak ones doze and dream!

12

—Ah, but the fresher faces! 'Is it true,'
Thou'lt ask, 'some eyes are beautiful and new?
   Some hair,—how can one choose but grasp such wealth?
And if a man would press his lips to lips
Fresh as the wilding hedge-rose-cup there slips
   The dew-drop out of, must it be by stealth?

13

'It cannot change the love still kept for Her,
More than if such a picture I prefer
   Passing a day with, to a room's bare side.
The painted form takes nothing she possessed,
Yet, while the Titian's Venus lies at rest,
   A man looks. Once more, what is there to chide?'

14

So must I see, from where I sit and watch,
My own self sell myself, my hand attach
   Its warrant to the very thefts from me—
Thy singleness of soul that made me proud,
Thy purity of heart I loved aloud,
   Thy man's-truth I was bold to bid God see!

15

Love, so, then, if thou wilt! Give all thou canst
Away to the new faces—disentranced—
   (Say it and think it) obdurate no more,
Re-issue looks and words from the old mint—
Pass them afresh, no matter whose the print
   Image and superscription once they bore!

16

Re-coin thyself and give it them to spend,—
It all comes to the same thing at the end,
   Since mine thou wast, mine art, and mine shalt be,
Faithful or faithless, sealing up the sum
Or lavish of my treasure, thou must come
   Back to the heart's place here I keep for thee!

17

Only, why should it be with stain at all?
Why must I, 'twixt the leaves of coronal,
   Put any kiss of pardon on thy brow?
Why need the other women know so much,
And talk together, 'Such the look and such
   The smile he used to love with, then as now!'

18

Might I die last and shew thee! Should I find
Such hardship in the few years left behind,
   If free to take and light my lamp, and go
Into thy tomb, and shut the door and sit,
Seeing thy face on those four sides of it
   The better that they are so blank, I know!

19

Why, time was what I wanted, to turn o'er
Within my mind each look, get more and more
   By heart each word, too much to learn at first,
And join thee all the fitter for the pause
'Neath the low door-way's lintel. That were cause
   For lingering, though thou calledst, if I durst!

20

And yet thou art the nobler of us two.
What dare I dream of, that thou canst not do,
    Outstripping my ten small steps with one stride?
I'll say then, here's a trial and a task—
Is it to bear?—if easy, I'll not ask—
    Though love fail, I can trust on in thy pride.

21

Pride?—when those eyes forestal the life behind
The death I have to go through!—when I find,
    Now that I want thy help most, all of thee!
What did I fear? Thy love shall hold me fast
Until the little minute's sleep is past
    And I wake saved.—And yet, it will not be!

343   Two in the Campagna

1

I WONDER do you feel to-day
    As I have felt since, hand in hand,
We sat down on the grass, to stray
    In spirit better through the land,
This morn of Rome and May?

2

For me, I touched a thought, I know,
    Has tantalized me many times,
(Like turns of thread the spiders throw
    Mocking across our path) for rhymes
To catch at and let go.

3

Help me to hold it: first it left
   The yellowing fennel, run to seed
There, branching from the brickwork's cleft,
   Some old tomb's ruin: yonder weed
Took up the floating weft,

4

Where one small orange cup amassed
   Five beetles,—blind and green they grope
Among the honey-meal,—and last,
   Everywhere on the grassy slope
I traced it. Hold it fast!

5

The champaign with its endless fleece
   Of feathery grasses everywhere!
Silence and passion, joy and peace,
   An everlasting wash of air—
Rome's ghost since her decease.

6

Such life here, through such lengths of hours,
   Such miracles performed in play,
Such primal naked forms of flowers,
   Such letting Nature have her way
While Heaven looks from its towers.

7

How say you? Let us, O my dove,
   Let us be unashamed of soul,
As earth lies bare to heaven above.
   How is it under our control
To love or not to love?

8

I would that you were all to me,
   You that are just so much, no more—
Nor yours, nor mine,—nor slave nor free!
   Where does the fault lie? what the core
Of the wound, since wound must be?

9

I would I could adopt your will,
   See with your eyes, and set my heart
Beating by yours, and drink my fill
   At your soul's springs,—your part, my part
In life, for good and ill.

10

No. I yearn upward—touch you close,
   Then stand away. I kiss your cheek,
Catch your soul's warmth,—I pluck the rose
   And love it more than tongue can speak—
Then the good minute goes.

11

Already how am I so far
   Out of that minute? Must I go
Still like the thistle-ball, no bar,
   Onward, whenever light winds blow,
Fixed by no friendly star?

12

Just when I seemed about to learn!
   Where is the thread now? Off again!
The old trick! Only I discern—
   Infinite passion, and the pain
Of finite hearts that yearn.

344 ## Love in a Life

1

ROOM after room,
I hunt the house through
We inhabit together.
Heart, fear nothing, for, heart, thou shalt find her,
Next time, herself!—not the trouble behind her
Left in the curtain, the couch's perfume!
As she brushed it, the cornice-wreath blossomed anew,—
Yon looking-glass gleamed at the wave of her feather.

2

Yet the day wears,
And door succeeds door;
I try the fresh fortune—
Range the wide house from the wing to the centre.
Still the same chance! she goes out as I enter.
Spend my whole day in the quest,—who cares?
But 'tis twilight, you see,—with such suites to explore,
Such closets to search, such alcoves to importune!

345 ## Life in a Love

ESCAPE me?
Never—
Beloved!
While I am I, and you are you,
So long as the world contains us both,
Me the loving and you the loth,
While the one eludes, must the other pursue.

My life is a fault at last, I fear—
  It seems too much like a fate, indeed!
    Though I do my best I shall scarce succeed—
But what if I fail of my purpose here?
It is but to keep the nerves at strain,
  To dry one's eyes and laugh at a fall,
And, baffled, get up and begin again,—
  So the chace takes up one's life, that's all.
While, look but once from your farthest bound
  At me so deep in the dust and dark,
No sooner the old hope goes to ground
  Than a new one, straight to the self-same mark,
            I shape me—
              Ever
            Removed!

346   Memorabilia

1

An, did you once see Shelley plain,
  And did he stop and speak to you?
And did you speak to him again?
  How strange it seems, and new!

2

But you were living before that,
  And also you are living after,
And the memory I started at—
  My starting moves your laughter!

3

I crossed a moor with a name of its own
  And a certain use in the world no doubt,
Yet a hand's-breadth of it shines alone
  'Mid the blank miles round about—

4

For there I picked up on the heather
  And there I put inside my breast
A moulted feather, an eagle-feather—
  Well, I forget the rest.

My Last Duchess

FERRARA

THAT'S my last Duchess painted on the wall,
Looking as if she were alive. I call
That piece a wonder, now: Frà Pandolf's hands
Worked busily a day, and there she stands.
Will't please you sit and look at her? I said
'Frà Pandolf' by design, for never read
Strangers like you that pictured countenance,
The depth and passion of its earnest glance,
But to myself they turned (since none puts by
The curtain I have drawn for you, but I)
And seemed as they would ask me, if they durst,
How such a glance came there; so, not the first
Are you to turn and ask thus. Sir, 'twas not
Her husband's presence only, called that spot
Of joy into the Duchess' cheek: perhaps
Frà Pandolf chanced to say 'Her mantle laps
Over my lady's wrist too much,' or 'Paint
Must never hope to reproduce the faint
Half-flush that dies along her throat:' such stuff
Was courtesy, she thought, and cause enough
For calling up that spot of joy. She had
A heart—how shall I say?—too soon made glad,
Too easily impressed; she liked whate'er
She looked on, and her looks went everywhere.

Sir, 'twas all one! My favour at her breast,
The dropping of the daylight in the West,
The bough of cherries some officious fool
Broke in the orchard for her, the white mule
She rode with round the terrace—all and each
Would draw from her alike the approving speech,
Or blush, at least. She thanked men,—good! but thanked
Somehow—I know not how—as if she ranked
My gift of a nine-hundred-years-old name
With anybody's gift. Who'd stoop to blame
This sort of trifling? Even had you skill
In speech—(which I have not)—to make your will
Quite clear to such an one, and say, 'Just this
Or that in you disgusts me; here you miss,
Or there exceed the mark'—and if she let
Herself be lessoned so, nor plainly set
Her wits to yours, forsooth, and made excuse,
—E'en then would be some stooping; and I choose
Never to stoop. Oh sir, she smiled, no doubt,
Whene'er I passed her; but who passed without
Much the same smile? This grew; I gave commands;
Then all smiles stopped together. There she stands
As if alive. Will't please you rise? We'll meet
The company below, then. I repeat,
The Count your master's known munificence
Is ample warrant that no just pretence
Of mine for dowry will be disallowed;
Though his fair daughter's self, as I avowed
At starting, is my object. Nay, we'll go
Together down, sir. Notice Neptune, though,
Taming a sea-horse, thought a rarity,
Which Claus of Innsbruck cast in bronze for me!

Bishop Blougram's Apology

No more wine? then we'll push back chairs and talk.
A final glass for me, though: cool, i' faith!
We ought to have our Abbey back, you see.
It's different, preaching in basilicas,
And doing duty in some masterpiece
Like this of brother Pugin's, bless his heart!
I doubt if they're half baked, those chalk rosettes,
Ciphers and stucco-twiddlings everywhere;
It's just like breathing in a lime-kiln: eh?
These hot long ceremonies of our church
Cost us a little—oh, they pay the price,
You take me—amply pay it! Now, we'll talk.

So, you despise me, Mr Gigadibs.
No deprecation,—nay, I beg you, sir!
Beside 'tis our engagement: don't you know,
I promised, if you'd watch a dinner out,
We'd see truth dawn together?—truth that peeps
Over the glasses' edge when dinner's done,
And body gets its sop and holds its noise
And leaves soul free a little. Now's the time:
Truth's break of day! You do despise me then.
And if I say, 'despise me,'—never fear!
I know you do not in a certain sense—
Not in my arm-chair, for example: here,
I well imagine you respect my place
(*Status, entourage*, worldly circumstance)
Quite to its value—very much indeed:
—Are up to the protesting eyes of you
In pride at being seated here for once—
You'll turn it to such capital account!
When somebody, through years and years to come,

Hints of the bishop,—names me—that's enough:
'Blougram? I knew him'—(into it you slide)
'Dined with him once, a Corpus Christi Day,
All alone, we two; he's a clever man:
And after dinner,—why, the wine you know,—
Oh, there was wine, and good!—what with the wine . . .
'Faith, we began upon all sorts of talk!
He's no bad fellow, Blougram; he had seen
Something of mine he relished, some review:
He's quite above their humbug in his heart,
Half-said as much, indeed—the thing's his trade.
I warrant, Blougram's sceptical at times:
How otherwise? I liked him, I confess!'
Che che, my dear sir, as we say at Rome,
Don't you protest now! It's fair give and take;
You have had your turn and spoken your home-truths:
The hand's mine now, and here you follow suit.

Thus much conceded, still the first fact stays—
You do despise me; your ideal of life
Is not the bishop's: you would not be I.
You would like better to be Goethe, now,
Or Buonaparte, or, bless me, lower still,
Count D'Orsay,—so you did what you preferred,
Spoke as you thought, and, as you cannot help,
Believed or disbelieved, no matter what,
So long as on that point, whate'er it was,
You loosed your mind, were whole and sole yourself.
—That, my ideal never can include,
Upon that element of truth and worth
Never be based! for say they make me Pope—
(They can't—suppose it for our argument!)
Why, there I'm at my tether's end, I've reached
My height, and not a height which pleases you:

An unbelieving Pope won't do, you say.
It's like those eerie stories nurses tell.
Of how some actor on a stage played Death,
With pasteboard crown, sham orb and tinselled dart,
And called himself the monarch of the world;
Then, going in the tire-room afterward,
Because the play was done, to shift himself,
Got touched upon the sleeve familiarly,
The moment he had shut the closet door,
By Death himself. Thus God might touch a Pope
At unawares, ask what his baubles mean,
And whose part he presumed to play just now.
Best be yourself, imperial, plain and true!

So, drawing comfortable breath again,
You weigh and find, whatever more or less
I boast of my ideal realized
Is nothing in the balance when opposed
To your ideal, your grand simple life,
Of which you will not realize one jot.
I am much, you are nothing; you would be all,
I would be merely much: you beat me there.

No, friend, you do not beat me: hearken why!
The common problem, yours, mine, every one's,
Is—not to fancy what were fair in life
Provided it could be,—but, finding first
What may be, then find how to make it fair
Up to our means: a very different thing!
No abstract intellectual plan of life
Quite irrespective of life's plainest laws,
But one, a man, who is man and nothing more,
May lead within a world which (by your leave)
Is Rome or London, not Fool's-paradise.

Embellish Rome, idealize away,
Make paradise of London if you can,
You're welcome, nay, you're wise.

         A simile!
We mortals cross the ocean of this world
Each in his average cabin of a life;
The best's not big, the worst yields elbow-room.
Now for our six months' voyage—how prepare?
You come on shipboard with a landsman's list
Of things he calls convenient: so they are!
An India screen is pretty furniture,
A piano-forte is a fine resource,
All Balzac's novels occupy one shelf,
The new edition fifty volumes long;
And little Greek books, with the funny type
They get up well at Leipsic, fill the next:
Go on! slabbed marble, what a bath it makes!
And Parma's pride, the Jerome, let us add!
'Twere pleasant could Correggio's fleeting glow
Hang full in face of one where'er one roams,
Since he more than the others brings with him
Italy's self,—the marvellous Modenese!—
Yet was not on your list before, perhaps.
—Alas, friend, here's the agent . . . is't the name?
The captain, or whoever's master here—
You see him screw his face up; what's his cry
Ere you set foot on shipboard? 'Six feet square!'
If you won't understand what six feet mean,
Compute and purchase stores accordingly—
And if, in pique because he overhauls
Your Jerome, piano, bath, you come on board
Bare—why, you cut a figure at the first
While sympathetic landsmen see you off;

Not afterward, when long ere half seas over,
You peep up from your utterly naked boards
Into some snug and well-appointed berth,
Like mine for instance (try the cooler jug—
Put back the other, but don't jog the ice!)
And mortified you mutter 'Well and good;
He sits enjoying his sea-furniture;
'Tis stout and proper, and there's store of it:
Though I've the better notion, all agree,
Of fitting rooms up. Hang the carpenter,
Neat ship-shape fixings and contrivances—
I would have brought my Jerome, frame and all!'
And meantime you bring nothing: never mind—
You've proved your artist-nature: what you don't
You might bring, so despise me, as I say.

Now come, let's backward to the starting-place.
See my way: we're two college friends, suppose.
Prepare together for our voyage, then;
Each note and check the other in his work—
Here's mine, a bishop's outfit; criticize!
What's wrong? why won't you be a bishop too?

Why first, you don't believe, you don't and can't,
(Not statedly, that is, and fixedly
And absolutely and exclusively)
In any revelation called divine.
No dogmas nail your faith; and what remains
But say so, like the honest man you are?
First, therefore, overhaul theology!
Nay, I too, not a fool, you please to think,
Must find believing every whit as hard:
And if I do not frankly say as much,
The ugly consequence is clear enough.

Now wait, my friend: well, I do not believe—
If you'll accept no faith that is not fixed,
Absolute and exclusive, as you say.
You're wrong—I mean to prove it in due time.
Meanwhile, I know where difficulties lie
I could not, cannot solve, nor ever shall,
So give up hope accordingly to solve—
(To you, and over the wine). Our dogmas then
With both of us, though in unlike degree,
Missing full credence—overboard with them!
I mean to meet you on your own premise:
Good, there go mine in company with yours!

And now what are we? unbelievers both,
Calm and complete, determinately fixed
To-day, to-morrow and for ever, pray?
You'll guarantee me that? Not so, I think!
In no wise! all we've gained is, that belief,
As unbelief before, shakes us by fits,
Confounds us like its predecessor. Where's
The gain? how can we guard our unbelief,
Make it bear fruit to us?—the problem here.
Just when we are safest, there's a sunset-touch,
A fancy from a flower-bell, some one's death,
A chorus-ending from Euripides,—
And that's enough for fifty hopes and fears
As old and new at once as nature's self,
To rap and knock and enter in our soul,
Take hands and dance there, a fantastic ring,
Round the ancient idol, on his base again,—
The grand Perhaps! We look on helplessly.
There the old misgivings, crooked questions are—
This good God,—what he could do, if he would,
Would, if he could—then must have done long since:

If so, when, where and how? some way must be,—
Once feel about, and soon or late you hit
Some sense, in which it might be, after all.
Why not, 'The Way, the Truth, the Life?'

                               —That way
Over the mountain, which who stands upon
Is apt to doubt if it be meant for a road;
While, if he views it from the waste itself,
Up goes the line there, plain from base to brow,
Not vague, mistakeable! what's a break or two
Seen from the unbroken desert either side?
And then (to bring in fresh philosophy)
What if the breaks themselves should prove at last
The most consummate of contrivances
To train a man's eye, teach him what is faith?
And so we stumble at truth's very test!
All we have gained then by our unbelief
Is a life of doubt diversified by faith,
For one of faith diversified by doubt:
We called the chess-board white,—we call it black.

  'Well,' you rejoin, 'the end's no worse, at least
We've reason for both colours on the board:
Why not confess then, where I drop the faith
And you the doubt, that I'm as right as you?'

  Because, friend, in the next place, this being so,
And both things even,—faith and unbelief
Left to a man's choice,—we'll proceed a step,
Returning to our image, which I like.

  A man's choice, yea—but a cabin-passenger's—
The man made for the special life o' the world—

Do you forget him? I remember though!
Consult our ship's conditions and you find
One and but one choice suitable to all;
The choice, that you unluckily prefer,
Turning things topsy-turvy—they or it
Going to the ground. Belief or unbelief
Bears upon life, determines its whole course,
Begins at its beginning. See the world
Such as it is,—you made it not, nor I;
I mean to take it as it is,—and you,
Not so you'll take it,—though you get nought else.
I know the special kind of life I like,
What suits the most my idiosyncrasy,
Brings out the best of me and bears me fruit
In power, peace, pleasantness and length of days.
I find that positive belief does this
For me, and unbelief, no whit of this.
—For you, it does, however?—that, we'll try!
'Tis clear, I cannot lead my life, at least,
Induce the world to let me peaceably,
Without declaring at the outset, 'Friends,
I absolutely and peremptorily
Believe!'—I say, faith is my waking life:
One sleeps, indeed, and dreams at intervals,
We know, but waking's the main point with us,
And my provision's for life's waking part.
Accordingly, I use heart, head and hand
All day, I build, scheme, study, and make friends;
And when night overtakes me, down I lie,
Sleep, dream a little, and get done with it,
The sooner the better, to begin afresh.
What's midnight doubt before the dayspring's faith?
You, the philosopher, that disbelieve,
That recognize the night, give dreams their weight—

To be consistent you should keep your bed,
Abstain from healthy acts that prove you man,
For fear you drowse perhaps at unawares!
And certainly at night you'll sleep and dream,
Live through the day and bustle as you please.
And so you live to sleep as I to wake,
To unbelieve as I to still believe?
Well, and the common sense o' the world calls you
Bed-ridden,—and its good things come to me.
Its estimation, which is half the fight,
That's the first cabin-comfort I secure:
The next . . . but you perceive with half an eye!
Come, come, it's best believing, if we may;
You can't but own that!

                  Next, concede again,
If once we choose belief, on all accounts
We can't be too decisive in our faith,
Conclusive and exclusive in its terms,
To suit the world which gives us the good things.
In every man's career are certain points
Whereon he dares not be indifferent;
The world detects him clearly, if he dare,
As baffled at the game, and losing life.
He may care little or he may care much
For riches, honour, pleasure, work, repose,
Since various theories of life and life's
Success are extant which might easily
Comport with either estimate of these;
And whoso chooses wealth or poverty,
Labour or quiet, is not judged a fool
Because his fellow would choose otherwise:
We let him choose upon his own account
So long as he's consistent with his choice.

But certain points, left wholly to himself,
When once a man has arbitrated on,
We say he must succeed there or go hang.
Thus, he should wed the woman he loves most
Or needs most, whatsoe'er the love or need—
For he can't wed twice. Then, he must avouch,
Or follow, at the least, sufficiently,
The form of faith his conscience holds the best,
Whate'er the process of conviction was:
For nothing can compensate his mistake
On such a point, the man himself being judge:
He cannot wed twice, nor twice lose his soul.

Well now, there's one great form of Christian faith
I happened to be born in—which to teach
Was given me as I grew up, on all hands,
As best and readiest means of living by;
The same on examination being proved
The most pronounced moreover, fixed, precise
And absolute form of faith in the whole world—
Accordingly, most potent of all forms
For working on the world. Observe, my friend!
Such as you know me, I am free to say,
In these hard latter days which hamper one,
Myself—by no immoderate exercise
Of intellect and learning, but the tact
To let external forces work for me,
—Bid the street's stones be bread and they are bread;
Bid Peter's creed, or rather, Hildebrand's,
Exalt me o'er my fellows in the world
And make my life an ease and joy and pride;
It does so,—which for me's a great point gained,
Who have a soul and body that exact
A comfortable care in many ways.

There's power in me and will to dominate
Which I must exercise, they hurt me else:
In many ways I need mankind's respect,
Obedience, and the love that's born of fear:
While at the same time, there's a taste I have,
A toy of soul, a titillating thing,
Refuses to digest these dainties crude.
The naked life is gross till clothed upon:
I must take what men offer, with a grace
As though I would not, could I help it, take!
An uniform I wear though over-rich—
Something imposed on me, no choice of mine;
No fancy-dress worn for pure fancy's sake
And despicable therefore! now folk kneel
And kiss my hand—of course the Church's hand.
Thus I am made, thus life is best for me,
And this that it should be I have procured;
And thus it could not be another way,
I venture to imagine.

                              You'll reply,
So far my choice, no doubt, is a success;
But were I made of better elements,
With nobler instincts, purer tastes, like you,
I hardly would account the thing success
Though it did all for me I say.

                              But, friend,
We speak of what is; not of what might be,
And how 'twere better if 'twere otherwise.
I am the man you see here plain enough:
Grant I'm a beast, why, beasts must lead beasts' lives!
Suppose I own at once to tail and claws;
The tailless man exceeds me: but being tailed
I'll lash out lion fashion, and leave apes

To dock their stump and dress their haunches up.
My business is not to remake myself,
But make the absolute best of what God made.
Or—our first simile—though you prove me doomed
To a viler berth still, to the steerage-hole,
The sheep-pen or the pigstye, I should strive
To make what use of each were possible;
And as this cabin gets upholstery,
That hutch should rustle with sufficient straw.
   But, friend, I don't acknowledge quite so fast
I fail of all your manhood's lofty tastes
Enumerated so complacently,
On the mere ground that you forsooth can find
In this particular life I choose to lead
No fit provision for them. Can you not?
Say you, my fault is I address myself
To grosser estimators than should judge?
And that's no way of holding up the soul,
Which, nobler, needs men's praise perhaps, yet knows
One wise man's verdict outweighs all the fools'—
Would like the two, but, forced to choose, takes that.
I pine among my million imbeciles
(You think) aware some dozen men of sense
Eye me and know me, whether I believe
In the last winking Virgin, as I vow,
And am a fool, or disbelieve in her
And am a knave,—approve in neither case,
Withhold their voices though I look their way:
Like Verdi when, at his worst opera's end
(The thing they gave at Florence,—what's its name?)
While the mad houseful's plaudits near outbang
His orchestra of salt-box, tongs and bones,
He looks through all the roaring and the wreaths
Where sits Rossini patient in his stall.

Nay, friend, I meet you with an answer here—
That even your prime men who appraise their kind
Are men still, catch a wheel within a wheel,
See more in a truth than the truth's simple self,
Confuse themselves. You see lads walk the street
Sixty the minute; what's to note in that?
You see one lad o'erstride a chimney-stack;
Him you must watch—he's sure to fall, yet stands!
Our interest's on the dangerous edge of things.
The honest thief, the tender murderer,
The superstitious atheist, demirep
That loves and saves her soul in new French books—
We watch while these in equilibrium keep
The giddy line midway: one step aside,
They're classed and done with. I, then, keep the line
Before your sages,—just the men to shrink
From the gross weights, coarse scales and labels broad
You offer their refinement. Fool or knave?
Why needs a bishop be a fool or knave
When there's a thousand diamond weights between?
So, I enlist them. Your picked twelve, you'll find,
Profess themselves indignant, scandalized
At thus being held unable to explain
How a superior man who disbelieves
May not believe as well: that's Schelling's way!
It's through my coming in the tail of time,
Nicking the minute with a happy tact.
Had I been born three hundred years ago
They'd say, 'What's strange? Blougram of course believes;'
And, seventy years since, 'disbelieves of course.'
But now, 'He may believe; and yet, and yet
How can he?' All eyes turn with interest.
Whereas, step off the line on either side—
You, for example, clever to a fault,

The rough and ready man who write apace,
Read somewhat seldomer, think perhaps even less—
You disbelieve! Who wonders and who cares?
Lord So-and-so—his coat bedropped with wax,
All Peter's chains about his waist, his back
Brave with the needlework of Noodledom—
Believes! Again, who wonders and who cares?
But I, the man of sense and learning too,
The able to think yet act, the this, the that,
I, to believe at this late time of day!
Enough; you see, I need not fear contempt.

   —Except it's yours! Admire me as these may,
You don't. But whom at least do you admire?
Present your own perfection, your ideal,
Your pattern man for a minute—oh, make haste,
Is it Napoleon you would have us grow?
Concede the means; allow his head and hand,
(A large concession, clever as you are)
Good! In our common primal element
Of unbelief (we can't believe, you know—
We're still at that admission, recollect!)
Where do you find—apart from, towering o'er
The secondary temporary aims
Which satisfy the gross taste you despise—
Where do you find his star?—his crazy trust
God knows through what or in what? it's alive
And shines and leads him, and that's all we want.
Have we aught in our sober night shall point
Such ends as his were, and direct the means
Of working out our purpose straight as his,
Nor bring a moment's trouble on success
With after-care to justify the same?
—Be a Napoleon, and yet disbelieve—

Why, the man's mad, friend, take his light away!
What's the vague good o' the world, for which you dare
With comfort to yourself blow millions up?
We neither of us see it! we do see
The blown-up millions—spatter of their brains
And writhing of their bowels and so forth,
In that bewildering entanglement
Of horrible eventualities
Past calculation to the end of time!
Can I mistake for some clear word of God
(Which were my ample warrant for it all)
His puff of hazy instinct, idle talk,
'The State, that's I,' quack-nonsense about crowns,
And (when one beats the man to his last hold)
A vague idea of setting things to rights,
Policing people efficaciously,
More to their profit, most of all to his own;
The whole to end that dismallest of ends
By an Austrian marriage, cant to us the Church,
And resurrection of the old *régime*?
Would I, who hope to live a dozen years,
Fight Austerlitz for reasons such and such?
No: for, concede me but the merest chance
Doubt may be wrong—there's judgement, life to come!
With just that chance, I dare not. Doubt proves right?
This present life is all?—you offer me
Its dozen noisy years, without a chance
That wedding an archduchess, wearing lace,
And getting called by divers new-coined names,
Will drive off ugly thoughts and let me dine,
Sleep, read and chat in quiet as I like!
Therefore I will not.

                   Take another case;
Fit up the cabin yet another way.

What say you to the poets? shall we write
Hamlet, Othello—make the world our own,
Without a risk to run of either sort?
I can't!—to put the strongest reason first.
'But try', you urge, 'the trying shall suffice;
The aim, if reached or not, makes great the life:
Try to be Shakespeare, leave the rest to fate!'
Spare my self-knowledge—there's no fooling me!
If I prefer remaining my poor self,
I say so not in self-dispraise but praise.
If I'm a Shakespeare, let the well alone;
Why should I try to be what now I am?
If I'm no Shakespeare, as too probable,—
His power and consciousness and self-delight
And all we want in common, shall I find—
Trying for ever? while on points of taste
Wherewith, to speak it humbly, he and I
Are dowered alike—I'll ask you, I or he,
Which in our two lives realizes most?
Much, he imagined—somewhat, I possess.
He had the imagination; stick to that!
Let him say, 'In the face of my soul's works
Your world is worthless and I touch it not
Lest I should wrong them'—I'll withdraw my plea.
But does he say so? look upon his life!
Himself, who only can, gives judgement there.
He leaves his towers and gorgeous palaces
To build the trimmest house in Stratford town;
Saves money, spends it, owns the worth of things,
Giulio Romano's pictures, Dowland's lute;
Enjoys a show, respects the puppets, too,
And none more, had he seen its entry once,
Than 'Pandulph, of fair Milan cardinal.'
Why then should I who play that personage,

The very Pandulph Shakespeare's fancy made,
Be told that had the poet chanced to start
From where I stand now (some degree like mine
Being just the goal he ran his race to reach)
He would have run the whole race back, forsooth,
And left being Pandulph, to begin write plays?
Ah, the earth's best can be but the earth's best!
Did Shakespeare live, he could but sit at home
And get himself in dreams the Vatican,
Greek busts, Venetian paintings, Roman walls,
And English books, none equal to his own,
Which I read, bound in gold (he never did).
—Terni's fall, Naples' bay and Gothard's top—
Eh, friend? I could not fancy one of these;
But, as I pour this claret, there they are:
I've gained them—crossed St. Gothard last July
With ten mules to the carriage and a bed
Slung inside; is my hap the worse for that?
We want the same things, Shakespeare and myself,
And what I want, I have: he, gifted more,
Could fancy he too had them when he liked,
But not so thoroughly that, if fate allowed,
He would not have them also in my sense.
We play one game; I send the ball aloft
No less adroitly that of fifty strokes
Scarce five go o'er the wall so wide and high
Which sends them back to me: I wish and get.
He struck balls higher and with better skill,
But at a poor fence level with his head,
And hit—his Stratford house, a coat of arms,
Successful dealings in his grain and wool,—
While I receive heaven's incense in my nose
And style myself the cousin of Queen Bess.
Ask him, if this life's all, who wins the game?

Believe—and our whole argument breaks up.
Enthusiasm's the best thing, I repeat;
Only, we can't command it; fire and life
Are all, dead matter's nothing, we agree:
And be it a mad dream or God's very breath,
The fact's the same,—belief's fire, once in us,
Makes of all else mere stuff to show itself:
We penetrate our life with such a glow
As fire lends wood and iron—this turns steel,
That burns to ash—all's one, fire proves its power
For good or ill, since men call flare success.
But paint a fire, it will not therefore burn.
Light one in me, I'll find it food enough!
Why, to be Luther—that's a life to lead,
Incomparably better than my own.
He comes, reclaims God's earth for God, he says,
Sets up God's rule again by simple means,
Re-opens a shut book, and all is done.
He flared out in the flaring of mankind;
Such Luther's luck was: how shall such be mine?
If he succeeded, nothing's left to do:
And if he did not altogether—well,
Strauss is the next advance. All Strauss should be
I might be also. But to what result?
He looks upon no future: Luther did.
What can I gain on the denying side?
Ice makes no conflagration. State the facts,
Read the text right, emancipate the world—
The emancipated world enjoys itself
With scarce a thank-you: Blougram told it first
It could not owe a farthing,—not to him
More than Saint Paul! 'twould press its pay, you think?
Then add there's still that plaguy hundredth chance
Strauss may be wrong. And so a risk is run—

For what gain? not for Luther's, who secured
A real heaven in his heart throughout his life,
Supposing death a little altered things.

'Ay, but since really you lack faith,' you cry,
'You run the same risk really on all sides,
In cool indifference as bold unbelief.
As well be Strauss as swing 'twixt Paul and him.
It's not worth having, such imperfect faith,
No more available to do faith's work
Than unbelief like mine. Whole faith, or none!'

Softly, my friend! I must dispute that point.
Once own the use of faith, I'll find you faith.
We're back on Christian ground. You call for faith:
I show you doubt, to prove that faith exists.
The more of doubt, the stronger faith, I say,
If faith o'ercomes doubt. How I know it does?
By life and man's free will, God gave for that!
To mould life as we choose it, shows our choice:
That's our one act, the previous work's his own.
You criticize the soul? it reared this tree—
This broad life and whatever fruit it bears!
What matter though I doubt at every pore,
Head-doubts, heart-doubts, doubts at my fingers' ends,
Doubts in the trivial work of every day,
Doubts at the very bases of my soul
In the grand moments when she probes herself—
If finally I have a life to show,
The thing I did, brought out in evidence
Against the thing done to me underground
By hell and all its brood, for aught I know?
I say, whence sprang this? shows it faith or doubt?
All's doubt in me; where's break of faith in this?

It is the idea, the feeling and the love,
God means mankind should strive for and show forth
Whatever be the process to that end,—
And not historic knowledge, logic sound,
And metaphysical acumen, sure!
'What think ye of Christ,' friend? when all's done and said,
Like you this Christianity or not?
It may be false, but will you wish it true?
Has it your vote to be so if it can?
Trust you an instinct silenced long ago
That will break silence and enjoin you love
What mortified philosophy is hoarse,
And all in vain, with bidding you despise?
If you desire faith—then you've faith enough:
What else seeks God—nay, what else seek ourselves?
You form a notion of me, we'll suppose,
On hearsay; it's a favourable one:
'But still' (you add), 'there was no such good man,
Because of contradiction in the facts.
One proves, for instance, he was born in Rome,
This Blougram; yet throughout the tales of him
I see he figures as an Englishman.'
Well, the two things are reconcileable.
But would I rather you discovered that,
Subjoining—'Still, what matter though they be?
Blougram concerns me nought, born here or there.'

Pure faith indeed—you know not what you ask!
Naked belief in God the Omnipotent,
Omniscient, Omnipresent, sears too much
The sense of conscious creatures to be borne.
It were the seeing him, no flesh shall dare.
Some think, Creation's meant to show him forth:
I say it's meant to hide him all it can,

And that's what all the blessed evil's for.
Its use in Time is to environ us,
Our breath, our drop of dew, with shield enough
Against that sight till we can bear its stress.
Under a vertical sun, the exposed brain
And lidless eye and disemprisoned heart
Less certainly would wither up at once
Than mind, confronted with the truth of him.
But time and earth case-harden us to live;
The feeblest sense is trusted most; the child
Feels God a moment, ichors o'er the place,
Plays on and grows to be a man like us.
With me, faith means perpetual unbelief
Kept quiet like the snake 'neath Michael's foot
Who stands calm just because he feels it writhe.
Or, if that's too ambitious,—here's my box—
I need the excitation of a pinch
Threatening the torpor of the inside-nose
Nigh on the imminent sneeze that never comes.
'Leave it in peace' advise the simple folk:
Make it aware of peace by itching-fits,
Say I—let doubt occasion still more faith!

You'll say, once all believed, man, woman, child,
In that dear middle-age these noodles praise.
How you'd exult if I could put you back
Six hundred years, blot out cosmogony,
Geology, ethnology, what not,
(Greek endings, each the little passing-bell
That signifies some faith's about to die),
And set you square with Genesis again,—
When such a traveller told you his last news,
He saw the ark a-top of Ararat
But did not climb there since 'twas getting dusk

And robber-bands infest the mountain's foot!
How should you feel, I ask, in such an age,
How act? As other people felt and did;
With soul more blank than this decanter's knob,
Believe—and yet lie, kill, rob, fornicate
Full in belief's face, like the beast you'd be!

No, when the fight begins within himself,
A man's worth something. God stoops o'er his head,
Satan looks up between his feet—both tug—
He's left, himself, i' the middle: the soul wakes
And grows. Prolong that battle through his life!
Never leave growing till the life to come!
Here, we've got callous to the Virgin's winks
That used to puzzle people wholesomely:
Men have outgrown the shame of being fools.
What are the laws of nature, not to bend
If the Church bid them?—brother Newman asks.
Up with the Immaculate Conception, then—
On to the rack with faith!—is my advice.
Will not that hurry us upon our knees,
Knocking our breasts, 'It can't be—yet it shall!
Who am I, the worm, to argue with my Pope?
Low things confound the high things!' and so forth.
That's better than acquitting God with grace
As some folk do. He's tried—no case is proved,
Philosophy is lenient—he may go!

You'll say, the old system's not so obsolete
But men believe still: ay, but who and where?
King Bomba's lazzaroni foster yet
The sacred flame, so Antonelli writes;
But even of these, what ragamuffin-saint
Believes God watches him continually,

As he believes in fire that it will burn,
Or rain that it will drench him? Break fire's law,
Sin against rain, although the penalty
Be just a singe or soaking? 'No,' he smiles;
'Those laws are laws that can enforce themselves.'

   The sum of all is—yes, my doubt is great,
My faith's still greater, then my faith's enough.
I have read much, thought much, experienced much,
Yet would die rather than avow my fear
The Naples liquefaction may be false,
When set to happen by the palace-clock
According to the clouds or dinner-time.
I hear you recommend, I might at least
Eliminate, decrassify my faith
Since I adopt it; keeping what I must
And leaving what I can—such points as this.
I won't—that is, I can't throw one away.
Supposing there's no truth in what I hold
About the need of trial to man's faith,
Still, when you bid me purify the same,
To such a process I discern no end.
Clearing off one excrescence to see two,
There's ever a next in size, now grown as big,
That meets the knife: I cut and cut again!
First cut the Liquefaction, what comes last
But Fichte's clever cut at God himself?
Experimentalize on sacred things!
I trust nor hand nor eye nor heart nor brain
To stop betimes: they all get drunk alike.
The first step, I am master not to take.

   You'd find the cutting-process to your taste
As much as leaving growths of lies unpruned,

Nor see more danger in it,—you retort.
Your taste's worth mine; but my taste proves more wise
When we consider that the steadfast hold
On the extreme end of the chain of faith
Gives all the advantage, makes the difference
With the rough purblind mass we seek to rule:
We are their lords, or they are free of us,
Just as we tighten or relax our hold.
So, other matters equal, we'll revert
To the first problem—which, if solved my way
And thrown into the balance, turns the scale—
How we may lead a comfortable life,
How suit our luggage to the cabin's size.

Of course you are remarking all this time
How narrowly and grossly I view life,
Respect the creature-comforts, care to rule
The masses, and regard complacently
'The cabin', in our old phrase. Well, I do.
I act for, talk for, live for this world now,
As this world prizes action, life and talk:
No prejudice to what next world may prove,
Whose new laws and requirements, my best pledge
To observe then, is that I observe these now,
Shall do hereafter what I do meanwhile.
Let us concede (gratuitously though)
Next life relieves the soul of body, yields
Pure spiritual enjoyment: well, my friend,
Why lose this life i' the meantime since its use,
May be to make the next life more intense?

Do you know, I have often had a dream
(Work it up in your next month's article)
Of man's poor spirit in its progress, still

Losing true life for ever and a day
Through ever trying to be and ever being—
In the evolution of successive spheres—
Before its actual sphere and place of life,
Halfway into the next, which having reached,
It shoots with corresponding foolery
Halfway into the next still, on and off!
As when a traveller, bound from North to South,
Scouts fur in Russia: what's its use in France?
In France spurns flannel: where's its need in Spain?
In Spain drops cloth, too cumbrous for Algiers!
Linen goes next, and last the skin itself,
A superfluity at Timbuctoo.
When, through his journey, was the fool at ease?
I'm at ease now, friend; worldly in this world,
I take and like its way of life; I think
My brothers, who administer the means,
Live better for my comfort—that's good too;
And God, if he pronounce upon such life,
Approves my service, which is better still.
If he keep silence,—why, for you or me
Or that brute beast pulled-up in to-day's 'Times,'
What odds is't, save to ourselves, what life we lead?

You meet me at this issue: you declare,—
All special-pleading done with—truth is truth,
And justifies itself by undreamed ways.
You don't fear but it's better, if we doubt,
To say so, act up to our truth perceived
However feebly. Do then,—act away!
'Tis there I'm on the watch for you. How one acts
Is, both of us agree, our chief concern:
And how you'll act is what I fain would see
If, like the candid person you appear,

You dare to make the most of your life's scheme
As I of mine, live up to its full law
Since there's no higher law that counterchecks.
Put natural religion to the test
You've just demolished the revealed with—quick,
Down to the root of all that checks your will
All prohibition to lie, kill and thieve,
Or even to be an atheistic priest!
Suppose a pricking to incontinence—
Philosophers deduce you chastity
Or shame, from just the fact that at the first
Whoso embraced a woman in the field,
Threw club down and forewent his brains beside,
So, stood a ready victim in the reach
Of any brother savage, club in hand;
Hence saw the use of going out of sight
In wood or cave to prosecute his loves:
I read this in a French book t'other day.
Does law so analysed coerce you much?
Oh, men spin clouds of fuzz where matters end,
But you who reach where the first thread begins,
You'll soon cut that!—which means you can, but won't,
Through certain instincts, blind, unreasoned out,
You dare not set aside, you can't tell why,
But there they are, and so you let them rule.
Then, friend, you seem as much a slave as I,
A liar, conscious coward and hypocrite,
Without the good the slave expects to get,
In case he has a master after all!
You own your instincts? why, what else do I,
Who want, am made for, and must have a God
Ere I can be aught, do aught?—no mere name
Want, but the true thing with what proves its truth,
To wit, a relation from that thing to me,

Touching from head to foot—which touch I feel,
And with it take the rest, this life of ours!
I live my life here; yours you dare not live.

   —Not as I state it, who (you please subjoin)
Disfigure such a life and call it names.
While, to your mind, remains another way
For simple men: knowledge and power have rights,
But ignorance and weakness have rights too
There needs no crucial effort to find truth
If here or there or anywhere about:
We ought to turn each side, try hard and see,
And if we can't, be glad we've earned at least
The right, by one laborious proof the more,
To graze in peace earth's pleasant pasturage.
Men are not angels, neither are they brutes:
Something we may see, all we cannot see.
What need of lying! I say, I see all,
And swear to each detail the most minute
In what I think a Pan's face—you, mere cloud:
I swear I hear him speak and see him wink,
For fear, if once I drop the emphasis,
Mankind may doubt there's any cloud at all.
You take the simple life—ready to see,
Willing to see (for no cloud's worth a face)- -
And leaving quiet what no strength can move,
And which, who bids you move? who has the right?
I bid you; but you are God's sheep, not mine:
'*Pastor est tui Dominus.*' You find
In this the pleasant pasture of our life
Much you may eat without the least offence,
Much you don't eat because your maw objects,
Much you would eat but that your fellow-flock
Open great eyes at you and even butt,

And thereupon you like your mates so well
You cannot please yourself, offending them;
Though when they seem exorbitantly sheep,
You weigh your pleasure with their butts and bleats
And strike the balance. Sometimes certain fears
Restrain you, real checks since you find them so;
Sometimes you please yourself and nothing checks:
And thus you graze through life with not one lie,
And like it best.

                But do you, in truth's name?
If so, you beat—which means you are not I—
Who needs must make earth mine and feed my fill
Not simply unbutted at, unbickered with,
But motioned to the velvet of the sward
By those obsequious wethers' very selves.
Look at me, sir; my age is double yours:
At yours, I knew beforehand, so enjoyed,
What now I should be—as, permit the word,
I pretty well imagine your whole range
And stretch of tether, twenty years to come.
We both have minds and bodies much alike:
In truth's name, don't you want my bishopric,
My daily bread, my influence and my state?
You're young. I'm old; you must be old one day;
Will you find then, as I do hour by hour,
Women their lovers kneel to, who cut curls
From your fat lap-dog's ear to grace a brooch—
Dukes, who petition just to kiss your ring—
With much beside you know or may conceive?
Suppose we die to-night: well, here am I,
Such were my gains, life bore this fruit to me,
While writing all the same my articles
On music, poetry, the fictile vase

Found at Albano, chess, Anacreon's Greek.
But you—the highest honour in your life,
The thing you'll crown yourself with, all your days,
Is—dining here and drinking this last glass
I pour you out in sign of amity
Before we part for ever. Of your power
And social influence, worldly worth in short,
Judge what's my estimation by the fact,
I do not condescend to enjoin, beseech,
Hint secrecy on one of all these words!
You're shrewd and know that should you publish one
The world would brand the lie—my enemies first,
Who'd sneer—'the bishop's an arch-hypocrite
And knave perhaps, but not so frank a fool.'
Whereas I should not dare for both my ears
Breathe one such syllable, smile one such smile,
Before the chaplain who reflects myself—
My shade's so much more potent than your flesh.
What's your reward, self-abnegating friend?
Stood you confessed of those exceptional
And privileged great natures that dwarf mine—
A zealot with a mad ideal in reach,
A poet just about to print his ode,
A statesman with a scheme to stop this war,
An artist whose religion is his art—
I should have nothing to object: such men
Carry the fire, all things grow warm to them,
Their drugget's worth my purple, they beat me.
But you,—you're just as little those as I—
You, Gigadibs, who, thirty years of age,
Write stately for Blackwood's Magazine,
Believe you see two points in Hamlet's soul
Unseized by the Germans yet—which view you'll print—
Meantime the best you have to show being still

That lively lightsome article we took
Almost for the true Dickens,—what's its name?
'The Slum and Cellar, or Whitechapel life
Limned after dark!' it made me laugh, I know,
And pleased a month, and brought you in ten pounds.
—Success I recognize and compliment,
And therefore give you, if you choose, three words
(The card and pencil-scratch is quite enough)
Which whether here, in Dublin or New York,
Will get you, prompt as at my eyebrow's wink,
Such terms as never you aspired to get
In all our own reviews and some not ours.
Go write your lively sketches! be the first
'Blougram, or The Eccentric Confidence'—
Or better simply say, 'The Outward-bound.'
Why, men as soon would throw it in my teeth
As copy and quote the infamy chalked broad
About me on the church-door opposite.
You will not wait for that experience though,
I fancy, howsoever you decide,
To discontinue—not detesting, not
Defaming, but at least—despising me!

Over his wine so smiled and talked his hour
Sylvester Blougram, styled *in partibus*
Episcopus, nec non—(the deuce knows what
It's changed to by our novel hierarchy)
With Gigadibs the literary man,
Who played with spoons, explored his plate's design,
And ranged the olive-stones about its edge,
While the great bishop rolled him out his mind.

For Blougram, he believed, say, half he spoke.
The other portion, as he shaped it thus

For argumentatory purposes,
He felt his foe was foolish to dispute.
Some arbitrary accidental thoughts
That crossed his mind, amusing because new,
He chose to represent as fixtures there,
Invariable convictions (such they seemed
Beside his interlocutor's loose cards
Flung daily down, and not the same way twice)
While certain hell-deep instincts, man's weak tongue
Is never bold to utter in their truth
Because styled hell-deep ('tis an old mistake
To place hell at the bottom of the earth)
He ignored these,—not having in readiness
Their nomenclature and philosophy:
He said true things, but called them by wrong names.
'On the whole,' he thought, 'I justify myself
On every point where cavillers like this
Oppugn my life: he tries one kind of fence,
I close, he's worsted, that's enough for him.
He's on the ground: if ground should break away
I take my stand on, there's a firmer yet
Beneath it, both of us may sink and reach.
His ground was over mine and broke the first:
So, let him sit with me this many a year!'

  He did not sit five minutes. Just a week
Sufficed his sudden healthy vehemence.
Something had struck him in the 'Outward-bound'
Another way than Blougram's purpose was:
And having bought, not cabin-furniture
But settler's-implements (enough for three)
And started for Australia—there, I hope,
By this time he has tested his first plough,
And studied his last chapter of St. John.

349 ## Rabbi Ben Ezra

1

GROW old along with me!
The best is yet to be,
The last of life, for which the first was made:
Our times are in His hand
Who saith 'A whole I planned,
Youth shows but half; trust God: see all, nor be afraid!'

2

Not that, amassing flowers,
Youth sighed 'Which rose make ours,
Which lily leave and then as best recall?'
Not that, admiring stars,
It yearned 'Nor Jove, nor Mars;
Mine be some figured flame which blends, transcends them all!'

3

Not for such hopes and fears
Annulling youth's brief years,
Do I remonstrate: folly wide the mark!
Rather I prize the doubt
Low kinds exist without,
Finished and finite clods, untroubled by a spark.

4

Poor vaunt of life indeed,
Were man but formed to feed
On joy, to solely seek and find and feast:
Such feasting ended, then
As sure an end to men;
Irks care the crop-full bird? Frets doubt the maw-crammed beast?

5

Rejoice we are allied
To That which doth provide
And not partake, effect and not receive!
A spark disturbs our clod;
Nearer we hold of God
Who gives, than of His tribes that take, I must believe.

6

Then, welcome each rebuff
That turns earth's smoothness rough,
Each sting that bids nor sit nor stand but go!
Be our joys three-parts pain!
Strive, and hold cheap the strain;
Learn, nor account the pang; dare, never grudge the throe!

7

For thence,—a paradox
Which comforts while it mocks,—
Shall life succeed in that it seems to fail:
What I aspired to be,
And was not, comforts me:
A brute I might have been, but would not sink i' the scale.

8

What is he but a brute
Whose flesh has soul to suit,
Whose spirit works lest arms and legs want play?
To man, propose this test—
Thy body at its best
How far can that project thy soul on its lone way?

9

Yet gifts should prove their use:
I own the Past profuse
Of power each side, perfection every turn:
Eyes, ears took in their dole,
Brain treasured up the whole;
Should not the heart beat once 'How good to live and learn?'

10

Not once beat 'Praise be Thine!
I see the whole design,
I, who saw power, see now Love perfect too:
Perfect I call Thy plan:
Thanks that I was a man!
Maker, remake, complete,—I trust what Thou shalt do!'

11

For pleasant is this flesh;
Our soul, in its rose-mesh
Pulled ever to the earth, still yearns for rest:
Would we some prize might hold
To match those manifold
Possessions of the brute,—gain most, as we did best!

12

Let us not always say
'Spite of this flesh to-day
I strove, made head, gained ground upon the whole!'
As the bird wings and sings,
Let us cry 'All good things
Are ours, nor soul helps flesh more, now, than flesh helps soul!'

13

Therefore I summon age
To grant youth's heritage,
Life's struggle having so far reached its term:
Thence shall I pass, approved
A man, for aye removed
From the developed brute; a god though in the germ.

14

And I shall thereupon
Take rest, ere I be gone
Once more on my adventure brave and new:
Fearless and unperplexed,
When I wage battle next,
What weapons to select, what armour to indue.

15

Youth ended, I shall try
My gain or loss thereby;
Be the fire ashes, what survives is gold:
And I shall weigh the same,
Give life its praise or blame:
Young, all lay in dispute; I shall know, being old.

16

For note, when evening shuts,
A certain moment cuts
The deed off, calls the glory from the grey:
A whisper from the west
Shoots—'Add this to the rest,
Take it and try its worth: here dies another day.'

17

So, still within this life,
Though lifted o'er its strife,
Let me discern, compare, pronounce at last,
'This rage was right i' the main,
That acquiescence vain:
The Future I may face now I have proved the Past.'

18

For more is not reserved
To man, with soul just nerved
To act to-morrow what he learns to-day:
Here, work enough to watch
The Master work, and catch
Hints of the proper craft, tricks of the tool's true play.

19

As it was better, youth
Should strive, through acts uncouth,
Toward making, than repose on aught found made;
So, better, age, exempt
From strife, should know, than tempt
Further. Thou waitedst age; wait death nor be afraid!

20

Enough now, if the Right
And Good and Infinite
Be named here, as thou callest thy hand thine own,
With knowledge absolute,
Subject to no dispute
From fools that crowded youth, nor let thee feel alone.

21

Be there, for once and all,
Severed great minds from small,
Announced to each his station in the Past!
Was I, the world arraigned,
Were they, my soul disdained,
Right? Let age speak the truth and give us peace at last!

22

Now, who shall arbitrate?
Ten men love what I hate,
Shun what I follow, slight what I receive;
Ten, who in ears and eyes
Match me: we all surmise,
They, this thing, and I, that: whom shall my soul believe?

23

Not on the vulgar mass
Called 'work,' must sentence pass,
Things done, that took the eye and had the price;
O'er which, from level stand,
The low world laid its hand,
Found straightway to its mind, could value in a trice:

24

But all, the world's coarse thumb
And finger failed to plumb,
So passed in making up the main account;
All instincts immature,
All purposes unsure,
That weighed not as his work, yet swelled the man's amount:

25

Thoughts hardly to be packed
Into a narrow act,
Fancies that broke through language and escaped;
All I could never be,
All, men ignored in me,
This, I was worth to God, whose wheel the pitcher shaped.

26

Ay, note that Potter's wheel,
That metaphor! and feel
Why time spins fast, why passive lies our clay,—
Thou, to whom fools propound,
When the wine makes its round,
'Since life fleets, all is change; the Past gone, seize to-day!'

27

Fool! All that is, at all,
Lasts ever, past recall;
Earth changes, but thy soul and God stand sure:
What entered into thee,
That was, is, and shall be:
Time's wheel runs back or stops: Potter and clay endure.

28

He fixed thee mid this dance
Of plastic circumstance,
This Present, thou, forsooth, wouldst fain arrest:
Machinery just meant
To give thy soul its bent,
Try thee and turn thee forth, sufficiently impressed.

29

What though the earlier grooves
Which ran the laughing loves
Around thy base, no longer pause and press?
What though, about thy rim,
Skull-things in order grim
Grow out, in graver mood, obey the sterner stress?

30

Look not thou down but up!
To uses of a cup,
The festal board, lamp's flash and trumpet's peal,
The new wine's foaming flow,
The Master's lips a-glow!
Thou, heaven's consummate cup, what needst thou with earth's
wheel?

31

But I need, now as then,
Thee, God, who mouldest men;
And since, not even while the whirl was worst,
Did I,—to the wheel of life
With shapes and colours rife,
Bound dizzily,—mistake my end, to slake Thy thirst:

32

So, take and use Thy work!
Amend what flaws may lurk,
What strain o' the stuff, what warpings past the aim!
My times be in Thy hand!
Perfect the cup as planned!
Let age approve of youth, and death complete the same!

350　　　　　　　Epilogue

AT the midnight in the silence of the sleeptime,
　　When you set your fancies free,
Will they pass to where—by death, fools think, imprisoned—
Low he lies who once so loved you, whom you loved so,
　　　　　—Pity me?

Oh to love so, be so loved, yet so mistaken!
　　What had I on earth to do
With the slothful, with the mawkish, the unmanly?
Like the aimless, helpless, hopeless, did I drivel
　　　　　—Being—who?

One who never turned his back but marched breast forward,
　　Never doubted clouds would break,
Never dreamed, though right were worsted, wrong would
　　triumph,
Held we fall to rise, are baffled to fight better,
　　　　　Sleep to wake.

No, at noonday in the bustle of man's worktime
　　Greet the unseen with a cheer!
Bid him forward, breast and back as either should be,
'Strive and thrive!' cry 'Speed,—fight on, fare ever
　　　　　There as here!'

AUBREY DE VERE

351　　　　　　[Spring]

　　ONCE more the cuckoo's call I hear;
　　　　I know, in many a glen profound,
　　The earliest violets of the year
　　　　Rise up like water from the ground.

The thorn I know once more is white;
　And, far down many a forest dale,
The anemones in dubious light
　Are trembling like a bridal veil.

By streams released that singing flow
　From craggy shelf through sylvan glades
The pale narcissus, well I know,
　Smiles hour by hour on greener shades.

The honeyed cowslip tufts once more
　The golden slopes; with gradual ray
The primrose stars the rock, and o'er
　The wood-path strews its milky way.

352　　　　　　Autumnal Ode

DEDICATED TO MY SISTER
OCTOBER, 1817

I

MINSTREL and Genius, to whose songs or sighs
　The round earth modulates her changeful sphere,
That bend'st in shadow from yon western skies,
　And lean'st, cloud-hid, along the woodlands sere,
　Too deep thy notes—too pure—for mortal ear!
　　Yet Nature hears them: without aid of thine
　　How sad were her decline!
From thee she learns with just and soft gradation
　Her dying hues in death to harmonize;
　Through thee her obsequies
A glory wear that conquers desolation.

Through thee she singeth, 'Faithless were the sighing
Breathed o'er a beauty only born to fleet:
A holy thing and precious is the dying
Of that whose life was innocent and sweet.'
From many a dim retreat
 Lodged on high-bosomed, echoing mountain lawn,
 Or chiming convent 'mid dark vale withdrawn,
From cloudy shrine or rapt oracular seat
Voices of loftier worlds that saintly strain repeat.

II

It is the Autumnal Epode of the year:
 The nymphs that urge the seasons on their round,
They to whose green lap flies the startled deer
 When bays the far off hound,
They that drag April by the rain-bright hair,
(Though sun-showers daze her and the rude winds scare)
 O'er March's frosty bound,
They by whose warm and furtive hand unwound
 The cestus falls from May's new-wedded breast—
Silent they stand beside dead Summer's bier,
 With folded palms, and faces to the West,
And their loose tresses sweep the dewy ground.

III

A sacred stillness hangs upon the air,
 A sacred clearness. Distant shapes draw nigh;
Glistens yon Elm-grove, to its heart laid bare,
 And all articulate in its symmetry,
 With here and there a branch that from on high
Far flashes washed as in a watery gleam:
Beyond, the glossy lake lies calm—a beam
Upheaved, as if in sleep, from its slow central stream.

IV

This quiet—is it Truth, or some fair mask?
  Is pain no more? Shall Sleep be lord, not Death?
Shall sickness cease to afflict and overtask
  The spent and laboring breath?
Is there 'mid all yon farms and fields, this day,
  No grey old head that drops? No darkening eye?
Spirits of Pity, lift your hands, and pray—
  Each hour, alas, men die!

V

The love songs of the Blackbird now are done;
  Upon the o'ergrown, loose, red-berried cover
The latest of late warblers sings as one
  That trolls at random when the feast is over:
  From bush to bush the dusk-bright cobwebs hover,
    Silvering the dried-up rill's exhausted urn;
No breeze is fluting o'er the green morass:
Nor falls the thistle-down: in deep-drenched grass,
    Now blue, now red, the shifting dew-gems burn.

VI

Mine ear thus torpid held, methinks mine eye
  Is armed the more with visionary power:
  As with a magnet's force each redd'ning bower
Compels me through the woodland pageantry:
Slowly I track the forest's skirt: emerging,
  Slowly I climb from pastoral steep to steep:
I see far mists from reedy valleys surging:
  I follow the procession of white sheep
    That fringe with wool old stock and ruined rath,
How staid to-day, how eager when the lambs
Went leaping round their dams!

I cross the leaf-choked stream from stone to stone,
  Pass the hoar ash tree, trace the upland path,
The furze-brake that in March all golden shone
  Reflected in the shy kingfisher's bath.

VII

No more from full-leaved woods that music swells
  Which in the summer filled the satiate ear:
A fostering sweetness still from bosky dells
  Murmurs; but I can hear
A harsher sound when down, at intervals,
The dry leaf rattling falls.
Dark as those spots which herald swift disease
The death-blot marks for death the leaf yet firm:
Beside the leaf down-trodden trails the worm:
  In forest depths the haggard, whitening grass
Repines at youth departed. Half-stripped trees
  Reveal, as one who says, 'Thou too must pass,'
Plainlier each day their quaint anatomies.
Yon Poplar grove is troubled! Bright and bold
Babbled his cold leaves in the July breeze
As though above our heads a runnel rolled:
  His mirth is o'er: subdued by old October
  He counts his lessening wealth, and, sadly sober,
Tinkles his minute tablets of wan gold.

VIII

Be still, ye sighs of the expiring year!
  A sword there is:—ye play but with the sheath!
Whispers there are more piercing, yet more dear
  Than yours, that come to me those boughs beneath;
And well-remembered footsteps known of old
  Tread soft the mildewed mould.

O magic memory of the things that were—
   Of those whose hands our childish locks carest,
Of one so angel-like in tender care,
   Of one in majesty so God-like drest—
O phantom faces painted on the air
   Of friend or sudden guest;—
I plead in vain:
The woods revere, but cannot heal my pain.
Ye sheddings from the Yew tree and the Pine,
   If on your rich and aromatic dust
I laid my forehead, and my hands put forth
In the last beam that warms the forest floor,
No answer to my yearnings would be mine,
To me no answer through those branches hoar
Would reach in noontide trance or moony gust!
   Her secret Heaven would keep, and mother Earth
Speak from her deep heart—'Where thou know'st
      not, trust!'

IX

That pang is past. Once more my pulses keep
   A tenor calm, that knows nor grief nor joy;
Once more I move as one that died in sleep,
   And treads, a Spirit, the haunts he trod, a boy,
And sees them like-unlike, and sees beyond:
Then earthly life comes back, and I despond.
All life, not life! Dim woods of crimsoned beech
   That swathe the hills in sacerdotal stoles,
Burn on, burn on! the year ere long will reach
   That day made holy to Departed Souls,
The day whereon man's heart, itself a priest,
   Descending to that Empire pale wherein
   Beauty and Sorrow dwell, but pure from Sin,
Holds with God's Church at once its fast and feast.

Dim woods, they, they alone your vaults should tread,
The sad and saintly Dead!
Your pathos those alone ungrieved could meet
    Who fit them for the Beatific Vision:
The things that as they pass us seem to cheat,
    To them would be a music-winged fruition,
    A cadence sweetest in the soft subsiding:
    Transience to them were dear;—for theirs the abiding—
Dear as that Pain which clears from fleshly film
    The spirit's eye, matures each spirit-germ,
    Frost-bound on earth, but at the appointed term
Mirror of Godhead in the immortal realm.

x

Lo there the regal exiles!—under shades
    Deeper than ours, yet in a finer air—
Climbing, successive, elders, youths, and maids,
    The penitential mountain's ebon stair:
    The earth-shadow clips that halo round their hair:
And as lone outcasts watch a moon that wanes,
Receding slowly o'er their native plains,
    Thus watch they, wistful, something far but fair.
      Serene they stand, and wait,
      Self-exiled by the ever-open gate:
Awhile self-exiled from the All-pitying Eyes,
Lest mortal stain should blot their Paradise.
Silent they pace, ascending high and higher
    The hills of God, a hand on every heart
That willing burns, a vase of cleansing fire
    Fed by God's love in souls from God apart.
Each lifted face with thirst of long desire
    Is pale; but o'er it grows a mystic sheen,
    Because on them God's face, by them unseen,
Is turned, through narrowing darkness hourly nigher.

XI

Sad thoughts, why roam ye thus in your unrest
    The bourne unseen? Why scorn our mortal bound?
Is it not kindly, Earth's maternal breast?
    Is it not fair, her head with vine-wreaths crowned?
Farm-yard and barn are heaped with golden store;
    High piled the sheaves illume the russet plain;
Hedges and hedge-row trees are yellowed o'er
    With waifs and trophies of the laboring wain:
Why murmur, 'Change is change, when downward ranging;
Spring's upward change but pointed to the unchanging?'
Yet, O how just your sorrow, if ye knew
The true grief's sanction true!
'Tis not the thought of parting youth that moves us;
    'Tis not alone the pang for friends departed:
The Autumnal pain that raises while it proves us
    Wells from a holier source and deeper-hearted!
For this a sadness swells above our birth;
    For this a bitter runs beneath the sweetness;
        The throne that shakes not is the Spirit's right;
        The heart and hope of Man are infinite;
Heaven is his home, and, exiled here on earth,
    Completion most betrays the incompleteness!

XII

Heaven is his home.—But hark! the breeze increases:
    The sunset forests, catching sudden fire,
    Flash, swell, and sing, a million-organed choir:
Roofing the West, rich clouds in glittering fleeces
        O'er-arch ethereal spaces and divine
        Of heaven's clear hyaline.
No dream is this! Beyond that radiance golden
    God's Sons I see, His armies bright and strong,

The ensanguined Martyrs here with palms high holden,
   The Virgins there, a lily-lifting throng!
The Splendors nearer draw. In choral blending
   The Prophets' and the Apostles' chaunt I hear;
I see the City of the Just descending
   With gates of pearl and diamond bastions sheer.
The walls are agate and chalcedony:
   On jacinth street and jasper parapet
The unwaning light is light of Deity,
   Not beam of lessening moon or suns that set.
That undeciduous forestry of spires
   Lets fall no leaf! those lights can never range:
Saintly fruitions and divine desires
   Are blended there in rapture without change.
—Man was not made for things that leave us,
   For that which goeth and returneth,
For hopes that lift us yet deceive us,
   For love that wears a smile yet mourneth;
Not for fresh forests from the dead leaves springing,
   The cyclic re-creation which, at best,
Yields us—betrayal still to promise clinging—
   But tremulous shadows of the realm of rest:
     For things immortal Man was made,
     God's Image, latest from His hand,
      Co-heir with Him, Who in Man's flesh arrayed
     Holds o'er the worlds the Heavenly-Human wand;
His portion this—sublime
To stand where access none hath Space or Time,
Above the starry host, the Cherub band,
To stand—to advance—and after all to stand!

CHARLOTTE BRONTË (*attributed to*)

Stanzas

OFTEN rebuked, yet always back returning
  To those first feelings that were born with me,
And leaving busy chase of wealth and learning
  For idle dreams of things which cannot be;

To-day, I will seek not the shadowy region;
  Its unsustaining vastness waxes drear;
And visions rising, legion after legion,
  Bring the unreal world too strangely near.

I'll walk, but not in old heroic traces,
  And not in paths of high morality,
And not among the half-distinguished faces,
  The clouded forms of long-past history.

I'll walk where my own nature would be leading:
  It vexes me to choose another guide:
Where the gray flocks in ferny glens are feeding;
  Where the wild wind blows on the mountain-side.

What have those lonely mountains worth revealing?
  More glory and more grief than I can tell:
The earth that wakes *one* human heart to feeling
  Can centre both the worlds of Heaven and Hell.

354   THE night is darkening round me,
       The wild winds coldly blow;
       But a tyrant spell has bound me
       And I cannot, cannot go.

       The giant trees are bending
       Their bare boughs weighed with snow,
       And the storm is fast descending,
       And yet I cannot go.

       Clouds beyond clouds above me,
       Wastes beyond wastes below;
       But nothing drear can move me;
       I will not, cannot go.

                                    November 1837

355   A LITTLE while, a little while,
       The noisy crowd are barred away,
       And I can sing and I can smile,
       A little while I've holyday!

       Where wilt thou go, my harassed heart?
       Full many a land invites thee now;
       And places near and far apart,
       Have rest for thee, my weary brow.

       There is a spot, 'mid barren hills,
       Where winter howls and driving rain,
       But, if the dreary tempest chills,
       There is a light that warms again.

The house is old, the trees are bare,
And moonless bends the misty dome;
But what on earth is half so dear,
So longed for as the hearth of home?

The mute bird sitting on the stone,
The dank moss dripping from the wall,
The garden-walk with weeds o'ergrown,
I love them—how I love them all!

Shall I go there? or shall I seek
Another clime, another sky,
Where tongues familiar music speak
In accents dear to memory?

Yes, as I mused, the naked room,
The flickering firelight died away,
And from the midst of cheerless gloom
I passed to bright, unclouded day—

A little and a lone green lane
That opened on a common wide;
A distant, dreamy, dim blue chain
Of mountains circling every side;

A heaven so clear, an earth so calm,
So sweet, so soft, so hushed an air
And, deepening still the dream-like charm,
Wild moor-sheep feeding everywhere—

That was the scene; I knew it well,
I knew the path-ways far and near,
That, winding o'er each billowy swell,
Marked out the tracks of wandering deer.

Could I have lingered but an hour,
It well had paid a week of toil;
But truth has banished fancy's power;
I hear my dungeon bars recoil—

Even as I stood with raptured eye,
Absorbed in bliss so deep and dear,
My hour of rest had fleeted by
And given me back to weary care.

4 December 1838

356 How still, how happy! These are words
That once would scarce agree together;
I loved the splashing of the surge,
The changing heaven, the breezy weather,

More than smooth seas and cloudless skies
And solemn, soothing, softened airs
That in the forest woke no sighs
And from the green spray shook no tears.

How still, how happy! Now I feel
Where silence dwells is sweeter far
Than laughing mirth's most joyous swell,
However pure its raptures are.

Come, sit down on this sunny stone:
'Tis wintry light o'er flowerless moors—
But sit—for we are all alone,
And clear expand heaven's breathless shores.

I could think in the withered grass
Spring's budding wreaths we might discern;
The violet's eye might shyly flash
And young leaves shoot among the fern.

It is but thought—full many a night
The snow shall clothe those hills afar,
And storms shall add a drearier blight
And winds shall wage a wilder war,

Before the lark may herald in
Fresh foliage twined with blossoms fair,
And summer days again begin
Their glory-haloed crown to wear.

Yet my heart loves December's smile
As much as July's golden beam;
Then let us sit and watch the while
The blue ice curdling on the stream.

7 December 1838

357   IF grief for grief can touch thee,
If answering woe for woe,
If any ruth can melt thee,
Come to me now!

I cannot be more lonely,
More drear I cannot be!
My worn heart throbs so wildly
'Twill break for thee.

And when the world despises,
When heaven repels my prayer,
Will not mine angel comfort?
Mine idol hear?

Yes, by the tears I've poured [thee],
By all my hours of pain,
O I shall surely win thee,
Beloved, again!

18 May 1840

EMILY BRONTË

358   The Old Stoic

RICHES I hold in light esteem,
And Love I laugh to scorn;
And lust of Fame was but a dream
That vanished with the morn—

And if I pray, the only prayer
That moves my lips for me
Is—'Leave the heart that now I bear,
And give me liberty.'

Yes, as my swift days near their goal,
'Tis all that I implore—
Through life and death, a chainless soul,
With courage to endure!

                                    1 March 1841

359   Song

THE linnet in the rocky dells,
The moor-lark in the air,
The bee among the heather-bells
That hide my lady fair:

The wild deer browse above her breast;
The wild birds raise their brood;
And they, her smiles of love caressed,
Have left her solitude!

I ween, that when the grave's dark wall
Did first her form retain,
They thought their hearts could ne'er recall
The light of joy again.

They thought the tide of grief would flow
Unchecked through future years;
But where is all their anguish now,
And where are all their tears?

Well, let them fight for Honour's breath,
Or Pleasure's shade pursue—
The Dweller in the land of Death
Is changed and careless too.

And if their eyes should watch and weep
Till sorrow's source were dry,
She would not, in her tranquil sleep,
Return a single sigh.

Blow, west wind, by the lonely mound,
And murmur, summer streams,
There is no need of other sound
To soothe my Lady's dreams.

1 May 1844

360   Remembrance

R[OSINA]. ALCONA TO J[ULIUS]. BRENZAIDA
COLD in the earth—and the deep snow piled above thee,
Far, far removed, cold in the dreary grave!
Have I forgot, my only Love, to love thee,
Severed at last by Time's all-severing wave?

Now, when alone, do my thoughts no longer hover
Over the mountains, on that northern shore,
Resting their wings where heath and fern-leaves cover
Thy noble heart for ever, ever more?

EMILY BRONTË

Cold in the earth—and fifteen wild Decembers
From those brown hills have melted into spring—
Faithful indeed is the spirit that remembers
After such years of change and suffering!

Sweet Love of youth, forgive if I forget thee
While the world's tide is bearing me along:
Other desires and other hopes beset me,
Hopes which obscure, but cannot do thee wrong!

No later light has lightened up my heaven;
No second morn has ever shone for me:
All my life's bliss from thy dear life was given—
All my life's bliss is in the grave with thee.

But, when the days of golden dreams had perished,
And even Despair was powerless to destroy,
Then did I learn how existence could be cherished,
Strengthened, and fed without the aid of joy;

Then did I check the tears of useless passion,
Weaned my young soul from yearning after thine;
Sternly denied its burning wish to hasten
Down to that tomb already more than mine!

And, even yet, I dare not let it languish,
Dare not indulge in Memory's rapturous pain;
Once drinking deep of that divinest anguish,
How could I seek the empty world again?

3 March 1845

361   Death

DEATH, that struck when I was most confiding
In my certain faith of joy to be,
Strike again, Time's withered branch dividing
From the fresh root of Eternity!

Leaves, upon Time's branch, were growing brightly,
Full of sap, and full of silver dew;
Birds, beneath its shelter, gathered nightly;
Daily, round its flowers, the wild bees flew.

Sorrow passed, and plucked the golden blossom,
Guilt stripped off the foliage in its pride;
But, within its parent's kindly bosom,
Flowed forever Life's restoring tide.

Little mourned I for the parted gladness,
For the vacant nest and silent song;
Hope was there and laughed me out of sadness,
Whispering, 'Winter will not linger long.'

And behold, with tenfold increase blessing,
Spring adorned the beauty-burdened spray;
Wind and rain and fervent heat caressing
Lavished glory on its second May.

High it rose; no winged grief could sweep it;
Sin was scared to distance with its shine:
Love and its own life had power to keep it
From all wrong, from every blight but thine!

Cruel Death, the young leaves droop and languish!
Evening's gentle air may still restore—
No: the morning sunshine mocks my anguish—
Time for me must never blossom more!

Strike it down, that other boughs may flourish
Where that perished sapling used to be;
Thus, at least, its mouldering corpse will nourish
That from which it sprung—Eternity.

10 April 1845

362   Anticipation

How beautiful the Earth is still
To thee—how full of Happiness;
How little fraught with real ill,
Or shadowy phantoms of distress;

How Spring can bring thee glory yet
And Summer win thee to forget
December's sullen time!
Why dost thou hold the treasure fast
Of youth's delight, when youth is past,
And thou art near thy prime?

When those who were thy own compeers,
Equal in fortune and in years,
Have seen their morning melt in tears,
To dull unlovely day;
Blest, had they died unproved and young,
Before their hearts were wildly wrung,—
Poor slaves, subdued by passions strong,
A weak and helpless prey!

'Because, I hoped while they enjoyed,
And by fulfilment, hope destroyed—
As children hope, with trustful breast,
I waited Bliss and cherished Rest.

'A thoughtful Spirit taught me soon
That we must long till life be done;
That every phase of earthly joy
Will always fade and always cloy—

'This I foresaw, and would not chase
The fleeting treacheries,
But with firm foot and tranquil face,
Held backward from that tempting race,
Gazed o'er the sands the waves efface
To the enduring seas—

'There cast my anchor of Desire
Deep in unknown Eternity;
Nor ever let my Spirit tire,
With looking for *What is to be*.

'It is Hope's spell that glorifies,
Like youth, to my maturer eyes
All Nature's million mysteries—
The fearful and the fair—

'Hope soothes me in the griefs I know,
She lulls my pain for others' woe
And makes me strong to undergo
What I am born to bear.

'Glad comforter, will I not brave,
Unawed, the darkness of the grave?
Nay, smile to hear Death's billows rave,
My Guide, sustained by thee?
The more unjust seems present fate,
The more my spirit swells elate,
Strong in thy strength, to anticipate
Rewarding Destiny!'

2 June 1845

363   The Visionary

SILENT is the house: all are laid asleep:
One alone looks out o'er the snow-wreaths deep,
Watching every cloud, dreading every breeze
That whirls the wildering drift, and bends the groaning trees.

Cheerful is the hearth, soft the matted floor;
Not one shivering gust creeps through pane or door;
The little lamp burns straight, its rays shoot strong and far:
I trim it well, to be the wanderer's guiding-star.

Frown, my haughty sire! chide, my angry dame;
Set your slaves to spy; threaten me with shame:
But neither sire nor dame, nor prying serf shall know,
What angel nightly tracks that waste of frozen snow.

What I love shall come like visitant of air,
Safe in secret power from lurking human snare;
What loves me, no word of mine shall e'er betray,
Though for faith unstained my life must forfeit pay.

Burn, then, little lamp; glimmer straight and clear—
Hush! a rustling wing stirs, methinks, the air:
He for whom I wait, thus ever comes to me;
Strange Power! I trust thy might; trust thou my constancy.

9 October 1845

364   from 'THE PRISONER'

A Fragment

'STILL, let my tyrants know, I am not doomed to wear
Year after year in gloom, and desolate despair;
A messenger of Hope comes every night to me,
And offers for short life, eternal liberty.

'He comes with western winds, with evening's wandering airs,
With that clear dusk of heaven that brings the thickest stars.
Winds take a pensive tone, and stars a tender fire,
And visions rise, and change, that kill me with desire.

'Desire for nothing known in my maturer years,
When Joy grew mad with awe, at counting future tears.
When, if my spirit's sky was full of flashes warm,
I knew not whence they came, from sun or thunder-storm.

'But, first, a hush of peace—a soundless calm descends;
The struggle of distress, and fierce impatience ends;
Mute music soothes my breast—unuttered harmony,
That I could never dream, till Earth was lost to me.

'Then dawns the Invisible; the Unseen its truth reveals;
My outward sense is gone, my inward essence feels:
Its wings are almost free—its home, its harbour found,
Measuring the gulf, it stoops and dares the final bound.

'O! dreadful is the check—intense the agony—
When the ear begins to hear, and the eye begins to see;
When the pulse begins to throb, the brain to think again;
The soul to feel the flesh, and the flesh to feel the chain.

'Yet I would lose no sting, would wish no torture less;
The more that anguish racks, the earlier it will bless;
And robed in fires of hell, or bright with heavenly shine,
If it but herald death, the vision is divine!'

9 October 1845

365 'The following are the last lines my sister Emily
    ever wrote.' [Note by Charlotte Brontë]

No coward soul is mine,
No trembler in the world's storm-troubled sphere:
I see Heaven's glories shine,
And faith shines equal, arming me from fear.

O God within my breast,
Almighty, ever-present Deity!
Life—that in me has rest,
As I—undying Life—have power in Thee!

Vain are the thousand creeds
That move men's hearts: unutterably vain;
Worthless as withered weeds,
Or idle froth amid the boundless main,

To waken doubt in one
Holding so fast by Thine infinity;
So surely anchored on
The steadfast rock of immortality.

With wide-embracing love
Thy spirit animates eternal years,
Pervades and broods above,
Changes, sustains, dissolves, creates, and rears.

Though earth and man were gone,
And suns and universes ceased to be,
And Thou were left alone,
Every existence would exist in Thee.

There is not room for Death,
Nor atom that his might could render void:
Thou—THOU art Being and Breath,
And what THOU art may never be destroyed.

2 January 1846

ARTHUR HUGH CLOUGH

366 ## The Latest Decalogue

THOU shalt have one God only; who
Would be at the expense of two?
No graven images may be
Worshipped, except the currency:
Swear not at all; for for thy curse
Thine enemy is none the worse:
At church on Sunday to attend
Will serve to keep the world thy friend:
Honour thy parents; that is, all
From whom advancement may befall:
Thou shalt not kill; but needst not strive
Officiously to keep alive:

Do not adultery commit;
Advantage rarely comes of it:
Thou shalt not steal; an empty feat,
When it's so lucrative to cheat:
Bear not false witness; let the lie
Have time on its own wings to fly:
Thou shalt not covet; but tradition
Approves all forms of competition.

The sum of all is, thou shalt love,
If any body, God above:
At any rate shalt never labour
More than thyself to love thy neighbour.

367 SAY not the struggle nought availeth,
  The labour and the wounds are vain,
The enemy faints not, nor faileth,
  And as things have been, they remain.

If hopes were dupes, fears may be liars;
  It may be, in yon smoke concealed,
Your comrades chase e'en now the fliers,
  And, but for you, possess the field.

For while the tired waves, vainly breaking,
  Seem here no painful inch to gain,
Far back through creeks and inlets making
  Comes, silent, flooding in, the main,

And not by eastern windows only,
  When daylight comes, comes in the light,
In front the sun climbs slow, how slowly,
  But westward, look, the land is bright.

368
    To spend uncounted years of pain,
    Again, again, and yet again,
    In working out in heart and brain
      The problem of our being here;
    To gather facts from far and near,
    Upon the mind to hold them clear,
    And, knowing more may yet appear,
    Unto one's latest breath to fear
    The premature result to draw—
    Is this the object, end and law,
      And purpose of our being here?

from 'AMOURS DE VOYAGE'

[I]

369   ['Ye Ancient Divine Ones']

YE, too, marvellous Twain, that erect on the Monte Cavallo
Stand by your rearing steeds in the grace of your motionless
    movement,
Stand with your upstretched arms and tranquil regardant faces,
Stand as instinct with life in the might of immutable manhood,—
O ye mighty and strange, ye ancient divine ones of Hellas,
Are ye Christian too? to convert and redeem [and renew] you,
Will the brief form have sufficed, that a Pope has set up on the
    apex
Of the Egyptian stone that o'ertops you, the Christian symbol?
    And ye, silent, supreme in serene and victorious marble,
Ye that encircle the walls of the stately Vatican chambers,
Juno and Ceres, Minerva, Apollo, the Muses and Bacchus,
Ye unto whom far and near come posting the Christian pilgrims,
Ye that are ranged in the halls of the mystic Christian Pontiff,

Are ye also baptized? are ye of the kingdom of Heaven?
Utter, O some one, the word that shall reconcile Ancient and
    Modern!
Am I to turn for this unto thee, great Chapel of Sixtus?

[II]

370   ['A Spirit from Perfecter Ages']

Is it illusion? or does there a spirit from perfecter ages,
    Here, even yet, amid loss, change, and corruption abide?
Does there a spirit we know not, though seek, though we find,
    comprehend not,
    Here to entice and confuse, tempt and evade us, abide?
Lives in the exquisite grace of the column disjointed and single,
    Haunts the rude masses of brick garlanded gayly with vine,
E'en in the turret fantastic surviving that springs from the ruin,
    E'en in the people itself? is it illusion or not?
Is it illusion or not that attracteth the pilgrim transalpine,
    Brings him a dullard and dunce hither to pry and to stare?
Is it illusion or not that allures the barbarian stranger,
    Brings him with gold to the shrine, brings him in arms to the
    gate?

[III]

371   ['Ah, that I were Far Away']

YET to the wondrous St. Peter's, and yet to the solemn Rotonda,
    Mingling with heroes and gods, yet to the Vatican walls,
Yet may we go, and recline, while a whole mighty world seems
                          above us
    Gathered and fixed to all time into one roofing supreme;

Yet may we, thinking on these things, exclude what is meaner
around us;
Yet, at the worst of the worst, books and a chamber remain;
Yet may we think, and forget, and possess our souls in resistance.—
Ah, but away from the stir, shouting, and gossip of war,
Where, upon Apennine slope, with the chestnut the oak-trees
immingle,
Where amid odorous copse bridle-paths wander and wind,
Where under mulberry-branches the diligent rivulet sparkles,
Or amid cotton and maize peasants their water-works ply,
Where, over fig-tree and orange in tier upon tier still repeated,
Garden on garden upreared, balconies step to the sky,—
Ah, that I were, far away from the crowd and the streets of the city,
Under the vine-trellis laid, O my beloved, with thee!

[IV]

372   ['Juxtaposition']

JUXTAPOSITION, in fine; and what is juxtaposition?
Look you, we travel along in the railway-carriage, or steamer,
And, *pour passer le temps*, till the tedious journey be ended,
Lay aside paper or book, to talk with the girl that is next one;
And, *pour passer le temps*, with the terminus all but in prospect,
Talk of eternal ties and marriages made in heaven.
  Ah, did we really accept with a perfect heart the illusion!
Ah, did we really believe that the Present indeed is the Only!
Or through all transmutation, all shock and convulsion of passion,
Feel we could carry undimmed, unextinguished, the light of our
knowledge!
  But for his funeral train which the bridegroom sees in the dis-
tance,

Would he so joyfully, think you, fall in with the marriage-
    procession?
But for that final discharge, would he dare enlist in that service?
But for that certain release, ever sign to that perilous contract?
But for that exit secure, ever bend to that treacherous doorway?—
Ah, but the bride, meantime,—do you think she sees it as he
    does?

But for the steady fore-sense of a freer and larger existence,
Think you that man could consent to be circumscribed here into
    action?
But for assurance within of a limitless ocean divine, o'er
Whose great tranquil depths unconscious the wind-tost surface
Breaks into ripples of trouble that come and change and endure
    not,—
But that in this, of a truth, we have our being, and know it,
Think you we men could submit to live and move as we do here?
Ah, but the women,—God bless them! they don't think at all
    about it.

    Yet we must eat and drink, as you say. And as limited beings
Scarcely can hope to attain upon earth to an Actual Abstract,
Leaving to God contemplation, to His hands knowledge con-
    fiding,
Sure that in us if it perish, in Him it abideth and dies not,
Let us in His sight accomplish our petty particular doings,—
Yes, and contented sit down to the victual that He has provided.
Allah is great, no doubt, and Juxtaposition his prophet.
Ah, but the women, alas! they don't look at it in that way.

    Juxtaposition is great;—but, my friend, I fear me, the maiden
Hardly would thank or acknowledge the lover that sought to
    obtain her,
Not as the thing he would wish, but the thing he must even put
    up with,—
Hardly would tender her hand to the wooer that candidly told her
That she is but for a space, an *ad interim* solace and pleasure,—

That in the end she shall yield to a perfect and absolute something
Which I then for myself shall behold, and not another,—
Which, amid fondest endearments, meantime I forget not, forsake
    not.
Ah, ye feminine souls, so loving and so exacting,
Since we cannot escape, must we even submit to deceive you?
Since so cruel is truth, sincerity shocks and revolts you,
Will you have us your slaves to lie to you, flatter and—leave
    you?

[v]

373   ['So Not Seeing I Sung']

TIBUR is beautiful, too, and the orchard slopes, and the Anio
Falling, falling yet, to the ancient lyrical cadence;
Tibur and Anio's tide; and cool from Lucretilis ever,
With the Digentian stream, and with the Bandusian fountain,
Folded in Sabine recesses, the valley and villa of Horace:—
So not seeing I sung; so seeing and listening say I,
Here as I sit by the stream, as I gaze at the cell of the Sibyl,
Here with Albunea's home and the grove of Tiburnus beside me;
Tivoli beautiful is, and musical, O Teverone,
Dashing from mountain to plain, thy parted impetuous waters!
Tivoli's waters and rocks; and fair under Monte Gennaro
(Haunt even yet, I must think, as I wander and gaze, of the
    shadows,
Faded and pale, yet immortal, of Faunus, the Nymphs, and the
    Graces),
Fair in itself, and yet fairer with human completing creations,
Folded in Sabine recesses the valley and villa of Horace:—
So not seeing I sung; so now—Nor seeing, nor hearing,
Neither by waterfall lulled, nor folded in sylvan embraces,
Neither by cell of the Sibyl, nor stepping the Monte Gennaro,

Seated on Anio's bank, nor sipping Bandusian waters,
But on Montorio's height, looking down on the tile-clad streets,
  the
Cupolas, crosses, and domes, the bushes and kitchen-gardens,
Which, by the grace of the Tiber, proclaim themselves Rome of
  the Romans,—
But on Montorio's height, looking forth to the vapoury moun-
  tains,
Cheating the prisoner Hope with illusions of vision and fancy,—
But on Montorio's height, with these weary soldiers by me,
Waiting till Oudinot enter, to reinstate Pope and Tourist.

374   from 'DIPSYCHUS'

    YET I could think, indeed, the perfect call
Should force the perfect answer. If the voice
Ought to receive its echo from the soul,
Wherefore this silence? If it *should* rouse my being,
Why this reluctance? Have not I thought o'ermuch
Of other men, and of the ways of the world?
But what they are, or have been, matters not.
To thine own self be true, the wise man says.
Are then my fears myself? O double self!
And I untrue to both. Oh, there are hours,
When love, and faith, and dear domestic ties,
And converse with old friends, and pleasant walks,
Familiar faces, and familiar books,
Study, and art, upliftings unto prayer,
And admiration of the noblest things,
Seem all ignoble only; all is mean,
And nought as I would have it. Then at others,
My mind is on her nest; my heart at home
In all around; my soul secure in place,

And the vext needle perfect to her poles.
Aimless and hopeless in my life I seem
To thread the winding byways of the town,
Bewildered, baffled, hurried hence and thence,
All at cross-purpose ever with myself,
Unknowing whence from whither. Then, in a moment,
At a step, I crown the Campanile's top,
And view all mapped below: islands, lagoon,
An hundred steeples and a million roofs,
The fruitful champaign, and the cloud-capt Alps,
And the broad Adriatic. Be it enough;
If I lose this, how terrible! No, no,
I am contented, and will not complain.
To the old paths, my soul! Oh, be it so!
I bear the workday burden of dull life
About these footsore flags of a weary world,
Heaven knows how long it has not been; at once,
Lo! I am in the Spirit on the Lord's day
With John in Patmos. Is it not enough,
One day in seven? and if this should go,
If this pure solace should desert my mind,
What were all else? I dare not risk this loss.

GEORGE ELIOT

375   O May I Join the Choir Invisible

> Longum illud tempus, quum non ero, magis me movet,
> quam hoc exiguum. CICERO, ad Att., xii. 18.

O MAY I join the choir invisible
Of those immortal dead who live again
In minds made better by their presence: live
In pulses stirred to generosity,

In deeds of daring rectitude, in scorn
For miserable aims that end with self,
In thoughts sublime that pierce the night like stars,
And with their mild persistence urge man's search
To vaster issues.
       So to live is heaven:
To make undying music in the world,
Breathing as beauteous order that controls
With growing sway the growing life of man.
So we inherit that sweet purity
For which we struggled, failed, and agonised
With widening retrospect that bred despair.
Rebellious flesh that would not be subdued,
A vicious parent shaming still its child
Poor anxious penitence, is quick dissolved;
Its discords, quenched by meeting harmonies,
Die in the large and charitable air.
And all our rarer, better, truer self,
That sobbed religiously in yearning song,
That watched to ease the burthen of the world,
Laboriously tracing what must be,
And what may yet be better—saw within
A worthier image for the sanctuary,
And shaped it forth before the multitude
Divinely human, raising worship so
To higher reverence more mixed with love—
That better self shall live till human Time
Shall fold its eyelids, and the human sky
Be gathered like a scroll within the tomb
Unread for ever.
       This is life to come,
Which martyred men have made more glorious
For us who strive to follow. May I reach
That purest heaven, be to other souls

The cup of strength in some great agony,
Enkindle generous ardour, feed pure love,
Beget the smiles that have no cruelty—
Be the sweet presence of a good diffused,
And in diffusion ever more intense.
So shall I join the choir invisible
Whose music is the gladness of the world.

1867

EBENEZER JONES

376   A Development of Idiotcy

FEARFUL the chamber's quiet; the veiled windows
Admit no breath of the out-door throbbing sunshine;
She moans in the bed's dusk;—some sharp revulsion
Shuddereth her lips as though she strives to cry,
But finds no voice: she draweth up her limbs,
They flutter fast and shake their covering.
Seven watch her, as might men a noonday sun,
Who vanishing backward in the top of heaven,
Leaves them all blindly staring through the dark;—
Physicians and servitors;—pryingly they bend,
While by her head kneels one in agony.
A gloom seems passing o'er her countenance,
As the shadow of a cloud across a field;
Perchance the ghastly expression of the horror
With which life ends: it darkened but a moment;
Now she turns white as stone, as fixed, as dead.
God! ten days hence she laughed out in thy sunshine!
Her filmed eyes looked, gestured happiness!—
They have no look at all.

The seven shuffle from the bed which hides
Her clutching fingers, and her doubled limbs,
So stiffening 'twixt its sheets; and one by one,
They coweringly glance towards her fallen mouth,
And all together hurry from out the room,
Not caring to leave it singly. All is still;
He rises from the ground, fast locks the door,
Breaks through her couch-clothes, feels about her heart;—
All there is motionless: he lifts her hand;—
There is nothing but dead form, it moves not, warms **not,**
It weighs, it slides away, it drops like lead,
Lies where it dropped: recoiling, the man gasps,
As though by ocean seized: his jaws contract,
He bounds, he rends the window; savagely
Looking right up into the broad blue sky,
No congruous curses aid him,—he is silent,
Save with his clenched hands, his writhing face,
His heaving chest.

          He was a force-filled man,
Whom the wise envy not; his passionate soul,
Being mighty to detect life's secret beauty,
Detecting, would display; and in his youth,
When first bright visions unveiled before his gaze
Their moral loveliness and physical grace,
With the sweet melody of affectionate clamour
He sang them to the world, and bade it worship:
But the world unrecognized his visions of goodness,
Or recognizing, hated them and him.
As some full cloud foregoes his native country
Of sublime hills, where bask'd he near to heaven,
And descends gently on his shadowy wings
Through the hot sunshine to refresh all creatures;
So came he to the world;—as the same cloud

Might slowly wend back to his Alpine home,
Unwatering the plain,—so left he men
Who knew not of their loss.

Yet sad was loneliness, and never beheld he
Aught beautiful amidst our world of beauty—
From sunsets flushing heaven with sudden crimson,
To the moth's wing that spots the poplar leaf;
Never developed he fact, or dreamed he glory,
Without being faint for sympathy,—that one
Might share with him his blissful adoration,
Loving even as he loved. This holy want
Wasted him unto sickness: then she came;
And while he hung above death's gloomy gulf,
Sternly considering its maddening stillness,
Measuring the plunge;—her soft voice called to him:
He turned; he saw her eyes his soul acquiring;
He saw her look of woman's infinite giving;
He saw her arms of eloquent entreaty,
Praying indeed to clasp him: yea, she saved;
And Oh! but he was happy, for her being
Loved all things as he loved, and thence to him
Came hope and rapturous quiet. Then no more
Lamented he the wingless minds of men,
Than pines the swan,—who down the midnight river,
Moves on considering the reflected stars—
Because dark reptiles burrowing in the ooze,
Care not for starry glories.

She is dead within that bed; and never more
Will she hearken to his dreams of paradise,
And wind her arms around him, sweetly paling
With excess of happiness.

Three days and nights he haunted a near mountain;
The sky was cloudless, and the sunshine strong,
And not one mournful breeze ever stole to him,
Loosening his tears. High on its top he stood;
His voice rose solemn, and loud, and fearlessly:—
The angels watching him midway in the air,
Rushed swift to heaven, and all heaven's shining group
Weepingly pleaded against his blasphemy;—
'Roll back! thou lying robe of halcyon blue!
And let me speak unto thy cowering Lord,
The slayer of my love, that I may tell him
My infinite hate, that he may slaughter me:
He has killed her: I will not have his life;—
Thou lying robe of halcyon blue! roll back!'
The peaks prolonged with echoings his defiance;
Still the sky stirred not—still the sunshine smiled,
And beneath the smile low rose a low wild sound:—
'And then my breast will be as cold as hers,—
My face as white—as signless.'

The fourth day, back he rushed into the chamber,
Where she lay coffined. None dared speak to him;
Great grief is majesty; he is alone.
Oh! is that she, or can it all be dreaming?
Fine lace is plaited round her countenance;
Her eyes are closed, as they would seem to say,
'My last farewell is taken.' Round her lips
Is fixed a sweet smile; her shrunken hands
Are clasped upon her bosom, their dark fingers
Cunningly hidden. Can it all be dreaming?
Striving to stare the mistiness from his eyes,
Griping his throat, he lightly presses her hand,—
The pressure of his fingers doth not vanish;—
Senseless he falls.

This singer of the beautiful, who retreated
Back from a scowling world; this force-filled man,
Who finding nothing whereunto he might sing,
Of power unuttered, and of passion unshared,
Nigh died; this gentle minister of love,
Who, hailed by loving sympathy, thrice lived
In singing his deities, and seeing them loved,
And loving their lover, and forgetting all else;—
Is now a thing that hideth most fair weathers,
Outwandering in most glooms,—after whose path
The village boys shout 'idiot', that some sport
His face may make them, when it turns enraged
With idiot rage, that slinks to empty smiles,
And tears, and laughter, empty. His chief habit
Is secretly rending piecemeal beauteous flowers;—
He ever shows when the groaning thunder toils,
And when the lightnings flash! and they who meet
His shrinking, shuddering, blank countenance,
Wonder to heaven with somewhat shaken trust.

377   A Winter Hymn—to the Snow

COME o'er the hills, and pass unto the wold,
And all things, as thou passest, in rest upfold,
   Nor all night long thy ministrations cease;
Thou succourer of young corn, and of each seed
In ploughed land sown, or lost on rooted mead,
   And bringer everywhere of exceeding peace!

Beneath the long interminable frost
Earth's landscapes all their excellent force have lost,
   And stripped and abject each alike appears;

Not now to adore can they exalt the soul,—
Panic, or anger, or unrest control,—
  Or aid the loosening of Affliction's tears.

No more doth Desolateness lovely sit
Lone on the moor; no more around her flit
  From far high-travelling heaven the sailing shades;
The shrunk grass shivers feebly; reed and sedge,
By frozen marsh, by rivulet's iron edge,
  Bow, blent into the ice, mixed stems and blades.

The mountains soar not, holding high in heaven
Their mighty kingdoms, but all downward driven
  Seem shrunken haggard ridges running low;
And all about stand drear upon the leas,
Like giant thorns, the frozen skeleton trees,
  Dead to the winds that ruining through them go.

The woodland rattles in the sudden gusts;
Frozen through frozen brakes the river thrusts
  His arm forth stiffly, like one slain and cold;
The glory from the horizon-line has fled;
One sullen formless gloom the skies are spread,
  And black the waters of the lakes are rolled.

Come! Daughter fair of Sire the sternest, come,
And bring the world relief! to the rivers numb
  Give garments, cover broadly the broad land;
All trees with thy resistless gentleness
Assume, and in thine own white vesture dress,
  And hush all nooks with thy persistings bland.

Come! making rugged gorge and rocky height
Even more than fur of ermine soft and white,
  And cover up and silence roads and lanes;

And, while the ravished wind sleeps hushed and still,
Wreaths, little infancy with glee to fill,
   Upheap at doorways and at casement-panes.

Fancy's most potent pandar! gentlest too:
Man, rising on the morn, the scene will view
   Thus, all transformed, with no less sweet surprise
Than stirreth him to whose half-doubting sight
Sudden appears belov'd friend, masquèd bright
   In not less fair than unexpected guise.

And some will think the earth, in white robes dressed,
Seems sinking fast in a great trance of rest,
   Beyond all further reach of wintry ill;
And some will say it seems as though a ghost
Appeared; and thus, on fancy's seas far tossed,
   With doubtful shadowy joys their spirits fill.

Thy task complete,—if to the amazing scene
With Night should come, full-orbed, Night's radiant Queen,
   How the whole race from out their homes will gaze!
Hard hearts will restless grow, and mean men sigh,
And wish they could be holier, and on high
   Some, whispering words of heaven, meek thanks will raise.

I, sweet celestial kisser! from croft home-crowned,
From ancient mead by stateliest trees girt round,
   From wilds where thou the earth lov'st all alone,
Shall watch thee shower thy kisses, and all the hours
Rapt worship solemnize, and bless the Powers
   That let thy loveliness to my soul be known!

In Utrumque Paratus

IF, in the silent mind of One all-pure
    At first imagin'd lay
The sacred world; and by procession sure
From those still deeps, in form and colour drest,
Seasons alternating, and night and day,
The long-mus'd thought to north south east and west
    Took then its all-seen way:

O waking on a world which thus-wise springs!
    Whether it needs thee count
Betwixt thy waking and the birth of things
Ages or hours: O waking on Life's stream!
By lonely pureness to the all-pure Fount
(Only by this thou canst) the colour'd dream
    Of Life remount.

Thin, thin the pleasant human noises grow;
    And faint the city gleams;
Rare the lone pastoral huts: marvel not thou!
The solemn peaks but to the stars are known,
But to the stars, and the cold lunar beams:
Alone the sun arises, and alone
    Spring the great streams.

But, if the wild unfather'd mass no birth
    In divine seats hath known:
In the blank, echoing solitude, if Earth,
Rocking her obscure body to and fro,
Ceases not from all time to heave and groan,
Unfruitful oft, and, at her happiest throe,
    Forms, what she forms, alone:

O seeming sole to awake, thy sun-bath'd head
    Piercing the solemn cloud
Round thy still dreaming brother-world outspread!
O man, whom Earth, thy long-vext mother, bare
Not without joy; so radiant, so endow'd—
(Such happy issue crown'd her painful care)
    Be not too proud!

O when most self-exalted most alone,
    Chief dreamer, own thy dream!
Thy brother-world stirs at thy feet unknown;
Who hath a monarch's hath no brother's part;
Yet doth thine inmost soul with yearning teem.
O what a spasm shakes the dreamer's heart—
    '*I too but seem!*'

379   To Marguerite

    YES: in the sea of life enisl'd,
    With echoing straits between us thrown,
    Dotting the shoreless watery wild,
    We mortal millions live *alone*.
    The islands feel the enclasping flow,
    And then their endless bounds they know.

    But when the moon their hollows lights
    And they are swept by balms of spring,
    And in their glens, on starry nights,
    The nightingales divinely sing,
    And lovely notes, from shore to shore,
    Across the sounds and channels pour;

Oh then a longing like despair
Is to their farthest caverns sent;
For surely once, they feel, we were
Parts of a single continent.
Now round us spreads the watery plain—
Oh might our marges meet again!

Who order'd, that their longing's fire
Should be, as soon as kindled, cool'd?
Who renders vain their deep desire?—
    A God, a God their severance ruled;
And bade betwixt their shores to be
The unplumb'd, salt, estranging sea.

380   The Scholar Gipsy

Go, for they call you, Shepherd, from the hill;
    Go, Shepherd, and untie the wattled cotes:
        No longer leave thy wistful flock unfed,
    Nor let thy bawling fellows rack their throats,
        Nor the cropp'd grasses shoot another head.
            But when the fields are still,
    And the tired men and dogs all gone to rest,
        And only the white sheep are sometimes seen
        Cross and recross the strips of moon-blanch'd green;
Come, Shepherd, and again renew the quest.

Here, where the reaper was at work of late,
    In this high field's dark corner, where he leaves
        His coat, his basket, and his earthen cruise,
    And in the sun all morning binds the sheaves,
        Then here, at noon, comes back his stores to use;

Here will I sit and wait,
While to my ear from uplands far away
The bleating of the folded flocks is borne;
With distant cries of reapers in the corn—
All the live murmur of a summer's day.

Screen'd is this nook o'er the high, half-reap'd field,
And here till sun-down, Shepherd, will I be.
Through the thick corn the scarlet poppies peep
And round green roots and yellowing stalks I see
Pale pink convolvulus in tendrils creep:
And air-swept lindens yield
Their scent, and rustle down their perfum'd showers
Of bloom on the bent grass where I am laid,
And bower me from the August sun with shade;
And the eye travels down to Oxford's towers:

And near me on the grass lies Glanvil's book—
Come, let me read the oft-read tale again,
The story of that Oxford scholar poor,
Of pregnant parts and quick inventive brain,
Who, tir'd of knocking at Preferment's door,
One summer morn forsook
His friends, and went to learn the Gipsy lore,
And roam'd the world with that wild brotherhood,
And came, as most men deem'd, to little good,
But came to Oxford and his friends no more.

But once, years after, in the country lanes,
Two scholars, whom at college erst he knew,
Met him, and of his way of life enquir'd.
Whereat he answer'd, that the Gipsy crew,
His mates, had arts to rule as they desir'd

The workings of men's brains;
And they can bind them to what thoughts they will:
'And I,' he said, 'the secret of their art,
When fully learn'd, will to the world impart:
But it needs heaven-sent moments for this skill.'

This said, he left them, and return'd no more,—
But rumours hung about the country side
That the lost Scholar long was seen to stray,
Seen by rare glimpses, pensive and tongue-tied,
In hat of antique shape, and cloak of grey,
The same the Gipsies wore.
Shepherds had met him on the Hurst in spring:
At some lone alehouse in the Berkshire moors,
On the warm ingle bench, the smock-frock'd boors
Had found him seated at their entering,

But, 'mid their drink and clatter, he would fly:
And I myself seem half to know thy looks,
And put the shepherds, Wanderer, on thy trace;
And boys who in lone wheatfields scare the rooks
I ask if thou hast pass'd their quiet place;
Or in my boat I lie
Moor'd to the cool bank in the summer heats,
Mid wide grass meadows which the sunshine fills,
And watch the warm green-muffled Cumner hills,
And wonder if thou haunt'st their shy retreats.

For most, I know, thou lov'st retired ground.
Thee, at the ferry, Oxford riders blithe,
Returning home on summer nights, have met
Crossing the stripling Thames at Bab-lock-hithe,
Trailing in the cool stream thy fingers wet,

As the slow punt swings round:
And leaning backward in a pensive dream,
    And fostering in thy lap a heap of flowers
    Pluck'd in shy fields and distant Wychwood bowers,
And thine eyes resting on the moonlit stream.

And then they land, and thou art seen no more.
    Maidens, who from the distant hamlets come
        To dance around the Fyfield elm in May,
    Oft through the darkening fields have seen thee roam,
        Or cross a stile into the public way.
            Oft thou hast given them store
    Of flowers—the frail-leaf'd, white anemone—
        Dark bluebells drench'd with dews of summer eves—
        And purple orchises with spotted leaves—
    But none has words she can report of thee.

And, above Godstow Bridge, when hay-time's here
    In June, and many a scythe in sunshine flames,
        Men who through those wide fields of breezy grass
    Where black-wing'd swallows haunt the glittering Thames,
        To bathe in the abandon'd lasher pass,
            Have often pass'd thee near
    Sitting upon the river bank o'ergrown:
        Mark'd thy outlandish garb, thy figure spare,
        Thy dark vague eyes, and soft abstracted air;
    But, when they came from bathing, thou wert gone.

At some lone homestead in the Cumner hills,
    Where at her open door the housewife darns,
        Thou hast been seen, or hanging on a gate
    To watch the threshers in the mossy barns.
        Children, who early range these slopes and late
            For cresses from the rills,

Have known thee watching, all an April day,
   The springing pastures and the feeding kine;
     And mark'd thee, when the stars come out and shine,
Through the long dewy grass move slow away.

In Autumn, on the skirts of Bagley Wood,
   Where most the Gipsies by the turf-edg'd way
     Pitch their smok'd tents, and every bush you see
With scarlet patches tagg'd and shreds of grey,
     Above the forest ground called Thessaly—
       The blackbird picking food
Sees thee, nor stops his meal, nor fears at all;
   So often has he known thee past him stray,
   Rapt, twirling in thy hand a wither'd spray,
And waiting for the spark from Heaven to fall.

And once, in winter, on the causeway chill
   Where home through flooded fields foot-travellers go,
     Have I not pass'd thee on the wooden bridge
Wrapt in thy cloak and battling with the snow,
     Thy face towards Hinksey and its wintry ridge?
       And thou hast climb'd the hill
And gain'd the white brow of the Cumner range,
   Turn'd once to watch, while thick the snow-flakes fall,
   The line of festal light in Christ-Church hall—
Then sought thy straw in some sequester'd grange.

But what—I dream! Two hundred years are flown
   Since first thy story ran through Oxford halls,
     And the grave Glanvil did the tale inscribe
That thou wert wander'd from the studious walls
     To learn strange arts, and join a Gipsy tribe:
       And thou from earth art gone

Long since, and in some quiet churchyard laid;
    Some country nook, where o'er thy unknown grave
    Tall grasses and white flowering nettles wave—
Under a dark red-fruited yew-tree's shade.

—No, no, thou hast not felt the lapse of hours.
    For what wears out the life of mortal men?
      'Tis that from change to change their being rolls:
    'Tis that repeated shocks, again, again,
      Exhaust the energy of strongest souls,
        And numb the elastic powers.
Till having us'd our nerves with bliss and teen,
    And tired upon a thousand schemes our wit,
    To the just-pausing Genius we remit
Our worn-out life, and are—what we have been.

Thou hast not lived, why should'st thou perish, so?
    Thou hadst *one* aim, *one* business, *one* desire:
      Else wert thou long since number'd with the dead—
    Else hadst thou spent, like other men, thy fire.
      The generations of thy peers are fled,
        And we ourselves shall go;
But thou possessest an immortal lot,
    And we imagine thee exempt from age
    And living as thou liv'st on Glanvil's page,
Because thou hadst—what we, alas, have not!

For early didst thou leave the world, with powers
    Fresh, undiverted to the world without,
      Firm to their mark, not spent on other things;
    Free from the sick fatigue, the languid doubt,
      Which much to have tried, in much been baffled, brings.
        O Life unlike to ours!

Who fluctuate idly without term or scope,
  Of whom each strives, nor knows for what he strives,
  And each half lives a hundred different lives;
Who wait like thee, but not, like thee, in hope.

Thou waitest for the spark from Heaven: and we,
  Vague half-believers of our casual creeds,
    Who never deeply felt, nor clearly will'd,
Whose insight never has borne fruit in deeds,
    Whose weak resolves never have been fulfill'd:
      For whom each year we see
Breeds new beginnings, disappointments new;
    Who hesitate and falter life away,
    And lose to-morrow the ground won to-day—
Ah! do not we, Wanderer! await it too?

Yes, we await it, but it still delays,
  And then we suffer; and amongst us One,
    Who most has suffer'd, takes dejectedly
His seat upon the intellectual throne;
    And all his store of sad experience he
      Lays bare of wretched days;
Tells us his misery's birth and growth and signs,
    And how the dying spark of hope was fed,
    And how the breast was sooth'd, and how the head,
And all his hourly varied anodynes.

This for our wisest: and we others pine,
  And wish the long unhappy dream would end,
    And waive all claim to bliss, and try to bear
With close-lipp'd Patience for our only friend,
    Sad Patience, too near neighbour to Despair:
      But none has hope like thine.

Thou through the fields and through the woods dost stray,
   Roaming the country side, a truant boy,
   Nursing thy project in unclouded joy,
And every doubt long blown by time away.

O born in days when wits were fresh and clear,
   And life ran gaily as the sparkling Thames;
    Before this strange disease of modern life,
   With its sick hurry, its divided aims,
    Its heads o'ertax'd, its palsied hearts, was rife—
     Fly hence, our contact fear!
   Still fly, plunge deeper in the bowering wood!
    Averse, as Dido did with gesture stern
    From her false friend's approach in Hades turn,
Wave us away, and keep thy solitude!

Still nursing the unconquerable hope,
   Still clutching the inviolable shade,
    With a free, onward impulse brushing through,
   By night, the silver'd branches of the glade—
    Far on the forest skirts, where none pursue,
     On some mild pastoral slope
   Emerge, and resting on the moonlit pales,
    Freshen thy flowers, as in former years,
    With dew, or listen with enchanted ears,
From the dark dingles, to the nightingales.

But fly our paths, our feverish contact fly!
   For strong the infection of our mental strife,
    Which, though it gives no bliss, yet spoils for rest;
   And we should win thee from thy own fair life,
    Like us distracted, and like us unblest.
     Soon, soon thy cheer would die,

Thy hopes grow timorous, and unfix'd thy powers,
    And thy clear aims be cross and shifting made:
    And then thy glad perennial youth would fade,
Fade, and grow old at last and die like ours.

Then fly our greetings, fly our speech and smiles!
    —As some grave Tyrian trader, from the sea,
    Descried at sunrise an emerging prow
Lifting the cool-hair'd creepers stealthily,
    The fringes of a southward-facing brow
        Among the Ægæan isles;
    And saw the merry Grecian coaster come,
    Freighted with amber grapes, and Chian wine,
    Green bursting figs, and tunnies steep'd in brine;
And knew the intruders on his ancient home,

The young light-hearted Masters of the waves;
    And snatch'd his rudder, and shook out more sail,
    And day and night held on indignantly
O'er the blue Midland waters with the gale,
    Betwixt the Syrtes and soft Sicily,
        To where the Atlantic raves
    Outside the Western Straits; and unbent sails
    There, where down cloudy cliffs, through sheets of foam,
    Shy traffickers, the dark Iberians come;
And on the beach undid his corded bales.

381 Thyrsis

A MONODY TO COMMEMORATE THE AUTHOR'S FRIEND,
ARTHUR HUGH CLOUGH, WHO DIED AT FLORENCE,
1861

> Thus yesterday, to-day, to-morrow come,
> They hustle one another and they pass;
> But all our hustling morrows only make
> The smooth to-day of God.
> > From LUCRETIUS, an unpublished Tragedy

How changed is here each spot man makes or fills!
    In the two Hinkseys nothing keeps the same;
        The village-street its haunted mansion lacks,
    And from the sign is gone Sibylla's name,
        And from the roofs the twisted chimney-stacks;
            Are ye too changed, ye hills?
    See, 'tis no foot of unfamiliar men
        To-night from Oxford up your pathway strays!
        Here came I often, often, in old days;
    Thyrsis and I; we still had Thyrsis then.

Runs it not here, the track by Childsworth Farm,
    Up past the wood, to where the elm-tree crowns
        The hill behind whose ridge the sunset flames?
    The signal-elm, that looks on Ilsley Downs,
        The Vale, the three lone weirs, the youthful Thames?—
            This winter-eve is warm,
    Humid the air; leafless, yet soft as spring,
        The tender purple spray on copse and briers;
        And that sweet City with her dreaming spires,
    She needs not June for beauty's heightening.

Lovely all times she lies, lovely to-night!
   Only, methinks, some loss of habit's power
     Befalls me wandering through this upland dim;
   Once pass'd I blindfold here, at any hour,
     Now seldom come I, since I came with him.
       That single elm-tree bright
   Against the west—I miss it! is it gone?
     We prized it dearly; while it stood, we said,
     Our friend, the Scholar-Gipsy, was not dead;
   While the tree lived, he in these fields lived on.

Too rare, too rare, grow now my visits here!
   But once I knew each field, each flower, each stick;
     And with the country-folk acquaintance made
   By barn in threshing-time, by new-built rick.
     Here, too, our shepherd-pipes we first assay'd.
       Ah me! this many a year
   My pipe is lost, my shepherd's-holiday!
     Needs must I lose them, needs with heavy heart
     Into the world and wave of men depart;
   But Thyrsis of his own will went away.

It irk'd him to be here, he could not rest.
   He loved each simple joy the country yields,
     He loved his mates; but yet he could not keep,
   For that a shadow lower'd on the fields,
     Here with the shepherds and the silly sheep.
       Some life of men unblest
   He knew, which made him droop, and fill'd his head.
     He went; his piping took a troubled sound
     Of storms that rage outside our happy ground;
   He could not wait their passing, he is dead!

So, some tempestuous morn in early June,
    When the year's primal burst of bloom is o'er,
      Before the roses and the longest day—
  When garden-walks, and all the grassy floor,
    With blossoms, red and white, of fallen May,
      And chestnut-flowers are strewn—
So have I heard the cuckoo's parting cry,
    From the wet field, through the vext garden-trees,
    Come with the volleying rain and tossing breeze:
The bloom is gone, and with the bloom go I.

Too quick despairer, wherefore wilt thou go?
    Soon will the high Midsummer pomps come on,
      Soon will the musk carnations break and swell,
  Soon shall we have gold-dusted snapdragon,
    Sweet-William with its homely cottage-smell,
      And stocks in fragrant blow;
Roses that down the alleys shine afar,
    And open, jasmine-muffled lattices,
    And groups under the dreaming garden-trees,
And the full moon, and the white evening-star.

He hearkens not! light comer, he is flown!
    What matters it? next year he will return,
      And we shall have him in the sweet spring-days,
  With whitening hedges, and uncrumpling fern,
    And blue-bells trembling by the forest-ways,
      And scent of hay new-mown.
But Thyrsis never more we swains shall see!
    See him come back, and cut a smoother reed,
    And blow a strain the world at last shall heed—
For Time, not Corydon, hath conquer'd thee.

Alack, for Corydon no rival now!—
    But when Sicilian shepherds lost a mate,
       Some good survivor with his flute would go,
    Piping a ditty sad for Bion's fate,
       And cross the unpermitted ferry's flow,
         And relax Pluto's brow,
    And make leap up with joy the beauteous head
       Of Proserpine, among whose crowned hair
       Are flowers, first open'd on Sicilian air,
    And flute his friend, like Orpheus, from the dead.

O easy access to the hearer's grace
    When Dorian shepherds sang to Proserpine!
       For she herself had trod Sicilian fields,
    She knew the Dorian water's gush divine,
       She knew each lily white which Enna yields,
         Each rose with blushing face;
    She loved the Dorian pipe, the Dorian strain.
       But ah, of our poor Thames she never heard!
       Her foot the Cumner cowslips never stirr'd!
    And we should tease her with our plaint in vain.

Well! wind-dispers'd and vain the words will be,
    Yet, Thyrsis, let me give my grief its hour
       In the old haunt, and find our tree-topp'd hill!
    Who, if not I, for questing here hath power?
       I know the wood which hides the daffodil,
         I know the Fyfield tree,
    I know what white, what purple fritillaries
       The grassy harvest of the river-fields,
       Above by Ensham, down by Sandford, yields,
    And what sedg'd brooks are Thames's tributaries;

I know these slopes; who knows them if not I?—
    But many a dingle on the loved hill-side,
      With thorns once studded, old, white-blossom'd trees,
    Where thick the cowslips grew, and, far descried,
      High tower'd the spikes of purple orchises,
        Hath since our day put by
    The coronals of that forgotten time.
      Down each green bank hath gone the ploughboy's team,
      And only in the hidden brookside gleam
    Primroses, orphans of the flowery prime.

Where is the girl, who, by the boatman's door,
    Above the locks, above the boating throng,
      Unmoor'd our skiff, when, through the Wytham flats,
    Red loosestrife and blond meadow-sweet among,
      And darting swallows, and light water-gnats,
        We track'd the shy Thames shore?
    Where are the mowers, who, as the tiny swell
      Of our boat passing heav'd the river-grass,
      Stood with suspended scythe to see us pass?—
    They all are gone, and thou art gone as well.

Yes, thou art gone! and round me too the night
    In ever-nearing circle weaves her shade.
      I see her veil draw soft across the day,
    I feel her slowly chilling breath invade
      The cheek grown thin, the brown hair sprent with grey;
        I feel her finger light
    Laid pausefully upon life's headlong train;
      The foot less prompt to meet the morning dew,
      The heart less bounding at emotion new,
    And hope, once crush'd, less quick to spring again.

And long the way appears, which seem'd so short
　　To the unpractis'd eye of sanguine youth;
　　　And high the mountain-tops, in cloudy air,
　　The mountain-tops where is the throne of Truth,
　　　Tops in life's morning-sun so bright and bare!
　　　　Unbreachable the fort
Of the long-batter'd world uplifts its wall.
　　　And strange and vain the earthly turmoil grows,
　　　And near and real the charm of thy repose,
And night as welcome as a friend would fall.

But hush! the upland hath a sudden loss
　　Of quiet;—Look! adown the dusk hillside,
　　　A troop of Oxford hunters going home,
　　As in old days, jovial and talking, ride!
　　　From hunting with the Berkshire hounds they come—
　　　　Quick, let me fly, and cross
Into yon further field!—'Tis done; and see,
　　　Back'd by the sunset, which doth glorify
　　　The orange and pale violet evening-sky,
Bare on its lonely ridge, the Tree! the Tree!

I take the omen! Eve lets down her veil,
　　The white fog creeps from bush to bush about,
　　　The west unflushes, the high stars grow bright,
　　And in the scatter'd farms the lights come out.
　　　I cannot reach the Signal-Tree to-night,
　　　　Yet, happy omen, hail!
Hear it from thy broad lucent Arno vale
　　　(For there thine earth-forgetting eyelids keep
　　　The morningless and unawakening sleep
Under the flowery oleanders pale),

Hear it, O Thyrsis, still our Tree is there!—
  Ah, vain! These English fields, this upland dim,
    These brambles pale with mist engarlanded,
That lone, sky-pointing tree, are not for him.
    To a boon southern country he is fled,
      And now in happier air,
Wandering with the great Mother's train divine
    (And purer or more subtle soul than thee,
     I trow, the mighty Mother doth not see!)
Within a folding of the Apennine,

Thou hearest the immortal strains of old.
  Putting his sickle to the perilous grain
    In the hot cornfield of the Phrygian king,
For thee the Lityerses song again
    Young Daphnis with his silver voice doth sing;
      Sings his Sicilian fold,
His sheep, his hapless love, his blinded eyes;
    And how a call celestial round him rang
    And heavenward from the fountain-brink he sprang,
And all the marvel of the golden skies.

There thou art gone, and me thou leavest here
  Sole in these fields; yet will I not despair;
    Despair I will not, while I yet descry
'Neath the soft canopy of English air
    That lonely Tree against the western sky.
     Still, still these slopes, 'tis clear,
Our Gipsy-Scholar haunts, outliving thee!
    Fields where soft sheep from cages pull the hay,
    Woods with anemonies in flower till May,
Know him a wanderer still; then why not me?

A fugitive and gracious light he seeks,
   Shy to illumine; and I seek it too.
      This does not come with houses or with gold,
    With place, with honour, and a flattering crew;
      'Tis not in the world's market bought and sold.
        But the smooth-slipping weeks
   Drop by, and leave its seeker still untired;
    Out of the heed of mortals he is gone,
    He wends unfollow'd, he must house alone;
  Yet on he fares, by his own heart inspired.

Thou too, O Thyrsis, on like quest wert bound,
   Thou wanderedst with me for a little hour;
      Men gave thee nothing, but this happy quest,
    If men esteem'd thee feeble, gave thee power,
      If men procured thee trouble, gave thee rest.
        And this rude Cumner ground,
   Its fir-topped Hurst, its farms, its quiet fields,
    Here cam'st thou in thy jocund youthful time,
    Here was thine height of strength, thy golden prime;
  And still the haunt beloved a virtue yields.

What though the music of thy rustic flute
   Kept not for long its happy, country tone,
      Lost it too soon, and learnt a stormy note
    Of men contention-tost, of men who groan,
      Which task'd thy pipe too sore, and tired thy throat—
        It fail'd, and thou wast mute;
   Yet hadst thou alway visions of our light,
    And long with men of care thou couldst not stay,
    And soon thy foot resumed its wandering way,
  Left human haunt, and on alone till night.

Too rare, too rare, grow now my visits here!
　'Mid city-noise, not, as with thee of yore,
　　Thyrsis, in reach of sheep-bells is my home!
　Then through the great town's harsh, heart-wearying **roar**,
　　Let in thy voice a whisper often come,
　　　To chase fatigue and fear:
　Why faintest thou? I wander'd till I died.
　　Roam on! the light we sought is shining still.
　　　Dost thou ask proof? Our Tree yet crowns the hill,
　Our Scholar travels yet the loved hillside.

382　　　　　　　　Dover Beach

THE sea is calm to-night,
The tide is full, the moon lies fair
Upon the Straits;—on the French coast, the light
Gleams, and is gone; the cliffs of England stand,
Glimmering and vast, out in the tranquil bay.
Come to the window, sweet is the night air!
Only, from the long line of spray
Where the ebb meets the moon-blanch'd sand,
Listen! you hear the grating roar
Of pebbles which the waves suck back, and fling,
At their return, up the high strand,
Begin, and cease, and then again begin,
With tremulous cadence slow, and bring
The eternal note of sadness in.

Sophocles long ago
Heard it on the Ægæan, and it brought
Into his mind the turbid ebb and flow
Of human misery; we
Find also in the sound a thought,
Hearing it by this distant northern sea.

The sea of faith
Was once, too, at the full, and round earth's shore
Lay like the folds of a bright girdle furl'd;
But now I only hear
Its melancholy, long, withdrawing roar,
Retreating to the breath
Of the night-wind down the vast edges drear
And naked shingles of the world.

Ah, love, let us be true
To one another! for the world, which seems
To lie before us like a land of dreams,
So various, so beautiful, so new,
Hath really neither joy, nor love, nor light,
Nor certitude, nor peace, nor help for pain;
And we are here as on a darkling plain
Swept with confused alarms of struggle and flight,
Where ignorant armies clash by night.

383   Palladium

SET where the upper streams of Simois flow
Was the Palladium, high 'mid rock and wood;
And Hector was in Ilium, far below,
And fought, and saw it not, but there it stood.

It stood; and sun and moonshine rain'd their light
On the pure columns of its glen-built hall.
Backward and forward roll'd the waves of fight
Round Troy; but while this stood, Troy could not fall.

So, in its lovely moonlight, lives the soul.
Mountains surround it, and sweet virgin air;
Cold plashing, past it, crystal waters roll;
We visit it by moments, ah! too rare.

Men will renew the battle in the plain
To-morrow; red with blood will Xanthus be;
Hector and Ajax will be there again;
Helen will come upon the wall to see.

Then we shall rust in shade, or shine in strife,
And fluctuate 'twixt blind hopes and blind despairs,
And fancy that we put forth all our life,
And never know how with the soul it fares.

Still doth the soul, from its lone fastness high,
Upon our life a ruling effluence send;
And when it fails, fight as we will, we die,
And while it lasts, we cannot wholly end.

384   The Last Word

CREEP into thy narrow bed,
Creep, and let no more be said!
Vain thy onset! all stands fast;
Thou thyself must break at last.

Let the long contention cease!
Geese are swans, and swans are geese.
Let them have it how they will!
Thou art tired; best be still!

They out-talk'd thee, hiss'd thee, tore thee.
Better men fared thus before thee;
Fired their ringing shot and pass'd,
Hotly charged—and broke at last.

Charge once more, then, and be dumb!
Let the victors, when they come,
When the forts of folly fall,
Find thy body by the wall.

WILLIAM JOHNSON CORY

385   Heraclitus

Εἶπέ τις, Ἡράκλειτε, τεὸν μόρον

THEY told me, Heraclitus, they told me you were dead;
They brought me bitter news to hear and bitter tears to shed.
I wept, as I remembered, how often you and I
Had tired the sun with talking and sent him down the sky.

And now that thou art lying, my dear old Carian guest,
A handful of grey ashes, long long ago at rest,
Still are thy pleasant voices, thy nightingales, awake,
For Death, he taketh all away, but them he cannot take.

386   A Dirge

NAIAD, hid beneath the bank
    By the willowy river-side,
Where Narcissus gently sank,
    Where unmarried Echo died,
Unto thy serene repose
Waft the stricken Anterôs.

Where the tranquil swan is borne,
    Imaged in a watery glass,
Where the sprays of fresh pink thorn
    Stoop to catch the boats that pass,
Where the earliest orchis grows,
Bury thou fair Anterôs.

Glide we by, with prow and oar:
  Ripple shadows off the wave,
And reflected on the shore
  Haply play about the grave.
Folds of summer-light enclose
All that once was Anterôs.

On a flickering wave we gaze,
  Not upon his answering eyes:
Flower and bird we scarce can praise,
  Having lost his sweet replies:
Cold and mute the river flows
With our tears for Anterôs.

387   A Separation

ΑΛΙΟΣ ΑΜΜΙ ΔΕΔΥΚΕ

I MAY not touch the hand I saw
  So nimbly weave the violet chain;
I may not see my artist draw
  That southward-sloping lawn again.
But joy brimmed over when we met,
Nor can I mourn our parting yet.

Though he lies sick and far away,
  I play with those that still are here,
Not honouring him the less, for they
  To me by loving him are dear:
They share, they soothe my fond regret,
Since neither they nor I forget.

His sweet strong heart so nobly beat
  With scorn and pity, mirth and zeal,
That vibrant hearts of ours repeat
  What they with him were wont to feel;
Still quiring in that higher key,
Till he take up the melody.

If there be any music here,
  I trust it will not fail, like notes
Of May-birds, when the waning year
  Abates their summer-wearied throats.
Shame on us, if we drudge once more
As dull and tuneless as before.

Without him I was weak and coarse,
  My soul went droning through the hours,
His goodness stirred a latent force
  That drew from others kindred powers.
Nor they nor I could think me base,
When with their prince I had found grace.

His influence crowns me, like a cloud
  Steeped in the light of a lost sun:
I reign, for willing knees are bowed
  And light behests are gladly done:
So Rome obeyed the lover-king,
Who drank at pure Egeria's spring.

Such honour doth my mind perplex:
  For, who is this, I ask, that dares
With manhood's wounds, and virtue's wrecks,
  And tangled creeds, and subtle cares,
Affront the look, or speak the name
Of one who from Elysium came.

And yet, though withered and forlorn,
  I had renounced what man desires,
I'd thought some poet might be born
  To string my lute with silver wires;
At least in brighter days to come
Such men as I would not lie dumb.

I saw the Sibyl's finger rest
  On fate's upturned imagined page,
Believed her promise, and was blest
  With dreams of that heroic age.
She sent me, ere my hope was cold,
One of the race that she foretold.

His fellows Time will bring, and they,
  In manifold affections free,
Shall scatter pleasures day by day
  Like blossoms rained from windy tree.
So let that garden bloom; and I,
Content with one such flower, will die.

COVENTRY PATMORE

388 ## The Tribute

Boon Nature to the woman bows;
  She walks in earth's whole glory clad,
And, chiefest far herself of shows,
  All others help her, and are glad:
No splendour 'neath the sky's proud dome
  But serves for her familiar wear;
The far-fetch'd diamond finds its home
  Flashing and smouldering in her hair;

For her the seas their pearls reveal;
  Art and strange lands her pomp supply
With purple, chrome, and cochineal,
  Ochre, and lapis lazuli;
The worm its golden woof presents;
  Whatever runs, flies, dives, or delves,
All doff for her their ornaments,
  Which suit her better than themselves;
And all, by this their power to give,
  Proving her right to take, proclaim
Her beauty's clear prerogative
  To profit so by Eden's blame.

389   The Revelation

An idle Poet, here and there,
  Looks round him, but, for all the rest,
The world, unfathomably fair,
  Is duller than a witling's jest.
Love wakes men, once a lifetime each;
  They lift their heavy lids, and look;
And, lo, what one sweet page can teach,
  They read with joy, then shut the book:
And some give thanks, and some blaspheme,
  And most forget; but, either way,
That and the Child's unheeded dream
  Is all the light of all their day.

390   A Farewell

With all my will, but much against my heart,
We two now part.
My Very Dear,
Our solace is, the sad road lies so clear.

It needs no art,
With faint, averted feet
And many a tear,
In our opposed paths to persevere.
Go thou to East, I West.
We will not say
There's any hope, it is so far away.
But, O, my Best,
When the one darling of our widowhead,
The nursling Grief,
Is dead,
And no dews blur our eyes
To see the peach-bloom come in evening skies,
Perchance we may,
Where now this night is day,
And even through faith of still averted feet,
Making full circle of our banishment,
Amazed meet;
The bitter journey to the bourne so sweet
Seasoning the termless feast of our content
With tears of recognition never dry.

391   Magna Est Veritas

HERE, in this little Bay,
Full of tumultuous life and great repose,
Where, twice a day,
The purposeless, glad ocean comes and goes,
Under high cliffs, and far from the huge town,
I sit me down.
For want of me the world's course will not fail:
When all its work is done, the lie shall rot;
The truth is great, and shall prevail,
When none cares whether it prevail or not.

Departure

IT was not like your great and gracious ways!
Do you, that have nought other to lament,
Never, my Love, repent
Of how, that July afternoon,
You went,
With sudden, unintelligible phrase,
And frighten'd eye,
Upon your journey of so many days,
Without a single kiss or a good-bye?
I knew, indeed, that you were parting soon;
And so we sate, within the low sun's rays,
You whispering to me, for your voice was weak,
Your harrowing praise.
Well, it was well,
To hear you such things speak,
And I could tell
What made your eyes a growing gloom of love,
As a warm South-wind sombres a March grove.
And it was like your great and gracious ways
To turn your talk on daily things, my Dear,
Lifting the luminous, pathetic lash
To let the laughter flash,
Whilst I drew near,
Because you spoke so low that I could scarcely hear.
But all at once to leave me at the last,
More at the wonder than the loss aghast,
With huddled, unintelligible phrase,
And frighten'd eye,
And go your journey of all days
With not one kiss or a good-bye,
And the only loveless look the look with which you pass'd:
'Twas all unlike your great and gracious ways.

393   Winter

I, SINGULARLY moved
To love the lovely that are not beloved,
Of all the Seasons, most
Love Winter, and to trace
The sense of the Trophonian pallor on her face.
It is not death, but plenitude of peace;
And the dim cloud that does the world enfold
Hath less the characters of dark and cold
Than warmth and light asleep;
And correspondent breathing seems to keep
With the infant harvest, breathing soft below
Its eider coverlet of snow.
Nor is in field or garden anything
But, duly look'd into, contains serene
The substance of things hoped for, in the Spring,
And evidence of Summer not yet seen.
On every chance-mild day
That visits the moist shaw,
The honeysuckle, 'sdaining to be crost
In urgence of sweet life by sleet or frost,
'Voids the time's law
With still increase
Of leaflet new, and little, wandering spray;
Often, in sheltering brakes,
As one from rest disturb'd in the first hour,
Primrose or violet bewilder'd wakes,
And deems 'tis time to flower;
Though not a whisper of her voice he hear,
The buried bulb does know
The signals of the year,
And hails far Summer with his lifted spear;
The gorse-field dark, by sudden, gold caprice,

Turns, here and there, into a Jason's fleece;
Lilies that, soon in Autumn, slipp'd their gowns of green
And vanish'd into earth,
And came again, ere Autumn died, to birth,
Stand full-array'd amidst the wavering shower,
And perfect for the Summer, less the flower;
In nook of pale or crevice of crude bark,
Thou canst not miss,
If close thou spy, to mark
The ghostly chrysalis,
That, if thou touch it, stirs in its dream dark;
And the flush'd Robin, in the evenings hoar,
Does of Love's Day, as if he saw it, sing;
But sweeter yet than dream or song of Summer or Spring
Are Winter's sometime smiles, that seem to well
From infancy ineffable;
Her wandering, languorous gaze,
So unfamiliar, so without amaze,
On the elemental, chill adversity,
The uncomprehended rudeness; and her sigh
And solemn, gathering tear,
And look of exile from some great repose, the sphere
Of ether, moved by ether only, or
By something still more tranquil.—

394   Arbor Vitae

    WITH honeysuckle, over-sweet, festoon'd;
    With bitter ivy bound;
    Terraced with funguses unsound;
    Deform'd with many a boss
    And closed scar, o'ercushion'd deep with moss;
    Bunch'd all about with pagan mistletoe;

And thick with nests of the hoarse bird
That talks, but understands not his own word;
Stands, and so stood a thousand years ago,
A single tree.
Thunder has done its worst among its twigs,
Where the great crest yet blackens, never pruned,
But in its heart, alway
Ready to push new verdurous boughs, whene'er
The rotting saplings near it fall and leave it air,
Is all antiquity and no decay.
Rich, though rejected by the forest-pigs,
Its fruit, beneath whose rough, concealing rind
They that will break it find
Heart-succouring savour of each several meat,
And kernell'd drink of brain-renewing power,
With bitter condiment and sour,
And sweet economy of sweet,
And odours that remind
Of haunts of childhood and a different day.
Beside this tree,
Praising no Gods nor blaming, sans a wish,
Sits, Tartar-like, the Time's civility,
And eats its dead-dog off a golden dish.

395   Saint Valentine's Day

WELL dost thou, Love, thy solemn Feast to hold
In vestal February,
Not rather choosing out some rosy day
From the rich coronet of the coming May,
When all things meet to marry!

O, quick, prævernal Power
That signall'st punctual through the sleepy mould
The Snowdrop's time to flower,
Fair as the rash oath of virginity
Which is first-love's first cry;
O, Baby Spring,
That flutter'st sudden 'neath the breast of Earth
A month before the birth;
Whence is the peaceful poignancy,
The joy contrite,
Sadder than sorrow, sweeter than delight,
That burthens now the breath of everything,
Though each one sighs as if to each alone
The cherish'd pang were known?
At dusk of dawn, on his dark spray apart,
With it the Blackbird breaks the young Day's heart;
In evening's hush
About it talks the heavenly-minded Thrush;
The hill with like remorse
Smiles to the Sun's smile in his westering course;
The fisher's drooping skiff
In yonder sheltering bay;
The choughs that call about the shining cliff;
The children, noisy in the setting ray,
Own the sweet season, each thing as it may;
Thoughts of strange kindness and forgotten peace
In me increase;
And tears arise
Within my happy, happy Mistress' eyes,
And, lo, her lips, averted from my kiss,
Ask from Love's bounty, much, much more than bliss.
    Is't the sequester'd and exceeding sweet
Of dear Desire electing his defeat?
Is't the waked Earth now to yon purpling cope

Uttering first-love's first cry,
Vainly renouncing, with a Seraph's sigh,
Love's natural hope?
Fair-meaning Earth, foredoom'd to perjury!
Behold, all amorous May,
With roses heap'd upon her laughing brows,
Avoids thee of thy vows!
Were it for thee, with her warm bosom near,
To abide the sharpness of the Seraph's sphere?
Forget thy foolish words;
Go to her summons gay,
Thy heart with dead, wing'd Innocencies fill'd,
Ev'n as a nest with birds
After the old ones by the hawk are kill'd.
   Well dost thou, Love, to celebrate
The noon of thy soft ecstasy,
Or e'er it be too late,
Or e'er the Snowdrop die!

SYDNEY DOBELL

396   Desolate

FROM the sad eaves the drip-drop of the rain!
The water washing at the latchel door;
A slow step plashing by upon the moor;
A single bleat far from the famished fold;
The clicking of an embered hearth and cold;
The rainy Robin tic-tac at the pane.

'So as it is with thee
Is it with me,
So as it is and it used not to be,

With thee used not to be,
Nor me.'
So singeth Robin on the willow tree,
The rainy Robin tic-tac at the pane.

Here in this breast all day
The fire is dim and low,
Within I care not to stay,
Without I care not to go.

A sadness ever sings
Of unforgotten things,
And the bird of love is patting at the pane;
But the wintry water deepens at the door,
And a step is plashing by upon the moor
Into the dark upon the darkening moor,
And alas, alas, the drip-drop of the rain!

397   A Nuptial Eve

[THE BALLAD OF KEITH OF RAVELSTON]

OH, happy, happy maid,
In the year of war and death
She wears no sorrow!
By her face so young and fair,
By the happy wreath
That rules her happy hair,
She might be a bride to-morrow!
She sits and sings within her moonlit bower,
Her moonlit bower in rosy June,
Yet ah, her bridal breath,

Like fragrance from some sweet night-blowing flower,
Moves from her moving lips in many a mournful tune!
She sings no song of love's despair,
She sings no lover lowly laid,
No fond peculiar grief
Has ever touched or bud or leaf
Of her unblighted spring.
She sings because she needs must sing;
She sings the sorrow of the air
Whereof her voice is made.
That night in Britain howsoe'er
On any chords the fingers strayed
They gave the notes of care.
A dim sad legend old
Long since in some pale shade
Of some far twilight told,
She knows not when or where,
She sings, with trembling hand on trembling lute-strings laid:—

> The murmur of the mourning ghost
>   That keeps the shadowy kine,
> 'Oh, Keith of Ravelston,
>   The sorrows of thy line!'

> Ravelston, Ravelston,
>   The merry path that leads
> Down the golden morning hill,
>   And thro' the silver meads;

> Ravelston, Ravelston,
>   The stile beneath the tree,
> The maid that kept her mother's kine,
>   The song that sang she!

She sang her song, she kept her kine,
　　She sat beneath the thorn
When Andrew Keith of Ravelston
　　Rode thro' the Monday morn,

His henchmen sing, his hawk-bells ring,
　　His belted jewels shine!
Oh, Keith of Ravelston,
　　The sorrows of thy line!

Year after year, where Andrew came,
　　Comes evening down the glade,
And still there sits a moonshine ghost
　　Where sat the sunshine maid.

Her misty hair is faint and fair,
　　She keeps the shadowy kine;
Oh, Keith of Ravelston,
　　The sorrows of thy line!

I lay my hand upon the stile,
　　The stile is lone and cold,
The burnie that goes babbling by
　　Says nought that can be told.

Yet, stranger! here, from year to year,
　　She keeps her shadowy kine;
Oh, Keith of Ravelston,
　　The sorrows of thy line!

Step out three steps, where Andrew stood—
　　Why blanch thy cheeks for fear?
The ancient stile is not alone,
　　'Tis not the burn I hear!

She makes her immemorial moan,
    She keeps her shadowy kine;
Oh, Keith of Ravelston,
    The sorrows of thy line!

398   He Loves and He Rides Away

'T WAS in that island summer where
They spin the morning gossamer,
And weave the evening mist,
That, underneath the hawthorn-tree,
I loved my love, and my love loved me,
And there we lay and kissed,
And saw the happy ships upon the yielding sea.

Soft my heart, and warm his wooing,
What we did seemed, while 'twas doing,
Beautiful and wise;
Wise, fairer, more in tune,
Than all else in that sweet June,
And sinless as the skies
That warmed the willing earth thro' all the languid noon.

Ah that fatal spell!
Ere the evening fell
I fled away to hide my frightened face,
And cried that I was born,
And sobbed with love and scorn,
And in the darkness sought a darker place,
And blushed, and wept, and blushed, and dared not think of
    morn.

Day and night, day and night,
And I saw no light,
Night and day, night and day,
And in my woe I lay
And dreamed the dreams they dream who cannot sleep:
My speech was withered, and I could not pray;
My tears were frozen, and I could not weep.

I saw the hawthorn rise
Between me and the skies,
I felt the shadow was from pole to pole,
I felt the leaves were shed,
I felt the birds were dead,
And on the earth I snowed the winter of my soul.

Like to the hare wide eyed,
That with her throbbing side
Pressed to the rock awaits the coming cry,
In my despair I sate
And waited for my fate;
And as the hunted hare returns to die,
And with her latest breath
Regains her native heath,
So, when I heard the feet of destiny
Near and more near, and caught the yelp of death,
Toward the sounding sea,
Toward my hawthorn-tree,
Under the ignorant stars I darkly crept:
'There,' I said, 'they'll find me dead,
Lying within my maidenhead.'
And at my own unwonted voice, I wept;
And for my great heart-ache,
Within a little brake
I lay me weary down and weary slept,
Nor ever oped mine eyes till morn had left the lake.

Her morning bath was o'er,
And on the golden shore
She stood like Flora with her floral train,
And all her track was seen
Among the watery sheen,
That blushed, and wished, and blushing wished again,
And parted still, and closed, with pleasure that had been.

Oh the happy isle,
The universal smile
That met, as love meets love, the smile of day,
And touched and lit delight
Within the common light,
Till all the joy of life was ecstacy,
And morn's wild maids ran each her flowery way,
And shook her dripping locks o'er hill, and dale, and lea!
'At least,' I said, 'my tree is sear and blight,
My tree, my hawthorn-tree!'

With downcast eyes of fear
I draw me near and near,
Dazed with the dewy glory of the hour,
Till under-foot I see
A flower too dear to me:
I pause, and raise my full eyes from the flower,
And lo! my hawthorn-tree!

As a white-limbed may,
In some illumined bay,
Flings round her shining charms in starry rain,
And with her body bright
Dazzles the waters white,
That fall from her fair form, and flee in vain,
Dyed with the dear unutterable sight,
And circle out her beauty thro' the circling main,

So my hawthorn-tree
Stood and seemed to me
The very face that smiled the summer smile:
All lesser light-bearers
Did light their lamps at hers—
She lit her own at heaven's, and looked the while
A purer sweeter sun,
Whence beauty was begun,
And blossomed from her blossoms thro' the blossoming isle.
Then I took heart, and as I looked upon
Her unstained white, I said, 'I am not wholly vile.'

Thus my hawthorn-tree
Was my witness unto me,
And so I answered my impleading sin
Till blossom-time was o'er,
And with the autumn roar
Mine unrebuked accuser entered in,
And I fell down convinced, and strove with shame no more.

Some time after came to me,
An image of the hawthorn-tree,
And bore the old sweet witness; and I heard,
And from among the dead
I lifted up my head,
As one lifts up to hear a little bird,
And finds the night is past and all the east is red.

Small and fair, choice and rare,
Snowy pale with moonlight hair,
My little one blossoms and springs!
Like joy with woe singing to it,
Like love with sorrow to woo it,

So my witty one so my pretty one sings!
And I see the white hawthorn-tree and the bright summer bird
    singing thro' it,
And my heart is prouder than kings!

While I look on her I seem
Once again in the sweet dream
Of that enchanted day,
When, underneath the hawthorn tree,
I loved my love, and my love loved me:
And lost in love we lay,
And saw the happy ships upon the yielding sea.

While I look on her I seem
Once again in that bright dream,
Beautiful and wise:
Wiser, fairer, more in tune,
Than all else in that sweet June,
And sinless as the skies
That warmed the willing earth thro' all the languid noon.

Like my hawthorn-tree,
She stands and seems to me
The very face that smiles the summer smile:
All lesser light-bearers
Do light their lamps at hers—
She lights her own at heaven's, and looks the while
A sweeter purer sun
Whence beauty is begun,
To blossom from that blossom thro' the blossoming isle.

Thou shalt not leave me, child!
Come weather fierce or mild,
My babe, my blossom! thou shalt never leave me!

Life shall never wean us,
Nor death shall e'er have room to come between us,
And time may grieve me but shall ne'er bereave me,
Nor see us more apart than he hath seen us.

For I will fall with thee,
As a bird from the tree
Falls with a butterfly petal whitely shed,
And falling—thou and I—
I shall not dread to die,
But like a child I'll take my flower to bed.
And when the long cold death-night hath gone by,
In the great darkness of the sepulchre
I'll feel and find thee near,
My babe, my white white blossom!
And when the trumpet cries,
I shall not fear to rise,
But wear thee o'er the spot upon my bosom,
And come out of my grave and bear the awful eyes.

399   The Orphan's Song

I HAD a little bird,
I took it from the nest;
I prest it, and blest it,
And nurst it in my breast.

I set it on the ground,
I danced round and round,
And sang about it so cheerly,
With 'Hey my little bird, and ho my little bird,
And ho but I love thee dearly!'

I make a little feast
Of food soft and sweet,
I hold it in my breast,
And coax it to eat;

I pit, and I pat,
I call it this and that,
And sing about it so cheerly,
With 'Hey my little bird, and ho my little bird,
And ho but I love thee dearly!'

I may kiss, I may sing,
But I can't make it feed,
It taketh no heed
Of any pleasant thing.

I scolded, and I socked,
But it minded not a whit,
Its little mouth was locked,
And I could not open it.

Tho' with pit, and with pat,
And with this, and with that,
I sang about it so cheerly,
And 'Hey my little bird, and ho my little bird,
And ho but I love thee dearly.'

But when the day was done,
And the room was at rest,
And I sat all alone
With my birdie in my breast,

And the light had fled,
And not a sound was heard,
Then my little bird
Lifted up its head,

And the little mouth
Loosed its sullen pride,
And it opened, it opened,
With a yearning strong and wide.

Swifter than I speak
I brought it food once more,
But the poor little beak
Was locked as before.

I sat down again,
And not a creature stirred,
I laid the little bird
Again where it had lain;

And again when nothing stirred,
And not a word I said,
Then my little bird
Lifted up its head,
And the little beak
Loosed its stubborn pride,
And it opened, it opened,
With a yearning strong and wide.

It lay in my breast,
It uttered no cry,
'T was famished, 't was famished,
And I could n't tell why.

I could n't tell why,
But I saw that it would die,
For all that I kept dancing round and round,
And singing above it so cheerly,
With 'Hey my little bird, and ho my little bird,
And ho but I love thee dearly!'

I never look sad,
I hear what people say,
I laugh when they are gay
And they think I am glad.

My tears never start,
I never say a word,
But I think that my heart
Is like that little bird.

Every day I read,
And I sing, and I play,
But thro' the long day
It taketh no heed.

It taketh no heed
Of any pleasant thing,
I know it doth not read,
I know it doth not sing.

With my mouth I read,
With my hands I play,
My shut heart is shut,
Coax it how you may.

You may coax it how you may
While the day is broad and bright,
But in the dead of night
When the guests are gone away,

And no more the music sweet
Up the house doth pass,
Nor the dancing feet
Shake the nursery glass;

And I've heard my aunt
Along the corridor,
And my uncle gaunt
Lock his chamber door;

And upon the stair
All is hushed and still,
And the last wheel
Is silent in the square;

And the nurses snore,
And the dim sheets rise and fall,
And the lamplight's on the wall,
And the mouse is on the floor;

And the curtains of my bed
Are like a heavy cloud,
And the clock ticks loud,
And sounds are in my head;

And little Lizzie sleeps
Softly at my side,
It opens, it opens,
With a yearning strong and wide!

It yearns in my breast,
It utters no cry,
'T is famished, 't is famished,
And I feel that I shall die,
I feel that I shall die,
And none will know why.
Tho' the pleasant life is dancing round and round
And singing about me so cheerly,
With 'Hey my little bird, and ho my little bird,
And ho but I love thee dearly!'

400 Spring

THE LOVER AND THE BIRDS

WITHIN a budding grove,
In April's ear sang every bird his best,
But not a song to pleasure my unrest,
Or touch the tears unwept of bitter love.
Some spake, methought, with pity, some as if in jest.
  To every word
  Of every bird
I listen'd, and replied as it behove.

Scream'd Chaffinch, 'Sweet, sweet, sweet!
Pretty lovey, come and meet me here!'
'Chaffinch,' quoth I, 'be dumb awhile, in fear
Thy darling prove no better than a cheat,
And never come, or fly when wintry days appear.'
  Yet from a twig
  With voice so big,
The little fowl his utterance did repeat.

Then I, 'The man forlorn
Hears Earth send up a foolish noise aloft.'
'And what'll *he* do? what'll *he* do?' scoff'd
The Blackbird, standing in an ancient thorn,
Then spread his sooty wings and flitted to the croft
  With cackling laugh:
  Whom I, being half
Enraged, call'd after, giving back his scorn.

Worse mock'd the Thrush, 'Die! die!
Oh, could he do it? could he do it? Nay!
Be quick! be quick! Here, here, here!' (went his lay)
   'Take heed! take heed!' then, 'Why? why? why? why? why?
See-ee now! see-ee now?' (he drawl'd). 'Back! back!
      back! R-r-r-run away!'
         O Thrush, be still!
         Or, at thy will,
Seek some less sad interpreter than I.

   'Air, air! blue air and white!
Whither I flee, whither, O whither, O whither I flee!'
(Thus the Lark hurried, mounting from the lea)
'Hills, countries, many waters glittering bright,
Whither I see, whither I see! deeper, deeper, deeper,
      whither I see, see, see!'
         'Gay Lark,' I said,
         'The song that's bred
In happy nest may well to heaven make flight.'

   'There's something, something sad,
I half remember'—piped a broken strain.
Well sung, sweet Robin! Robin sung again,
'Spring's opening cheerily, cheerily! be we glad!'
Which moved, I wist not why, me melancholy mad,
         Till now, grown meek,
         With wetted cheek,
Most comforting and gentle thoughts I had.

401   Meadowsweet

THROUGH grass, through amber'd cornfields, our slow Stream—
   Fringed with its flags and reeds and rushes tall,
   And Meadowsweet, the chosen from them all
By wandering children, yellow as the cream
Of those great cows—winds on as in a dream
   By mill and footbridge, hamlet old and small
(Red roofs, gray tower), and sees the sunset gleam
   On mullion'd windows of an ivied Hall.

There, once upon a time, the heavy King
   Trod out its perfume from the Meadowsweet,
   Strown like a woman's love beneath his feet,
In stately dance or jovial banqueting,
When all was new; and in its wayfaring
   Our Streamlet curved, as now, through grass and wheat.

DANTE GABRIEL ROSSETTI

402   The Blessed Damozel

THE blessed damozel leaned out
   From the gold bar of Heaven;
Her eyes were deeper than the depth
   Of waters stilled at even;
She had three lilies in her hand,
   And the stars in her hair were seven.

Her robe, ungirt from clasp to hem,
   No wrought flowers did adorn,
But a white rose of Mary's gift,

For service meetly worn;
Her hair that lay along her back
    Was yellow like ripe corn.

Herseemed she scarce had been a day
    One of God's choristers;
The wonder was not yet quite gone
    From that still look of hers;
Albeit, to them she left, her day
    Had counted as ten years.

(To one, it is ten years of years.
    . . . Yet now, and in this place,
Surely she leaned o'er me—her hair
    Fell all about my face. . . .
Nothing: the autumn-fall of leaves.
    The whole year sets apace.)

It was the rampart of God's house
    That she was standing on;
By God built over the sheer depth
    The which is Space begun;
So high, that looking downward thence
    She scarce could see the sun.

It lies in Heaven, across the flood
    Of ether, as a bridge.
Beneath, the tides of day and night
    With flame and darkness ridge
The void, as low as where this earth
    Spins like a fretful midge.

Heard hardly, some of her new friends
   Amid their loving games,
Spake evermore among themselves
   Their virginal chaste names;
And the souls mounting up to God
   Went by her like thin flames.

And still she bowed herself and stooped
   Out of the circling charm;
Until her bosom must have made
   The bar she leaned on warm,
And the lilies lay as if asleep
   Along her bended arm.

From the fixed place of Heaven she saw
   Time like a pulse shake fierce
Through all the worlds. Her gaze still strove
   Within the gulf to pierce
Its path; and now she spoke as when
   The stars sang in their spheres.

The sun was gone now; the curled moon
   Was like a little feather
Fluttering far down the gulf; and now
   She spoke through the still weather.
Her voice was like the voice the stars
   Had when they sang together.

(Ah sweet! Even now, in that bird's song,
   Strove not her accents there,
Fain to be hearkened? When those bells
   Possessed the mid-day air,
Strove not her steps to reach my side
   Down all the echoing stair?)

'I wish that he were come to me,
   For he will come,' she said.
'Have I not prayed in Heaven?—on earth,
   Lord, Lord, has he not pray'd?
Are not two prayers a perfect strength?
   And shall I feel afraid?

'When round his head the aureole clings,
   And he is clothed in white,
I'll take his hand and go with him
   To the deep wells of light;
We will step down as to a stream,
   And bathe there in God's sight.

'We two will stand beside that shrine,
   Occult, withheld, untrod,
Whose lamps are stirred continually
   With prayers sent up to God;
And see our old prayers, granted, melt
   Each like a little cloud.

'We two will lie i' the shadow of
   That living mystic tree
Within whose secret growth the Dove
   Is sometimes felt to be,
While every leaf that His plumes touch
   Saith His Name audibly.

'And I myself will teach to him,
   I myself, lying so,
The songs I sing here; which his voice
   Shall pause in, hushed and slow,
And find some knowledge at each pause,
   Or some new thing to know.'

(Alas! we two, we two, thou say'st!
  Yea, one wast thou with me
That once of old. But shall God lift
  To endless unity
The soul whose likeness with thy soul
  Was but its love for thee?)

'We two,' she said, 'will seek the groves
  Where the lady Mary is,
With her five handmaidens, whose names
  Are five sweet symphonies,
Cecily, Gertrude, Magdalen,
  Margaret and Rosalys.

'Circlewise sit they, with bound locks
  And foreheads garlanded;
Into the fine cloth white like flame
  Weaving the golden thread,
To fashion the birth-robes for them
  Who are just born, being dead.

'He shall fear, haply, and be dumb:
  Then will I lay my cheek
To his, and tell about our love,
  Not once abashed or weak:
And the dear Mother will approve
  My pride, and let me speak.

'Herself shall bring us, hand in hand,
  To Him round whom all souls
Kneel, the clear-ranged unnumbered heads
  Bowed with their aureoles:
And angels meeting us shall sing
  To their citherns and citoles.

'There will I ask of Christ the Lord
　　Thus much for him and me:—
Only to live as once on earth
　　With Love,—only to be,
As then awhile, for ever now
　　Together, I and he.'

She gazed and listened and then said,
　　Less sad of speech than mild,—
'All this is when he comes.' She ceased.
　　The light thrilled towards her, fill'd
With angels in strong level flight.
　　Her eyes prayed, and she smil'd.

(I saw her smile.) But soon their path
　　Was vague in distant spheres:
And then she cast her arms along
　　The golden barriers,
And laid her face between her hands,
　　And wept. (I heard her tears.)

403　　　　　　　　Even so

　　So it is, my dear.
All such things touch secret strings
　　For heavy hearts to hear.
　　So it is, my dear.

　　Very like indeed:
Sea and sky, afar, on high,
　　Sand and strewn seaweed,—
　　Very like indeed.

But the sea stands spread
As one wall with the flat skies,
Where the lean black craft like flies
Seem well-nigh stagnated,
Soon to drop off dead.

Seemed it so to us
When I was thine and thou wast mine,
And all these things were thus,
But all our world in us?

Could we be so now?
Not if all beneath heaven's pall
Lay dead but I and thou,
Could we be so now!

404   Sudden Light

I HAVE been here before,
    But when or how I cannot tell:
I know the grass beyond the door,
    The sweet keen smell,
The sighing sound, the lights around the shore.

You have been mine before,—
    How long ago I may not know:
But just when at that swallow's soar
    Your neck turned so,
Some veil did fall,—I knew it all of yore.

Then, now,—perchance again! ...
    O round mine eyes your tresses shake!
Shall we not lie as we have lain
    Thus for Love's sake,
And sleep, and wake, yet never break the chain?

405 The Woodspurge

THE wind flapped loose, the wind was still,
Shaken out dead from tree and hill:
I had walked on at the wind's will,—
I sat now, for the wind was still.

Between my knees my forehead was,—
My lips, drawn in, said not Alas!
My hair was over in the grass,
My naked ears heard the day pass.

My eyes, wide open, had the run
Of some ten weeds to fix upon;
Among those few, out of the sun,
The woodspurge flowered, three cups in one.

From perfect grief there need not be
Wisdom or even memory:
One thing then learnt remains to me,—
The woodspurge has a cup of three.

from 'THE HOUSE OF LIFE'

406 Love Enthroned

I MARKED all kindred Powers the heart finds fair:—
    Truth, with awed lips; and Hope, with eyes upcast;
    And Fame, whose loud wings fan the ashen Past
To signal-fires, Oblivion's flight to scare;
And Youth, with still some single golden hair
    Unto his shoulder clinging, since the last
    Embrace wherein two sweet arms held him fast;
And Life, still wreathing flowers for Death to wear.

Love's throne was not with these; but far above
   All passionate wind of welcome and farewell
He sat in breathless bowers they dream not of;
     Though Truth foreknow Love's heart, and Hope foretell,
     And Fame be for Love's sake desirable,
And Youth be dear, and Life be sweet to Love.

407   Lovesight

WHEN do I see thee most, beloved one?
   When in the light the spirits of mine eyes
   Before thy face, their altar, solemnize
The worship of that Love through thee made known?
Or when in the dusk hours (we two alone,)
   Close-kissed and eloquent of still replies
   Thy twilight-hidden glimmering visage lies,
And my soul only sees thy soul its own?

O love, my love! if I no more should see
Thyself, nor on the earth the shadow of thee,
   Nor image of thine eyes in any spring,—
How then should sound upon Life's darkening slope
The ground-whirl of the perished leaves of Hope,
   The wind of Death's imperishable wing?

408   Silent Noon

YOUR hands lie open in the long fresh grass,—
   The finger-points look through like rosy blooms:
   Your eyes smile peace. The pasture gleams and glooms
'Neath billowing skies that scatter and amass.

All round our nest, far as the eye can pass,
   Are golden kingcup-fields with silver edge
   Where the cow-parsley skirts the hawthorn-hedge.
'Tis visible silence, still as the hour-glass.

Deep in the sun-searched growths the dragon-fly
Hangs like a blue thread loosened from the sky:—
   So this wing'd hour is dropt to us from above.
Oh! clasp we to our hearts, for deathless dower,
This close-companioned inarticulate hour
   When twofold silence was the song of love.

409   Pride of Youth

EVEN as a child, of sorrow that we give
   The dead, but little in his heart can find,
   Since without need of thought to his clear mind
Their turn it is to die and his to live:—
Even so the winged New Love smiles to receive
   Along his eddying plumes the auroral wind,
   Nor, forward glorying, casts one look behind
Where night-rack shrouds the Old Love fugitive.

There is a change in every hour's recall,
   And the last cowslip in the fields we see
   On the same day with the first corn-poppy.
Alas for hourly change! Alas for all
The loves that from his hand proud Youth lets fall,
   Even as the beads of a told rosary!

410 ## Without Her

WHAT of her glass without her? The blank grey
  There where the pool is blind of the moon's face.
  Her dress without her? The tossed empty space
Of cloud-rack whence the moon has passed away.
Her paths without her? Day's appointed sway
  Usurped by desolate night. Her pillowed place
  Without her? Tears, ah me! for love's good grace,
And cold forgetfulness of night or day.

What of the heart without her? Nay, poor heart,
  Of thee what word remains ere speech be still?
  A wayfarer by barren ways and chill,
Steep ways and weary, without her thou art,
Where the long cloud, the long wood's counterpart,
  Sheds doubled darkness up the labouring hill.

411 ## Barren Spring

ONCE more the changed year's turning wheel returns:
  And as a girl sails balanced in the wind,
  And now before and now again behind
Stoops as it swoops, with cheek that laughs and burns,—
So Spring comes merry towards me here, but earns
  No answering smile from me, whose life is twin'd
  With the dead boughs that winter still must bind,
And whom to-day the Spring no more concerns.

Behold, this crocus is a withering flame;
  This snowdrop, snow; this apple-blossom's part
  To breed the fruit that breeds the serpent's art.
Nay, for these Spring-flowers, turn thy face from them,
Nor stay till on the year's last lily-stem
  The white cup shrivels round the golden heart.

412

A Superscription

LOOK in my face; my name is Might-have-been;
  I am also called No-more, Too-late, Farewell;
  Unto thine ear I hold the dead-sea shell
Cast up thy Life's foam-fretted feet between;
Unto thine eyes the glass where that is seen
  Which had Life's form and Love's, but by my spell
  Is now a shaken shadow intolerable,
Of ultimate things unuttered the frail screen.

Mark me, how still I am! But should there dart
  One moment through thy soul the soft surprise
  Of that winged Peace which lulls the breath of sighs,—
Then shalt thou see me smile, and turn apart
Thy visage to mine ambush at thy heart
  Sleepless with cold commemorative eyes.

413

Chimes

I

HONEY-flowers to the honey-comb
And the honey-bee's from home.

A honey-comb and a honey-flower,
And the bee shall have his hour.

A honeyed heart for the honey-comb,
And the humming bee flies home.

A heavy heart in the honey-flower,
And the bee has had his hour.

II

A honey-cell's in the honeysuckle,
And the honey-bee knows it well.

The honey-comb has a heart of honey,
And the humming bee's so bonny.

A honey-flower's the honeysuckle,
And the bee's in the honey-bell.

The honeysuckle is sucked of honey,
And the bee is heavy and bonny.

III

Brown shell first for the butterfly
And a bright wing by and by.

Butterfly, good-bye to your shell,
And, bright wings, speed you well.

Bright lamplight for the butterfly
And a burnt wing by and by.

Butterfly, alas for your shell,
And, bright wings, fare you well.

IV

Lost love-labour and lullaby,
And lowly let love lie.

Lost love-morrow and love-fellow
And love's life lying low.

Lovelorn labour and life laid by
And lowly let love lie.

Late love-longing and life-sorrow
And love's life lying low.

V

Beauty's body and benison
With a bosom-flower new blown.

Bitter beauty and blessing bann'd
With a breast to burn and brand.

Beauty's bower in the dust o'erblown
With a bare white breast of bone.

Barren beauty and bower of sand
With a blast on either hand.

VI

Buried bars in the breakwater
And bubble of the brimming weir.

Body's blood in the breakwater
And a buried body's bier.

Buried bones in the breakwater
And bubble of the brawling weir.

Bitter tears in the breakwater
And a breaking heart to bear.

VII

Hollow heaven and the hurricane
And hurry of the heavy rain.

Hurried clouds in the hollow heaven
And a heavy rain hard-driven.

The heavy rain it hurries amain
And heaven and the hurricane.

Hurrying wind o'er the heaven's hollow
And the heavy rain to follow.

GEORGE MEREDITH

from 'MODERN LOVE'

414 'I PLAY for Seasons; not Eternities!'
Says Nature, laughing on her way. 'So must
All those whose stake is nothing more than dust!'
And lo, she wins, and of her harmonies
She is full sure! Upon her dying rose
She drops a look of fondness, and goes by,
Scarce any retrospection in her eye;
For she the laws of growth most deeply knows,
Whose hands bear, here, a seed-bag; there, an urn.
Pledged she herself to aught, 'twould mark her end!
This lesson of our only visible friend,
Can we not teach our foolish hearts to learn?
Yes! yes!—but oh, our human rose is fair
Surpassingly! Lose calmly Love's great bliss,
When the renew'd forever of a kiss
Whirls life within the shower of loosened hair!

*

415   Mark where the pressing wind shoots javelin-like
Its skeleton shadow on the broad-back'd wave!
Here is a fitting spot to dig Love's grave;
Here where the ponderous breakers plunge and strike,
And dart their hissing tongues high up the sand:
In hearing of the ocean, and in sight
Of those ribb'd wind-streaks running into white.
If I the death of Love had deeply plann'd,
I never could have made it half so sure,
As by the unbless'd kisses which upbraid
The full-waked sense; or, failing that, degrade!
'Tis morning: but no morning can restore
What we have forfeited. I see no sin:
The wrong is mix'd. In tragic life, God wot,
No villain need be! Passions spin the plot:
We are betray'd by what is false within.

★

416   We saw the swallows gathering in the sky,
And in the osier-isle we heard them noise.
We had not to look back on summer joys,
Or forward to a summer of bright dye.
But in the largeness of the evening earth
Our spirits grew as we went side by side.
The hour became her husband, and my bride.
Love that had robb'd us so, thus bless'd our dearth!
The pilgrims of the year wax'd very loud
In multitudinous chatterings, as the flood
Full brown came from the West, and like pale blood
Expanded to the upper crimson cloud.
Love that had robb'd us of immortal things,
This little moment mercifully gave,
Where I have seen across the twilight wave
The swan sail with her young beneath her wings.

★

417   THUS piteously Love closed what he begat:
The union of this ever-diverse pair!
These two were rapid falcons in a snare,
Condemn'd to do the flitting of a bat.
Lovers beneath the singing sky of May,
They wander'd once; clear as the dew on flowers:
But they fed not on the advancing hours:
Their hearts held cravings for the buried day.
Then each applied to each that fatal knife,
Deep questioning, which probes to endless dole.
Ah, what a dusty answer gets the soul
When hot for certainties in this our life!—
In tragic hints here see what evermore
Moves dark as yonder midnight ocean's force,
Thundering like ramping hosts of warrior horse,
To throw that faint thin line upon the shore!

418   The Orchard and the Heath

I CHANCED upon an early walk to spy
A troop of children through an orchard gate:
  The boughs hung low, the grass was high;
  They had but to lift hands or wait
For fruits to fill them; fruits were all their sky.

They shouted, running on from tree to tree,
And played the game the wind plays, on and round.
  'Twas visible invisible glee
  Pursuing; and a fountain's sound
Of laughter spouted, pattering fresh on me.

I could have watched them till the daylight fled,
Their pretty bower made such a light of day.
   A small one tumbling sang, 'Oh! head!'
    The rest to comfort her straightway
Seized on a branch and thumped down apples red.

The tiny creature flashing through green grass,
And laughing with her feet and eyes among
   Fresh apples, while a little lass
    Over as o'er breeze-ripples hung:
That sight I saw, and passed as aliens pass.

My footpath left the pleasant farms and lanes,
Soft cottage-smoke, straight cocks a-crow, gay flowers;
   Beyond the wheel-ruts of the wains,
    Across a heath I walked for hours,
And met its rival tenants, rays and rains.

Still in my view mile-distant firs appeared,
When, under a patched channel-bank enriched
   With foxglove whose late bells drooped seared,
    Behold, a family had pitched
Their camp, and labouring the low tent upreared.

Here, too, were many children, quick to scan
A new thing coming; swarthy cheeks, white teeth:
   In many-coloured rags they ran,
    Like iron runlets of the heath.
Dispersed lay broth-pot, sticks, and drinking-can.

Three girls, with shoulders like a boat at sea
Tipp'd sideways by the wave (their clothing slid
   From either ridge unequally),
    Lean, swift and voluble, bestrid
A starting-point, unfrocked to the bent knee.

They raced; their brothers yelled them on, and broke
In act to follow, but as one they snuffed
   Wood-fumes, and by the fire that spoke
   Of provender, its pale flame puffed,
And rolled athwart dwarf furzes grey-blue smoke.

Soon on the dark edge of a ruddier gleam,
The mother-pot perusing, all, stretched flat,
   Paused for its bubbling-up supreme:
   A dog upright in circle sat,
And oft his nose went with the flying steam.

I turned and looked on heaven awhile, where now
The moor-faced sunset broaden'd with red light;
   Threw high aloft a golden bough,
   And seemed the desert of the night
Far down with mellow orchards to endow.

419   Lucifer in Starlight

On a starred night Prince Lucifer uprose.
Tired of his dark dominion swung the fiend
Above the rolling ball in cloud part screened,
Where sinners hugged their spectre of repose.
Poor prey to his hot fit of pride were those.
And now upon his western wing he leaned,
Now his huge bulk o'er Africa careened,
Now the black planet shadowed Arctic snows.
Soaring through wider zones that pricked his scars
With memory of the old revolt from Awe,
He reached a middle height, and at the stars,
Which are the brain of heaven, he looked, and sank.
Around the ancient track marched, rank on rank,
The army of unalterable law.

420 The Thrush in February

I KNOW him, February's thrush,
And loud at eve he valentines
On sprays that paw the naked bush
Where soon will sprout the thorns and bines.

Now ere the foreign singer thrills
Our vale his plain-song pipe he pours,
A herald of the million bills;
And heed him not, the loss is yours.

My study, flanked with ivied fir
And budded beech with dry leaves curled,
Perched over yew and juniper,
He neighbours, piping to this world:—

The wooded pathways dank on brown,
The branches on grey cloud a web,
The long green roller of the down,
An image of the deluge-ebb:—

And farther, they may hear along
The stream beneath the poplar row.
By fits, like welling rocks, the song
Spouts of a blushful Spring in flow.

But most he loves to front the vale
When waves of warm South-western rains
Have left our heavens clear in pale,
With faintest beck of moist red veins:

Vermilion wings, by distance held
To pause aflight while fleeting swift:
And high aloft the pearl inshelled
Her lucid glow in glow will lift;

A little south of coloured sky;
Directing, gravely amorous,
The human of a tender eye
Through pure celestial on us.

Remote, not alien; still, not cold;
Unraying yet, more pearl than star;
She seems a while the vale to hold
In trance, and homelier makes the far.

Then Earth her sweet unscented breathes;
An orb of lustre quits the height;
And like broad iris-flags, in wreaths
The sky takes darkness, long ere quite.

His Island voice then shall you hear,
Nor ever after separate
From such a twilight of the year
Advancing to the vernal gate.

He sings me, out of Winter's throat,
The young time with the life ahead;
And my young time his leaping note
Recalls to spirit-mirth from dead.

Imbedded in a land of greed,
Of mammon-quakings dire as Earth's,
My care was but to soothe my need;
At peace among the littleworths.

To light and song my yearning aimed;
To that deep breast of song and light
Which men have barrenest proclaimed;
As 'tis to senses pricked with fright.

So mine are these new fruitings rich
The simple to the common brings;
I keep the youth of souls who pitch
Their joy in this old heart of things:

Who feel the Coming young as aye,
Thrice hopeful on the ground we plough;
Alive for life, awake to die;
One voice to cheer the seedling Now.

Full lasting is the song, though he,
The singer, passes: lasting too,
For souls not lent in usury,
The rapture of the forward view.

With that I bear my senses fraught
Till what I am fast shoreward drives.
They are the vessel of the Thought.
The vessel splits, the Thought survives.

Nought else are we when sailing brave,
Save husks to raise and bid it burn.
Glimpse of its livingness will wave
A light the senses can discern

Across the river of the death,
Their close. Meanwhile, O twilight bird
Of promise! bird of happy breath!
I hear, I would the City heard.

The City of the smoky fray;
A prodded ox, it drags and moans:
Its Morrow no man's child; its Day
A vulture's morsel beaked to bones.

It strives without a mark for strife;
It feasts beside a famished host:
The loose restraint of wanton life,
That threatened penance in the ghost!

Yet there our battle urges; there
Spring heroes many: issuing thence,
Names that should leave no vacant air
For fresh delight in confidence.

Life was to them the bag of grain,
And Death the weedy harrow's tooth.
Those warriors of the sighting brain
Give worn Humanity new youth.

Our song and star are they to lead
The tidal multitude and blind
From bestial to the higher breed
By fighting souls of love divined.

They scorned the ventral dream of peace,
Unknown in nature. This they knew:
That life begets with fair increase
Beyond the flesh, if life be true.

Just reason based on valiant blood,
The instinct bred afield would match
To pipe thereof a swelling flood,
Were men of Earth made wise in watch.

Though now the numbers count as drops
An urn might bear, they father Time.
She shapes anew her dusty crops;
Her quick in their own likeness climb.

Of their own force do they create;
They climb to light, in her their root.
Your brutish cry at muffled fate
She smites with pangs of worse than brute.

She, judged of shrinking nerves, appears
A Mother whom no cry can melt;
But read her past desires and fears,
The letters on her breast are spelt.

A slayer, yea, as when she pressed
Her savage to the slaughter-heaps,
To sacrifice she prompts her best:
She reaps them as the sower reaps.

But read her thought to speed the race,
And stars rush forth of blackest night:
You chill not at a cold embrace
To come, nor dread a dubious might.

Her double visage, double voice,
In oneness rise to quench the doubt.
This breath, her gift, has only choice
Of service, breathe we in or out.

Since Pain and Pleasure on each hand
Led our wild steps from slimy rock
To yonder sweeps of gardenland,
We breathe but to be sword or block.

The sighting brain her good decree
Accepts; obeys those guides, in faith,
By reason hourly fed, that she,
To some the clod, to some the wraith,

Is more, no mask; a flame, a stream.
Flame, stream, are we, in mid career
From torrent source, delirious dream,
To heaven-reflecting currents clear.

And why the sons of Strength have been
Her cherished offspring ever; how
The Spirit served by her is seen
Through Law; perusing love will show.

Love born of knowledge, love that gains
Vitality as Earth it mates,
The meaning of the Pleasures, Pains,
The Life, the Death, illuminates.

For love we Earth, then serve we all;
Her mystic secret then is ours:
We fall, or view our treasures fall,
Unclouded, as beholds her flowers

Earth, from a night of frosty wreck,
Enrobed in morning's mounted fire,
When lowly, with a broken neck,
The crocus lays her cheek to mire.

421   Dirge in Woods

A WIND sways the pines,
            And below
Not a breath of wild air;
Still as the mosses that glow
On the flooring and over the lines
Of the roots here and there.

The pine-tree drops its dead;
They are quiet, as under the sea.
Overhead, overhead
Rushes life in a race,
As the clouds the clouds chase;
  And we go,
And we drop like the fruits of the trees,
   Even we,
   Even so.

422   Hymn to Colour

I

WITH Life and Death I walked when Love appeared,
And made them on each side a shadow seem.
Through wooded vales the land of dawn we neared,
Where down smooth rapids whirls the helmless dream
To fall on daylight; and night puts away
  Her darker veil for grey.

II

In that grey veil green grassblades brushed we by;
We came where woods breathed sharp, and overhead
Rocks raised clear horns on a transforming sky:
Around, save for those shapes, with him who led
And linked them, desert varied by no sign
  Of other life than mine.

III

By this the dark-winged planet, raying wide,
From the mild pearl-glow to the rose upborne,
Drew in his fires, less faint than far descried,

Pure-fronted on a stronger wave of morn:
And those two shapes the splendour interweaved
  Hung web-like, sank and heaved.

IV

Love took my hand when hidden stood the sun
To fling his robe on shoulder-heights of snow.
Then said: There lie they, Life and Death in one.
Whichever is, the other is: but know,
It is thy craving self that thou dost see,
  Not in them seeing me.

V

Shall man into the mystery of breath
From his quick beating pulse a pathway spy?
Or learn the secret of the shrouded death,
By lifting up the lid of a white eye?
Cleave thou thy way with fathering desire
  Of fire to reach to fire.

VI

Look now where Colour, the soul's bridegroom, makes
The house of heaven splendid for the bride.
To him as leaps a fountain she awakes,
In knotting arms, yet boundless: him beside,
She holds the flower to heaven, and by his power
  Brings heaven to the flower.

VII

He gives her homeliness in desert air,
And sovereignty in spaciousness; he leads
Through widening chambers of surprise to where
Throbs rapture near an end that aye recedes,
Because his touch is infinite and lends
  A yonder to all ends.

VIII

Death begs of Life his blush; Life Death persuades
To keep long day with his caresses graced.
He is the heart of light, the wing of shades,
The crown of beauty: never soul embraced
Of him can harbour unfaith; soul of him
  Possessed walks never dim.

IX

Love eyed his rosy memories: he sang:
O bloom of dawn, breathed up from the gold sheaf
Held springing beneath Orient! that dost hang
The space of dewdrops running over leaf;
Thy fleetingness is bigger in the ghost
  Than Time with all his host!

X

Of thee to say behold, has said adieu:
But love remembers how the sky was green,
And how the grasses glimmered lightest blue;
How saint-like grey took fervour: how the screen
Of cloud grew violet; how thy moment came
  Between a blush and flame.

XI

Love saw the emissary eglantine
Break wave round thy white feet above the gloom;
Lay finger on thy star; thy raiment line
With cherub wing and limb; wed thy soft bloom,
Gold-quivering like sunrays in thistle-down,
  Earth under rolling brown.

XII

They do not look through love to look on thee,
Grave heavenliness! nor know they joy of sight,
Who deem the wave of rapt desire must be
Its wrecking and last issue of delight.
Dead seasons quicken in one petal-spot
      Of colour unforgot.

XIII

This way have men come out of brutishness
To spell the letters of the sky and read
A reflex upon earth else meaningless.
With thee, O fount of the Untimed! to lead;
Drink they of thee, thee eyeing, they unaged
      Shall on through brave wars waged.

XIV

More gardens will they win than any lost;
The vile plucked out of them, the unlovely slain.
Not forfeiting the beast with which they are crossed,
To stature of the Gods will they attain.
They shall uplift their Earth to meet her Lord,
      Themselves the attuning chord!

XV

The song had ceased; my vision with the song.
Then of those Shadows, which one made descent
Beside me I knew not: but Life ere long
Came on me in the public ways and bent
Eyes deeper than of old: Death met I too,
      And saw the dawn glow through.

Spring

FROST-locked all the winter,
Seeds, and roots, and stones of fruits,
What shall make their sap ascend
That they may put forth shoots?
Tips of tender green,
Leaf, or blade, or sheath;
Telling of the hidden life
That breaks forth underneath,
Life nursed in its grave by Death.

Blows the thaw-wind pleasantly,
Drips the soaking rain,
By fits looks down the waking sun:
Young grass springs on the plain;
Young leaves clothe early hedgerow trees;
Seeds, and roots, and stones of fruits,
Swollen with sap put forth their shoots;
Curled-headed ferns sprout in the lane;
Birds sing and pair again.

There is no time like Spring,
When life's alive in everything,
Before new nestlings sing,
Before cleft swallows speed their journey back
Along the trackless track—
God guides their wing,
He spreads their table that they nothing lack,—
Before the daisy grows a common flower,
Before the sun has power
To scorch the world up in his noontide hour.

There is no time like Spring,
Like Spring that passes by;
There is no life like Spring-life born to die,—
Piercing the sod,
Clothing the uncouth clod,
Hatched in the nest,
Fledged on the windy bough,
Strong on the wing:
There is no time like Spring that passes by,
Now newly born, and now
Hastening to die.

424   Remember

REMEMBER me when I am gone away,
   Gone far away into the silent land;
    When you can no more hold me by the hand,
Nor I half turn to go yet turning stay.
Remember me when no more day by day
    You tell me of our future that you planned:
    Only remember me; you understand
It will be late to counsel then or pray.
Yet if you should forget me for a while
    And afterwards remember, do not grieve:
    For if the darkness and corruption leave
    A vestige of the thoughts that once I had,
Better by far you should forget and smile
    Than that you should remember and be sad.

425 A Summer Wish

LIVE all thy sweet life thro',
  Sweet Rose, dew-sprent,
Drop down thine evening dew
To gather it anew
When day is bright:
  I fancy thou wast meant
Chiefly to give delight.

Sing in the silent sky,
  Glad soaring bird;
Sing out thy notes on high
To sunbeam straying by
Or passing cloud;
  Heedless if thou art heard
Sing thy full song aloud.

Oh that it were with me
  As with the flower;
Blooming on its own tree
For butterfly and bee
Its summer morns:
  That I might bloom mine hour
A rose in spite of thorns.

Oh that my work were done
  As birds' that soar
Rejoicing in the sun:
That when my time is run
And daylight too,
  I so might rest once more
Cool with refreshing dew.

426   An Apple Gathering

I PLUCKED pink blossoms from mine apple-tree
    And wore them all that evening in my hair:
Then in due season when I went to see
    I found no apples there.

With dangling basket all along the grass
    As I had come I went the selfsame track:
My neighbours mocked me while they saw me pass
    So empty-handed back.

Lilian and Lilias smiled in trudging by,
    Their heaped-up basket teased me like a jeer;
Sweet-voiced they sang beneath the sunset sky,
    Their mother's home was near.

Plump Gertrude passed me with her basket full,
    A stronger hand than hers helped it along;
A voice talked with her through the shadows cool
    More sweet to me than song.

Ah Willie, Willie, was my love less worth
    Than apples with their green leaves piled above?
I counted rosiest apples on the earth
    Of far less worth than love.

So once it was with me you stooped to talk
    Laughing and listening in this very lane:
To think that by this way we used to walk
    We shall not walk again!

I let my neighbours pass me, ones and twos
    And groups; the latest said the night grew chill,
And hastened: but I loitered, while the dews
    Fell fast I loitered still.

427 Echo

COME to me in the silence of the night;
    Come in the speaking silence of a dream;
Come with soft rounded cheeks and eyes as bright
    As sunlight on a stream;
        Come back in tears,
O memory, hope, love of finished years.

Oh dream how sweet, too sweet, too bitter sweet,
    Whose wakening should have been in Paradise,
Where souls brimfull of love abide and meet;
    Where thirsting longing eyes
        Watch the slow door
That opening, letting in, lets out no more.

Yet come to me in dreams, that I may live
    My very life again though cold in death:
Come back to me in dreams, that I may give
    Pulse for pulse, breath for breath:
        Speak low, lean low,
As long ago, my love, how long ago!

428 A Pause of Thought

I LOOKED for that which is not, nor can be,
    And hope deferred made my heart sick in truth:
But years must pass before a hope of youth
    Is resigned utterly.

I watched and waited with a steadfast will:
    And though the object seemed to flee away
That I so longed for, ever day by day
    I watched and waited still.

Sometimes I said: This thing shall be no more;
  My expectation wearies and shall cease;
  I will resign it now and be at peace:
    Yet never gave it o'er.

Sometimes I said: It is an empty name
  I long for; to a name why should I give
  The peace of all the days I have to live?—
    Yet gave it all the same.

Alas, thou foolish one! alike unfit
  For healthy joy and salutary pain:
  Thou knowest the chase useless, and again
    Turnest to follow it.

429   Twilight Calm

    OH, pleasant eventide!
    Clouds on the western side
Grow grey and greyer hiding the warm sun:
The bees and birds, their happy labours done,
    Seek their close nests and bide.

    Screened in the leafy wood
    The stock-doves sit and brood:
The very squirrel leaps from bough to bough
But lazily; pauses; and settles now
    Where once he stored his food.

    One by one the flowers close,
    Lily and dewy rose
Shutting their tender petals from the moon:
The grasshoppers are still; but not so soon
    Are still the noisy crows.

The dormouse squats and eats
    Choice little dainty bits
Beneath the spreading roots of a broad lime;
Nibbling his fill he stops from time to time
    And listens where he sits.

From far the lowings come
    Of cattle driven home:
From farther still the wind brings fitfully
The vast continual murmur of the sea,
    Now loud, now almost dumb.

The gnats whirl in the air,
    The evening gnats; and there
The owl opes broad his eyes and wings to sail
For prey; the bat wakes; and the shell-less snail
    Comes forth, clammy and bare.

Hark! that's the nightingale,
    Telling the selfsame tale
Her song told when this ancient earth was young:
So echoes answered when her song was sung
    In the first wooded vale.

We call it love and pain
    The passion of her strain;
And yet we little understand or know:
Why should it not be rather joy that so
    Throbs in each throbbing vein?

In separate herds the deer
    Lie; here the bucks, and here
The does, and by its mother sleeps the fawn:
Through all the hours of night until the dawn
    They sleep, forgetting fear.

The hare sleeps where it lies,
　　With wary half-closed eyes;
The cock has ceased to crow, the hen to cluck:
Only the fox is out, some heedless duck
　　Or chicken to surprise.

Remote, each single star
　　Comes out, till there they are
All shining brightly: how the dews fall damp!
While close at hand the glow-worm lights her lamp
　　Or twinkles from afar.

But evening now is done
　　As much as if the sun
Day-giving had arisen in the East:
For night has come; and the great calm has ceased,
　　The quiet sands have run.

430　　　　　　The One Certainty

VANITY of vanities, the Preacher saith,
　　All things are vanity. The eye and ear
　　Cannot be filled with what they see and hear.
Like early dew, or like the sudden breath
Of wind, or like the grass that withereth,
　　Is man, tossed to and fro by hope and fear:
　　So little joy hath he, so little cheer,
Till all things end in the long dust of death.
To-day is still the same as yesterday,
　　To-morrow also even as one of them;
And there is nothing new under the sun:
Until the ancient race of Time be run,
　　The old thorns shall grow out of the old stem,
And morning shall be cold and twilight grey.

431   Rest

O EARTH, lie heavily upon her eyes;
    Seal her sweet eyes weary of watching, Earth;
    Lie close around her; leave no room for mirth
With its harsh laughter, nor for sound of sighs.
She hath no questions, she hath no replies,
    Hushed in and curtained with a blessèd dearth
    Of all that irked her from the hour of birth;
With stillness that is almost Paradise.
Darkness more clear than noon-day holdeth her,
    Silence more musical than any song;
Even her very heart has ceased to stir:
Until the morning of Eternity
Her rest shall not begin nor end, but be;
    And when she wakes she will not think it long.

432   Up-hill

DOES the road wind up-hill all the way?
    Yes, to the very end.
Will the day's journey take the whole long day?
    From morn to night, my friend.

But is there for the night a resting-place?
    A roof for when the slow dark hours begin.
May not the darkness hide it from my face?
    You cannot miss that inn.

Shall I meet other wayfarers at night?
    Those who have gone before.
Then must I knock, or call when just in sight?
    They will not keep you standing at that door.

Shall I find comfort, travel-sore and weak?
    Of labour you shall find the sum.
Will there be beds for me and all who seek?
    Yea, beds for all who come.

433   Old and New Year Ditties. III

PASSING away, saith the World, passing away:
Chances, beauty and youth sapped day by day:
Thy life never continueth in one stay.
Is the eye waxen dim, is the dark hair changing to grey
That hath won neither laurel nor bay?
I shall clothe myself in Spring and bud in May:
Thou, root-stricken, shalt not rebuild thy decay
On my bosom for aye.
Then I answered: Yea.

Passing away, saith my Soul, passing away:
With its burden of fear and hope, of labour and play;
Hearken what the past doth witness and say:
Rust in thy gold, a moth is in thine array,
A canker is in thy bud, thy leaf must decay.
At midnight, at cockcrow, at morning, one certain day
Lo, the Bridegroom shall come and shall not delay:
Watch thou and pray.
Then I answered: Yea.

Passing away, saith my God, passing away:
Winter passeth after the long delay:
New grapes on the vine, new figs on the tender spray,
Turtle calleth turtle in Heaven's May.
Though I tarry wait for Me, trust Me, watch and pray.
Arise, come away, night is past and lo it is day.
My love, My sister, My spouse, thou shalt hear Me say.
Then I answered: Yea.

713

434   Twice

I TOOK my heart in my hand
   (O my love, O my love),
I said: Let me fall or stand,
   Let me live or die,
But this once hear me speak—
   (O my love, O my love)—
Yet a woman's words are weak;
   You should speak, not I.

You took my heart in your hand
   With a friendly smile,
With a critical eye you scanned,
   Then set it down,
And said: It is still unripe,
   Better wait awhile;
Wait while the skylarks pipe,
   Till the corn grows brown.

As you set it down it broke—
   Broke, but I did not wince;
I smiled at the speech you spoke,
   At your judgment that I heard:
But I have not often smiled
   Since then, nor questioned since,
Nor cared for corn-flowers wild,
   Nor sung with the singing bird.

I take my heart in my hand,
   O my God, O my God,
My broken heart in my hand:
   Thou hast seen, judge Thou.

My hope was written on sand,
  O my God, O my God:
Now let Thy judgment stand—
  Yea, judge me now.

This contemned of a man,
  This marred one heedless day,
This heart take Thou to scan
  Both within and without:
Refine with fire its gold,
  Purge Thou its dross away—
Yea, hold it in Thy hold,
  Whence none can pluck it out.

I take my heart in my hand—
  I shall not die, but live—
Before Thy face I stand;
  I, for Thou callest such:
All that I have I bring,
  All that I am I give,
Smile Thou and I shall sing,
  But shall not question much.

435   The Bourne

UNDERNEATH the growing grass,
Underneath the living flowers,
Deeper than the sound of showers:
  There we shall not count the hours
By the shadows as they pass.

Youth and health will be but vain,
  Beauty reckoned of no worth:
There a very little girth
  Can hold round what once the earth
Seemed too narrow to contain.

Memory

436

I

I NURSED it in my bosom while it lived,
    I hid it in my heart when it was dead;
In joy I sat alone, even so I grieved
    Alone and nothing said.

I shut the door to face the naked truth,
    I stood alone—I faced the truth alone,
Stripped bare of self-regard or forms or ruth
    Till first and last were shown.

I took the perfect balances and weighed;
    No shaking of my hand disturbed the poise;
Weighed, found it wanting: not a word I said,
    But silent made my choice.

None know the choice I made; I make it still.
    None know the choice I made and broke my heart,
Breaking mine idol: I have braced my will
    Once, chosen for once my part.

I broke it at a blow, I laid it cold,
    Crushed in my deep heart where it used to live.
My heart dies inch by inch; the time grows old,
    Grows old in which I grieve.

437

II

I HAVE a room whereinto no one enters
    Save I myself alone:
    There sits a blessed memory on a throne,
There my life centres.

While winter comes and goes—oh tedious comer!—
    And while its nip-wind blows;
      While bloom the bloodless lily and warm rose
Of lavish summer.

If any should force entrance he might see there
    One buried yet not dead,
      Before whose face I no more bow my head
Or bend my knee there;

But often in my worn life's autumn weather
    I watch there with clear eyes,
      And think how it will be in Paradise
When we're together.

Monna Innominata

438

    Vien dietro a me e lascia dir le genti. DANTE
    Contando i casi della vita nostra. PETRARCA

MANY in aftertimes will say of you
'He loved her'—while of me what will they say?
    Not that I loved you more than just in play,
For fashion's sake as idle women do.
Even let them prate; who know not what we knew
    Of love and parting in exceeding pain,
    Of parting hopeless here to meet again,
Hopeless on earth, and heaven is out of view.
But by my heart of love laid bare to you,
    My love that you can make not void nor vain,
Love that foregoes you but to claim anew
      Beyond this passage of the gate of death,
    I charge you at the Judgment make it plain
      My love of you was life and not a breath.

★

439 E la Sua Volontade è nostra pace. DANTE
     Sol con questi pensier, con altre chiome. PETRARCA

YOUTH gone, and beauty gone if ever there
    Dwelt beauty in so poor a face as this;
    Youth gone and beauty, what remains of bliss?
I will not bind fresh roses in my hair,
To shame a cheek at best but little fair,—
    Leave youth his roses, who can bear a thorn,—
I will not seek for blossoms anywhere,
    Except such common flowers as blow with corn.
Youth gone and beauty gone, what doth remain?
    The longing of a heart pent up forlorn,
    A silent heart whose silence loves and longs;
    The silence of a heart which sang its songs
    While youth and beauty made a summer morn,
Silence of love that cannot sing again.

440   Passing and Glassing

              ALL things that pass
              Are woman's looking-glass;
          They show her how her bloom must fade,
              And she herself be laid
              With withered roses in the shade;
              With withered roses and the fallen peach,
              Unlovely, out of reach
                  Of summer joy that was.

              All things that pass
              Are woman's tiring-glass;
          The faded lavender is sweet,
              Sweet the dead violet
          Culled and laid by and cared for yet;

                        718

The dried-up violets and dried lavender
  Still sweet, may comfort her,
    Nor need she cry Alas!

    All things that pass
    Are wisdom's looking-glass;
  Being full of hope and fear, and still
  Brimful of good or ill,
According to our work and will;
    For there is nothing new beneath the sun;
    Our doings have been done,
      And that which shall be was.

441   The Thread of Life

THE irresponsive silence of the land,
  The irresponsive sounding of the sea,
  Speak both one message of one sense to me:—
Aloof, aloof, we stand aloof, so stand
Thou too aloof bound with the flawless band
  Of inner solitude; we bind not thee;
  But who from thy self-chain shall set thee free?
What heart shall touch thy heart? what hand thy hand?—
And I am sometimes proud and sometimes meek,
  And sometimes I remember days of old
When fellowship seemed not so far to seek
  And all the world and I seemed much less cold,
  And at the rainbow's foot lay surely gold,
And hope felt strong and life itself not weak.

JEAN INGELOW

442
from 'DIVIDED'

A DAPPLED sky, a world of meadows,
   Circling above us the black rooks fly
Forward, backward; lo their dark shadows
   Flit on the blossoming tapestry.

Flit on the beck, for her long grass parteth
   As hair from a maid's bright eyes blown back;
And lo, the sun like a lover darteth
   His flattering smile on her wayward track.

Sing on! we sing in the glorious weather
   Till one steps over the tiny strand,
So narrow, in sooth, that still together
   On either brink we go hand in hand.

The beck grows wider, the hands must sever.
   On either margin, our songs all done,
We move apart, while she singeth ever,
   Taking the course of the stooping sun.

He prays, 'Come over'—I may not follow;
   I cry, 'Return'—but he cannot come:
We speak, we laugh, but with voices hollow;
   Our hands are hanging, our hearts are numb.

443
Seven Times One. Exultation

THERE's no dew left on the daisies and clover,
   There's no rain left in heaven:
I've said my 'seven times' over and over,
   Seven times one are seven.

JEAN INGELOW

I am old, so old, I can write a letter;
    My birthday lessons are done;
The lambs play always, they know no better;
    They are only one times one.

O moon! in the night I have seen you sailing
    And shining so round and low;
You were bright! ah bright! but your light is failing—
    You are nothing now but a bow.

You moon, have you done something wrong in heaven
    That God has hidden your face?
I hope if you have you will soon be forgiven,
    And shine again in your place.

O velvet bee, you're a dusty fellow,
    You've powdered your legs with gold!
O brave marsh marybuds, rich and yellow,
    Give me your money to hold!

O columbine, open your folded wrapper,
    Where two twin turtle-doves dwell!
O cuckoopint, toll me the purple clapper
    That hangs in your clear green bell!

And show me your nest with the young ones in it;
    I will not steal them away;
I am old! you may trust me, linnet, linnet—
    I am seven times one to-day.

THOMAS EDWARD BROWN

444   Ibant Obscuræ

To-night I saw three maidens on the beach,
     Dark-robed descending to the sea,
So slow, so silent of all speech,
     And visible to me
Only by that strange drift-light, dim, forlorn,
Of the sun's wreck and clashing surges born.
Each after other went,
     And they were gathered to his breast—
It seemed to me a sacrament
     Of some stern creed unblest;
As when to rocks, that cheerless girt the bay,
They bound thy holy limbs, Andromeda.

445   Wesley in Heaven

When Wesley died, the Angelic orders
     To see him at the state
Pressed so incontinent that the warders
     Forgot to shut the gate.
So I, that hitherto had followed
     As one with grief o'ercast,
Where for the doors a space was hollowed
     Crept in, and heard what passed.
And God said—'Seeing thou hast given
     Thy life to my great sounds,
Choose thou through all the cirque of Heaven
     What most of bliss redounds.'

Then Wesley said—'I hear the thunder
    Low growling from Thy seat—
Grant me that I may bind it under
    The trampling of my feet.'
And Wesley said—'See, lightning quivers
    Upon the presence walls—
Lord, give me of it four great rivers,
    To be my manuals.'
And then I saw the thunder chidden
    As slave to his desire;
And then I saw the space bestridden
    With four great bands of fire:
And stage by stage, stop stop subtending,
    Each lever strong and true,
One shape inextricable blending,
    The awful organ grew.
Then certain angels clad the Master
    In very marvellous wise,
Till clouds of rose and alabaster
    Concealed him from mine eyes.
And likest to a dove soft brooding,
    The innocent figure ran;
So breathed the breath of his preluding,
    And then the fugue began—
Began; but, to his office turning,
    The porter swung his key;
Wherefore, although my heart was yearning,
    I had to go; but he
Played on; and, as I downward clomb,
    I heard the mighty bars
Of thunder-gusts that shook heaven's dome,
    And moved the balanced stars.

446   ## To K. H.

O FAR withdrawn into the lonely West,
  To whom those Irish hills are as a grave
    Cairn-crowned, the dead sun's monument,
And this fair English land but vaguely guessed—
  Thee, lady, by the melancholy wave
    I greet, where salt winds whistle through the bent,
And harsh sea-holly buds beneath thy foot are pressed.

What is thy thought? 'Tis not the obvious scene
  That holds thee with its grand simplicity
    Of natural forms. Thou musest rather
What larger life may be, what richer sheen
  Of social gloss in lands beyond the sea,
    What nobler cult than where, around thy father,
The silent fishers pray in chapel small and mean.

Yes, thou art absent far—thy soul has slipt
  The visual bond, and thou art lowly kneeling
    Upon a pavement with the sacred kisses
Of emerald and ruby gleamings lipped;
  And down the tunnelled nave the organ, pealing,
    Blows music-storm, and with far-floating blisses
Gives tremor to the bells, and shakes the dead men's crypt.

This is thy thought; for this thou heav'st the sigh.
  Yet, lady, look around thee! hast thou not
    The life of real men, the home,
The tribe, and for a temple that old sky,
  Whereto the sea intones the polyglot
    Of water-pipes antiphonal, and the dome,
Round-arched, goes up to God in lapis lazuli?

from 'ROMAN WOMEN'

O ENGLISHWOMAN on the Pincian,
I love you not, nor ever can—
Astounding woman on the Pincian!
I know your mechanism well-adjusted,
I see your mind and body have been trusted
To all the proper people:
I see you straight as is a steeple;
I see you are not old;
I see you are a rich man's daughter;
I see you know the use of gold,
But also know the use of soap-and-water;
And yet I love you not, nor ever can—
Distinguished woman on the Pincian!

You have no doubt of your preëminence,
Nor do I make pretence
To challenge it for my poor little slattern,
Whose costume dates from Saturn—
My wall-flower with the long, love-draggled fringes:
But then the controversy hinges
On higher forms; and you must bear
Comparisons more noble. Stare, yes, stare—
I love you not, nor ever can,
You peerless woman on the Pincian.

No, you'll not see her on the Pincian,
My Roman woman, wife of Roman man!
Elsewhere you may—
And she is bright as is the day;
And she is sweet, that honest workman's wife
Fulfilled with bounteous life:
Her body balanced like a spring

In equipoise of perfect natural grace;
Her soul unquestioning
Of all but genial cares; her face,
Her frock, her attitude, her pace
The confluence of absolute harmonies—
And you, my Lady Margaret,
Pray what have you to set
'Gainst splendours such as these?
No, I don't love you, and I never can,
Pretentious woman on the Pincian!

But morals—beautiful serenity
Of social life, the sugar and the tea,
The flannels and the soup, the coals,
The patent recipes for saving souls,
And other things: the chill dead sneer
Conventional, the abject fear
Of form-transgressing freedom—I admit
That you have these; but love you not a whit
The more, nor ever can,
Alarming female on the Pincian!

Come out, O woman, from this blindness!
Rome, too, has women full of loving-kindness,
Has noble women, perfect in all good
That makes the glory of great womanhood—
But they are Women! I have seen them bent
On gracious errand; seen how goodness lent
The grave, ineffable charm
That guards from possibility of harm
A creature so divinely made,
So softly swayed
With native gesture free—
The melting-point of passionate purity.

Yes—soup and flannels too,
And tickets for them—just like you—
Tracts, books, and all the innumerable channels
Through which your bounty acts—
Well—not the tracts,
But certainly the flannels—
Her I must love, but you I never can,
Unlovely woman on the Pincian.

And yet—
Remarkable woman on the Pincian!—
We owe a sort of debt
To you, as having gone with us of old
To those bleak islands, cold
And desolate and grim,
Upon the Ocean's rim,
And shared their horrors with us—not that then
Our poor bewildered ken
Could catch the further issues, knowing only
That we were very lonely!
Ah well, you did us service in your station;
And how the progress of our civilisation
Has made you quite so terrible
It boots not ask; for still
You gave us stalwart scions,
Suckled the young sea-lions,
And smiled infrequent, glacial smiles
Upon the sulky isles—
For this and all His mercies—stay at home!
Here are the passion-flowers!
Here are the sunny hours!
O Pincian woman, do not come to Rome!

727

C. L. DODGSON (LEWIS CARROLL)

448 THE HUNTING OF THE SNARK

Fit the First

THE LANDING

'Just the place for a Snark!' the Bellman cried,
    As he landed his crew with care;
Supporting each man on the top of the tide
    By a finger entwined in his hair.

'Just the place for a Snark! I have said it twice:
    That alone should encourage the crew.
Just the place for a Snark! I have said it thrice:
    What I tell you three times is true.'

The crew was complete: it included a Boots—
    A maker of Bonnets and Hoods—
A Barrister, brought to arrange their disputes—
    And a Broker, to value their goods.

A Billiard-marker, whose skill was immense,
    Might perhaps have won more than his share—
But a Banker, engaged at enormous expense,
    Had the whole of their cash in his care.

There was also a Beaver, that paced on the deck,
    Or would sit making lace in the bow:
And had often (the Bellman said) saved them from wreck,
    Though none of the sailors knew how.

C. L. DODGSON (LEWIS CARROLL)

There was one who was famed for the number of things
    He forgot when he entered the ship:
His umbrella, his watch, all his jewels and rings,
    And the clothes he had bought for the trip.

He had forty-two boxes, all carefully packed,
    With his name painted clearly on each:
But, since he omitted to mention the fact,
    They were all left behind on the beach.

The loss of his clothes hardly mattered, because
    He had seven coats on when he came,
With three pair of boots——but the worst of it was,
    He had wholly forgotten his name.

He would answer to 'Hi!' or to any loud cry,
    Such as 'Fry me!' or 'Fritter my wig!'
To 'What-you-may-call-um!' or 'What-was-his-name!'
    But especially 'Thing-um-a-jig!'

While, for those who preferred a more forcible word,
    He had different names from these:
His intimate friends called him 'Candle-ends',
    And his enemies 'Toasted-cheese'.

'His form is ungainly——his intellect small——'
    (So the Bellman would often remark)
'But his courage is perfect! And that, after all,
    Is the thing that one needs with a Snark.'

He would joke with hyænas, returning their stare
    With an impudent wag of the head:
And he once went a walk, paw-in-paw, with a bear,
    'Just to keep up its spirits,' he said.

He came as a Baker: but owned, when too late—
    And it drove the poor Bellman half-mad—
He could only bake Bridecake——for which, I may state,
    No materials were to be had.

The last of the crew needs especial remark,
    Though he looked an incredible dunce:
He had just one idea——but, that one being 'Snark',
    The good Bellman engaged him at once.

He came as a Butcher: but gravely declared,
    When the ship had been sailing a week,
He could only kill Beavers. The Bellman looked scared,
    And was almost too frightened to speak:

But at length he explained, in a tremulous tone,
    There was only one Beaver on board;
And that was a tame one he had of his own,
    Whose death would be deeply deplored.

The Beaver, who happened to hear the remark,
    Protested, with tears in its eyes,
That not even the rapture of hunting the Snark
    Could atone for that dismal surprise!

It strongly advised that the Butcher should be
    Conveyed in a separate ship:
But the Bellman declared that would never agree
    With the plans he had made for the trip;

Navigation was always a difficult art,
    Though with only one ship and one bell:
And he feared he must really decline, for his part,
    Undertaking another as well.

C. L. DODGSON (LEWIS CARROLL)

The Beaver's best course was, no doubt, to procure
    A second-hand dagger-proof coat——
So the Baker advised it——and next, to insure
    Its life in some Office of note:

This the Ba[n]ker suggested, and offered for hire
    (On moderate terms), or for sale,
Two excellent Policies, one Against Fire,
    And one Against Damage From Hail.

Yet still, ever after that sorrowful day,
    Whenever the Butcher was by,
The Beaver kept looking the opposite way,
    And appeared unaccountably shy.

FIT THE SECOND

THE BELLMAN'S SPEECH

The Bellman himself they all praised to the skies——
    Such a carriage, such ease and such grace!
Such solemnity, too! One could see he was wise,
    The moment one looked in his face!

He had bought a large map representing the sea,
    Without the least vestige of land:
And the crew were much pleased when they found it to be
    A map they could all understand.

'What's the good of Mercator's North Poles and Equators,
    Tropics, Zones, and Meridian Lines?'
So the Bellman would cry: and the crew would reply
    'They are merely conventional signs!

'Other maps are such shapes, with their islands and capes!
    But we've got our brave Captain to thank'
(So the crew would protest) 'that he's bought us the best——
    A perfect and absolute blank!'

This was charming, no doubt: but they shortly found out
  That the Captain they trusted so well
Had only one notion for crossing the ocean,
  And that was to tingle his bell.

He was thoughtful and grave——but the orders he gave
  Were enough to bewilder a crew.
When he cried 'Steer to starboard, but keep her head larboard!'
  What on earth was the helmsman to do?

Then the bowsprit got mixed with the rudder sometimes:
  A thing, as the Bellman remarked,
That frequently happens in tropical climes,
  When a vessel is, so to speak, 'snarked'.

But the principal failing occurred in the sailing,
  And the Bellman, perplexed and distressed,
Said he *had* hoped, at least, when the wind blew due East
  That the ship would *not* travel due West!

But the danger was past——they had landed at last,
  With their boxes, portmanteaus, and bags:
Yet at first sight the crew were not pleased with the view,
  Which consisted of chasms and crags.

The Bellman perceived that their spirits were low,
  And repeated in musical tone
Some jokes he had kept for a season of woe——
  But the crew would do nothing but groan.

He served out some grog with a liberal hand,
  And bade them sit down on the beach:
And they could not but own that their Captain looked grand,
  As he stood and delivered his speech.

C. L. DODGSON (LEWIS CARROLL)

'Friends, Romans, and countrymen, lend me your ears!'
  (They were all of them fond of quotations:
So they drank to his health, and they gave him three cheers,
  While he served out additional rations).

'We have sailed many months, we have sailed many weeks
  (Four weeks to the month you may mark),
But never as yet ('tis your Captain who speaks)
  Have we caught the least glimpse of a Snark!

'We have sailed many weeks, we have sailed many days
  (Seven days to the week I allow),
But a Snark, on the which we might lovingly gaze,
  We have never beheld till now!

'Come, listen, my men, while I tell you again
  The five unmistakable marks
By which you may know, wheresoever you go,
  The warranted genuine Snarks.

'Let us take them in order. The first is the taste,
  Which is meagre and hollow, but crisp:
Like a coat that is rather too tight in the waist,
  With a flavour of Will-o'-the-wisp.

'Its habit of getting up late you'll agree
  That it carries too far, when I say
That it frequently breakfasts at five-o'clock tea,
  And dines on the following day.

'The third is its slowness in taking a jest,
  Should you happen to venture on one,
It will sigh like a thing that is deeply distressed:
  And it always looks grave at a pun.

'The fourth is its fondness for bathing-machines,
    Which it constantly carries about,
And believes that they add to the beauty of scenes——
    A sentiment open to doubt.

'The fifth is ambition. It next will be right
    To describe each particular batch:
Distinguishing those that have feathers, and bite,
    From those that have whiskers, and scratch.

'For, although common Snarks do no manner of harm,
    Yet, I feel it my duty to say,
Some are Boojums——' The Bellman broke off in alarm,
    For the Baker had fainted away.

FIT THE THIRD

THE BAKER'S TALE

They roused him with muffins—they roused him with ice—
    They roused him with mustard and cress—
They roused him with jam and judicious advice—
    They set him conundrums to guess.

When at length he sat up and was able to speak,
    His sad story he offered to tell;
And the Bellman cried 'Silence! not even a shriek!'
    And excitedly tingled his bell.

There was silence supreme! Not a shriek, not a scream,
    Scarcely even a howl or a groan,
As the man they called 'Ho!' told his story of woe
    In an antediluvian tone.

'My father and mother were honest, though poor——'
  'Skip all that!' cried the Bellman in haste.
'If it once becomes dark, there's no chance of a Snark——
  We have hardly a minute to waste!'

'I skip forty years,' said the Baker, in tears,
  'And proceed without further remark
To the day when you took me aboard of your ship
  To help you in hunting the Snark.

'A dear uncle of mine (after whom I was named)
  Remarked, when I bade him farewell——'
'Oh, skip your dear uncle!' the Bellman exclaimed,
  As he angrily tingled his bell.

'He remarked to me then,' said that mildest of men,
  '"If your Snark be a Snark, that is right:
Fetch it home by all means——you may serve it with greens,
  And it's handy for striking a light.

'"You may seek it with thimbles—and seek it with care;
  You may hunt it with forks and hope;
You may threaten its life with a railway-share;
  You may charm it with smiles and soap—"'

('That's exactly the method,' the Bellman bold
  In a hasty parenthesis cried,
'That's exactly the way I have always been told
  That the capture of Snarks should be tried!')

'"But oh, beamish nephew, beware of the day,
  If your Snark be a Boojum! For then
You will softly and suddenly vanish away,
  And never be met with again!"'

'It is this, it is this that oppresses my soul,
  When I think of my uncle's last words:
And my heart is like nothing so much as a bowl
  Brimming over with quivering curds!

'It is this, it is this——' 'We have had that before!'
  The Bellman indignantly said.
And the Baker replied 'Let me say it once more.
  It is this, it is this that I dread!

'I engage with the Snark——every night after dark——
  In a dreamy delirious fight:
I serve it with greens in those shadowy scenes,
  And I use it for striking a light;

'But if ever I meet with a Boojum, that day,
  In a moment (of this I am sure),
I shall softly and suddenly vanish away—
  And the notion I cannot endure!'

FIT THE FOURTH

THE HUNTING

The Bellman looked uffish, and wrinkled his brow.
  'If only you'd spoken before!
It's excessively awkward to mention it now,
  With the Snark, so to speak, at the door!

'We should all of us grieve, as you well may believe,
  If you never were met with again——
But surely, my man, when the voyage began,
  You might have suggested it then?

'It's excessively awkward to mention it now—
  As I think I've already remarked.'
And the man they called 'Hi!' replied, with a sigh,
  'I informed you the day we embarked.

'You may charge me with murder—or want of sense—
  (We are all of us weak at times):
But the slightest approach to a false pretence
  Was never among my crimes!

'I said it in Hebrew—I said it in Dutch—
  I said it in German and Greek;
But I wholly forgot (and it vexes me much)
  That English is what you speak!'

''Tis a pitiful tale,' said the Bellman, whose face
  Had grown longer at every word;
'But, now that you've stated the whole of your case,
  More debate would be simply absurd.

'The rest of my speech' (he explained to his men)
  'You shall hear when I've leisure to speak it.
But the Snark is at hand, let me tell you again!
  'Tis your glorious duty to seek it!

'To seek it with thimbles, to seek it with care;
  To pursue it with forks and hope;
To threaten its life with a railway-share;
  To charm it with smiles and soap!

'For the Snark's a peculiar creature, that won't
  Be caught in a commonplace way.
Do all that you know, and try all that you don't:
  Not a chance must be wasted to-day!

'For England expects——I forbear to proceed:
　'Tis a maxim tremendous, but trite:
And you'd best be unpacking the things that you need
　To rig yourselves out for the fight.'

Then the Banker endorsed a blank cheque (which he crossed),
　And changed his loose silver for notes.
The Baker with care combed his whiskers and hair,
　And shook the dust out of his coats.

The Boots and the Broker were sharpening a spade—
　Each working the grindstone in turn;
But the Beaver went on making lace, and displayed
　No interest in the concern:

Though the Barrister tried to appeal to its pride,
　And vainly proceeded to cite
A number of cases, in which making laces
　Had been proved an infringement of right.

The maker of Bonnets ferociously planned
　A novel arrangement of bows:
While the Billiard-marker with quivering hand
　Was chalking the tip of his nose.

But the Butcher turned nervous, and dressed himself fine,
　With yellow kid gloves and a ruff——
Said he felt it exactly like going to dine,
　Which the Bellman declared was all 'stuff'.

'Introduce me, now there's a good fellow,' he said,
　'If we happen to meet it together!'
And the Bellman, sagaciously nodding his head,
　Said 'That must depend on the weather'.

C. L. DODGSON (LEWIS CARROLL)

The Beaver went simply galumphing about,
  At seeing the Butcher so shy:
And even the Baker, though stupid and stout,
  Made an effort to wink with one eye.

'Be a man!' said the Bellman in wrath, as he heard
  The Butcher beginning to sob.
'Should we meet with a Jubjub, that desperate bird,
  We shall need all our strength for the job!'

Fit the Fifth

the beaver's lesson

They sought it with thimbles, they sought it with care;
  They pursued it with forks and hope;
They threatened its life with a railway-share;
  They charmed it with smiles and soap.

Then the Butcher contrived an ingenious plan
  For making a separate sally;
And had fixed on a spot unfrequented by man,
  A dismal and desolate valley.

But the very same plan to the Beaver occurred:
  It had chosen the very same place;
Yet neither betrayed, by a sign or a word,
  The disgust that appeared in his face.

Each thought he was thinking of nothing but 'Snark'
  And the glorious work of the day;
And each tried to pretend that he did not remark
  That the other was going that way.

But the valley grew narrow and narrower still,
   And the evening got darker and colder,
Till (merely from nervousness, not from goodwill)
   They marched along shoulder to shoulder.

Then a scream, shrill and high, rent the shuddering sky,
   And they knew that some danger was near:
The Beaver turned pale to the tip of its tail,
   And even the Butcher felt queer.

He thought of his childhood, left far far behind—
   That blissful and innocent state—
The sound so exactly recalled to his mind
   A pencil that squeaks on a slate!

"Tis the voice of the Jubjub!' he suddenly cried.
   (This man, that they used to call 'Dunce'.)
'As the Bellman would tell you,' he added with pride,
   'I have uttered that sentiment once.

"Tis the note of the Jubjub! Keep count, I entreat;
   You will find I have told it you twice.
'Tis the song of the Jubjub! The proof is complete,
   If only I've stated it thrice.'

The Beaver had counted with scrupulous care,
   Attending to every word:
But it fairly lost heart, and outgrabe in despair,
   When the third repetition occurred.

It felt that, in spite of all possible pains,
   It had somehow contrived to lose count,
And the only thing now was to rack its poor brains
   By reckoning up the amount.

'Two added to one—if that could but be done,'
  It said, 'with one's fingers and thumbs!'
Recollecting with tears how, in earlier years,
  It had taken no pains with its sums.

'The thing can be done,' said the Butcher, 'I think.
  The thing must be done, I am sure.
The thing shall be done! Bring me paper and ink,
  The best there is time to procure.'

The Beaver brought paper, portfolio, pens,
  And ink in unfailing supplies:
While strange creepy creatures came out of their dens,
  And watched them with wondering eyes.

So engrossed was the Butcher, he heeded them not,
  As he wrote with a pen in each hand,
And explained all the while in a popular style
  Which the Beaver could well understand.

'Taking Three as the subject to reason about——
  A convenient number to state——
We add Seven, and Ten, and then multiply out
  By One Thousand diminished by Eight.

'The result we proceed to divide, as you see,
  By Nine Hundred and Ninety and Two:
Then subtract Seventeen, and the answer must be
  Exactly and perfectly true.

'The method employed I would gladly explain,
  While I have it so clear in my head,
If I had but the time and you had but the brain——
  But much yet remains to be said.

'In one moment I've seen what has hitherto been
    Enveloped in absolute mystery,
And without extra charge I will give you at large
    A Lesson in Natural History.'

In his genial way he proceeded to say
    (Forgetting all laws of propriety,
And that giving instruction, without introduction,
    Would have caused quite a thrill in Society),

'As to temper the Jubjub's a desperate bird,
    Since it lives in perpetual passion:
Its taste in costume is entirely absurd——
    It is ages ahead of the fashion:

'But it knows any friend it has met once before:
    It never will look at a bribe:
And in charity-meetings it stands at the door,
    And collects——though it does not subscribe.

'Its flavour when cooked is more exquisite far
    Than mutton, or oysters, or eggs:
(Some think it keeps best in an ivory jar,
    And some, in mahogany kegs:)

'You boil it in sawdust: you salt it in glue:
    You condense it with locusts and tape:
Still keeping one principal object in view——
    To preserve its symmetrical shape.'

The Butcher would gladly have talked till next day,
    But he felt that the Lesson must end,
And he wept with delight in attempting to say
    He considered the Beaver his friend.

While the Beaver confessed, with affectionate looks
    More eloquent even than tears,
It had learnt in ten minutes far more than all books
    Would have taught it in seventy years.

They returned hand-in-hand, and the Bellman, unmanned
    (For a moment) with noble emotion,
Said 'This amply repays all the wearisome days
    We have spent on the billowy ocean!'

Such friends, as the Beaver and Butcher became,
    Have seldom if ever been known;
In winter or summer, 'twas always the same——
    You could never meet either alone.

And when quarrels arose——as one frequently finds
    Quarrels will, spite of every endeavour——
The song of the Jubjub recurred to their minds,
    And cemented their friendship for ever!

Fit the Sixth

THE BARRISTER'S DREAM

They sought it with thimbles, they sought it with care;
    They pursued it with forks and hope;
They threatened its life with a railway-share;
    They charmed it with smiles and soap.

But the Barrister, weary of proving in vain
    That the Beaver's lace-making was wrong,
Fell asleep, and in dreams saw the creature quite plain
    That his fancy had dwelt on so long.

C. L. DODGSON (LEWIS CARROLL)

He dreamed that he stood in a shadowy Court,
    Where the Snark, with a glass in its eye,
Dressed in gown, bands, and wig, was defending a pig
    On the charge of deserting its sty.

The Witnesses proved, without error or flaw,
    That the sty was deserted when found:
And the Judge kept explaining the state of the law
    In a soft under-current of sound.

The indictment had never been clearly expressed,
    And it seemed that the Snark had begun,
And had spoken three hours, before any one guessed
    What the pig was supposed to have done.

The Jury had each formed a different view
    (Long before the indictment was read),
And they all spoke at once, so that none of them knew
    One word that the others had said.

'You must know——' said the Judge: but the Snark
    exclaimed 'Fudge!
    That statute is obsolete quite!
Let me tell you, my friends, the whole question depends
    On an ancient manorial right.

'In the matter of Treason the pig would appear
    To have aided, but scarcely abetted:
While the charge of Insolvency fails, it is clear,
    If you grant the plea "never indebted".

'The fact of Desertion I will not dispute:
    But its guilt, as I trust, is removed
(So far as relates to the costs of this suit)
    By the Alibi which has been proved.

'My poor client's fate now depends on your votes.'
    Here the speaker sat down in his place,
And directed the Judge to refer to his notes
    And briefly to sum up the case.

But the Judge said he never had summed up before;
    So the Snark undertook it instead,
And summed it so well that it came to far more
    Than the Witnesses ever had said!

When the verdict was called for, the Jury declined,
    As the word was so puzzling to spell;
But they ventured to hope that the Snark wouldn't mind
    Undertaking that duty as well.

So the Snark found the verdict, although as it owned,
    It was spent with the toils of the day:
When it said the word 'GUILTY!' the Jury all groaned,
    And some of them fainted away.

Then the Snark pronounced sentence, the Judge being quite
    Too nervous to utter a word:
When it rose to its feet, there was silence like night,
    And the fall of a pin might be heard.

'Transportation for life' was the sentence it gave,
    'And *then* to be fined forty pound.'
The Jury all cheered, though the Judge said he feared
    That the phrase was not legally sound.

But their wild exultation was suddenly checked
    When the jailer informed them, with tears,
Such a sentence would have not the slightest effect,
    As the pig had been dead for some years.

The Judge left the Court, looking deeply disgusted:
    But the Snark, though a little aghast,
As the lawyer to whom the defence was intrusted,
    Went bellowing on to the last.

Thus the Barrister dreamed, while the bellowing seemed
    To grow every moment more clear:
Till he woke to the knell of a furious bell,
    Which the Bellman rang close at his ear.

FIT THE SEVENTH

THE BANKER'S FATE

They sought it with thimbles, they sought it with care;
    They pursued it with forks and hope;
They threatened its life with a railway-share;
    They charmed it with smiles and soap.

And the Banker, inspired with a courage so new
    It was matter for general remark,
Rushed madly ahead and was lost to their view
    In his zeal to discover the Snark.

But while he was seeking with thimbles and care,
    A Bandersnatch swiftly drew nigh
And grabbed at the Banker, who shrieked in despair,
    For he knew it was useless to fly.

He offered large discount—he offered a cheque
    (Drawn 'to bearer') for seven-pounds-ten:
But the Bandersnatch merely extended its neck
    And grabbed at the Banker again.

Without rest or pause—while those frumious jaws
  Went savagely snapping around—
He skipped and he hopped, and he floundered and flopped,
  Till fainting he fell to the ground.

The Bandersnatch fled as the others appeared:
  Led on by that fear-stricken yell:
And the Bellman remarked 'It is just as I feared!'
  And solemnly tolled on his bell.

He was black in the face, and they scarcely could trace
  The least likeness to what he had been:
While so great was his fright that his waistcoat turned white—
  A wonderful thing to be seen!

To the horror of all who were present that day,
  He uprose in full evening dress,
And with senseless grimaces endeavoured to say
  What his tongue could no longer express.

Down he sank in a chair—ran his hands through his hair—
  And chanted in mimsiest tones
Words whose utter inanity proved his insanity,
  While he rattled a couple of bones.

'Leave him here to his fate—it is getting so late!'
  The Bellman exclaimed in a fright.
'We have lost half the day. Any further delay,
  And we sha'n't catch a Snark before night!'

FIT THE EIGHTH

THE VANISHING

They sought it with thimbles, they sought it with care;
  They pursued it with forks and hope;
They threatened its life with a railway-share;
  They charmed it with smiles and soap.

They shuddered to think that the chase might fail,
   And the Beaver, excited at last,
Went bounding along on the tip of its tail,
   For the daylight was nearly past.

'There is Thingumbob shouting!' the Bellman said.
   'He is shouting like mad, only hark!
He is waving his hands, he is wagging his head,
   He has certainly found a Snark!'

They gazed in delight, while the Butcher exclaimed
   'He was always a desperate wag!'
They beheld him—their Baker—their hero unnamed—
   On the top of a neighbouring crag,

Erect and sublime, for one moment of time.
   In the next, that wild figure they saw
(As if stung by a spasm) plunge into a chasm,
   While they waited and listened in awe.

'It's a Snark!' was the sound that first came to their ears,
   And seemed almost too good to be true.
Then followed a torrent of laughter and cheers:
   Then the ominous words 'It's a Boo—'

Then, silence. Some fancied they heard in the air
   A weary and wandering sigh
That sounded like '—jum!' but the others declare
   It was only a breeze that went by.

They hunted till darkness came on, but they found
   Not a button, or feather, or mark,
By which they could tell that they stood on the ground
   Where the Baker had met with the Snark.

In the midst of the word he was trying to say
   In the midst of his laughter and glee,
He had softly and suddenly vanished away——
   For the Snark *was* a Boojum, you see.

RICHARD WATSON DIXON

449 from 'LOVE'S CONSOLATION'

ALL who have loved, be sure of this from me,
That to have touched one little ripple free
Of golden hair, or held a little hand
Very long since, is better than to stand
Rolled up in vestures stiff with golden thread,
Upon a throne o'er many a bowing head
Of adulators; yea, and to have seen
Thy lady walking in a garden green,
'Mid apple blossoms and green twisted boughs,
Along the golden gravel path, to house
Herself, where thou art watching far below,
Deep in thy bower impervious, even though
Thou never give her kisses after that,
Is sweeter than to never break the flat
Of thy soul's rising, like a river tide
That never foams; yea, if thy lady chide
Cruelly thy service, and indeed becomes
A wretch, whose false eyes haunt thee in all rooms,
'Tis better so, than never to have been
An hour in love; than never to have seen
Thine own heart's worthiness to shrink and shake,
Like silver quick, all for thy lady's sake,
Weighty with truth, with gentleness as bright.
    Moreover, let sad lovers take delight
In this, that time will bring at last their peace:
We watch great passions in their huge increase,
Until they fill our hearts, so that we say,
'Let go this, and I die'; yet nay and nay,
We find them leave us strangely quiet then,
When they must quit; one lion leaves the den,
Another enters; wherefore thus I cross
All lovers pale and starving with their loss.

450   The Judgment of the May

    COME to the judgment, golden threads
        Upon golden hair in rich array;
    Many a chesnut shakes its heads,
        Many a lupine at this day,
    Many a white rose in our beds
        Waits the judgment of the May.

    Oh, like white roses, great white queen,
        Come to the judgment, come to-day.
    The white stars on thy robes of green
        Are like white roses on trees in May:
    By me thy stars and flowers are seen,
        But now thou seemest far away.

451   By the Sea

    IN tottering row, like shadows, silently
    The old pier-timbers struggle from the sea;
    Strained in old storms by those wild waves that creep
    So gently now, no longer do they keep
    The pier that on them rested long ago,
    But stand as driven piles in tottering row.
    The sky sails downward, upward creeps the wave,
    For countless clouds toward the sun's bright grave
    Move curiously with grey and misty wing;
    So thickly all the sky environing,
    That only by one pale bright spot is known
    Where still the sunken light is upward thrown,
    And lately sunk the weary king of day:
    Still on the sands below in stealthy play

Arise the billows of the nightly tide;
Each with its own clear layer doth override
The spreaded calm where its last brother rolled;
Each upon other rippling draws the fold
Of its thin edge along the soakèd sand,
And stirs the spongy foam 'twixt sea and land,
And lifts the dark waifs higher on the shore.
Yet in this quietness resides the roar
Of ocean floods; one rising of that wind,
And those slow clouds would leave the night behind
In bitter clearness; those cold waves would roll
In snarling billows white. So of the soul.

452   Song

THE feathers of the willow
Are half of them grown yellow
    Above the swelling stream;
And ragged are the bushes,
And rusty now the rushes,
    And wild the clouded gleam.

The thistle now is older,
His stalk begins to moulder,
    His head is white as snow;
The branches all are barer,
The linnet's song is rarer,
    The robin pipeth now.

453   Ode: The Spirit Wooed

ART thou gone so far,
Beyond the poplar tops, beyond the sunset-bar,
Beyond the purple cloud that swells on high
In the tender fields of sky?

RICHARD WATSON DIXON

Leanest thou thy head
On sunset's golden breadth? is thy wide hair spread
To his solemn kisses? Yet grow thou not pale
As he pales and dies: nor more my eyes avail
To search his cloud-drawn bed.

O come thou again!
Be seen on the falling slope: let thy footsteps pass
Where the river cuts with his blue scythe the grass:
Be heard in the voice that across the river comes
From the distant wood, even when the stilly rain
Is made to cease by light winds: come again,
As out of yon grey glooms,
When the cloud grows luminous and shiftily riven,
Forth comes the moon, the sweet surprise of heaven:
And her footfall light
Drops on the multiplied wave: her face is seen
In evening's pallor green:
And she waxes bright
With the death of the tinted air: yea, brighter grows
In sunset's gradual close.
To earth from heaven comes she,
So come thou to me.

Oh, lay thou thy head
On sunset's breadth of gold, thy hair bespread
In his solemn kisses: but grow thou not pale
As he pales and dies, lest eye no more avail
To search thy cloud-drawn bed.

Can the weeping eye
Always feel light through mists that never dry?
Can empty arms alone for ever fill
Enough the breast? Can echo answer still,
When the voice has ceased to cry?

454 ## Unrest

DAY is again begun
By the unresting sun:
Morning o'er all the lands
Rises with clasped hands:
And in the increasing light
Sickens the Moon of night:
For darkness leaves her there
To linger pale and bare,
Till fullest light, more kind,
From view her form shall wind.
  But in this rising morn
Muse not on things forlorn,
Knowing thyself the thrall
Of life beyond them all.
Another day shall pass
Like yesterday that was;
Another night shall come,
Like the last perished gloom:
And thou shalt never rest,
Nor yet attain thy quest:
But, like thy very earth,
Betwixt dark death, dark birth,
Speed, and not know thy speed,
While days and nights recede:
Thy seeming rest to be
Gyres in immensity;
The paces of thy strength
Small measures of fate's length:
Thy waste or use of powers
Predestined to their hours:
And thou thyself?—The sob
Of pallid lips, the throb

Of every heart this day,
By which life ebbs away,
And yet by which life lives,—
Ah, this thy emblem gives.

JAMES THOMSON (B.V.)

455 from 'THE CITY OF DREADFUL NIGHT'

1870:1874

Proem

Lo, thus, as prostrate, 'In the dust I write
   My heart's deep languor and my soul's sad tears.'
Yet why evoke the spectres of black night
   To blot the sunshine of exultant years?
Why disinter dead faith from mouldering hidden?
Why break the seals of mute despair unbidden,
   And wail life's discords into careless ears?

Because a cold rage seizes one at whiles
   To show the bitter old and wrinkled truth
Stripped naked of all vesture that beguiles,
   False dreams, false hopes, false masks and modes of youth;
Because it gives some sense of power and passion
In helpless impotence to try to fashion
   Our woe in living words howe'er uncouth.

Surely I write not for the hopeful young,
   Or those who deem their happiness of worth,
Or such as pasture and grow fat among
   The shows of life and feel nor doubt nor dearth,
Or pious spirits with a God above them
To sanctify and glorify and love them,
   Or sages who foresee a heaven on earth.

For none of these I write, and none of these
   Could read the writing if they deigned to try:
So may they flourish, in their due degrees,
   On our sweet earth and in their unplaced sky.
If any cares for the weak words here written,
It must be some one desolate, Fate-smitten,
   Whose faith and hope are dead, and who would die.

Yes, here and there some weary wanderer
   In that same city of tremendous night,
Will understand the speech, and feel a stir
   Of fellowship in all-disastrous fight;
'I suffer mute and lonely, yet another
Uplifts his voice to let me know a brother
   Travels the same wild paths though out of sight.'

O sad Fraternity, do I unfold
   Your dolorous mysteries shrouded from of yore?
Nay, be assured; no secret can be told
   To any who divined it not before:
None uninitiate by many a presage
Will comprehend the language of the message,
   Although proclaimed aloud for evermore.

[1]

The City is of Night; perchance of Death,
   But certainly of Night; for never there
Can come the lucid morning's fragrant breath
   After the dewy dawning's cold grey air;
The moon and stars may shine with scorn or pity;
The sun has never visited that city,
   For it dissolveth in the daylight fair.

Dissolveth like a dream of night away;
　　Though present in distempered gloom of thought
And deadly weariness of heart all day.
　　But when a dream night after night is brought
Throughout a week, and such weeks few or many
Recur each year for several years, can any
　　Discern that dream from real life in aught?

For life is but a dream whose shapes return,
　　Some frequently, some seldom, some by night
And some by day, some night and day: we learn,
　　The while all change and many vanish quite,
In their recurrence with recurrent changes
A certain seeming order; where this ranges
　　We count things real; such is memory's might.

A river girds the city west and south,
　　The main north channel of a broad lagoon,
Regurging with the salt tides from the mouth;
　　Waste marshes shine and glister to the moon
For leagues, then moorland black, then stony ridges;
Great piers and causeways, many noble bridges,
　　Connect the town and islet suburbs strewn.

Upon an easy slope it lies at large,
　　And scarcely overlaps the long curved crest
Which swells out two leagues from the river marge.
　　A trackless wilderness rolls north and west,
Savannahs, savage woods, enormous mountains,
Bleak uplands, black ravines with torrent fountains;
　　And eastward rolls the shipless sea's unrest.

The city is not ruinous, although
  Great ruins of an unremembered past,
With others of a few short years ago
  More sad, are found within its precincts vast.
The street-lamps always burn; but scarce a casement
In house or palace front from roof to basement
  Doth glow or gleam athwart the mirk air cast.

The street-lamps burn amidst the baleful glooms,
  Amidst the soundless solitudes immense
Of rangèd mansions dark and still as tombs.
  The silence which benumbs or strains the sense
Fulfils with awe the soul's despair unweeping:
Myriads of habitants are ever sleeping,
  Or dead, or fled from nameless pestilence!

Yet as in some necropolis you find
  Perchance one mourner to a thousand dead,
So there; worn faces that look deaf and blind
  Like tragic masks of stone. With weary tread,
Each wrapt in his own doom, they wander, wander,
Or sit foredone and desolately ponder
  Through sleepless hours with heavy drooping head.

Mature men chiefly, few in age or youth,
  A woman rarely, now and then a child:
A child! If here the heart turns sick with ruth
  To see a little one from birth defiled,
Or lame or blind, as preordained to languish
Through youthless life, think how it bleeds with anguish
  To meet one erring in that homeless wild.

They often murmur to themselves, they speak
  To one another seldom, for their woe
Broods maddening inwardly and scorns to wreak
  Itself abroad; and if at whiles it grow

To frenzy which must rave, none heeds the clamour,
Unless there waits some victim of like glamour,
   To rave in turn, who lends attentive show.

The City is of Night, but not of Sleep;
   There sweet sleep is not for the weary brain;
The pitiless hours like years and ages creep,
   A night seems termless hell. This dreadful strain
Of thought and consciousness which never ceases,
Or which some moments' stupor but increases,
   This, worse than woe, makes wretches there insane.

They leave all hope behind who enter there:
   One certitude while sane they cannot leave;
One anodyne for torture and despair;
   The certitude of Death, which no reprieve
Can put off long; and which, divinely tender,
But waits the outstretched hand to promptly render
   That draught whose slumber nothing can bereave.[1]

[11]

Although lamps burn along the silent streets;
   Even when moonlight silvers empty squares
The dark holds countless lanes and close retreats;
   But when the night its sphereless mantle wears
The open spaces yawn with gloom abysmal,
The sombre mansions loom immense and dismal,
   The lanes are black as subterranean lairs.

[1] Though the Garden of thy life be wholly waste, the sweet flowers withered, the fruit-trees barren, over its wall hang ever the rich dark clusters of the Vine of Death, within easy reach of thy hand, which may pluck of them when it will.

And soon the eye a strange new vision learns:
 The night remains for it as dark and dense,
Yet clearly in this darkness it discerns
 As in the daylight with its natural sense;
Perceives a shade in shadow not obscurely,
Pursues a stir of black in blackness surely,
 Sees spectres also in the gloom intense.

The ear, too, with the silence vast and deep
 Becomes familiar though unreconciled;
Hears breathings as of hidden life asleep,
 And muffled throbs as of pent passions wild,
Far murmurs, speech of pity or derision;
But all more dubious than the things of vision,
 So that it knows not when it is beguiled.

No time abates the first despair and awe,
 But wonder ceases soon; the weirdest thing
Is felt least strange beneath the lawless law
 Where Death-in-Life is the eternal king;
Crushed impotent beneath this reign of terror,
Dazed with such mysteries of woe and error,
 The soul is too outworn for wondering.

[III]

Some say that phantoms haunt those shadowy streets,
 And mingle freely there with sparse mankind;
And tell of ancient woes and black defeats,
 And murmur mysteries in the grave enshrined:
But others think them visions of illusion,
Or even men gone far in self-confusion;
 No man there being wholly sane in mind.

759

And yet a man who raves, however mad,
   Who bares his heart and tells of his own fall,
Reserves some inmost secret good or bad:
   The phantoms have no reticence at all:
The nudity of flesh will blush though tameless,
The extreme nudity of bone grins shameless,
   The unsexed skeleton mocks shroud and pall.

I have seen phantoms there that were as men
   And men that were as phantoms flit and roam;
Marked shapes that were not living to my ken,
   Caught breathings acrid as with Dead Sea foam:
The City rests for man so weird and awful,
That his intrusion there might seem unlawful,
   And phantoms there may have their proper home.

[IV]

It is full strange to him who hears and feels,
   When wandering there in some deserted street,
The booming and the jar of ponderous wheels,
   The trampling clash of heavy ironshod feet:
Who in this Venice of the Black Sea rideth?
Who in this city of the stars abideth
   To buy or sell as those in daylight sweet?

The rolling thunder seems to fill the sky
   As it comes on; the horses snort and strain,
The harness jingles, as it passes by;
   The hugeness of an overburthened wain:
A man sits nodding on the shaft or trudges
Three parts asleep beside his fellow-drudges:
   And so it rolls into the night again.

What merchandise? whence, whither, and for whom?
   Perchance it is a Fate-appointed hearse,
Bearing away to some mysterious tomb
   Or Limbo of the scornful universe
The joy, the peace, the life-hope, the abortions
Of all things good which should have been our portions,
   But have been strangled by that City's curse.

[v]

What men are they who haunt these fatal glooms,
   And fill their living mouths with dust of death,
And make their habitations in the tombs,
   And breathe eternal sighs with mortal breath,
And pierce life's pleasant veil of various error
To reach that void of darkness and old terror
   Wherein expire the lamps of hope and faith?

They have much wisdom yet they are not wise,
   They have much goodness yet they do not well,
(The fools we know have their own Paradise,
   The wicked also have their proper Hell);
They have much strength but still their doom is stronger,
Much patience but their time endureth longer,
   Much valour but life mocks it with some spell.

They are most rational and yet insane:
   An outward madness not to be controlled;
A perfect reason in the central brain,
   Which has no power, but sitteth wan and cold,
And sees the madness, and foresees as plainly
The ruin in its path, and trieth vainly
   To cheat itself refusing to behold.

And some are great in rank and wealth and power,
　　And some renowned for genius and for worth;
And some are poor and mean, who brood and cower
　　And shrink from notice, and accept all dearth
Of body, heart and soul, and leave to others
All boons of life: yet these and those are brothers,
　　The saddest and the weariest men on earth.

[vi]

Of all things human which are strange and wild
　　This is perchance the wildest and most strange,
And showeth man most utterly beguiled,
　　To those who haunt that sunless City's range;
That he bemoans himself for aye, repeating
How Time is deadly swift, how life is fleeting,
　　How nought is constant on the earth but change.

The hours are heavy on him and the days;
　　The burden of the months he scarce can bear;
And often in his secret soul he prays
　　To sleep through barren periods unaware,
Arousing at some longed-for date of pleasure;
Which having passed and yielded him small treasure,
　　He would outsleep another term of care.

Yet in his marvellous fancy he must make
　　Quick wings for Time, and see it fly from us;
This Time which crawleth like a monstrous snake,
　　Wounded and slow and very venomous;
Which creeps blindwormlike round the earth and ocean,
Distilling poison at each painful motion,
　　And seems condemned to circle ever thus.

And since he cannot spend and use aright
   The little time here given him in trust,
But wasteth it in weary undelight
   Of foolish toil and trouble, strife and lust,
He naturally claimeth to inherit
The everlasting Future, that his merit
   May have full scope; as surely is most just.

O length of the intolerable hours,
   O nights that are as æons of slow pain,
O Time, too ample for our vital powers,
   O Life, whose woeful vanities remain
Immutable for all of all our legions
Through all the centuries and in all the regions,
   Not of your speed and variance *we* complain.

We do not ask a longer term of strife,
   Weakness and weariness and nameless woes;
We do not claim renewed and endless life
   When this which is our torment here shall close,
An everlasting conscious inanition!
We yearn for speedy death in full fruition,
   Dateless oblivion and divine repose.

[VII]

How the moon triumphs through the endless nights!
   How the stars throb and glitter as they wheel
Their thick processions of supernal lights
   Around the blue vault obdurate as steel!
And men regard with passionate awe and yearning
The mighty marching and the golden burning,
   And think the heavens respond to what they feel.

Boats gliding like dark shadows of a dream,
   Are glorified from vision as they pass
The quivering moonbridge on the deep black stream;
   Cold windows kindle their dead glooms of glass
To restless crystals; cornice, dome, and column
Emerge from chaos in the splendour solemn;
   Like faëry lakes gleam lawns of dewy grass.

With such a living light these dead eyes shine,
   These eyes of sightless heaven, that as we gaze
We read a pity, tremulous, divine,
   Or cold majestic scorn in their pure rays:
Fond man! they are not haughty, are not tender;
There is no heart or mind in all their splendour,
   They thread mere puppets all their marvellous maze.

If we could near them with the flight unflown,
   We should but find them worlds as sad as this,
Or suns all self-consuming like our own
   Enringed by planet worlds as much amiss:
They wax and wane through fusion and confusion;
The spheres eternal are a grand illusion,
   The empyréan is a void abyss.

[VIII]

The mighty river flowing dark and deep,
   With ebb and flood from the remote sea-tides
Vague-sounding through the City's sleepless sleep,
   Is named the River of the Suicides;
For night by night some lorn wretch overweary
And shuddering from the future yet more dreary,
   Within its cold secure oblivion hides.

JAMES THOMSON (B.V.)

One plunges from a bridge's parapet,
  As by some blind and sudden frenzy hurled;
Another wades in slow with purpose set
  Until the waters are above him furled;
Another in a boat with dreamlike motion
Glides drifting down into the desert ocean,
  To starve or sink from out the desert world.

They perish from their suffering surely thus,
  For none beholding them attempts to save,
The while each thinks how soon, solicitous,
  He may seek refuge in the self-same wave.
Some hour when tired of ever-vain endurance
Impatience will forerun the sweet assurance
  Of perfect peace eventual in the grave.

When this poor tragic-farce has palled us long,
  Why actors and spectators do we stay?—
To fill our so-short *rôles* out right or wrong;
  To see what shifts are yet in the dull play
For our illusion; to refrain from grieving
Dear foolish friends by our untimely leaving:
  But those asleep at home, how blest are they!

Yet it is but for one night after all:
  What matters one brief night of dreary pain?
When after it the weary eyelids fall
  Upon the weary eyes and wasted brain;
And all sad scenes and thoughts and feelings vanish
In that sweet sleep no power can ever banish,
  That one best sleep which never wakes again.

[IX]

I sat me weary on a pillar's base,
    And leaned against the shaft; for broad moonlight
O'erflowed the peacefulness of cloistered space,
    A shore of shadow slanting from the right:
The great cathedral's western front stood there,
A wave-worn rock in that calm sea of air.

Before it, opposite my place of rest,
    Two figures faced each other, large, austere;
A couchant sphinx in shadow to the breast,
    An angel standing in the moonlight clear;
So mighty by magnificence of form,
They were not dwarfed beneath that mass enorm.

Upon the cross-hilt of a naked sword
    The angel's hands, as prompt to smite, were held;
His vigilant, intense regard was poured
    Upon the creature placidly unquelled,
Whose front was set at level gaze which took
No heed of aught, a solemn trance-like look.

And as I pondered these opposèd shapes
    My eyelids sank in stupor, that dull swoon
Which drugs and with a leaden mantle drapes
    The outworn to worse weariness. But soon
A sharp and clashing noise the stillness broke,
And from the evil lethargy I woke.

The angel's wings had fallen, stone on stone,
    And lay there shattered; hence the sudden sound:
A warrior leaning on his sword alone
    Now watched the sphinx with that regard profound;
The sphinx unchanged looked forthright, as aware
Of nothing in the vast abyss of air.

Again I sank in that repose unsweet,
  Again a clashing noise my slumber rent;
The warrior's sword lay broken at his feet:
  An unarmed man with raised hands impotent
Now stood before the sphinx, which ever kept
Such mien as if with open eyes it slept.

My eyelids sank in spite of wonder grown;
  A louder crash upstartled me in dread;
The man had fallen forward, stone on stone,
  And lay there shattered, with his trunkless head
Between the monster's large quiescent paws,
Beneath its grand front changeless as life's laws.

The moon had circled westward full and bright,
  And made the temple-front a mystic dream,
And bathed the whole enclosure with its light,
  The sworded angel's wrecks, the sphinx supreme:
I pondered long that cold majestic face
Whose vision seemed of infinite void space.

[x]

Anear the centre of that northern crest
  Stands out a level upland bleak and bare,
From which the city east and south and west
  Sinks gently in long waves; and thronèd there
An Image sits, stupendous, superhuman,
The bronze colossus of a wingèd Woman,
  Upon a graded granite base foursquare.

Low-seated she leans forward massively,
  With cheek on clenched left hand, the forearm's might
Erect, its elbow on her rounded knee;
  Across a clasped book in her lap the right

767

Upholds a pair of compasses; she gazes
With full set eyes, but wandering in thick mazes
   Of sombre thought beholds no outward sight.

Words cannot picture her; but all men know
   That solemn sketch the pure sad artist wrought
Three centuries and threescore years ago,
   With phantasies of his peculiar thought:
The instruments of carpentry and science
Scattered about her feet, in strange alliance
   With the keen wolf-hound sleeping undistraught;

Scales, hour-glass, bell, and magic-square above;
   The grave and solid infant perched beside,
With open winglets that might bear a dove,
   Intent upon its tablets, heavy-eyed;
Her folded wings as of a mighty eagle,
But all too impotent to lift the regal
   Robustness of her earth-born strength and pride;

And with those wings, and that light wreath which seems
   To mock her grand head and the knotted frown
Of forehead charged with baleful thoughts and dreams,
   The household bunch of keys, the housewife's gown
Voluminous, indented, and yet rigid
As if a shell of burnished metal frigid,
   The feet thick-shod to tread all weakness down;

The comet hanging o'er the waste dark seas,
   The massy rainbow curved in front of it
Beyond the village with the masts and trees;
   The snaky imp, dog-headed, from the Pit,
Bearing upon its batlike leathern pinions
Her name unfolded in the sun's dominions,
   The 'MELENCOLIA' that transcends all wit.

Thus has the artist copied her, and thus
   Surrounded to expound her form sublime,
Her fate heroic and calamitous;
   Fronting the dreadful mysteries of Time,
Unvanquished in defeat and desolation,
Undaunted in the hopeless conflagration
   Of the day setting on her baffled prime.

Baffled and beaten back she works on still,
   Weary and sick of soul she works the more,
Sustained by her indomitable will:
   The hands shall fashion and the brain shall pore,
And all her sorrow shall be turned to labour,
Till Death the friend-foe piercing with his sabre
   That mighty heart of hearts ends bitter war.

But as if blacker night could dawn on night,
   With tenfold gloom on moonless night unstarred,
A sense more tragic than defeat and blight,
   More desperate than strife with hope debarred,
More fatal than the adamantine Never
Encompassing her passionate endeavour,
   Dawns glooming in her tenebrous regard:

The sense that every struggle brings defeat
   Because Fate holds no prize to crown success;
That all the oracles are dumb or cheat
   Because they have no secret to express;
That none can pierce the vast black veil uncertain
Because there is no light beyond the curtain;
   That all is vanity and nothingness.

Titanic from her high throne in the north,
    That City's sombre Patroness and Queen,
In bronze sublimity she gazes forth
    Over her Capital of teen and threne,
Over the river with its isles and bridges,
The marsh and moorland, to the stern rock-ridges,
    Confronting them with a coëval mien.

The moving moon and stars from east to west
    Circle before her in the sea of air;
Shadows and gleams glide round her solemn rest.
    Her subjects often gaze up to her there:
The strong to drink new strength of iron endurance,
The weak new terrors; all, renewed assurance
    And confirmation of the old despair.

WILLIAM MORRIS

456   Golden Wings

MIDWAYS of a walled garden,
    In the happy poplar land,
    Did an ancient castle stand,
With an old knight for a warden.

Many scarlet bricks there were
    On its walls, and old grey stone;
    Over which red apples shone
At the right time of the year.

On the bricks the green moss grew,
    Yellow lichen on the stone,
    Over which red apples shone;
Little war that castle knew.

770

Deep green water fill'd the moat,
    Each side had a red-brick lip,
    Green and mossy with the drip
Of dew and rain; there was a boat

Of carven wood, with hangings green
    About the stern; it was great bliss
    For lovers to sit there and kiss
In the hot summer noons, not seen.

Across the moat the fresh west wind
    In very little ripples went;
    The way the heavy aspens bent
Towards it, was a thing to mind.

The painted drawbridge over it
    Went up and down with gilded chains,
    'Twas pleasant in the summer rains
Within the bridge-house there to sit.

There were five swans that ne'er did eat
    The water-weeds, for ladies came
    Each day, and young knights did the same,
And gave them cakes and bread for meat.

They had a house of painted wood,
    A red roof gold-spiked over it,
    Wherein upon their eggs to sit
Week after week; no drop of blood,

Drawn from men's bodies by sword-blows,
    Came ever there, or any tear;
    Most certainly from year to year
'Twas pleasant as a Provence rose.

The banners seem'd quite full of ease,
   That over the turret-roofs hung down;
   The battlements could get no frown
From the flower-moulded cornices.

Who walked in the garden there?
   Miles and Giles and Isabeau,
   Tall Jehane du Castel beau,
Alice of the golden hair,

Big Sir Gervaise, the good knight,
   Fair Ellayne le Violet,
   Mary, Constance fille de fay,
Many dames with footfall light.

Whosoever wander'd there,
   Whether it be dame or knight,
   Half of scarlet, half of white
Their raiment was; of roses fair

Each wore a garland on the head,
   At Ladies' Gard the way was so:
   Fair Jehane du Castel beau
Wore her wreath till it was dead.

Little joy she had of it,
   Of the raiment white and red,
   Or the garland on her head,
She had none with whom to sit

In the carven boat at noon;
   None the more did Jehane weep,
   She would only stand and keep
Saying, 'He will be here soon.'

Many times in the long day
　　Miles and Giles and Gervaise past,
　　Holding each some white hand fast,
Every time they heard her say:

'Summer cometh to an end,
　　Undern cometh after noon;
　　Golden wings will be here soon,
What if I some token send?'

Wherefore that night within the hall,
　　With open mouth and open eyes,
　　Like some one listening with surprise,
She sat before the sight of all.

Stoop'd down a little she sat there,
　　With neck stretch'd out and chin thrown **up**,
　　One hand around a golden cup;
And strangely with her fingers fair

She beat some tune upon the gold;
　　The minstrels in the gallery
　　Sung: 'Arthur, who will never die,
In Avallon he groweth old.'

And when the song was ended, she
　　Rose and caught up her gown and ran;
　　None stopp'd her eager face and wan
Of all that pleasant company.

Right so within her own chamber
　　Upon her bed she sat; and drew
　　Her breath in quick gasps; till she knew
That no man follow'd after her:

She took the garland from her head,
  Loosed all her hair, and let it lie
  Upon the coverlit; thereby
She laid the gown of white and red;

And she took off her scarlet shoon,
  And bared her feet; still more and more
  Her sweet face redden'd; evermore
She murmur'd: 'He will be here soon;

'Truly he cannot fail to know
  My tender body waits him here;
  And if he knows, I have no fear
For poor Jehane du Castel beau.'

She took a sword within her hand,
  Whose hilts were silver, and she sung,
  Somehow like this, wild words that rung
A long way over the moonlit land:—

    Gold wings across the sea!
    Grey light from tree to tree,
    Gold hair beside my knee,
    I pray thee come to me,
    Gold wings!

        The water slips,
    The red-bill'd moorhen dips.
    Sweet kisses on red lips;
    Alas! the red rust grips,
    And the blood-red dagger rips,
    Yet, O knight, come to me!

Are not my blue eyes sweet?
The west wind from the wheat
Blows cold across my feet;
Is it not time to meet
Gold wings across the sea?

White swans on the green moat,
Small feathers left afloat
By the blue-painted boat;
Swift running of the stoat;
Sweet gurgling note by note
Of sweet music.

          O gold wings,
Listen how gold hair sings,
And the Ladies' Castle rings
Gold wings across the sea.

I sit on a purple bed,
Outside the wall is red,
Thereby the apple hangs,
And the wasp, caught by the fangs,

Dies in the autumn night.
And the bat flits till light,
And the love-crazed knight

Kisses the long wet grass:
The weary days pass,—
Gold wings across the sea!

Gold wings across the sea!
Moonlight from tree to tree,
Sweet hair laid on my knee,
O sweet knight, come to me!

Gold wings, the short night slips,
The white swan's long neck drips,
I pray thee, kiss my lips,
Gold wings across the sea.

No answer through the moonlight night;
No answer in the cold grey dawn;
No answer when the shaven lawn
Grew green, and all the roses bright.

Her tired feet look'd cold and thin,
Her lips were twitch'd, and wretched tears,
Some, as she lay, roll'd past her ears,
Some fell from off her quivering chin.

Her long throat, stretch'd to its full length,
Rose up and fell right brokenly;
As though the unhappy heart was nigh
Striving to break with all its strength.

And when she slipp'd from off the bed,
Her cramp'd feet would not hold her; she
Sank down and crept on hand and knee,
On the window-sill she laid her head.

There, with crooked arm upon the sill,
She look'd out, muttering dismally:
'There is no sail upon the sea,
No pennon on the empty hill.

'I cannot stay here all alone,
Or meet their happy faces here,
And wretchedly I have no fear;
A little while, and I am gone.'

Therewith she rose upon her feet,
　　And totter'd; cold and misery
　　Still made the deep sobs come, till she
At last stretch'd out her fingers sweet,

And caught the great sword in her hand;
　　And, stealing down the silent stair,
　　Barefooted in the morning air,
And only in her smock, did stand

Upright upon the green lawn grass;
　　And hope grew in her as she said:
　　'I have thrown off the white and red,
And pray God it may come to pass

'I meet him; if ten years go by
　　Before I meet him; if, indeed,
　　Meanwhile both soul and body bleed,
Yet there is end of misery.

'And I have hope. He could not come,
　　But I can go to him and show
　　These new things I have got to know,
And make him speak, who has been dumb.'

O Jehane! the red morning sun
　　Changed her white feet to glowing gold,
　　Upon her smock, on crease and fold,
Changed that to gold which had been dun.

O Miles, and Giles, and Isabeau,
　　Fair Ellayne le Violet,
　　Mary, Constance fille de fay!
Where is Jehane du Castel beau?

O big Gervaise ride apace!
   Down to the hard yellow sand,
   Where the water meets the land.
This is Jehane by her face;

Why has she a broken sword?
   Mary! she is slain outright;
   Verily a piteous sight;
Take her up without a word!

Giles and Miles and Gervaise there,
   Ladies' Gard must meet the war;
   Whatsoever knights these are,
Man the walls withouten fear!

Axes to the apple-trees,
   Axes to the aspens tall!
   Barriers without the wall
May be lightly made of these.

O poor shivering Isabeau;
   Poor Ellayne le Violet,
   Bent with fear! we miss to-day
Brave Jehane du Castel beau.

O poor Mary, weeping so!
   Wretched Constance fille de fay!
   Verily we miss today
Fair Jehane du Castel beau.

The apples now grow green and sour
   Upon the mouldering castle-wall,
   Before they ripen there they fall:
There are no banners on the tower.

The draggled swans most eagerly eat
   The green weeds trailing in the moat;
   Inside the rotting leaky boat
You see a slain man's stiffen'd feet.

457   The Haystack in the Floods

HAD she come all the way for this,
To part at last without a kiss?
Yea, had she borne the dirt and rain
That her own eyes might see him slain
Beside the haystack in the floods?

Along the dripping leafless woods,
The stirrup touching either shoe,
She rode astride as troopers do;
With kirtle kilted to her knee,
To which the mud splash'd wretchedly;
And the wet dripp'd from every tree
Upon her head and heavy hair,
And on her eyelids broad and fair;
The tears and rain ran down her face.
By fits and starts they rode apace,
And very often was his place
Far off from her; he had to ride
Ahead, to see what might betide
When the roads cross'd; and sometimes, when
There rose a murmuring from his men,
Had to turn back with promises;
Ah me! she had but little ease;
And often for pure doubt and dread
She sobb'd, made giddy in the head
By the swift riding; while, for cold
Her slender fingers scarce could hold

The wet reins; yea, and scarcely, too,
She felt the foot within her shoe
Against the stirrup; all for this,
To part at last without a kiss
Beside the haystack in the floods.

For when they near'd that old soak'd hay,
They saw across the only way
That Judas, Godmar, and the three
Red running lions dismally
Grinn'd from his pennon, under which,
In one straight line along the ditch,
They counted thirty heads.

                    So then,
While Robert turn'd round to his men,
She saw at once the wretched end,
And, stooping down, tried hard to rend
Her coif the wrong way from her head,
And hid her eyes; while Robert said:
'Nay, love, 'tis scarcely two to one,
At Poictiers where we made them run
So fast—why, sweet my love, good cheer.
The Gascon frontier is so near,
Nought after this.'

                But, 'O,' she said,
'My God! my God! I have to tread
The long way back without you; then
The court at Paris; those six men;
The gratings of the Chatelet;
The swift Seine on some rainy day
Like this, and people standing by,
And laughing, while my weak hands try
To recollect how strong men swim.
All this, or else a life with him,

For which I should be damned at last,
Would God that this next hour were past!'

He answer'd not, but cried his cry,
'St. George for Marny!' cheerily;
And laid his hand upon her rein.
Alas! no man of all his train
Gave back that cheery cry again;
And, while for rage his thumb beat fast
Upon his sword-hilts, some one cast
About his neck a kerchief long,
And bound him.

       Then they went along
To Godmar; who said: 'Now, Jehane,
Your lover's life is on the wane
So fast, that, if this very hour
You yield not as my paramour,
He will not see the rain leave off—
Nay, keep your tongue from gibe and scoff,
Sir Robert, or I slay you now.'

She laid her hand upon her brow,
Then gazed upon the palm, as though
She thought her forehead bled, and—'No,'
She said, and turn'd her head away,
As there were nothing else to say,
And everything were settled: red
Grew Godmar's face from chin to head:
'Jehane, on yonder hill there stands
My castle, guarding well my lands:
What hinders me from taking you,
And doing that I list to do
To your fair wilful body, while
Your knight lies dead?'

                    A wicked smile
Wrinkled her face, her lips grew thin,
A long way out she thrust her chin:
'You know that I should strangle you
While you were sleeping; or bite through
Your throat, by God's help—ah!' she said,
'Lord Jesus, pity your poor maid!
For in such wise they hem me in,
I cannot choose but sin and sin,
Whatever happens: yet I think
They could not make me eat or drink,
And so should I just reach my rest.'
'Nay, if you do not my behest,
O Jehane! though I love you well,'
Said Godmar, 'would I fail to tell
All that I know.' 'Foul lies,' she said.
'Eh? lies my Jehane? by God's head,
At Paris folks would deem them true!
Do you know, Jehane, they cry for you,
"Jehane the brown, Jehane the brown!
Give us Jehane to burn or drown!"—
Eh—gag me Robert!—sweet my friend,
This were indeed a piteous end
For those long fingers, and long feet,
And long neck, and smooth shoulders sweet;
An end that few men would forget
That saw it—So, an hour yet:
Consider, Jehane, which to take
Of life or death!'

                    So, scarce awake,
Dismounting, did she leave that place,
And totter some yards: with her face
Turn'd upward to the sky she lay,

Her head on a wet heap of hay,
And fell asleep: and while she slept,
And did not dream, the minutes crept
Round to the twelve again; but she,
Being waked at last, sigh'd quietly,
And strangely childlike came, and said:
'I will not.' Straightway, Godmar's head,
As though it hung on strong wires, turn'd
Most sharply round, and his face burn'd.

For Robert—both his eyes were dry.
He could not weep, but gloomily
He seem'd to watch the rain; yea, too,
His lips were firm; he tried once more
To touch her lips; she reach'd out, sore
And vain desire so tortured them,
The poor grey lips, and now the hem
Of his sleeve brush'd them.

                    With a start
Up Godmar rose, thrust them apart;
From Robert's throat he loosed the bands
Of silk and mail; with empty hands
Held out, she stood and gazed, and saw,
The long bright blade without a flaw
Glide out from Godmar's sheath, his hand
In Robert's hair; she saw him bend
Back Robert's head; she saw him send
The thin steel down; the blow told well,
Right backward the knight Robert fell,
And moan'd as dogs do, being half dead,
Unwitting, as I deem: so then
Godmar turn'd grinning to his men,
Who ran, some five or six, and beat
His head to pieces at their feet.

Then Godmar turn'd again, and said:
'So, Jehane, the first fitte is read!
Take note, my lady, that your way
Lies backward to the Chatelet!'
She shook her head and gazed awhile
At her cold hands with a rueful smile,
As though this thing had made her mad.

This was the parting that they had
Beside the haystack in the floods.

458   Summer Dawn

PRAY but one prayer for me 'twixt thy closed lips,
    Think but one thought of me up in the stars.
The summer night waneth, the morning light slips,
    Faint and grey 'twixt the leaves of the aspen,
        betwixt the cloud-bars,
That are patiently waiting there for the dawn:
    Patient and colourless, though Heaven's gold
Waits to float through them along with the sun.
Far out in the meadows, above the young corn,
    The heavy elms wait, and restless and cold
The uneasy wind rises; the roses are dun;
Through the long twilight they pray for the dawn,
Round the lone house in the midst of the corn.
    Speak but one word to me over the corn,
    Over the tender, bow'd locks of the corn.

WILLIAM MORRIS

459 AN APOLOGY [for] *THE EARTHLY PARADISE*

Of Heaven or Hell I have no power to sing,
I cannot ease the burden of your fears,
Or make quick-coming death a little thing,
Or bring again the pleasure of past years,
Nor for my words shall ye forget your tears,
Or hope again for aught that I can say,
The idle singer of an empty day.

But rather, when aweary of your mirth,
From full hearts still unsatisfied ye sigh,
And, feeling kindly unto all the earth,
Grudge every minute as it passes by,
Made the more mindful that the sweet days die—
Remember me a little then I pray,
The idle singer of an empty day.

The heavy trouble, the bewildering care
That weighs us down who live and earn our bread,
These idle verses have no power to bear;
So let me sing of names remembered,
Because they, living not, can ne'er be dead,
Or long time take their memory quite away
From us poor singers of an empty day.

Dreamer of dreams, born out of my due time,
Why should I strive to set the crooked straight?
Let it suffice me that my murmuring rhyme
Beats with light wing against the ivory gate,
Telling a tale not too importunate
To those who in the sleepy region stay,
Lulled by the singer of an empty day.

Folk say, a wizard to a northern king
At Christmas-tide such wondrous things did show,
That through one window men beheld the spring,
And through another saw the summer glow,
And through a third the fruited vines a-row,
While still, unheard, but in its wonted way,
Piped the drear wind of that December day.

So with this Earthly Paradise it is,
If ye will read aright, and pardon me,
Who strive to build a shadowy isle of bliss
Midmost the beating of the steely sea,
Where tossed about all hearts of men must be;
Whose ravening monsters mighty men shall slay,
Not the poor singer of an empty day.

460   [The Road of Life]

Two gates unto the road of life there are,
And to the happy youth both seem afar,
Both seem afar; so far the past one seems,
The gate of birth, made dim with many dreams,
Bright with remembered hopes, beset with flowers;
So far it seems he cannot count the hours
That to this midway path have led him on
Where every joy of life now seemeth won—
So far, he thinks not of the other gate,
Within whose shade the ghosts of dead hopes wait
To call upon him as he draws anear,
Despoiled, alone, and dull with many a fear,
'Where is thy work? how little thou hast done,
Where are my friends, why art thou so alone?'

How shall he weigh his life? slow goes the time
The while the fresh dew-sprinkled hill we climb,
Thinking of what shall be the other side,
Slow pass perchance the minutes we abide
On the gained summit, blinking at the sun;
But when the downward journey is begun
No more our feet may loiter, past our ears
Shrieks the harsh wind scarce noted midst our fears,
And battling with the hostile things we meet
Till, ere we know it, our weak shrinking feet
Have brought us to the end and all is done.

461   October

O LOVE, turn from the unchanging sea, and gaze
Down these grey slopes upon the year grown old,
A-dying mid the autumn-scented haze,
That hangeth o'er the hollow in the wold,
Where the wind-bitten ancient elms infold
Grey church, long barn, orchard, and red-roofed stead,
Wrought in dead days for men a long while dead.

    Come down, O love; may not our hands still meet,
Since still we live to-day, forgetting June,
Forgetting May, deeming October sweet—
—O hearken, hearken! through the afternoon,
The grey tower sings a strange old tinkling tune!
Sweet, sweet, and sad, the toiling year's last breath,
Too satiate of life to strive with death.

    And we too—will it not be soft and kind,
That rest from life, from patience and from pain,
That rest from bliss we know not when we find,

That rest from Love which ne'er the end can gain?—
Hark, how the tune swells, that erewhile did wane!
Look up, love!—ah, cling close and never move!
How can I have enough of life and love?

462   A Garden by the Sea

I KNOW a little garden-close,
Set thick with lily and red rose,
Where I would wander if I might
From dewy morn to dewy night,
And have one with me wandering.

And though within it no birds sing,
And though no pillared house is there,
And though the apple-boughs are bare
Of fruit and blossom, would to God
Her feet upon the green grass trod,
And I beheld them as before.

There comes a murmur from the shore,
And in the close two fair streams are,
Drawn from the purple hills afar,
Drawn down unto the restless sea:
Dark hills whose heath-bloom feeds no bee,
Dark shore no ship has ever seen,
Tormented by the billows green
Whose murmur comes unceasingly
Unto the place for which I cry.
For which I cry both day and night,
For which I let slip all delight,
Whereby I grow both deaf and blind,
Careless to win, unskilled to find,
And quick to lose what all men men seek.

Yet tottering as I am and weak,
Still have I left a little breath
To seek within the jaws of death
An entrance to that happy place,
To seek the unforgotten face,
Once seen, once kissed, once reft from me
Anigh the murmuring of the sea.

463   The Message of the March Wind

FAIR now is the springtide, now earth lies beholding
    With the eyes of a lover the face of the sun;
Long lasteth the daylight, and hope is enfolding
    The green-growing acres with increase begun.

Now sweet, sweet it is through the land to be straying
    Mid the birds and the blossoms and the beasts of the field;
Love mingles with love, and no evil is weighing
    On thy heart or mine, where all sorrow is healed.

From township to township, o'er down and by tillage
    Far, far have we wandered and long was the day,
But now cometh eve at the end of the village,
    Where over the grey wall the church riseth grey.

There is wind in the twilight; in the white road before us
    The straw from the ox-yard is blowing about;
The moon's rim is rising, a star glitters o'er us,
    And the vane on the spire-top is swinging in doubt.

Down there dips the highway, toward the bridge crossing over
    The brook that runs on to the Thames and the sea.
Draw closer, my sweet, we are lover and lover;
    This eve art thou given to gladness and me.

789

Shall we be glad always? Come closer and hearken:
   Three fields further on, as they told me down there,
When the young moon has set, if the March sky should darken,
   We might see from the hill-top the great city's glare.

Hark, the wind in the elm-boughs! From London it bloweth,
   And telling of gold, and of hope and unrest;
Of power that helps not; of wisdom that knoweth,
   But teacheth not aught of the worst and the best.

Of the rich men it telleth, and strange is the story
   How they have, and they hanker, and grip far and wide;
And they live and they die, and the earth and its glory
   Has been but a burden they scarce might abide.

Hark! the March wind again of a people is telling;
   Of the life that they live there, so haggard and grim,
That if we and our love amidst them had been dwelling
   My fondness had faltered, thy beauty grown dim.

This land we have loved in our love and our leisure
   For them hangs in heaven, high out of their reach;
The wide hills o'er the sea-plain for them have no pleasure,
   The grey homes of their fathers no story to teach.

The singers have sung and the builders have builded,
   The painters have fashioned their tales of delight;
For what and for whom hath the world's book been gilded,
   When all is for these but the blackness of night?

How long and for what is their patience abiding?
   How oft and how oft shall their story be told,
While the hope that none seeketh in darkness is hiding
   And in grief and in sorrow the world groweth old?

Come back to the inn, love, and the lights and the fire,
   And the fiddler's old tune and the shuffling of feet;
For there in a while shall be rest and desire,
   And there shall the morrow's uprising be sweet.

Yet, love, as we wend the wind bloweth behind us
   And beareth the last tale it telleth to-night,
How here in the springtide the message shall find us;
   For the hope that none seeketh is coming to light.

Like the seed of midwinter, unheeded, unperished,
   Like the autumn-sown wheat 'neath the snow lying green,
Like the love that o'ertook us, unawares and uncherished,
   Like the babe 'neath thy girdle that groweth unseen,

So the hope of the people now buddeth and groweth—
   Rest fadeth before it, and blindness and fear;
It biddeth us learn all the wisdom it knoweth;
   It hath found us and held us, and biddeth us hear:

For it beareth the message: 'Rise up on the morrow
   And go on your ways toward the doubt and the strife;
Join hope to our hope and blend sorrow with sorrow,
   And seek for men's love in the short days of life.'

But lo, the old inn, and the lights and the fire,
   And the fiddler's old tune and the shuffling of feet;
Soon for us shall be quiet and rest and desire,
   And tomorrow's uprising to deeds shall be sweet.

JOHN LEICESTER WARREN,
LORD DE TABLEY

The Churchyard on the Sands

My Love lies in the gates of foam,
    The last dear wreck of shore;
The naked sea-marsh binds her home,
    The sand her chamber door.

The gray gull flaps the written stones,
    The ox-birds chase the tide;
And near that narrow field of bones
    Great ships at anchor ride.

Black piers with crust of dripping green,
    One foreland, like a hand,
O'er intervals of grass between
    Dim lonely dunes of sand.

A church of silent weathered looks,
    A breezy reddish tower,
A yard whose mounded resting-nooks
    Are tinged with sorrel flower.

In peace the swallow's eggs are laid
    Along the belfry walls;
The tempest does not reach her shade,
    The rain her silent halls.

But sails are sweet in summer sky,
    The lark throws down a lay;
The long salt levels steam and dry,
    The cloud-heart melts away.

But patches of the sea-pink shine,
  The pied crows poise and come;
The mallow hangs, the bindweeds twine,
  Where her sweet lips are dumb.

The passion of the wave is mute;
  No sound or ocean shock;
No music save the rilling flute
  That marks the curlew flock.

But yonder when the wind is keen,
  And rainy air is clear,
The merchant city's spires are seen,
  The toil of men grows near.

Along the coast-way grind the wheels
  Of endless carts of coal;
And on the sides of giant keels
  The shipyard hammers roll.

The world creeps here upon the shout,
  And stirs my heart in pain;
The mist descends and blots it out,
  And I am strong again.

Strong and alone, my dove, with thee;
  And, tho' mine eyes be wet,
There 's nothing in the world to me
  So dear as my regret.

I would not change my sorrow, sweet,
  For others' nuptial hours;
I love the daisies at thy feet
  More than their orange flowers.

My hand alone shall tend thy tomb
From leaf-bud to leaf-fall,
And wreathe around each season's bloom
Till autumn ruins all.

Let snowdrops, early in the year,
Droop o'er her silent breast;
And bid the later cowslip rear
The amber of its crest.

Come hither, linnets tufted-red,
Drift by, O wailing tern;
Set pure vale lilies at her head,
At her feet lady-fern.

Grow, samphire, at the tidal brink,
Wave, pansies of the shore,
To whisper how alone I think
Of her for evermore.

Bring blue sea-hollies thorny, keen,
Long lavender in flower;
Gray wormwood like a hoary queen,
Stanch mullein like a tower.

O sea-wall mounded long and low
Let iron bounds be thine;
Nor let the salt wave overflow
That breast I held divine.

Nor float its sea-weed to her hair,
Nor dim her eyes with sands:
No fluted cockle burrow where
Sleep folds her patient hands.

Tho' thy crest feel the wild sea's breath,
　Tho' tide-weight tear thy root,
Oh, guard the treasure house, where Death
　Has bound my darling mute.

Tho' cold her pale lips to reward
　With love's own mysteries,
Ah, rob no daisy from her sward,
　Rough gale of eastern seas!

Ah, render sere no silent bent,
　That by her head-stone waves;
Let noon and golden summer blent
　Pervade these ocean graves.

And, ah, dear heart, in thy still nest,
　Resign this earth of woes,
Forget the ardours of the west,
　Neglect the morning glows.

Sleep, and forget all things but one,
　Heard in each wave of sea,—
How lonely all the years will run
　Until I rest by thee.

ALGERNON CHARLES SWINBURNE

465　　　　　A Leave-taking

LET us go hence, my songs; she will not hear.
Let us go hence together without fear;
Keep silence now, for singing-time is over,
And over all old things and all things dear.
She loves not you nor me as all we love her.
Yea, though we sang as angels in her ear,
　　She would not hear.

Let us rise up and part; she will not know.
Let us go seaward as the great winds go,
Full of blown sand and foam, what help is here?
There is no help, for all these things are so,
And all the world is bitter as a tear.
And how these things are, though ye strove to show,
  She would not know.

Let us go home and hence; she will not weep.
We gave love many dreams and days to keep,
Flowers without scent, and fruits that would not grow,
Saying 'If thou wilt, thrust in thy sickle and reap.'
All is reaped now; no grass is left to mow;
And we that sowed, though all we fell on sleep,
  She would not weep.

Let us go hence and rest; she will not love.
She shall not hear us if we sing hereof,
Nor see love's ways, how sore they are and steep.
Come hence, let be, lie still; it is enough.
Love is a barren sea, bitter and deep;
And though she saw all heaven in flower above,
  She would not love.

Let us give up, go down; she will not care.
Though all the stars made gold of all the air,
And the sea moving saw before it move
One moon-flower making all the foam-flowers fair;
Though all those waves went over us, and drove
Deep down the stifling lips and drowning hair,
  She would not care.

Let us go hence, go hence; she will not see.
Sing all once more together; surely she,
She too, remembering days and words that were,
Will turn a little toward us, sighing; but we,
We are hence, we are gone, as though we had not been there.
Nay, and though all men seeing had pity on me,
      She would not see.

466   Hymn to Proserpine

AFTER THE PROCLAMATION IN ROME OF THE CHRISTIAN FAITH

Vicisti, Galilæe

I HAVE lived enough, having seen one thing, that love hath an end;
Goddess and maiden and queen, be near me now and befriend.
Thou art more than the day or the morrow, the seasons that
    laugh or that weep;
For these give joy and sorrow; but thou, Proserpina, sleep.
Sweet is the treading of wine, and sweet the feet of the dove;
But a goodlier gift is thine than foam of the grapes or love.
Yea, is not even Apollo, with hair and harpstring of gold,
A bitter God to follow, a beautiful God to behold?
I am sick of singing: the bays burn deep and chafe: I am fain
To rest a little from praise and grievous pleasure and pain.
For the Gods we know not of, who give us our daily breath,
We know they are cruel as love or life, and lovely as death.
O Gods dethroned and deceased, cast forth, wiped out in a day!
From your wrath is the world released, redeemed from your
    chains, men say.
New Gods are crowned in the city; their flowers have broken
    your rods;
They are merciful, clothed with pity, the young compassionate
    Gods.

But for me their new device is barren, the days are bare;
Things long past over suffice, and men forgotten that were.
Time and the Gods are at strife; ye dwell in the midst thereof,
Draining a little life from the barren breasts of love.
I say to you, cease, take rest; yea, I say to you all, be at peace
Till the bitter milk of her breast and the barren bosom shall cease.
Wilt thou yet take all, Galilean? but these thou shalt not take,
The laurel, the palms and the pæan, the breasts of the nymphs in
    the brake;
Breasts more soft than a dove's, that tremble with tenderer
    breath;
And all the wings of the Loves, and all the joy before death;
All the feet of the hours that sound as a single lyre,
Dropped and deep in the flowers, with strings that flicker like
    fire.
More than these wilt thou give, things fairer than all these things?
Nay, for a little we live, and life hath mutable wings.
A little while and we die; shall life not thrive as it may?
For no man under the sky lives twice, outliving his day.
And grief is a grievous thing, and a man hath enough of his tears:
Why should he labour, and bring fresh grief to blacken his years?
Thou hast conquered, O pale Galilean; the world has grown grey
    from thy breath;
We have drunken of things Lethean, and fed on the fullness of
    death.
Laurel is green for a season, and love is sweet for a day;
But love grows bitter with treason, and laurel outlives not May.
Sleep, shall we sleep after all? for the world is not sweet in the end;
For the old faiths loosen and fall, the new years ruin and rend.
Fate is a sea without shore, and the soul is a rock that abides;
But her ears are vexed with the roar and her face with the foam of
    the tides.
O lips that the live blood faints in, the leavings of racks and rods!
O ghastly glories of saints, dead limbs of gibbeted Gods!

Though all men abase them before you in spirit, and all knees bend,
I kneel not neither adore you, but standing, look to the end.
All delicate days and pleasant, all spirits and sorrows are cast
Far out with the foam of the present that sweeps to the surf of the
    past:
Where beyond the extreme sea-wall, and between the remote sea-
    gates,
Waste water washes, and tall ships founder, and deep death waits:
Where, mighty with deepening sides, clad about with the seas as
    with wings,
And impelled of invisible tides, and fulfilled of unspeakable things,
White-eyed and poisonous-finned, shark-toothed and serpentine-
    curled,
Rolls, under the whitening wind of the future, the wave of the
    world.
The depths stand naked in sunder behind it, the storms flee away;
In the hollow before it the thunder is taken and snared as a prey;
In its sides is the north-wind bound; and its salt is of all men's
    tears:
With light of ruin, and sound of changes, and pulse of years:
With travail of day after day, and with trouble of hour upon hour;
And bitter as blood is the spray; and the crests are as fangs that
    devour:
And its vapour and storm of its steam as the sighing of spirits to be;
And its noise as the noise in a dream; and its depth as the roots of
    the sea:
And the height of its heads as the height of the utmost stars of the
    air:
And the ends of the earth at the might thereof tremble, and time
    is made bare.
Will ye bridle the deep sea with reins, will ye chasten the high sea
    with rods?
Will ye take her to chain her with chains, who is older than all ye
    Gods?

All ye as a wind shall go by, as a fire shall ye pass and be past;

Ye are Gods, and behold, ye shall die, and the waves be upon you
at last.

In the darkness of time, in the deeps of the years, in the changes of
things,

Ye shall sleep as a slain man sleeps, and the world shall forget you
for kings.

Though the feet of thine high priests tread where thy lords and our
forefathers trod,

Though these that were Gods are dead, and thou being dead art a
God,

Though before thee the throned Cytherean be fallen, and hidden
her head,

Yet thy kingdom shall pass, Galilean, thy dead shall go down to
thee dead.

Of the maiden thy mother men sing as a goddess with grace clad
around;

Thou art throned where another was king; where another was
queen she is crowned.

Yea, once we had sight of another: but now she is queen, say these.

Not as thine, not as thine was our mother, a blossom of flowering
seas,

Clothed round with the world's desire as with raiment, and fair
as the foam,

And fleeter than kindled fire, and a goddess, and mother of Rome.

For thine came pale and a maiden, and sister to sorrow; but ours,

Her deep hair heavily laden with odour and colour of flowers,

White rose of the rose-white water, a silver splendour, a flame,

Bent down unto us that besought her, and earth grew sweet with
her name.

For thine came weeping, a slave among slaves, and rejected; but
she

Came flushed from the full-flushed wave, and imperial, her foot
on the sea.

And the wonderful waters knew her, the winds and the viewless ways.

And the roses grew rosier, and bluer the sea-blue stream of the bays.

Ye are fallen, our lords, by what token? we wist that ye should not fall.

Ye were all so fair that are broken; and one more fair than ye all.

But I turn to her still, having seen she shall surely abide in the end;

Goddess and maiden and queen, be near me now and befriend.

O daughter of earth, of my mother, her crown and blossom of birth,

I am also, I also, thy brother; I go as I came unto earth.

In the night where thine eyes are as moons are in heaven, the night where thou art,

Where the silence is more than all tunes, where sleep overflows from the heart,

Where the poppies are sweet as the rose in our world, and the red rose is white,

And the wind falls faint as it blows with the fume of the flowers of the night,

And the murmur of spirits that sleep in the shadow of Gods from afar

Grows dim in thine ears and deep as the deep dim soul of a star,

In the sweet low light of thy face, under heavens untrod by the sun,

Let my soul with their souls find place, and forget what is done and undone.

Thou art more than the Gods who number the days of our temporal breath;

For these give labour and slumber; but thou, Proserpina, death.

Therefore now at thy feet I abide for a season in silence. I know

I shall die as my fathers died, and sleep as they sleep; even so.

For the glass of the years is brittle wherein we gaze for a span;

A little soul for a little bears up this corpse which is man.[1]
So long I endure, no longer; and laugh not again, neither weep.
For there is no God found stronger than death; and death is a
    sleep.

          [1] ψυχάριον εἶ βαστάζον νεκρόν. Epictetus.

467   The Garden of Proserpine

    HERE, where the world is quiet;
      Here, where all trouble seems
    Dead winds' and spent waves' riot
      In doubtful dreams of dreams;
    I watch the green field growing
    For reaping folk and sowing,
    For harvest-time and mowing,
      A sleepy world of streams.

    I am tired of tears and laughter,
      And men that laugh and weep;
    Of what may come hereafter
      For men that sow to reap:
    I am weary of days and hours,
    Blown buds of barren flowers,
    Desires and dreams and powers
      And everything but sleep.

    Here life has death for neighbour,
      And far from eye or ear
    Wan waves and wet winds labour,
      Weak ships and spirits steer;
    They drive adrift, and whither
    They wot not who make thither;
    But no such winds blow hither,
      And no such things grow here.

No growth of moor or coppice,
   No heather-flower or vine,
But bloomless buds of poppies,
   Green grapes of Proserpine,
Pale beds of blowing rushes
Where no leaf blooms or blushes
Save this whereout she crushes
   For dead men deadly wine.

Pale, without name or number,
   In fruitless fields of corn,
They bow themselves and slumber
   All night till light is born;
And like a soul belated,
In hell and heaven unmated,
By cloud and mist abated
   Comes out of darkness morn.

Though one were strong as seven,
   He too with death shall dwell,
Nor wake with wings in heaven,
   Nor weep for pains in hell;
Though one were fair as roses,
His beauty clouds and closes;
And well though love reposes,
   In the end it is not well.

Pale, beyond porch and portal,
   Crowned with calm leaves, she stands
Who gathers all things mortal
   With cold immortal hands;
Her languid lips are sweeter
Than love's who fears to greet her
To men that mix and meet her
   From many times and lands.

She waits for each and other,
   She waits for all men born;
Forgets the earth her mother,
   The life of fruits and corn;
And spring and seed and swallow
Take wing for her and follow
Where summer song rings hollow
   And flowers are put to scorn.

There go the loves that wither,
   The old loves with wearier wings;
And all dead years draw thither,
   And all disastrous things;
Dead dreams of days forsaken,
Blind buds that snows have shaken,
Wild leaves that winds have taken,
   Red strays of ruined springs.

We are not sure of sorrow,
   And joy was never sure;
To-day will die to-morrow;
   Time stoops to no man's lure;
And love, grown faint and fretful,
With lips but half regretful
Sighs, and with eyes forgetful
   Weeps that no loves endure.

From too much love of living,
   From hope and fear set free,
We thank with brief thanksgiving
   Whatever gods may be
That no life lives for ever;
That dead men rise up never;
That even the weariest river
   Winds somewhere safe to sea.

Then star nor sun shall waken,
 Nor any change of light:
Nor sound of waters shaken,
 Nor any sound or sight:
Nor wintry leaves nor vernal,
Nor days nor things diurnal;
Only the sleep eternal
 In an eternal night.

468   Hesperia

OUT of the golden remote wild west where the sea without shore
 is,
 Full of the sunset, and sad, if at all, with the fulness of joy,
As a wind sets in with the autumn that blows from the region of
 stories,
 Blows with a perfume of songs and of memories beloved from a
 boy,
Blows from the capes of the past oversea to the bays of the
 present,
 Filled as with shadow of sound with the pulse of invisible feet,
Far out to the shallows and straits of the future, by rough ways or
 pleasant,
 Is it thither the wind's wings beat? is it hither to me, O my
 sweet?
For thee, in the stream of the deep tide-wind blowing in with the
 water,
 Thee I behold as a bird borne in with the wind from the west,
Straight from the sunset, across white waves whence rose as a
 daughter
 Venus thy mother, in years when the world was a water at rest.

Out of the distance of dreams, as a dream that abides after slumber,
    Strayed from the fugitive flock of the night, when the moon
        overhead
Wanes in the wan waste heights of the heaven, and stars without
    number
    Die without sound, and are spent like lamps that are burnt by
        the dead,
Comes back to me, stays by me, lulls me with touch of forgotten
    caresses,
    One warm dream clad about with a fire of life that endures;
The delight of thy face, and the sound of thy feet, and the wind
    of thy tresses,
    And all of a man that regrets, and all of a maid that allures.
But thy bosom is warm for my face and profound as a manifold
    flower,
    Thy silence as music, thy voice as an odour that fades in a flame;
Not a dream, not a dream is the kiss of thy mouth, and the
    bountiful hour
    That makes me forget what was sin, and would make me forget
        were it shame.
Thine eyes that are quiet, thine hands that are tender, thy lips that
    are loving,
    Comfort and cool me as dew in the dawn of a moon like a
        dream;
And my heart yearns baffled and blind, moved vainly toward thee,
    and moving
    As the refluent seaweed moves in the languid exuberant stream,
Fair as a rose is on earth, as a rose under water in prison,
    That stretches and swings to the slow passionate pulse of the
        sea,
Closed up from the air and the sun, but alive, as a ghost rearisen,
    Pale as the love that revives as a ghost rearisen in me.
From the bountiful infinite west, from the happy memorial places
    Full of the stately repose and the lordly delight of the dead,

Where the fortunate islands are lit with the light of ineffable faces,
  And the sound of a sea without wind is about them, and sunset
    is red,
Come back to redeem and release me from love that recalls and
    represses,
  That cleaves to my flesh as a flame, till the serpent has eaten his
    fill;
From the bitter delights of the dark, and the feverish, the furtive
    caresses
  That murder the youth in a man or ever his heart have its will.
Thy lips cannot laugh and thine eyes cannot weep; thou art pale
    as a rose is,
  Paler and sweeter than leaves that cover the blush of the bud;
And the heart of the flower is compassion, and pity the core it
    encloses,
  Pity, not love, that is born of the breath and decays with the
    blood.
As the cross that a wild nun clasps till the edge of it bruises her
    bosom,
  So love wounds as we grasp it, and blackens and burns as a flame;
I have loved overmuch in my life; when the live bud bursts with
    the blossom,
  Bitter as ashes or tears is the fruit, and the wine thereof shame.
As a heart that its anguish divides is the green bud cloven asunder;
  As the blood of a man self-slain is the flush of the leaves that
    allure;
And the perfume as poison and wine to the brain, a delight and a
    wonder;
  And the thorns are too sharp for a boy, too slight for a man, to
    endure.
Too soon did I love it, and lost love's rose; and I cared not for
    glory's:
  Only the blossoms of sleep and of pleasure were mixed in my
    hair.

Was it myrtle or poppy thy garland was woven with, O my
Dolores?
Was it pallor of slumber, or blush as of blood, that I found in
thee fair?
For desire is a respite from love, and the flesh not the heart is her
fuel;
She was sweet to me once, who am fled and escaped from the
rage of her reign;
Who behold as of old time at hand as I turn, with her mouth
growing cruel,
And flushed as with wine with the blood of her lovers, Our
Lady of Pain.
Low down where the thicket is thicker with thorns than with
leaves in the summer,
In the brake is a gleaming of eyes and a hissing of tongues that
I knew;
And the lithe long throats of her snakes reach round her, their
mouths overcome her,
And her lips grow cool with their foam, made moist as a desert
with dew.
With the thirst and the hunger of lust though her beautiful lips
be so bitter,
With the cold foul foam of the snakes they soften and redden
and smile;
And her fierce mouth sweetens, her eyes wax wide and her eye-
lashes glitter,
And she laughs with a savour of blood in her face, and a savour
of guile.
She laughs, and her hands reach hither, her hair blows hither and
hisses,
As a low-lit flame in a wind, back-blown till it shudder and leap;
Let her lips not again lay hold on my soul, nor her poisonous kisses,
To consume it alive and divide from thy bosom, Our Lady of
Sleep.

Ah daughter of sunset and slumber, if now it return into prison,
    Who shall redeem it anew? but we, if thou wilt, let us fly;
Let us take to us, now that the white skies thrill with a moon
    unarisen,
    Swift horses of fear or of love, take flight and depart and not die.
They are swifter than dreams, they are stronger than death; there
    is none that hath ridden,
    None that shall ride in the dim strange ways of his life as we ride;
By the meadows of memory, the highlands of hope, and the
    shore that is hidden,
    Where life breaks loud and unseen, a sonorous invisible tide;
By the sands where sorrow has trodden, the salt pools bitter and
    sterile,
    By the thundering reef and the low sea-wall and the channel of
    years,
Our wild steeds press on the night, strain hard through pleasure
    and peril,
    Labour and listen and pant not or pause for the peril that nears;
And the sound of them trampling the way cleaves night as an
    arrow asunder,
    And slow by the sand-hill and swift by the down with its
    glimpses of grass,
Sudden and steady the music, as eight hoofs trample and thunder,
    Rings in the ear of the low blind wind of the night as we pass;
Shrill shrieks in our faces the blind bland air that was mute as a
    maiden,
    Stung into storm by the speed of our passage, and deaf where
    we past;
And our spirits too burn as we bound, thine holy but mine heavy-
    laden,
    As we burn with the fire of our flight; ah love, shall we win at
    the last?

469   The Sundew

A LITTLE marsh-plant, yellow green,
And pricked at lip with tender red.
Tread close, and either way you tread
Some faint black water jets between
Lest you should bruise the curious head.

A live thing maybe; who shall know?
The summer knows and suffers it;
For the cool moss is thick and sweet
Each side, and saves the blossom so
That it lives out the long June heat.

The deep scent of the heather burns
About it; breathless though it be,
Bow down and worship; more than we
Is the least flower whose life returns,
Least weed renascent in the sea.

We are vexed and cumbered in earth's sight
With wants, with many memories;
These see their mother what she is,
Glad-growing, till August leave more bright
The apple-coloured cranberries.

Wind blows and bleaches the strong grass,
Blown all one way to shelter it
From trample of strayed kine, with feet
Felt heavier than the moorhen was,
Strayed up past patches of wild wheat.

You call it sundew; how it grows,
If with its colour it have breath,
If life taste sweet to it, if death
Pain its soft petal, no man knows:
Man has no sight or sense that saith.

My sundew, grown of gentle days,
In these green miles the spring begun
Thy growth ere April had half done
With the soft secret of her ways
Or June made ready for the sun.

O red-lipped mouth of marsh-flower,
I have a secret halved with thee.
The name that is love's name to me
Thou knowest, and the face of her
Who is my festival to see.

The hard sun, as thy petals knew,
Coloured the heavy moss-water:
Thou wert not worth green midsummer
Nor fit to live to August blue,
O sundew, not remembering her.

470   A Forsaken Garden

IN a coign of the cliff between lowland and highland,
    At the sea-down's edge between windward and lee,
Walled round with rocks as an inland island,
    The ghost of a garden fronts the sea.
A girdle of brushwood and thorn encloses
    The steep square slope of the blossomless bed
Where the weeds that grew green from the graves of its roses
                Now lie dead.

The fields fall southward, abrupt and broken,
   To the low last edge of the long lone land.
If a step should sound or a word be spoken,
   Would a ghost not rise at the strange guest's hand?
So long have the grey bare walks lain guestless,
   Through branches and briars if a man make way,
He shall find no life but the sea-wind's, restless
       Night and day.

The dense hard passage is blind and stifled
   That crawls by a track none turn to climb
To the strait waste place that the years have rifled
   Of all but the thorns that are touched not of time.
The thorns he spares when the rose is taken;
   The rocks are left when he wastes the plain.
The wind that wanders, the weeds wind-shaken,
       These remain.

Not a flower to be prest of the foot that falls not;
   As the heart of a dead man the seed-plots are dry;
From the thicket of thorns whence the nightingale calls **not,**
   Could she call, there were never a rose to reply.
Over the meadows that blossom and wither
   Rings but the note of a sea-bird's song;
Only the sun and the rain come hither
       All year long.

The sun burns sere and the rain dishevels
   One gaunt black blossom of scentless breath.
Only the wind here hovers and revels
   In a round where life seems barren as death.
Here there was laughing of old, there was weeping,
   Haply, of lovers none ever will know,
Whose eyes went seaward a hundred sleeping
       Years ago.

Heart handfast in heart as they stood, 'Look thither,'
   Did he whisper? 'look forth from the flowers to the sea;
For the foam-flowers endure when the rose-blossoms wither,
   And men that love lightly may die—but we?'
And the same wind sang and the same waves whitened,
   And or ever the garden's last petals were shed,
In the lips that had whispered, the eyes that had lightened,
       Love was dead.

Or they loved their life through, and then went whither?
   And were one to the end—but what end who knows?
Love deep as the sea as a rose must wither,
   As the rose-red seaweed that mocks the rose.
Shall the dead take thought for the dead to love them?
   What love was ever as deep as a grave?
They are loveless now as the grass above them
       Or the wave.

All are at one now, roses and lovers,
   Not known of the cliffs and the fields and the sea.
Not a breath of the time that has been hovers
   In the air now soft with a summer to be.
Not a breath shall there sweeten the seasons hereafter
   Of the flowers or the lovers that laugh now or weep,
When as they that are free now of weeping and laughter
       We shall sleep.

Here death may deal not again for ever;
   Here change may come not till all change end.
From the graves they have made they shall rise up never,
   Who have left nought living to ravage and rend.
Earth, stones, and thorns of the wild ground growing,
   While the sun and the rain live, these shall be;
Till a last wind's breath upon all these blowing
       Roll the sea.

Till the slow sea rise and the sheer cliff crumble,
    Till terrace and meadow the deep gulfs drink,
Till the strength of the waves of the high tides humble
    The fields that lessen, the rocks that shrink,
Here now in his triumph where all things falter,
    Stretched out on the spoils that his own hand spread,
As a god self-slain on his own strange altar,
        Death lies dead.

471   Ave Atque Vale

IN MEMORY OF CHARLES BAUDELAIRE

> Nous devrions pourtant lui porter quelques fleurs;
> Les morts, les pauvres morts, ont de grandes douleurs,
> Et quand Octobre souffle, émondeur des vieux arbres,
> Son vent mélancolique à l'entour de leurs marbres,
> Certe, ils doivent trouver les vivants bien ingrats.
>
> *Les Fleurs du Mal*

I

SHALL I strew on thee rose or rue or laurel,
    Brother, on this that was the veil of thee?
    Or quiet sea-flower moulded by the sea,
Or simplest growth of meadow-sweet or sorrel,
    Such as the summer-sleepy Dryads weave,
    Waked up by snow-soft sudden rains at eve?
Or wilt thou rather, as on earth before,
    Half-faded fiery blossoms, pale with heat
    And full of bitter summer, but more sweet
To thee than gleanings of a northern shore
    Trod by no tropic feet?

II

For always thee the fervid languid glories
    Allured of heavier suns in mightier skies;
    Thine ears knew all the wandering watery sighs
Where the sea sobs round Lesbian promontories,
    The barren kiss of piteous wave to wave
    That knows not where is that Leucadian grave
Which hides too deep the supreme head of song.
    Ah, salt and sterile as her kisses were,
    The wild sea winds her and the green gulfs bear
Hither and thither, and vex and work her wrong,
    Blind gods that cannot spare.

III

Thou sawest, in thine old singing season, brother,
    Secrets and sorrows unbeheld of us:
    Fierce loves, and lovely leaf-buds poisonous,
Bare to thy subtler eye, but for none other
    Blowing by night in some unbreathed-in clime;
    The hidden harvest of luxurious time,
Sin without shape, and pleasure without speech;
    And where strange dreams in a tumultuous sleep
    Make the shut eyes of stricken spirits weep;
And with each face thou sawest the shadow on each,
    Seeing as men sow men reap.

IV

O sleepless heart and sombre soul unsleeping,
    That were athirst for sleep and no more life
    And no more love, for peace and no more strife!
Now the dim gods of death have in their keeping
    Spirit and body and all the springs of song,
    Is it well now where love can do no wrong,

Where stingless pleasure has no foam or fang
    Behind the unopening closure of her lips?
    Is it not well where soul from body slips
And flesh from bone divides without a pang
    As dew from flower-bell drips?

V

It is enough; the end and the beginning
    Are one thing to thee, who art past the end.
    O hand unclasped of unbeholden friend,
For thee no fruits to pluck, no palms for winning,
    No triumph and no labour and no lust,
    Only dead yew-leaves and a little dust.
O quiet eyes wherein the light saith nought,
    Whereto the day is dumb, nor any night
    With obscure finger silences your sight,
Nor in your speech the sudden soul speaks thought,
    Sleep, and have sleep for light.

VI

Now all strange hours and all strange loves are over,
    Dreams and desires and sombre songs and sweet,
    Hast thou found place at the great knees and feet
Of some pale Titan-woman like a lover,
    Such as thy vision here solicited,
    Under the shadow of her fair vast head,
The deep division of prodigious breasts,
    The solemn slope of mighty limbs asleep,
    The weight of awful tresses that still keep
The savour and shade of old-world pine-forests
    Where the wet hill-winds weep?

VII

Hast thou found any likeness for thy vision?
    A gardener of strange flowers, what bud, what bloom,
    Hast thou found sown, what gathered in the gloom?
What of despair, of rapture, of derision,
    What of life is there, what of ill or good?
    Are the fruits grey like dust or bright like blood?
Does the dim ground grow any seed of ours,
    The faint fields quicken any terrene root,
    In low lands where the sun and moon are mute
And all the stars keep silence? Are there flowers
    At all, or any fruit?

VIII

Alas, but though my flying song flies after,
    O sweet strange elder singer, thy more fleet
    Singing, and footprints of thy fleeter feet,
Some dim derision of mysterious laughter
    From the blind tongueless warders of the dead,
    Some gainless glimpse of Proserpine's veiled head,
Some little sound of unregarded tears
    Wept by effaced unprofitable eyes,
    And from pale mouths some cadence of dead sighs—
These only, these the hearkening spirit hears,
    Sees only such things rise.

IX

Thou art far too far for wings of words to follow,
    Far too far off for thought or any prayer.
    What ails us with thee, who art wind and air?
What ails us gazing where all seen is hollow?
    Yet with some fancy, yet with some desire,
    Dreams pursue death as winds a flying fire,

Our dreams pursue our dead and do not find.
    Still, and more swift than they, the thin flame flies,
    The low light fails us in elusive skies,
Still the foiled earnest ear is deaf, and blind
    Are still the eluded eyes.

X

Not thee, O never thee, in all time's changes,
    Not thee, but this the sound of thy sad soul,
    The shadow of thy swift spirit, this shut scroll
I lay my hand on, and not death estranges
    My spirit from communion of thy song—
    These memories and these melodies that throng
Veiled porches of a Muse funereal—
    These I salute, these touch, these clasp and fold
    As though a hand were in my hand to hold,
Or through mine ears a mourning musical
    Of many mourners rolled.

XI

I among these, I also, in such station
    As when the pyre was charred, and piled the sods,
    And offering to the dead made, and their gods,
The old mourners had, standing to make libation,
    I stand, and to the gods and to the dead
    Do reverence without prayer or praise, and shed
Offering to these unknown, the gods of gloom,
    And what of honey and spice my seedlands bear,
    And what I may of fruits in this chilled air,
And lay, Orestes-like, across the tomb
    A curl of severed hair.

XII

But by no hand nor any treason stricken,
    Not like the low-lying head of Him, the King,
    The flame that made of Troy a ruinous thing,
Thou liest, and on this dust no tears could quicken
    There fall no tears like theirs that all men hear
    Fall tear by sweet imperishable tear
Down the opening leaves of holy poets' pages.
    Thee not Orestes, not Electra mourns;
    But bending us-ward with memorial urns
The most high Muses that fulfil all ages
    Weep, and our God's heart yearns.

XIII

For, sparing of his sacred strength, not often
    Among us darkling here the lord of light
    Makes manifest his music and his might
In hearts that open and in lips that soften
    With the soft flame and heat of songs that shine.
    Thy lips indeed he touched with bitter wine,
And nourished them indeed with bitter bread;
    Yet surely from his hand thy soul's food came,
    The fire that scarred thy spirit at his flame
Was lighted, and thine hungering heart he fed
    Who feeds our hearts with fame.

XIV

Therefore he too now at thy soul's sunsetting,
    God of all suns and songs, he too bends down
    To mix his laurel with thy cypress crown,
And save thy dust from blame and from forgetting.
    Therefore he too, seeing all thou wert and art,
    Compassionate, with sad and sacred heart,

Mourns thee of many his children the last dead,
    And hallows with strange tears and alien sighs
    Thine unmelodious mouth and sunless eyes,
And over thine irrevocable head
    Sheds light from the under skies.

XV

And one weeps with him in the ways Lethean,
    And stains with tears her changing bosom chill:
    That obscure Venus of the hollow hill,
That thing transformed which was the Cytherean,
    With lips that lost their Grecian laugh divine
    Long since, and face no more called Erycine;
A ghost, a bitter and luxurious god.
    Thee also with fair flesh and singing spell
    Did she, a sad and second prey, compel
Into the footless places once more trod,
    And shadows hot from hell.

XVI

And now no sacred staff shall break in blossom,
    No choral salutation lure to light
    A spirit sick with perfume and sweet night
And love's tired eyes and hands and barren bosom.
    There is no help for these things; none to mend
    And none to mar; not all our songs, O friend,
Will make death clear or make life durable.
    Howbeit with rose and ivy and wild vine
    And with wild notes about this dust of thine
At least I fill the place where white dreams dwell
    And wreathe an unseen shrine.

XVII

Sleep; and if life was bitter to thee, pardon,
    If sweet, give thanks; thou hast no more to live;
    And to give thanks is good, and to forgive.
Out of the mystic and the mournful garden
    Where all day through thine hands in barren braid
    Wove the sick flowers of secrecy and shade,
Green buds of sorrow and sin, and remnants grey,
    Sweet-smelling, pale with poison, sanguine-hearted,
    Passions that sprang from sleep and thoughts that started,
Shall death not bring us all as thee one day
    Among the days departed?

XVIII

For thee, O now a silent soul, my brother,
    Take at my hands this garland, and farewell.
    Thin is the leaf, and chill the wintry smell,
And chill the solemn earth, a fatal mother,
    With sadder than the Niobean womb,
    And in the hollow of her breasts a tomb.
Content thee, howsoe'er, whose days are done;
    There lies not any troublous thing before,
    Nor sight nor sound to war against thee more,
For whom all winds are quiet as the sun,
    All waters as the shore.

THOMAS HARDY

472   In a Wood

PALE beech and pine-tree blue,
        Set in one clay,
    Bough to bough cannot you
        Live out your day?

When the rains skim and skip,
Why mar sweet comradeship,
Blighting with poison-drip
    Neighbourly spray?

Heart-halt and spirit-lame,
    City-opprest,
Unto this wood I came
    As to a nest;
Dreaming that sylvan peace
Offered the harrowed ease—
Nature a soft release
    From men's unrest.

But, having entered in,
    Great growths and small
Show them to men akin—
    Combatants all!
Sycamore shoulders oak,
Bines the slim sapling yoke,
Ivy-spun halters choke
    Elms stout and tall.

Touches from ash, O wych,
    Sting you like scorn!
You, too, brave hollies, twitch
    Sidelong from thorn.
Even the rank poplars bear
Illy a rival's air,
Cankering in black despair
    If overborne.

Since, then, no grace I find
    Taught me of trees,
Turn I back to my kind,
    Worthy as these.
There at least smiles abound,
There discourse trills around,
There, now and then, are found
    Life-loyalties.

1887 : 1896

473   Zermatt

TO THE MATTERHORN

(June–July 1897)

THIRTY-two years since, up against the sun,
Seven shapes, thin atomies to lower sight,
Labouringly leapt and gained thy gabled height,
And four lives paid for what the seven had won.

They were the first by whom the deed was done,
And when I look at thee, my mind takes flight
To that day's tragic feat of manly might,
As though, till then, of history thou hadst none.

Yet ages ere men topped thee, late and soon
Thou didst behold the planets lift and lower;
Saw'st, maybe, Joshua's pausing sun and moon,
And the betokening sky when Caesar's power
Approached its bloody end; yea, even that Noon
When darkness filled the earth till the ninth hour.

THOMAS HARDY

474   The Darkling Thrush

I LEANT upon a coppice gate
    When Frost was spectre-gray,
And Winter's dregs made desolate
    The weakening eye of day.
The tangled bine-stems scored the sky
    Like strings of broken lyres,
And all mankind that haunted nigh
    Had sought their household fires.

The land's sharp features seemed to be
    The Century's corpse outleant,
His crypt the cloudy canopy,
    The wind his death-lament.
The ancient pulse of germ and birth
    Was shrunken hard and dry,
And every spirit upon earth
    Seemed fervourless as I.

At once a voice arose among
    The bleak twigs overhead
In a full-hearted evensong
    Of joy illimited;
An aged thrush, frail, gaunt, and small,
    In blast-beruffled plume,
Had chosen thus to fling his soul
    Upon the growing gloom.

So little cause for carollings
    Of such ecstatic sound
Was written on terrestrial things
    Afar or nigh around,

That I could think there trembled through
    His happy good-night air
Some blessed Hope, whereof he knew
    And I was unaware.

December 1900

475   The Self-unseeing

HERE is the ancient floor,
Footworn and hollowed and thin,
Here was the former door
Where the dead feet walked in.

She sat here in her chair,
Smiling into the fire;
He who played stood there,
Bowing it higher and higher.

Childlike, I danced in a dream;
Blessings emblazoned that day;
Everything glowed with a gleam;
Yet we were looking away!

476   A Trampwoman's Tragedy

(182–)

I

FROM Wynyard's Gap the livelong day,
    The livelong day,
We beat afoot the northward way
    We had travelled times before.
The sun-blaze burning on our backs,
Our shoulders sticking to our packs,
By fosseway, fields, and turnpike tracks
    We skirted sad Sedge-Moor.

II

Full twenty miles we jaunted on,
 We jaunted on,—
My fancy-man, and jeering John,
 And Mother Lee, and I.
And, as the sun drew down to west,
We climbed the toilsome Polden crest,
And saw, of landskip sights the best,
 The inn that beamed thereby.

III

For months we had padded side by side,
 Ay, side by side
Through the Great Forest, Blackmoor wide,
 And where the Parret ran.
We'd faced the gusts on Mendip ridge,
Had crossed the Yeo unhelped by bridge,
Been stung by every Marshwood midge,
 I and my fancy-man.

IV

Lone inns we loved, my man and I,
 My man and I;
'King's Stag', 'Windwhistle' high and dry,
 'The Horse' on Hintock Green,
The cozy house at Wynyard's Gap,
'The Hut' renowned on Bredy Knap,
And many another wayside tap
 Where folk might sit unseen.

V

Now as we trudged—O deadly day,
 O deadly day!—
I teased my fancy-man in play
 And wanton idleness.

I walked alongside jeering John,
I laid his hand my waist upon;
I would not bend my glances on
    My lover's dark distress.

VI

Thus Poldon top at last we won,
    At last we won,
And gained the inn at sink of sun
    Far-famed as 'Marshal's Elm'.
Beneath us figured tor and lea,
From Mendip to the western sea—
I doubt if finer sight there be
    Within this royal realm.

VII

Inside the settle all a-row—
    Ay, all a-row
We sat, I next to John, to show
    That he had wooed and won.
And then he took me on his knee,
And swore it was his turn to be
My favoured mate, and Mother Lee
    Passed to my former one.

VIII

Then in a voice I had never heard,
    I had never heard,
My only Love to me: 'One word,
    My doxy, if you please!
Whose is the child you are like to bear?—
His? After all my months o' care?'
God knows 'twas not! But, O despair!
    I nodded—still to tease.

IX

Then up he sprung, and with his knife—
 And with his knife
He let out jeering Johnny's life,
 Yes, there, at set of sun.
The slant ray through the window nigh
Gilded John's blood and glazing eye,
Ere scarcely Mother Lee and I
 Knew that the deed was done.

X

The taverns tell the gloomy tale,
 The gloomy tale,
How that at Ivel-chester jail
 My Love, my sweetheart swung;
Though stained till now by no misdeed
Save one horse ta'en in time o' need;
(Blue Jimmy stole right many a steed
 Ere his last fling he flung.)

XI

Thereaft I walked the world alone,
 Alone, alone!
On his death-day I gave my groan
 And dropt his dead-born child.
'Twas nigh the jail, beneath a tree.
None tending me; for Mother Lee
Had died at Glaston, leaving me
 Unfriended on the wild.

XII

And in the night as I lay weak,
 As I lay weak,
The leaves a-falling on my cheek,
 The red moon low declined—

The ghost of him I'd die to kiss
Rose up and said: 'Ah, tell me this!
Was the child mine, or was it his?
Speak, that I rest may find!'

XIII

O doubt not but I told him then,
    I told him then,
That I had kept me from all men
    Since we joined lips and swore.
Whereat he smiled, and thinned away
As the wind stirred to call up day . . .
—'Tis past! And here alone I stray
    Haunting the Western Moor.

April 1902

477   On the Departure Platform

WE kissed at the barrier; and passing through
She left me, and moment by moment got
Smaller and smaller, until to my view
    She was but a spot;

A wee white spot of muslin fluff
That down the diminishing platform bore
Through hustling crowds of gentle and rough
    To the carriage door.

Under the lamplight's fitful glowers,
Behind dark groups from far and near,
Whose interests were apart from ours,
    She would disappear,

Then show again, till I ceased to see
That flexible form, that nebulous white;
And she who was more than my life to me
    Had vanished quite. . . .

We have penned new plans since that fair fond day,
And in season she will appear again—
Perhaps in the same soft white array—
    But never as then!

—'And why, young man, must eternally fly
A joy you'll repeat, if you love her well?'
    —O friend, nought happens twice thus; why,
      I cannot tell!

478   He Abjures Love

AT last I put off love,
    For twice ten years
The daysman of my thought,
    And hope, and doing;
Being ashamed thereof,
    And faint of fears
And desolations, wrought
    In his pursuing,

Since first in youthtime those
    Disquietings
That heart-enslavement brings
    To hale and hoary,
Became my housefellows,
    And, fool and blind,
I turned from kith and kind
    To give him glory.

I was as children be
  Who have no care;
I did not shrink or sigh,
  I did not sicken;
But lo, Love beckoned me
  And I was bare,
And poor, and starved, and dry,
  And fever-stricken.

Too many times ablaze
  With fatuous fires,
Enkindled by his wiles
  To new embraces,
Did I, by wilful ways
  And baseless ires,
Return the anxious smiles
  Of friendly faces.

No more will now rate I
  The common rare,
The midnight drizzle dew,
  The gray hour golden,
The wind a yearning cry,
  The faulty fair,
Things dreamt, of comelier hue
  Than things beholden! . . .

—I speak as one who plumbs
  Life's dim profound,
One who at length can sound
  Clear views and certain.
But—after love what comes?
  A scene that lours,
A few sad vacant hours,
  And then, the Curtain.

1883

831

479　　　　　　At Casterbridge Fair

FORMER BEAUTIES

THESE market-dames, mid-aged, with lips thin-drawn,
　　　And tissues sere,
Are they the ones we loved in years agone,
　　　And courted here?

Are these the muslined pink young things to whom
　　　We vowed and swore
In nooks on summer Sundays by the Froom,
　　　Or Budmouth shore?

Do they remember those gay tunes we trod
　　　Clasped on the green;
Aye; trod till moonlight set on the beaten sod
　　　A satin sheen?

They must forget, forget! They cannot know
　　　What once they were,
Or memory would transfigure them, and show
　　　Them always fair.

1902

480　　　　　In Front of the Landscape

PLUNGING and labouring on in a tide of visions,
　　　Dolorous and dear,
Forward I pushed my way as amid waste waters
　　　Stretching around,
Through whose eddies there glimmered the customed landscape
　　　Yonder and near,

Blotted to feeble mist. And the coomb and the upland
      Coppice-crowned,
Ancient chalk-pit, milestone, rills in the grass-flat
      Stroked by the light,
Seemed but a ghost-like gauze, and no substantial
      Meadow or mound.

What were the infinite spectacles bulking foremost
      Under my sight,
Hindering me to discern my paced advancement
      Lengthening to miles;
What were the re-creations killing the daytime
      As by the night?

O they were speechful faces, gazing insistent,
      Some as with smiles,
Some as with slow-born tears that brinily trundled
      Over the wrecked
Cheeks that were fair in their flush-time, ash now with anguish,
      Harrowed by wiles.

Yes, I could see them, feel them, hear them, address them—
      Halo-bedecked—
And, alas, onwards, shaken by fierce unreason,
      Rigid in hate,
Smitten by years-long wryness born of misprision,
      Dreaded, suspect.

Then there would breast me shining sights, sweet seasons
      Further in date;
Instruments of strings with the tenderest passion
      Vibrant, beside
Lamps long extinguished, robes, cheeks, eyes with the earth's
      crust
      Now corporate.

Also there rose a headland of hoary aspect
      Gnawed by the tide,
Frilled by the nimb of the morning as two friends stood there
      Guilelessly glad—
Wherefore they knew not—touched by the fringe of an ecstasy
      Scantly descried.

Later images too did the day unfurl me,
      Shadowed and sad,
Clay cadavers of those who had shared in the dreams,
      Laid now at ease,
Passions all spent, chiefest the one of the broad brow
      Sepulture-clad.

So did beset me scenes miscalled of the bygone,
      Over the leaze,
Past the clump, and down to where lay the beheld ones;
      —Yea, as the rhyme
Sung by the sea-swell, so in their pleading dumbness
      Captured me these.

For, their lost revisiting manifestations
      In their live time
Much had I slighted, caring not for their purport,
      Seeing behind
Things more coveted, reckoned the better worth calling
      Sweet, sad, sublime.

Thus do they now show hourly before the intenser
      Stare of the mind
As they were ghosts avenging their slights by my bypast
      Body-borne eyes,
Show, too, with fuller translation than rested upon them
      As living kind.

Hence wag the tongues of the passing people, saying
      In their surmise,
'Ah—whose is this dull form that perambulates, seeing nought
      Round him that looms
Whithersoever his footsteps turn in his farings,
      Save a few tombs?'

481   After the Visit

            (TO F. E. D.)

      COME again to the place
Where your presence was as a leaf that skims
Down a drouthy way whose ascent bedims
      The bloom on the farer's face.

      Come again, with the feet
That were light on the green as a thistledown ball,
And those mute ministrations to one and to all
      Beyond a man's saying sweet.

      Until then the faint scent
Of the bordering flowers swam unheeded away,
And I marked not the charm in the changes of day
      As the cloud-colours came and went.

      Through the dark corridors
Your walk was so soundless I did not know
Your form from a phantom's of long ago
      Said to pass on the ancient floors,

      Till you drew from the shade,
And I saw the large luminous living eyes
Regard me in fixed inquiring-wise
      As those of a soul that weighed,

Scarce consciously,
The eternal question of what Life was,
And why we were here, and by whose strange laws
That which mattered most could not be.

482   To Meet, or Otherwise

WHETHER to sally and see thee, girl of my dreams,
Or whether to stay
And see thee not! How vast the difference seems
Of Yea from Nay
Just now. Yet this same sun will slant its beams
At no far day
On our two mounds, and then what will the difference weigh!

Yet I will see thee, maiden dear, and make
The most I can
Of what remains to us amid this brake
Cimmerian
Through which we grope, and from whose thorns we ache,
While still we scan
Round our frail faltering progress for some path or plan.

By briefest meeting something sure is won;
It will have been:
Nor God nor Daemon can undo the done,
Unsight the seen,
Make muted music be as unbegun,
Though things terrene
Groan in their bondage till oblivion supervene.

So, to the one long-sweeping symphony
    From times remote
Till now, of human tenderness, shall we
    Supply one note,
Small and untraced, yet that will ever be
    Somewhere afloat
Amid the spheres, as part of sick Life's antidote.

483   Beyond the Last Lamp

NEAR TOOTING COMMON

I

WHILE rain, with eve in partnership,
Descended darkly, drip, drip, drip,
Beyond the last lone lamp I passed
    Walking slowly, whispering sadly,
    Two linked loiterers, wan, downcast:
Some heavy thought constrained each face,
And blinded them to time and place.

II

The pair seemed lovers, yet absorbed
In mental scenes no longer orbed
By love's young rays. Each countenance
    As it slowly, as it sadly
    Caught the lamplight's yellow glance,
Held in suspense a misery
At things which had been or might be.

III

When I retrod that watery way
Some hours beyond the droop of day,

Still I found pacing there the twain
   Just as slowly, just as sadly,
     Heedless of the night and rain.
One could but wonder who they were,
And what wild woe detained them there.

IV

Though thirty years of blur and blot
Have slid since I beheld that spot,
And saw in curious converse there
    Moving slowly, moving sadly
     That mysterious tragic pair,
Its olden look may linger on—
All but the couple; they have gone.

V

Whither? Who knows, indeed. . . . And yet
To me, when nights are weird and wet,
Without those comrades there at tryst
    Creeping slowly, creeping sadly,
     That lone lane does not exist.
There they seem brooding on their pain,
And will, while such a lane remain.

484   My Spirit Will not Haunt the Mound

MY spirit will not haunt the mound
    Above my breast,
But travel, memory-possessed,
To where my tremulous being found
    Life largest, best.

My phantom-footed shape will go
　　When nightfall grays
Hither and thither along the ways
I and another used to know
　　In backward days.

And there you'll find me, if a jot
　　You still should care
For me, and for my curious air;
If otherwise, then I shall not,
　　For you, be there.

485　　　　　　Wessex Heights

(1896)

THERE are some heights in Wessex, shaped as if by a kindly hand
For thinking, dreaming, dying on, and at crises when I stand,
Say, on Ingpen Beacon eastward, or on Wylls-Neck westwardly,
I seem where I was before my birth, and after death may be.

In the lowlands I have no comrade, not even the lone man's
　　friend—
Her who suffereth long and is kind; accepts what he is too weak
　　to mend:
Down there they are dubious and askance; there nobody thinks as I,
But mind-chains do not clank where one's next neighbour is the
　　sky.

In the towns I am tracked by phantoms having weird detective
　　ways—
Shadows of beings who fellowed with myself of earlier days:
They hang about at places, and they say harsh heavy things—
Men with a wintry sneer, and women with tart disparagings.

Down there I seem to be false to myself, my simple self that was,
And is not now, and I see him watching, wondering what crass
    cause
Can have merged him into such a strange continuator as this,
Who yet has something in common with himself, my chrysalis.

I cannot go to the great grey Plain; there's a figure against the
    moon,
Nobody sees it but I, and it makes my breast beat out of tune;
I cannot go to the tall-spired town, being barred by the forms now
    passed
For everybody but me, in whose long vision they stand there fast.

There's a ghost at Yell'ham Bottom chiding loud at the fall of the
    night,
There's a ghost in Froom-side Vale, thin lipped and vague, in a
    shroud of white,
There is one in the railway train whenever I do not want it near,
I see its profile against the pane, saying what I would not hear.

As for one rare fair woman, I am now but a thought of hers,
I enter her mind and another thought succeeds me that she pre-
    fers;
Yet my love for her in its fulness she herself even did not know;
Well, time cures hearts of tenderness, and now I can let her go.

So I am found on Ingpen Beacon, or on Wylls-Neck to the west,
Or else on homely Bulbarrow, or little Pilsdon Crest,
Where men have never cared to haunt, nor women have walked
    with me,
And ghosts then keep their distance; and I know some liberty.

486   ## Your Last Drive

HERE by the moorway you returned,
And saw the borough lights ahead
That lit your face—all undiscerned
To be in a week the face of the dead,
And you told of the charm of that haloed view
That never again would beam on you.

And on your left you passed the spot
Where eight days later you were to lie,
And be spoken of as one who was not;
Beholding it with heedless eye
As alien from you, though under its tree
You soon would halt everlastingly.

I drove not with you. . . . Yet had I sat
At your side that eve I should not have seen
That the countenance I was glancing at
Had a last-time look in the flickering sheen,
Nor have read the writing upon your face,
'I go hence soon to my resting-place;

'You may miss me then. But I shall not know
How many times you visit me there,
Or what your thoughts are, or if you go
There never at all. And I shall not care.
Should you censure me I shall take no heed
And even your praises no more shall need.'

True: never you'll know. And you will not mind.
But shall I then slight you because of such?
Dear ghost, in the past did you ever find
The thought 'What profit', move me much?
Yet the fact indeed remains the same,—
You are past love, praise, indifference, blame.

                                    December 1912

487   The Voice

WOMAN much missed, how you call to me, call to me,
Saying that now you are not as you were
When you had changed from the one who was all to me,
But as at first, when our day was fair.

Can it be you that I hear? Let me view you, then,
Standing as when I drew near to the town
Where you would wait for me: yes, as I knew you then,
Even to the original air-blue gown!

Or is it only the breeze, in its listlessness
Travelling across the wet mead to me here,
You being ever dissolved to wan wistlessness,
Heard no more again far or near?

        Thus I; faltering forward,
        Leaves around me falling,
Wind oozing thin through the thorn from norward,
        And the woman calling.

                                        December 1912

488   After a Journey

HERETO I come to view a voiceless ghost;
    Whither, O whither will its whim now draw me?
Up the cliff, down, till I'm lonely, lost,
    And the unseen waters' ejaculations awe me.
Where you will next be there's no knowing,
    Facing round about me everywhere,
        With your nut-coloured hair,
And gray eyes, and rose-flush coming and going.

Yes: I have re-entered your olden haunts at last;
   Through the years, through the dead scenes I have tracked you;
What have you now found to say of our past—
   Scanned across the dark space wherein I have lacked you?
Summer gave us sweets, but autumn wrought division?
   Things were not lastly as firstly well
      With us twain, you tell?
But all's closed now, despite Time's derision.

I see what you are doing: you are leading me on
   To the spots we knew when we haunted here together,
The waterfall, above which the mist-bow shone
   At the then fair hour in the then fair weather,
And the cave just under, with a voice still so hollow
   That it seems to call out to me from forty years ago,
      When you were all aglow,
And not the thin ghost that I now fraily follow!

Ignorant of what there is flitting here to see,
   The waked birds preen and the seals flop lazily,
Soon you will have, Dear, to vanish from me,
   For the stars close their shutters and the dawn whitens hazily.
Trust me, I mind not, though Life lours,
   The bringing me here; nay, bring me here again!
      I am just the same as when
Our days were a joy, and our paths through flowers.

Pentargan Bay

489   Beeny Cliff

March 1870–March 1913

I

O THE opal and the sapphire of that wandering western sea,
And the woman riding high above with bright hair flapping free—
The woman whom I loved so, and who loyally loved me.

II

The pale mews plained below us, and the waves seemed far away
In a nether sky, engrossed in saying their ceaseless babbling say,
As we laughed light-heartedly aloft on that clear-sunned March
    day.

III

A little cloud then cloaked us, and there flew an irised rain,
And the Atlantic dyed its levels with a dull misfeatured stain,
And then the sun burst out again, and purples prinked the main.

IV

—Still in all its chasmal beauty bulks old Beeny to the sky,
And shall she and I not go there once again now March is nigh,
And the sweet things said in that March say anew there by and by?

V

What if still in chasmal beauty looms that wild weird western
    shore,
The woman now is—elsewhere—whom the ambling pony bore,
And nor knows nor cares for Beeny, and will laugh there never-
    more.

490   At Castle Boterel

    As I drive to the junction of lane and highway,
      And the drizzle bedrenches the waggonette,
    I look behind at the fading byway,
      And see on its slope, now glistening wet,
        Distinctly yet

Myself and a girlish form benighted
    In dry March weather. We climb the road
Beside a chaise. We had just alighted
    To ease the sturdy pony's load
        When he sighed and slowed.

What we did as we climbed, and what we talked of
    Matters not much, nor to what it led,—
Something that life will not be balked of
    Without rude reason till hope is dead,
        And feeling fled.

It filled but a minute. But was there ever
    A time of such quality, since or before,
In that hill's story? To one mind never,
    Though it has been climbed, foot-swift, foot-sore,
        By thousands more.

Primaeval rocks form the road's steep border,
    And much have they faced there, first and last,
Of the transitory in Earth's long order;
    But what they record in colour and cast
        Is—that we two passed.

And to me, though Time's unflinching rigour,
    In mindless rote, has ruled from sight
The substance now, one phantom figure
    Remains on the slope, as when that night
        Saw us alight.

I look and see it there, shrinking, shrinking,
    I look back at it amid the rain
For the very last time; for my sand is sinking,
    And I shall traverse old love's domain
        Never again.

March 1913

491   Afterwards

WHEN the Present has latched its postern behind my tremulous
     stay,
   And the May month flaps its glad green leaves like wings,
Delicate-filmed as new-spun silk, will the neighbours say,
   'He was a man who used to notice such things'?

If it be the dusk when, like an eyelid's soundless blink,
   The dewfall-hawk comes crossing the shades to alight
Upon the wind-warped upland thorn, a gazer may think,
   'To him this must have been a familiar sight.'

If I pass during some nocturnal blackness, mothy and warm,
   When the hedgehog travels furtively over the lawn,
One may say, 'He strove that such innocent creatures should come
     to no harm,
   But he could do little for them; and now he is gone.'

If, when hearing that I have been stilled at last, they stand at the
     door,
   Watching the full-starred heavens that winter sees,
Will this thought rise on those who will meet my face no more,
   'He was one who had an eye for such mysteries'?

And will any say when my bell of quittance is heard in the gloom,
   And a crossing breeze cuts a pause in its outrollings,
Till they rise again, as they were a new bell's boom,
   'He hears it not now, but used to notice such things'?

WILFRID SCAWEN BLUNT

from 'ESTHER'

HE who has once been happy is for aye
  Out of destruction's reach. His fortune then
Holds nothing secret, and Eternity,
  Which is a mystery to other men,
Has like a woman given him its joy.
  Time is his conquest. Life, if it should fret,
Has paid him tribute. He can bear to die.
  He who has once been happy! When I set
The world before me and survey its range,
  Its mean ambitions, its scant fantasies,
The shreds of pleasure which for lack of change
  Men wrap around them and call happiness,
The poor delights which are the tale and sum
Of the world's courage in its martyrdom,

When I hear laughter from a tavern door,
  When I see crowds agape and in the rain
Watching on tiptoe and with stifled roar
  To see a rocket fired or a bull slain,
When misers handle gold, when orators
  Touch strong men's hearts with glory till they weep,
When cities deck their streets for barren wars
  Which have laid waste their youth, and when I keep
Calmly the count of my own life and see
  On what poor stuff my manhood's dreams were fed
Till I too learned what dole of vanity
  Will serve a human soul for daily bread,
—Then I remember that I once was young
And lived with Esther the world's gods among.

AUSTIN DOBSON

493   ## A Garden Song

HERE, in this sequestered close
Bloom the hyacinth and rose;
Here beside the modest stock
Flaunts the flaring hollyhock;
Here, as everywhere, one sees
Ranks, condition, and degrees.

All the seasons run their race
In this quiet resting place;
Peach, and apricot, and fig
Here will ripen, and grow big;
Here is store and overplus,—
More had not Alcinous!

Here, in alleys cool and green,
Far ahead the thrush is seen;
Here along the southern wall
Keeps the bee his festival;
All is quiet else—afar
Sounds of toil and turmoil are.

Here be shadows large and long;
Here be spaces meet for song;
Grant, O garden-god, that I,
Now that mood and moment please,
Find the fair Pierides!

MATHILDE BLIND

494 from 'LOVE IN EXILE'

DOST thou remember ever, for my sake,
When we two rowed upon the rock-bound lake?
How the wind-fretted waters blew their spray
About our brows like blossom-falls of May
     One memorable day?

Dost thou remember the glad mouth that cried—
'Were it not sweet to die now side by side,
To lie together tangled in the deep
Close as the heart-beat to the heart—so keep
     The everlasting sleep?'

Dost thou remember? Ah, such death as this
Had set the seal upon my heart's young bliss!
But, wrenched asunder, severed and apart,
Life knew a deadlier death; the blighting smart
     Which only kills the heart.

495 The After-Glow

IT is a solemn evening, golden-clear—
    The Alpine summits flame with rose-lit snow
  And headlands purpling on wide seas below,
And clouds and woods and arid rocks appear
Dissolving in the sun's own atmosphere
    And vast circumference of light, whose slow
    Transfiguration—glow and after-glow—
Turns twilight earth to a more luminous sphere.

O heart, I ask, seeing that the orb of day
Has sunk below, yet left to sky and sea
　　His glory's spiritual after-shine:
I ask if Love, whose sun hath set for thee,
May not touch grief with his memorial ray,
　　And lend to loss itself a joy divine?

ARTHUR O'SHAUGHNESSY

496

Song

I WENT to her who loveth me no more,
　　And prayed her bear with me, if so she might;
For I had found day after day too sore,
　　And tears that would not cease night after night.
And so I prayed her, weeping, that she bore
To let me be with her a little; yea,
　　To soothe myself a little with her sight,
Who loved me once, ah! many a night and day.

Then she who loveth me no more, maybe
　　She pitied somewhat: and I took a chain
To bind myself to her, and her to me;
　　Yea, so that I might call her mine again.
Lo! she forbade me not; but I and she
Fettered her fair limbs, and her neck more fair,
　　Chained the fair wasted white of love's domain,
And put gold fetters on her golden hair.

Oh! the vain joy it is to see her lie
　　Beside me once again; beyond release,
Her hair, her hand, her body, till she die,
　　All mine, for me to do with as I please!

For, after all, I find no chain whereby
To chain her heart to love me as before,
   Nor fetter for her lips, to make them cease
From saying still she loveth me no more.

497   Silences

'Tis a world of silences. I gave a cry
   In the first sorrow my heart could not withstand;
I saw men pause, and listen, and look sad,
As though an answer in their hearts they had;
   Some turned away, some came and took my hand,
For all reply.

I stood beside a grave. Years had passed by;
   Sick with unanswered life I turned to death,
And whispered all my question to the grave,
And watched the flowers desolately wave,
   And grass stir on it with a fitful breath,
For all reply.

I raised my eyes to heaven; my prayer went high
   Into the luminous mystery of the blue;
My thought of God was purer than a flame
And God it seemed a little nearer came,
   Then passed; and greater still the silence grew,
For all reply.

But you! If I can speak before I die,
   I spoke to you with all my soul, and when
I look at you 'tis still my soul you see.
Oh, in your heart was there no word for me?
   All would have answered had you answered then
With even a sigh.

GERARD MANLEY HOPKINS

498 ## Heaven-haven

A NUN TAKES THE VEIL

I HAVE desired to go
Where springs not fail,
To fields where flies no sharp and sided hail
And a few lilies blow.

And I have asked to be
Where no storms come,
Where the green swell is in the havens dumb,
And out of the swing of the sea.

499 ## The Wreck of the Deutschland

*To the
happy memory of five Franciscan Nuns
exiles by the Falk Laws
drowned between midnight and morning of
Dec. 7th, 1875*

PART THE FIRST

I

THOU mastering me
God! giver of breath and bread;
World's strand, sway of the sea;
Lord of living and dead;
Thou hast bound bones and veins in me, fastened me flesh,
And after it almost unmade, what with dread,
Thy doing: and dost thou touch me afresh?
Over again I feel thy finger and find thee.

2

I did say yes
O at lightning and lashed rod;
Thou heardst me truer than tongue confess
Thy terror, O Christ, O God;
Thou knowest the walls, altar and hour and night:
The swoon of a heart that the sweep and the hurl of thee trod
Hard down with a horror of height:
And the midriff astrain with leaning of, laced with fire of stress.

3

The frown of his face
Before me, the hurtle of hell
Behind, where, where was a, where was a place?
I whirled out wings that spell
And fled with a fling of the heart to the heart of the Host.
My heart, but you were dovewinged, I can tell,
Carrier-witted, I am bold to boast.
To flash from the flame to the flame then, tower from the grace to
the grace.

4

I am soft sift
In an hourglass—at the wall
Fast, but mined with a motion, a drift,
And it crowds and it combs to the fall;
I steady as a water in a well, to a poise, to a pane,
But roped with, always, all the way down from the tall
Fells or flanks of the voel, a vein
Of the gospel proffer, a pressure, a principle, Christ's gift.

853

5

I kiss my hand
To the stars, lovely-asunder
Starlight, wafting him out of it; and
Glow, glory in thunder;
Kiss my hand to the dappled-with-damson west:
Since, tho' he is under the world's splendour and wonder,
His mystery must be instressed, stressed;
For I greet him the days I meet him, and bless when I understand.

6

Not out of his bliss
Springs the stress felt
Nor first from heaven (and few know this)
Swings the stroke dealt—
Stroke and a stress that stars and storms deliver,
That guilt is hushed by, hearts are flushed by and melt—
But it rides time like riding a river
(And here the faithful waver, the faithless fable and miss).

7

It dates from day
Of his going in Galilee;
Warm-laid grave of a womb-life grey;
Manger, maiden's knee;
The dense and the driven Passion, and frightful sweat;
Thence the discharge of it, there its swelling to be,
Though felt before in high flood yet—
What none would have known of it, only the heart, being hard
at bay,

8

Is out with it! Oh,
We lash with the best or worst
Word last! How a lush-kept plush-capped sloe
Will, mouthed to flesh-burst,
Gush!—flush the man, the being with it, sour or sweet
Brim, in a flash, full!—Hither then, last or first,
To hero of Calvary, Christ,'s feet—
Never ask if meaning it, wanting it, warned of it—men go.

9

Be adored among men,
God, three-numberèd form;
Wring thy rebel, dogged in den,
Man's malice, with wrecking and storm.
Beyond saying sweet, past telling of tongue,
Thou art lightning and love, I found it, a winter and warm;
Father and fondler of heart thou hast wrung;
Hast thy dark descending and most art merciful then.

10

With an anvil-ding
And with fire in him forge thy will
Or rather, rather then, stealing as Spring
Through him, melt him but master him still:
Whether at once, as once at a crash Paul,
Or as Austin, a lingering out swéet skíll,
Make mercy in all of us, out of us all
Mastery, but be adored, but be adored King.

GERARD MANLEY HOPKINS

PART THE SECOND

11

'Some find me a sword; some
    The flange and the rail; flame,
Fang, or flood' goes Death on drum,
    And storms bugle his fame.
But wé dream we are rooted in earth — Dust!
Flesh falls within sight of us, we, though our flower the same,
    Wave with the meadow, forget that there must
The sour scythe cringe, and the blear share come.

12

On Saturday sailed from Bremen,
    American-outward-bound,
Take settler and seamen, tell men with women,
    Two hundred souls in the round—
O Father, not under thy feathers nor ever as guessing
The goal was a shoal, of a fourth the doom to be drowned;
    Yet did the dark side of the bay of thy blessing
Not vault them, the millions of rounds of thy mercy not reeve
    even them in?

13

Into the snows she sweeps,
    Hurling the haven behind,
The Deutschland, on Sunday; and so the sky keeps,
    For the infinite air is unkind,
And the sea flint-flake, black-backed in the regular blow,
Sitting Eastnortheast, in cursed quarter, the wind;
    Wiry and white-fiery and whirlwind-swivellèd snow
Spins to the widow-making unchilding unfathering deeps.

14

She drove in the dark to leeward,
    She struck—not a reef or a rock
  But the combs of a smother of sand: night drew her
    Dead to the Kentish Knock;
And she beat the bank down with her bows and the ride of
    her keel:
The breakers rolled on her beam with ruinous shock;
    And canvas and compass, the whorl and the wheel
Idle for ever to waft her or wind her with, these she endured.

15

Hope had grown grey hairs,
    Hope had mourning on,
  Trenched with tears, carved with cares,
    Hope was twelve hours gone;
And frightful a nightfall folded rueful a day
Nor rescue, only rocket and lightship, shone,
    And lives at last were washing away:
To the shrouds they took,—they shook in the hurling and horrible
    airs.

16

One stirred from the rigging to save
    The wild woman-kind below,
  With a rope's end round the man, handy and brave—
    He was pitched to his death at a blow,
For all his dreadnought breast and braids of thew:
They could tell him for hours, dandled the to and fro
    Through the cobbled foam-fleece, what could he do
With the burl of the fountains of air, buck and the flood of the
    wave?

17

They fought with God's cold—
And they could not and fell to the deck
  (Crushed them) or water (and drowned them) or rolled
    With the sea-romp over the wreck.
Night roared, with the heart-break hearing a heart-broke
  rabble,
The woman's wailing, the crying of child without check—
    Till a lioness arose breasting the babble,
A prophetess towered in the tumult, a virginal tongue told.

18

Ah, touched in your bower of bone
Are you! turned for an exquisite smart,
  Have you! make words break from me here all alone,
    Do you!—mother of being in me, heart.
O unteachably after evil, but uttering truth,
  Why tears! is it? tears; such a melting, a madrigal start!
    Never-eldering revel and river of youth,
What can it be, this glee? the good you have there of your own?

19

Sister, a sister calling
A master, her master and mine!—
  And the inboard seas run swirling and hawling;
    The rash smart sloggering brine
Blinds her; but she that weather sees one thing, one;
  Has one fetch in her: she rears herself to divine
    Ears, and the call of the tall nun
To the men in the tops and the tackle rode over the storm's
  brawling.

20

She was first of a five and came
Of a coifèd sisterhood.
(O Deutschland, double a desperate name!
O world wide of its good!
But Gertrude, lily, and Luther, are two of a town,
Christ's lily and beast of the waste wood:
From life's dawn it is drawn down,
Abel is Cain's brother and breasts they have sucked the same.)

21

Loathed for a love men knew in them,
Banned by the land of their birth,
Rhine refused them. Thames would ruin them;
Surf, snow, river and earth
Gnashed: but thou art above, thou Orion of light;
Thy unchancelling poising palms were weighing the worth,
Thou martyr-master: in thy sight
Storm flakes were scroll-leaved flowers, lily showers—sweet
heaven was astrew in them.

22

Five! the finding and sake
And cipher of suffering Christ.
Mark, the mark is of man's make
And the word of it Sacrificed.
But he scores it in scarlet himself on his own bespoken,
Before-time-taken, dearest prizèd and priced—
Stigma, signal, cinquefoil token
For lettering of the lamb's fleece, ruddying of the rose-flake.

23

Joy fall to thee, father Francis,
Drawn to the Life that died;
With the gnarls of the nails in thee, niche of the lance, his
Lovescape crucified
And seal of his seraph-arrival! and these thy daughters
And five-livèd and leavèd favour and pride,
Are sisterly sealed in wild waters,
To bathe in his fall-gold mercies, to breathe in his all-fire glances.

24

Away in the loveable west,
On a pastoral forehead of Wales,
I was under a roof here, I was at rest,
And they the prey of the gales;
She to the black-about air, to the breaker, the thickly
Falling flakes, to the throng that catches and quails
Was calling 'O Christ, Christ, come quickly':
The cross to her she calls Christ to her, christens her wild-worst
Best.

25

The majesty! what did she mean?
Breathe, arch and original Breath.
Is it love in her of the being as her lover had been?
Breathe, body of lovely Death.
They were else-minded then, altogether, the men
Woke thee with a *we are perishing* in the weather of Gen-
nesareth.
Or is it that she cried for the crown then,
The keener to come at the comfort for feeling the combating
keen?

26

For how to the heart's cheering
    The down-dugged ground-hugged grey
Hovers off, the jay-blue heavens appearing
    Of pied and peeled May!
Blue-beating and hoary-glow height; or night, still higher,
With belled fire and the moth-soft Milky Way,
    What by your measure is the heaven of desire,
The treasure never eyesight got, nor was ever guessed what for the
    hearing?

27

No, but it was not these.
    The jading and jar of the cart,
Time's tasking, it is fathers that asking for ease
    Of the sodden-with-its-sorrowing heart,
Nor danger, electrical horror; then further it finds
The appealing of the Passion is tenderer in prayer apart:
    Other, I gather, in measure her mind's
Burden, in wind's burly and beat of endragonèd seas.

28

But how shall I . . . make me room there:
    Reach me a . . . Fancy, come faster—
Strike you the sight of it? look at it loom there,
    Thing that she . . . there then! the Master,
Ipse, the only one, Christ, King, Head:
He was to cure the extremity where he had cast her;
    Do, deal, lord it with living and dead;
Let him ride, her pride, in his triumph, despatch and have done
    with his doom there.

29

Ah! there was a heart right!
There was single eye!
Read the unshapeable shock night
And knew the who and the why;
Wording it how but by him that present and past,
Heaven and earth are word of, worded by?—
The Simon Peter of a soul! to the blast
Tarpeian-fast, but a blown beacon of light.

30

Jesu, heart's light,
Jesu, maid's son,
What was the feast followed the night
Thou hadst glory of this nun?—
Feast of the one woman without stain.
For so conceivèd, so to conceive thee is done;
But here was heart-throe, birth of a brain,
Word, that heard and kept thee and uttered thee outright.

31

Well, she has thee for the pain, for the
Patience; but pity of the rest of them!
Heart, go and bleed at a bitterer vein for the
Comfortless unconfessed of them—
No not uncomforted: lovely-felicitous Providence
Finger of a tender of, O of a feathery delicacy, the breast of the
Maiden could obey so, be a bell to, ring of it, and
Startle the poor sheep back! is the shipwrack then a harvest,
does tempest carry the grain for thee?

32

I admire thee, master of the tides,
　　Of the Yore-flood, of the year's fall;
　The recurb and the recovery of the gulf's sides,
　　The girth of it and the wharf of it and the wall;
Stanching, quenching ocean of a motionable mind;
Ground of being, and granite of it: past all
　　Grasp God, throned behind
Death with a sovereignty that heeds but hides, bodes but abides;

33

With a mercy that outrides
　　The all of water, an ark
　For the listener; for the lingerer with a love glides
　　Lower than death and the dark;
A vein for the visiting of the past-prayer, pent in prison,
The-last-breach penitent spirits—the uttermost mark
　　Our passion-plungèd giant risen,
The Christ of the Father compassionate, fetched in the storm of
　his strides.

34

Now burn, new born to the world,
　　Doubled-naturèd name,
　The heaven-flung, heart-fleshed, maiden-furled
　　Miracle-in-Mary-of-flame,
Mid-numbered He in three of the thunder-throne!
Not a dooms-day dazzle in his coming nor dark as he came;
　　Kind, but royally reclaiming his own;
A released shower, let flash to the shire, not a lightning of fire
　hard-hurled.

35

    Dame, at our door
    Drowned, and among our shoals,
Remember us in the roads, the heaven-haven of the
      Reward:
    Our King back, oh, upon English souls!
Let him easter in us, be a dayspring to the dimness of us, be
    a crimson-cresseted east,
More brightening her, rare-dear Britain, as his reign rolls,
    Pride, rose, prince, hero of us, high-priest,
Our hearts' charity's hearth's fire, our thoughts' chivalry's throng's
    Lord.

500   Spring

NOTHING is so beautiful as spring—
    When weeds, in wheels, shoot long and lovely and lush;
    Thrush's eggs look little low heavens, and thrush
Through the echoing timber does so rinse and wring
The ear, it strikes like lightnings to hear him sing;
    The glassy peartree leaves and blooms, they brush
    The descending blue; that blue is all in a rush
With richness; the racing lambs too have fair their fling.

What is all this juice and all this joy?
    A strain of the earth's sweet being in the beginning
      In Eden garden.—Have, get, before it cloy,
    Before it cloud, Christ, lord, and sour with sinning,
Innocent mind and Mayday in girl and boy,
    Most, O maid's child, thy choice and worthy the winning.

501 The Windhover

TO CHRIST OUR LORD

I CAUGHT this morning morning's minion, king-
　　dom of daylight's dauphin, dapple-dawn-drawn Falcon, in
　　　his riding
　Of the rolling level underneath him steady air, and striding
High there, how he rung upon the rein of a wimpling wing
In his ecstacy! then off, off forth on swing,
　　As a skate's heel sweeps smooth on a bow-bend: the hurl and
　　　gliding
　Rebuffed the big wind. My heart in hiding
Stirred for a bird,—the achieve of, the mastery of the thing!

Brute beauty and valour and act, oh, air, pride, plume, here
　Buckle! AND the fire that breaks from thee then, a billion
Times told lovelier, more dangerous, O my chevalier!

　No wonder of it: shéer plód makes plough down sillion
Shine, and blue-bleak embers, ah my dear,
　Fall, gall themselves, and gash gold-vermilion.

502 Pied Beauty

　　GLORY be to God for dappled things—
　　　For skies of couple-colour as a brinded cow;
　　　　For rose-moles all in stipple upon trout that swim;
　　Fresh-firecoal chestnut-falls; finches' wings;
　　　Landscape plotted and pieced—fold, fallow, and plough;
　　　And áll trádes, their gear and tackle and trim.

All things counter, original, spare, strange;
   Whatever is fickle, freckled (who knows how?)
    With swift, slow; sweet, sour; adazzle, dim;
He fathers-forth whose beauty is past change:
     Praise him.

503   Felix Randal

FELIX RANDAL the farrier, O he is dead then? my duty all ended,
Who have watched his mould of man, big-boned and hardy-
    handsome
Pining, pining, till time when reason rambled in it and some
Fatal four disorders, fleshed there, all contended?

Sickness broke him. Impatient he cursed at first, but mended
Being anointed and all; though a heavenlier heart began some
Months earlier, since I had our sweet reprieve and ransom
Tendered to him. Ah well, God rest him all road ever he offended!

This seeing the sick endears them to us, us too it endears.
My tongue had taught thee comfort, touch had quenched thy
    tears,
Thy tears that touched my heart, child, Felix, poor Felix Randal;

How far from then forethought of, all thy more boisterous years,
When thou at the random grim forge, powerful amidst peers,
Didst fettle for the great grey drayhorse his bright and battering
    sandal!

504 God's Grandeur

THE world is charged with the grandeur of God.
   It will flame out, like shining from shook foil;
   It gathers to a greatness, like the ooze of oil
Crushed. Why do men then now not reck his rod?
Generations have trod, have trod, have trod;
   And all is seared with trade; bleared, smeared with toil;
   And wears man's smudge and shares man's smell: the soil
Is bare now, nor can foot feel, being shod.

And for all this, nature is never spent;
   There lives the dearest freshness deep down things;
And though the last lights off the black West went
   Oh, morning, at the brown brink eastward, springs—
Because the Holy Ghost over the bent
   World broods with warm breast and with ah! bright wings.

505 The Leaden Echo and the Golden Echo

(*Maidens' song from St. Winefred's Well*)

THE LEADEN ECHO

How to kéep—is there ány any, is there none such, nowhere
   known some, bow or brooch or braid or brace, láce, latch or
   catch or key to keep
Back beauty, keep it, beauty, beauty, beauty, . . . from vanishing
   away?
Ó is there no frowning of these wrinkles, rankèd wrinkles deep,
Dówn? no waving off of these most mournful messengers, still
   messengers, sad and stealing messengers of grey?

No there's none, there's none, O no there's none,
Nor can you long be, what you now are, called fair,
Do what you may do, what, do what you may,
And wisdom is early to despair:
Be beginning; since, no, nothing can be done
To keep at bay
Age and age's evils, hoar hair,

Ruck and wrinkle, drooping, dying, death's worst, winding sheets,
    tombs and worms and tumbling to decay;
So be beginning, be beginning to despair.
O there's none; no no no there's none:
Be beginning to despair, to despair,
Despair, despair, despair, despair.

THE GOLDEN ECHO

    Spare!
There is one, yes I have one (Hush there!);
Only not within seeing of the sun,
Not within the singeing of the strong sun,
Tall sun's tingeing, or treacherous the tainting of the earth's air,
Somewhere elsewhere there is ah well where! one,
Ońe. Yes I cán tell such a key, I dó know such a place,
Where whatever's prized and passes of us, everything that's fresh
    and fast flying of us, seems to us sweet of us and swiftly away
    with, done away with, undone,
Úndone, done with, soon done with, and yet dearly and danger-
    ously sweet
Of us, the wimpled-water-dimpled, not-by-morning-matchèd
    face,
The flower of beauty, fleece of beauty, too too apt to, ah! to fleet,
Never fleets móre, fastened with the tenderest truth
To its own best being and its loveliness of youth: it is an ever-
    lastingness of, O it is an all youth!

Come then, your ways and airs and looks, locks, maiden gear,
    gallantry and gaiety and grace,
Winning ways, airs innocent, maiden manners, sweet looks, loose
    locks, long locks, lovelocks, gaygear, going gallant, girlgrace—
Resign them, sign them, seal them, send them, motion them with
    breath,
And with sighs soaring, soaring síghs deliver
Them; beauty-in-the-ghost, deliver it, early now, long before
    death
Give beauty back, beauty, beauty, beauty, back to God, beauty's
    self and beauty's giver.
See; not a hair is, not an eyelash, not the least lash lost; every hair
Is, hair of the head, numbered.
Nay, what we had lighthanded left in surly the mere mould
Will have waked and have waxed and have walked with the wind
    what while we slept,
This side, that side hurling a heavyheaded hundredfold
What while we, while we slumbered.
O then, weary then whý should we tread? O why are we so
    haggard at the heart, so care-coiled, care-killed, so fagged,
    so fashed, so cogged, so cumbered,
When the thing we freely fórfeit is kept with fonder a care,
Fonder a care kept than we could have kept it, kept
Far with fonder a care (and we, we should have lost it) finer,
    fonder
A care kept.—Where kept? Do but tell us where kept, where.—
Yonder.—What high as that! We follow, now we follow.—
    Yonder, yes, yonder, yonder,
Yonder.

506 [Sonnets]

NOT, I'll not, carrion comfort, Despair, not feast on thee;
Not untwist—slack they may be—these last strands of man
In me ór, most weary, cry *I can no more*. I can;
Can something, hope, wish day come, not choose not to be.
But ah, but O thou terrible, why wouldst thou rude on me
Thy wring-world right foot rock? lay a lionlimb against me? scan
With darksome devouring eyes my bruisèd bones? and fan,
O in turns of tempest, me heaped there; me frantic to avoid thee
     and flee?

   Why? That my chaff might fly; my grain lie, sheer and clear.
Nay in all that toil, that coil, since (seems) I kissed the rod,
Hand rather, my heart lo! lapped strength, stole joy, would laugh,
     chéer.
Cheer whom though? the hero whose heaven-handling flung me,
     fóot tród
Me? or me that fought him? O which one? is it each one? That
     night, that year
Of now done darkness I wretch lay wrestling with (my God!)
     my God.

                              *

507

No worst, there is none. Pitched past pitch of grief,
More pangs will, schooled at forepangs, wilder wring.
Comforter, where, where is your comforting?
Mary, mother of us, where is your relief?
My cries heave, herds-long; huddle in a main, a chief
Woe, wórld-sorrow; on an age-old anvil wince and sing—
Then lull, then leave off. Fury had shrieked 'No ling-
ering! Let me be fell: force I must be brief'.

O the mind, mind has mountains; cliffs of fall
Frightful, sheer, no-man-fathomed. Hold them cheap
May who ne'er hung there. Nor does long our small
Durance deal with that steep or deep. Here! creep,
Wretch, under a comfort serves in a whirlwind: all
Life death does end and each day dies with sleep.

★

508 PATIENCE, hard thing! the hard thing but to pray,
But bid for, Patience is! Patience who asks
Wants war, wants wounds; weary his times, his tasks;
To do without, take tosses, and obey.
    Rare patience roots in these, and, these away,
Nowhere. Natural heart's ivy, Patience masks
Our ruins of wrecked past purpose. There she basks
Purple eyes and seas of liquid leaves all day.

We hear our hearts grate on themselves: it kills
To bruise them dearer. Yet the rebellious wills
Of us we do bid God bend to him even so.
    And where is he who more and more distils
Delicious kindness?—He is patient. Patience fills
His crisp combs, and that comes those ways we know.

ANDREW LANG

509   The Odyssey

As one that for a weary space has lain
    Lull'd by the song of Circe and her wine
    In gardens near the pale of Proserpine,
Where that Ægæan isle forgets the main,

And only the low lutes of love complain,
    And only shadows of wan lovers pine—
      As such an one were glad to know the brine
Salt on his lips, and the large air again—
So gladly from the songs of modern speech
    Men turn, and see the stars, and feel the free
      Shrill wind beyond the close of heavy flowers,
      And through the music of the languid hours
They hear like Ocean on a western beach
    The surge and thunder of the Odyssey.

ROBERT BRIDGES

510   ['I will not let thee go']

    I WILL not let thee go.
Ends all our month-long love in this?
    Can it be summed up so,
    Quit in a single kiss?
    I will not let thee go.

    I will not let thee go.
If thy words' breath could scare thy deeds,
    As the soft south can blow
    And toss the feathered seeds,
    Then might I let thee go.

    I will not let thee go.
Had not the great sun seen, I might;
    Or were he reckoned slow
    To bring the false to light,
    Then might I let thee go.

       I will not let thee go.
The stars that crowd the summer skies
      Have watched us so below
      With all their million eyes,
      I dare not let thee go.

       I will not let thee go.
Have we not chid the changeful moon,
      Now rising late, and now
      Because she set too soon,
      And shall I let thee go?

       I will not let thee go.
Have not the young flowers been content,
      Plucked ere their buds could blow,
      To seal our sacrament?
      I cannot let thee go.

       I will not let thee go.
I hold thee by too many bands:
      Thou sayest farewell, and lo!
      I have thee by the hands,
      And will not let thee go.

511   A Passer-by

Whither, O splendid ship, thy white sails crowding,
    Leaning across the bosom of the urgent West,
That fearest nor sea rising, nor sky clouding,
    Whither away, fair rover, and what thy quest?
    Ah! soon, when Winter has all our vales opprest,
When skies are cold and misty, and hail is hurling,
    Wilt thou glide on the blue Pacific, or rest
In a summer haven asleep, thy white sails furling.

I there before thee, in the country that well thou knowest,
 Already arrived am inhaling the odorous air:
I watch thee enter unerringly where thou goest,
 And anchor queen of the strange shipping there,
 Thy sails for awnings spread, thy masts bare;
Nor is aught from the foaming reef to the snow-capped, grandest
 Peak, that is over the feathery palms more fair
Than thou, so upright, so stately, and still thou standest.

And yet, O splendid ship, unhailed and nameless,
 I know not if, aiming a fancy, I rightly divine
That thou hast a purpose joyful, a courage blameless,
 Thy port assured in a happier land than mine.
 But for all I have given thee, beauty enough is thine,
As thou, aslant with trim tackle and shrouding,
 From the proud nostril curve of a prow's line
In the offing scatterest foam, thy white sails crowding.

512   London Snow

WHEN men were all asleep the snow came flying,
 In large white flakes falling on the city brown,
Stealthily and perpetually settling and loosely lying,
 Hushing the latest traffic of the drowsy town;
Deadening, muffling, stifling its murmurs failing;
Lazily and incessantly floating down and down:
 Silently sifting and veiling road, roof and railing;
Hiding difference, making unevenness even,
Into angles and crevices softly drifting and sailing.
 All night it fell, and when full inches seven
It lay in the depth of its uncompacted lightness,
The clouds blew off from a high and frosty heaven;

And all woke earlier for the unaccustomed brightness
Of the winter dawning, the strange unheavenly glare:
The eye marvelled—marvelled at the dazzling whiteness;
 The ear hearkened to the stillness of the solemn air;
No sound of wheel rumbling nor of foot falling,
And the busy morning cries came thin and spare.

 Then boys I heard, as they went to school, calling,
They gathered up the crystal manna to freeze
Their tongues with tasting, their hands with snowballing;
 Or rioted in a drift, plunging up to the knees;
Or peering up from under the white-mossed wonder,
'O look at the trees!' they cried, 'O look at the trees!'

 With lessened load a few carts creak and blunder,
Following along the white deserted way,
A country company long dispersed asunder:
 When now already the sun, in pale display
Standing by Paul's high dome, spread forth below
His sparkling beams, and awoke the stir of the day.

 For now doors open, and war is waged with the snow;
And trains of sombre men, past tale of number,
Tread long brown paths, as toward their toil they go:
 But even for them awhile no cares encumber
Their minds diverted; the daily word is unspoken,
The daily thoughts of labour and sorrow slumber
At the sight of the beauty that greets them, for the charm
  they have broken.

513   On a Dead Child

PERFECT little body, without fault or stain on thee,
 With promise of strength and manhood full and fair!
  Though cold and stark and bare,
The bloom and the charm of life doth awhile remain on thee.

Thy mother's treasure wert thou;—alas! no longer
  To visit her heart with wondrous joy; to be
      Thy father's pride;—ah, he
Must gather his faith together, and his strength make stronger.

To me, as I move thee now in the last duty,
  Dost thou with a turn or gesture anon respond;
      Startling my fancy fond
With a chance attitude of the head, a freak of beauty.

Thy hand clasps, as 'twas wont, my finger, and holds it:
  But the grasp is the clasp of Death, heartbreaking and stiff;
      Yet feels to my hand as if
'Twas still thy will, thy pleasure and trust that enfolds it.

So I lay thee there, thy sunken eyelids closing,—
  Go lie thou there in thy coffin, thy last little bed!—
      Propping thy wise, sad head,
Thy firm, pale hands across thy chest disposing.

So quiet! doth the change content thee?—Death, whither hath he
    taken thee?
  To a world, do I think, that rights the disaster of this?
      The vision of which I miss,
Who weep for the body, and wish but to warm thee and awaken
    thee?

Ah! little at best can all our hopes avail us
  To lift this sorrow, or cheer us, when in the dark,
      Unwilling, alone we embark,
And the things we have seen and have known and have heard of,
    fail us.

514   Nightingales

BEAUTIFUL must be the mountain whence ye come,
And bright in the fruitful valleys the streams, wherefrom
          Ye learn your song:
Where are those starry woods? O might I wander there,
   Among the flowers, which in that heavenly air
          Bloom the year long!

Nay, barren are those mountains and spent the streams:
Our song is the voice of desire, that haunts our dreams,
          A throe of the heart,
Whose pining visions dim, forbidden hopes profound,
   No dying cadence nor long sigh can sound,
          For all our art.

Alone, aloud in the raptured ear of men
We pour our dark nocturnal secret; and then,
          As night is withdrawn
From these sweet-springing meads and bursting boughs of May,
   Dream, while the innumerable choir of day
          Welcome the dawn.

515   The South Wind

THE south wind rose at dusk of the winter day,
   The warm breath of the western sea
Circling wrapp'd the isle with his cloke of cloud,
And it now reach'd even to me, at dusk of the day,
   And moan'd in the branches aloud:
While here and there, in patches of dark space,
   A star shone forth from its heavenly place
As a spark that is borne in the smoky chase;
   And, looking up, there fell on my face—

Could it be drops of rain
Soft as the wind, that fell on my face?
Gossamers light as threads of the summer dawn,
Suck'd by the sun from midmost calms of the main,
From groves of coral islands secretly drawn,
O'er half the round of earth to be driven,
Now to fall on my face
In silky skeins spun from the mists of heaven.

   Who art thou, in wind and darkness and soft rain
Thyself that robest, that bendest in sighing pines
To whisper thy truth? that usest for signs
A hurried glimpse of the moon, the glance of a star
In the rifted sky?
Who art thou, that with thee I
Woo and am wooed?
That robing thyself in darkness and soft rain
Choosest my chosen solitude,
Coming so far
To tell thy secret again,
As a mother to her child, in her folding arm
Of a winter night by a flickering fire,
Telleth the same tale o'er and o'er
With gentle voice, and I never tire,
So imperceptibly changeth the charm,
As Love on buried ecstasy buildeth his tower,
—Like as the stem that beareth the flower
By trembling is knit to power;—
Ah! long ago
In thy first rapture I renounced my lot,
The vanity, the despondency and the woe,
And seeking thee to know
Well was't for me, and evermore
I am thine, I know not what.

For me thou seekest ever, me wondering a day
In the eternal alternations, me
Free for a stolen moment of chance
To dream a beautiful dream
In the everlasting dance
Of speechless worlds, the unsearchable scheme,
To me thou findest the way,
Me and whomsoe'er
I have found my dream to share
Still with thy charm encircling; even to-night
To me and my love in darkness and soft rain
Under the sighing pines thou comest again,
And staying our speech with mystery of delight,
Of the kiss that I give a wonder thou makest,
And the kiss that I take thou takest.

516   November

THE lonely season in lonely lands, when fled
Are half the birds, and mists lie low, and the sun
Is rarely seen, nor strayeth far from his bed;
The short days pass unwelcomed one by one.

Out by the ricks the mantled engine stands
Crestfallen, deserted,—for now all hands
Are told to the plough,—and ere it is dawn appear
The teams following and crossing far and near,
As hour by hour they broaden the brown bands
Of the striped fields; and behind them firk and prance
The heavy rooks, and daws grey-pated dance:
As awhile, surmounting a crest, in sharp outline
(A miniature of toil, a gem's design,)
They are pictured, horses and men, or now near by

Above the lane they shout lifting the share,
By the trim hedgerow bloom'd with purple air;
Where, under the thorns, dead leaves in huddle lie
Packed by the gales of Autumn, and in and out
The small wrens glide
With a happy note of cheer,
And yellow amorets flutter above and about,
Gay, familiar in fear.

And now, if the night shall be cold, across the sky
Linnets and twites, in small flocks helter-skelter,
All the afternoon to the gardens fly,
From thistle-pastures hurrying to gain the shelter
Of American rhododendron or cherry-laurel:
And here and there, near chilly setting of sun,
In an isolated tree a congregation
Of starlings chatter and chide,
Thickset as summer leaves, in garrulous quarrel:
Suddenly they hush as one,—
The tree top springs,—
And off, with a whirr of wings,
They fly by the score
To the holly-thicket, and there with myriads more
Dispute for the roosts; and from the unseen nation
A babel of tongues, like running water unceasing,
Makes live the wood, the flocking cries increasing,
Wrangling discordantly, incessantly,
While falls the night on them self-occupied;
The long dark night, that lengthens slow,
Deepening with Winter to starve grass and tree,
And soon to bury in snow
The Earth, that, sleeping 'neath her frozen stole,
Shall dream a dream crept from the sunless pole
Of how her end shall be.

ALICE MEYNELL

517   Renouncement

I MUST not think of thee; and, tired yet strong,
   I shun the thought that lurks in all delight—
   The thought of thee—and in the blue Heaven's height,
And in the dearest passage of a song.

Oh, just beyond the fairest thoughts that throng
   This breast, the thought of thee waits hidden, yet bright;
   But it must never, never come in sight;
I must stop short of thee the whole day long.

But when sleep comes to close each difficult day,
   When night gives pause to the long watch I keep,
   And all my bonds I needs must loose apart,
Must doff my will as raiment laid away,—
   With the first dream that comes with the first sleep
   I run, I run, I am gathered to thy heart.

DIGBY MACKWORTH DOLBEN

518

WE hurry on, nor passing note
   The rounded hedges white with May;
   For golden clouds before us float
   To lead our dazzled sight astray.
   We say, 'they shall indeed be sweet
   'The summer days that are to be'—
   The ages murmur at our feet
   The everlasting mystery.

We seek for Love to make our own,
But clasp him not for all our care
Of outspread arms; we gain alone
The flicker of his yellow hair
Caught now and then through glancing vine,
How rare, how fair, we dare not tell;
We know those sunny locks entwine
With ruddy-fruited asphodel.

A little life, a little love,
Young men rejoicing in their youth,
A doubtful twilight from above,
A glimpse of Beauty and of Truth,—
And then, no doubt, spring-loveliness
Expressed in hawthorns white and red,
The sprouting of the meadow grass,
But churchyard weeds about our head.

519   A Song

THE world is young today:
        Forget the gods are old,
        Forget the years of gold
When all the months were May.

A little flower of Love
        Is ours, without a root,
        Without the end of fruit,
Yet—take the scent thereof.

There may be hope above,
        There may be rest beneath;
        We see them not, but Death
Is palpable—and Love.

WILLIAM ERNEST HENLEY

from 'LIFE AND DEATH'

(ECHOES)

520   [1]

Out of the night that covers me,
    Black as the pit from pole to pole,
I thank whatever gods may be
    For my unconquerable soul.

In the fell clutch of circumstance
    I have not winced nor cried aloud.
Under the bludgeonings of chance
    My head is bloody, but unbowed.

Beyond this place of wrath and tears
    Looms but the Horror of the shade,
And yet the menace of the years
    Finds, and shall find, me unafraid.

It matters not how strait the gate,
    How charged with punishments the scroll,
I am the master of my fate:
    I am the captain of my soul.

                                                    1875

521   [11]

I am the Reaper.
All things with heedful hook
Silent I gather.
Pale roses touched with spring,
Tall corn in summer,
Fruits rich with autumn, and frail winter blossoms—
Reaping, still reaping—
All things with heedful hook
Timely I gather.

I am the Sower.
All the unbodied life
Runs through my seed-sheet.
Atom with atom wed,
Each quickening the other,
Fall through my hands, ever changing, still changeless.
Ceaselessly sowing,
Life, incorruptible life,
Flows from my seed-sheet.

Maker and breaker,
I am the ebb and the flood,
Here and Hereafter.
Sped through the tangle and coil
Of infinite nature,
Viewless and soundless I fashion all being.
Taker and giver,
I am the womb and the grave,
The Now and the Ever.

1875

522

[III]

Margaritæ Sorori, I. M.

A LATE lark twitters from the quiet skies;
And from the west,
Where the sun, his day's work ended,
Lingers as in content,
There falls on the old, gray city
An influence luminous and serene,
A shining peace.

The smoke ascends
In a rosy-and-golden haze. The spires
Shine, and are changed. In the valley
Shadows rise. The lark sings on. The sun,
Closing his benediction,
Sinks, and the darkening air
Thrills with a sense of the triumphing night—
Night, with her train of stars
And her great gift of sleep.

So be my passing!
My task accomplished and the long day done,
My wages taken, and in my heart
Some late lark singing,
Let me be gathered to the quiet west,
The sundown splendid and serene,
Death.

1876

523   [IV]

    ON the way to Kew,
    By the river old and gray,
    Where in the Long Ago
    We laughed and loitered so,
    I met a ghost to-day,
    A ghost that told of you,
    A ghost of low replies
    And sweet inscrutable eyes,
        Coming up from Richmond,
    As you used to do.

By the river old and gray,
The enchanted Long Ago
Murmured and smiled anew.
On the way to Kew,
March had the laugh of May,
The bare boughs looked aglow,
And old immortal words
Sang in my breast like birds,
    Coming up from Richmond,
As I used with you.

With the life of Long Ago
Lived my thought of you.
By the river old and gray
Flowing his appointed way,
As I watched, I knew
What is so good to know:
Not in vain, not in vain,
I shall look for you again,
    Coming up from Richmond,
On the way to Kew.

524 Rondel

BESIDE THE IDLE SUMMER SEA

BESIDE the idle summer sea,
And in the vacant summer days,
Light Love came fluting down the ways
Where you were loitering with me.

Who has not welcomed even as we
That jocund minstrel and his lays
Beside the idle summer sea,
And in the vacant summer days?

We listened, we were fancy-free;
And lo! in terror and amaze,
We stood alone—alone at gaze
With an implacable memory,
Beside the idle summer sea.

PHILIP BOURKE MARSTON

525   Too Late

LOVE has its morn, its noon, its eve, and night.
    We never had the noontide, never knew
    The deep, intense, illimitable blue
Of fervid, mid-day heavens, making bright
With princely liberality of light
Waters the water-lily trembles through;
But, in the evening's shadow did we two
Set out to gain Love's farthest, fairest height.
    O love! too late, too late for this we met;
    The goal was near, the nightfall nearer yet.
One star of Memory lightens in our track,
And all the rest is dark; I will go back—
    Back to the paths we walked in, and there stay,
    Until I change them for the silent way.

526   The Old Churchyard of Bonchurch

*(This old churchyard has been for many years slipping toward the sea
which it is expected will ultimately engulf it.)*

THE churchyard leans to the sea with its dead—
It leans to the sea with its dead so long.
Do they hear, I wonder, the first bird's song,
When the winter's anger is all but fled,
The high, sweet voice of the west wind,
The fall of the warm, soft rain,
When the second month of the year
Puts heart in the earth again?

Do they hear, through the glad April weather,
The green grasses waving above them?
Do they think there are none left to love them,
They have lain for so long there, together?
Do they hear the note of the cuckoo,
The cry of the gulls on the wing,
The laughter of winds and waters,
The feet of the dancing Spring?

Do they feel the old land slipping seaward,
The old land, with its hills and its graves,
As they gradually slide to the waves
With the wind blowing on them from leeward?
Do they know of the change that awaits them,
The sepulchre vast and strange?
Do they long for the days to go over,
And bring that miraculous change?

Or love they their night with no moonlight,
With no starlight, no dawn to its gloom?
Do they sigh—' 'Neath the snow, or the bloom
Of the wild things that wave from our night,

888

We are warm, through winter and summer;
We hear the winds rave, and we say—
"The storm-wind blows over our heads,
But we, here, are out of its way" '?

Do they mumble low, one to another,
With a sense that the waters that thunder
Shall ingather them all, draw them under,
'Ah! how long to our moving, brother?
How long shall we quietly rest here,
In graves of darkness and ease?
The waves, even now, may be on us,
To draw us down under the seas!'

Do they think 't will be cold when the waters
That they love not, that neither can love them,
Shall eternally thunder above them?
Have they dread of the sea's shining daughters,
That people the bright sea-regions
And play with the young sea-kings?
Have they dread of their cold embraces,
And dread of all strange sea-things?

But their dread or their joy—it is bootless:
They shall pass from the breast of their mother;
They shall lie low, dead brother by brother,
In a place that is radiant and fruitless,
And the folk that sail over their heads
In violent weather
Shall come down to them, haply, and all
They shall lie there, together.

Ungathered Love

WHEN the autumn winds go wailing
   Through branches yellow and brown,
When the grey, sad light is failing,
   And the day is going down,
I hear the desolate evening sing
Of a love that bloomed in the early Spring,
And which no heart had for gathering.

I and my lover, we dwell apart—
   We twain may never be one;
We shall never stand heart to heart;
   Then what can be said or done,
When winds and waters and song-birds sing
Of a love that bloomed in the early Spring,
And which no heart had for gathering?

When day is over and night descends,
   And dank mists circle and rise,
I fall asleep, and slumber befriends,
   For I dream of April skies;
But I wake to hear the silence sing
Of a love that bloomed in the early Spring,
And which no heart had for gathering.

When the dawn comes in with wind and rain,
   And birds awake in the eaves,
And raindrops smite the window-pane,
   And drench the eddying leaves,
I hear the voice of the daybreak sing
Of a love that bloomed in the early Spring,
And which no heart had for gathering.

528   To K[atharine]. de M[attos].

A LOVER of the moorland bare
And honest country winds, you were;
The silver-skimming rain you took;
And loved the floodings of the brook,
Dew, frost and mountains, fire and seas,
Tumultuary silences,
Winds that in darkness fifed a tune,
And the high-riding, virgin moon.

And as the berry, pale and sharp,
Springs on some ditch's counterscarp
In our ungenial, native north—
You put your frosted wildings forth,
And on the heath, afar from man,
A strong and bitter virgin ran.

The berry ripened keeps the rude
And racy flavour of the wood.
And you that loved the empty plain
All redolent of wind and rain,
Around you still the curlew sings—
The freshness of the weather clings—
The maiden jewels of the rain
Sit in your dabbled locks again.

529   Henry James

WHO comes to-night? We ope the doors in vain.
Who comes? My bursting walls, can you contain
The presences that now together throng
Your narrow entry, as with flowers and song,

As with the air of life, the breath of talk?
Lo, how these fair immaculate women walk
Behind their jocund maker; and we see
Slighted *De Mauves*, and that far different she,
Gressie, the trivial sphynx; and to our feast
Daisy and *Barb* and *Chancellor* (she not least!)
With all their silken, all their airy kin,
Do like unbidden angels enter in.
But he, attended by these shining names,
Comes (best of all) himself—our welcome James.

530   Requiem

UNDER the wide and starry sky,
Dig the grave and let me lie.
Glad did I live and gladly die,
 And I laid me down with a will.

This be the verse you grave for me:
Here he lies where he longed to be;
Home is the sailor, home from sea,
 And the hunter home from the hill.

531

SAY not of me that weakly I declined
The labours of my sires, and fled the sea,
The towers we founded and the lamps we lit,
To play at home with paper like a child.
But rather say: *In the afternoon of time*
A strenuous family dusted from its hands
The sand of granite, and beholding far
Along the sounding coast its pyramids
And tall memorials catch the dying sun,
Smiled well content, and to this childish task
Around the fire addressed its evening hours.

from 'SONGS OF TRAVEL'

532

[I]

BRIGHT is the ring of words
  When the right man rings them,
Fair the fall of songs
  When the singer sings them.
Still they are carolled and said—
  On wings they are carried—
After the singer is dead
  And the maker buried.

Low as the singer lies
  In the field of heather,
Songs of his fashion bring
  The swains together.
And when the west is red
  With the sunset embers,
The lover lingers and sings
  And the maid remembers.

533

[II]

If this were Faith

GOD, if this were enough,
That I see things bare to the buff
And up to the buttocks in mire;
That I ask nor hope nor hire,
Nut in the husk,
Nor dawn beyond the dusk,
Nor life beyond death:
God, if this were faith?

Having felt thy wind in my face
Spit sorrow and disgrace,
Having seen thine evil doom
In Golgotha and Khartoum,
And the brutes, the work of thine hands,
Fill with injustice lands
And stain with blood the sea:
If still in my veins the glee
Of the black night and the sun
And the lost battle, run:
If, an adept,
The iniquitous lists I still accept
With joy, and joy to endure and be withstood,
And still to battle and perish for a dream of good:
God, if that were enough?

If to feel, in the ink of the slough,
And the sink of the mire,
Veins of glory and fire
Run through and transpierce and transpire,
And a secret purpose of glory in every part,
And the answering glory of battle fill my heart;
To thrill with the joy of girded men
To go on for ever and fail and go on again,
And be mauled to the earth and arise,
And contend for the shade of a word and a thing not
    seen with the eyes:
With the half of a broken hope for a pillow at night
That somehow the right is the right
And the smooth shall bloom from the rough:
Lord, if that were enough?

534

[III]

To S. R. Crockett

ON RECEIVING A DEDICATION

BLOWS the wind today, and the sun and the rain are flying,
  Blows the wind on the moors today and now,
Where about the graves of the martyrs the whaups are crying,
  My heart remembers how!

Grey recumbent tombs of the dead in desert places,
  Standing-stones on the vacant wine-red moor,
Hills of sheep, and the howes of the silent vanished races,
  And winds, austere and pure.

Be it granted me to behold you again in dying,
  Hills of home! and to hear again the call;
Hear about the graves of the martyrs the peewees crying,
  And hear no more at all.

OSCAR WILDE

535   Requiescat

TREAD lightly, she is near
  Under the snow,
Speak gently, she can hear
  The daisies grow.

All her bright golden hair
   Tarnished with rust,
She that was young and fair
   Fallen to dust.

Lily-like, white as snow,
   She hardly knew
She was a woman, so
   Sweetly she grew.

Coffin-board, heavy stone,
   Lie on her breast,
I vex my heart alone
   She is at rest.

Peace, Peace, she cannot hear
   Lyre or sonnet,
All my life's buried here,
   Heap earth upon it.

536 from *THE BALLAD OF READING GAOL*

He did not wear his scarlet coat,
   For blood and wine are red,
And blood and wine were on his hands
   When they found him with the dead,
The poor dead woman whom he loved,
   And murdered in her bed.

He walked amongst the Trial Men
   In a suit of shabby gray;
A cricket cap was on his head,
   And his step seemed light and gay;
But I never saw a man who looked
   So wistfully at the day.

I never saw a man who looked
  With such a wistful eye
Upon that little tent of blue
  Which prisoners call the sky,
And at every drifting cloud that went
  With sails of silver by.

I walked, with other souls in pain,
  Within another ring,
And was wondering if the man had done
  A great or little thing,
When a voice behind me whispered low,
  '*That fellow's got to swing.*'

Dear Christ! the very prison walls
  Suddenly seemed to reel,
And the sky above my head became
  Like a casque of scorching steel;
And, though I was a soul in pain,
  My pain I could not feel.

I only knew what hunted thought
  Quickened his step, and why
He looked upon the garish day
  With such a wistful eye;
The man had killed the thing he loved,
  And so he had to die.

*

Yet each man kills the thing he loves,
  By each let this be heard,
Some do it with a bitter look,
  Some with a flattering word,
The coward does it with a kiss,
  The brave man with a sword!

Some kill their love when they are young,
  And some when they are old;
Some strangle with the hands of Lust,
  Some with the hands of Gold:
The kindest use a knife, because
  The dead so soon grow cold.

Some love too little, some too long,
  Some sell, and others buy;
Some do the deed with many tears,
  And some without a sigh:
For each man kills the thing he loves,
  Yet each man does not die.

*

He does not die a death of shame
  On a day of dark disgrace,
Nor have a noose about his neck,
  Nor a cloth upon his face,
Nor drop feet foremost through the floor
  Into an empty space.

He does not sit with silent men
  Who watch him night and day;
Who watch him when he tries to weep,
  And when he tries to pray;
Who watch him lest himself should rob
  The prison of its prey.

He does not wake at dawn to see
  Dread figures throng his room,
The shivering Chaplain robed in white,
  The Sheriff stern with gloom,
And the Governor all in shiny black,
  With the yellow face of Doom.

He does not rise in piteous haste
    To put on convict-clothes,
While some coarse-mouthed Doctor gloats, and notes
    Each new and nerve-twitched pose,
Fingering a watch whose little ticks
    Are like horrible hammer-blows.

He does not feel that sickening thirst
    That sands one's throat, before
The hangman with his gardener's gloves
    Comes through the padded door,
And binds one with three leathern thongs,
    That the throat may thirst no more.

He does not bend his head to hear
    The Burial Office read
Nor, while the anguish of his soul
    Tells him he is not dead,
Cross his own coffin, as he moves
    Into the hideous shed.

He does not stare upon the air
    Through a little roof of glass:
He does not pray with lips of clay
    For his agony to pass;
Nor feel upon his shuddering cheek
    The kiss of Caiaphas.

537   London

ATHWART the sky a lowly sigh
  From west to east the sweet wind carried;
The sun stood still on Primrose Hill;
  His light in all the city tarried:
The clouds on viewless columns bloomed
Like smouldering lilies unconsumed.

'Oh sweetheart, see! how shadowy,
  Of some occult magician's rearing,
Or swung in space of heaven's grace
  Dissolving, dimly reappearing,
Afloat upon ethereal tides
St Paul's above the city rides!'

A rumour broke through the thin smoke
  Enwreathing abbey, tower, and palace,
The parks, the squares, the thoroughfares,
  The million-peopled lanes and alleys,
An ever-muttering prisoned storm,
The heart of London beating warm.

538   Thirty Bob a Week

I COULDN'T touch a stop and turn a screw,
  And set the blooming world a-work for me
Like such as cut their teeth—I hope, like you—
  On the handle of a skeleton gold key;
I cut mine on a leek, which I eat it every week:
  I'm a clerk at thirty bob as you can see.

But I don't allow it's luck and all a toss;
　　There's no such thing as being starred and crossed;
It's just the power of some to be a boss,
　　And the bally power of others to be bossed:
I face the music, sir; you bet I ain't a cur;
　　Strike me lucky if I don't believe I'm lost!

For like a mole I journey in the dark,
　　A-travelling along the underground
From my Pillar'd Halls and broad Suburbean Park,
　　To come the daily dull official round;
And home again at night with my pipe all alight,
　　A-scheming how to count ten bob a pound.

And it's often very cold and very wet,
　　And my missis stitches towels for a hunks;
And the Pillar'd Halls is half of it to let—
　　Three rooms about the size of travelling trunks.
And we cough, my wife and I, to dislocate a sigh,
　　When the noisy little kids are in their bunks.

But you never hear her do a growl or whine,
　　For she's made of flint and roses, very odd;
And I've got to cut my meaning rather fine,
　　Or I'd blubber, for I'm made of greens and sod:
So p'r'aps we are in Hell for all that I can tell,
　　And lost and damn'd and served up hot to God.

I ain't blaspheming, Mr Silver-tongue;
　　I'm saying things a bit beyond your art:
Of all the rummy starts you ever sprung,
　　Thirty bob a week's the rummiest start!
With your science and your books and your the'ries about spooks,
　　Did you ever hear of looking in your heart?

I didn't mean your pocket, Mr, no:
　　I mean that having children and a wife,
With thirty bob on which to come and go,
　　Isn't dancing to the tabor and the fife:
When it doesn't make you drink, by Heaven! it makes you think,
　　And notice curious items about life.

I step into my heart and there I meet
　　A god-almighty devil singing small,
Who would like to shout and whistle in the street,
　　And squelch the passers flat against the wall;
If the whole world was a cake he had the power to take,
　　He would take it, ask for more, and eat it all.

And I meet a sort of simpleton beside,
　　The kind that life is always giving beans;
With thirty bob a week to keep a bride
　　He fell in love and married in his teens:
At thirty bob he stuck; but he knows it isn't luck:
　　He knows the seas are deeper than tureens.

And the god-almighty devil and the fool
　　That meet me in the High Street on the strike,
When I walk about my heart a-gathering wool,
　　Are my good and evil angels if you like.
And both of them together in every kind of weather
　　Ride me like a double-seated bike.

That's rough a bit and needs its meaning curled.
　　But I have a high old hot un in my mind—
A most engrugious notion of the world,
　　That leaves your lightning 'rithmetic behind—
I give it at a glance when I say 'There ain't no chance,
　　Nor nothing of the lucky-lottery kind.'

And it's this way that I make it out to be:
  No fathers, mothers, countries, climates—none;
Not Adam was responsible for me,
  Nor society, nor systems, nary one:
A little sleeping seed, I woke—I did, indeed—
  A million years before the blooming sun.

I woke because I thought the time had come;
  Beyond my will there was no other cause;
And everywhere I found myself at home,
  Because I chose to be the thing I was;
And in whatever shape of mollusc or of ape
  I always went according to the laws.

I was the love that chose my mother out;
  I joined two lives and from the union burst;
My weakness and my strength without a doubt
  Are mine alone for ever from the first:
It's just the very same with a difference in the name
  As 'Thy will be done.' You say it if you durst!

They say it daily up and down the land
  As easy as you take a drink, it's true;
But the difficultest go to understand,
  And the difficultest job a man can do,
Is to come it brave and meek with thirty bob a week,
  And feel that that's the proper thing for you.

It's a naked child against a hungry wolf;
  It's playing bowls upon a splitting wreck;
It's walking on a string across a gulf
  With millstones fore-and-aft about your neck;
But the thing is daily done by many and many a one;
  And we fall, face forward, fighting, on the deck.

539 A Northern Suburb

NATURE selects the longest way,
  And winds about in tortuous grooves;
A thousand years the oaks decay;
  The wrinkled glacier hardly moves.

But here the whetted fangs of change
  Daily devour the old demesne—
The busy farm, the quiet grange,
  The wayside inn, the village green.

In gaudy yellow brick and red,
  With rooting pipes, like creepers rank,
The shoddy terraces o'erspread
  Meadow, and garth, and daisied bank.

With shelves for rooms the houses crowd,
  Like draughty cupboards in a row—
Ice-chests when wintry winds are loud,
  Ovens when summer breezes blow.

Roused by the fee'd policeman's knock,
  And sad that day should come again,
Under the stars the workmen flock
  In haste to reach the workmen's train.

For here dwell those who must fulfil
  Dull tasks in uncongenial spheres,
Who toil through dread of coming ill,
  And not with hope of happier years—

The lowly folk who scarcely dare
  Conceive themselves perhaps misplaced,
Whose prize for unremitting care
  Is only not to be disgraced.

540 War Song

In anguish we uplift
    A new unhallowed song:
The race is to the swift;
    The battle to the strong.

Of old it was ordained
    That we, in packs like curs,
Some thirty million trained
    And licensed murderers,

In crime should live and act,
    If cunning folk say sooth
Who flay the naked fact
    And carve the heart of truth.

The rulers cry aloud,
    'We cannot cancel war,
The end and bloody shroud
    Of wrongs the worst abhor,
And order's swaddling band:
    Know that relentless strife
Remains by sea and land
    The holiest law of life.
From fear in every guise,
    From sloth, from lust of pelf,
By war's great sacrifice
    The world redeems itself.
War is the source, the theme
    Of art; the goal, the bent
And brilliant academe
    Of noble sentiment;

The augury, the dawn
    Of golden times of grace;
The true catholicon,
    And blood-bath of the race.'

We thirty million trained
    And licensed murderers,
Like zanies rigged, and chained
    By drill and scourge and curse
In shackles of despair
    We know not how to break—
What do we victims care
    For art, what interest take
In things unseen, unheard?
    Some diplomat no doubt
Will launch a heedless word,
    And lurking war leap out!

We spell-bound armies then,
    Huge brutes in dumb distress,
Machines compact of men
    Who once had consciences,
Must trample harvests down—
    Vineyard, and corn and oil;
Dismantle town by town,
    Hamlet and homestead spoil
On each appointed path,
    Till lust of havoc light
A blood-red blaze of wrath
    In every frenzied sight.

In many a mountain-pass,
    Or meadow green and fresh,
Mass shall encounter mass
    Of shuddering human flesh;

Opposing ordnance roar
  Across the swaths of slain,
And blood in torrents pour
  In vain—always in vain,
    For war breeds war again!

The shameful dream is past,
  The subtle maze untrod:
We recognize at last
  That war is not of God.
Wherefore we now uplift
  Our new unhallowed song:
The race is to the swift,
  The battle to the strong.

541　　　　In the Isle of Dogs

WHILE the water-wagon's ringing showers
Sweetened the dust with a woodland smell,
'Past noon, past noon, two sultry hours,'
Drowsily fell
From the schoolhouse clock
In the Isle of Dogs by Millwall Dock.

Mirrored in shadowy windows draped
With ragged net or half-drawn blind
Bowsprits, masts, exactly shaped
To woo or fight the wind,
Like monitors of guilt
By strength and beauty sent,
Disgraced the shameful houses built
To furnish rent.

From the pavements and the roofs
In shimmering volumes wound
The wrinkled heat;
Distant hammers, wheels and hoofs,
A turbulent pulse of sound,
Southward obscurely beat,
The only utterance of the afternoon,
Till on a sudden in the silent street
An organ-man drew up and ground
The Old Hundredth tune.

Forthwith the pillar of cloud that hides the past
Burst into flame,
Whose alchemy transmuted house and mast,
Street, dockyard, pier and pile:
By magic sound the Isle of Dogs became
A northern isle—
A green isle like a beryl set
In a wine-coloured sea,
Shadowed by mountains where a river met
The ocean's arm extended royally.

There also in the evening on the shore
An old man ground the Old Hundredth tune,
An old enchanter steeped in human lore,
Sad-eyed, with whitening beard, and visage lank:
Not since and not before,
Under the sunset or the mellowing moon,
Has any hand of man's conveyed
Such meaning in the turning of a crank.

Sometimes he played
As if his box had been
An organ in an abbey richly lit;
For when the dark invaded day's demesne,

And the sun set in crimson and in gold;
When idlers swarmed upon the esplanade,
And a late steamer wheeling towards the quay
Struck founts of silver from the darkling sea,
The solemn tune arose and shook and rolled
Above the throng,
Above the hum and tramp and bravely knit
All hearts in common memories of song.

Sometimes he played at speed;
Then the Old Hundredth like a devil's mass
Instinct with evil thought and evil deed,
Rang out in anguish and remorse. Alas!
That men must know both Heaven and Hell!
Sometimes the melody
Sang with the murmuring surge;
And with the winds would tell
Of peaceful graves and of the passing bell.
Sometimes it pealed across the bay
A high triumphal dirge,
A dirge
For the departing undefeated day.

A noble tune, a high becoming mate
Of the capped mountains and the deep broad firth;
A simple tune and great,
The fittest utterance of the voice of earth.

WILLIAM WATSON

542

Wordsworth's Grave

I

THE old rude church, with bare, bald tower, is here;
  Beneath its shadow high-born Rotha flows;
Rotha, remembering well who slumbers near,
  And with cool murmur lulling his repose.

Rotha, remembering well who slumbers near.
  His hills, his lakes, his streams are with him yet.
Surely the heart that read her own heart clear
  Nature forgets not soon: 'tis we forget.

We that with vagrant soul his fixity
  Have slighted; faithless, done his deep faith wrong;
Left him for poorer loves, and bowed the knee
  To misbegotten strange new gods of song.

Yet, led by hollow ghost or beckoning elf
  Far from her homestead to the desert bourn,
The vagrant soul returning to herself
  Wearily wise, must needs to him return.

To him and to the powers that with him dwell:—
  Inflowings that divulged not whence they came;
And that secluded spirit unknowable,
  The mystery we make darker with a name;

The Somewhat which we name but cannot know,
  Ev'n as we name a star and only see
His quenchless flashings forth, which ever show
  And ever hide him, and which are not he.

II

Poet who sleepest by this wandering wave!
　　When thou wast born, what birth-gift hadst thou then?
To thee what wealth was that the Immortals gave,
　　The wealth thou gavest in thy turn to men?

Not Milton's keen, translunar music thine;
　　Not Shakespeare's cloudless, boundless human view;
Not Shelley's flush of rose on peaks divine;
　　Nor yet the wizard twilight Coleridge knew.

What hadst thou that could make so large amends
　　For all thou hadst not and thy peers possessed,
Motion and fire, swift means to radiant ends —
　　Thou hadst, for weary feet, the gift of rest.

From Shelley's dazzling glow or thunderous haze,
　　From Byron's tempest-anger, tempest-mirth,
Men turned to thee and found—not blast and blaze,
　　Tumult of tottering heavens, but peace on earth.

Nor peace that grows by Lethe, scentless flower,
　　There in white languors to decline and cease;
But peace whose names are also rapture, power,
　　Clear sight, and love: for these are parts of peace.

III

I hear it vouched the Muse is with us still;—
　　If less divinely frenzied than of yore,
In lieu of feelings she has wondrous skill
　　To simulate emotion felt no more.

Not such the authentic Presence pure, that made
  This valley vocal in the great days gone!—
In *his* great days, while yet the spring-time played
  About him, and the mighty morning shone.

No word-mosaic artificer, he sang
  A lofty song of lowly weal and dole.
Right from the heart, right to the heart it sprang,
  Or from the soul leapt instant to the soul.

He felt the charm of childhood, grace of youth,
  Grandeur of age, insisting to be sung.
The impassioned argument was simple truth
  Half-wondering at its own melodious tongue.

Impassioned? ay, to the song's ecstatic core!
  But far removed were clangour, storm and feud;
For plenteous health was his, exceeding store
  Of joy, and an impassioned quietude.

IV

A hundred years ere he to manhood came,
  Song from celestial heights had wandered down,
Put off her robe of sunlight, dew and flame,
  And donned a modish dress to charm the Town.

Thenceforth she but festooned the porch of things;
  Apt at life's lore, incurious what life meant.
Dextrous of hand, she struck her lute's few strings,
  Ignobly perfect, barrenly content.

Unflushed with ardour and unblanched with awe,
  Her lips in profitless derision curled,
She saw with dull emotion—if she saw—
  The vision of the glory of the world.

The human masque she watched, with dreamless eyes
  In whose clear shallows lurked no trembling shade:
The stars, unkenned by her, might set and rise,
  Unmarked by her, the daisies bloom and fade.

The age grew sated with her sterile wit.
  Herself waxed weary on her loveless throne.
Men felt life's tide, the sweep and surge of it,
  And craved a living voice, a natural tone.

For none the less, though song was but half true,
  The world lay common, one abounding theme.
Man joyed and wept, and fate was ever new,
  And love was sweet, life real, death no dream.

In sad stern verse the rugged scholar-sage
  Bemoaned his toil unvalued, youth uncheered.
His numbers wore the vesture of the age,
  But, 'neath it beating, the great heart was heard.

From dewy pastures, uplands sweet with thyme,
  A virgin breeze freshened the jaded day.
It wafted Collins' lonely vesper-chime,
  It breathed abroad the frugal note of Gray.

It fluttered here and there, nor swept in vain
  The dusty haunts where futile echoes dwell,—
Then, in a cadence soft as summer rain,
  And sad from Auburn voiceless, drooped and fell.

It drooped and fell, and one 'neath northern skies,
  With southern heart, who tilled his father's field,
Found Poesy a-dying, bade her rise
  And touch quick nature's hem and go forth healed.

On life's broad plain the ploughman's conquering share
   Upturned the fallow lands of truth anew,
And o'er the formal garden's trim parterre
   The peasant's team a ruthless furrow drew.

Bright was his going forth, but clouds ere long
   Whelmed him; in gloom his radiance set, and those
Twin morning stars of the new century's song,
   Those morning stars that sang together, rose.

In elfish speech the *Dreamer* told his tale
   Of marvellous oceans swept by fateful wings.—
The *Seër* strayed not from earth's human pale,
   But the mysterious face of common things

He mirrored as the moon in Rydal Mere
   Is mirrored, when the breathless night hangs blue:
Strangely remote she seems and wondrous near,
   And by some nameless difference born anew.

v

Peace—peace—and rest! Ah, how the lyre is loth,
   Or powerless now, to give what all men seek!
Either it deadens with ignoble sloth
   Or deafens with shrill tumult, loudly weak.

Where is the singer whose large notes and clear
   Can heal and arm and plenish and sustain?
Lo, one with empty music floods the ear,
   And one, the heart refreshing, tires the brain.

And idly tuneful, the loquacious throng
   Flutter and twitter, prodigal of time,
And little masters make a toy of song
   Till grave men weary of the sound of rhyme.

And some go prankt in faded antique dress,
  Abhorring to be hale and glad and free;
And some parade a conscious naturalness,
  The scholar's not the child's simplicity.

Enough;—and wisest who from words forbear.
  The kindly river rails not as it glides;
And suave and charitable, the winning air
  Chides not at all, or only him who chides.

VI

Nature! we storm thine ear with choric notes.
  Thou answerest through the calm great nights and days,
'Laud me who will: not tuneless are your throats;
  Yet if ye paused I should not miss the praise.'

We falter, half-rebuked, and sing again.
  We chant thy desertness and haggard gloom,
Or with thy splendid wrath inflate the strain,
  Or touch it with thy colour and perfume.

One, his melodious blood aflame for thee,
  Wooed with fierce lust, his hot heart world-defiled.
One, with the upward eye of infancy,
  Looked in thy face, and felt himself thy child.

Thee he approached without distrust or dread—
  Beheld thee throned, an awful queen, above—
Climbed to thy lap and merely laid his head
  Against thy warm wild heart of mother-love.

He heard that vast heart beating—thou didst press
  Thy child so close, and lov'dst him unaware.
Thy beauty gladdened him; yet he scarce less
  Had loved thee, had he never found thee fair!

For thou wast not as legendary lands
   To which with curious eyes and ears we roam.
Nor wast thou as a fane mid solemn sands,
   Where palmers halt at evening. Thou wast home.

And here, at home, still bides he; but he sleeps;
   Not to be wakened even at thy word;
Though we, vague dreamers, dream he somewhere keeps
   An ear still open to thy voice still heard,—

Thy voice, as heretofore, about him blown,
   For ever blown about his silence now;
Thy voice, though deeper, yet so like his own
   That almost, when he sang, we deemed 'twas thou!

VII

Behind Helm Crag and Silver Howe the sheen
   Of the retreating day is less and less.
Soon will the lordlier summits, here unseen,
   Gather the night about their nakedness.

The half-heard bleat of sheep comes from the hill.
   Faint sounds of childish play are in the air.
The river murmurs past. All else is still.
   The very graves seem stiller than they were.

Afar though nation be on nation hurled,
   And life with toil and ancient pain depressed,
Here one may scarce believe the whole wide world
   Is not at peace, and all man's heart at rest.

Rest! 'twas the gift *he* gave; and peace! the shade
   He spread, for spirits fevered with the sun.
To him his bounties are come back—here laid
   In rest, in peace, his labour nobly done.

FRANCIS THOMPSON

543

Daisy

WHERE the thistle lifts a purple crown
  Six foot out of the turf,
And the harebell shakes on the windy hill—
  O the breath of the distant surf!—

The hills look over on the South
  And southward dreams the sea;
And, with the sea-breeze hand in hand
  Came innocence and she.

Where 'mid the gorse the raspberry
  Red for the gatherer springs,
Two children did we stray and talk
  Wise, idle, childish things.

She listened with big-lipped surprise,
  Breast-deep 'mid flower and spine:
Her skin was like a grape whose veins
  Run snow instead of wine.

She knew not those sweet words she spake,
  Nor knew her own sweet way;
But there's never a bird, so sweet a song
  Thronged in whose throat that day!

Oh, there were flowers in Storrington
  On the turf and on the spray;
But the sweetest flower on Sussex hills
  Was the Daisy-flower that day!

Her beauty smoothed earth's furrowed face!
   She gave me tokens three:—
A look, a word of her winsome mouth,
   And a wild raspberry.

A berry red, a guileless look,
   A still word,—strings of sand!
And yet they made my wild, wild heart
   Fly down to her little hand.

For standing artless as the air,
   And candid as the skies,
She took the berries with her hand,
   And the love with her sweet eyes.

The faintest things have fleetest end;
   Their scent survives their close,
But the rose's scent is bitterness
   To him that loved the rose!

She looked a little wistfully,
   Then went her sunshine way:—
The sea's eye had a mist on it,
   And the leaves fell from the day.

She went her unremembering way,
   She went and left in me
The pang of all the partings gone,
   And partings yet to be.

She left me marvelling why my soul
   Was sad that she was glad;
At all the sadness in the sweet,
   The sweetness in the sad.

Still, still I seemed to see her, still
    Look up with soft replies,
And take the berries with her hand,
    And the love with her lovely eyes.

Nothing begins, and nothing ends,
    That is not paid with moan;
For we are born in others' pain,
    And perish in our own.

544   from 'ODE TO THE SETTING SUN'

Now that the red glare of thy fall is blown
    In smoke and flame about the windy sky,
Where are the wailing voices that should meet
    From hill, stream, grove, and all of mortal shape
Who tread thy gifts, in vineyards as stray feet
    Pulp the globed weight of juiced Iberia's grape?
            Where is the threne o' the sea?
            And why not dirges thee
The wind, that sings to himself as he makes stride
    Lonely and terrible on the Andéan height?
        Where is the Naiad 'mid her sworded sedge?
    The Nymph wan-glimmering by her wan fount's verge?
The Dryad at timid gaze by the wood-side?
            The Oread jutting light
    On one up-strainèd sole from the rock-ledge?
            The Nereid tip-toe on the scud o' the surge,
With whistling tresses dank athwart her face,
And all her figure poised in lithe Circean grace?

Why withers their lament?
Their tresses tear-besprent,
Have they sighed hence with trailing garment-hem?
O sweet, O sad, O fair!
I catch your flying hair,
Draw your eyes down to me, and dream on them!

545   from 'CONTEMPLATION'

NATURE one hour appears a thing unsexed,
Or to such serene balance brought
That her twin natures cease their sweet alarms,
And sleep in one another's arms.
The sun with resting pulses seems to brood,
And slacken its command upon my unurged blood.

The river has not any care
Its passionless water to the sea to bear;
The leaves have brown content;
The wall to me has freshness like a scent,
And takes half-animate the air,
Making one life with its green moss and stain;
And life with all things seems too perfect blent
For anything of life to be aware.
The very shades on hill, and tree, and plain,
Where they have fallen doze, and where they doze
    remain.

No hill can idler be than I;
No stone its inter-particled vibration
Investeth with a stiller lie;
No heaven with a more urgent rest betrays
The eyes that on it gaze.

We are too near akin that thou shouldst cheat
Me, Nature, with thy fair deceit.
In poets floating like a water-flower
Upon the bosom of the glassy hour,
In skies that no man sees to move,
Lurk untumultuous vortices of power,
For joy too native, and for agitation
Too instant, too entire for sense thereof,
Motion like gnats when autumn suns are low,
Perpetual as the prisoned feet of love
On the heart's floors with painèd pace that go.
From stones and poets you may know,
Nothing so active is, as that which least seems so.

ALFRED EDWARD HOUSMAN

546   On Wenlock Edge the wood's in trouble;
          His forest fleece the Wrekin heaves;
      The gale, it plies the saplings double,
          And thick on Severn snow the leaves.

      'Twould blow like this through holt and hanger
          When Uricon the city stood:
      'Tis the old wind in the old anger,
          But then it threshed another wood.

      Then, 'twas before my time, the Roman
          At yonder heaving hill would stare:
      The blood that warms an English yeoman,
          The thoughts that hurt him, they were there.

There, like the wind through woods in riot,
  Through him the gale of life blew high;
The tree of man was never quiet:
  Then 'twas the Roman, now 'tis I.

The gale, it plies the saplings double,
  It blows so hard, 'twill soon be gone:
To-day the Roman and his trouble
  Are ashes under Uricon.

547   O N the idle hill of summer,
               Sleepy with the flow of streams,
           Far I hear the steady drummer
               Drumming like a noise in dreams.

           Far and near and low and louder
               On the roads of earth go by,
           Dear to friends and food for powder,
               Soldiers marching, all to die.

           East and west on fields forgotten
               Bleach the bones of comrades slain,
           Lovely lads and dead and rotten;
               None that go return again.

           Far the calling bugles hollo,
               High the screaming fife replies,
           Gay the files of scarlet follow:
               Woman bore me, I will rise.

548

Be still, my soul, be still; the arms you bear are brittle,
  Earth and high heaven are fixt of old and founded strong.
Think rather,—call to thought, if now you grieve a little,
  The days when we had rest, O soul, for they were long.

Men loved unkindness then, but lightless in the quarry
  I slept and saw not; tears fell down, I did not mourn;
Sweat ran and blood sprang out and I was never sorry:
  Then it was well with me, in days ere I was born.

Now, and I muse for why and never find the reason,
  I pace the earth, and drink the air, and feel the sun.
Be still, be still, my soul; it is but for a season:
  Let us endure an hour and see injustice done.

Ay, look: high heaven and earth ail from the prime foundation;
  All thoughts to rive the heart are here, and all are vain:
Horror and scorn and hate and fear and indignation—
  O why did I awake? when shall I sleep again?

549

Tell me not here, it needs not saying,
    What tune the enchantress plays
  In aftermaths of soft September
    Or under blanching mays,
  For she and I were long acquainted
    And I knew all her ways.

  On russet floors, by waters idle,
    The pine lets fall its cone;
  The cuckoo shouts all day at nothing
    In leafy dells alone;
  And traveller's joy beguiles in autumn
    Hearts that have lost their own.

On acres of the seeded grasses
   The changing burnish heaves;
Or marshalled under moons of harvest
   Stand still all night the sheaves;
Or beeches strip in storms for winter
   And stain the wind with leaves.

Possess, as I possessed a season,
   The countries I resign,
Where over elmy plains the highway
   Would mount the hills and shine,
And full of shade the pillared forest
   Would murmur and be mine.

For nature, heartless, witless nature,
   Will neither care nor know
What stranger's feet may find the meadow
   And trespass there and go,
Nor ask amid the dews of morning
   If they are mine or no.

MARY COLERIDGE

550   Gone

ABOUT the little chambers of my heart
Friends have been coming—going—many a year.
   The doors stand open there.
Some, lightly stepping, enter; some depart.

Freely they come and freely go, at will.
The walls give back their laughter; all day long
   They fill the house with song.
One door alone is shut, one chamber still

551 'He Knoweth Not that the Dead are Thine'

THE weapon that you fought with was a word,
And with that word you stabbed me to the heart.
Not once but twice you did it, for the sword
    Made no blood start.

They have not tried you for your life. You go
Strong in such innocence as men will boast.
They have not buried me. They do not know
    Life from its ghost.

552   Jealousy

'THE myrtle bush grew shady
    Down by the ford.'—
'Is it even so?' said my lady.
    'Even so!' said my lord.
'The leaves are set too thick together
    For the point of a sword.'

'The arras in your room hangs close,
    No light between!
You wedded one of those
    That see unseen.'—
'Is it even so?' said the King's Majesty.
    'Even so!' said the Queen.

553 ## Unwelcome

WE were young, we were merry, we were very very wise,
    And the door stood open at our feast,
When there passed us a woman with the West in her eyes,
    And a man with his back to the East.

O, still grew the hearts that were beating so fast,
    The loudest voice was still.
The jest died away on our lips as they passed,
    And the rays of July struck chill.

The cups of red wine turned pale on the board,
    The white bread black as soot.
The hound forgot the hand of her lord,
    She fell down at his foot.

Low let me lie, where the dead dog lies,
    Ere I sit me down again at a feast,
When there passes a woman with the West in her eyes,
    And a man with his back to the East.

554 ## Awake

THE wailing wind doth not enough despair;
    The sea, for all her sobbing, hath the moon,
I cannot find my heart's cry anywhere,
    Fain to complain alone.

The whistle of the train that, like a dart,
    Pierces the darkness as it hurries by,
Hath not enough of sadness, and my heart
    Is stifled for a cry.

555   ## Where a Roman Villa Stood, above Freiburg

On alien ground, breathing an alien air,
    A Roman stood, far from his ancient home,
And gazing, murmured, 'Ah, the hills are fair,
    But not the hills of Rome!'

Descendant of a race to Romans kin,
    Where the old son of Empire stood, I stand.
The self-same rocks fold the same valley in,
    Untouched of human hand.

Over another shines the self-same star,
    Another heart with nameless longing fills,
Crying aloud, 'How beautiful they are,
    But not our English hills!'

556   ## From my Window

An old man leaning on a gate
Over a London mews—to contemplate—
Is it the sky above—the stones below?
    Is it remembrance of the years gone by,
    Or thinking forward to futurity
That holds him so?

Day after day he stands,
Quietly folded are the quiet hands,
Rarely he speaks.
    Hath he so near the hour when Time shall end,
    So much to spend?
What is it he seeks?

Whate'er he be,
He is become to me
A form of rest.
   I think his heart is tranquil, from it springs
   A dreamy watchfulness of tranquil things,
And not unblest.

RUDYARD KIPLING

557   ## By the Hoof of the Wild Goat

By the hoof of the Wild Goat up-tossed
From the Cliff where She lay in the Sun,
   Fell the Stone
To the Tarn where the daylight is lost;
So She fell from the light of the Sun,
   And alone.

Now the fall was ordained from the first,
With the Goat and the Cliff and the Tarn,
   But the Stone
Knows only Her life is accursed,
As She sinks in the depths of the Tarn,
   And alone.

Oh, Thou who hast builded the world!
Oh, Thou who hast lighted the Sun!
Oh, Thou who hast darkened the Tarn!
   Judge Thou
The sin of the Stone that was hurled
By the Goat from the light of the Sun,
As She sinks in the mire of the Tarn,
   Even now—even now—even now!

558   Recessional

(AFTER QUEEN VICTORIA'S JUBILEE, JUNE 22, 1897)

GOD of our fathers, known of old,
   Lord of our far-flung battle-line,
Beneath whose awful Hand we hold
   Dominion over palm and pine—
Lord God of Hosts, be with us yet,
Lest we forget—lest we forget!

The tumult and the shouting dies,
   The captains and the kings depart:
Still stands Thine ancient sacrifice,
   An humble and a contrite heart.
Lord God of Hosts, be with us yet,
Lest we forget—lest we forget!

Far-call'd, our navies melt away;
   On dune and headland sinks the fire:
Lo, all our pomp of yesterday
   Is one with Nineveh and Tyre!
Judge of the Nations, spare us yet,
Lest we forget—lest we forget!

If, drunk with sight of power, we loose
   Wild tongues that have not Thee in awe,
Such boastings as the Gentiles use,
   Or lesser breeds without the Law—
Lord God of Hosts, be with us yet,
Lest we forget—lest we forget!

For heathen heart that puts her trust
  In reeking tube and iron shard,
All valiant dust that builds on dust,
  And, guarding, calls not Thee to guard—
For frantic boast and foolish word—
  Thy Mercy on Thy People, Lord!

559   Cities and Thrones and Powers

CITIES and Thrones and Powers
  Stand in Time's eye,
Almost as long as flowers,
  Which daily die:
But, as new buds put forth
  To glad new men,
Out of the spent and unconsidered Earth
  The Cities rise again.

This season's Daffodil,
  She never hears
What change, what chance, what chill,
  Cut down last year's;
But with bold countenance,
  And knowledge small,
Esteems her seven days' continuance
  To be perpetual.

So Time that is o'er-kind
  To all that be,
Ordains us e'en as blind,
  As bold as she:
That in our very death,
  And burial sure,
Shadow to shadow, well persuaded, saith,
  'See how our works endure!'

560   Harp Song of the Dane Women

WHAT is a woman that you forsake her,
And the hearth-fire and the home-acre,
To go with the old grey Widow-maker?

She has no house to lay a guest in—
But one chill bed for all to rest in,
That the pale suns and the stray bergs nest in.

She has no strong white arms to fold you,
But the ten-times-fingering weed to hold you—
Out on the rocks where the tide has rolled you.

Yet, when the signs of summer thicken,
And the ice breaks, and the birch-buds quicken
Yearly you turn from our side, and sicken—

Sicken again for the shouts and the slaughters.
You steal away to the lapping waters,
And look at your ship in her winter-quarters.

You forget our mirth, and talk at the tables,
The kine in the shed and the horse in the stables—
To pitch her sides and go over her cables.

Then you drive out where the storm-clouds swallow,
And the sound of your oar-blades, falling hollow,
Is all we have left through the months to follow.

Ah, what is Woman that you forsake her,
And the hearth-fire and the home-acre,
To go with the old grey Widow-maker?

561   ## The Way through the Woods

THEY shut the road through the woods
  Seventy years ago.
Weather and rain have undone it again,
  And now you would never know
There was once a road through the woods
  Before they planted the trees:
It is underneath the coppice and heath,
  And the thin anemones.
  Only the keeper sees
That, where the ring-dove broods
  And the badgers roll at ease,
There was once a road through the woods.

Yet, if you enter the woods
  Of a summer evening late,
When the night-air cools on the trout-ring'd pools
  Where the otter whistles his mate
(They fear not men in the woods
  Because they see so few),
You will hear the beat of a horse's feet
  And the swish of a skirt in the dew,
  Steadily cantering through
The misty solitudes,
  As though they perfectly knew
The old lost road through the woods. . . .
But there is no road through the woods.

562 Rebirth

IF any God should say
  'I will restore
The world her yesterday
  Whole as before
My Judgment blasted it'—who would not lift
Heart, eye, and hand in passion o'er the gift?

If any God should will
  To wipe from mind
The memory of this ill
  Which is mankind
In soul and substance now—who would not bless
Even to tears His loving-tenderness?

If any God should give
  Us leave to fly
These present deaths we live,
  And safely die
In those lost lives we lived ere we were born—
What man but would not laugh the excuse to scorn?

For we are what we are—
  So broke to blood
And the strict works of war—
  So long subdued
To sacrifice, that threadbare Death commands
Hardly observance at our busier hands.

Yet we were what we were,
  And, fashioned so,
It pleases us to stare
  At the far show
Of unbelievable years and shapes that flit,
In our own likeness, on the edge of it.

ARTHUR SYMONS

563   At Dieppe: Rain on the Down

NIGHT, and the down by the sea,
And the veil of rain on the down;
And she came through the mist and the rain to me
From the safe warm lights of the town.

The rain shone in her hair,
And her face gleamed in the rain;
And only the night and the rain were there
As she came to me out of the rain.

564   Emmy

EMMY'S exquisite youth and her virginal air,
Eyes and teeth in the flash of a musical smile,
Come to me out of the past, and I see her there
As I saw her once for a while.

Emmy's laughter rings in my ears, as bright,
Fresh and sweet as the voice of a mountain brook,
And still I hear her telling us tales that night,
Out of Boccaccio's book.

There, in the midst of the villainous dancing-hall,
Leaning across the table, over the beer,
While the music maddened the whirling skirts of the ball,
As the midnight hour drew near,

There with the women, haggard, painted and old,
One fresh bud in a garland withered and stale,
She, with her innocent voice and her clear eyes, told
Tale after shameless tale.

And ever the witching smile, to her face beguiled,
Paused and broadened, and broke in a ripple of fun,
And the soul of a child looked out of the eyes of a child,
Or ever the tale was done.

O my child, who wronged you first, and began
First the dance of death that you dance so well?
Soul for soul: and I think the soul of a man
Shall answer for yours in hell.

Berlin, July 1891

565   ## At Dawn

She only knew the birth and death
Of days, when each that died
Was still at morn a hope, at night
A hope unsatisfied.

The dark trees shivered to behold
Another day begin;
She, being hopeless, did not weep
As the grey dawn came in.

566   ## Amoris Exsul

IN THE BAY

The sea-gulls whiten and dip,
Crying their lonely cry,
At noon in the blue of the bay;
And I hear the slow oars drip,
As the fisherman's boat drifts by,
And the cuckoo calls from the hillside far away.

The white birds cry for the foam,
O white birds crying to me
The cry of my heart evermore,
By perilous seas to roam
To a shore far over the sea,
And I would that my ship went down within sight of
   the shore!

567   On an Air of Rameau

TO ARNOLD DOLMETSCH

A MELANCHOLY desire of ancient things
Floats like a faded perfume out of the wires;
Pallid lovers, what unforgotten desires,
Whispered once, are retold in your whisperings?

Roses, roses, and lilies with hearts of gold,
These you plucked for her, these she wore in her breast;
Only Rameau's music remembers the rest,
The death of roses over a heart grown cold.

But these sighs? Can ghosts then sigh from the tomb?
Life then wept for you, sighed for you, chilled your breath?
It is the melancholy of ancient death
The harpsichord dreams of, sighing in the room.

568   In Ireland: By the Pool at the Third Rosses

I HEARD the sighing of the reeds
In the grey pool in the green land,
The sea-wind in the long reeds sighing
Between the green hill and the sand.

ARTHUR SYMONS

I heard the sighing of the reeds
Day after day, night after night;
I heard the whirring wild ducks flying,
I saw the sea-gulls' wheeling flight.

I heard the sighing of the reeds
Night after night, day after day,
And I forgot old age, and dying,
And youth that loves, and love's decay.

I heard the sighing of the reeds
At noontide and at evening,
And some old dream I had forgotten
I seemed to be remembering.

I hear the sighing of the reeds:
Is it in vain, is it in vain
That some old peace I had forgotten
Is crying to come back again?

569   A Tune

A FOOLISH rhythm turns in my idle head
As a wind-mill turns in the wind on an empty sky.
Why is it when love, which men call deathless, is dead,
That memory, men call fugitive, will not die?
Is love not dead? yet I hear that tune if I lie
Dreaming awake in the night on my lonely bed,
And an old thought turns with the old tune in my head
As a wind-mill turns in the wind on an empty sky.

JOHN GRAY

The Flying Fish. II

OF the birds that fly in the farthest sea
six are stranger than others be:
under its tumble, among the fish,
six are a marvel passing wish.

First is a hawk, exceeding great;
he dwelleth alone; he hath no mate;
his neck is wound with a yellow ring;
on his breast is the crest of a former king.

The second bird is exceeding pale,
from little head to scanty tail;
she is striped with black on either wing,
which is rose-lined, like a princely thing.

Though small the bulk of the brilliant third,
of all blue birds 'tis the bluest bird;
they fly in bands; and, seen by day,
by the side of them the sky is grey.

I mind the fifth, I forget the fourth,
unless that it comes from the east by north.
The fifth is an orange white-billed duck;
he diveth for fish, like the god of Luck;

he hath never a foot on which to stand;
for water yields and he loves not land.
This is the end of many words
save one, concerning marvellous birds.

JOHN GRAY

The great-faced dolphin is first of fish;
he is devil-eyed and devilish;
of all the fishes is he most brave,
he walks the sea like an angry wave.

The second the fishes call their lord;
himself a bow, his face is a sword;
his sword is armed with a hundred teeth,
fifty above and fifty beneath.

The third hath a scarlet suit of mail;
the fourth is naught but a feeble tail;
the fifth is a whip with a hundred strands,
and every arm hath a hundred hands.

The last strange fish is the last strange bird;
of him no sage hath ever heard;
he roams the sea in a gleaming horde
in fear of the dolphin and him of the sword.

He leaps from the sea with a silken swish;
he beats the air does the flying fish.
His eyes are round with excess of fright,
bright as the drops of his pinions' flight.

In sea and sky he hath no peace;
for the five strange fish are his enemies;
and the five strange fowls keep watch for him;
they know him well by his crystal gleam.

Oftwhiles, sir Sage, on my junk's white deck
have I seen this fish-bird come to wreck,
oftwhiles (fair deck) 'twixt bow and poop
have I seen this piteous sky-fish stoop.

Scaled bird, how his snout and gills dilate,
all quivering and roseate:
he pants in crystal and mother-of-pearl
while his body shrinks and his pinions furl.

His beauty passes like bubbles blown;
the white bright bird is a fish of stone;
the bird so fair, for its putrid sake,
is flung to the dogs in the junk's white wake.

.

571 The Night Nurse goes her Round

DROOP under doves' wings silent, breathing shapes
white coverlids dissimulate; in hope
of opiate aid to round the ledge where gapes
the sootblack gulf in which obtuse minds grope

for very nothing, vast and undefined,
in starless depths no astrolabe can probe.
The moving form, as doomed to pass and wind,
unwind and pass anew, in sleep-dyed robe

of firmamental silence more than hue,
watches the doorway of the tired's escape
only. Fatigue gone on; I left behind

with moths' feet, wordless whispering; or find
reality, white coiffe and scarlet cape;
and dreams are what a dream should be, or true.

ERNEST DOWSON

572   Non sum qualis eram bonae sub regno
Cynarae

LAST night, ah, yesternight, betwixt her lips and mine
There fell thy shadow, Cynara! thy breath was shed
Upon my soul between the kisses and the wine;
And I was desolate and sick of an old passion,
    Yea, I was desolate and bowed my head:
I have been faithful to thee, Cynara! in my fashion.

All night upon mine heart I felt her warm heart beat,
Night-long within mine arms in love and sleep she lay;
Surely the kisses of her bought red mouth were sweet;
But I was desolate and sick of an old passion,
    When I awoke and found the dawn was gray:
I have been faithful to thee, Cynara! in my fashion.

I have forgot much, Cynara! gone with the wind,
Flung roses, roses riotously with the throng,
Dancing, to put thy pale, lost lilies out of mind;
But I was desolate and sick of an old passion,
    Yea, all the time, because the dance was long:
I have been faithful to thee, Cynara! in my fashion.

I cried for madder music and for stronger wine,
But when the feast is finished and the lamps expire,
Then falls thy shadow, Cynara! the night is thine;
And I am desolate and sick of an old passion,
    Yea, hungry for the lips of my desire:
I have been faithful to thee, Cynara! in my fashion.

573 ## Autumnal

FOR ALEXANDER TEIXEIRA DE MATTOS

PALE amber sunlight falls across
　　The reddening October trees,
　　That hardly sway before a breeze
As soft as summer: summer's loss
　　Seems little, dear! on days like these!

Let misty autumn be our part!
　　The twilight of the year is sweet:
　　Where shadow and the darkness meet
Our love, a twilight of the heart
　　Eludes a little time's deceit.

Are we not better and at home
　　In dreamful Autumn, we who deem
　　No harvest joy is worth a dream?
A little while and night shall come,
　　A little while, then, let us dream.

Beyond the pearled horizons lie
　　Winter and night: awaiting these
　　We garner this poor hour of ease,
Until love turn from us and die
　　Beneath the drear November trees.

574 ## The Garden of Shadow

LOVE heeds no more the sighing of the wind
Against the perfect flowers: thy garden's close
Is grown a wilderness, where none shall find
One strayed, last petal of one last year's rose.

O bright, bright hair! O mouth like a ripe fruit!
Can famine be so nigh to harvesting?
Love, that was songful, with a broken lute
In grass of graveyards goeth murmuring.

Let the wind blow against the perfect flowers,
And all thy garden change and glow with spring:
Love is grown blind with no more count of hours,
Nor part in seed-time nor in harvesting.

575   De Amore

SHALL one be sorrowful because of love,
    Which hath no earthly crown,
    Which lives and dies, unknown?
Because no words of his shall ever move
    Her maiden heart to own
    Him lord and destined master of her own:
Is Love so weak a thing as this,
    Who can not lie awake,
    Solely for his own sake,
For lack of the dear hands to hold, the lips to kiss,
        A mere heart-ache?

Nay, though love's victories be great and sweet,
    Nor vain and foolish toys,
    His crowned, earthly joys,
Is there no comfort then in love's defeat?
    Because he shall defer,
    For some short span of years all part in her,
    Submitting to forego
    The certain peace which happier lovers know;

Because he shall be utterly disowned,
    Nor length of service bring
    Her least awakening:
Foiled, frustrate and alone, misunderstood, discrowned,
        Is Love less King?

Grows not the world to him a fairer place,
    How far soever his days
    Pass from his lady's ways,
From mere encounter with her golden face?
    Though all his sighing be vain,
    Shall he be heavy-hearted and complain?
Is she not still a star,
Deeply to be desired, worshipped afar,
    A beacon-light to aid
    From bitter-sweet delights, Love's masquerade?
Though he lose many things,
    Though much he miss:
The heart upon his heart, the hand that clings,
    The memorable first kiss;
Love that is love at all,
Needs not an earthly coronal;
Love is himself his own exceeding great reward,
        A mighty lord!

Lord over life and all the ways of breath,
    Mighty and strong to save
    From the devouring grave;
Yes, whose dominion doth out-tyrant death,
    Thou who art life and death in one,
    The night, the sun;
Who art, when all things seem:
    Foiled, frustrate and forlorn, rejected of today
    Go with me all my way,
And let me not blaspheme.

576   Breton Afternoon

HERE, where the breath of the scented-gorse floats through the
    sun-stained air,
On a steep hill-side, on a grassy ledge, I have lain hours long and
    heard
Only the faint breeze pass in a whisper like a prayer,
And the river ripple by and the distant call of a bird.

On the lone hill-side, in the gold sunshine, I will hush me and
    repose,
And the world fades into a dream and a spell is cast on me;
And what was all the strife about, for the myrtle or the rose,
And why have I wept for a white girl's paleness passing ivory!

Out of the tumult of angry tongues, in a land alone, apart,
In a perfumed dream-land set betwixt the bounds of life and death,
Here will I lie while the clouds fly by and delve an hole where my
    heart
May sleep deep down with the gorse above and red, red earth
    beneath.

Sleep and be quiet for an afternoon, till the rose-white angelus
Softly steals my way from the village under the hill:
Mother of God, O Misericord, look down in pity on us,
The weak and blind who stand in our light and wreak ourselves such ill.

LIONEL JOHNSON

By the Statue of King Charles at Charing Cross

TO WILLIAM WATSON

Sombre and rich, the skies;
Great glooms, and starry plains.
Gently the night wind sighs;
Else a vast silence reigns.

The splendid silence clings
Around me: and around
The saddest of all kings
Crowned, and again discrowned.

Comely and calm, he rides
Hard by his own Whitehall:
Only the night wind glides:
No crowds, nor rebels, brawl.

Gone, too, his Court: and yet,
The stars his Courtiers are:
Stars in their stations set;
And every wandering star.

Alone he rides, alone,
The fair and fatal king;
Dark night is all his own,
That strange and solemn thing.

Which are more full of fate:
The stars; or those sad eyes?
Which are more still and great:
Those brows; or the dark skies?

Although his whole heart yearn
In passionate tragedy:
Never was face so stern
With sweet austerity.

Vanquished in life, his death
By beauty made amends:
The passing of his breath
Won his defeated ends.

Brief life, and hapless? Nay:
Through death, life grew sublime.
Speak after sentence? Yea:
And to the end of time.

Armoured he rides, his head
Bare to the stars of doom:
He triumphs now, the dead,
Beholding London's gloom.

Our wearier spirit faints,
Vexed in the world's employ:
His soul was of the saints;
And art to him was joy.

King, tried in fires of woe!
Men hunger for thy grace;
And through the night I go,
Loving thy mournful face.

Yet, when the city sleeps;
When all the cries are still:
The stars and heavenly deeps
Work out a perfect will.

578   In Memory. II

        Ah! fair face gone from sight,
            with all its light
        of eyes, that pierced the deep
            of human night!
        Ah! fair face calm in sleep.

        Ah! fair lips hushed in death!
            Now their glad breath
        Breathes not upon our air
            Music, that saith
        Love only, and things fair.

        Ah! lost brother! Ah! sweet
            still hands and feet!
        May those feet haste to reach,
            Those hands to greet,
        Us, where love needs no speech.

                                        1886

579   Dead

          TO OLIVIER GEORGES DESTRÉE

    In Merioneth, over the sad moor
        Drives the rain, the cold wind blows:
        Past the ruinous church door,
    The poor procession without music goes.

    Lonely she wandered out her hour, and died.
        Now the mournful curlew cries
        Over her, laid down beside
    Death's lonely people: lightly down she lies.

In Merioneth, the wind lives and wails,
  On from hill to lonely hill:
  Down the loud, triumphant gales,
A spirit cries *Be strong!* and cries *Be still!*

1887

580   Oxford

TO ARTHUR GALTON

OVER, the four long years! And now there rings
One voice of freedom and regret: *Farewell !*
Now old remembrance sorrows, and now sings:
But song from sorrow, now, I cannot tell.

City of weathered cloister and worn court;
Gray city of strong towers and clustering spires:
Where art's fresh loveliness would first resort;
Where lingering art kindled her latest fires.

Where on all hands, wondrous with ancient grace,
Grace touched with age, rise works of goodliest men:
Next Wykeham's art obtain their splendid place
The zeal of Inigo, the strength of Wren.

Where at each coign of every antique street,
A memory hath taken root in stone:
There, Raleigh shone; there, toil'd Franciscan feet;
There, Johnson flinch'd not, but endured alone.

There, Shelley dream'd his white Platonic dreams;
There, classic Landor throve on Roman thought;
There, Addison pursued his quiet themes;
There, smiled Erasmus, and there, Colet taught.

And there, O memory more sweet than all!
Lived he, whose eyes keep yet our passing light;
Whose crystal lips Athenian speech recall;
Who wears Rome's purple with least pride, most right.

That is the Oxford, strong to charm us yet:
Eternal in her beauty and her past.
What, though her soul be vexed? She can forget
Cares of an hour: only the great things last.

Only the gracious air, only the charm,
And ancient might of true humanities:
These, nor assault of man, nor time, can harm;
Not these, nor Oxford with her memories.

Together have we walked with willing feet
Gardens of plenteous trees, bowering soft lawn:
Hills whither Arnold wandered; and all sweet
June meadows, from the troubling world withdrawn:

Chapels of cedarn fragrance, and rich gloom
Poured from empurpled panes on either hand:
Cool pavements, carved with legends of the tomb;
Grave haunts, where we might dream, and understand.

Over, the four long years! And unknown powers
Call to us, going forth upon our way:
Ah! turn we, and look back upon the towers,
That rose above our lives, and cheered the day.

Proud and serene, against the sky, they gleam:
Proud and secure, upon the earth, they stand:
Our city hath the air of a pure dream,
And hers indeed is an Hesperian land.

Think of her so! the wonderful, the fair,
The immemorial, and the ever young:
The city, sweet with our forefathers' care;
The city, where the Muses all have sung.

Ill times may be; she hath no thought of time:
She reigns beside the waters yet in pride.
Rude voices cry: but in her ears the chime
Of full, sad bells brings back her old springtide.

Like to a queen in pride of place, she wears
The splendour of a crown in Radcliffe's dome.
Well fare she, well! As perfect beauty fares;
And those high places, that are beauty's home.

1890

INDEX OF FIRST LINES

First lines of extracts are printed in italics.
The numbers refer to the pages

INDEX OF FIRST LINES

INDEX OF FIRST LINES

INDEX OF FIRST LINES

INDEX OF FIRST LINES

INDEX OF FIRST LINES

INDEX OF FIRST LINES

INDEX OF FIRST LINES

INDEX OF FIRST LINES

INDEX OF FIRST LINES

INDEX OF FIRST LINES

INDEX OF AUTHORS

The references are to the numbers of the poems

INDEX OF AUTHORS

PRINTED IN GREAT BRITAIN
AT THE UNIVERSITY PRESS, OXFORD
BY VIVIAN RIDLER
PRINTER TO THE UNIVERSITY